MAY 26 2005

Y0-CWP-591

Property of
Fargo Public Library

TO THINK LIKE GOD

TO THINK LIKE GOD

Pythagoras and Parmenides
The Origins Of Philosophy

ARNOLD HERMANN

PARMENIDES
PUBLISHING

PARMENIDES PUBLISHING
Las Vegas 89109
© 2004 by Parmenides Publishing

All rights reserved. Published 2004
Printed in the United States of America

ISBN: 1-930972-00-8

Publisher's Cataloging-In-Publication Data

Hermann, Arnold, 1953–
   To think like God : Pythagoras and Parmenides :
the origins of philosophy / Arnold Hermann.

   p. : ill. ; cm.

   Includes bibliographical references and index.
   ISBN: 1-930972-00-8

1. Philosophy, Ancient.   2. Parmenides—Influence.
3. Pythagoras—Influence.   4. Xenophanes, ca.
580-ca. 478 B.C.—Influence.   5. Evidence.   I. Title.

B188.H47 2004
182

182
H552t
c 1

Excerpts from LORE AND SCIENCE IN ANCIENT PYTHAGOREANISM by Walter Burkert, translated by Edwin L. Minar, Jr., are reprinted throughout this work by permission of the publisher, Harvard University Press, Cambridge, Mass., Copyright © 1972 by the President and Fellows of Harvard College. English edition translated, with revisions, from WEISHEIT UND WISSENSCHAFT: STUDIEN ZU PYTHAGORAS, PHILOLAOS UND PLATON, Copyright © 1962 by Verlag Hans Carl, Nürnberg.

www.tothinklikegod.com
www.parmenides.com

Only a philosopher's mind grows wings,
since its memory always keeps it as close as possible
to those realities by being close to which
the gods are divine.

—Plato, *Phaedrus* 249c

Contents

Preface	xiii
Acknowledgments	xxi
A Note on References, Translations, Citations, Notes, Bibliography, and Some Idiosyncrasies	xxv
Abbreviations	xxix
INTRODUCTION	1

I. PYTHAGORAS — 15
The Search for a Way Out — 15
One of the Oldest Questions: What Do All Things Have in Common? — 15
The Seeker of Wisdom — 17
Separating Pythagoreanism into Early, Middle, and Late Periods — 21
The Search for Proof — 25
Euphorbus' Shield — 25
Relying on Reasoning — 27
A Science for the Intangible, Abstract — 29

II. THE PYTHAGOREANS — 31
Tradition Versus the Historical Account — 31
Conflicting Reports and Forgeries — 31
Almost No Mention of Pythagoras in Plato and Aristotle — 33
The Main Sources of Pythagorean Lore — 34
The Pythagorean Agenda — 41
Croton before Pythagoras — 41
The Lecturer and Miracle-Worker — 42
The Four Speeches — 44
Earth as a Prison — 47

The Politics of Pythagoreanism	50
The Making of a Religious Political Conspiracy	50
Becoming a Member in the Pythagorean Society	52
Secrecy and Anti-Democracy	55
The Gods; and the Ruling of the Many by the Few	56
Signs of a Pythagorean Police State?	58
Beans and Politics	59
A Religious-Political-Economic Dictatorship?	60
War and Luxury	63
Sybaris—the Antipode of Pythagoreanism	63
The War	65
Why was Sybaris Destroyed?	67
The Revolts Against the Pythagorean Political Elite	71
The Growing Hatred of the Non-Pythagoreans	71
The First Revolt	73
Pythagoras' Death	75
A Return to Power and the Second Revolt	77
The Gradual End of the Movement	78
Those Who Listen and Those Who Learn	80
A Split in the Order	80
The Listeners: Teaching by Passwords, Tokens, and Maxims	82
The Emergence of Scientist Pythagoreans	86
Hippasus, the All-around Thinker	88
Aristotle's "Those Called Pythagoreans"	90
III. IN WANT OF A MATHEMATICS FOR THE SOUL	93
The Source Code of the Universe	93
The Music of the Spheres	99
Conquering the Unlimited	99
The Sound of Order	101
Order and Proportion	102
Harmony and the Soul	104
Numerology—Deriving Philosophy from Number?	107
Confusing Numbers with Things and Things with Numbers	107
Number Symbolism	110
The Counter-Earth	112

IV.	PYTHAGORIZING VERSUS PHILOSOPHIZING	115
	Truth After Death?	115
	An Exercise in Apprehending the True Nature of Things	117
	Purification or Reasoning as a Way to Truth?	118
	Calibrating the Ability to Reason	121
V.	PARMENIDES	127
	The Lawmaker	127
	The Poet's Challenge and the Lawgiver's Response	132
	Xenophanes and the Truth Available to Mortals	132
	The Need for Reliable Criteria	139
	The Senses, Reason, and Proof	141
	Early Lawmaking and Analytic Problem Solving	144
	The Ways of Proof and Disproof	147
VI.	THE POEM OF PARMENIDES	151
	A Quick Guide to the Poem's Ordering	151
	The Poem, a Translation	155
	The Proem	155
	The Ways of Inquiry for Thinking	156
	The Reliable or Evidential Account	158
	DOXA—The Deceptive Order of Words, *or the Plausible Ordering*	160
VII.	THE POEM'S MOST DIFFICULT POINTS EXPLAINED	163
	What Is the Significance of the Proem?	163
	The Realm of the Nameless Goddess	163
	The Curriculum	167
	How Opinion Would Be Judged If Truth Did Not Exist	168
	Dokimos—What is Genuinely Reliable Because Proven as Such	170
	Doxa: the Positive Versus the Negative Read	172
	A Call for a Unified Approach?	174
	The Problem of Contradictory Formulas	178
	A Unity of Formula	181
	"Esti" or "IS": The Parmenidean Object	184
	Verb or Subject?	184

	Way or Destination?	186
	The Object of Judgment	188
	The Naked IS	189
	The IS as the Universe: An Old Misconception	191
	The Dead World	191
	A Fateful Misunderstanding?	192
	Proving Motion Versus Proving a Proper Understanding of Motion	194
	Julian Barbour's The End of Time	196
	What Does the Concept of Truth Signify for Parmenides?	198
	The Question of IS NOT	200
	Doxa: Opinion or Appearance?	204
	Are There Advantages to Rearranging the Fragments?	209
VIII.	**GUIDELINES FOR AN EVIDENTIAL ACCOUNT**	211
	Delimiting the Object of Judgment	211
	Twelve Provisos for the Evidential Account	218
IX.	**METHODS OF PROOF AND DISPROOF**	225
	Like according to Like	225
	The Way of the Daemon	225
	Aiming for Conceptual Correspondence	227
	A Unity of Corresponding Landmarks	230
	What Do Falling Millet Seeds Have in Common?	232
	Sufficient Reason, Contradiction, and Infinite Regress	234
	Sufficient Reason	240
	Contradiction	242
	Infinite Regress	244
	Summation of Parmenides' Doctrine	245
X.	**IRRATIONALS AND THE PERFECT PREMISE**	251
	Philosophy: An Exercise in Infallibility	251
	A Perfect Premise	253
	To Drown in a Sea of Non-Identity	256
	Irrationality and the Pythagorean Theorem	260
	The Indirect Proof of Odd Being Even	262

XI. **MIND AND UNIVERSE: TWO REALMS, TWO SEPARATE APPROACHES**   267
    Two Ways of Looking at Things   267
    What We Think Fits with What We Think, but Not Necessarily with the Universe   269
    Renouncing Thinking's Dependency upon Sense-Experience   273

APPENDIX   279
    The Info to Certainty Sequence, Part I   279
    The Info to Certainty Sequence, Part II   287

Subdivided Bibliography   297
Index Locorum   341
General Index   353

Preface

The questions of how philosophy came about and why it began in pre-classical Greece at exactly that particular place and time—and not earlier, later, somewhere else, or not at all—have an intrinsic relation to one of the most disarming arguments in Parmenides' Poem (masked as a simple inquiry into the genesis of "what is"), and they seem just as unsolvable: "What necessity would have impelled it to grow later rather than earlier, if it began from nothing?" (fr. 8.9–10) Still, philosophy's *raison d'être* has preoccupied my mind since the time I first picked up the works of Kant and Hegel in my later teens—admittedly, my earliest, rather clumsy encounters with the subject, and not the wisest choices for a novice. Nonetheless, how my own interest in philosophy came about, and why then and not at a different time, I can easily answer. While this interest did not begin from nothing, it was not stirred by a particular book, a moving lecture, or an inspiring professor, but by some very special music. The year was 1970. I was 17 years old, and I found myself at a summer rock festival, dragged there by friends who eventually had evaporated into the smothering crowd. Unwittingly thrust toward the stage, I was suddenly pummeled by the most complex, confounding, indeed kaleidoscopic sounds. The music was a magnetic vortex—everywhere, completely erratic, yet at the same time soothing, massive, collapsing, like a towering wall rushing to crush—but the ravaging blow never comes. The band, I soon learned, was called Van Der Graaf Generator, and its sound was produced by a stoical keyboard player operating some kind of hybrid mutated Hammond organ, the syncopated thunder of a sizable drum kit mastered by an intense-looking drummer, and surprisingly, a self-absorbed saxophone player who had wrapped himself in an array of saxophones of different shapes and sizes, gleaming in the light like a brass armor, and who was playing two of them at the same time! But most striking was the sudden appearance of a lone singer, his voice lashing out boldly through the noise, mercilessly slicing it like a jagged blade, commanding, overpowering, mercurial, like a burst of lighting in a midnight storm. And then the words (one can hardly call them lyrics) . . . he sang of fiery universes beyond the edge of thought; of vacant time, living antimatter, and the angst of hyperspace travelers above the speed of light; of thinking about thinking, and refugees from fate; of houses with walls but no doors, where only time can enter or escape; of killers, angels, acolytes, and the silence at humanity's end. The singer's name is Peter Hammill, and I consider him the greatest musical genius of my generation, a generation that was blessed with not a small number of geniuses. Peter is one of the most creative artists imaginable, with more than sixty records or CDs to date—yes, he is still very much active—and it is the only music, in my view, that really merits being called philosophical. I still listen to it today, and some of it played often in the background while I researched this work. In any case, Peter Hammill's influence was decisive in my desire to become a philosopher, which is why I need to pay tribute to him in this form.

As to the question of how or why philosophy came about when it did, this book is an attempt to shed a tentative if somewhat unorthodox light on the matter. I say "tentative" because no subject in philosophy can be deemed as categorically resolved, particularly not the manifold issues of ancient philosophy, which are further handicapped by a dearth of extant material. Nor has the evolution of *To Think Like God* been a straight development from A to B, instead encompassing a time span of some fifteen years or more. The somewhat impenetrable subject matter made the whole project more akin to a philosophical odyssey than a critical examination, which is very difficult to express as a linear narrative. Still, one of the functions of a preface is to give an account of a work's development; nevertheless, I will try to be brief.

Due to reasons that will become clearer in the course of this book, *To Think Like God* attempts to address three distinct audiences: (1) experts on the Presocratics, particularly interpreters of the extant Pythagorean and Eleatic material; (2) scholars with broader classicist interests, philosophers in general, and students of classics or ancient philosophy, as well as the history of law; and (3) nonscholars who have developed an interest in the matters discussed. Having noticed in recent years an increased curiosity regarding both Pythagoras and Parmenides among the latter group, I have sought to update the overall picture for the general public in a way that is much more in line with the present state of inquiry, and which so far has been only available to experts. Of course, to satisfy these sometimes divergent demands has not been an easy task, and it had a great impact on the character and form of my presentation and arguments. It is much more difficult to explain a philosophical point in conventional language than with technical expressions. On the other hand, if specialized terms are completely avoided, other scholars have no means by which to assess, indeed calibrate, the meaning of my claims. Thus, all in all, *To Think Like God* has been a venturous balancing act.

The project itself began close to two decades ago, during a detailed study of Hegelian method and the history of dialectics. More by accident than design, I was suddenly confronted with what is generally considered Plato's most inaccessible dialogue, the *Parmenides*. Needless to say, my first efforts to make sense of this work were rather ill-fated. However, I became very much intrigued with the dialogue's titular character, Parmenides, and I wanted to know more about the enigmatic figure who seemed to have inspired Plato to this most difficult work. Increasingly, what was originally intended as a cursory background inquiry became a full-time occupation.

Yet Parmenides is so difficult to interpret that for the first five to six years, I scored failure after failure. By the time I had exhausted various possibilities—the cosmological, existential, mystical, metaphysical, and so forth—my writings on the subject had ballooned to an unwieldy 4,000 pages, with a 1,200-page introduction. It was not so much a manuscript as it was a logbook of various failures to achieve a consistent interpretation that did justice to the whole Poem and not to only a few select parts. But I had also made some progress. What turned out to be fruitful was the investigation of Parmenides' impact on other Presocratics, and furthermore the exploration of Plato's so-called Eleatic dialogues, in particular the reexamination of the abovementioned *Parmenides*. (In due course, I completed an entirely new interpretation of the dialogue itself, which will be released subsequently to this present work under the title *Above Being*.) Also, my research focused increasingly on the logical/veridical aspects of Parmenides' Poem. Additionally, I tried to trace Parmenidean thought across 2,500 years, in a kind of encyclopedic attempt to show how various thinkers approached the problems that can be drawn from his doctrine. Of course, the first part of my study dwelled upon the period before Parmenides; thus, it examined the Milesians, Xenophanes, Pythagoras, and Heraclitus.

Various significant things happened at this stage. First, I made contact with Néstor-Luis Cordero, one of the most knowledgeable Parmenidean experts and the author of *Les deux chemins de Parménide*. His criticism and advice brought much-needed depth and consistency to my work. The second important event was a connection with Richard McKirahan, whose general study on the Presocratics—*Philosophy Before Socrates*—offers an insightful and to-the-point examination of Parmenides, as well as of Pythagoreanism. I sent him not only my draft on the pre-Parmenideans, but also parts from *The Naked IS*—as I was calling my book on Parmenides—together with samples of some of my other works. Richard dissected everything meticulously, argument by argument, and supplied me with his advice and criticism, which had an invaluable effect on the overall quality of my work.

At this point in my research, finding no convincing evidence that Parmenides was either influenced by or reacting against the Milesians or Heraclitus, I narrowed my focus on the Pythagoreans and Xenophanes and investigated these subjects for another three years. In addition to the possibility of a link between Pythagoreanism and Parmenides—which, like others, I have failed to prove convincingly—there are quite a few facets to the movement that have not been explored by others to the extent I thought necessary, especially the group's characteristics as a cult—a phenomenon I was particularly interested in and had studied for many years. The most authoritative work on the Pythagoreans is undoubtedly Walter Burkert's *Lore and Science in Ancient Pythagoreanism*, which inspired me to connect the dots in a more nuanced way, one that could bring their political agenda—which was unreservedly anti-democratic—in context with their cultism and their deification of Pythagoras, together with a cogent motive for their war against Sybaris, a city that, due to its unbridled luxury and richness, was not only a religious thorn in the side of the movement, but was also governed democratically. The volatile combination of fanatical cult with dictatorial political aspirations supplied more than enough motive for the repeated anti-Pythagorean uprisings that gripped most of Southern Italy.

The opportunity to tell this story also provided me with a plausible background and a contrast to the peaceful life of the Eleatics, as the events in question—including the conflict with Sybaris, the death of Pythagoras, and both anti-Pythagorean revolts—all occurred within Parmenides' lifetime. Moreover, I was fascinated by the story of how the Crotonian army under Pythagorean command had engineered the catastrophic flooding of Sybaris, and so, as part of my research, I decided to see for myself the place where the course of the river Crati had been changed such a long time ago. To my knowledge, this was the first use of a weapon of mass destruction in history. Wandering through what little is left of the ruins—where allegedly hundreds of thousands had been killed—to the dried old riverbed not far away was a somewhat disquieting experience. I also visited other historical sites with links to Pythagoreanism, including Croton, Locri, Reggio di Calabria, and indeed Metapontum—much as Cicero did two millennia ago, when he desired to come to the Temple of the Muses in order to see, in his words, "the very place where Pythagoras breathed his last and the seat he sat in."[1] Visiting these places and seeing some of the archeological evidence, gravestone markings, coins, and so forth, had some influence on my understanding of Pythagoreanism, and I felt it necessary to expand the section in the book that dealt with the historical aspects. (In light of the often conflicting doxographical material on Pythagorean lore, a cursory demonstration of my approach toward sorting some of it out is provided in the Appendix.)

Around the same time, Cordero and I visited Velia on the western shores of Southern Italy, the historical site of Parmenides' Elea. This experience also affected my writing in a profound way, as did my innumerable talks with Cordero about Parmenides' activity as a lawgiver—and how his legislation would have to be formulated to match his doctrine—which caused me to spend yet another year trying to explore some of these issues. The legislative angle allowed me to revisit the question of Xenophanes and what role he might have played for Parmenides in the formulation of his doctrine—with particular emphasis on the evidentiary argumentative methods—subjects, I found, that were not explored by others as much as they arguably deserved. As to the further details of my visit to Velia, I spent many days among the ruins—I even took a helicopter ride to survey the entire site from air—and hiked most of the surrounding countryside while taking a multitude of photographs. I was allowed free access to Parmenides' head—a marble representation of the great thinker that has been found among Velia's ruins—as well as to other archeological findings. For this, I am grateful to the friendly officials who manage the archeological excavations.[2]

In due course, I was afforded the opportunity to submit the manuscripts for review to Walter Burkert himself. To my astonishment, he found the whole project worthwhile, and he encouraged me to continue in the direction I had begun and complete the general thesis. Also around this time, Patricia Curd, whose book *The Legacy of Parmenides* represents a milestone of interpretation, agreed to review what I had written, and she advised me to keep a detailed analysis of interpretative problems regarding Parmenides, as she thought it would be useful to students. Thus, I decided to rework *The Naked IS* and release it later as a study for experts. I still wanted to explore a general treatment of Parmenides, together with the Pythagorean

---

1 **Cicero** [153] *De finibus bonorum et malorum* 5.2.4.
2 For further details, please see my acknowledgments at the beginning of the book.

material, in one more easily accessible book on the origins of philosophy, and that became *To Think Like God* in its present form.

Perhaps I should offer a clarifying word on Parmenides' object of inquiry: for years, my own interpretations had been repeatedly plagued by inconsistencies, a realization that forced me one day to restart my whole research into Parmenides' Poem from scratch. I was seeking to avoid any kind of a priori approach, focusing only on the verses themselves. It was during this time that I developed the notion of the "Naked IS," meaning the essential object of discourse of fragment 8, without resorting to anything else to compare this concept to—no other doctrine or argumentative devices. I have likened this process to removing Christmas decorations from a Christmas tree. The question is, how many decorations can a Christmas tree afford to lose and still be considered a Christmas tree? After dispensing with subsequent interpretations and comparisons regarding the object of fragment 8, I proceeded to play around with its *semata*, that is, its "signs" or "landmarks" (8.2), removing them one by one, adding others, in an attempt to see how this might affect the *esti* or IS. Of great assistance was a construct Patricia Curd had introduced through her work, namely that of a "theoretically fundamental entity."[3] Other approaches that gave me much food for thought included Richard McKirahan's stripping of the object of discourse to the bare "IT is"[4] and some of Montgomery Furth's deductions, such as "of what is, only one thing can be said" and "the only true thought is the thought that it is."[5] Correspondence with Cordero about the *"esti dénudé"* were also very helpful. As a test, I even subjected the object of inquiry to Plato's exercises in the *Parmenides*—the eight hypotheses found in the second half of the dialogue—not as the "One" as Plato did, of course, but simply as "IS."

One thing became increasingly clear: whatever "tree" it was that Parmenides introduced—if I can continue with the analogy—it only became a Christmas tree in the hands of subsequent writers, each one adding or removing whatever decorations matched or opposed a favorite theory. In this sense, Parmenides' object of discourse became all things for all people. With only a few modifications, it could be an entity, a force or element, an atom, a Form, a First Principle, a Mind, and so forth. Indeed, it could provide any speculative object with all the characteristics or attributes of an absolute,

---

3   **Curd** [297] *The Legacy of Parmenides* 47–48, 97.
4   **McKirahan** [67] *Philosophy Before Socrates (PBS)* 170–172.
5   **Furth** [334] 'Elements of Eleatic Ontology' 127–129.

whether this absolute was the most basic, not further divisible particle or atom; the overall universe; all of existence; or even a Supreme Being. It seemed that Parmenides had stumbled upon the perfect premise, one that could be transformed by others into a perfect entity.

Arguably, the above theory can only explain what effect it had on others, or how it was received, but the larger question was, what did Parmenides himself think of the object of his Poem? What did it mean for him, and why did he write about it? Eventually, having no other place to go—in true Parmenidean fashion—I had to focus on what, according to the Poem, remained of this bare idea, the IS. What could not be removed from Parmenides' overall approach were concepts like "the unshaking heart of well-rounded truth" (1.29),[6] "the only ways of inquiry for thinking or knowing" (2.2), and statements like "behold things which, although absent, are yet securely present to the mind" (4.1), "speaking and thinking must be of What IS, for it can be" (6.1), "judge by reasoning [and not the senses] the much-contested disproof" (7.5), and "for without What IS, in which it is expressed, you will not find thinking or knowing" (8.35–36). What all these statements have in common can be summarized to this: Parmenides was speaking of something that was of great importance for *thought* and *discourse*, something that should be examined by reasoning and not by the senses. In short, it was something for the mind or of the mind, connected to knowledge and, above all, truth. I found myself coming closer and closer to Charles Kahn's read of the IS, as he puts it, "the object of knowing, what is or can be known" or "the knowable, the object of cognition."[7] To this day, I find that a reading of the Poem that focuses on its veridical, epistemic, and logical aspects is the most consistent of all, providing one coherent message that does justice to the work both in part and as a whole. And it also does justice to Doxa.

Finally, another year and a half later, the outcome of this long but fascinating journey was once again reviewed by Burkert, Cordero, Curd, and

---

6 Throughout the work, reference numbers in parentheses pertain to the fragment and line numbering of Parmenides' Poem in accordance with Diels/Kranz. They refer to the so-called "B" fragments. Other Presocratic material is cited in full.

7 **Kahn** [395] 'The Thesis of Parmenides' 710, 712. I have also found much common ground with **Long**'s [448] veridical/noetical approach (see 'Parmenides and Thinking Being'). What is particularly compelling is Long's fourfold distinction of those Presocratic subjects of inquiry that are commonly neglected by modern scholarship, e.g. "methodology," "second-order inquiry," "mind" and the "relation of knower to the known." (129 and *passim*) It is precisely these kinds of issues that I have sought to give prominence to in this book. Regrettably I have obtained Long's paper when the manuscript was practically finished. I did manage to address some points in the notes, but not as much or as detailed as I would have liked.

McKirahan—all of whom must be fed up with my ideas by now—and this became *To Think Like God* in its final form. (However, whatever shortcomings, flaws, or inaccuracies the work may still have are entirely my own.) As any Parmenidean scholar can surely attest, this kind of research does not move from Truth to Truth, but from "Doxa" to "Doxa." As a definitive interpretation of Parmenides is beyond our grasp, the best one can hope for is a more "plausible ordering of words." If *To Think Like God* achieves this, then at least some yet-to-be-defined part of my odyssey is complete.

Arnold Hermann
June 4, 2004

Acknowledgments

Being entirely social without having to be mutual is what makes gratitude a rather peculiar emotion. Unthinkable without relations to others, it is nevertheless free from reciprocation, and if genuine, it never comes to an end. This is the sense of appreciation that I feel towards the persons named below, who, I am sure, have no idea how much their help, encouragement, influence, or kind words have meant to me, and without whom I would have never summoned the nerve or the stamina to carry out such a totally absorbing project.

The untiring efforts of my "staff"—assistants, longtime friends, et al.—were all-important: the countless nights and weekends spent hunting down, comparing, and updating a myriad of articles and books (even transcribing or translating some) provided me with a much broader field of inquiry. Some have formed different groups according to various tasks, such as the "Capizzi Sisters," a name first adopted by those who transcribed and translated Capizzi's *La porta di Parmenide* in time for me to complete an important inquiry. The name stuck, and for many years Laura (Bea) Dobler, Jutta Geisenberger, Claudia Zanvit, Claudia Volker, Moni Sauerteig, Cornelia Frieden, and Eliza Tutellier have supplied the project with a continuous stream of dependable material, which was much needed and appreciated. I am also thankful to René Schön, whose command of French has helped me repeatedly with difficult material; to Denise Senn, who has always been on call for anything I might need; and furthermore to Ev Michalek, Angela Harris, and Susanne Waldburger for their general assistance.

I would like to express my special gratitude to Barbara Meier, who proficiently keeps track of all the research material as well as the library, both virtual and real; and likewise to Gale Carr, whose knowledge of the field and personal contacts with other scholars have been very important. (She also helped track down many elusive or out-of-print articles or books within the U.S.A.) I am also very grateful to her European counterpart, the imaginative Regula Suter, who has organized such things as hard-to-come-by photographs of Pythagoras' busts and who is regularly informed on what's going on in Velia. Last but not least are Mats Scholz and Stefan Schrott. They have been part of this great effort right from the start. They have dreamed the dream and held the fort, and without their wholehearted support, much of what was accomplished would not have been possible. Thank you again.

I deeply appreciate the tireless work of my editor Jennifer Morgan, who had to put up with draft after draft, change after change, and who still managed to be both tolerant and unforgiving. I would also like to thank Jean Blackburn for being so patient and accommodating in the process of giving the manuscript its final shape. In addition, I want to mention Laura Brenneman, as well as Leonard Rosenbaum for their meticulous work on the indexes.

I am much indebted to Néstor-Luis Cordero for his encouragement and advice in solving difficult issues regarding Parmenides. His unparalleled expertise, contagious enthusiasm, and deep devotion to the subject mark him as the ultimate Parmenidean in my judgment. (His new work, *By Being, It Is,* is a must-read.) It was the endless talks with Néstor which gave me confidence to go beyond what I had originally aspired. He urged me to take a stand, to aim for a fresh or original theory.

Richard McKirahan's patient but relentless line-by-line criticisms and very high standards I value immensely. His sweeping understanding of ancient philosophy, paired with his uncompromising demands, affected more than anything else the quality of my research. (Richard's translation of *Parmenides' Poem* is exemplary, and his *Philosophy Before Socrates* is also a must-read.) There simply is no better or tougher reviewer one could ask for, and I learned a lot from him.

I have always considered Walter Burkert's *Lore and Science in Ancient Pythagoreanism* as the paragon of scholarly achievement. The extant material is piecemeal, intricate, duplicitous, and above all, vast, and it is hard to understand how anyone can know so much about such a difficult subject, let alone organize it in a cogent way. Thus the submission of my manuscripts to Walter Burkert was accompanied with an understandable sense of trepidation. To my relief, he not only accepted them, but his synopsis of the entire work—not only with regard to Pythagoras but also to Parmenides—was so precise and to the point that it laid bare the very heart of what I was trying to express. I have never felt so fully understood, which added wings to my efforts.

Patricia Curd's *The Legacy of Parmenides* is a seminal work, and I believe that future Parmenidean scholars will be speaking more about some of the issues she has brought to the forefront than about those of many other interpretations. Also, her insights into how Parmenides was received by the post-Parmenidean Presocratics set me on a different course of inquiry, which proved invaluable. On a personal note, I very much appreciate her candid advice to find or to speak in my own voice, to express more boldly what I wanted to say and not to try to please everyone. It transformed decisively my approach to the subject, which to that point had been too cautious and discursive.

Furthermore, I am grateful to Mitchell Miller for his outspoken, knowledgeable, and very original views regarding both the historical Parmenides and Plato's *Parmenides,* and for the opportunities we have had to debate some of the issues. They set my interpretation of the Proem in a new direction. Likewise, I want to express my appreciation to David Yount, who, with his expertise in Plotinus, has afforded me many opportunities to explore Parmenides in context with Plato and the Neoplatonists. And I am indebted to both Debra Petersen and Stanley Lombardo for their advice regarding the Poem's translation.

I am thankful to Dott.ssa Giuliana Tocco (Soprintendenza di Salerno) and to Dott.ssa Antonella Fiammenghi (in charge of the Elea/Velia excavations) for their generosity in allowing us an unhindered examination of the archeological sites and artifacts and for their permission to photograph as much as I wanted. We (Néstor, his wife Estela, Sara and I) have also appreciated the hospitality of Dott.ssa Giovanna Greco, the invitations to the University of Naples as well as to her home, and the hours of intriguing discussions on Parmenides. I am much indebted to Dr. Verena Gassner of the University of Vienna—who accompanied us in our explorations and always put in a good word for us—for her untiring and detailed explanations, for unfettered access to many of the findings, and above all for her time and patience. And I must also thank Elio de Magistris for helping us with so many details during our visit.

A special expression of gratitude should be conveyed to Ill. Douglas Lemons, 33°, Sovereign Grand Inspector General of the Orient of California, as well as to the Supreme Council, 33°, Ancient & Accepted Scottish Rite of Freemasonry, Southern Jurisdiction, USA, Mother Council of the World, for graciously opening the doors to various research libraries, archives, museums, ritualistic collections and studies, and so forth. This helped me tremendously in retracing many elusive strands of lore that either stem from or are associable with Pythagoreanism, as well as understanding into what other esoteric doctrines these might have metamorphosed within the last centuries.

The wonderful Hopi people have a special place in my mind and heart. I have learned so much about their reverent way of life, their ceremonies, and their unique view of the world. The people of Old Oraibi, especially, should know how much Sara and I value their friendliness and hospitality. And above all, to my Hopi mother Virginia Taylor and my Hopi brother Hubert Taylor, I want to express my affection and respect. Knowing them and understanding the Hopi way have given me so many new understandings of other things, insights that for the rest of us may have been lost or obscured by time and the veneer of Western culture.

Above all, I am exceedingly grateful to my wife Sara Hermann for being an inspiring and driving force, and who, as the publisher of Parmenides Publishing, has participated in every aspect of this book. To say that my appreciation is endless would be inappropriate in a work about Parmenides; it is rather "like a perfect sphere."

Finally, I want to thank Peter Hammill again. I have mentioned his music and his words (see the beginning of the Preface) and the seeds these planted in my consciousness so long ago. But what I am really in awe of is not just that he went out on a limb in his quest, but how far he went. Whenever I thought I had lost sight of my own way, or ends became unintelligible, I fancied that there was still someone out there, that there was still an IS to be thought, or to be expressed. There is always, it seems, some vantage point thinkable, some "out there" position, from where one can speak of even such things as "universes," "being," "reality," "existence," or "mind" as if from the externalized point of view of the observer—before one is sucked back into the role of participant. Perhaps it is what we do in these rare depersonalized moments that denotes what philosophy is all about.

A Note on References, Translations, Citations, Notes, Bibliography, and Some Idiosyncrasies

Regarding the extant Presocratic material the usual Diels/Kranz (DK), numbering has been followed. When needed, secondary references have been provided, such as Wehrli's ordering (*Die Schule des Aristoteles*), or Rose's arrangement of the fragments of Aristotle. Each DK reference is generally spelled out in full, e.g., **Xenophanes, DK** 21B11. The only exception is Parmenides, whose "B" references are written in the shortened form such as fr. 8, and frs. 2–7 when referring to whole fragments, or as 7.5, 8.15–18, when a particular line or sequence of lines is discussed. References to Parmenides' "A" testimonia are reproduced in full, i.e., **Parmenides, DK** 28A12. Other forms of referencing such as "A7" or "B8" are avoided (unless they are part of a quotation from other works in order to maintain accuracy).

The translation of Parmenides' Poem is found in Chapter VI. Each line is individually numbered, again following the DK ordering. (However, an alternative if speculative rearrangement of fragments 2 through 8.1 is offered in Chapter VII, preserving nonetheless the line numbering according to DK.) The Greek text on which the translation is based is largely David Gallop's [340], cf., *Parmenides of Elea: Fragments*. In select parts the translation observes emendations that others have suggested—such as Néstor-Luis Cordero's [277] read of 6.3, cf., *Les deux chemins de Parménide*—which are indicated in the notes. Additional reproductions of the Greek text have also been consulted, notably Diels/Kranz [3]; Leonardo Tarán [569] *Parmenides*; Alexander Mourelatos [480] *The Route of Parmenides*; David Sider and Henry W. Johnstone [544] *The Fragments of Parmenides*; and Scott Austin [199] *Parmenides: Being, Bounds, and Logic*.

All translations are my own unless otherwise indicated. Additionally, and except where noted differently, passages quoted from ancient texts are from the following translations:

Aristotle: Jonathan Barnes [618] ed., *The Complete Works of Aristotle: The Revised Oxford Translation.* (2 vols. Princeton: Princeton University Press, 1991)

Diodorus Siculus: C. H. Oldfather [633] trans. (et al.) *Diodorus Siculus: The Library of History.* (Loeb Classical Library. 12 vols. Cambridge, MA: Harvard University Press, 1933–1967)

Diogenes Laertius: R. D. Hicks [634] *Diogenes Laertius: Lives of Eminent Philosophers.* (Loeb Classical Library. 2 vols. Cambridge, MA: Harvard University Press, 1925)

Iamblichus: Gillian Clark [639] *Iamblichus: On the Pythagorean Life.* (Liverpool: Liverpool University Press, 1989)

Plato: John Cooper [652] ed., *Plato: Complete Works.* (Indianapolis: Hackett Publishing, 1997)

Porphyry: Hadas Moses [660] and Morton Smith, *Heroes and Gods: Spiritual Biographies in Antiquity.* (New York: Harper & Row, 1965)

In notes, the main goal was to make citations and references to other authors as clear and discernible as possible. The last names of authors are rendered in bold type, followed by the bibliographical reference number in square brackets, and the work cited. (An author's name in a general discussion, or without a direct reference to a particular work, remains in regular type.) I have taken the unusual step of providing both a bibliographical reference number as well as the title of the work in question to spare the reader the effort of going back and forth between text and bibliography. Works which are often cited are indicated with a shortened title. However, the first time a work is mentioned in a note the full title is reproduced, together with the reference number, and the subsequent abbreviation or short form of the title.

Largely due to its size and the divergence of its subjects, the bibliography is subdivided and each relevant item is numbered in sequence. (See also the separate index prefacing the bibliography.) As is customary, more listings are enumerated than directly cited in the main body, the intent being to provide a comprehensive background of the topics discussed. Abbreviations are listed separately at the beginning of the book. Bibliographical information for certain works of reference, such as for *RE* (*Realencyclopädie*) or *OED* (*Oxford English Dictionary*), is cited only in the Abbreviations.

Parmenides' Poem is always written with a capital "P," to differentiate it from other Presocratic works, as is his Goddess with a capital "G", to differentiate her from other goddesses. Reviewers have asked me why "gods" is generally written in lowercase throughout the work, but "God" is capitalized. As in other matters, my answer is for instant recognition. The lowercase "gods" usually pertains to Homeric deities and similar divinities, immortals, etc. The capitalized "God" refers to the kind of absolute deity Xenophanes had in mind, and which in my view belongs epistemologically to an entirely different category. (As well as for other reasons, such as being unanthropomorphic, unmoving, all-seeing, eternal; yet these are secondary considerations in the context of this book. Furthermore, my approach is not without precedent, see e.g., Popper [72] 'Back to the Presocratics.') I make the same distinction for Aristotle's God.

Abbreviations

DK   Diels [3], Hermann, and Walther Kranz. *Die Fragmente der Vorsokratiker: griechisch und deutsch.* 6th ed. 3 vols., 1951. Reprint, Zurich: Weidmann, 1996.

D.L.   Diogenes Laertius. (See bibliography s.v. Diogenes Laertius, Hicks [634])

DNP   Cancik, Hubert, and Helmuth Schneider, eds. *Der neue Pauly: Enzyklopädie der Antike.* 15 vols. Stuttgart: J. B. Metzler, 1996.

DPdG   Zeller [89], Eduard. *Die Philosophie der Griechen in ihrer geschichtlichen Entwicklung.* 6 vols. Hildesheim: Georg Olms, 1990.

EPP   Minar [160], Edwin L. Jr. *Early Pythagorean Politics.* Baltimore: Waverly Press, 1942. Reprint, Ann Arbor: UMI, 2001.

FGrHist Jacoby [2], Felix. *Die Fragmente der griechischen Historiker.* Leiden: E. J. Brill, 1923.

HGP   Guthrie [43], W. K. C. *History of Greek Philosophy.* 6 vols. Cambridge: Cambridge University Press, 1962–1981.

KRS   Kirk [56], G. S., J. E. Raven, and M. Schofield. *The Presocratic Philosophers.* 2nd ed. Cambridge: Cambridge University Press, 1983.

LSJ   Liddell, Henry George, and Robert Scott. *A Greek–English Lexicon.* 9th ed. Revised by Henry Stuart Jones. Oxford: Clarendon Press, 1948, 1996.

OCD   Hornblower, Simon, and Antony Spawforth, eds. *The Oxford Classical Dictionary.* 3rd ed. Oxford: Oxford University Press, 1996.

OED   *Oxford English Dictionary* (CD-ROM, version 3.00). Oxford: Oxford University Press, 2002.

PBS   McKirahan [67], Richard, Jr. *Philosophy Before Socrates.* Indianapolis: Hackett Publishing, 1994.

PEP	Philip [163], J. A. *Pythagoras and Early Pythagoreanism.* Toronto: University of Toronto Press, 1966.
PPSI	von Fritz [122], Kurt. *Pythagorean Politics in Southern Italy.* New York: Octagon Books, 1977.
RE	Wissowa, Georg. *Paulys' Realencyclopädie der classischen Altertumswissenschaft.* Stuttgart: J. B. Metzler, 1995.
TAPA	*Transactions of the American Philological Association.*
TPP	Barnes [9], Jonathan. *The Presocratic Philosophers.* Rev. ed. New York: Routledge, 1982.

Iamblichus *VP* *De vita Pythagorica.*
Porphyry *VP*   *Vita Pythagorae.*

TO THINK LIKE GOD

Introduction

> But the first to use the term [philosophy], and to call himself a philosopher or lover of wisdom, was Pythagoras; for, said he, no man is wise, but God alone.
> —Diogenes Laertius[8]

> Parmenides' logic must have seemed to him ... a path beyond the limits of mortality." A mortal must think mortal, not immortal, thoughts," had been the common belief. And mortal thoughts never strike certainty; by common consent this was the privilege of the gods. Yet in his doctrine of Being, Parmenides found certitude and security such as no god could surpass.
> —Gregory Vlastos[9]

Gods know. They enjoy an immediate, unfettered access to truth, a truth that is certain, errorless, and complete. Mortals, on the other hand, are not capable of attaining the same; they can only express opinion, not truth. This view was held by some of the earliest pioneers of philosophy, Greek thinkers who theorized that knowledge came in two forms, divine and human. This twofold distinction was quite a novelty at the time, a shift in thinking which challenged Homer's and Hesiod's depictions of the gods as flawed or depraved beings, obsessed only with their Machiavellian ploys and their insatiable sexual appetites.

While some changes are so obvious that no one questions them, a few, perhaps the really momentous ones, pass by without notice, but, irreversibly, humanity's course has been altered. This was the case with the concept of deity in ancient Greece. Between the sixth and fifth centuries B.C., the concept underwent a subtle yet significant modification when a handful of thinkers argued for a more sublime characterization of the divine, one that was less human or anthropomorphic. It was a most revolutionary idea, and

---

8 **D.L.**, 1.12.
9 **Vlastos** [594], 'Parmenides' Theory of Knowledge,' (*TAPA* 77) 75.

its outcome surely surpassed the expectations of its originators. Who would have thought that by stripping the gods of human weaknesses or traits, qualities would be revealed in their purest form, qualities that could be examined and defined independently? Abstracted, these qualities eventually gave us our first genuinely hypothetical concepts or ideas. Liberated from having to be personified as individual deities, concepts such as Love, Strife, Being, Change, Mind, Justice, Good, and Necessity became principles, even causes that managed the universe, without requiring a pantheon or needing to be worshiped by humans. Who could have thought that by not humanizing the gods, and by not deifying their qualities, we would be left with ideas in their most fundamental form, objects of pure speculation, which would become the building blocks of theoretical science, or as it was originally known, *philosophia*? Literally meaning the "love of wisdom," philosophy is that special contrivance of human reasoning which, in its highest form, concerns itself with knowing the causes of things, and often just with knowing—that is, knowledge for its own sake.

Undoubtedly, those who are considered philosophy's earliest contributors had no idea what they would bequeath to the rest of us, much less that their introspective musings would prompt such a fundamental change in thinking and in our civilization as a whole. They all had their own problems to contend with, and whatever advances we cherish as ingenious or monumental were nothing more than the first attempts at finding generally acceptable solutions. Even Aristotle, one to two centuries later, was still too close to the originators to appreciate this subtle shift in thinking,[10] attributing the dawning of philosophy to even earlier speculators, who, in his view, had their curiosity aroused by the heavenly bodies:

> For it is owing to their wonder that men both now begin and at first began to philosophize; they wondered originally at the obvious difficulties, then advanced little by little and stated difficulties about the greater matters, e.g. about the phenomena of the moon and those of the sun and the stars, and about the genesis of the universe. And a man who is puzzled and wonders thinks himself ignorant; therefore since they philosophized in order to escape from ignorance, evidently they were pursuing science in order to know.[11]

---

10 Even though, not so subtly, Socrates had to pay the ultimate price for his novel view of deity, one of the main charges against him being impiety for introducing "new gods" not recognized by the state, **D.L.**, 2.40. (Even if these were trumped-up charges, the real reasons being political in nature, cf. **Guthrie** [43] *HGP* 3.382.)

11 **Aristotle**, *Metaphysics* 982b12.

To deem philosophy a quest for knowledge is certainly appropriate, even if we, like Aristotle, tend to include wondering about the stars or the cosmos in its original mandate. Of course, Aristotle was only trying to justify his own quite legitimate interests in the natural sciences. Thus, when he speaks of the men who "first began to philosophize," he largely has the Milesians in mind: Thales, Anaximander, and Anaximenes, natives of sixth-century B.C. Miletus, in Asia Minor. These men were the first thinkers—at least that we know of—to venture claims about the makeup of the world, and due to Aristotle's endorsement they are traditionally viewed as the earliest natural philosophers.[12] Each proposed a different prime substance for the material source of the universe: Thales chose water; Anaximander, the boundless; and Anaximenes, air.

However, Aristotle does not explain why the "escape from ignorance" suddenly became a concentrated, systematic effort just a few generations before his time, instead of remaining what it had always been: a spell of curiosity or interest, which, as a basic human impulse, is far too random and ordinary to be justified as a genuine vocation, much less a movement or a science. Arguably, people have wondered about the stars and the universe even before the dawn of recorded history, and elaborate cosmologies have been around since the heydays of Egypt or Babylon, yet none of these efforts are deemed genuinely philosophical. Why a *methodical* form of speculation began specifically in ancient Greece is a much-debated subject among experts. Some theories contend that a handful of thinkers became tired of the prevailing mythological explanations, and so attempted a more reasoned approach: one based not on faith or belief but on cogent argumentation and reflection. Thus the inventive speculations of the aforementioned Milesians, for example, are judged as a first attempt to attribute the creation of the world to a physical substance, instead of to a whim of the gods.[13]

Yet an abrupt disillusionment with mythology is too superficial an answer, especially because most, if not all, pioneers of philosophy—collectively, if prosaically, termed the Presocratics[14]—did not avoid references to

---

12 **Aristotle**, *Metaphysics* 983b20, 984a5, 1053b14. Yet even Aristotle is equivocal as to who should be credited with being the first to postulate a material cause, cf. 983b29–984a4.

13 Cf. **De Santillana** [76] *The Origins of Scientific Thought* 21–22, **Guthrie** [43] *HGP* 1.28–31, and **McKirahan** [67] *PBS* 19. For a well-balanced discussion, see **Barnes** [9] *The Presocratic Philosophers* (*TPP*) 4–5.

14 The name "Presocratics" is misleading because it implies that these philosophers lived before Socrates, when in fact many of them were his contemporaries, and some even outlived him.

gods, immortals, the soul, and other such intangibles. In fact, the fundamental change I have mentioned was first presaged in their very teachings, many of which were dedicated to such esoteric questions. What these works actually show is an increasing determination to abstract the concept of deity, paired with the rejection of Homer's and Hesiod's tales. This trend is particularly noticeable in Southern Italy, where thinkers like Pythagoras (c. 570–c. 500 B.C.), Xenophanes (c. 570–c. 478 B.C.), and Parmenides (c. 515– after 450 B.C.) exhibited a different understanding of the divine. Xenophanes, a gifted poet in his own right, attacked Homer and Hesiod because they ascribed to the Olympian gods traits that even among mortals are deemed disgraceful, such as deceitfulness, adultery and thievery.[15] That which was divine had to stand above human concerns, meaning it had to be in every conceivable way *other* than fallible—hence, it had to be all-seeing and all-knowing.[16] Thus, Xenophanes was obliged to condemn any attempt to portray God as human, whether in corporeal shape or character.[17]

But what is most noteworthy, in our context, is the linkage of this un-Homeric view of deity to the subject of *truth*, whether we call it knowledge, wisdom, or certainty. While the powerful Olympians were commonly viewed as being better informed than the most knowledgeable human, their relationship with truth was volatile; otherwise they would not have been so readily deceived by the schemes of their peers. The tales of Homer and Hesiod are full of such examples of gods plotting against gods, always jostling for power, prestige, or other advantages. Thus, the original mythological blueprint appeared to support a threefold division of truth: the least dependable kind belonging to man; the somewhat more comprehensive, but still incomplete, truth belonging to the gods; and last, the pure truth. Oddly, the latter belonged to no one at all. This design was problematic, of course, because it suggested that the absolute truth was not accessible by anyone, god or man; in other words, it was totally unknowable. However, this difficulty could perhaps be circumvented if the threefold distinction was reduced to two possibilities. This simpler solution allowed for the genuine truth to remain unchallenged in the custody of the divine, while a lesser, more duplicitous version could be allotted to mortals, who, after all, suffered from unruly passions, undependable senses, forgetfulness, and a

---

15 Xenophanes, DK 21B11.
16 Xenophanes, DK 21B23, B24, B25, B26.
17 Xenophanes, DK 21A12, B14, B15, B16.

limited life span—which made them fitting candidates for any inferior sort of truth.

The lines, therefore, needed to be clearly drawn: gods on one side, mortals on the other. All that the divine was required to relinquish was an all-too-human personification, with its many foibles and liabilities. It had to become as ideal and absolute as the truth in its charge. And if such a twofold distinction held, then Pythagoras could afford to teach that he himself was only a philosopher—in other words, a *seeker*, not an owner, of wisdom—because true wisdom belonged only to God.[18] The dual approach to wisdom allowed an improved epistemological order to take hold that had tremendous consequences—and not only for a new understanding of the gods. It eventually allowed a proper classification for all ideal or intelligible things, whether they were objects of thought, abstracts, universals, Platonic Forms, or Aristotelian First Principles.

Per this new view, for example, there could be no hierarchy among the divine, no god the master of all others.[19] (Of course, this line of reasoning had to lead eventually to monotheism, the first signs of which we can see in Xenophanes' thoughts.) Quite obviously, between all-powerful indestructible beings, the only advantages to be gained were in the realm of knowledge and truth. Thus, distinctions in rank would have introduced subjectivity to a domain that had to be absolute to be at all. In short, deity—whether it was one being or many—had to *know*, and had to know *objectively*; it was obliged to maintain a direct, uninhibited kinship with truth, in contrast to mortals, who could only express their subjective opinions. This was the new epistemological blueprint, which was particularly well-represented among the Presocratic thinkers of Southern Italy.

However, this did not mean that there was smooth sailing from that point to mainstream philosophy. The "Greatest Difficulty," as Plato later called it, still lay ahead. The first thinker to have an inkling of that difficulty was, once again, Xenophanes,[20] who authored perhaps the most pivotal

---

18 The story originated with **Heraclides Ponticus**, cf. **D.L.**, 1.12; cf. also 8.8. See motto of this chapter.

19 **Xenophanes**, DK 21A32.

20 *Mutatis mutandis*, of course, see **Plato**, *Parmenides* 133b–c, 134a–c. Yet the basic problem that **Xenophanes** addresses (DK 21B34, see fragment below) is the same, i.e., the unbridgeable gap between opinion and truth, or in Plato's case, the sensible and intelligible world. Plato develops the theme further, resulting in the "argument too strange" (134d–e), which contends—based on our inability to know the intelligible world—that, by the same token, God is deprived from knowing our sensible world.

statement at the dawn of philosophy—a statement that, as all such milestones must, introduced an apparently unsolvable dilemma. It seems that there was something quite unmanageable about a twofold distinction of knowledge or truth—at least insofar as mortal affairs were concerned—especially if one distinction had to be absolute for the other to be subjective:

> No man has seen nor will anyone know
> the truth about the gods and all the things I speak of.
> For even if a person should in fact say what is absolutely the case,
> nevertheless he himself does not know, but belief is fashioned over all things.[21]

The basic question here is *how do we know that we know*, if all things are susceptible to *opinion*—including ourselves, as well as our understanding of what we know? There are many memorable statements that can be considered critical for our comprehension of what philosophy is about, but none goes to its heart like this one. Perhaps "going for the jugular" is a more appropriate description, because, as the argument implies, even if by chance we should stumble upon truth, we have no way of knowing that we are dealing with the genuine article. Indeed, we may study the universe as much as we want and still not be entirely confident that what we *think* of it actually matches what is "out there"—particularly if we have no means of proving or confirming our contentions.

In one fell swoop, through Xenophanes' remarks, even the most acclaimed advances in the natural sciences had become undone. The Milesians, in other words, were stopped dead in their tracks. They could assert that the universe was made from water, the boundless, or air with the deepest conviction, yet in the end, all that they had to offer were unsubstantiated claims.[22] This means that even if the conclusions of modern scholarship are accurate and the first thinkers sought refuge from a traditional approach by adopting physical rather than mythological solutions, Xenophanes put them right back in the mythological box. He simply attacked the weakest link in their chain of reasoning, that is, the epistemological one:

---

21 **Xenophanes, DK** 21B34 (trans. **McKirahan** [67] *PBS* 66–67. McKirahan adds in brackets at the end of line 4, "or, in the case of all persons."

22 In spite of Aristotle's charitable categorization of the Milesians as philosophers, their claims were not more credible than those of any cultic or religious cosmology, because they offered no reasoned proof for their theories—Anaximander may be an exception—in contrast to Parmenides and most of the post-Parmenideans. The adoption of some natural substance like water or air as *prima materia* is not enough, in my opinion, to merit the title of philosopher, certainly not after Parmenides. Only those who substantiate their claims with proofs through argument and reasoning deserve such distinction.

Introduction 7

how, in fact, *did* they *know* what the universe was made of if, as mortals, they had no means of escaping their own beliefs?

The critique was brilliant. It simply showed that any gap between absolute and relative truth would have to be utterly unbridgeable—in Xenophanes' view, as unbridgeable as the one between God and man.[23] It is quite interesting that, although Xenophanes relied on what could be deemed a mythological, hence religious, contrast between divinity and mortality, he managed to presage a thoroughly scientific dilemma, one that eventually, as we shall see further on, not only undermined Pythagorean number theory, but still preoccupied the minds of prominent twentieth-century thinkers like Albert Einstein and Karl Popper.[24] And, if no one had risen up in the sixth to fifth centuries B.C. to challenge Xenophanes' troublesome remarks, it is quite conceivable that the novel field of philosophy would have been stillborn. It did not matter whether the gods enjoyed the absolute truth; so far as mortals were concerned, they themselves stood no chance of ever approaching same, much less of developing any kind of dependable science.

Once again the time had come for a novel approach. And fortunately, a different type of thinker had joined the debate, namely Parmenides of Elea (a minor Greek settlement on the western shores of Southern Italy). A renowned legislator traditionally considered to be close to Xenophanes, Parmenides must have been unsettled by the older man's words, and particularly by the effect they would have upon the reliability of discourse, not to mention the integrity of law, which, after all, was formulated and interpreted by man, not God. Even the best, most infallible piece of legislation was only as sound as the opinions of those who read or enforced it. If the sanctity of giving dependable testimony was to be preserved, some means or method needed to be developed by which one could gauge whether a person was accurately expressing a state of affairs, as opposed to a mere supposition or a statement of belief. Parmenides' approach to the problem was revolutionary; in fact, it was a stroke of pure genius. He discovered that even for mortals there was a way of determining whether they were dealing with genuine truth or only a semblance of it, a way that allowed for a certainty not inferior to that of the gods. The key was the phenomenon of *contradiction*, or to be more precise, the vital role contradiction plays in

---

23 Again, revisited by **Plato** in the *Parmenides* 133b–134c; see note 20.
24 Incompatibilities, for example, as between geometry and arithmetic, or theoretic and reality-oriented mathematical statements. See Chapter XI, "Mind and Universe: Two Realms, Two Separate Approaches."

thinking, allowing the mind to ascertain with complete confidence the veracity of a statement.

By exploiting this extremely powerful tool, Parmenides came up with surefire techniques for examining a claim or an opinion by simply testing how it was put together—he referred to opinion as a "deceptive ordering of words"[25]—and, most importantly, to what conclusions it may lead. In other words, was an explanation, in the end, *self-refuting*? For example, he could take a given statement on "something being the case"—like the kind of statement Xenophanes said a person could express without actually knowing whether it was true—and force it toward contradiction. One very effective method was to treat any belief first as if it were the bona fide truth, if only to determine what consequences would follow if it were actually so. If a self-negation ensued—or an inherent impossibility became exposed—then, obviously, what was initially assumed to be true could be discarded as false. This technique is known as Indirect Proof, and Parmenides relies almost exclusively upon such rational or argumentative devices. This is why many have called him the father of logic.

The mechanism of contradiction was so dependable that even if one knew nothing of the matter discussed, one could still immediately recognize whether a claim was sound or self-defeating. Without this propensity of the mind to fasten on inconsistencies, on assertions that are mutually exclusive, our entire jury system, for example, would collapse. In trying to resolve difficulties that cannot be judged by using one's own eyes or ears—the events in question having occurred in the past—a judge or jury has to rely on the testimony of others. Thus, the system is based solely upon a decision-making process that must be performed by ordinary mortals, not gods—indeed, by laypeople whose job it is to digest a whole host of largely contradicting accounts, including the reports of experts. Fortunately, one does not have to be an authority in a particular field to recognize when a statement is in conflict with itself.

Was it perhaps the art of dealing with questionable statements, common to any court system, that inspired the lawmaker's answer to Xenophanes' challenge? We cannot say for certain. But because of Parmenides' new way of arguing a position, the world of speculation was dramatically changed. Methods of proof and disproof became critical to any scientific approach—particularly if empirical examination was not possible and one

---

25 **Parmenides**, fr. 8.52.

had only reasoning to rely upon. This, then, signifies the true onset of philosophy as a *systematic* pursuit instead of merely wanton speculation.

And so, once and for all, the question of whether human beings were capable of certainty in thought and discourse seemed settled. I emphasize "thought and discourse" because Parmenides did not provide us with means to make sense-perception accurate or our experiences objective. Quite likely, he considered that an impossible task. Instead he chose to focus exclusively on reasoning itself and the way it composes a statement or account. However, his approach did allow the testing of the veracity of an opinion, which in turn, quite obviously, may have been derived from perception or experience. If it passed the test of contradiction—or allowed itself to be modified until it passed—it then could be confidently accepted as truth. With this innovation, the foundations of logic were set, and philosophy, as the art of managing knowledge, was off to a promising start.

However, this does not mean that Parmenides' conclusions were received with open arms. His only work known to us, a poem in hexameter verse containing the bulk of his logical methods, was generally misinterpreted as a cosmological manifesto—in the vein, for example, of the Milesian declarations. Two central parts distinguish it, an ordering that corresponds to the new understanding I have mentioned, that of subdividing knowledge into what is certain as opposed to what is questionable. The first part of the Poem is largely an outlining of his methods, together with several demonstrations of how to use them properly. Its entire import is purely rational, meant to show the makeup of a *reliable account* and the evidentiary criteria that govern it. Today, we would call this a logical exercise. The second part of the Poem is an inventory of various subjects that together represent the so-called "opinions of mortals." It is only among these topics that we find anything like a cosmological theory.

Yet many thinkers have had, at best, a love-hate relationship with Parmenides. The trouble is that when interpreted cosmologically, some of his claims seem unbelievably unworldly and provocative. He annoyed people. (At one point Aristotle even likens Parmenides and his followers to lunatics.[26]) Here was someone who could be read as denying the existence of the most elemental things, such as change, movement, plurality, coming-to-be and passing-away, and even time and space—notions which are obvious, even to a child. He seemed such an easy target; his ideas literally begged to

---

26 **Aristotle**, *On Generation and Corruption* 325a18–23.

be disproved. The funny thing was that the more one tried to prove him wrong, the more difficult this turned out to be. Fortunately, more and more philosophy was created in the process. One can compare Parmenides' effect upon the speculative world to that of the proverbial grain of sand upon the oyster. He may have been the most uncompromising thinker of all, but the beautiful pearl that ensued from his irritating approach is simply philosophy as we know it.

While the outcome of Parmenides' arguments was often rejected, most thinkers nevertheless adopted his compelling logical techniques. Whether they liked it or not, his way of arguing set a new standard that eventually no one could avoid without appearing foolish. To boot, it raised the general expectations regarding the reliability of knowledge. If knowledge was to be judged dependable, that qualifier had to be earned, thus rigorously worked for, not merely assumed or taken for granted. Explanations could be challenged, which meant that they had to be defended; their acceptance by others was not simply a foregone conclusion. In other words, learning how to compose a properly reasoned or convincing argument became just as important as learning how to guard against one. And the best way to defend a claim was to advance it together with the evidential arguments or proofs supporting it, which was most aptly demonstrated by Parmenides himself.

If the beginning of philosophy as a general movement is to be sought anywhere, then it is precisely here, in the increasingly popular rehearsing of how to attack and defend by argumentative means. This fad spread rapidly throughout the Greek world of the fifth century B.C., coincidentally, it may be noted, with the emergence of democracy, or government by argument. Schools of rhetoric seemed to sprout everywhere, and Sophists like Gorgias (c. 485–c. 380 B.C.) not only adopted techniques in the style of Parmenides and his followers, but flaunted them in front of mass audiences, giant events where people would pay exorbitant fees to witness the most dazzling rhetorical performances. Not unlike a modern rock star, Gorgias would tour from city to city, often engaging the public in a kind of "stump the orator" sport, which meant accepting impromptu questions on any given subject.

The art of persuasion had turned into a fashionable parlor game, a phenomenon that would have far-reaching consequences. While for the Sophists, absolute truth was unattainable by mortals—they preferred instead to attain persuasion by *bending* opinion,[27] rather than removing any likely inherent in-

---

27 Following here **McKirahan**'s [67] phrasing, which I find quite poignant, cf. *PBS* 378.

consistences, as Parmenides suggested—philosophy moved on. There was an increasing demand for a higher kind of knowledge, the kind that allowed *defensible* conclusions, not just oratorical bravado. To seek the sort of first-rate truth the gods had always enjoyed became neither an uncommon nor an inordinate desire.[28]

Naturally this trend included the Pythagoreans, particularly those contemporary with Parmenides or after him, who also aimed for a demonstrable truth. Before the Eleatic's Poem, there was no such thing as a nonempirical, or purely rational, attempt to prove anything, not even in mathematics. It has been pointed out that some in the mathematical professions took pride in the fact that the exactness of their calculations could be corroborated in the physical world, by measurement, for example.[29] It was only when difficulties emerged that could not be solved by strict empirical means that certain thinkers recalled the utterly rational proofs introduced by Parmenides, and mathematics took a theoretical turn.

In this sense, the majority of Pythagorean advances that can be characterized as philosophical transpired after Parmenides. Our best witness is Aristotle himself, the main source for most of what is known about their doctrine. Pythagoras, the purported founder of the movement, wrote nothing, and what he really taught his immediate disciples is unknown, as one ancient commentator remarked, so exceptional was the secrecy of his followers.[30] The first book to lay out Pythagorean doctrine was by Philolaus of Croton (c. 470–385 B.C.).[31] Written perhaps sixty to eighty years after Pythagoras' death, the work seems to have also served as Aristotle's main source on the movement. This means that Philolaus came of age after Parmenides, and most scholars agree that Philolaus was influenced by the older man. Thus, we have no idea what a pre-Parmenidean philosophy of the Pythagoreans looked like, nor even if there was such a thing. Nonetheless, in this book we shall deal with Pythagoreanism first before we take up Parmenides, due in part to the following reasons: (1) to show the evolution of the movement; (2) to provide a panoramic view of the sixth and fifth centuries in Southern Italy, with particular focus on the political agenda of the

---

28 Indeed, by Plato's time, this particular trend had evolved to the point that subsequent thinkers could justly summarize Plato's philosophical aim as "becoming like god." (E.g. **Alcinous**, *Handbook* chapter 28; and others, according to **Annas** [672]. See 'Becoming like God' 52–71, particularly 52n1, n2, n3. Cf. also **Sedley** [693] 'The Ideal of Godlikeness' 309–328.)

29 **Szabó** [772] *The Beginnings of Greek Mathematics* 216–218.

30 **Dicaearchus**, according to **Porphyry**, *VP* 19.

31 I rely here on what is, in my view, currently the most authoritative work on Philolaus, namely, **Huffman**'s [135] *Philolaus of Croton* 8.

society, its conspiracies, and the anti-Pythagorean revolts; and (3) to acquaint ourselves with some of the shortcomings of their speculative system—as much of it would affect other philosophical directions—if only to appreciate the profoundness of Parmenides' solutions to such problems. After all, the Pythagoreans were the first to strive for a unified theory of everything, including knowledge and existence. In other words, they tried to avoid the twofold distinction in knowledge and truth I have mentioned, by seeking to uncover some principle that was common to *both* epistemological domains, mind and universe—a daunting task that seemed doomed from the beginning. This may also answer why Parmenides' two differing approaches to giving an account—the evidential[32] versus the merely plausible—have passed the test of time and, modified into scientific methods, are still valid today—as attested to by our distinctions between a theoretical and an empirical approach in science. In the end, philosophy is not about resolving all incompatibilities, but about finding ways to manage them. And in this, Parmenides, was the first to succeed.

---

32 Cf. **Parmenides**, fr. 8.50, concerning the account which is said to end there, conventionally translated as "reliable" or "trustworthy." I have opted for "evidential" because, as the argumentative methods demonstrated in fr. 8 show, this account is not merely a collection of unchallenged claims or pronouncements, but a series of statements and conclusions that adhere to strict rules and logical principles, such as Like according to Like, Non-Contradiction, Excluded Third, Sufficient Reason, etc. Above all, Parmenides seeks to *prove* his assertions. Furthermore, his terminology indicates a possible link to his legislative background, which may also have served as inspiration for his methods. Thus, my use of "evidential" for this type of approach should be understood as not substantially different from the way **Heidel** [51] uses the term "forensic argumentation" for the same (cf. 'On Certain Fragments of the Pre-Socratics' 718); or **Mansfeld**'s [455] use of "forensic rhetoric." (*Die Offenbarung des Parmenides und die menschliche Welt* 105, cf. also 270–271) See also Chapter VI, "The Poem," note 464, also VII, subhead "What Is the Significance of the Proem," and note 491.

We ought to fly away from earth to heaven as quickly as we can;
and to fly away is to become like God, as far as this is possible;
and to become like Him, is to become holy, just, and wise.

—Plato, *Theaetetus* 176b

CHAPTER I

Pythagoras

THE SEARCH FOR A WAY OUT

> This is what Heraclides of Pontus tells us [Pythagoras] used to say about himself: that he had once been Aethalides and was accounted to be Hermes' son, and Hermes told him he might choose any gift he liked except immortality; so he asked to retain through life and through death a memory of his experiences. Hence in life he could recall everything, and when he died he still kept the same memories.
> —Diogenes Laertius[33]

One of the Oldest Questions: What Do All Things Have in Common?

From its earliest beginnings, philosophy has always been on the lookout for the perfect premise, that whole and wholesome rationale with enough persuasive power to end all further questions. Its function would also be that of a reliable standard or criterion against which everything else is measurable, and which, no matter what, remains universally valid. To be generally acceptable, the perfect premise must be both stable and pliable enough to facilitate the adjustment, or indeed the *calibration*, of reasoning and discourse, so that we may think and speak of the same thing, and know that we did. Finally, the most perfect premise has to be able to be used by anyone to explain anything.

The Pythagoreans may have been the first to seek such dependable devices to substantiate their explanations. This is without a doubt why they turned to arithmetic and geometry, which, when compared to other studies, have a uniquely persuasive effect upon the mind. There is not much to argue about the fact that 2 + 2 is 4, or that 3, 5, 7, and 9 are odd numbers. In some ways, the study of number is a study of both the rules for thinking

---

33 D.L., 8.4–5.

and the laws that govern the universe. For the Pythagoreans—who dreamed of a unified theory—the two were one and the same. They thought that the relationships between *numbers* were equivalent to the relationships between *things*; thus to understand one is to understand the other. Furthermore, because these relations were considered most fundamental and applicable to all things, they were deemed invariable, inasmuch as the rules that organize mathematics are applicable to all numbers while being utterly consistent. Accordingly, the study of number was equally the study of *order* and *cosmos*—concepts that for the Pythagoreans were interchangeable, for they used the word "cosmos" for a "set of ordered things"—such as a universe, for example.[34]

What provided stability to the numerical order was the nature of its most fundamental constituent, the *unit*. By being the base for everything, it was the Pythagorean version of the perfect premise. Accordingly, their doctrines centered around the concept of Unit, One, or Monad, from which not only the number series proceeded, but in effect, the very nature of things—as long as these were expressible in numerical relationships. In fact, according to Aristotle, certain Pythagoreans believed that things either *were* numbers, or were *made* of numbers.[35] In this sense, the unit, as the facilitator of order, was a very pliable concept, able to be the base or fountainhead but also the building block or constituent in any conceivable combination. Best of all, it was that single factor that was common to all; that made all things *alike*.

Even if broken down, the "principle of unit" was not lost, because, as mathematics showed, the ensuing fractions were also odd or even—thus, bona fide numbers. And when they were put together again, the result was once more a perfect unit—not more, nor less, nor something else. In the same way, if a thing was disassembled, its parts kept the unitary nature by being units themselves, and when reassembled they transferred that nature right back to the whole. The unit, then, stood justifiably at the center of things, because everything could be added up to it, or subtracted from it, or returned to it. Thus it fulfilled quite nicely one of the essentials for a perfect premise: anyone could use it for practically anything. In fact, even today, whether or not an explanation works depends largely on the proper formulation of what kind of unit or units one is talking about. In short, things are expressible as units, interact as units, can be broken down into constituent

---

[34] D.L., 8.48.
[35] **Aristotle**, *Metaphysics* 986a20, 987a20, 1083b11.

units, and can be rebuilt again into units. Here, for all intents and purposes, was a solid, incorruptible base or standard by which to calibrate all reasoning—the most perfect of premises, or so the Pythagoreans thought. (Eventually they were to find out that the unit could not deliver everything they would demand of it, but we will examine these difficulties later.)

If the idea of the unit—with all its ramifications—was Pythagoras' personal contribution to philosophy, then it was truly a worthy achievement, positively superior to the theorem that bears his name or any theory on music he may have introduced. Unfortunately, we cannot tie the sage himself to its conception. The best we can do is associate it with a caste of "scientific" Pythagoreans whom some have called the *Mathematikoi*—meaning "those who study" or "the learned ones"—who came to prominence a considerable time after his death.[36] It is these thinkers who developed a respectable number theory and whose philosophical ideas had a momentous influence on Plato and his followers. In truth, we cannot credit the founder of the Pythagorean movement with any of its philosophical advances, unless we consider the transmigration of the soul, immortality, musical harmony, magic, vegetarianism, purification rites, and initiations to be proper philosophical pursuits. If anything, it is only these rather esoteric interests that can be traced to the Great Sage.

The Seeker of Wisdom

One of the most mysterious figures in antiquity, Pythagoras was originally a native of the island of Samos in the Aegean Sea, only a stone's throw from Asia Minor or modern Turkey today. While there are no exact dates available, most levelheaded estimates put his birth at c. 570 B.C. and his death at c. 500 B.C. He is known to have emigrated to the Greek colony of Croton, in Southern Italy, sometime after 530 B.C., and there he founded a movement that was both religious and political, with some of its tenets having a significant influence on subsequent thinkers. We have no firsthand accounts regarding his character or life, and the only contemporary voices to speak of him are rather contemptuous, even describing him as a charlatan.[37]

Without a doubt, Pythagoras aimed for the viewpoint of the divine, and the opinions he expressed were taken by his followers as sacred revelations.

---

36 **Porphyry,** *VP* 37; **Iamblichus,** *VP* 81. See also Chapter II, subhead "Those Who Listen and Those Who Learn," and notes 234, 269, 270.

37 Viz. **Xenophanes, DK** 21B7; and **Heraclitus, DK** 22B40, B129.

To find an acceptable justification for their master's exemplary insight—and lacking the means by which to emulate it—his supporters sought refuge in the only explanation they could think of, namely that he was of divine origin. In other words, without some technique by which to learn to think like God, the next best thing was to descend from God. And so the tales abound that characterize Pythagoras as either the son of a god, or the incarnation of a god, or even as a third kind of being apart from mortals and gods.[38] Naturally, this makes it very difficult to accurately ascertain what his teachings were, because his admirers tended to attribute to him every great or interesting idea they had ever heard of. This was an odd but widespread practice, and we find not only Plato's doctrines being ascribed to Pythagoras, but also accusations that he and Aristotle had stolen them in the first place.[39] This trend continued on and off for some 800 years and included the Neoplatonists in the third century A.D., who are largely to be credited—or blamed—for the great reputation the Samian enjoys even today.

What, then, can be said about Pythagoras' very own teachings that is conclusive? Very little, I'm afraid. In truth, we know hardly anything that is more than rumor or hearsay. Aside from the damage done by the romanticized embellishments of a much later date, there are a number of insurmountable difficulties that stem perhaps from the original makeup of his society, two of which I have already mentioned: the proverbial secrecy everyone observed, and that he never wrote anything down—at least nothing that escaped his inner circle.[40] To make matters worse, many of Pythagoras' followers attributed their own contributions to their leader, a custom that was still practiced long after he was gone,[41] and one which leaves us with no trustworthy testimony that can be linked to him at all, nor an accurate assessment of the state or achievements of the society itself during his lifetime. Accordingly, when we speak of the Samian's beliefs, we must keep in mind that these are most likely the inventions of later Pythagoreans or their sympathizers.

---

38   For being the son of a god, i.e., Hermes; see motto of this chapter, **D.L.**, 8.4–5. On being counted among the gods, as an Olympian, or as the Hyperborean Apollo, see **Iamblichus**, *VP* 30 (also **Aristotle**, fr. 191 R on the latter). On the third type of being besides gods and mortals, see **Aristotle**, fr. 192 R, **Iamblichus**, *VP* 31.

39   See **Aristoxenus**, fr. 67 (**Wehrli** [626] *Die Schule des Aristoteles*) = **D.L.**, 3.37 and fr. 68 (Wehrli), **Porphyry**, *VP* 53.

40   See **Burkert** [100] *Lore and Science in Ancient Pythagoreanism* 218–220; **Kirk, Raven, Schofield** [56] *The Presocratic Philosophers* (**KRS**) 216; **Barnes** [9] *TPP* 100, 604n2. For **D. L.**'s questionable listing of works attributed to Pythagoras, see **D.L.**, 8.6–8.

41   See **Cornford** [21] on all inventions being inspired by Pythagoras: *From Religion to Philosophy* 203; also **Guthrie** [43] *HGP* 1.149, 155.

The Seeker of Wisdom

With this disclaimer out of the way, there are a few claims we can make. For example, there is no reason to doubt that the subject of *metempsychosis*, or the transmigration of the soul, was central to his teachings.[42] Yet so far as we can gather, this does not suggest that the Pythagoreans practiced some kind of introspective "soul-searching," much less the type of past-life recollection "therapies" popular today with the New Age enthusiast. Aside from a few anecdotes regarding the master's own incarnations, there is no evidence that his followers dwelled upon the past. In fact, the movement seemed much more preoccupied with the future fate of the soul than with its previous exploits. The main concern for a Pythagorean was the attainment of a hopefully joyful afterlife.[43] Naturally, the key to the future can only be forged in the present. Thus, *to live rightly* was very important to the follower of this inherently optimistic doctrine—optimistic, I say, insofar as one's existence beyond this world was concerned. Accordingly, the life of the common Pythagorean was governed by strict rules and routines that covered a wide range of issues, everything from dietary restrictions to purification rites to religious taboos to the observance of decorous behavior, not to mention a host of magical practices.[44]

Pythagoras himself, apparently, was the very model for the godly life he advocated. Depicted as a tall, imposing figure dressed in faultless white, he had a dignified, even solemn demeanor. It is said that he avoided all inappropriate conduct, such as overeating, being drunk, jesting, or even laughing.[45] "Nothing in excess" might very well have been his motto, a trait

---

42 E.g., **Iamblichus**, *VP* 134: "[Pythagoras] knew his own soul and from where it had come to his body, and his previous lives, and gave clear evidence of this."

43 I have called this section "The Search for a Way Out" instead of "A Search for Immortality" because **McKirahan** [67] (*PBS* 114) has rightfully pointed out that the older Pythagoreans were so convinced of their immortality that it would not have occurred to them to seek it. Why seek what you already have? Instead, as McKirahan contends, they sought ways to *use* their immortality; that is, by leading the best of lives, one could use this current sojourn on Earth to secure one's eventual divinization. **Guthrie** [43] concludes: "Philosophy for Pythagoras and his followers had to be first and foremost the basis for a way of life: more than that, for a way of eternal salvation." (*HGP* 1.182) However, **Burkert** [100] argues that among the later scholarly Pythagoreans (i.e., *mathematikoi*), "there is not a trace of the idea of science as *an escape from the world*." (*Lore* 212; emphasis added). In fact, as Burkert continues, "the idea of purification through science was apparently not ascribed to Pythagoras before the time of Iamblichus." Nonetheless, if we remind ourselves of the teachings of Empedocles, which owe to Pythagoreanism as much as they owe to Parmenides, there is enough evidence that an escapist theory was widespread long before Iamblichus. In fact, it must have been made public not long after Pythagoras' death, as the dates of Empedocles' life confirm: c. 492–432 B.C.

44 **D.L.**, 8.34–36; 2:349–351; **Aristotle**, frs. 194–197; **Porphyry**, *VP* 42; **Iamblichus**, *VP* 82, 85, 86.

45 **D.L.**, 8.20.

he shared with other Greek thinkers.[46] Allegedly, he inspired his disciples to hesitate a moment at the door whenever they returned home to ask themselves the following: "Where did I trespass? What have I achieved? What duties did I leave unfulfilled?"[47]

We can say that by minding the teachings of his school, a Pythagorean was put in charge of his own soul. He alone was responsible for its well-being and care. Life and soul were essentially two different things, and only the soul, due to its exalted origin, was deemed immortal, because, as we are told: "That from which it is detached is immortal."[48] Nonetheless, the soul could be contaminated, largely because of the corrupting effect that corporal confinement causes. As a result, a host of impurities bind it to the cyclical returns known as the wheel of rebirth, and only the best of lives—that of a "lover of wisdom"—allows it to escape this fate, so that it may rejoin its divine origin.

This, in essence, seems to be what philosophy—if we can call it that—meant to the early Pythagoreans. Those who were wise enough to understand its calling made use of the opportunities offered by their earthly sojourn to purify the soul of all its ills and imperfections. These then, were the "philosophers," and to them only belonged an afterlife of their own choosing. To attain this miraculous state the followers of Pythagoras dedicated themselves to a life of study, which blended a wide variety of interests, most of which we would call esoteric or occult. What is extraordinary is how well-coordinated this effort appears, no less because it represents the first known attempt of a mass movement striving to educate its members in an organized fashion. On the other hand, we should keep in mind that they never developed beyond being a cult; the religious subtext of their teaching as well as the makeup of their organization suggests this. Of course, I am not the first researcher to point this out.[49] In fact, the Pythagoreans fit the

---

46 D.L., 8.9: "[Pythagoras] discountenances all excess, saying that no one should go beyond due proportion either in drinking or in eating." (Loeb 2.329)
47 D.L., 8.22.
48 D.L., 8.27.
49 Scholars have debated the issue of Pythagoras' role as a cultic leader versus educator or politician. I believe Pythagoras was all of these, including being the founder of a conspiracy that aimed to take over governments by converting public servants to his society (cf. **Minar** [160] *Early Pythagorean Politics in Practice and Theory* [EPP] 27). The least evidence available is of him as a philosopher. This characterization, as understood from Plato onwards, is awarded *postmortem* to the Samian sage. For a concise discussion of Pythagoras as protophilosopher vs. leader of a cult, see **Barnes** [9] *TPP* 101–102. For a neutral analysis, see **Guthrie** [43] *HGP* 1. For a critical review of him as a philosopher, see **Reinhardt** [520] *Parmenides und die Geschichte der griechischen Philosophie* 231–241. On being more akin to a shaman, see **Burkert** [100] *Lore* 120–165, 285, 357. (For dissenting views, which defend Pythagoras as a philosopher, see **van der**

Separating Pythagoreanism into Early, Middle, and Late Periods

classic definition of "escapist" belief if there ever was one,[50] not only trying to free themselves from the bonds of their earthly exile, but renouncing anything that might become an impediment to their quest. To this end, they were obsessed with avoiding luxury or pleasure at all costs, believing that such pursuits would chain a person more solidly to a worldly existence. And not only did these have to be shunned, but as we shall see further on, hardship and difficulty were to be actively sought, because as one Pythagorean saying implied, if we were sentenced to this world to be punished, any avoidance of punishment only prolonged our stay.[51]

Separating Pythagoreanism into Early, Middle, and Late Periods

The above synopsis cannot do justice to all of Pythagoreanism; for example, there are indications that later adherents may have had difficulties with the notion of an immortal soul.[52] Thus, if we want to gain a more accurate view of the movement as a whole, we must distinguish different stages in its development. There is the early stage, which begins after 530 B.C. with Pythagoras' arrival in Croton and ends with his death some thirty years later. That later date, around 500 B.C., also coincides with the onset of the first popular revolt against the Pythagoreans, which forced many members to flee the colony and seek refuge in other cities. The middle phase begins with the return of the exiled Pythagoreans not only to Croton but also to

---

Waerden [183] *Pythagoreer*, and **de Vogel** [180] *Pythagoras and Early Pythagoreanism*, who considers Pythagoras an "enlightened educator of the masses" (64–65, 159–175, particularly 245–246 against Burkert). For Pythagoras as political leader, see **von Fritz** [122] *Pythagorean Politics in Southern Italy (PPSI)*, and **Minar** [160] *EPP*. For a read that attempts to reconcile these various notions, see **Kahn** [146] 'Pythagorean Philosophy Before Plato,' and [147] *Pythagoras*.

50   I may be in disagreement with Burkert regarding this point; see note 43 above. However, I would not call Pythagorean speculation "science," not before Archytas, and definitely not before Hippasus, if what is said of his contributions is accurate.

51   **Iamblichus**, *VP* 85; see Chapter II, subhead "The Pythagorean Agenda."

52   I am alluding to the discrepancy between accepting the soul as a *harmonia* or attunement on one hand, and its immortality as an incomposite on the other; see **Plato**'s dramatization (*Phaedo* 88d; see also the arguments in 86a–d) of Echecrates of Phlius' doubts (he was purportedly one of the Last Pythagoreans; see **Aristoxenus**, fr. 19, [Wehrli], D.L., 8.46; **Iamblichus**, *VP* 251). For an interesting discussion of the subject, see **Guthrie** [43] *HGP* 1.309–319. Further food for thought is provided by Aristoxenus, who is affiliated with the Last Pythagoreans (**de Vogel** [180] *Pythagoras* 11, labels him one of them, i.e., a "mathematician," as in *Mathematikoi*). **Burnet** [14] *Early Greek Philosophy* 277, points out that Xenophilus was his teacher; while for **Minar** [160] he is "a reliable representative of the Pythagorean tradition" (*EPP* 98). Aristoxenus referred to the soul as a "harmony," thus discrediting its immortality and perhaps even denying its existence. (**Cicero** [629] our source, attests to both possibilities; see *Tusculan Disputations* 1.10.19 and 1.22.51, respectively, **Aristoxenus**, frs. 118, 120a; **Wehrli** [626] *Schule* II, cf. also 84–85.)

political power, and it lasted approximately forty to fifty years, only to end abruptly with a second, much larger revolt. The final phase covers the prolonged exodus of the surviving Pythagoreans after 450 B.C. and concludes with the gradual disappearance of the remnants of the society, including the demise of the so-called Last Pythagoreans, after 365 B.C.[53]

In regard to the first phase of its development, Pythagoreanism may undoubtedly be classified as a cult, albeit one with pronounced political aspirations. By the end of this early stage, it operated as a genuine political party with enough clout to exert actual control upon the government of Croton, a large colony of a few hundred thousand inhabitants. The middle phase—after the overthrow of the Pythagorean faction—was not only characterized by its return to power, but also by the expansion of its political influence over other cities throughout Southern Italy, creating what may be considered a veritable empire. Thus, by mid-century, a number of colonies seem to have been governed by the society's secretive initiates. In some ways, this was the golden age of Pythagoreanism,[54] marked above all by their political successes, and yet there is virtually no evidence of any philosophical accomplishments or even pursuits.[55] Whether they still operated as a cult or only as a political association, we do not know. Perhaps it was a mix of both, if only to retain control of their membership through the bonds of initiation. In any case, after the second revolt, Pythagoreanism was utterly eliminated as a political force, marking the beginning of the third phase. Among the survivors there were a few who seemed more interested in the speculative side of Pythagoreanism than in usurping governments, and for the first time, we have some indications of a genuine Pythagorean philosophy. Thinkers like Philolaus of Croton or Archytas of Tarentum (fl. 400–350 B.C.) display an impressive command of the speculative crafts and may rightfully be considered bona fide philosophers. (There will be more on Pythagorean history and tradition in subsequent chapters.)

Thus, regarding the question of whether Pythagoreanism was a cult, order, fraternal organization, political party, or philosophical school, my view

---

53 Chronology based roughly on **Jacoby**'s [617] reconstruction of **Apollodorus** (*Apollodor's Chronik* 215–227, particularly 218). See also **von Fritz**'s [122] time line including second revolt and exodus, *PPSI* 92. On the "Last Pythagoreans," the date recorded is 366/365 B.C., according to **Diodorus**, 15.76.4. For further references, see the Appendix section titled "The Info to Certainty Sequence, Part 1."

54 I agree here with **Minar**'s [160] assessment based on Aristoxenus' report (*EPP* 75).

55 The only exception may be Hippasus of Metapontum, yet his achievements are a matter of dispute. See subheads "The Revolts Against the Pythagorean Political Elite" and

is that at some time or another it was all of these[56] (with the exception of a fraternity, in the strict sense of the word, as it seems that women were allowed to participate[57]). Therefore, in this work, I will use such terms as "order" or "cult" when I allude to the early phase, and "political party" or "secret society" for the ruling faction that was the focus of the revolts. A characterization as a "philosophical school" is only warranted for the activities or doctrines attributed to the later or Last Pythagoreans, the likes of Philolaus, as well as those mentioned by Aristotle, which in all likelihood were one and the same group.

Returning to the doctrinal differences between early and late Pythagoreanism, many of the original preoccupations may rightfully be judged arcane or even occult. However, we should not think of all followers as navel-gazing mystics. Eventually, some of the best thinkers found their way to the movement, which also attracted powerful politicians, administrators, and lawgivers. In time, this loose group that we rightly or wrongly call Pythagoreans—even Aristotle seems occasionally unsure[58]—became associated with numerous scientific achievements. For example, in the fifth century B.C., we can see how mathematics and geometry are increasingly transformed into genuine sciences of the abstract, a development that is commonly attributed to the influence of the society. The difficulties with identi-

---

"Those Who Listen and Those Who Learn" in this chapter, as well as Chapter X, subhead "To Drown in a Sea of Nonidentity."

56 **Philip** [163] doubts that Pythagoreanism was set up as a "quasi-monastic order governed by a rule imposed by its founder." (*Pythagoras and Early Pythagoreanism* [PEP] 147) Philip considers characterizations such as "brotherhood" or "sect" to be products of Iamblichus' imagination (135), and the notion of a religious-political association an invention of Timaeus (143–145). Yet Philip compares Pythagoras to other thinkers, "the cast of whose thought was religious" (175), and counts Pythagoreanism among religious movements, albeit one that became a philosophy (177). (For the latter, however, he cites no proof that Pythagoras had anything to do with this development.) Furthermore, Philip concedes, as above, that they were a "political association," also calling them a "loosely organized political *hetaireia*" (club, association) (147). My point: Why is it wrong to call such a religious/political movement a cult or order, particularly when it is so utterly dedicated to its visionary founder that all doctrines and every advancement are attributed to him, and when the organization complies to stringent rules simply *because* they were issued by this one authority, who, to boot, was considered divine? All this surely cannot be the invention of Timaeus and Iamblichus.

57 It is possible that women belonged only to the branch of listeners—called *Akousmatikoi*—that frequented the discourses but were not part of the scholarly insiders who became the *Mathematikoi*. (See **Iamblichus**, *VP* 30.) It is unknown whether the list of the most illustrious Pythagorean women (267) contains female *Mathematikoi*. But the list's origins are dubious; for example, the inclusion of the lawmakers Zaleucus and Charondas suggests that it relied—at least partially—upon forgeries.

58 E.g., **Aristotle**, *Metaphysics* 985b23, 989b30, regarding "those called Pythagoreans."

fying the genuine accomplishments of this later group are the same as those regarding its original founder: too many successes have been accredited to them by their enthusiastic fans centuries after their demise, each trying to outdo the other in their starry-eyed glorifications.[59] But there is no reason to doubt that due to their fascination with number, some of the later Pythagoreans can be counted among the first thinkers to experiment with *proof* and *demonstration*, even if such practice was confined to the mathematical arts. Thus, all things considered, it seems reasonable to claim that a handful of third-phase Pythagoreans may have made some worthy contributions to the burgeoning field of philosophy; at least, their views were to have a profound effect upon Plato and his teachings.

Yet the question remains: was what the great Pythagoras himself practiced—whatever it may have been—already qualified to be called philosophy? In other words, do any of the subjects usually identified with his brand of early Pythagoreanism, such as the transmigration of the soul, the afterlife, asceticism, supernatural abilities, magic, astrology, numerology, and so forth, have merit as philosophical pursuits?

Where am I going with all of this? Am I trying to prove that there is a general misunderstanding of what philosophy is about? My point is quite simple, but it can make all the difference: Philosophy is about *reasoned proof*. Yet whatever can be attributed to early Pythagorean speculation only amounts to *contention*, not proof. While it is undeniable that the above-mentioned subjects have something intriguing about them, the conclusions they offer can only be described as opinions, beliefs, allegations, claims, or conjectures. There are many more things we can call such speculations, but we cannot call them a *reliable account*. Thus, the words "test," "evidence," "verification," and "certainty" were alien to early Pythagoreanism, nor in fact were they required if, as a movement, it was mainly religious or even political. Yet genuine philosophical inquiry cannot accept any approach that in the end is less than a reasoned approach—in other words, a *demonstration* or *proving by thinking*. There is no evidence that this most critical contribution to philosophy was supplied by Pythagoras or his followers. To better understand the distinction, the following section is an attempt to explain—in a Pythagorean context—how proof by thinking is different from proof by other means.

---

59 As **Philip** [163] puts it, "The Pythagorean tradition annexed for itself all scientific discoveries of a mathematical character, and systematically attributed them to their founder, obscuring both the time and the nature of the discoveries." (*PEP* 125)

THE SEARCH FOR PROOF

> [Pythagoras] himself used to say that he remembered being, in Trojan times, Euphorbus, Panthus' son, who was killed by Menelaus. They say that once when he was staying at Argos, he saw a shield from the spoils of Troy nailed up, and burst into tears. When the Argives asked him the reason for his emotion, he said that he himself had borne that shield at Troy when he was Euphorbus. They did not believe him and judged him to be mad, but he said he would provide a true sign that it was indeed the case: on the inside of the shield there had been inscribed in archaic lettering EUPHORBUS. Because of the extraordinary nature of his claim, they all urged that the shield be taken down—and it turned out that on the inside the inscription was found.
> —Diodorus[60]

Euphorbus' Shield

Diodorus' tale of the shield of Euphorbus provides us with a splendid example of the kind of lore required to turn Pythagoras into a man of wonder. Once again we are witnessing a great sage being challenged by a horde of doubting Thomases. Naturally, he shames these unwitting louts by an act of unparalleled bravura, yet without abandoning the graciousness and modesty of those who truly know. Pythagoras does not boast, he merely *demonstrates* the truth. He did not provoke the situation, nor the criticisms of the crowd; he merely revealed a strong if emotional reaction to what must have been a very personal and difficult experience. Obviously, one is not often accorded the chance to recall one's own death. Thus Pythagoras does not appear angered by the accusations of the mob, harboring instead only that special compassion the wise man reserves for the truly ignorant.

Regrettably, no one really knows if this tale is genuinely Pythagorean, much less if it originates with the master himself. In all likelihood it was created after his death, as scholars contend, perhaps to bolster the credibility of the society and its beliefs.[61] But even if the account is absolutely true, we must nonetheless ask: what is its place in philosophy? Admittedly, it is a demonstration of challenge and proof, but is it fit to be called a *philosophi-*

---

60 **Diodorus**, 10.5.1–3 (trans. **Barnes** [8] *Early Greek Philosophy* 87).
61 **Barnes** [9] *TPP* 110. Iamblichus and Porphyry seek to omit lore that is related to the shield "as being of very popular nature," that is, a myth. See **Iamblichus**, *VP* 63 and **Porphyry**, *VP* 27.

cal approach? If it shows anything, then it is only that philosophy is not about *thinking* but about turning things around with one's hands so we can take a good look at their backsides. This may sound facetious, but the "method" used by Pythagoras in this story does not teach us anything about the transmigration of the soul, much less about how to remember such transmigrations. At best, it teaches us that it is really fortunate to have a generous god—like Hermes—as one's father. What, then, must a common mortal do if he seeks to learn of a previous existence—turn old things around, hoping to find inscriptions that appear somehow familiar? In a more serious vein, is it unjustified to ask by what means can the average person ascertain the truth? (And by "average," I mean not a deity or a descendant of one.) For that matter, what is truth?

Truth is commonly defined as "agreement with reality," "conformity with fact," or the "accurate representation of something." With respect to philosophy, it is often quite useful to regard "what is true" simply as "what is the case." For example, an accurate representation of "what is the case" is called a *reliable* account by Parmenides. For an account to be truly reliable it cannot aim for the tentative or provisional, and thus reflect the mere possibility that something is the case. Nor can truth be *relative* or *conditional*, meaning dependent upon a situation or a person. In other words, no one can have a monopoly upon truth, nor even the benefit of some personal shortcut to it.[62] In this sense, Parmenides introduces a truly bold idea, namely, that for God and man the *reliable* account is one and the same, *if* both use reason.

In any case, for us as humans, it is very important to realize as early as possible in our development what the concept of truth means—not only because the ability to determine "what is the case" is beneficial to our survival, but also because we begin to understand that truth is *unambiguous* and *unvarying*. Thus, for us, "What is the case?" takes on the meaning, "What can we rely upon?" Curiously, this lesson also acquaints us with concepts that are actually foreign to this endlessly *changing* and therefore

---

[62] As stated by **Heraclitus** of Ephesus, there are no *private* accounts of truth. See **DK** 22B2: "For this reason it is necessary to follow what is common. But although the *logos* is common, most people live as if they had their own private understanding." (Trans. **McKirahan** [67] *PBS* 116). This is why it is inappropriate to speak of a person's "personal philosophy." See also **DK** 22B114 on those who speak with understanding having to rely on what is common to all. Or as former U.S. Senator Patrick **Moynahan** used to say: "We are all entitled to our own opinions, we are not entitled to our own facts."

unpredictable medium we call universe[63]; concepts such as justice, love, trust, and loyalty seem to refer to a different, far more reliable place. We are dealing here with what seems to be an irreconcilable gap: the arbitrariness of the world versus our need for dependable conditions. Yet somehow this gap must be bridged, and whatever we rely upon to bridge this gap must *earn* our trust; the truth will not just present itself *as is* or *prima facie*. It must be developed in some way or distilled. This, as we shall see, is where Parmenides' idea of a *methodical* approach to truth and knowledge comes in; with it, step by step, the gap is indeed overcome.

Relying on Reasoning

If our benchmark is *reliability*, then every method must be *as* reliable as the object it pursues. This also implies that the same method must achieve the same result *time after time*. And when the method is taught to others, and they follow it, then they also have to arrive at that very same result. Nor should the fact that a method is for *thinking* make it less reliable or call for exceptions. Accordingly, "to prove something by thought alone" means precisely this and not something else—namely, that a truth or a fact was tested and proved only by thinking, without having to rely upon other means for validation or support. This, in essence, must be what philosophy is about, and to provide this option is why it came to be. In this context the story of Euphorbus' shield clearly demonstrates that Pythagoras' way of "providing a true sign" cannot be deemed a philosophical method.

I suppose that some might object to such a narrow definition of philosophy, but allow me to submit the following question: if philosophy is not about "proof alone by thinking," what, then, is its main objective? It is difficult to justify philosophy's existence, in part because many of the subjects commonly associated with it can be successfully addressed by other fields of inquiry—including physics, biology, mathematics, astronomy, theology, religion, medicine, sociology, law, and the arts. Long before philosophy's arrival, many of these interests were driven by their own necessities, meaning they had to develop their own validation procedures, while others, like

---

63 In this book, I usually avoid the definite article "the" before "universe" when I speak of it as a medium such as "air" or "water." Philosophically, it is often more conducive to call it an environment, even an intermediate agency or conduit, which allows the conveyance not only of force but also of ideas. In short, it is a facilitating environment whose defining function is to allow communion, even among contraries.

religion, are usually assumed exempt from proof. In short, none of these matters needed philosophy in order to become fields of study in their own right. As a matter of fact, it had to be the other way around: it was philosophy that required such interests to preexist if it was to evolve.

My suggestion is that the link between philosophy and all the other fields of study can only be explained if philosophy was able to provide certain benefits or services that were otherwise hard to come by or simply unavailable. If other disciplines produced their own methods of verification, then the scope of each method was determined largely by the properties of their particular objects of inquiry. For example, if I need to measure a piece of wood to make a shelf, I obviously need a means of measurement that is appropriate. Naturally, the means cannot be too large or too small, or generally incompatible with the properties of my object. It would be silly to try to measure the length of wood with a thermometer. Furthermore, whatever system or instrument I choose must not only be able to perform the task, but must do it reliably and repeatedly. In my case, this means that whenever I measure the piece of wood using the same means I must obtain the same results. It is up to me to find such a method, one that is agreeable with the task and the kind of object I am inquiring about.

When dealing with physical objects of inquiry, the search for the right method and its application may be a fairly straightforward task. By observation and a process of trial and error called experimentation, we can adjust the means to suit both the task and the object we are inquiring about. In philosophy, we call this type of inquiry *empirical*—that is, conducted by means of observation and experimentation. The word originates from the Greek *empeiria*, which means "experience." *Empeiria* is itself derived from the root word *peira*, which signifies trial, attempt, test, or experiment. So it's no surprise that we also find *peira* in the word *experience* itself, as well as in *experiment*.

The *empirical* approach is most appropriate for tangible things that can be perceptively observed and experimented upon. Yet how may we develop a method of observation and proving if the object we are curious about is not at all physical, but only an object of thought? I cannot *see*, much less experiment with, other people's objects of thought, and contemplating my own with the mind's eye is not the same as seeing or feeling them.

Must we not develop other methods of measurement or discernment whenever we are dealing with nontangible, intelligible things—methods that are *agreeable* to them? Is the same not also true for the means by which we calibrate our methods? Yet how can we *calibrate thinking* so that its results or conclusions are just as reliable as those of any outward instrument we might construe, if not even more so? In fact, can reasoning be taught not to err? Does it have the capacity to arrive at the right decision time after time? In my view it is right here, with the very object of these questions, that the jurisdiction *and* justification of philosophy begins. Its specialty is to address itself to all issues that may fall under the category of "proof by thinking." I see no other possibility than to recognize that *this* is philosophy's true *raison d'être*.

A Science for the Intangible, Abstract

Returning to the question of Pythagoras' former existence as Euphorbus, we realize that the shield does not prove that he was a particular warrior previously, nor that he was at the battle of Troy, but only that when he came face to face with it in the temple, he somehow knew (or guessed) that the name "Euphorbus" was inscribed on the side that was hidden from view. That is the only demonstrable indication that we actually have, namely, that Pythagoras possessed a bit of information that was neither shared by others nor visible to anyone else.[64] As for his having been Euphorbus, no empirical approach will establish this until the existence of the soul itself—the actual object of inquiry in this case—is confirmed by empirical means, that is, observed and tested. Furthermore, even if we could step into a time machine and travel back to Troy to meet Euphorbus, we would have no way of determining that his individual soul would one day become Pythagoras. We could actually jump back and forth, from one to the other, comparing their behavior, their likes and dislikes, and so on, and still not know conclusively that we are dealing with the very same soul, or even that there *is* such a soul. Therefore, to deal with such an intangible subject as the soul—which is clearly not accessible by ordinary means—a different approach is needed if it is to be *accounted* for: a method or discipline perhaps not unlike mathematics, as that field, too, focuses on intangibles. Thus, we would need a mathematics not for numbers but for abstract ideas—a mathematics for the soul.

---

64 In want of empirical proof for claims that do not belong in philosophy but to religion, one had to settle upon miracles as substitutes for proof. As **Burkert** [100] explains: "If the historical Pythagoras taught metempsychosis, this same historical Pythagoras must have claimed superhuman wisdom, he had to use his own life as an example and find himself in the Trojan War. And if he wanted to make this credible, he had to—perform miracles." *(Lore* 147)

This, then, was philosophy, and to pose and answer these special questions became its burden: to test those things that were not suitable objects of inquiry for our eyes and ears.[65] That sooner or later some Pythagoreans sought to subscribe to this idea is without question; however, there is no evidence that Pythagoras himself saw it this way.

Yet what about him as a historical figure? Was there really such a person, and if there was, how accessible is he for us? If he was not really a philosopher, why did his society exert such a mesmerizing effect upon other thinkers, many of whom were genuine philosophers? These are very difficult questions. To better understand the background of what eventually became "Pythagorean" philosophy, it is best to explore as much as we can about the man who allegedly inspired it, his life and death, his influence, his politics, and the organization he established, even the wars or uprisings he may have been responsible for. Some of the testimony will clash with what we think great sages ought to be like, and some of it may seem quite disturbing, but we should keep in mind that practically everything we know of Pythagoras, from antiquity forward, was written by those most favorable to him or his group. Our authors are either Pythagorean wannabes or strong admirers who are intrigued by his exploits. Thus, even if they paint him once in a while in colors we may consider unfavorable, our ancient commentators did not necessarily judge matters the way we do. In fact, things that can make us cringe, they may find praiseworthy, even boasting with the details. But if we can accept the testimonies in question with both an open mind and a certain amount of reserve, we should be able to recognize a fascinating picture of the Great Sage and the remarkable times he lived in. Moreover, the events that mark this period in Southern Italy may give us an interesting background for both Xenophanes' and Parmenides' lives, and perhaps reveal some clues as to why "methodical reasoning" came about in that part of the world.

---

65 Cf. **Parmenides**, fr. 7.3–6.

CHAPTER II

The Pythagoreans

TRADITION VERSUS THE HISTORICAL ACCOUNT

> In the history of the south Italian colonies, scanty as it is, there is a strong element of fancy, almost of myth. . . . In a word, scarcely an event in early south Italian history is not tinged with romantic or miraculous colour.
>
> —T. J. Dunbabin[66]

Conflicting Reports and Forgeries

To present a reliable account of Pythagoras' life, death, and the anti-Pythagorean revolts is an almost impossible task. This is certainly not due to a lack of available testimony; on the contrary, we seem flooded with far too many versions of the same events. If we take only the circumstances of how Pythagoras' death relates to the uprisings, we are confronted with the following, often contradictory testimony[67]:

- Pythagoras was in Croton during the revolt.
- No, he was not present because he foresaw the coming difficulties and managed to move quietly to Metapontum.
- No, not only was he present, but he was inside a burning Pythagorean meetinghouse and just barely escaped.
- No, he was not in the meetinghouse, but he was in Croton, where he fled to the harbor, subsequently traveling from city to city in desperate search for shelter, only to be turned away repeatedly.
- No, he went only as far as a field of beans, where he was caught.
- No, he made it to Metapontum, but starved to death in the Temple of the Muses, beleaguered by his foes.
- No, he refused to eat on purpose, being heartbroken over the terrible fate of his followers.

---

66 **Dunbabin** [704] *The Western Greeks* 372, 373.
67 For the appropriate textual references, please consult the Appendix titled "The Info to Certainty Sequence, Part II."

- No, that is not the way he died; he had his throat cut after being captured near the field of beans.
- No, he was not even in Italy at that time, having journeyed abroad to take care of his old teacher, who was ill.
- No, his teacher had passed away a long time ago, and Pythagoras had moved to Metapontum some twenty years before these difficulties emerged.
- No, Pythagoras himself was long dead when all of this transpired.
- And so on.

These conflicting versions have come to be called the "traditional account" of Pythagoras' fate—that is, traditional as opposed to historical. Even though most of these stories contradict each other, they are all part of the legend surrounding him, both in antiquity as well as today. This makes it quite impossible for the modern researcher to separate fact from myth. And the same difficulties hinder us from discovering more about the development of his society or the circumstances surrounding its demise. At best, one can speak of a "historical tradition," with strong emphasis on the latter. A traditional account need not differentiate between verifiable events, legend and lore, and the "improvements" by subsequent writers. It need only pass on whatever stories were typical at the time on a given subject, usually those individual anecdotes that were most memorable. The popularity of little cookie-cutter sayings, or sound bites, is certainly not just a modern phenomenon, nor is the type of romanticism that feeds on the legendary, the larger-than-life.

Still, this kind of starry-eyed favoritism is not the worst thing to befall the documentation of Pythagoreanism, which is particularly evident when dealing with its "philosophical" doctrine. The sad truth is that much of what among nonexpert publications are indiscriminately propounded as genuine Pythagorean teachings are nothing but forgeries. The list of the spurious includes works such as *The Golden Verses of Pythagoras, The Sacred Discourse, The Pythagorean Notebooks, On the Nature of the Cosmos and the Soul by Timaeus of Locri,* and *On the Nature of the Universe by Ocellus Lucanus.*[68] The trend to propagate counterfeit Pythagorean works for profit or prestige may have arisen as early as the third century B.C.,[69] some 300 years after Py-

---

68 For a representative listing of pseudonymous and pseudepigraphical writings, see **Thesleff** [178] *An Introduction to the Pythagorean Writings of the Hellenistic Period* 8–24.

69 Cf. **Thesleff** [178] *Introduction* 99; **Kahn** [147] *Pythagoras* 77. The practice of forgery was not only reserved for the alleged writings of Pythagoras, but also targeted such later Pythagoreans as Archytas. Cf. also **Burkert** [100] *Lore* 218–227. Check **van der Waerden** [183] *Pythagoreer* 148–158, for a benevolent commentary on the admittedly neo-Pythagorean "Golden Verses."

thagoras, and it continued unabated well into the new millennium. We even hear of attempts to mass-produce such fakes, as in the case of King Juba II of Mauretania (early first century A.D.), himself a well-educated author who had amassed a vast library of speculative texts, but who was widely known for being a passionate collector of Pythagoras' writings.[70] The laws of supply and demand seem to have motivated multitudinous attempts to accommodate this need. Perhaps quite a few "suppliers" were suddenly surprised to find the lost books of Pythagoras in their grandmother's attic. In any case, the total number of questionable works is undoubtedly in the hundreds.[71]

Almost No Mention of Pythagoras in Plato and Aristotle

Our first quasi-biographical data on Pythagoras originates after Plato and Aristotle, and it is conveyed by sources that are far less reliable. Oddly, these two philosophers barely mention him by name. Plato cites him only once in the *Republic*, and only to point out that the Samian had gifted his followers with a unique way of living—the so-called "Pythagorean life"—which made them stand out from the rest of mankind.[72] And Aristotle, otherwise our best source on Pythagorean teachings, rarely mentions their alleged originator.[73] When Aristotle refers to the followers of this doctrine, he sometimes speaks of them as "those called Pythagoreans," as if in quotation marks; the reason behind this qualification is still largely unresolved today.[74] Some have speculated that he intended to differentiate between the political party and the "philosophical" school.[75] It is unfortunate that the work that Aristotle specifically dedicated to Pythagoreanism is irrecover-

---

70 **Olympiodorus** [650] *Commentaria in Aristotelem Graeca* 12.13.13 (**Busse**) and **Elias** [635] *Commentaria in Aristotelem Graeca* 18.128.5 (**Busse**). Cf. **Thesleff**'s [178] comments on King Juba II regarding the above passages (*Introduction* 31–32, 51, 54–55), as well as **Zeller** [89] *Die Philosophie der Griechen in ihrer geschichtlichen Entwicklung* (*DPdG*) III/2.112–113, 112n2, 113n1, and **Jacoby** [139] (*RE* IX,2.2387.60).

71 Cf. **Zeller** [89] *DPdG* I/1.366–378; **Thesleff** [178] *Introduction*. **Kahn** [147] (*Pythagoras* 76) muses that the number of eighty works for Pythagoras and 200 for his followers may be exaggerated.

72 **Plato**, *Republic* X.600b. See **Burkert** [100] for inspiring my particular phrasing of this idea (*Lore* 84).

73 The statement in *Metaphysics* 986a30 that "Alcmaeon lived during the old age of Pythagoras" is not accepted by all scholars. Interestingly, **Burkert** [100] believes that Aristotle's "studious avoidance of Pythagoras' name" was intentional. (*Lore* 30)

74 E.g., **Aristotle**, *Metaphysics* 985b23, 989b29, and *On the Heavens* 284b7. (See also **Ross** [624] *Aristotle's Metaphysics* 1.143; and **Burkert** [100] *Lore* 30, 30n8.)

75 E.g., **Zeller** [89] *DPdG* 1/1.446n1; **Minar** [160] *EPP* 22.

ably lost.[76] Only a few references to it are preserved in the works of other, less dependable writers. The one historical statement that can be linked to Aristotle—very loosely, I might add—that has anything relevant to say about Pythagoras is a claim that the Samian foretold to his followers the coming of political strife, a hunch that supposedly compelled him to leave the city ahead of time and move secretly to Metapontum, a neighboring colony to the north of Croton.[77] All the other information preserved by Aristotle deals with Pythagorean doctrine or belief, but most, if not all, of it involves late fifth-century Pythagoreanism.[78] Whether a few of these ideas may have their roots in the early teachings—that is, to the old sage himself—cannot be ascertained.[79] So, lacking input from Plato and Aristotle, we have no choice but to turn to the testimony of subsequent biographers.

The Main Sources of Pythagorean Lore

There are six principal sources for the Pythagorean tradition (I have, as we have seen, no other way to refer to it). Three are from the fourth and third centuries B.C.: Aristoxenus of Tarentum, Dicaearchus and Timaeus of Tauromenium. The other three are much later and belong to the second and third centuries A.D.: Diogenes Laertius, Porphyry, and Iamblichus.[80]

Aristoxenus of Tarentum (b. c. 370 B.C.[81]), a famous writer and musician, was a pupil of Aristotle. He is considered one of our most knowledgeable sources, largely because of his own claim that he was personally ac-

---

76 I.e., "On the Pythagoreans." See **Philip** [163] on the classification of the work as originally two separate monographs, *PEP* 5, 7, 23n15.

77 **Aristotle**, fr. 191 R, **Apollonius**, historiae mirabiles 6.

78 Cf. **Ross** [624] *Aristotle's Metaphysics* 1.143. Ross identifies Aristotle's Pythagoreans as those at the end of the fifth century, such as Philolaus. See also **Guthrie** [43] *HGP* 1.233, who speaks of middle–fifth century Pythagoreanism, and **Barnes** [9] who generously remarks: "The Pythagorean views that Aristotle reports belong as a whole to the fifth century." (*TPP* 379) In other words, none of Aristotle's sources have anything to do with Pythagoras.

79 This is why some testimonies are not commented upon in this book, in case some readers wonder why I do not address every known aspect of the Pythagorean belief system. As so much of this material is post-Parmenidean, it is not relevant to our present inquiry. But Chapter III, "In Want of a Mathematics for the Soul," contains the most important information on Pythagorean belief.

80 Of course, there are many more commentators on the Pythagorean historical tradition—e.g., Polybius, Neanthes, Cicero, Diodorus, Pompeius Trogus, Apollonius of Tyana, etc.—but most of their sources are either Aristoxenus, Dicaearchus and Timaeus, or perhaps even some version of Aristotle's book. Nor have I forgotten Heraclides Ponticus, Speusippus, Xenocrates, Theophrastus, Posidonius, Aetius, Nicomachus, et al., but it appears that they are more concerned with the speculative material—i.e., their ideas of Pythagoreanism as a philosophical doctrine—and less with its history.

81 376 B.C. or right after, according to *DNP* 1; 370 B.C., according to *OCD*.

quainted with the so-called Last Pythagoreans, a group of exiles, or their descendants, who had eventually migrated to mainland Greece. However, some speculate that he had an axe to grind with Plato and Aristotle—he criticizes them severely—and therefore, might have had an ulterior motive to make Pythagoreanism appear in the best possible light, if only to show how aberrant other philosophical directions were, or how much some of these other schools had "stolen" from Pythagoras.[82] One of the most egregious falsities that goes back to Aristoxenus is the inclusion of two legendary lawmakers, Zaleucus and Charondas, in the ranks of the Pythagoreans. Both lived close to a century *before* Pythagoras, yet they are portrayed as willing followers of the wise master, who, seemingly, was so versed in all things that he even taught these legislators the art of lawmaking before he was born.[83] (Perhaps he did so in a previous life?)

Dicaearchus (b. c. 375?[84]) was not only a fellow Aristotelian student but also a famous explorer, writer, and universal scholar who entertained a particular interest in the history of Pythagorean politics. His assessments seem a bit more objective than those of Aristoxenus.[85] He focuses largely on Pythagoras' activity as a politician and public educator. Regarding the anti-Pythagorean uprisings, he seems to speak mostly of the events of the second revolt, and from him we have the much-quoted phrase that "everywhere [in Southern Italy] there were great riots, which even now the inhabitants of these places remember and tell about, calling them the riots in the time of the Pythagoreans."[86] He is one of the principal sources on Pythagoreanism for Cicero (106–43 B.C.), the famous Roman philosopher/statesman, who mentions, as he is writing, that he has a sizeable stack of Dicaearchus' books right in front of him.[87]

Timaeus (350–260 B.C.[88]) is a much-referred-to Greek historian of Sicil-

---

82 See **Aristoxenus**, fr. 67 (Wehrli) (= **D.L.**, 3.37) and fr. 68 (**Porphyry**, *VP* 53) on Plato. Also fr. 68 and fr. 1 on Aristotle. I am largely indebted to **Philip**'s [163] analysis, *PEP* 13–16, and **Burkert** [100] *Lore* 225–227, on the allegations against Plato, and of course, **Wehrli**'s [626] comments, *Schule* II 67–68.

83 **Aristoxenus**, fr. 17 (Wehrli) (**Porphyry**, *VP* 21–22; **Iamblichus**, *VP* 33, see also 104, 130) and fr. 43 (Wehrli) (**D.L.**, 8.16). Cf. **Burkert** [100] *Lore* 108, 110n4.

84 According to *DNP*. **Philip** [163] sets birth at c. 360–340 B.C., *PEP* 140. *Flourit* latest 310 according to *RE* V,1.547.24.

85 Cf. **Kahn** [147] *Pythagoras* 69.

86 **Dicaearchus**, fr. 34 (**Wehrli** [632]), **Porphyry**, *VP* 56.

87 **Cicero** [631] *Letters to Atticus* 22 (II.2). See also 305 (XIII.32): Cicero bids Atticus to send him **Dicaearchus**' two books *On the Soul*. In a subsequent letter (309 [XIII.33]), Cicero conveys that he has received one book of Dicaearchus.

88 *OCD*; also **Sandys** [787] *A History of Classical Scholarship* 1:164.

ian origin who was exiled from Southern Italy in his youth and forced to spend the next fifty years in Athens. There he focused largely on preserving the history of his homeland, compiling an extensive body of work in the process. Many who wrote on the critical Pythagorean events relied on Timaeus' material, and he seems to be the source for what is considered a significant historical fact—namely, that the so-called clubhouses of the Pythagoreans were set on fire all over Southern Italy[89]—as well as for other meaningful data about the revolts. Furthermore, he is noted for supplying such details as the qualifications for Pythagorean membership, the testing of the initiates, the structure of the order, and so forth, and he is also thought to be the source for the famous four speeches of Pythagoras.[90] The downside on Timaeus, however, is the fact that he was so thoroughly removed by banishment from the very object of his inquiry—Southern Italy and Sicily—for most of his life. Several scholars have theorized he might have maintained some form of correspondence with the old colonies—an exchange of letters or couriers, perhaps—and acquired his information in this way.[91] Others believe that he merely scoured the libraries of Athens, maintaining only an academic grasp of the events that had transpired.[92] There are a few troublesome hints that perhaps, due to his patriotic sentiments, he might have bent the truth occasionally to favor the Pythagoreans. For example, Walter Burkert points to the repeated connections between Pythagoras and the city of Tauromenium (Timaeus' hometown in Sicily)—that are traceable to the historian. However, as Burkert also reminds us, Tauromenium was not founded until 403 B.C., around a century after the death of the old sage.[93]

Be that as it may, I believe that the reliability of all of these sources was compromised by the great time span that separated them from the actual events, a time span that even by the most optimistic estimates was still one and a half to two centuries; hence, we have no reason to believe that any of these authors were able to distinguish between actual history and what al-

---

89 Preserved by **Polybius**, *The Histories* 2.39, 1–4. Cf. **von Fritz** [122] *PPSI* 86; **de Vogel** [180] *Pythagoras* 5.
90 Cf. **de Vogel** [180] *Pythagoras* 7, 65–66; **van der Waerden** [183] *Pythagoreer* 186, 188–189. See also **Burkert** [100] *Lore* 104n37, for an evenhanded treatment of the issue.
91 E.g., **von Fritz** [122] *PPSI* 35, 65–67; **de Vogel** [180] *Pythagoras* 5, 8, 65, 66, 68–69, 303; **van der Waerden** [183] *Pythagoreer* 21, 189.
92 **Polybius**, 12.28.5–7, 405; **Philip** [163] *PEP* 143
93 **Burkert** [100] *Lore* 104n37. Also see 455, on Timaeus showing "a local patriotic partiality to Pythagoras."

ready had become accepted tradition. And if we have such difficulties with our earliest sources, one can imagine how hard it is to sort out the intricate accounts of our other group of biographers, who wrote some six centuries later—seven to eight centuries after the events in question. Diogenes Laertius, for example, is a self-styled biographer of philosophers, a mysterious man of whom nothing, not even his place of origin, is conclusively known. (The guess that he lived around the mid-third century A.D., is based entirely on the latest thinkers referred to in his work, *The Lives of Eminent Philosophers*.[94]) Then we have the Neoplatonist writer Porphyry (A.D. 234–c. 305/10, originally from Tyre), who composed a condensed report on the Pythagorean movement and its founder titled *Life of Pythagoras*. And finally, there is Porphyry's pupil Iamblichus (c. A.D. 245–c. 325), also of Syrian origin, who offers us a much more detailed exposé called *On the Pythagorean Life*.[95]

Unfortunately, it is only the lack of better source material that has turned these often questionable accounts into authoritative works. They are largely cut-and-paste operations, particularly the ones of Diogenes Laertius and Iamblichus. In their writings we find many jumbled reports carelessly thrown together, often contradicting one another. Furthermore, by the time the anecdotes in question had come into the possession of these writers, they had passed through so many hands that a reconstruction of the original sources is virtually impossible. By original sources I do not mean the aforementioned Aristoxenus, Dicaearchus, and Timaeus—all of whom were much used by the latter three—but truly firsthand accounts by people who were actually taught by Pythagoras himself, or who at least witnessed the persecutions of the society.[96] In this sense, the difficulty of composing a

---

94 For dates on **D.L.**, see *DNP* 3; on **Iamblichus**, *VP* 5 (b. A.D. 240); on **Porphyry**, *VP* 10; and generally *OCD*.

95 I.e., **Porphyry**'s *Vita Pythagorae* and **Iamblichus**' *De vita Pythagorica*. See Bibliography for details on available translations. In the main text, however, I usually refer to these works by their English titles, viz. *Life of Pythagoras* and *On the Pythagorean Life*, respectively (while abbreviating both as *VP* in the notes).

96 For any data on Pythagoras' death to come to Iamblichus—via the *postulated* axis Lysis-Aristoxenus—someone had to tell Lysis, who was conceivably twenty years old when he escaped the burning meetinghouse, some fifty to sixty years after Pythagoras' death. It is not unreasonable to posit at least *two* conduits between one event and the other. For any information regarding Pythagoras' arrival in Croton thirty years earlier, we have to add at least one additional source. Also, Lysis had to pass the info to the Last Pythagoreans, possibly via his pupil Epaminondas (see **von Fritz** [122] *PPSI* 28–29, 78–79) or Philolaus, and these in turn had to relay it to Aristoxenus. Afterward, it had to make its way to Nicomachus or Apollonius—possibly via Neanthes—and finally to Iamblichus. This would be the shortest route imaginable—hence, at least seven to eight conduits.

coherent picture from a motley collection of anecdotes[97] is best summarized by Walter Burkert:

> One is tempted to say that there is not a single detail in the life of Pythagoras that stands uncontradicted. It is possible, from a more or less critical selection of the data, to construct a plausible account; but it is bound to rest on shaky foundations, for no documentary evidence has appeared.... No [ancient] author seems to use documentary evidence; everything depends on oral tradition, in which "Pythagoras" quickly comes to mean "the Pythagoreans."[98]

If there is one thing that is most perplexing for the modern researcher, it is the fact that not one of the ancient historians or biographers appears aware that there were *two* anti-Pythagorean uprisings, or at least, no such specific conclusion is preserved in the extant works.[99] In other words, our sources believe they are speaking of the same catastrophic event; thus they are forced to merge widely diverging episodes, which results, of course, in the wildest chronological absurdities. In the end—as we have seen earlier with the varying opinions on Pythagoras' death—there are just as many plausible accounts linking him to the revolts as there are denials of such a link. It is only due to the untiring work of many modern interpreters that the mixups have begun to become disentangled.[100]

Why is it important to make sense of all these contradictions? Because in order to understand Pythagoras' relevance to philosophy, we should not only ascertain what roles he may have played, but also rule out the impossible ones. This brings up the next question: is there any way to sum up the historical tradition so that we may obtain at least *some* coherent picture of what happened? In other words, does Burkert's idea of a *"plausible* account"

---

97 For a contrary position—which I consider too charitable—cf. **de Vogel** [180] *Pythagoras*, and **van der Waerden** [183] *Pythagoreer*. However, I recommend **Kahn**'s [147] *Pythagoras* for its balanced, reasoned approach.

98 **Burkert** [100] *Lore* 100, 117.

99 Perhaps Timaeus (see **von Fritz** [122] *PPSI* 87), whose account of the two revolts might have been jumbled by subsequent writers, is an exception. However, **Delatte** [111] holds that Timaeus may have failed to distinguish two separate incidents (*Essay sur la Politique Pythagoricienne* 213–218). As for the others, cf. **Minar** [160]: "We can see clearly that Iamblichus himself thought of only one attack" (*EPP* 58); and "as early as Neanthes ... the disturbances of the last years of the sixth century (c. 509 B.C.) were being misunderstood and mixed with those of sixty years later. Neanthes and many others after him assumed that there was only one revolution" (*EPP* 52); as well as **van der Waerden** [183]: "Obviously, Porphyry did not know that there were two anti-Pythagorean revolts." (*Pythagoreer* 214)

100 E.g., **Delatte** [111] *Politique*; **von Fritz** [122] *PPSI*; **Minar** [160] *EPP*; **Burkert** [100] *Lore*. Also **Lévy** [155] *Recherches sur les Sources de la Légende de Pythagore* (on ancient sources, not on the duality of the revolts).

stand a chance? I believe that it does (even if my optimism is somewhat tentative, largely because compiling it is a tremendously demanding project that still may not satisfy all experts). Of course, this present work was never intended as an encyclopedic study of Pythagoreanism, but only as an attempt to shed light upon some factors that have contributed to the development of philosophy in general, and metaphysics and logic in particular. We should also keep in mind that Pythagoreanism as a movement was fairly unique (inasmuch as its achievements surpassed those of its founder), and its real heroes are still largely unknown, as are some of the key circumstances surrounding its fate. For example, there is the enigmatic Pythagorean innovator, Hippasus; the splintering of the order into separate sects; the background of its dabbling in politics, together with its anti-democratic platform; its makeup as a cult; its purported savageness in war; and the reasons behind the revolts—subjects that are practically never discussed outside the academic community.

It is unfortunate that Southern Italy usually takes the backseat in the history of philosophy while everyone's attention is focused on glorious Athens, bedazzled by Socrates' argumentative fireworks. While there is nothing essentially wrong with that, what is often overlooked is that Socrates' activity took place largely during the last quarter of the fifth century, while Pythagoras' death, the uprisings, and Parmenides' life all belonged to the first half. So, 500–430 B.C. is, historically speaking, a virtual black hole for most philosophic research. Yet what transpired during this very period laid the groundwork for all philosophy to come. It is especially fruitful to investigate how Pythagorean lore has been utilized by subsequent writers to support their individual agendas. Years, even centuries, after Plato and Aristotle, people were still probing the mysteries of Pythagoreanism.

A note to the reader regarding the method used to assemble a coherent picture of the historical tradition: I had to approach the problem in three ways. First, I needed to develop cohesiveness, striving to meet Burkert's call for a "plausible account," albeit one that could appeal to experts and nonexperts alike. The storyline itself spans the next five sections of this chapter: "The Pythagorean Agenda," "The Politics of Pythagoreanism," "War and Luxury," "The Revolts Against the Pythagorean Political Elite," and "Those Who Listen and Those Who Learn." Second, I did have to satisfy scholarly demands, as well as my own standards, for a transparent, well-documented account. This explains the at times abundant notes, as well as some special elaborations in the appendix. Third, I had to evaluate the findings, that is, bring the data into some kind of correspondence with itself, thereby creating a framework of priorities by which information could be examined. The result is as follows: within the present chapters, all belonging to the narrative part of the book, I will seek to render as much of a comprehensive image as I can. However, scholars—or other readers who enjoy exploring various plotlines, versions, and so on—may find two particular sections in the appendix useful. These sections are titled "The Info to Certainty Sequence, Parts I and II," and they represent the so-called framework of priorities I have mentioned.

THE PYTHAGOREAN AGENDA

> Dicaearchus says that when [Pythagoras] set foot in Italy and arrived in Croton, he was received as a man of remarkable powers and experience after his many travels, and as someone well supplied by fortune with regard to his personal characteristics. For his manner was grand and liberal, and in his voice, his character and everything else about him there was grace and harmony in abundance. Consequently he was able so to organize the city of Croton that, when he had persuaded the governing council of elders by many noble discourses, at the behest of the government he then delivered to the young men appropriate exhortations, and after that he addressed the boys, collected together from their schools, and then the women, since he had called a meeting of women too.
>
> —Porphyry, *Life of Pythagoras*[101]

Croton before Pythagoras

How did the end begin? What factors led to a Pythagorean *Götterdämmerung*? The quick answer is envy, greed, power struggles, secret conspiracies, war and quarrels over its spoils, fear of dictatorship, and mass propaganda—in one word, *politics*. There is also an important lesson here: the mixing of religion, commerce, and politics will certainly not amount to *philosophy*, but rather to a combination more akin to a powder keg ready to explode. Adding the makeup of a secret society to this formula—with all of its elitist trappings, backroom deals, and subterfuge—is tantamount to lighting the fuse. If we can, after all this time, pinpoint that one individual most likely to have held *the* burning match in his hand, then without a doubt, Pythagoras is our best candidate.

The story begins with the Great Sage's arrival in Southern Italy, sometime after 530 B.C.[102] As he came to the great colony of Croton, the Samian expatriate found it lingering in a state of despondency, oddly coupled with luxurious living and wanton decadence—an admittedly peculiar mix. Croton's citizens were still deeply affected by having lost an important war against neighboring Locri, a circumstance that was all the more dispiriting

---

101 **Dicaearchus**, fr. 33 (Wehrli); **Porphyry**, *VP* 18 (**DK** 14,8a). Quoted from **KRS** [39] 226–227.

102 According to **Aristoxenus**, 532/531 B.C. is the date when Pythagoras leaves Samos to avoid the tyrant Polycrates: fr. 16 (Wehrli). A date adopted by Apollodorus (**Jacoby** [2] *FGrHist* II.D 244F338–339, and *Kommentar* under 244), see **Burkert** [100] *Lore* 110, 110n4. Cf. **Philip** [163] *PEP* 195; **de Vogel** [180] *Pythagoras* 24.

because the Locrians had been entirely outnumbered. Tradition has it that sometime between 550 and 530 B.C.,[103] a small but determined force of 15,000 Locrian fighters repelled an aggressively attacking Crotonian army, some 130,000 strong. Although the numbers seem inflated today, in antiquity, with odds at almost 9 : 1, the battle's outcome became proverbial for "events which are unexpected."[104]

We are told that the proud Locrians would rather have died than surrendered, so after resigning themselves to the inevitable, they fought as if they had nothing to lose but their honor. "To have given up all hope" was afterwards considered the victory's most decisive factor.[105] Even the Sons of Zeus,[106] the twin giants Castor and Pollux, are said to have personally honored such a death-defying stance by fighting alongside the Locrians, their scarlet capes and white stallions visible to the end.[107]

Reportedly, this shameful defeat had a devastating effect upon the morale and psyche of the Crotonians. They abandoned all military training and athletic competitions, and even refrained from sending participants to the Olympic Games. Instead they drowned their humiliation in a life of luxury, sensual pleasures, extravagant clothes, and lavish entertainment. Curiously, having lost a war did not affect their wealth, which they were now determined to enjoy in the full. This, we are assured, was the scene upon Pythagoras' arrival, and it was something he felt compelled to change rather drastically.[108]

The Lecturer and Miracle-Worker

According to legend, Pythagoras proceeded to give a series of speeches to the populace of Croton, each one aimed at a different focus group, such as the young men of the gymnasium, the council, the women, and even the children. To grab everyone's attention, Pythagoras made use of a ploy that today would be called a public relations stunt.

---

103 *DNP* 6, under Kroton: "548" B.C.; **Minar** [160]: "530–520" (*EPP* 8); **Burkert** [100]: "530" (*Lore* 115n40); **Dunbabin** [704]: "550–540" (*Western Greeks* 359–360).

104 **Dunbabin** [704] *Western Greeks* 359.

105 **Justin (Pompeius Trogus)**, 20.3.5–6. "They considered themselves victorious if they did not die unavenged. But in seeking merely to die with honour, they succeeded in gaining a victory, and it was only their desperation that brought them their success." (Trans. **Yardley** [659] *Justin* 167.) Cf. **de Vogel** [180] *Pythagoras* 58–59, and **van der Waerden** [183] *Pythagoreer* 205.

106 I.e., the Spartan *Dioscuri*.

107 **Justin**, 20.2.12–3.8; **Diodorus**, 8.32. For details, see **Dunbabin** [704] *Western Greeks* 358–360; **Minar** [160] *EPP* 8–9; **de Vogel** [180] *Pythagoras* 58–60.

108 **Justin**, 20.4.1. Cf. **Dunbabin** [704] *Western Greeks* 360.

The tale unfolds as follows: en route to his destination, Pythagoras met a few fishermen and he excited their interest by claiming to know the exact number of fish they had caught that day. Intrigued, the men counted their catch, and to everyone's surprise, the result matched precisely what Pythagoras foretold. The fish not only survived this ordeal, but Pythagoras convinced everyone to return their catch to the sea. As the fish swam happily away, he recompensed the fishermen for their loss and continued on his way toward Croton. News of this miraculous feat preceded his arrival, and soon his name was known in every household.[109]

Only a few days later we have Pythagoras strolling to the gymnasium, prepared to launch his very first speech.[110] His intended audience was the young men who frequented the facility for their workouts. The lecture was a great success, compelling the young men to relate its content to their fathers, who, as fate would have it, were members of the city council. At once, the governing body invited Pythagoras to speak to them—and, as they say, the rest is history (or at least a good yarn).

Some scholars view Pythagoras as a mesmerizing public speaker with a mission.[111] His aim? To educate the Crotonian public and reinvigorate their decadent, luxury-craving elite. The suggestion is that Croton's rise to a position of dominance over Southern Italy was largely due to the sage's edifying influence, and that his well-executed curriculum of public lectures impelled the citizenry to change their ways. That is not, however, what the surviving *evidence* allows us to conclude. In reality, only four speeches are preserved by Iamblichus—considered verbatim by the same scholars, I might add, although they were recorded an astonishing 800 years after the fact, if there ever was such a fact. It is presupposed that the motivating im-

---

109   **Iamblichus**, *VP* 36; **Porphyry**, *VP* 25.
110   This passage in **Iamblichus** (*VP* 37) is unclear, as it seems to contradict an earlier report (*VP* 30) where Pythagoras' first speech upon his arrival is described as directed at the assembled populace of Croton. At this talk, the report says, he made 2,000 recruits on the spot, which might have included women and children.
111   E.g., **de Vogel** [180] *Pythagoras* 68: "There was indeed a direct education of the people by Pythagoras.... This education was not so much concerned with political influence, but with *character training* in a social context, with 'Sozialpaedagogik.' ... [I]n other terms: it was a kind of *mission*." Also, 2, 67–69, 159–191, 245–246. She regards the four speeches of Pythagoras as genuine and treats them as literal transcripts. The same applies to **van der Waerden**'s [183] general position, (*Pythagoreer* 190–201), and in addition, (a) he sees their effect as proof of Pythagoras' vocation; (b) he believes that Timaeus recorded them whole, accurate, and verbatim—or at least very close to the original; and (c) he believes that they were transmitted in such a mint condition to Apollonius, i.e., Iamblichus' direct source. Even **Dunbabin** [704] is led to conclude: "The moral regeneration which [Pythagoras] wrought was the necessary condition of Krotoniate expansion, political and otherwise." (*Western Greeks* 361)

pact of these very teachings constituted the backbone of Croton's revival, justifying, in effect, Pythagoras' claim to fame as the architect of its golden age.

Yet even the most cursory perusal of the speeches' content reveals them as being mind-numbingly dull; they are a collection of homespun homilies which would be too embarrassing to be claimed by a third-rate Sunday school teacher, never mind awaken a nation. And from what should the Crotonians be awakened? The so-called "good life," perhaps, in exchange for a monastic one? Shall we really believe—as we are told—that the rich relinquished their luxurious life voluntarily, or the women their jewels and gold-threaded clothes? Yet that is precisely what we are supposed to believe, according to some of our earlier sources, such as the historian Pompeius Trogus (first century B.C.), who reports that the Crotonian women cast aside their lavish adornments recognizing these as mere "instruments of luxury." Instead of these, he claims, they were content to wear their chastity as the "true ornament of womanhood."[112]

What seems even more difficult to grasp is how all this "public education" would instigate an unavoidable chain of events, ultimately propelling Croton into yet another war, advocated by, of all people, Pythagoras himself. And not just any ordinary war, but a most savage and murderous conflict, on a scale unequaled in Greek history.[113] This time the enemy was not little undermanned Locri, but mighty Sybaris, the capital of a sprawling empire.

The Four Speeches

In any case, the so-called First Speech[114]—the one given to the young men in the gymnasium—stresses the importance of honoring one's parents and the need to respect elders in general. Pythagoras' argument centers around the idea that we should venerate things that come earlier, or are prior, instead of those that come later. So, for example, the gods should be worshiped because, as immortal beings, they are certainly prior to man. Accordingly, as the teaching further explains, the East is more respectable than the West, sunrise more important than sunset, beginning better than end, and growth preferable to decay. However, this simplistic metaphor

---

112 **Justin**, 20.4.10–12.
113 **Minar** [160] *EPP* 9. **Dunbabin** [704] *Western Greeks* 364.
114 **Iamblichus**, *VP* 37.

The Four Speeches 45

quickly becomes pretentious with Pythagoras' suggestion that natives are more honorable than emigrants because they are prior. (Odd. Was he not a foreigner himself, having just arrived to their city?) Pursuing the argument to its end, Pythagoras eventually concludes that it is the ancestors who are in fact responsible for the achievements of their descendants.

Then, bringing up friendship, the Samian declares that one should treat all enemies as future friends, and friends never as enemies, and above all, people must train themselves in self-control. Youth, he continues, is nature's way of testing the individual, because it marks the time when one's desires are most overwhelming. Next Pythagoras stresses the importance of education as opposed to concern for the body, comparing the latter to a disloyal friend who deserts us in a pinch, contrary to education, which not only lasts a lifetime, but may even foster eternal fame. (I wonder, doesn't the body also last a lifetime?)

Iamblichus' account also states that Pythagoras bolsters his claims with many examples, some from history, others from philosophy. Pythagoras then concludes his lecture with a bit of xenophobic/elitist diatribe, claiming that it is education that marks the difference between Greek and barbarian, human and beast, free men and slaves, philosopher and common folk.

As soon as the city's leaders heard of the speech, they summoned Pythagoras to the Council of the Thousand—a body akin to a large senate—and asked for advice.[115] What followed then was another speech allowing Pythagoras to unfold his agenda.[116] In it he first advocates the construction of a temple for the Muses. Then he points out that the nation is a trust, consigned to the administrators by the people themselves, and that their primary duty is to ensure that the trust will be passed on to future generations. After extolling the benefits of justice, Pythagoras implores his listeners to manage their private lives in accordance with their own political principles. Men should be faithful to their wives, so as not to give them reasons to retaliate against their indiscretions by "adulterating the family line," that is, by covertly creating offspring with outsiders as an act of revenge. After more tidbits like these, Pythagoras reminds his listeners that the job of the politician is not to impede his opponents, but to help his own supporters. Lastly, he points out that praise is better than advice, because only humans need to be counseled, while the gods need to be praised. (Sorry, I can't fig-

---

115 According to **Dunbabin** [704], the supreme council of a thousand at Croton may be post-Pythagoras, and the result of a Pythagorean imitation of the council of Locri (*Western Greeks* 72).

116 **Iamblichus**, *VP* 45.

ure this out. I can only get as far as gods, who by being immortal and all-knowing, do not need advice, because, in contrast to mortals, they know all things. Yet why these gods *need* to be praised by the very same mortals whose advice they spurn admittedly strains my powers of reasoning.) Allegedly, the members of the council were so moved by this speech that they immediately commissioned the creation of a temple of the Muses, dismissed their concubines, and became faithful to their wives.[117] Furthermore, they begged Pythagoras to also speak to their women and children, and the old sage seems to have foreseen this request.

He began his speech to the children by admonishing them never to start a fight or a quarrel.[118] After repeating his hymn on education, he warned the youngsters that it is easy for good children to *remain* good for the rest of their life, but that no one can finish well after a bad start—in other words, whoever begins bad will also end bad. Moreover, he claimed that the gods listen most readily to children, which is why whenever times are difficult, such as in a drought, the youngest are usually used as messengers to the gods to implore them for rain. Children must also learn to listen so that they may be able to speak, and by respecting their elders, they will, in turn, earn the respect of those who are even younger than they are. We are told that the people were so impressed with this particular speech that afterward they begin to avoid Pythagoras' name and only speak of "that man" or "the Divine."

In his speech to the women of Croton, Pythagoras' first advice is on how to sacrifice and properly pray to the gods.[119] Then he counsels them not to oppose their husbands. In fact, women should mark it as a personal victory every time they "give in" to their spouses. Moreover, he admonishes them to be faithful, and he declares that a woman who sleeps with any man not her husband can never again go to the temples. Pythagoras also informs the women that as long as they live, they must keep in mind to say as little as possible, and then only voice cheerful things, and that they should always strive to have others say only good things about them. He also reminds the women that they are by nature much more pious than men, which is why the sacred oracles, like those of Delphi, always used women to communicate to the world. Apparently, Pythagoras' call for modesty and piety had such a tremendous effect upon his female listeners that they rid

---

117   Iamblichus, *VP* 48, 50, 132.
118   Iamblichus, *VP* 51.
119   Iamblichus, *VP* 54.

themselves at once of their extravagant clothes, donating them in the tens of thousands to the temple of Hera, the mother goddess.[120]

Earth as a Prison

As I have pointed out, it is hard to imagine that these tedious speeches could move anyone to anything, much less to the abandonment of a peaceful and opulent life in exchange for poverty, abstinence, and most significantly, as we shall see, yet another bloody adventure inspired—even demanded—by Pythagoras. But this is precisely what tradition wants us to believe. What are we to make of the claim that his rants against wealth and extravagance awakened a mass movement? More importantly, what was the intention behind this extraordinary political platform? Was Pythagoras' strategy based on some requisite religious doctrine or at least a shrewd political agenda? Or was he instead obsessed with something? Some clues may be found in Pompeius Trogus' historical account:

> [Pythagoras] came to Croton and there by his authority called the people who had fallen into luxury back to the practice of sobriety. Every day he praised virtue and summed up the wrongs of luxury and the fate of states that had been ruined by that plague; and he induced so great a zeal for sobriety among the masses that it seemed incredible that some of them should live in luxury.[121]

And another ancient historian, Diodorus Siculus (first century B.C.), insists:

> Whoever associated with him he converted from their ways of extravagance and luxury, whereas all men, because of their wealth, were giving themselves over without restraint to indulgence and an ignoble dissipation of body and soul.[122]

If this image is accurate, and so far we have no reason to believe otherwise, then the first and foremost effect produced by Pythagoras upon the Crotonians had nothing to do with higher education, sacred mystical science, or the secrets of the universe. His agenda is depicted as not much more than a political manifesto wrapped in religious bromides.

The celebrated "Pythagorean life" is certainly not a happy life, and in fact, under no circumstances can it ever be a happy life, because—in Py-

---

120 **Iamblichus**, *VP* 56. **Justin**, 20.4.10–12; **de Vogel** [180] *Pythagoras* 136.
121 **Justin**, 20.4.6–12. Quote from **de Vogel** [180] *Pythagoras* 61, 62.
122 **Diodorus** 10.3.3.

thagoras' view—mortals were not put on this Earth to enjoy themselves, but only to suffer. This dogma was pivotal for his movement, and it was as much political platform as it was religious doctrine. In fact, regardless of who its real author may have been, one thing is certain: he or she either could not or would not differentiate between the two. Politics had to be religion and religion, politics.[123] We could say that Pythagoreanism aimed for the perfect blend of church and state.

We cannot know if Pythagoras himself was in fact the driving force behind this agenda, or whether it was a later contribution of a fervent supporter.[124] Nonetheless, another clue is provided by one peculiar saying, also attributed to him:

> [Hard] labours are good, but pleasures are in every respect bad. For as we came into the present life for the purpose of punishment, it is necessary that we should be punished.[125]

Thus, for the faithful Pythagorean, a life of luxury was the ultimate offense against the very powers who have condemned us to our terrestrial stay.

Earth was regarded as a prison, with the body as our individual jail cell, and only by embracing our punishment are we fulfilling the terms of our sentence. Naturally, such a radical outlook is far too sweeping to be separated from politics, religion, or any other human interest. Indeed, it holds sway over every aspect of our earthly existence, because whatever we do—or is done to us—must reflect not only the reality that we are here for our punishment, but also the fact *that we are presently undergoing it*. This basic notion becomes exploited to such extremes in Pythagoreanism that any act which ameliorates our stay must be condemned.[126] Hence, only deeds that *increase* a person's punishment are to be encouraged—as aptly demon-

---

123 **Minar** [160] points out: "The Pythagorean Society was not the same as the ordinary political club. It was bound together by religious as well as by political and social ties and much more closely organized than the often ephemeral groups which made their influence felt in the political field." (*EPP* 22)

124 **Burkert** [100]: "Even the later "mathematical" Pythagoreans conceded that the *acusmata* came from Pythagoras." (*Lore* 189) Also **Aristotle**, fr. 196 R (**Porphyry**, *VP* 41) cites such examples.

125 **Iamblichus**, *VP* 85 (trans. **Taylor** [646] *Iamblichus on the Mysteries of the Egyptians, Chaldeans, and Assyrians; Life of Pythagoras* 231).

126 Granted, this radical interpretation may well be a romanticized neo-Pythagorean posture, or even entirely the invention of wannabe Pythagoreans such as Apollonius or Iamblichus (the latter being our immediate source). But we have enough support for such ideas in the early, pythagorizing **Plato** (see the *Phaedo*), with its contempt for the corporeal gratifications or pursuits, and its idea of the body as a prison.

strated by another Pythagorean saying: "Do not assist a man in laying a burden down; for it is not proper to be the cause of not labouring [also translated as 'idleness' or 'lack of effort']; but assist him in taking it up."[127] How curiously twisted this is: to make someone's life easier is to *lessen* the punishment, which means that one is doing a disservice to the person because it prolongs their earthly exile. Hence, the more we enjoy ourselves, the less likely we are to be paroled from our jail sentence.

Be that as it may, we are supposed to believe that this kind of talk was exactly the bitter medicine required by Croton if it was to become the dominant force of Southern Italy.[128] That is somewhat of a tough sell... and it leads one to wonder why no one tossed Pythagoras out on his ear. However, it is possible that he didn't rely on mere eloquence to sway the average Crotonians, but also developed a secret instrument to control the populace, namely, a *political conspiracy*. It is one thing to have lofty ideas, but it's quite another to infuse them with real political power.

---

[127] **Iamblichus**, *VP* 84 (trans. **Taylor** [646] *Iamblichus* 230).
[128] **De Vogel** [180] even ventures: "Of course, Pythagoras could be called 'the founder of all political education.'" (*Pythagoras* 147)

THE POLITICS OF PYTHAGOREANISM

> The Pythagorean organizations were unions of people, the members of which had accepted certain principles and doctrines, and who lived, thought, and acted *collectively*, and whose acts were dictated or related to the beliefs that they had accepted. Moreover, as all the sources testify, the chief characteristic of the Pythagorean movement was *secrecy*. Experience had taught Pythagoras that small but secretly and well-organized forces could have great results.
> —Konstantine I. Boudouris[129]

The Making of a Religious Political Conspiracy

There is a somber side to Pythagoreanism that is often overlooked or minimized by some writers, who, it seems, would rather try to make sense of its teachings than to examine its politics. Yet the ancient commentators insist that Pythagoras did more than wear out the soapbox; he set up a secret society with extremely rigorous standards for membership and far-reaching goals. In time, the group attained control of the Crotonian council, and as their influence grew, it extended also to other city-states. By mid–fifth century B.C., the order seems to have had clubhouses all over Southern Italy.[130]

While the overall tone of Pythagoras' teaching appears concerned with morality, virtue, and religious piety, the mission of the secret group seems to have been the infiltration and takeover of the government.[131] Thus, it functioned as a political conspiracy on the one hand, while on the other projecting the outward appearance of a bona fide political association. Of course, the ultimate goal of Pythagoreanism may in fact have been entirely religious—yet in its *organized form* it cunningly used *political* means to achieve its ends.[132] As Walter Burkert points out, "there is no inconsistency between [its politics] and the religious and ritual side of Pythagoreanism. In

---

129 **Boudouris** [96] 'The Pythagorean Community: Creation, Development and Downfall' 51, 59.

130 A conclusion based in part on **Polybius**, 2.39: "In the district of Italy, then known as Greater Hellas, the clubhouses of the Pythagoreans" . . . and **Dicaearchus**, fr. 34 (Wehrli), in **Porphyry**, *VP* 56: "the riots were everywhere."

131 Cf. **Justin**, 20.4.14; see note 136 below. Cf. also **Minar** [160] *EPP* 27, on how this pattern was repeated by the Pythagoreans in other cities in order to subvert and seize control over them.

132 **Dunbabin** [704] points out: "[Pythagoras'] political influence was, however, a secondary consequence of his teaching." (*Western Greeks* 361)

fact, cult society and political club are in origin virtually identical."[133] One of the reasons for the affinity between cult and political union has to do with the fact that both groups usually start out similarly, that is, as a nucleus of resistance against a prevailing system. We might call this a "seed of otherness"—which is only the natural reaction to an established norm by a minority that wants to preserve its distinctiveness.

One of the most effective mechanisms for reinforcing *otherness* is secrecy.[134] It protects a less powerful minority from being smothered by a majority that cannot but strive for totality. However, it seems that the Pythagoreans did not realize soon enough that they, in fact, had become mainstream, perhaps because they had attained such standing through intrigue. Having achieved genuine political power, they should have grown more inclusive, perhaps opening their doors to everyone.[135] Instead, they continued to behave like a cult, one that opted only to manipulate a system, but not to fully submit to its rules. It is precisely this kind of self-absorption—while dangerously dabbling in politics—that sparked the revolts and hastened the order's demise. Being far too aloof and out of touch, they simply did not recognize how left out other people felt.

We can draw upon the account of Pompeius Trogus for a compelling portrayal of the Pythagorean "insider club" and its eventual fate:

> But three hundred of the young men bound themselves by oath to a fraternal association, and lived (together with their comrades) apart from the rest of the citizens, as if they were the assembly of a secret conspiracy. This association achieved control of the state, and the other citizens determined, when they were assembled in one house, to burn down [house and] brotherhood within it. In that fire sixty members perished and the rest went into exile.[136]

There is no indication here that the citizenry rose up against religious ideas, but merely that they resisted what was perceived as a burgeoning dictator-

---

133 **Burkert** [100] *Lore* 119.

134 **Minar** [160] *EPP* 26: "There may be reason to suppose that a great part of the vaunted 'silence' and mystification of Pythagoreanism concealed political secrets."

135 Ibid., 17: "Beginning with 'influence on the established powers' the society grew in importance until it finally was able to assume actual and probably also titular control of the governmental functions. Pythagorean control is too definite and absolute to be regarded as merely semi-official. The adherents of the society from the first were the aristocrats, and there was no need of a reform or revolution." The need for reform is emphasized by **Boudouris** [96] in 'The Pythagorean Community' 64.

136 **Justin**, 20.4.4 (trans. **Philip** [163] *PEP* 144). This account, according to most scholars, depicts the second revolt, c. 450 B.C. However, Pythagoras' success in galvanizing his followers in the council of Croton against surrendering the Sybarite aristocrats—even if this meant a bloody conflict—only demonstrates that a nucleus of willing conspirators was already in oper-

ship. Furthermore, Pompeius is not our only source for the common Crotonian's view of Pythagoreanism. The biographer Diogenes Laertius preserves this assessment:

> [The meetinghouse of the Pythagoreans] was set ablaze out of jealousy by one of the people who were not accounted worthy of admittance to [Pythagoras'] presence, though some say it was the work of the inhabitants of Croton anxious to safeguard themselves against the setting-up of a tyranny.[137]

The jealousy of the rejected ones—in concert with the popular opinion that they aimed for a dictatorship—would come to haunt the Pythagoreans. Yet what precisely was the political outlook of early Pythagoreanism? From what we can tell, it was virulently anti-democratic, often characterized by our sources as totalitarianism by an anointed elite, and thus an *aristocracy* in the most literal sense, that is, "government by the best."[138] A number of superb works have been written on the subject, and this is not the place to rehash political theory.[139] Perhaps it is best to take a different approach, namely to focus on the excruciating Pythagorean requirements for membership, which will tell us not only that the makeup of the society was indistinguishable from a cult, but, by extension, reveal its true political orientation.

Becoming a Member in the Pythagorean Society

According to Iamblichus' *On the Pythagorean Life*, each candidate had to undergo a series of tests, meted out over several stages.[140] The author prefaces the listing of requirements with a quasi-religious exposition of Pythagoras' supernatural ability to heal *ignorance*—"the soul's most tenacious affliction." The means he offers is *purification*, and its aim is to restore sight to the soul, so that it may "redirect toward the object of thought its divine

---

ation before the war against Sybaris. The order of the three hundred only perpetrated this set pattern, even if their particular organizational form had coalesced after the master's death. For the number of 300 adherents in government, see also **D.L.**, 8.3.

137 **D.L.**, 8.39.
138 Greek: *aristos* = best + *kratia* = rule. See **D.L.**, 8.3.
139 E.g., **Zeller** [89] *DPdG* I/1; **Lévy** [155] *Sources*; **Delatte** [111] *Politique*; **Corssen** [106] 'Die Sprengung des pythagoreischen Bundes' 332–352; **von Fritz** [122] *PPSI*; **Minar** [160] *EPP*; **Dunbabin** [704] *Western Greeks*; **Burkert** [100] *Lore*; **de Vogel** [180] *Pythagoras*; **Philip** [163] *PEP*; **van der Waerden** [183] *Pythagoreer*; **Boudouris** [96] 'The Pythagorean Community.'
140 **Iamblichus**, *VP* 70–74. Possibly sourced by Timaeus. See also **Iamblichus**, *VP* 94, on Pythagorean testing and training. **Minar** [160] gives a to-the-point brief of the whole process (*EPP* 28–29).

eye—that eye, as Plato says, whose safeguarding is more important than that of a thousand corporeal eyes." We are then informed that Pythagoras not only trained his mind-purification techniques upon this lofty goal, but also employed a *system of education* of his own design.[141] Yet, instead of acquainting us with further details about this enticing program, Iamblichus only introduces the requirements for admission to it, saying, "Since this was the education he could offer his disciples, he would not immediately accept young men who came and wanted to study with him, until he had put them through an examination and made a judgment."[142]

This examination began with a background check of the petitioner; inquiries were conducted into his personal life and the state of his relationships with family, friends, and so forth.[143] Then the person's behavior was scrutinized. Did he talk too much or laugh on the wrong occasions? How did he get along with other students? What, for example, made him happy or sad? Next followed a physical inspection, which included an evaluation of the shape and gait of the applicant's body, allegedly for assessing the state or habits of his soul. If a candidate passed these preliminaries, he graduated to the next phase, in which he was simply sent away for three years and utterly ignored. The idea was to test the person's resolve, that is, how strong was his desire to learn. However, unbeknownst to the aspirant, he remained under constant, if covert, observation in an attempt to determine whether he craved status or recognition, instead of displaying scorn for such lowly impulses.

If a petitioner survived this phase, a greater trial still lay ahead: a five-year period of absolute silence awaited those still determined to belong. The objective was to test the person's self-control, particularly his capacity to keep his mouth shut—the most difficult of trials, according to Iamblichus.[144]

A candidate who entered this phase had to turn over his belongings—money, properties, income—to the order, where it was held by trustees

---

141 However, the doctrine of redirecting one's vision upon the intelligible is obviously Plato's own, which is probably why he is mentioned. This is yet another typically Neoplatonist example of the attempt to merge the two thinkers. As **Burkert** [100] reminds us: "It was Iamblichus who set the direction for the later Neoplatonists, toward a definite equation of Platonism and Pythagoreanism." (*Lore* 98) Hence we must take these particular statements with a good measure of reserve.
142 **Iamblichus**, *VP* 71.
143 **Iamblichus**, *VP* 71.
144 **Iamblichus**, *VP* 72. **Minar** [160] suggests that the "rule of silence may have been largely symbolic, or have referred only to certain rites or occasions." (*EPP* 28n58)

called "politicians," "economists," and "legislators."[145] These elite Pythagoreans managed the financial affairs of the group and made the necessary decisions, probably paid the bills, settled debts, and the like. If the candidate survived the ordeal and was still found worthy to join, he was raised to the rank of *esoteric* and allowed to the inner circle. This meant that from that moment on, the associate was authorized to see the *face* of Pythagoras, who, so far, had only lectured from behind a curtain. To be admitted "inside the veil"—as it was called—constituted the highest honor, bestowed only upon those few who had navigated all trials.[146]

The unlucky ones, on the other hand, who—for whatever reason—did not make the grade, not only had their investment returned, but were paid double the amount by the order before they were summarily dismissed. The expulsion was definitive. In fact, not only did the Pythagoreans never grant a second chance to those who failed, but they also entertained the controversial custom of building a grave—complete with a tombstone—for these unfortunates, as if they had died.[147] If an upstanding Pythagorean encountered such an outcast accidentally, he had to treat the other as a complete stranger. Seemingly, there was no exception to the rule that whoever was dismissed was irrevocably dead. In some weird sense, no one could get out of Pythagoreanism alive. Of course, these kinds of cultist attitudes did not go over well with the rest of the population. On this point, Iamblichus' reports are unanimous.[148]

What seems most amazing in this context is Pythagoras' inability—or that of his political advisers—to anticipate the disastrous results that would ensue from any attempt to convert religious custom to political policy.[149] And if the old sage is not to blame, because, let's say, all these practices were implemented after his death, then the responsibility still lies with those he personally selected or trained. To set up rules that exclude people from an order is one thing, but to not recognize that the very same restrictions—if applied politically—will only end up barring an *ever-increasing majority* of citizens from civic power and political office is the peak of blinding arrogance and self-righteousness, peculiar only to the most narrow-

---

145 *Politikoi, oikonomikoi, nomothetikoi*, **Iamblichus**, *VP* 72.11–12. See also *VP* 257 for the membership of prominent Pythagoreans in the assembly of the Thousand, i.e., the government of Croton.
146 **Iamblichus**, *VP* 72, 89.
147 **Iamblichus**, *VP* 73, 74.
148 **Iamblichus**, *VP* 252, 254, 255, 257, 259, 260, 261, 262.
149 **Boudouris** [96]: "[Pythagoras] did not foresee that soon his Community would clash with the state that he sincerely wished to serve." ('The Pythagorean Community' 62)

minded of cults. Early Pythagoreanism is a case study as to why cults in general cannot handle political power well.

Secrecy and Anti-Democracy

The notion that Pythagoras founded a movement whose mission was the "education or enlightenment of the masses" is wonderfully romantic,[150] yet the very sources who have sought to convey this impression have also preserved old sayings that paint a very different picture. It seems that Pythagoras (or whoever of his immediate followers epitomized this view) fostered a deep mistrust of the general public, even contempt, as the original teachings show, which defined the order in every conceivable way as anti-majority.[151] And public opinion was spurned for precisely that reason: it represented the belief of the many. Iamblichus offers us the rationale behind this policy:

> [The Pythagoreans say] it is silly to adhere to any and every belief, especially if it is widely held, for only a few are capable of having the right beliefs and opinions: these, evidently, are the ones who know, and they are few, so it is clear that this capacity cannot extend to the many.[152]

And Porphyry explains that one of Pythagoras' most mystifying admonitions—namely, "not to walk the highways"—was a coded instruction forbidding his disciples to follow the opinions of the majority. Likewise, all

---

150 I am reproducing **de Vogel** [180] here, who ardently champions this idea (*Pythagoras* 66–69, 147, 159, 246, and *passim*). See **van der Waerden** [183] (*Pythagoreer*) for a sympathetic view. See also **Anton**'s [93] 'The Pythagorean Way of Life: Morality and Religion' 28–38. However, Anton seems to restrict Pythagoras' contributions to education to the edification of the members of the society.

151 This is even admitted by **de Vogel** [180] (*Pythagoras* 160, 174–175), yet without her ever realizing that her beautiful theory of Pythagoras as the public educator set on educating the *masses* has herewith collapsed. In fact, she defends the old maxims as genuinely "of early Pythagorean origin" (175), even remarking on the similarities to **Plato**'s Socrates in the *Crito*, who advocates a similar anti-masses position. As she forcefully argues, why should not this "have been a Pythagorean principle before it became a Socratic one?" However, Pythagoras either educated the many or the few. Now, I am not advocating that Pythagoras never interacted with the common populace, for the testimony on his initial public lectures speaks otherwise. However, that was before his exclusive society had taken hold. Moreover, once the organization was established, access to his teachings was restricted to those "inside" and "outside the veil" who, in both cases, were members of the order. There is also testimony that it was his neglect of the public through associating only with his disciples that generated the wide resentment among the masses that eventually sparked the revolt (cf. **Iamblichus**, *VP* 254).

152 **Iamblichus**, *VP* 200.

Pythagoreans were advised to avoid intercourse with the mass public, and particularly to shun public discussions.[153]

Cornelia de Vogel sees in this "practice of apartness" a motive for why the 300 conspirators—the core of the Pythagorean political faction—had to be sequestered from "the majority of the citizens in whose midst they lived."[154] Not only during their preparation as the council's future leaders, but even after they had seized control, Iamblichus tells us, the Pythagorean elite maintained their separation from the rest of the city, "which was not governed by the same customs and practices as they were."[155] Secrecy separates, and in power, the unapproachable otherness remained emphasized—in much the same way Pythagoras used the veil.

This systematic partitioning of people, things, or conditions into distinct classes was very much in accord with the basic Pythagorean doctrines on harmony, number theory, and numerology. One cannot have relationships or proportions without things keeping their distances from each other. The idea of apartness also helped to distinguish the *prior* from the *subsequent* (consider the message of the "First Speech to the young men," ascribed to the master himself). Segregation also facilitated the famous threefold classification of rational beings—"gods, mortals, and beings like Pythagoras"—preserved by Aristotle.[156] It differentiated immortals from mortals, the divine from the mundane, the earthly convicts from the powers that convicted them. In politics, it also separated the rulers from the ruled, and in the order itself, the ones "inside the veil" from those outside of it. This particular distinction is actually made by Iamblichus, who speaks of "those divided into 'inside' and 'outside.'"[157]

The Gods; and the Ruling of the Many by the Few

It goes without saying that the Pythagorean political symmetry was not complete without the gods—a factor that irreversibly imbued their politics with religion. Indeed, we are informed that:

---

153 **Porphyry**, *VP* 42, on the "walk on highways" saying, and 32 on the "public discussion." **Iamblichus** mentions that "Leave the highway and use the footpaths" was one of many coded phrases not meant to be deciphered by the uninitiated (*VP* 105).

154 See de Vogel [180] *Pythagoras* 175, to whom I am grateful for pointing out the parallels between sequestered life of the common Pythagorean (i.e., **Iamblichus**, *VP* 96–100), and **Apollonius'** account on the isolation of the governing elite in **Iamblichus**, *VP* 254. (See also **de Vogel** [180] *Pythagoras* 189–190.)

155 **Iamblichus**, *VP* 254.

156 **Aristotle**, fr. 192 R = **Iamblichus**, *VP* 31.

157 **Iamblichus**, *VP* 89.

> All their decisions about what to do or not to do aimed at being in accord with the divine. This is the principle; all of life is so ordered as to follow the god, and the rationale of this philosophy is that people behave absurdly when they seek the good anywhere but from the gods.[158]

Thus, the Pythagorean approach to thinking like God was to subordinate everything, even the most banal aspects of day-to-day life, to divine principles. Naturally, this had to include the legislative field. As Iamblichus assures us, it is from the rule of the gods that Pythagoras derived the laws to govern society.[159] Hence, according to the aforementioned principle that "what comes first must be more honored than what comes later," rulers must take heed of the will of the gods—who are obviously prior to them—and not the will of the people, as they are merely subsequent. By the same token, the ruled have to follow the rulers; it was the only way to follow the gods.[160] In other words, the Pythagoreans' justification for being anti-democratic was bolstered by this very premise, which for them reflected the cosmic order: the majority is subsequent to all; the ruling minority is prior to the majority, but subsequent to the gods; and the gods are prior to all, thus they follow no one.

There is an important fragment, attributed to Archytas (the Pythagorean ruler of Tarentum and friend of Plato), that defines the distinction between ruler and ruled and the common bond that binds them:

> All actions are made by the interweaving of ruling, being ruled, and controlling. To rule belongs to the better, to be ruled belongs to the worse, and to control is proper to both. For the rational part of the soul rules, the irrational is ruled, and both control the passions. For from the attunement of these two comes virtue, and it leads the soul away from pleasures and pains to peace and freedom from passion.[161]

The greatest enemy of the Pythagorean state is anarchy. It is the antithesis of their pyramidal arrangement that validated their laws—the gods on top, then the minority of rulers, followed by the majority of the ruled. This

---

158   Iamblichus, *VP* 137. Source is possibly Aristoxenus; cf. **Guthrie** [43] *HGP* 1.199, 199n2.
159   Iamblichus, *VP* 174.
160   This was pointed out by **Minar** [160]: "Rulers are in no real sense responsible to the people, but only to the gods. If the government is regarded as a trust it is not as a result of any 'social contract' theory but the trust consists in the fact that they alone can interpret properly the will of the gods." (*EPP* 101 and 102) Thus, "men are guided on this earth by those who are able to interpret to them the will of the gods." (*EPP* 100)
161   Archytas was an atypical Pythagorean, a democrat who respected the election process by which he himself came to power. In many ways the above fragment—if it is really his—betrays a maturity of thinking missing in early Pythagoreanism. I doubt it reflects sixth-

is why in the Pythagorean order of things even slaves had their rightful place. According to Iamblichus, the Pythagoreans believed that the human race must be given a type of government against which it feels unwilling to rebel, and that, in their view, was only *government by the divine*. (We should not forget here that Pythagoras was also considered divine.) The idea of divine government was intrinsically connected with the idea of salvation. This we see in the Pythagorean rationale against anarchy preserved by Iamblichus, namely that human beings cannot be saved if there is no one to exercise control over them.[162] Accordingly, it was characteristic for the Pythagoreans to demand that "a human being should never be allowed to do as he likes. There should always be a government, a lawful and decorous authority, to which each citizen is subject."[163]

Signs of a Pythagorean Police State?

The adoration of precedence and conformity also explains the Pythagorean relationship to existing laws. They thought that it was better to follow a law that was ancestral or conventional—hence, prior—even if it was not a good law, than to experiment with new law or have no law at all. Thus, to love the law was imperative for the Pythagoreans, as one of the most famous sayings attributed to Pythagoras attests: "To help the law, fight against lawlessness." Every day, a Pythagorean had to repeat this maxim shortly after the ceremonial evening meal.[164]

Could this instruction lead to the establishment of a Pythagorean police state? Armand Delatte offers an interesting interpretation. He believes the saying pertains to the "civic duty of denunciation," which should be understood in light of Plato's demand that the "duty of every citizen is to report acts of lawlessness to the magistrates."[165] Following Delatte, E. L. Minar concludes that "the necessity for spying and delation in the Pythagorean state was obvious." He continues: "If people were not sufficiently impres-

---

or even fifth-century thinking. Yet the principle of division it refers to may be much older. The fragment is of **Stobaeus**, Fl. 43.132, fr. 2c, in accordance with **Minar** [160] (*EPP* 112), to whom I am indebted for this passage. See also **Delatte** [111] *Politique* 85–86, for the French rendition and comments. (I believe he is Minar's source.)

162 **Iamblichus**, *VP* 174–175. See also **Minar's** [160] comments: "The basis of relations between men in society ... was considered by the earliest Pythagoreans to be the absolute rule of the gods" and "divine guidance in human affairs corresponded to an innate need of man." (*EPP* 110, also 99–100)

163 **Iamblichus**, *VP* 203.
164 **Iamblichus**, *VP* 100, 171, 223.
165 **Delatte** [111] *Politique* 49–50. On **Plato**, *Laws* IX.856.b–c. Cf. **Minar** [160] *EPP* 101–102.

sed with the fact that Pythagoras was a god and the pronouncements of his followers in effect divine commands, the arm of the law must be ready. The idea of disobedience must not be allowed to spread in the populace."[166]

And there is one additional, often ignored detail on how the Pythagoreans kept tabs on each other. Diodorus Siculus reports that as soon as they got up in the morning, the members were required to disclose to one another a detailed account of the activities and events of the previous day. Supposedly, this exercise had a twofold aim: to train a person's memory and to teach him to assess his conduct, in order to, as Diodorus says, "gain knowledge and judgment in all matters." Perhaps; but such practice may well have furnished the leadership with a continuous stream of information on the state of mind of each and every member.[167]

Beans and Politics

A somewhat amusing hint concerning the order's political orientation may also be drawn from a curious connection between *beans* and democracy. In question is one of Pythagoras' most arcane ordinances, which required his followers to "avoid beans."[168] This remarkable demand provoked widespread speculation in antiquity. Some have blamed the ban on the unusual shape of beans, namely, they looked like genitals, or the gates of Hades, or even resembled the shape of the universe, and so on. Other interpretations rate beans as unhealthy or destructive, or perceive certain sexual implications. However, one version persists that considers the taboo a *political* directive—this on the authority of Aristotle, no less: it was a warning against participation in a democratic election process.[169] As it turns out, beans were used as counters for the type of political elections that were decided not by direct vote—for example, a show of hands—but by *sortition*, the casting or drawing of lots: in other words, a lottery. Usually, the highest offices were *allotted* by such methods of chance, which, together with strict

---

166 **Minar** [160] *EPP* 103.

167 **Diodorus**, 10.5.1. For parallels see **Iamblichus**, *VP* 165, where it is not specified that members had to perform this exercise with one another, but only that they did not get up in the morning until they had recalled the events of the previous day. See also *VP* 256.

168 **Porphyry**, *VP* 43–44: "Abstain from beans as if from human flesh." Parallels: **Iamblichus**, *VP* 109; D.L., 8.19 and 34 = **Aristotle**, fr. 195 R; **Cicero** [628] *De Divinatione* 2.58.119.

169 **Aristotle**, fr. 195 R. Also according to **Hippolytus**: "Do not accept office in the government. For they used beans for the elections to offices in those days." (*Refutation* 6, 154 W 27.5, **Osborne** [638] *Rethinking Early Greek Philosophy: Hippolytus of Rome and the Presocratics* 271). See also Ninon's speech against Pythagoreanism in **Iamblichus**, *VP* 260: "Fight against beans, for they are lords of the lot, and of putting into office those chosen by lot."

rules delimiting reelections, assured a perpetual rotation of officeholders. W. K. C. Guthrie explains that in this manner the ban on beans was rationalized in a political sense: "It was said to symbolize the oligarchic tendencies of Pythagoras."[170]

Above all else, Pythagoras seems to have abhorred every form of factionalism in politics, striving to eliminate it completely in the cities of Southern Italy. This is according to Porphyry, who attributes the following saying to the sage:

> One must drive out by every device, and with fire and sword and all means whatever cut off from the body disease, from the soul ignorance, from the belly luxury, from the city factionalism, from the household dissidence, and from all at once disproportion.[171]

A Religious-Political-Economic Dictatorship?

In light of the above, the movement's political views might have looked something like this:

- Power is to be held unequivocally in the hands of an anointed elite.
- This elite must always be a minority because "only the few know best."
- Measures by which the multitude expresses its will are prohibited; thus the *uninitiated* majority is invariably excluded from any decision process.
- The social order is maintained by the rigid enforcement of classes consisting of rulers and ruled, each with its own obligations. This is most poignantly demonstrated by a particular fragment of Stobaeus (early fifth century A.D.): "They said that rulers should be not only wise, but also lovers of mankind; while the ruled should be not only obedient, but lovers of rulers."[172]
- Any way one cuts it, Pythagoreanism is fiercely anti-democratic, at least when implemented as above, that is, as a *political* movement. Moreover, because the members held the form of a cult *in spite* of having political power, they were much more than a mere political party. The ramifications of their agenda exceeded the usual political boundaries and invaded all aspects of life, particularly family and social relations, as well as *economics*.
- For all their respect for the law, the ruling Pythagorean elite operated on different principles when compared to the rest of the population. For instance, this powerful minority pooled its possessions and managed them, in a sense, as a giant private trust. In fact, Iamblichus insists, "Everything was in common and the same for all: *no-one had any private property.*"[173]

---

170 **Guthrie** [43] *HGP* 1.185.
171 **Porphyry**, *VP* 22.
172 **Stobaeus**, fr. 18. (Fl. 4.1.40 H; F.H.G. 2.278, after **Minar** [160] *EPP* 102, 102n30.)
173 **Iamblichus**, *VP* 168; see also 72, 257. By alluding to friendship, the saying in **Porphyry**, *VP* 33, serves as a moral justification for the abolishment of individual ownership: "What friends own, they own in common."

- All non-Pythagoreans, naturally, did not benefit from this arrangement. Again, we see the separation principle at work. Nonetheless, we should not seek to recognize within this mythical portrait of Pythagoras reflections of an early Karl Marx, even though the disciples were obliged to relinquish all individual ownership. Pythagoras' target audience was the aristocracy, not the "proletariat"—that is, the rulers, not the ruled. Thus, we can at best speak of an "aristocratic communism."[174]
- The early Pythagoreans, who allegedly set out to create a utopia—in their view, a state run by a true *aristocracy*, as in "government by the *best*," rather than adopting a *meritocracy*, or "rule by the most educated"—ended up installing an imbalanced *oligarchy*, or "rule by the few."[175]

Pythagoras never created a new ruling class through *education* (as some modern scholars like to believe) but instead recruited his followers from an existing *hereditary* aristocracy: the privileged sons of the governing elite, who have their future council positions firmly assured.[176] Thus, in spite of Pythagoras' praise of frugality and abstinence or his condemnation of wealth and luxury, the order focused its recruitment efforts entirely upon the rich and powerful; the nonaffluent powerless majority was shunned.[177]

And yet, the stringent membership requirements—which initially assisted Pythagoras in forging a loyal and cohesive body of willing conspirators—eventually turned into a liability for the order. Sooner or later, the friends or family members of the anointed would fail to make the grade, and, given enough time, an increasingly large contingent of Crotonian citizens, otherwise perfectly qualified to lead, ended up barred forever from the ranks of the order—and, thus, from civic power.[178] To make matters worse, because of the order's rigid policies regulating friendship, the governing Pythagoreans stopped caring for non-Pythagoreans, and, as we have seen, from interacting with failed candidates.

---

174 See **Minar** [160] on the "large number of initiates who were members of the 'communistic' group" (*EPP* 30) and "the Society and its 'communistic' organization" (55).

175 **Dunbabin** [704]: "Their direction, like that of political clubs elsewhere in Greece, was oligarchic." (*Western Greeks* 361) And **von Fritz** [122]: "The Pythagorean order with its hierarchical tendencies was admirably fitted to become a supporter of aristocratic government in the time of rising democratic tendencies." (*PPSI* 98)

176 **Iamblichus**, *VP* 45; **Justin**, 20.4.14. See **Minar** [160]: "There is no record of a *coup d'état* by which the Pythagoreans seized power. This was unnecessary, it seems certain, because the Pythagoreans were members of the ruling class, and the growth of Pythagorean influence is in fact a process of 'boring from within.'" (*EPP* 8)

177 **Minar** [160] states: "The membership of the clubs was made up mainly of nobles, the rich and well-born citizens who could afford such activities and were most interested in the advantages they could bring." (*EPP* 25)

178 **Iamblichus**, *VP* 73, 74, 95: "But if [Pythagoras] saw that someone was not suited, he expelled him as a stranger and an alien."

In summary, whenever the order's political elite got hold of power, they formed a convincing dictatorship of cultic fundamentalists whose only commitment was to the gods, Pythagoras, and each other. The closest analogy to it would be the junta of a banana republic—one that is based not on anything even remotely resembling "philosophy," but on the notion of a religiously tainted personality cult.

In fairness, the Pythagorean faction within the ruling council should not be considered a monolithic political bloc, at least not as far as its political orientation is concerned. There are reports, not less credible than the rest, that the Pythagorean party split into conservative oligarchists on one side and democrats on the other, with the latter being in the minority. The likely representative of the democrats was a controversial thinker named Hippasus, and it is only when he and like-minded members sided with the popular forces that the Pythagorean traditionalists lost power. However, as we cannot associate this split accurately with either anti-Pythagorean revolt, we cannot time the emergence of a democratic orientation within Pythagoreanism. It is safe to assume that the split transpired between 500 and 450 B.C., after the founder's death.

In any case, we now have some *plausible* insight into the political climate in Croton as events gradually snowballed toward the popular uprisings—whether we are dealing with the first, the second, or both.

But first we should focus on the catastrophic event that may have set the revolts in motion: the savage war against Sybaris.

WAR AND LUXURY

> When in former times the Greeks had founded Sybaris in Italy, the city had enjoyed a rapid growth because of the fertility of the land. For lying as the city did between two rivers, the Crathis and the Sybaris, from which it derived its name, its inhabitants, who tilled an extensive and fruitful countryside, came to possess great riches. And since they kept granting citizenship to many aliens, they increased to such an extent that they were considered to be far the first among the inhabitants of Italy.
> —Diodorus Siculus (first century B.C.)[179]

Sybaris—the Antipode of Pythagoreanism

Before the war with Croton, Sybaris was the wealthiest, most powerful, and most advanced city of Southern Italy, with a population of perhaps 500,000.[180] It was known, above all, for two things: its beauty and its luxury. In his critical work, *The Western Greeks* (to which I am much indebted), T. J. Dunbabin recounts the literary tradition that mentions Sybaris' "great banquets and splendid public festivals, its elegant youth, the shaded streets and well-tilled fields, the care for health and comfort, the pride in wine and cuisine," and he speaks of its metropolitan flair as something akin to a Parisian ambience. Most noteworthy was the unparalleled wealth manifested in the city's temples, in the bridges spanning its rivers, and even in its popular Turkish baths, which are said to have originally been invented by the Sybarites. Allegedly, they planted trees alongside the roads leading from the city so that when visiting the countryside all Sybarites could enjoy traveling in the shade—a blessing in the sweltering climate of Southern Italy, but also, it would seem, an incredible logistical feat. (One wonders how they managed to water all the trees.) The city's banquets were so elaborate that the attending women were notified a year in advance to have time to arrange for their dresses. The Sybarites were most proud of their magnificent cavalry: the well-trained horses were renowned for their ability to dance to the music of flutes. Some citizens were so wealthy that one particular aristocrat is mentioned as traveling with a thousand cooks; the same individual complained to everyone that his bed of roses gave him blis-

---

179 **Diodorus**, 12.9.1–2.
180 Including noncitizens, slaves, and the greater surroundings. See **Dunbabin** [704] *Western Greeks* 77, 365. According to **Diodorus**, 12.9.2, there were 300,000 citizens.

ters.[181] These kinds of stories were popular in antiquity. The historian Diodorus Siculus lists one example after another, proving that to many Sybaris was a synonym for unbridled extravagance, concluding, "The Sybarites are slaves to their belly and lovers of luxury."[182]

Eventually, Sybaris came to a collision course with Croton, to the south, when a new ruler, Telys, seized control over the city, seemingly against the will of the entrenched aristocrats.[183] He mobilized the popular masses, causing some of his opponents to seek sanctuary in Croton. By one account some 500 of the wealthiest citizens left, and subsequently, their estates were confiscated. Yet apparently Telys was not satisfied with the status quo, so he sent ambassadors to Croton to demand the return of the expatriates. The regular Crotonians—as well as some undetermined faction of their governing body—were inclined to return the exiled aristocrats. Ultimately, it was only Pythagoras' personal intervention with the assembly that averted such action.[184] Iamblichus specifies that when the citizens of Croton became uncertain of how to handle the affair, Pythagoras instructed his disciples to reject Sybaris' request. One of the reasons given was that in Telys' struggle for power, his followers had supposedly killed a few aristocrats who were also Pythagoreans. What the state of Pythagoreanism was among the Sybarites, we are not told; there are no other indications that, at this time, the Samian had further extended his missionary work or his political influence so as to include Sybaris.[185] Be that as it may, it appears that Pythagoras refused to negotiate with the "murderous" ambassadors, and that the Crotonians retained the expatriates at his behest, accepting the now-inevitable war. Such

---

181 **Dunbabin** [704] *Western Greeks* 76, 78–83. (On the "thousand cooks" reference, see **Timaeus**, fr. 9 (Athen. 12, 58, p. 541), *FGrHist* 566 (IIIB, p. 595). Some parallels on luxury are in **Diodorus**, 8.18–20.

182 **Diodorus**, 8.18.

183 See **Diodorus**, 12.9–10. **Dunbabin** [704] *Western Greeks* 362.

184 **Diodorus**, 12.9; **Minar** [160]: "Although the people wished to give back the fugitives, the influence of Pythagoras in the senate prevented it." (*EPP* 13)

185 **Iamblichus**, *VP* 177, only states that some of Pythagoras' students had been killed by those who had come as Sybarite ambassadors. Cf. **Minar** [160] *EPP* 13. But Minar also finds convincing reasons as to why Pythagoras refuses to give up the exiled aristocrats, i.e., because they too were Pythagoreans. (38) Yet by a different account, the other Pythagoreans, the ones allegedly murdered in Sybaris, were not Sybarite citizens at all, but belonged to a Crotonian delegation of thirty emissaries who had come on a goodwill mission—perhaps a last-ditch effort to avert the war. Apparently, the Sybarites slaughtered this entire group, according to **van der Waerden** [183] (*Pythagoreer* 206) in reference to **Athenaios** (*Deipnosophistai* 12.521). **Dunbabin** [704] also indicates this same version of events: "The immediate cause, one of the greatest impieties of which the Greeks were capable, was that [the Sybarites] killed thirty envoys from Kroton, who had come perhaps bearing the refusal to surrender the Sybarite exiles." (*Western Greeks* 363)

sway only demonstrates that the council of Croton was firmly in Pythagorean hands.[186]

The War

Finally, in the year 510 B.C., the opposing armies met for one decisive battle. Reportedly, there were 300,000 Sybarites against 100,000 Crotonians.[187] The latter were aided, however, by an uncertain number of mercenaries—originally settlers en route to Sicily—led by the Spartan prince, Dorieus.[188] The overall command over the Crotonian force was held by the famous Olympic athlete Milo, the Pythagorean general. An awe-inspiring figure draped in lion skin and complete with battle club, Milo represented the consummate impersonation of Heracles, Croton's mythical founder.[189]

A savage battle ensued, but the Crotonians gained the upper hand with a most clever strategy. Aware of the musical conditioning of the Sybarite horses, they hid a group of flute players along the path of the enemy's onrushing cavalry.[190] As soon as the horses heard the flutes, the whole attack was thrown into disarray. Taking advantage of the confusion, the Crotonians, in a burst of unmitigated anger, refused to accept prisoners and slaughtered their foes without discrimination. Most of the Sybarites perished. The victors moved on to the city itself, and after a short siege overran it completely. Telys and his supporters sought refuge in the temple, but to no avail. They were soon found and mercilessly killed. The Crotonians then

---

186 **Minar** [160]: "Pythagoras gave his advice "to the associates" and the action was obviously that of a [political] club, but it is impossible to say just what were the concrete devices used." (*EPP* 27) **Dunbabin** [704] infers that the revolts themselves "indicate sufficiently clearly that real power was in [the] hands [of the Pythagoreans]." (*Western Greeks* 361) And **von Fritz** [122] concludes: "The lasting enmity between the Pythagoreans and Sybaris as well as the character of the earliest Alliance coins, which can scarcely be dated later than about 500, indicates that the order must have played some part in politics as far back as the destruction of Sybaris in 510." (*PPSI* 91) Also: "These [Pythagorean] societies . . . seem to have taken a strong hand in active politics as far back as the great struggle between Kroton and her mighty neighbor Sybaris in 510." (99)

187 **Diodorus**, 12.9.5–10.1.

188 Possibly 1,000 fighters or thereabouts—estimated by **Dunbabin** [704] *Western Greeks* 363; see **Herodotus**, *Histories* 5.44.

189 **Diodorus** (4.24.7) relates the story of a man named Croton whom Heracles had accidentally killed. The mythical hero was traveling through Italy at the time on one of his famous quests. Full of remorse, Heracles accorded the dead man a majestic funeral and erected a huge tomb in his honor, promising the natives that one day a famous city would arise on the spot and it would bear the dead man's name. See **Dunbabin** [704] (*Western Greeks* 27) for comments on Crotonian coins commemorating this account.

190 **Dunbabin** [704] *Western Greeks* 364.

plundered the city and set it on fire, but even this, it seems, was not enough. Displaying an almost inhuman ruthlessness, they came up with a plan to erase Sybaris from the face of the Earth. Managing to divert the course of a nearby river, the Crotonians flooded what was left of the city—an act labeled by scholars as the worst atrocity in Greek history.[191] Sybaris was literally washed away, its riches and beauty irretrievably lost.

From an archeologist's perspective, Dunbabin reserves some hope that one day we may catch a glimpse of her past glory. As he wrote in 1948:

> In the luxuriant fever-stricken forest near the mouth of the [river] Crati, perhaps 20 feet under one of its abandoned stony beds, still lies what the Krotoniates left after its sack; a harvest of archaic Greek art which has always excited the hopes of scholars. Perhaps some day the wealth and skill needed for its discovery will be united, to produce the richest and most valuable reward which a Greek archaeologist can imagine.[192]

Unfortunately, only very little of the original city has been uncovered today. There were some efforts to rebuild it after its fall, yet the results were insignificant compared with what was destroyed. Eventually, two cities were built on top of Sybaris' ruins, first Thuri, an Athenian effort, some seventy years later, and then Copia, a Roman colony in 193 B.C. There are only a few places where all three layers are exposed to view, sitting on top of each other some four to five feet apart. The archeological site is not small, yet it is negligible when compared with how large Sybaris must have been. The excavations continue, yet to my knowledge they focus mainly on the Roman remains and on Thuri, wherever these sites are readily exposed. The lowest level, Sybaris proper, is so far mostly untouched.

As is usual in such cases, no one wants to destroy two well-preserved layers, even if there is the probability of a worthwhile third layer below them. Furthermore, the entire area is largely marshland. The ground is still quite wet, and the first thing that strikes the visitor is the network of aboveground pipes that crisscross the site. These pipes are fed by powerful pumps designed to drain the land, if only to ameliorate the situation for the resident team of archeologists. In any case, the landscape has an old feel about it; "detached" and "solitary" are also words that come to mind. There

---

191 *RE* IV A1,1008.26; **Dunbabin** [704] *Western Greeks* 364. On the magnitude of Sybaris' destruction, see **Minar** [160]: "Worst disaster that had ever befallen a Greek city at the hands of another" (*EPP* 9); also **Burkert** [100]: "The destruction of Sybaris was the worst atrocity wrought by Greeks against a Greek city in that era." (*Lore* 116)

192 **Dunbabin** [704] *Western Greeks* 364.

Why was Sybaris Destroyed? 67

are some scatterings of bushes and trees, all thick and tough-looking, but also wide spaces as far as one can see. Both the new and old riverbeds are still there, perhaps a couple of miles away, the latter as stony as remembered by Dunbabin, but characterized here and there by rich orange groves, and watered on one end by a tiny rivulet which, intriguingly, may have worked its way back from where it was banished so long ago. The Crati itself, though not far off, runs its course quietly; its waters move slow enough that, watching it, one wonders how long it took the Crotonians to flood the city. It still amazes me that a site so peaceful and serene may have witnessed so much death and despair—destruction on a scale that defies the imagination.

Why was Sybaris Destroyed?

Perhaps we might ask ourselves why this particular war developed such horrendous dimensions. But if there is truth to the story of Pythagorean involvement, as the ancient sources attest, then it is not unjustified to ask: what factors could have motivated such an army—commanded, no less, by a Pythagorean general, under the authority of a Pythagorean-controlled council, and guided by a principled leader like Pythagoras—to commit such all-out atrocities, perhaps even genocide, culminating in the obliteration of a thriving metropolis by a means that, in this case, was nothing less than a weapon of mass destruction? So far, only a few answers have been forwarded, none of which seem satisfying. Admittedly, we are navigating a speculative domain, appearing to some to be closer to lore than to history, which is perhaps why there is some reluctance among scholars to tackle this question.[193] Yet if Croton's rise to power is linked to this catastrophe—by making it the dominant colony of Southern Italy[194]—and if its af-

---

193 **Van der Waerden** [183] does conclude that the Pythagoreans share in the responsibility for the terrible savagery that destroyed Sybaris: "Allerdings begingen die Krotoniaten am Anfang dieser Periode eine furchtbare Gewalttat, für welche die Pythagoreer wohl mitverantwortlich waren: die Vernichtung von Sybaris." (*Pythagoreer* 192) As for Pythagoras' role, **van der Waerden** ventures that we do not know if he is equally responsible for this horrifying bloody deed, but that certainly the Pythagoreans were involved: "Ob Pythagoras für diese entsetzliche Bluttat mit verantwortlich war, das wissen wir nicht. Sicherlich waren die Pythagoreer mit dabei." (206) My point is, considering Pythagoras' godlike status within the order, how could he not be responsible?

194 **Dunbabin** [704]: "Kroton was now unquestionably the first power in south Italy for a generation" (*Western Greeks* 367) and "For the greater part of the first half of the fifth century [the Pythagoreans] appear to have had control of the affairs of Kroton." (369) Also **Burkert** [100]: "From that time on, according to the evidence of coins, Croton exercised some kind of hegemony in Southern Italy. It clearly ended, suddenly, about 450 B.C." (*Lore* 115; the date, of

tereffects are also to be blamed for the Pythagorean society's eventual demise, it is not improper to seek out those factors that might have played a significant role.

The reasons usually cited for this conflict are not different from those postulated for other wars: rivalry in commerce, blocked trade routes, political disputes, and unholy alliances, such as between the Pythagorean aristocrats of Croton and their counterparts in Sybaris, or between Sybaris' ruling democrats and the anti-Pythagorean minority in Croton. It has been argued that the reasons above could have forced both sides to opt for war.[195]

While these grounds may constitute some of the motives for the conflict itself, what they do not explain is why, *after* the battle was won, Sybaris had to be wiped off the map. What has not been reconciled so far is the inconsistency between trying to protect the lives *and* the interests of the Sybarite aristocracy—who, reportedly, had their properties confiscated by Telys—and fighting a war that irrevocably destroyed the very possessions of which they had been deprived. If the Crotonite engagement was a reaction against a democratic coup d'état, why did they not stop their attack once Telys and his supporters were killed and restore the deposed Sybarite aristocrats without much ado to their original stations? An alliance of both cities—the mightiest combination imaginable—under the hegemony of an "international" Pythagorean council would have given the order almost inconceivable power.

Moreover, the bitterness over the distribution of Sybarite spoils would have been avoided. There would have been no demands to allocate a part of it to the common people, because the possessions would not have changed hands; they would have remained under the control of the original aristocratic owners. Obviously, where there are no spoils, there are no claims. Eventually, the Pythagoreans, with their communal policies on personal possessions, could have "owned" it all unchallenged. It seems to me that one might expect such a strategy if the Pythagoreans were headed by an ambitious politician, a military conqueror, or at least some shrewd businessman. Yet apparently, Pythagoras did not react in such a predictable manner.

---

course, is coincidental with that of the widespread second revolt against the order, which put a definitive end to its political rule, and with that, also ended Croton's preeminent role. This only goes to show how the power and prestige of the Pythagoreans were intertwined with Croton's status.)

195 Mentioned by **Minar** [160] *EPP* 11, 12–13, 27.

Here I must speculate, but only because, to my knowledge, the following possibility has never been fully explored: is it not thinkable that Pythagoras, true to the mission he inaugurated upon his arrival in Italy, allowed Sybaris to be wiped out precisely *because* it was the absolute embodiment of luxury? Was such a gleaming diamond of unbridled extravagance not an unbearable sight in Pythagoras' eyes, an affront to everything he stood for? Sybaris was a city whose very name had become synonymous with lavishness, wealth, and pleasure seeking throughout the world! Even for us today the term "sybarite" suggests a person devoted to luxury and pleasure. Could Sybaris not have been Pythagoras' equivalent to Sodom and Gomorrah, his very own Babylon forever taunting his authority or beliefs? If the Samian considered it his duty to expedite everyone's "jail term" here on Earth—by depriving them of the pleasures that would make them want to linger on—what would he think of a city which, by its sheer opulence, might forever prevent its inhabitants from being punished *enough* for their sentences to be fulfilled?

The contrasts between the two cities could not have been more extreme. On one hand, the Sybarites indulged themselves in the most exorbitant and opulent banquets imaginable, while the Pythagoreans, we are told, only set up delicious feasts as a test of their ascetic resolve, and after carefully taking in the sight and smell of each dish, to better incite their desires, they returned the food to the servants without taking a taste.[196] We've seen that the Sybarite women required a full year for the creation of their lavish garments and flaunted everywhere their precious jewelry, while the Crotonian women were forced to give up their gold-threaded dresses and were banned from wearing gold, lest they be mistaken for prostitutes.[197] There are many more examples.

In the end, the differences between both political systems must have signified the worst of all threats for the order. Here, all were subjected to the most rigorous rule, exercised authoritarian and elitist from the top down, while prescriptions and regulations governed every waking moment of a follower; there, democracy reigned from the bottom up, according to the power of the masses. For Pythagoras, this must have been equivalent to anarchy, with everyone doing what they wanted. Hence, without an enforceable political/religious system, the Sybarites fell prey to the pursuit of

---

196 **Iamblichus**, *VP* 187.
197 Ibid.

worldly pleasures and self-gratifications. This attitude, coupled with their incomparable wealth and their commercial dominance in Southern Italy, must have constituted a never-ending threat to Pythagoras' mission and the standing of his society, not to mention Croton's position.

We do have some hints from Iamblichus himself as to what Pythagoras' attitude was toward fighting a war: namely, to wage it *ruthlessly* and as a *holy struggle*. Yes, the Great Sage does recommend not to become hostile against "those not wholly bad";[198] however, if enmity is justified, then, as Iamblichus explains:

> Once assumed, however, hatred should be carried out mercilessly, unless the opponent reforms. War is in such a situation a holy thing: "One should fight not with words but with deeds, and war is a lawful and a holy thing, if they fight as man against man."[199]

Perhaps, in Pythagoras' view, there was no chance for Sybaris to reform—not as long as it was under popular or democratic control—and certainly not if reform meant to relinquish its wealth and luxurious living. This concern might also have applied to any of the returning Sybarite aristocrats. The temptation to bring back the "good life" could have been considered too great, particularly if one had been forcefully deprived of it. In any case, Sybaris was probably a lost cause for the Pythagoreans, one that had to be eliminated, lest it should rise again.

---

198 **Iamblichus**, *VP* 232.
199 **Minar's** [160] rendition of **Iamblichus**, *VP* 232 (*EPP* 103).

THE REVOLTS AGAINST THE PYTHAGOREAN POLITICAL ELITE

> But when they conquered Sybaris, and that one (Pythagoras) departed, and they (the Pythagoreans) administered the captured land, but did not divide it by lot according to the desire of the multitude, the people's silent hatred broke out, and they formed a faction against them. And those who stood closest to the Pythagoreans in ties of kinship and friendship became leaders of the dissension.... But their relatives were especially indignant because the Pythagoreans gave the right hand as a pledge of good faith only to Pythagoreans, and to no other relatives except parents; also because they offered their possessions in common to one another, but excluded their relatives. When these started the dissension, the rest readily fell in with their enmity.
> —Iamblichus, *On the Pythagorean Life*[200]

The Growing Hatred of the Non-Pythagoreans

If the above testimony is accurate, the destruction of Sybaris may have hounded the Pythagoreans for years, eventually playing a role in the order's demise as a political force. The troubles began, as they often do, with the spoils of war and their distribution. It was up to the governing council—firmly controlled by the Pythagorean faction—to lawfully divide the vast estates of the Sybarites and to disperse them fairly. Yet the majority of the population resented the proposed partitioning and took sides with the anti-Pythagorean opposition. The latter, not surprisingly, consisted of relatives and former friends of the Pythagorean elite who had been shut out from the privileges enjoyed by those accepted into the order.[201] We hear of a silent hatred that must have festered for some time; the fact that a fair amount of people "had been given up" by the society "as beyond hope" did not help the situation. Those rejected certainly felt ridiculed by the Pythagoreans. Declaring people dead or erecting their graves—only for failing the candidate tests—was not the smartest public relations policy. We must keep in mind that such disgrace could befall anyone aspiring to join the group, even if the transgression was only that the person was a slow learner.[202]

---

200 **Iamblichus**, *VP* 255–257 (trans. **Dillon** and **Hershbell** [641] *Iamblichus: On the Pythagorean Way of Life*).
201 **Iamblichus**, *VP* 255; **Minar** [160]: "But the decisive factor in bringing the discontent to a head was the refusal of the ruling oligarchy to divide the newly-acquired territory according to the pleasure of the populace.... The growth of large estates and the expansion of the aristocratic landed interests were driving the small farmers and laborers to the wall." (*EPP* 61)
202 **Iamblichus**, *VP* 74. On "given up as hopeless" and "subjected to ridicule," see *VP* 252.

To nonmembers the Pythagoreans must have seemed like the most incomprehensible of cults. For example, their obsession with secrecy led them to communicate in code words or enigmatic symbols when outsiders were present; as Iamblichus reports, they used "secret devices to exclude the uninitiated."[203] The outward behavior of the followers became increasingly unnatural the longer they belonged to the order, or at least that must have been the impression upon those familiar with them. Members were obliged to abstain from displays of emotion, and particularly frowned upon was laughing, showing sympathy, and acting out of anger. In fact, no Pythagorean would punish a slave while angry; he would wait until he had recovered his poise and then punish him.[204] Pythagoras himself was renowned for never laughing or jesting, but always maintaining a solemn demeanor. This behavior was called "holding one's peace." Pythagoreans had to wear only white clothing, and, as we have seen, advanced candidates were sworn to five years of absolute silence. Such conduct must have been quite irritating to their family and friends.[205]

Furthermore, as all personal possessions of the initiates were converted to common property, we can appreciate what a humongous can of worms the Pythagoreans had opened when their leaders began partitioning the land of vanquished Sybaris. Finding themselves shut out and treated as absolute strangers, those most neglected by the Pythagoreans—their relatives and former friends—were the first to conspire against them.[206] Yet in their arrogance, the members ignored these troubling signs, behaving more like the typical members of a boneheaded cult than students of human nature.

An additional reason for widespread dissatisfaction with the Pythagorean regime may have been the desire of the public to return to the kind of "good life" that prevailed before the Samian sage had reached their shores. There are some indications that after the victory over Sybaris, the Crotonians were soon fed up with the harsh frugality propagated by the Pythago-

---

203 Iamblichus, *VP* 104. On covert communications, see also 105, 227; **Porphyry**, *VP* 57.
204 Iamblichus, *VP* 197. See also the example on Archytas, who told his slaves that the reason that they did not receive punishment for certain misdeeds was because they had made him angry; also **Diodorus**, 10.7.4.
205 On repressing emotion: **Iamblichus**, *VP* 196–198, 225–226. On not punishing in anger: **Iamblichus**, *VP* 197–198; **D.L.**, 8.20; **Diodorus**, 10.7.4. On Pythagoras never laughing or jesting: **D.L.**, 8.19; **Porphyry**, *VP* 35. On "holding one's peace": **Iamblichus**, *VP* 68, 104, 226; sought by Pythagoras when testing candidates, **Iamblichus**, *VP* 94. On wearing white: **Iamblichus**, *VP* 100, 149.
206 On common property and ignoring their kinfolk: **Iamblichus**, *VP* 72, 257.

rean faction and yearned for more self-gratification, wealth, and luxurious living.[207]

The First Revolt

The details that follow these increasing difficulties are quite murky, and the events of the second revolt are repeatedly mixed up with the first. Moreover, the narrative, which shares more affinities with a Shakespearean tragedy than with a historical account, seems to suffer from a peculiar affliction: the more comprehensive the attempt to present it in a cogent way, the more inconsistencies and contradictions one encounters.[208]

There are a number of important players involved in this ensuing drama, such as Cylon, a leading aristocrat who applied for membership to the society, only to be turned down by Pythagoras himself because the latter detected certain signs in his physical appearance that betrayed a tyrannical disposition. Rebuffed, Cylon mobilized his supporters and began to conspire against the hapless Pythagoreans. However, a different report names Cylon as the commander of Sybaris, possibly functioning as Croton's governor of the vanquished city—conceivably the man who would administer the spoils, including the captured real estate.[209] Perhaps the whole altercation arose from a land deal gone sour.

---

207 **Timaeus**, fr. 44 (*FGrHist* 566F44, Athen. 12, 22 p. 522 A). Cf. **Minar** [160] *EPP* 73–74 and **Burkert** [100] *Lore* 116–117 for further comments. (See also *FGrHist* IIIB, 297–607 *Kommentar, TEXT* p. 560.)

208 The author of one such attempt is Apollonius of Tyana (first century A.D.), preserved in **Iamblichus**, *VP* 254, and referred to by **von Fritz** [122] as a "large-scale fresco painting." (*PPSI* 61) A mystic, prophet, and miracle man, Apollonius allegedly thought of himself as the reincarnation of Pythagoras (see **Philip** [163] *PEP* 17). While it is believed that he had genuine source material at his disposal, the picture drawn by Apollonius is commonly taken with a few grains of salt. Naturally, I also make use of other passages in Iamblichus, Porphyry, and D.L., as well as Polybius, Diodorus, Pompeius Trogus, Cicero, and Plutarch, to render as much of a panoramic view as possible.

209 On Cylon, see **Iamblichus**, *VP* 248–258; **Porphyry**, *VP* 54–55; **Diodorus**, 10.11. On Cylon and Sybaris: **Iamblichus**, *VP* 74, where he is titled the *exarchos* of Sybaris; also **Dunbabin's** [704] *Western Greeks* 366. See **Zeller** [89] *DPdG* I/1.420n2 (422–423), on the possibility that an internal quarrel—resulting from Cylon's dismissal—beset the order, developing eventually into the so-called Cylonian movement. Most important is **Corssen's** [106] analysis ('Die Sprengung des pythagoreischen Bundes' 340–344) on the discrepancies between the accounts of Iamblichus-Nicomachus and Porphyry. According to Porphyry, Cylon was never admitted to the Pythagorean society, while the way Iamblichus-Nicomachus speak of him indicates that he must have been expelled from the order. See also **Corssen's** [106] reference to **Olympiodorus'** scholia on the *Phaedo*, p. 61D, according to which *Gylon* (Cylon?) sought revenge for being kicked out of the Pythagorean auditorium (343). See the section in the Appendix titled "The Info to Certainty Sequence, Part II" for details.

Another powerful protagonist is Ninon, a somewhat enigmatic figure. While depicted as a public agitator—by those sympathetic to the Pythagoreans—he seems to be the representative of the democratic faction. As a resolute opponent of dictatorship, he rallied the masses to join the anti-Pythagorean movement.

As for the main Pythagorean players, they seem to be split into two camps. There is the alliance of Hippasus, Diodorus, and Theages, who urged their fellow members to allow all citizens equal and open access to the assembly. They advocated that government officials should be accountable to those who represent the people, as they are elected by lot from the whole citizen body.

However, Hippasus and the others are opposed by a very powerful group of Pythagoreans, all of whom are arch-conservatives, thus, true believers in "government by the best," not "by the most." Their names are Alkimachos, Deinarchos, Meton, and Demokedes, and they charge that the changes proposed by the pro-democrats would destroy the inherited constitution. Thus, they are followers of the Pythagorean dictum that old law, even if it is bad law, is better than new law. (They seem to adhere to Pythagoras' teaching in the First Speech that what is prior is preferable to what is subsequent.)

The drama appears to unfold first at the general assembly, the governing body of the Thousand. But soon the speeches seem to be directed at a larger audience; perhaps, in time, access to the debate was granted to all citizens. The decisive speech is attributed to Ninon, who fires charge after charge against the elitist persuasions of the Pythagoreans. As a coup de grâce he offers insight into a secret work, allegedly by Pythagoras, which he obtained clandestinely. It is called the *Sacred Discourse,* and Ninon makes use of certain inflammatory passages in order to expose to the general public the real intentions of the society. One critical verse has Pythagoras saying that one should treat friends as one would treat the gods, but anyone else should be handled like wild beasts. This notion is further substantiated by a saying from Homer that refers to a "shepherd of the people." The idea, as Ninon states, was praised by Pythagoras because it was oligarchic: it demonstrated that the common folk are merely cattle. Another quote from the book refers to the notorious beans, saying, "Fight against beans, for they are lords of the lot, and of putting into office those chosen by lot."[210] Ninon

---

210 **Iamblichus,** *VP* 259.

then offers a synopsis of Pythagorean doctrine, denouncing it as a conspiracy against democracy.

The events that follow are somewhat confusing, again due to a failure to distinguish between the revolts. Tradition has it that these proceedings lasted a number of days until the people, all fired up by further anti-Pythagorean revelations, turned into a revengeful mob. From that point on, the reports vary considerably, often conflicting with each other. By some accounts, the Pythagoreans were forewarned, and when the attack commenced, they all fled to an inn. By other accounts, the citizens caught the leaders of the order as they met at the gathering house to deliberate the political situation. The exits were blocked as the house was set on fire, and some sixty members perished in the flames. However, this particular testimony appears to address the events of the second revolt, where there is an apparent consensus between accounts that certain "meeting houses were burned."[211] Furthermore, tradition maintains that only two Pythagoreans escaped the blaze: Lysis and Archippos, young lads who were strong enough to force their way out. But it is particularly the escape of Lysis—who in his old age became the teacher of Epaminondas (d. 362 B.C.), one of Greece's most celebrated generals—that helps us narrow down the date of the burning. There is some accord among scholars that Lysis had to be in his twenties during the second revolt, c. 450 B.C., if he was still around as Epaminondas' instructor in c. 385 B.C.[212]

Pythagoras' Death

What was Pythagoras' role in all of this? The reports range from total involvement to no role whatsoever. The more credible ones, such as Aristotle's, have him moving to Metapontum ahead of time, after he "foretells his followers of the coming political strife."[213] By other accounts, he barely escaped Croton, and in his desperation, wandered from city to city in search of sanctuary, only to be turned away at the gates. The Locrians, for example, informed him that their laws need no improvement, thank you

---

211 See **Minar** [160] regarding the events being mixed up: "The destruction *by fire* and all subsequent details belong properly to the second great catastrophe." (*EPP* 68)

212 Cf. **von Fritz** [122] on Lysis: "Considering ... that he could not have died before 390 or 385 ... the very earliest date [of his flight] would be about 455. But it seems more likely that the catastrophe happened some years later." (*PPSI* 79) Also **Minar** [160] *EPP* 92; **Burkert** [100] *Lore* 115–16; **van der Waerden** [183] *Pythagoreer* 220, 269.

213 **Aristotle**, fr. 191 R.

very much, and he had better move on. (An indication that they considered Pythagoras a lawgiver and politician, not a philosopher.) And when he arrived at Tarentum, we are told that "he encountered similar misfortunes as in Croton"[214]—whatever that may mean. No one, it seems, wanted the old sage. Eventually, Pythagoras made his way to the Temple of Muses in Metapontum. Dismayed by what had transpired, he died there after forty days of starvation. This version of Pythagoras' death is deemed most credible by scholars.[215]

As mentioned earlier, though, a separate report places Pythagoras squarely inside the meetinghouse as it was set on fire. Bravely, his followers threw their bodies into the inferno, in a desperate attempt to create a bridge for their master. He even managed to escape, yet was so dismayed by their deaths that he died of grief. Other versions have him being caught while trying to avoid crossing a field of beans, and getting his throat cut, or being killed after a battle, while his followers were burned at the stake. As for the story that he was traveling abroad at the time—to visit his old teacher, Pherecydes, in Delos, aiming to cure him of lice—it seems that Pherecydes had died much earlier (long before the tragedies ensued), whether from lice or otherwise. And some even believe that Pythagoras had also passed away when all this transpired. The theory is not implausible, particularly if we are thinking of the second revolt.[216]

Returning to the sequence of events, we are told that the end of the first revolt came about when the interested parties sought help from foreign mediators. And some representatives were indeed sent by other cities to help even things out. It also appears that a group of surviving Pythagoreans, after escaping to other cities, demanded a public trial. Surprisingly, this was granted by the arbitrators, although the ensuing verdict turned out against them. Having been found guilty, their expatriation was pronounced permanent. However, the report continues, the mediators might have been bribed, or it is also possible that they were only recompensed for their efforts by the Crotonians. This particular detail, as well as the verdict, was entered into the Crotonian records. Lastly, the victorious democrats exiled everyone who was dissatisfied with their form of government, at the same time cancelling all existing debts and redistributing the land.

---

214 **Porphyry**, *VP* 56, according to **Dicaearchus**.
215 The references are **Dicaearchus** fr. 35a + b (Wehrli): **Porphyry**, *VP* 57: **D.L.**, 8.40. For comments, see **Cicero** [630] *De finibus* 5.2.4; **Guthrie** [43] *HGP* I.179; **McKirahan** [67] *PBS* 79.
216 Cf. **Zeller** [89] *DPdG* I/1.420n2, on 422–423. He adopts **Corssen**'s [106] supposition ('Die Sprengung des pythagoreischen Bundes' 344).

A Return to Power and the Second Revolt

As it happens, the expatriation of the Pythagoreans was not permanent after all. The Crotonians had a change of heart and invited all those expelled to rejoin the citizenry. This reconciliation turned out to be so favorable for the returning Pythagoreans that they not only reclaimed their former status, but they managed to expand their influence exponentially, once again gaining control of the government. For the next decades, Croton remained unchallenged as the most powerful city in Southern Italy, commanding a veritable commonwealth.

Then, all of a sudden, history seems to repeat itself. Except this time, the anti-Pythagorean uprising was much more violent and widespread. Not only was the notorious meetinghouse in Croton set on fire, but throughout Southern Italy—then known as Greater Greece—the Pythagorean *synedria*, or clubhouses, were burning. The famous historian Polybius (c. 200–c. 120 B.C.) reports that as these events started taking place:

> ...there ensued, as was natural, a general revolutionary movement, the leading citizens of each city having thus unexpectedly perished, and in all the Greek towns of the district murder, sedition, and every kind of disturbance were rife.[217]

This great revolt of 450 B.C. (approximately) finally put an end to all political aspirations of the Pythagoreans. Too many were lost, especially the ones trained in governmental work. As for the survivors, they felt betrayed by those cities that had disregarded their plight. Cast out, alone, and abandoned, most sought to leave Italy for good. Some gathered in Rhegium (Reggio di Calabria, at the southernmost tip of Italy's boot) to practice their ways, and this seemed to work for a while. But soon a new tyrant, Dionysius, loomed, and his commanding influence could not be ignored. By the end of the century, some hundred years after Pythagoras' death, practically all those who considered themselves his followers were gone from Southern Italy.

There was one notable exception: Archytas, the leader of Tarentum, a city that flourished beyond Dionysius' grasp.[218] Archytas was described as a most unusually wise and benign Pythagorean, and in contrast to the origi-

---

217 **Polybius**, 2.39. (Trans. **Paton** [658] *Polybius: The Histories*. Loeb 1.337.)
218 Cf. **von Fritz** [122] (*PPSI*) for comments, e.g.: "The Pythagoreans...promoted strong resistance against [Dionysius'] advance," and "Tarentum never came under the supremacy of Dionysius." (76)

nal followers, he chose to abide unconditionally by Tarentum's democratic constitution. Hence, Archytas was nothing more than an *elected* official, even though the office he held was that of *strategos*—in effect, commander-in-chief—a position that by law could be bestowed only once and only for one year. Archytas' reputation as a military commander was legendary, and it was said that he never lost a battle, a fact that seemed to compel his fellow citizens to waive the limits of his term repeatedly. They elected him an unprecedented seven times.[219] We hear of no other notable Pythagoreans in Southern Italy.

The Gradual End of the Movement

As for mainland Greece, there are only a few anecdotes that have been passed down regarding the society's fate. We are told that Lysis, after his narrow escape from the burning meetinghouse, was fed up with Italy and eventually wound up in Thebes.[220] Other Pythagoreans took his lead, and in time we hear of Pythagorean activities in Thebes and Phlius from no lesser authority than Plato himself.[221] As an old man, Lysis took under his wing Epaminondas, who later in life broke almost singlehandedly Sparta's iron grip on its neighbors by being the first general ever to execute a successful incursion upon her soil. Three times he managed to invade the Spartan heartland, ending her 300-year hegemony in the Peloponnese. While Epaminondas' successes were generally attributed to his shrewdness paired with his nobility of character, credit was equally given to Lysis' philosophical training.[222]

Then there is the eminent Pythagorean thinker, Philolaus of Croton—allegedly himself a pupil of Lysis[223]—who taught for a number of years in Thebes. Among his students were Archytas and Eurytus, the inventor of "pebble arithmetic." Eurytus also joined the teaching profession, and both he and Philolaus were celebrated for instructing the so-called Last Pythago-

---

219 D.L., 8.79, 82.
220 **Iamblichus**, *VP* 250; **Plutarch**, *Moralia* 583.B.
221 **Plato**'s *Phaedo* 57a, on Echecrates and Phlius, one of Aristoxenus' "Last Pythagoreans"; 59c, on Simmias of Thebes; and 61e, on Philolaus staying with the Theban group.
222 **Diodorus**, 10.1.2. Diodorus mentions that Lysis even became Epaminondas' father through adoption because of the affection he had for him. On Epaminondas' shrewd strategies, see **Vidal-Naquet**, [727] *The Black Hunter* 61–69.
223 Philolaus as Lysis' pupil is based on a not-too-credible account; see **DNP** 9 (on **DK** 44A1a) and **Huffman** [135] *Philolaus* 4n3, on comments on the same passage from **Olympiodorus**' scholia on the *Phaedo*. It is likely that Lysis and Philolaus were about the same age—not that this has to mean anything, one way or another.

The Gradual End of the Movement

reans of Aristoxenus. Some of these belonged to a group that Plato associates with Phlius, a city in the Peloponnese not far from Corinth. Thus, there are at least two Pythagorean centers where ostensibly speculative activities were carried out long into the fourth century B.C.—up to 150 years after Pythagoras' death.

But they lingered to no avail; the Pythagorean order slowly faded out, and after Aristoxenus' claim to have personally known the very last ones (around 365 B.C., according to the historian Diodorus), nothing more is heard of any scholarly pursuits.[224] Only the obscure group called the Pythagorists abides for a while in the public's awareness, cultist drifters who seem to roam the land while stubbornly maintaining their mysterious ways. Depicted as unwashed ascetics and made fun of in popular plays, they were possibly remnants from an earlier schism within the movement. And they too disappeared.

With a moving eulogy to Pythagoras' disciples, Porphyry captures their final days with the following words:

> When this catastrophe seized upon the men, the knowledge likewise came to an end with them, since it had been kept as a secret in their breasts until that time, only the enigmatic symbols being mentioned when outsiders were present, and since there was no written work by Pythagoras. But those who escaped, Lysis and Archippus and such as happened to be out of the country, preserved a few sparks of the philosophy, but obscure and difficult to grasp. For having been isolated and despairing at what had happened, they were scattered hither and thither, avoiding association with men. However, fearing lest the name of philosophy should wholly perish from men and lest they should be hated by the gods themselves for this reason, they collected the writings of the elders and such things as they remembered, and they composed summary memoranda which they left behind, each where he happened to die, commanding sons or daughters or wives to give these to no one outside the family. And their descendants in succession kept this injunction for a long time, giving the same commandment to their offspring.[225]

And Iamblichus adds: "They maintained the original customs and doctrines, though the school was diminishing, until they died out with dignity."[226]

To better understand the transition from middle to late Pythagoreanism and the philosophies, particularly to Parmenides' Eleaticism and Platonism, we will next review the split in the order and the possible outlook of the Last Pythagoreans.

---

224 **Diodorus**, 15.76.4. Parallels in **Iamblichus**, *VP* 251.
225 **Porphyry**, *VP* 57–58. See parallel in **Iamblichus**, *VP* 253.
226 **Iamblichus**, *VP* 251.

THOSE WHO LISTEN AND THOSE WHO LEARN

> The genius of Pythagoras must have possessed both a rational and a religious quality such as are rarely united in the same man. It is not surprising that he and his school attracted two different types, on the one hand enthusiasts for the promotion of mathematical philosophy and on the other religious devotees whose ideal was the 'Pythagorean way of life', the life of a religious sect strongly resembling that of the Orphics and justifying its practices by a similar system of mystical beliefs. The philosophical wing inevitably neglected, or secretly despised, the simple superstitious faith of the devotees, but could not deny that it had played a part in the foundations laid by Pythagoras.
> —W. K. C. Guthrie[227]

A Split in the Order

As devastating as the effects of the anti-Pythagorean revolts were to the movement, they did not affect all members equally. We can assume this was largely due to the way the order was organized, together with the emerging rift within its membership. The structuring of the society[228] relied on certain essential positions or functions required to administer its membership. These were the so-called "politicians," "economists," and "legislators"—trustees who managed the affairs of the society. These designations, however, were not restricted to internal functions only; for example, members of the ruling counsel were also referred to as *politikoi*, as were the leading Pythagoreans of other cities. The meaning of *"politikoi"* is somewhat different than "politician" in our conventional sense and is often translated as civil servant or administrator.[229] Furthermore, *politikoi* seems to be a generic term that embraced a variety of responsibilities—as demonstrated by Iamblichus, who also uses it for lawmakers.[230]

---

227 **Guthrie** [43] *HGP* 1.192.
228 The best exposition is **Delatte**'s [111] *Politique* 22–35, followed by **Minar**'s [160] *EPP* 17–35, which leans considerably on Delatte.
229 **Iamblichus**, *VP* 72, 108, 129 (council members or political leaders, i.e., *politikoi kai archikoi*), and 150. *Politikoi* as "civil-servants": **Clark** [639] *Iamblichus* 31, on *VP* 72. For "administrators," see **Minar** [160] *EPP* 31, 35. As "politicians" and "those who were concerned with the human problems of everyday life": **Boudouris** [96] 'The Pythagorean Community' 55. De Vogel [180] considers the duties of "managers and legislators" to be different from the *politikoi*—and says regarding *VP* 97: "One may conclude that not all members are *politikoi*." (*Pythagoras* 189) Curiously, **Photius** explains *politikoi* as business people, *Bibliotheka* 438b19–23.
230 **Iamblichus**, *VP* 108.16. **Deubner** [640]: '*politikon tois nomothetais*,' "civil-servants of such kind as the legislators." (**Clark** [639] *Iamblichus* 48, translates the passage as "He also instructed the 'legislators' among the civil servants...") The use of *politikoi* as a generic term is

A Split in the Order

There are many more distinctions that have been used for the members of the society, most of which do not concern us at the moment.[231] There are a few, however, that merit a closer look, such as the status of *esoteric*, the title bestowed upon the few who passed the trial of silence and were received "inside the veil." This particular differentiation between "inside" and "outside the veil" is quite helpful when attempting to sort out the various offices or "grades" within Pythagoreanism.[232] The members who were allowed into the inner circle had one thing in common: absolute trust. Hence, we may safely assume that in addition to the esoterics, the trustees who handled finances, made the rules, or administered the order also belonged to the "insider club." Conceivably, all were called esoterics upon initiation, and only received the other titles afterwards, depending upon their individual duties.

The distinction of "inside" or "outside the veil" is also important because, in time, it may have led to an overall division of the membership, spawning two basic camps. One belonged to those allowed to hear the master but not see him; the other involved the esoterics, who could do both. It seems that over time, the followers who were admitted only to *hearing* the teachings became mostly privy to tidbits of information, while the insiders were free to observe Pythagoras in his rituals or techniques, and even engage him in face-to-face discussions.[233] Both Porphyry and Iamblichus attest that such differentiation was practiced, referring to those who only attended certain lectures as *Akousmatikoi*, or Listeners, as opposed to the select few who actually studied with the master, calling them *Mathematikoi*, or Learners.[234] Oddly, Iamblichus alleges that Pythagoras referred to the Listeners also as *Pythagorists*, and not as "Pythagoreans"; the latter designation appears to have been reserved for the Learners, the so-called "genuine followers."[235]

---

pointed out by **Delatte** [111] *Politique* 25, followed by **Minar** [160] who concludes: "Some [initiates] were treasurers or stewards, others legislators, others (probably) administrators of various sorts; and all seem to have been included in the general designation of *politikoi*." (EPP 35)

231   See note 732 in the section of the Appendix titled "The Info to Certainty Sequence, Part II."

232   See **Iamblichus**, *VP* 89, where such a differentiation is suggested.

233   **Minar** [160] *EPP* 29.

234   **Porphyry**, *VP* 37; **Iamblichus**, *VP* 30, 81, 82, 87, 88, 150 and *De Communi Mathematica Scientia* 25 (**Festa** [643] 76.18–19).

235   **Iamblichus**, *VP* 80. See also **Clark's** [639] translation (*Iamblichus* 35): "The distinction of names appropriately marked out some as real followers and some as aspirants to their status." In a nutshell, as formulated by **Clark**: "The groups inside and outside the veil (72), like the Pythagoreans and the Pythagorisers (80) are meant to correspond to Learners and Hearers respectively (89)." (*Iamblichus* 35n80)

The term *Akousmatikoi* means "those eager to hear."[236] The word *akoustikos*, or "hearing," from which we derive *acoustic*, is related to it, as is also *akousma*, or "thing heard."[237] Some older translations refer to this group as *auditors*.[238] We are told that whenever the *Akousmatikoi* gathered, they received only summarized versions of the master's teachings, without the benefit of elaborate expositions. This abbreviated version of Pythagorean teaching consisted largely of colorful aphorisms called *akousmata*.[239] Attributed to Pythagoras, the *akousmata* are short oral instructions, maxims at best, and their topics are usually proper conduct, taboos, or advice. The *Akousmatikoi* considered all sayings by the master as divine revelations and strove to learn them by heart. Even the most banal recommendation had to be embraced without argument or need for proof. That particular qualifier, "to be accepted on faith" or "without needing proof," became important, and it marked the increasing rift between one group and the other. Such a rift, of course, is a natural result whenever someone establishes two classes of knowledge. The infamous ban on beans is a typical example of the sayings that belong to the *akousmata*. It's a command, not a demonstrative argument or a reasoned proof.

The Listeners: Teaching by Passwords, Tokens, and Maxims

A different name for *akousmata* is *symbola*,[240] a term that means "passwords" or "tokens." It comes from the singular, *symbolon*, from which we derive the word "symbol." As Walter Burkert explains: "In the realm of mystery religion, *symbola* are 'passwords'—specified formulas ... which are given the initiate and which provide him assurance that by his fellows, and especially by the gods, his new, special status will be recognized."[241]

---

236 **LSJ**.
237 Ibid.; also **McKirahan** [67] *PBS* 89.
238 E.g., **Taylor** [646] *Iamblichus* 210, 214.
239 **Porphyry**, *VP* 37; **Iamblichus**, *VP* 82. See **Burkert** [100] *Lore* 166–192, 196–197; **van der Waerden** [183] *Pythagoreer*, 64–77. Also **Delatte** [111] *Politique* 22–27; **Minar** [160] *EPP* 31–34; **Philip** [163] *PEP* 28, 145–146; **Guthrie** [43] *HGP* 1.191–193; **Clark** [639] *Iamblichus* 34n80; and particularly **McKirahan** [67] *PBS* 89–91, for a concise but to-the-point presentation.
240 **Iamblichus**, *VP* 103–105; *Protrepticus* 21.104.27, 105.6, 106.8; **Porphyry**, *VP* 41–42. According to **Burkert** [100] (*Lore* 196–197), the term *akousmata*—found only in **Iamblichus**—traces back to Aristotle, while non-Aristotelian sources use *symbola* instead. Burkert recognizes here a hint that the report of the schism may originate with Aristotle.
241 **Burkert** [100] *Lore* 176. He mentions **Aristoxenus**, fr. 43 (Wehrli) = **D.L.**, 8.15, where *symbolon* is specifically used as a password. And **Hicks** [634] (*D.L.*, Loeb 2..335) has settled on the following translation: "When [Pythagoras] found his own *watchwords* adopted by anyone ..." (emphasis added).

The Pythagoreans often conveyed the *symbola* as a question-and-answer formula, not dissimilar to the way Freemasons or equivalent societies employ their own pass-phrases when testing a candidate's proficiency or the authenticity of foreign membership. Even though some questions take the form of a riddle, the answer is intended to communicate more than the right of entry; it should transmit a deeper meaning, particularly when educating the initiate. Thus, questions and answers like "From where have you traveled?" "From the East," are not meant to impart some geographical information, but rather to arouse some profound revelation in the candidate's mind. In much the same way, the Pythagoreans made use of *symbola* or *akousmata* to communicate their essential tenets.

Iamblichus informs us that there were three types of *akousmata*: the first asking for "what something is," the second "what is the best or most" of something, and the third focusing on regulations or taboos, such as "what should, or should not be done."[242] A few examples of the first category include the following:

- Q.: What are the islands of the Blest? A.: The Sun and Moon.
- Q.: What is the oracle at Delphi? A.: The tetractys, which is the harmony in which the Sirens sing.[243]
- Q.: Who are you, Pythagoras? A.: The Hyperborean Apollo.[244]

Some *akousmata* on the most or best include these:[245]

- Q.: What is the most just? A.: Sacrifice.
- Q.: What is wisest? A.: Number. And the second wisest is the one who gave names to things.
- Q.: What is most beautiful? A.: Harmony.
- Q.: What is strongest? A.: Insight.
- Q.: What is most true? A.: That people are wicked.

Most of the *akousmata* concerning recommendations or taboos are preserved not as questions and answers, but as ordinances or directives:

- One should never give advice except with the best intent, for advice is sacred.
- Do not digress from the way to the temple, for God should not be made an incidental task.

---

242 **Iamblichus**, *VP* 82.

243 Allusions to the Harmony of the Spheres, the sirens in **Plato**'s *Republic* X.617b, the invention of the counter-Earth to conform to the numerologically perfect ten: **Aristotle**, *Metaphysics* 986a2–12. See also Chapter III, subhead "The Music of the Spheres," and notes 312, 313.

244 **Iamblichus**, *VP* 140. See **Burkert** [100] *Lore* 168), who points to the *akousma* character of this saying.

245 All sayings are from **Iamblichus**, *VP* 82–86, unless otherwise noted.

- One must beget children, for it is our duty to leave behind someone to worship the gods.
- Do not speak without a light.[246]
- Do not use public baths.[247]
- One should point a sharp knife in the other direction.[248]
- When rising, one should straighten out the bed sheets to remove the imprint of the body.[249]
- Do not seek to have children by a woman who wears gold jewelry.[250]

There are additional *akousmata* that appear to fall outside the above categories, a medley of wise sayings, common proverbs, sibylline admonitions, or just odd observations:

- Friendship is harmonious equality.[251]
- A friend is a second self.[252]
- One should touch the ground when it thunders.[253]
- An earthquake is a mass meeting of the dead.[254]
- White represents the nature of good, black the nature of evil.[255]
- The rainbow is the reflected splendor of the Sun.[256]
- Happiness consists in knowledge of the perfection of the numbers of the soul.[257]
- Choose the noblest way of living; habit will make it enjoyable.[258]
- Mind sees and hears all: the rest are dumb and blind.[259]
- Above all tell the truth, for only this can make man be like God.[260]

Other *akousmata* are transmitted to us complete with clarifications—I have alluded to a few in previous chapters, such as the dictum to avoid highways or not to assist someone to put a burden down. Porphyry offers a list of such sayings, for example:[261]

---

246 Interpreted as not to speak of Pythagoreanism in the dark: see **Iamblichus**, *VP* 105.
247 Because we might be sharing a bath with someone not pure: **Iamblichus**, *VP* 83.
248 **Iamblichus**, *Protrepticus* 21.107.6 (**Pistelli** [645]). Phrasing after **Burkert** [100] *Lore* 173.
249 **Iamblichus**, *Protrepticus* 21.108.3 (**Pistelli** [645]). Cf. **Burkert** [100] *Lore* 173, and **McKirahan** [67] *PBS* 91.
250 Usually understood as a warning that a rich woman will not take her motherly duties seriously. However, I read this saying in light of Pythagoras' abhorrence for luxury, and the likening of women who wear jewelry to prostitutes.
251 **Timaeus**, *FGrHist* 566F13. After **Burkert** [100] *Lore* 171, 171n37.
252 **Porphyry**, *VP* 33.
253 **Guthrie** [43] *HGP* 1.183.
254 **Aelianus**, 4.17. According to **Burkert** [100] *Lore* 170.
255 D.L., 8.34.
256 **Aelianus**, 4.17, after **Burkert** [100] *Lore* 170.
257 **Heraclides Ponticus**, fr. 44 (Wehrli) = **Clemens**, *Stromateis* 2.84 St.; **Guthrie** [43] *HGP* 1.164.
258 **Cicero** [627] *Rhetorica ad Herennium* 4.17.24. Attributed to Pythagoras: Loeb 1.289ne.
259 **Iamblichus**, *VP* 228.
260 **Porphyry**, *VP* 41.
261 **Porphyry**, *VP* 41–45.

- "Do not turn around when going on a journey" meant not to cling to this life when dying.
- "Do not poke a fire with a knife," that is, do not excite with sharp words someone swelling with anger.
- "Do not eat the heart" meant do not torment yourself with griefs or sorrows—in other words, mental pain, remorse, etc.
- "Do not wear rings with images of gods," that is, do not flaunt your religious beliefs or turn them into public affairs.[262]
- "Do not threaten the stars" signified not to be angry with one's superiors.[263]
- "Do not place a candle against the wall," that is, stop trying to enlighten the stupid.[264]

The above represent but a sample of Pythagorean precepts or maxims. Iamblichus assures us that most are guidelines for subjects like the appropriate sacrifice for every occasion, how to honor the gods, escaping Earth by transmigration, and the observation of proper burial methods. For the Listeners, collecting *akousmata* constituted an exceptionally honorable pursuit, and those who could commit the most to memory were considered the wisest among them. But the one defining characteristic of this branch of Pythagoreanism was the members' resolve not to add anything of their own to their master's teaching. Accordingly, the *Akousmatikoi* claimed never to say anything of their own invention, considering all innovations wrong. The work of Pythagoras was too perfect to be improved upon. In fact, it was godly, as Iamblichus informs us: "They took their laws and ordinances from Pythagoras as if they were divine commands, and did nothing except by them ... and they counted him among the gods as a good and kindly spirit."[265] Increasingly, this attitude not only forced the *Akousmatikoi* to reject any improvement of Pythagorean doctrine, but condemned them to a life of superstitious pursuits. This characterization does not fit the picture usually drawn of the Pythagoreans as sagacious, well-educated philosophers. As Richard McKirahan notes: "[The Akousmatikoi's] acceptance of the akousmata unproved and unargued is unphilosophical and unscientific."[266]

Iamblichus conveys a rather intriguing theory of how the *Akousmatikoi* became content with simplistic sound bites, as opposed to solid argumenta-

---

262 Also **Iamblichus**, *VP* 84, and *Protrepticus* 21.107, which also includes the succinct "Do not wear a ring." In general, there are many parallels between Pythagoreanism and the Greek initiatory cults. **Burkert** [100] mentions that the worshipers in Delos not only approach the deity barefoot and clad in white, but they also abstain from sex, meat, and the wearing of metal implements, such as "iron rings, keys, belts, purses or weapons." (*Lore* 177)

263 **Guthrie**, K. [124] *The Pythagorean Sourcebook and Library* 161.

264 Ibid.

265 **Iamblichus**, *VP* 30. See also *VP* 82. See the parallel to Iamblichus in **Porphyry**, *VP* 20.

266 **McKirahan** [67] *PBS* 91.

tion or proof: in the beginning, Pythagoras had indeed provided the necessary demonstrations along with his instructions, yet because eventually these had to be conveyed to an increasingly larger following, most of whom were sluggish in their reasoning, the proofs were soon left out and only the unsubstantiated claims were passed on.[267]

The Emergence of Scientist Pythagoreans

The other branch of Pythagoreanism, the *Mathematikoi*, were rather sophisticated followers, who supposedly "mastered the deepest and most fully worked out parts of [Pythagoras'] wisdom."[268] In contrast to the Listeners, these individuals had a scholarly outlook. By seeking further answers, they committed themselves to a life of research, not recollection. The word *mathema* means "a study"—not necessarily the study of mathematics, but learning in general. Accordingly, the *Mathematikoi* are described as "those concerned with the subjects of learning," and in the words of Walter Burkert, "They do not want 'hearsay,' but the comprehension of truth."[269] This distinction is very important because it puts Pythagorean advances in the proper perspective. It is evident that only the *Mathematikoi* deserve to be called *philosophers*, as they are the ones who defended the continual investigation into the nature of things, and to them we owe most, if not all, advancements that are commonly labeled as "Pythagorean."

A listing of achievements that can be attributed to the *Mathematikoi* can help us appreciate that at least *some* of the so-called Pythagoreans were not just the equivalent of underpaid staffers of a psychic hotline:

- The society is credited with making significant advances in geometry. In fact, of *The Elements*, Euclid's geometrical bible, the entirety of Book IV and very likely Book II are considered Pythagorean, as are a number of individual theorems throughout the work.[270]

---

267   **Iamblichus**, *VP* 87.
268   **Porphyry**, *VP* 37; phrasing by **Guthrie** [43] *HGP* 1.192.
269   **Burkert** [100] *Lore* 207n80 (cf. also for the above definition of *Mathematikoi*).
270   For **Euclid** Book II and IV (Scholium 4.2), see **Heath** [636] *Euclid: The Thirteen Books of the Elements* 1.414 and 2.97; also **Heath** [745] *A History of Greek Mathematics*, vol. I, 143–169, and **van der Waerden** [183] *Pythagoreer* 337–363, for a comprehensive representation. (**Burkert** [100] remarks that Book IV depends upon constructions in Book II; see *Lore* 452. Cf. also 449–453 for further comments on Books I–IV.) As for other books in **Euclid**'s *Elements* containing or corresponding to Pythagorean material, see **Heath** [745] *A History of Greek Mathematics*, vol. I, 167–169. For **Euclid**, IX.21–34, see **Becker** [730] 'Die Lehre vom Geraden und Ungeraden im Neunten Buch der Euklidischen Elemente' 533–553, and [732] *Das Mathematische Denken der Antike* 47–74. (For a short review on **Becker**, see **Burkert** [100] *Lore* 434–437.)

- One example is the theorem "every triangle has its interior angles equal to two right angles."[271] Another is the famous Pythagorean theorem, that is, that in a right-angled triangle, the sum of the squares of the lengths of the two sides is equal to the square of the length of the hypotenuse, also known as $a^2 + b^2 = c^2$. (There are some questions, however, as to whether the Samian discovered the theorem that bears his name. Evidence that this principle was independently known can be found in early Babylonian, Chinese, and Indian writings.)[272]
- A significant discovery, also attributed to the Pythagoreans, is the application of areas[273] and the special use this has in the determination of the Golden Section.
- Worth mentioning is also the construction of the pentagon, and possibly the mathematical justification for the pentagram, the five-pointed star.[274]
- Nor should we forget the mathematical determination of the diatonic, chromatic, and enharmonic musical scales, particularly in relation to the contributions of Archytas of Tarentum.[275]
- Considered especially important is Archytas' number theory and his much lauded attempt to solve the problem of doubling the cube.[276]
- Last but not least are the contributions to philosophy by Philolaus of Croton, particularly his outlining of the two principles called *limiters* and *unlimiteds*. His doctrines are a shining jewel in the Pythagorean crown.[277]

Without a doubt, there are more achievements that can be associated with the Pythagoreans. Those that we know of have one thing in common: they worked, meaning that the steps necessary to prove each claim could be readily retraced and the theorems *demonstrated*. Of this, Euclid's celebrated *Elements* provides ample proof. And the best theories, as we shall see, are those that can be verified by thought alone.

We have to assume that by the time the *Mathematikoi* conducted their most intense inquiries, the division throughout the order had become so great that it is hardly possible to speak of one movement, much less a ho-

---

271 See **Proclus**, *In Euclidem* I.32. (379 Friedlein = **DK** 58B21. Cf. also **Morrow** [663] *Proclus: A Commentary on the First Book of Euclid's Elements* 298; and **KRS** [39] 334–335.)

272 **Heath** [636] *Euclid: The Elements* 1.349–352; **Guthrie** [43] *HGP* 1.217–218; and Burkert [100] *Lore* 428–430, 429n9, 462, 472.

273 **Proclus** *In Euclidem* I.44 (419.15 **Friedlein**). **Eudemus**, fr. 137; **DK** 58B20. See also Burkert [100] *Lore* 450, 452, 454.

274 **Euclid**, Book IV. See also **Burkert** [100] *Lore* 452.

275 **Archytas** extrapolated the ratios from the tetrachord. On this and other accomplishments, cf. **Freeman** [31] *The Pre-Socratic Philosophers: A Companion to Diels, Fragmente der Vorsokratiker* 238. See also **DK** 47B1, B2, and B3.

276 Both the doubling of the cube and the numerical ratios of the aforementioned scales originate with Archytas. For detailed information, see **Heath** [745] *A History of Greek Mathematics* and **Guthrie** [43] *HGP* 1; the doubling of the cube is particularly well presented in **Huffman**'s [138] paper, 'Doubling the Cube: Plato's Criticism of Archytas.'

277 I highly recommend **Huffman**'s [135] *Philolaus of Croton*, a most meticulously researched work that is a must for any researcher into Pythagorean thought. Of course, *Lore and Science*, **Burkert**'s [100] work on all things Pythagorean, is still indispensable; the sections on Philolaus are a must-read.

mogeneous organization. In other words, most of this development must have transpired *after* the last revolts. If, following the master's death, Pythagoreanism ever had a central command—and the Committee of the Three Hundred seems to have been the closest thing to such a body—the last upheavals irrevocably put an end to any organizational structure the order might have enjoyed. Gone were the functions of legislator, economist, and above all, *politikoi*. The latter seemed most affected by the turmoil, and what was left of the society appeared unable to weather such a substantial deficiency in leadership. Too many were dead, we are told, too great was "the loss of those best suited to govern."[278] With this statement, Iamblichus refers to the cities, suggesting this as the reason the Pythagoreans relinquished control of their administrations. However, if it is true that the members abstained from political involvement because too many well-trained administrators had been killed, then we have to believe that the order, internally, must have suffered from the same lack of qualified officials.

In the final analysis, what killed organized Pythagoreanism was not the indiscriminate persecution of its membership. There are no reports that the *Akousmatikoi* and the *Mathematikoi*—or their precursors—were even touched. In fact, with the notable exception of the *politikoi*, none of the "behind the veil" esoterics seems to have been targeted. We may conclude, therefore, that the final revolts were all about getting rid of one particular group of politicians who happened to be members of the Pythagorean party, and not about a wholesale extermination of Pythagoreanism. And not even every politically active Pythagorean was targeted, but only the diehard oligarchs—the commissars, if you will—not unlike the apparatchiks who make up the central committee of Marxist regimes. We have no reports that pro-democracy Pythagoreans were harmed in any way. In fact, the untimely fate of Hippasus, the most prominent of the latter group, was probably "facilitated" by his fellow associates, or as tradition has it, by divine retribution for betraying Pythagoreanism.

Hippasus, the All-around Thinker

Hippasus of Metapontum (early fifth century B.C.) was a most unusual Pythagorean, a brilliant yet also tragic man, an almost mythical figure, and the order's earliest thinker—outside of Pythagoras—that we know by name. Hippasus' role was always considered very controversial, and thus quite

---

278 Iamblichus, *VP* 250.

Hippasus, the All-around Thinker

difficult to write about. Practically everything we know about him is imbued with legend, and the reports are not only hearsay five to six times removed, but they are also conveyed mainly by unfriendly commentators. Hence, I must alert the reader that many comments regarding him (my own included) should be taken with a grain of salt. Despite the controversy, Hippasus is probably the most intriguing figure in all of Pythagoreanism. Thus, if the myths surrounding him hold only a kernel of truth, they are still worth investigating, or at least thinking about.

There is the possibility that Hippasus' attempt to revolutionize Pythagoreanism—to turn it into a genuine science—went beyond anything its cultish founder could have imagined. On the other hand, he may also have sabotaged it fatally. It is all a question of perspective, and of whom we want to believe. One of the fascinating things about Hippasus is that he was the ultimate esoteric, belonging both to the *Mathematikoi* and to the *politikoi*—he is explicitly called a member of the Council of the Thousand.[279] And he may not only have been the first Pythagorean scientist, as well as the speaker of the democratic faction, but he is also credited—or blamed—for the very split within the movement that resulted in the *Mathematikoi* and *Akousmatikoi*. In fact, each side appears to condemn the other for following Hippasus instead of the master, at least according to Iamblichus (who, unfortunately, forwards a handful of confusing reports).[280]

Whether the split is Hippasus' fault, we do not know. In fact, it seems reasonable to look for an earlier cause for the eventual division, namely, to Pythagoras himself. The *Mathematikoi*—or their precursors—must have been pooled from followers "inside the veil." On the other hand, the Listeners, or *Akousmatikoi*, are commonly identified with the laypeople—ardent believers, but not full-time associates. They still had families and outside jobs. If there was no intention of initiating these followers to the inner circle, they were necessarily barred from knowing all the passwords and the meaning of symbols, not to mention the hidden or speculative doctrines. Thus the very same communication or message, coming either from Py-

---

279 **Iamblichus**, *VP* 257. The only other *Mathematikoi* to achieve a prominent political position was Archytas, but that was as much as a century later. Curiously, what these two rather unusual Pythagoreans have in common is that they were both for a democratic form of government.

280 For **Iamblichus'** contradictory accounts, see *VP* 81, where the *Mathematikoi* discount the *Akousmatikoi* as the followers of Hippasus, versus *De Communi Mathematica Scientia* 25 (Festa [643] 76), which claims the reverse. However, the mix-up may be Iamblichus' own, or by his design; see **Burkert** [100] *Lore* 193–195, and **Philip** [163] *PEP* 28–29. **Van der Waerden** [183] (*Pythagoreer* 66–70) offers a clear and to-the-point exposition.

thagoras or from whoever succeeded him, may easily have had a double meaning: an obvious one for the laypeople and a coded one for the esoterics. For example, the ban on beans may have been received by the Listeners as a simple dietary rule, while at the same time serving as a covert signal to the *politikoi* to abstain from democratic elections. Under such conditions a split is only natural, and it can very well predate any political or scientific/religious debate. It is the simple result of subdividing the membership into "insiders" and "outsiders." In other words, whoever instituted the veil is to blame, because from that moment on there were two realities, two truths, and two bodies of teaching, all within the same society.[281] There were certainly two sets of laws, two sets of religious precepts, and two economic or proprietary systems, demonstrated by the fact that the "outsiders" kept their private property, as well as their families,[282] as opposed to the esoterics, who had to give up both. (Laypeople were also freed from certain dietary restrictions.)

Aristotle's "Those Called Pythagoreans"

If we want to seek genuine philosophical ideas in Pythagoreanism, we must turn to the later *Mathematikoi*. They were the ones who had received the unvarnished doctrines, or even created them in the first place. This group inspired Plato, and their ideas are preserved by Aristotle.[283] Neither Pythagoras nor the *Akousmatikoi* are relevant in any way. Conceivably, the Great Sage may have encouraged speculation, but the emphasis was strongly on the arcane arts, such as divination, astrology, numerology, symbolism, and so forth. Without a doubt, Pythagoras' religious-political movement provided the wherewithal for these types of pursuits, perhaps functioning as an umbrella or a raison d'être. They may have played an integral

---

281 **Iamblichus**: "Those inside and outside the veil, those who hear and see and those who hear without seeing, and those divided into 'inside' and 'outside' are to be equated with the two groups I have described" (i.e., the *Akousmatikoi* and the *Mathematikoi*) (*VP* 89).

282 Specifically pointed out by **Iamblichus** in *VP* 81. However, he seems to contradict himself with *VP* 30, where he carelessly indicates that "'they' had their properties in common, as Pythagoras had told them." On dietary freedoms, see also *VP* 108–109.

283 For the Last Pythagoreans' classification as *Mathematikoi*, see **Burkert** [100] *Lore* 198, and **Guthrie** [43] *HGP* 191, 193; **de Vogel** [180] even considers Aristoxenus himself a *Mathematikoi* (*Pythagoras* 11). For non-Pythagorists, see **van der Waerden** [183] *Pythagoreer* 19. As for Aristotle's source material, quite a few notable scholars have embraced the idea that it came from Philolaus; cf. **Burkert** [100] *Lore* 47, 234–238; **Huffman** [135] *Philolaus* 28–35. However, **Barnes** [9] expresses doubts, *TPP* 379, and **Philip** [163] is contra, *PEP* 119–122.

part in his overall strategy, possibly as a way of attracting potential recruits or as a means of indoctrination and initiation.

This is not to suggest that speculative pursuits were just a front for early Pythagoreanism. There is no reason to doubt its founder's genuine interest in such matters. However, the occult or magical—even when it dabbles in geometry, arithmetic, or musical theory—is so far removed from anything even resembling philosophy that we should not associate Pythagoras with the latter. For this we have good precedent—in fact, none better than Aristotle himself, who never mentions the Samian by name in context with the doctrines of those he designates the "so-called Pythagoreans," or "those called Pythagoreans."[284] Perhaps, with this unusual distinction, he meant to set the Learners apart not only from the boorish *Akousmatikoi*— who, as self-centered fundamentalists, denied everyone else the claim of being true Pythagoreans—but also from the teachings of the one who (rightly or wrongly) lent his name to the overall movement. As W. D. Ross points out, "for Aristotle [Pythagoras] seems to be little if anything more than a legendary figure; there is a set of people commonly called Pythagoreans, but Aristotle will not vouch for the origin of any of their doctrines in Pythagoras himself."[285]

Admittedly, Aristotle has also preserved many of the group's superstitious ideas, digressions into numerology, and the like—burdens that the *Mathematikoi* inherited from early Pythagoreanism—and, as we shall see, he rightfully criticizes these. But there are other teachings that he treats as legitimate philosophical concerns. It is to these we can now turn—having clarified things—to ascertain not only the philosophical merit of the ideas held by the "so-called Pythagoreans" but also whether they had created a workable "mathematics for the soul" as a method of proof, and most important, if this kind of "mathematics" was based on a sound premise, meaning a defensible one.

---

284 καλούμενοι Πυθαγόρειοι, **Aristotle**, *Metaphysics* 985b23. (Also translated as "the Pythagoreans, as they are called." It has been argued that Aristotle's designation is tantamount to putting the term Pythagoreans in quotation marks, and thus may indicate some reservation on his part. See the next note for additional details and references.)

285 **Ross** [624] *Aristotle's Metaphysics* 1.143. Cf. **Burkert** [100] *Lore* 46–47, who mentions that Aristotle purposefully avoids Pythagoras' name, perhaps because the "Pythagoreans" belong to the later Presocratics. (For a brief discussion of the term, see also *Lore* 30, 30n8.) **Zeller** [89] *DPdG* I/1.446n1, speculates that "Pythagorean" was less of a philosophical designation than a religious or political one, perhaps introduced by their enemies, seeing here a possible motive for Aristotle's need to differentiate between the two. **Minar** [160] *EPP* 22, supports this interpretation. But a must-read is **Huffman**'s [135] condensed but excellent discussion of this subject (*Philolaus* 31–34).

CHAPTER III

In Want of a Mathematics for the Soul

THE SOURCE CODE OF THE UNIVERSE

> The Pythagoreans, having devoted themselves to mathematics, and admiring the accuracy of its reasonings, because it alone among human activities knows of proofs... they deemed these (facts of mathematics) and their principles to be, generally, causative of existing things, so that whoever wishes to comprehend the true nature of existing things should turn his attention to... numbers... and proportions, because it is by them that everything is made clear.
>
> —Iamblichus[286]

According to the *Oxford English Dictionary*, the word "superstition" is traced etymologically to the Latin *superstitio*, which perhaps can be interpreted as "standing over a thing in amazement and awe." Of course, to be amazed by something is not necessarily wrong; after all, both Plato and Aristotle have taught us that philosophy begins with a sense of wonder. Yet all awe and amazement must eventually give way if we are to gain reliable knowledge of a thing. Thus, we may conclude that superstition ends where proof begins.

Philosophy as the art of proving dawned for the Pythagoreans with music. They found it an ideal evidential medium, one that allowed them ready access to its most basic constituents—not notes but *numbers*—and also a graceful way to express their theories. The original idea of looking to number for universal answers seems to have been hatched by the old sage himself, and it came, we are told, from his study of harmony.[287] What Py-

---

286 Iamblichus, *De Communi Mathematica Scientia* 25 (**Festa** [643] 78.8–18). (Quote is from **Burkert** [100] *Lore* 447–448.)
287 Iamblichus, *VP* 115–121.

thagoras discovered was that the differences in vibration that characterize the notes of a musical scale can be calculated. Each individual tone is determined by the number of times a particular sound-producing medium—such as the strings of a lyre or guitar—oscillates in a given time. Of course, no one at that time could calculate the number of vibrations, but what they could measure was the length of the string. The shorter the string or stronger the tension, the faster the vibration. And the faster the vibration, the higher the tone. Harmony is produced when a certain number of vibrations corresponds to the number of other vibrations; for example, when a string is halved, the sound produced is precisely one octave higher than that of the whole string. When the sounds are played together they agree with each other, and the result of such union is called a "chord." The ratio for the octave is 1:2, because the string that is half as long will move twice as fast as the other string. Additional intervals are set at the ratio of 3:2 for the fifth, and 4:3 for the fourth.[288] Thus, the basic intervals of a musical scale were expressible in only four numbers: 1, 2, 3, and 4.[289] When 1 + 2 + 3 + 4 are added up, we arrive at 10, the number considered by the Pythagoreans as most perfect and divine.[290]

The discernment between agreeable or disagreeable sounds was no longer the exclusive domain of one's ears. One also could determine these ratios by entirely *intelligible* means. The noted middle-Platonist writer Plutarch (c. A.D. 45–c. 125) captures this liberating innovation with these poignant words:

> The grave Pythagoras rejected the judging of music by the sense of hearing, asserting that its excellence must be apprehended by the mind. This is why he did not judge it by the ear, but by the scale based on the proportions, and considered it sufficient to pursue the study no further than the octave.[291]

The idea was truly revolutionary. Not only was music capable of being reduced to number—an intriguing notion in itself—but more significant was the reverse approach, that is, that from simple number ratios alone one

---

288 See **Philolaus**, **DK** 44B6, respectively, 6a as in **Huffman**'s [135] *Philolaus* 145–147. Also **Aristotle**, fr. 203 R (**Alexander**, *Commentarius in Metaphysica* 39.20–23).

289 Cf. **Burnet** [15] *Greek Philosophy* 1.45–49; **Guthrie** [43] *HGP* 1.222–225; **Burkert** [100] *Lore* 40, 72. For a discussion of the pros and cons regarding Archytas' contribution to the mathematical foundation for the basic ratios, see *Lore* 384–386. And for a general exposition on music, harmony, scales, ratios, and Pythagoreanism, see *The Manual of Harmonics of Nicomachus the Pythagorean*, translation and commentary by **Levin** [649].

290 **DK** 44B11; **Aristotle**, *Metaphysics* 986a7.

291 **Plutarch**, *On Music* (*Moralia* 1145.37). (Trans. **Einarson** and **De Lacy** [657] *Plutarch: Moralia*. Loeb 14.441.)

could evoke tones that were rich, colorful, and above all, real, not abstract. Thus, instead of composing a song by ear, voice, or the aid of a musical instrument—means which are all empirical—one could arrange harmonic relationships just by playing with numbers. This was a major breakthrough. Thought could come up with hypothetical constructs that could be converted *reliably* into meaning. Numbers, then, proved that music was more than just a pleasing noise; it reflected a hidden but rigorous order. And this order allowed itself to be revealed. Even if ignorant of number, by way of music, a person could still be made to grasp its underlying *logos*—that is, its message or structure. And if music could be regulated by numerical relationships, then why, the Pythagoreans asked, couldn't *all* relationships be governed by the same harmonious principles?[292]

If one of the roles of philosophy is to reveal the imperceptible similarities and distinctions between things, then certainly the study of number is useful to anyone who seeks to reduce the relationships of things to graspable dimensions, hence to *objects of thought*. Numbers help us *unitize*, meaning "to make a unit out of something"—which, incidentally, is a vital function of the mind. Our ability to unitize allows us to *recognize* and *verify* each thing as an individuated entity—thus, to supply it with a "format" that is distinctive, dependable, and complete. And the same applies, naturally, to its *relationships* to other entities. By also being recognizable as unitary, the relationships themselves become things or entities in their own right. As all entities can be organized as units, number allows us to treat the things themselves as little units of proof. Someone, it seems, had finally stumbled upon a workable means to calibrate one's thinking. If this someone was not Pythagoras himself, then perhaps it was an unknown yet unassuming member of the order, who may have deferred all credit to his master.

But the question remains: did number live up to what was expected of it? Was it indeed the long-sought panacea that could cure the ills of reasoning? Did it prove *what* things are, and was such proof attainable by thinking alone? To find a satisfactory answer here, we should first realize that Pythagoreanism entertained ideas on number that differ from our own. In fact, some notions may appear today to be rather strange. For instance, even though the numeral unit itself is obviously not grasped by sense perception, some Pythagoreans did not regard number as something *abstract*, or at least that is what Aristotle tells us. According to him, they thought

---

292 **Aristotle**, *Metaphysics* 985b23–986a6.

each number had some spatial magnitude.[293] Moreover, numbers were not *separate* from the sensible substances, but all things were supposed to be formed out of them. In effect, numbers were not just the formula of what things are composed of, such as the ratio, perhaps, of constituent parts, but they themselves were like little bits of prime matter.[294] Thus, they fulfilled a vital function for these ancient speculators: they were a *universal solvent*—an answer to everything. As Aristotle puts it, "[The Pythagoreans] construct the whole universe out of numbers."[295] One way they could justify this theory was by equating geometrical *points* with numbers. This is best demonstrated by the tetractys, their symbolic representation of the sacred number ten:

•

• •

• • •

• • • •

The number ten was thought to be perfect because it "comprised the whole nature of numbers."[296] It also contained the formula for the line, surface, and solid.[297] The four tiers in the tetractys represented in progression the first four integers—1, 2, 3, 4—and from these basic constituents the Pythagoreans generated not only the musical scales but also the things themselves.

---

293 See **Aristotle**, *Metaphysics* 1080b17–21, 32; also 1083b11. But in *Metaphysics* 989b30, he seems to contradict this claim: "[The Pythagoreans] got the principles from non-sensible things, for the objects of mathematics, except those of astronomy, are of the class of things without movement."

294 For bits that are units, see **Raven** [516] *Pythagoreans and Eleatics* 59–60, particularly for a discussion of Aristotle's evaluation of the Pythagoreans' belief that "things are numbers," and "numbers as formula." Raven addresses Aristotle's critique that the Pythagoreans do not specify whether numbers for them constitute the material that things are composed of or the formula—i.e., a ratio of the mix of their constituents.

295 **Aristotle**, *Metaphysics* 1080b19.

296 **Aristotle**, *Metaphysics* 986a8.

297 Paraphrasing **Guthrie** [43] *HGP* 1.260. The idea is preserved in **Speusippus**, F28 **Tarán** [667] (fr. 4 Lang = DK 44A13), respectively **Iamblichus**, *Theologumena Arithmeticae* 82.10 ff. For further comments, see **Burkert** [100] *Lore* 69, 69n106; **McKirahan** [67] *PBS* 100–101; **Barnes** [9] *TPP* 381. For translation of this passage, see **Waterfield** [647] *The Theology of Arithmetic* 112–114 (whole) and **Huffman** [135] *Philolaus* 359–360 (parts).

If, for example, the number 1, as a single geometrical point, was linked to another point, the two points could be coupled by a line.

If we add a third point and allow it to be linked to the other two by lines, we have three points connected by three lines—in other words, a triangle, which is the first plane figure.

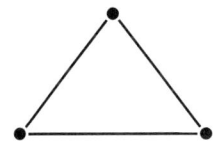

And if we connect point number four to the triangle, we have a pyramid, which is the first solid figure, a three-dimensional body.

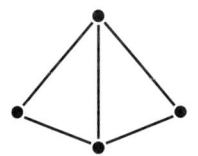

Thus, we can see that if we equate numbers to geometrical points, and then construct all manner of shapes just by connecting them—by bringing them into *relation* with each other—we might come to the conclusion that the things which *result* from such construction are essentially *made of* numbers, and *brought about* by them. To provide convincing proof for this belief was paramount for some Pythagoreans.

One particular member of the group, Eurytus,[298] chose a different way to demonstrate this principle. He would take as many pebbles as required, and, on a floor or wall, lay out the figures of a man or a horse with them. If one considered each such pebble a unit, counting them, he thought, would reveal the specific formula for man or horse.[299] The idea was as original as it

---

298 Eurytus is possibly a pupil of Philolaus. The account of Eurytus using pebbles goes back to Archytas. (See **Aristotle**, *Metaphysics* 1092b10; **Theophrastus**, *Metaphysics* 6a19.) For a crude and dubious account of this method, see **Pseudo-Alexander**, DK 45A3. For comments see **Guthrie** [43] *HGP* 1.274, and **Barnes** [9] *TPP* 390–391.

299 Naturally, my account here has to be overly brief and simplistic. For a more detailed discussion of Eurytus and "pebble arithmetic," see **Burnet** [14] *Early Greek Philosophy* 99–107;

was naive. It only works if we equate number not just with geometrical points but with irreducible units of some sort that nonetheless have magnitude—a kind of "atomic marble," perhaps.[300] This means that although this type of ultimate entity is a solid three-dimensional body, it cannot be cut or reduced any further into something that is *less* than it is.[301] Only when this last requirement is assured can number serve as the *most basic* constituent for all things, because there is nothing less, lower, or more basic than it. However, this, as we shall see, will turn out to be a quite problematic proposition.

Of course, the motive behind this sort of reasoning is obvious: If the things themselves are *made* of numbers—whether as points or as irreducible units—then we can know a thing if we know its number.[302] With this approach, the Pythagoreans thought they had finally discovered the key for deciphering what everything is. All one had to do was learn the number of a thing and relate it to the numbers of other things, and *voilà*, there was the source code of the universe, or even the formula of the soul. One account has Pythagoras saying that happiness consists of knowing the perfection of the numbers of the soul.[303] Moreover, God surely knew the number to everything, so if one would study these numerical interrelationships among things, one could learn to think like God. On account of these ideas alone, a full-fledged mathematics for the soul seemed to be just around the corner.

Guthrie [43] *HGP* 1.259, 273–275; **Barnes** [9] *TPP* 390–391; **Huffman** [135] *Philolaus* 185–186; **Raven** [516] *Pythagoreans and Eleatics* 103–105.

300 For **Aristotle**'s criticisms, see *Metaphysics* 990a12–22, 1083b7–19, and 1092b8–25.

301 For **Burkert**'s [100] comments on the "extended monad," "the materialized point as a kind of atom," "point-atoms," and "atom-points-units," see *Lore* 41. Cf. also **Raven** [516] *Pythagoreans and Eleatics*, on no distinction between "the unit, the point and the atom." (178) Also **Cornford** [282] *Plato and Parmenides* 13.

302 See **Philolaus**, fr. 4: "And indeed all the things that are known have number. For it is not possible that anything whatsoever be understood or known without this." DK 44B4 (trans. **Huffman** [135] *Philolaus* 172).

303 **Heraclides Ponticus**, fr. 44 (Wehrli) = **Clemens** *Stromateis* 2.21.130, 3: "Heraclides attributes to Pythagoras the statement that happiness consists in knowledge of the perfection of the numbers of the soul." (Trans. **Guthrie** [43] *HGP* 1.164, who states the reference as fr. 44 Clem. *Strom.* 2.84 St.)

THE MUSIC OF THE SPHERES

> ... having made a profound study of the nature of number [Pythagoras] asserted that the cosmos sings and it is harmoniously constructed, and he was the first to reduce the motion of the seven planets to rhythm and melody.
>
> —Hippolytus[304]

Conquering the Unlimited

Let us reflect for a moment on what it meant to be an initiate of the Pythagorean order, to realize that it is *correspondence* and *proportion* that rule the world—a world of rigorous laws, sustained by a numerical network, that, although hidden, spans all of creation. If all things are subjected to these rules, then injustice is an impossibility when viewed on a universal scale, because only one principle, that of number, regulates the constitution and behavior of each thing. There was finally one measure for all things, be it for man or God, Sun or Moon, a drop of rain or a grain of sand. And most miraculously, although this agreement among things was hidden from view, it was willing to be revealed to those initiated to its secret ways.

This discovery must have seemed like humanity's greatest achievement, or at least the gods' most generous gift. With it the world could be understood as *cosmos,* a word that, according to legend, was first used by Pythagoras to describe the universe.[305] Cosmos meant "order," "world order," or an "ordered world," as opposed to disorder or chaos. Furthermore, for the Pythagoreans the *ordering of the world* had a beginning.[306] The *cosmos* began when a seed of order was introduced into a vastness of disorder—or as described by one scholar, "the planting of a unit in the infinite."[307]

The Pythagoreans had an innovative view of the *unit* as the foundation of creation. The unit was not passive, but active. In other words, the unit

---

304 **Hippolytus**, *Refutation* 1.2.2. *Doxographi graeci* [1] p. 555. Quote is from **Guthrie** [43] *HGP* 1.298.

305 **Aetius**, 2.1, 1 (D. 327, 8); **DK** 14, 21; **D.L.**, 8.48. The idea is disputed, see **Peters** [784] *Greek Philosophical Terms* 108.

306 **Aristotle**, *Metaphysics* 1091a13–20, 1092a32. Aristotle is greatly annoyed by this, i.e., that what is eternal can be considered as having a beginning.

307 **Guthrie** [126] 'Pythagoras and Pythagoreanism' 39. Note **Raven**'s [516] description of the process: " . . . this principle of Unity or Limit was conceived as having started the whole Pythagorean cosmogony by somehow injecting 'the first unit with magnitude' like a seed into the womb of the Unlimited." (*Pythagoreans and Eleatics* 115) See **Burkert** [100]: "In Aristotle's account the origin of the One from seed is at least mentioned as a possibility." (*Lore* 37) See also **McKirahan**'s [67] discourse of the subject (*PBS* 102–103).

did something: it *unitized*. As mentioned, to unitize means to make a unit out of something, to unite, to make one. The unit, which itself is the quintessence of what limit is, converted the unlimited to unity and finiteness simply by imposing limits or boundaries upon it.[308] And the unlimited proved to be a compliant medium, as it allowed itself to be delimited, thus unitized. In the *Metaphysics*, Aristotle describes this process from the point of view of the Pythagoreans: as soon as the unit was introduced to the unlimited—whether it was constructed or had grown like a seed—immediately the "nearest part" of the unlimited began to be drawn in and ended up being limited by it.[309]

We do not know what mysterious power the unit had over the unlimited, or why the latter was attracted to it. (There are enough problems with this statement as it is—for example, how can we speak of a "part" or "near" with regard to a medium that is not yet partitioned and thus cannot be differentiated as being close or far?) One explanation passed on to us by Aristotle is that the unlimited or void was "breathed in" by the unit.[310] In all likelihood, the proof of the unit's authority over the unlimited was consid-

---

308 See **D.L.**, 8.24 (**DK** 58B1a): "The principle of all things is the monad or unit; arising from this monad the undefined dyad or two serves as material substratum to the monad, which is cause." For the unit as a synthesis of the Unlimited and the Limited, see **Aristotle**, *Metaphysics* 986a18–21, 987a15–20) or only as the Limit principle, *Metaphysics* 1091a18. Other distinctions are the Limit-Odd (implied, see **Aristotle**, *Physics* 203a10 = **DK** 58B28); the Even-Odd (*Metaphysics* 986a20, fr. 199); or just the Odd (*Physics* 203a11). For the Odd being ungenerated, hence as a *first principle*, see **Aristotle**, *Metaphysics* 1091a23. (The nature of the prime unit has been exhaustively discussed by scholars. The following listing is but a small sample.) For a comprehensive deliberation, see **Raven**'s [516] *Pythagoreans and Eleatics* 114–124, particularly on the two Pythagorean views of the Unit—i.e., as Limit in early or pre-Parmenidean Pythagoreanism, and as a mix of both fundamental principles in later Pythagoreanism. Important also are **Burkert**'s [100] encyclopedic evaluations of Aristotle's take, as well as that of modern interpreters: *Lore* 32–37, 40, 42–43, 45n91, 46, 265–266; quotes (all *Lore* 36): "The One had its origin from Limit and Unlimited together," "The One has a share in each of the opposite forces," "The One becomes a Two as the Unlimited penetrates it." As far as I can tell, Burkert prefers the "One from both principles" version (see 34), and takes Limit and Unlimited as "first principles" (35). See also the comparison of the Pythagoreans' cosmogony to Leucippus' own because it is also based on two initial "entities," i.e., the atoms and the void that facilitates their separation (35). As to the equivalence of One and *peras*, Burkert says, it "would seem natural to any later, Platonic-minded reader" (36n38). Recommendable are also **Guthrie**'s [43] comments, *HGP* 1.239–251, 261, 272–273, 276–281. See also **Philip** [163] (*PEP* 60–70), particularly on the One as a product of the imposition of Limit on the Unlimited (61); the One "is also the cosmos that is product of *peras* and *apeiron*" (67). Cf. **Cornford** [282] *Plato and Parmenides* 16–22, and on confusing the two senses for the One, 3–7. See **McKirahan** [67] *PBS* 96–97, 101, 103, for a focus upon **DK** 58B1a; **D.L.**, 8.24; and **Aristotle**, fr. 201 R.

309 **Aristotle**, *Metaphysics* 1091a15.

310 For further elucidations or analogies to the unit, see also the world or heaven "inhaling the void," **Aristotle**, *Physics* 213b22; or "the heaven as one," **Aristotle**, fr. 201 R. In *Physics* 203a10–15 it is the "one"—the principle of *odd*—that cuts off and shuts in the infinite *even*.

ered self-evident; it is so typical for our minds to function this way. (However, the universe seems to always have a few surprises up its sleeve.) The reasoning is all too obvious: by simply being what it was—namely, finite—the unit put an end to the infinite. All it had to do was take a position. In any case, an alluring idea was taking shape: that what is finite must have precedence or dominion over what is not finite.

Accordingly, the overall mission of order was to conquer the unordered, and from the unit at its center a wave of unification increasingly spread throughout the unlimited, converting it thereby to *cosmos*. And the cosmos sang.

The Sound of Order

If there is one Pythagorean idea that has stirred the imagination, it is that of a music-producing universe. Known alternately as the Harmony of the Spheres or the Music of the Spheres, this theory, together with that of the unit, presents us with a wondrous image: expanding from the primordial unit, a filigree of order expresses itself in a melodious way.

Aristotle has preserved this particular idea in his work *On the Heavens*, explaining that due to the movement of heavenly bodies, sound had to be generated—or so the Pythagoreans thought.[311] The sounds were supposed to vary in accordance with the sizes of the stars and planets, their distances to the listener, and the velocity of their movement. The law was not unlike that which applies to the sound produced by musical instruments: the faster the movement, the higher the pitch. The distance between the astral

---

Oddly, in *Metaphysics* 1091a15 **Aristotle** speaks of a constructed one. Interpreting Aristotle, **Raven** [516] mentions a "first unit," i.e., " . . . that first unit, which began forthwith to breathe in and limit the Unlimited" (*Pythagoreans and Eleatics* 115–116). Similarly **Kahn** [146] 'Pythagorean Philosophy Before Plato' 183. See **Philip** [163] for "The One *qua* universe" that "breathes in from the infinite void that surrounds it" (*PEP* 71n4). He also explains that "This One . . . did not use up the Unlimited, some of which remained outside the cosmos as a void, which the One breathed it in to fill the space between things" (*PEP* 61). See **Guthrie** [43] on the "unit-seed," and on "the fiery unit" which feeds on air or breath (*HGP* 1.281). Cf. **Burkert** [100] *Lore* 36, for "the One" as "the world before its further evolution," and as "heaven" (35). Quote: "The One begins to breathe, and, as the breath flows in, it assumes a more complicated structure" (*Lore* 37). See **Cornford** [282] on "the one," the "unit of arithmetic," the "seed," and "fiery seed" (*Plato and Parmenides* 19–21).

311 **Aristotle**, *On the Heavens*, 290b12; also *Metaphysics* 986a2: "They supposed . . . the whole heaven to be a musical scale and a number." See also *Metaphysics* 1093a5, 1093b2. See also **Plato**, *Republic* X.617b, for a lyric account on the sirens as the voices of planets, each representing a note on the solar system's musical scale. Most informative are **Alexander**'s commentaries on Aristotle's *Metaphysics*, **Aristotle**, fr. 203 R.

bodies was very important, because each was positioned in accordance to a numerical *proportion* that *corresponded* exactly to the ratios of the musical scale. Thus, the sounds that the stars made were concordant, meaning they resulted in harmony.[312]

We do not know to which Pythagoreans Aristotle attributes this theory—he is highly critical of it—nor does he tell us if those who upheld it were early or late members of the society.[313] Yet one thing is quite clear: these people believed that the difference between order and disorder was also an acoustic one.[314] This brings up the next question: what, in terms of sound, was the opposite of cosmic harmony? Was it dissonance or silence? No one has related to us a satisfactory description of what the sound of the stars is like. There have been some speculations about its nature, from Aristotle's account of it as "a harmony" and "a concordant sound" to Plato's imaginative rendition of eight singing sirens located on or above the so-called spheres—that is, the bodies of the solar system—each one giving voice to only a single note of the musical scale. According to him, the eight tones together resulted in "the concord of a single harmony."[315] However, the difficulties of conceiving a musical scale whose notes, when played in *unison,* still produce a harmony are all too obvious. There are other subsequent accounts that attempt to remedy this problem, but these are of no concern to us at the moment.[316] What we are interested in is the Pythagorean mind-set, which had to subject everything to some proper proportion or ratio. From this point of view, the result of the sound of the stars must obviously have been some kind of chord.

Order and Proportion

This typical Pythagorean outlook—relegating all things to their proper positions—is important to us because (1) it presages some of the problems that fatefully affected the evolution of philosophy, and (2) it might have

---

312 For an edifying exposition on the Harmony of the Spheres, I recommend **Burkert** [100] *Lore* 350–368. Not to be missed is also **Guthrie**'s [43] account, *HGP* 1.296–301. See also **Philip** [163] *PEP* 122–128, particularly his comprehensive notes, 128–133.

313 One of the best presentations of the Harmony of the Spheres, and a thought-provoking argumentation that seeks to link the theory to Pythagoras himself, can be found in **Kahn**'s [146] 'Pythagorean Philosophy Before Plato,' esp. 176–185.

314 **Guthrie** [43] *HGP* 1.295–301, esp. 299.

315 **Plato**, *Republic* X.617b.

316 See **Burkert** [100] *Lore* 352, 354–355, on the harmonical problems of the theory, and 355 on the alternative interpretation of the number of tones involved. Also **Guthrie** [43] *HGP* 1.299–301; **Philip** [163] *PEP* 123, 125, 127.

Order and Proportion

been a contributing factor in the demise of their system. Thus, if, as the Pythagoreans believed, the distances between the spheres were regulated by the laws of proportion—which, as dictated by the musical scale, had to be harmonic intervals—and if the result, as maintained by Aristotle and Plato, was a concord, then dissonance per se appears impossible. And I do not necessarily mean *acoustic* discord, such as the sound that emerges when various notes are played simultaneously, but the kind of incongruity that results when order is abandoned. For the Pythagoreans, it was important that whatever notes were played by the cosmos were planted firmly upon the musical scale. In this sense, any departure from it meant a departure from order. Each note, like a number, had to have a specific and unique character in the order of things, but it also had to have the right *separation* from other notes in order to preserve this character. This *distance between notes*—that is, the difference of pitch known as an interval—constituted their exact limitation, being the factor that gave them individuality and distinction—in other words, this was the very principle that allowed them to remain unitized. The Pythagoreans could not permit the notes to drift into a kind of "no man's land" between them; each had to be relegated to its rightful place, governed by a fundamental law that was best exemplified by the regularity of the planetary orbits.

A "no man's land" of disorder, where things were indeterminate—thus lacking some kind of discernible border or limit—had to be avoided at all costs, particularly, as we shall see, apropos their basic universal building block: number. For example, was a number that could not be determined as either odd or even *still a number*? Such concerns may sound spurious or artificial, but they represent a very important dilemma, one that we must take up later, especially because of its often overlooked relevance for the birth of logic and metaphysics. The problem of odd and even versus neither odd nor even or both odd and even certainly helped in the demonstration of "reasoned proof."

Returning to the music of the spheres, for discord to occur, the heavenly bodies would be required to enter the "no man's land" of the indeterminate, that is, they would have to either break out of their orderly positions with regard to one another or arbitrarily accelerate or slow down their movement. To the Pythagoreans, these were in effect the same thing, because they believed that the farther from Earth a body was, the faster it moved.[317] But if it is the principle of *limit* that facilitates the distinctiveness

---

317   **Aristotle**, fr. 203 R (**Alexander**, 39.22–40.9); cf. **Philip** [163] *PEP* 129.

of each thing, then the following conclusion is unavoidable: if *accord* was introduced to the unlimited by means of a delimiting nucleus, so also must *discernible sound* have been introduced, together with all other things that are equally dependent upon limit to be perceptible, such as sight, taste, and so on. Therefore, if sound had to be introduced by order, the "original" state of the infinite had to be soundlessness.[318] In other words, the idea of an expanding cosmos makes us think of the universe as a lonely yet polyphonic voice extending itself through unfathomable silence.

But if it is true that the universe sings, then why are the stars themselves mute? We are, after all, surrounded by them, and yet their sound escapes us. Whatever happened to this fabled music of the spheres; what must we do to hear it? To meet these questions, the Pythagoreans devised an intriguing solution: we have been hearing the stars all along, they say. In fact, from the moment of our birth, our ears have been bombarded by their song. However, due to its uninterrupted presence, we have grown so accustomed to the noise that it eludes us—just as someone who lives near a waterfall eventually ceases to pay attention to its roar.[319] Oddly enough, we would only become aware of all the omnipresent sounds if they were to stop completely. When suddenly confronted by absolute silence, we could come to appreciate the music that is *universe*. Only then would we miss the sound of its mellifluous voice rushing through the darkness.

Harmony and the Soul

There is one more point to be made regarding the music of the spheres: for the Pythagoreans, it was intrinsically connected with the fate of the soul, its proper place in the order of things, and especially its life hereafter.[320] Music lifted the soul to the divine, its rightful home. As Walter Burkert explains, "The soul that in ecstasy, or dream, or trance, travels to heaven, hears there the music of the universe, and its mysterious structure immediately becomes clear to him."[321] It is said that Pythagoras' last wish before dying was to hear the song of the lyre, claiming that souls cannot ascend

---

318 Moreover, if the heavenly bodies produce sound by moving, then of course if something did not move, it made no sound.
319 The waterfall analogy is **Cicero**'s own. See *Scipio's Dream* (*The Republic* VI.18.19) on people who spend their whole life close to the cataracts of the Nile, and as a result have lost their awareness of the sound produced by them. Cf. also **Guthrie**'s [43] comments, HGP 1.297.
320 See **Burkert** [100] *Lore* 357, on the eschatological character of the belief.
321 Ibid.

without music.[322] Thus, for his followers music became a healing medium, and in the words of Cornelia de Vogel, it effectively "restores the soul to a state in which it can return to the stars, the realm of the blessed."[323]

What better medium than music to manifest the invisible rapport between things, not only to the mind, philosophy's domain, but directly to the soul? Music, as philosophy's companion, became a viable bridge between the inner and outer cosmos, stirring not just the soul but the stars. Similar thoughts must have inspired Plutarch to conclude his work on music with the following words:

> But in fact, my friends, the greatest consideration, one that particularly reveals music as most worthy of all reverence, has been omitted. It is that the revolution of the universe and the courses of the stars are said by Pythagoras, Archytas, Plato, and the rest of the ancient philosophers not to come into being or to be maintained without the influence of music; for they assert that God has shaped all things in a framework based on harmony.... Nothing is more important or more in the spirit of music than to assign to all things their proper measure.[324]

Certain Pythagoreans had a grand design for the order of things. Their speculations on correspondence and relation presaged what would eventually become philosophy's greatest strength: *the reflection upon relationships and their consequences.*

Let's reduce the above arguments to specific points, with emphasis on the type of reasoning that shall prove essential to philosophy and its subaltern fields:

- The principle of proportion was embedded in the universe, revealing itself in many ways, one of them being harmony.
- The song of the cosmos was maintained if each "sphere," large or small, stayed in its proper orbit.
- Any deviation would cause a tear in the fabric of interrelation, with unforeseen consequences.
- In order to have a cosmos, the proper *closeness* between things must be maintained just as rigorously as the proper *distance*.
- Our field of study becomes essentially the management of the proper *relations* between things, allowing them neither to disconnect nor to merge.

---

322 Ibid.
323 **De Vogel** [180] *Pythagoras* 165; also on the therapeutic powers of music and more on the harmony of the spheres, 162–166.
324 **Plutarch**, *On Music (Moralia* 1147.44). (Trans. **Einarson** and **De Lacy** [657] *Plutarch: Moralia.* Loeb 14.453)

- This was the key to existence as well as apprehension by the mind: the right proportion and correspondence meant that each thing could maintain its individuality not only in the presence of other things, but *because* of the *regulated* presence of other things. (This conclusion, surprisingly, reappears in Plato's most formidable work, the *Parmenides*, and provides a crucial element for reconciliation of its most difficult hypothesis.)

In essence, the Pythagoreans tried to substantiate the following premise: not only is the unit that a thing *is* important, but equally so is the unit that stands for its *relation* with other things. In other words, a thing is unitary, as is the nature of its relation with others. Things express themselves as units, if that which is between them is also expressible in units. It was a revolutionary idea, or perhaps the most self-evident of all. What it meant for the Pythagoreans, however, is that they had to assure the integrity of the unit at all costs. And that, as we shall see, may have come back to haunt them.

Thus if we sum up what numerical philosophy meant to the Pythagoreans, we might call it two things: (1) "the study of suitable proportion," and (2) the "defense of the integrity of the unit." This also meant that they had staked their beliefs upon the *commensurability* of things, in other words, upon the existence of a *common standard* by which all things could be *measured*.

As appealing as it may have seemed, this outlook was to have unwelcome consequences for the Pythagoreans. Some have ventured that it might have played a part in the demise of the order as a philosophical school. We shall return to these matters after examining Parmenides. For now, we can say that their headaches began when they chose to seek a *common* measure for both thinking and the universe within the realm of *number*. (Curiously, it is that medium which is commonly considered the most dependable.)

Was number, as a system, robust and reliable enough to assure the Pythagoreans a unified theory of things? Regrettably, the universe is not always the neat and tidy place our minds want it to be. Things cannot always be resolved into what is expected of them, nor do they fit perfectly. All too often they fall through the cracks—if only, perhaps, through the cracks of our understanding. At times, to accommodate the inexplicable, number theory was contorted into symbology, from where it degenerated quickly into numerology. We realize that for the Pythagoreans, science and superstition not only lived side by side, but were indistinguishable from each other.

NUMEROLOGY—DERIVING PHILOSOPHY FROM NUMBER?

> How indeed can qualities—white, sweet, hot—be numbers?
> —Aristotle[325]

Confusing Numbers with Things and Things with Numbers

What were the drawbacks of the Pythagorean belief system, particularly when viewed as a philosophical approach? Without question, their number-dependent religious doctrine suffered from vulnerabilities that are an impediment to philosophical inquiry. It is also true that Aristotle credits the Pythagoreans very generously with being the first to advance the study of mathematics, yet modern scholarship holds that the progress in both arithmetic and geometry was due to an overall Greek effort, and not simply the result of the musings of a handful of initiates.[326]

We should also keep in mind that the Pythagoreans' romance with number was not without ulterior motive, particularly if it was tied to the agenda of early Pythagoreanism, namely, advancement to the next world.[327] The blending of arithmetic and religion was still in fashion with the later Pythagoreans, and this set their pursuits apart from those of other thinkers. Yet number, as it turned out, was not the most suitable foundation to base philosophy on, and digressions into magic and symbolism were facilitated instead of averted. To make matters worse, the Pythagoreans, as devotees of the esoteric and the occult, seemed unable to realize the liabilities in their approach. They never learned to differentiate between mathematics and numerology, the esoteric significance assigned to number. This flaw also included the later, more enlightened members, and even Plato seemed occasionally unable to conceal a somewhat unhealthy fascination with the mystical side of numbers.

The notion that all things can be reduced to number is quite absurd. Not everything we inquire into can suffer the transition to a purely numerical representation or allow itself to be validated by such means. This led Aristotle to question this specific aspect of Pythagorean belief, asking, as quoted above: "How indeed can qualities—white, sweet, hot—be num-

---

325 **Aristotle**, *Metaphysics* 1092b15.
326 **Aristotle**, *Metaphysics* 985b23. For a general discussion on the Pythagorean contribution versus the Ionians, see **Guthrie** [43] *HGP* 1.217–220; **KRS** [39] 335–336; **Burkert** [100] *Lore*, esp. 449 on geometry, and in general, 401–465.
327 Cf. **Guthrie** [43] *HGP* 1.181–182.

bers?" Some modern interpreters nonetheless find grounds to disagree with his reasoning. For example, W. K. C. Guthrie appears to defend the Pythagoreans:

> Looking back, it seems as if it was Aristotle who was leading science on to the wrong track. Today the scientific description of everything in the physical world takes the form of numerical equations. What we perceive as physical qualities—colour, heat, light, sound—disappear and are replaced by numbers representing wave-lengths and masses.[328]

I do believe, however, that Aristotle was onto something. He seems to have a better grasp of what is scientifically possible or necessary than his critics. My point is that just because we can calculate ratios that for us translate into something being considered as "hot," "sweet," or "white"—as opposed to something less hot, less sweet, or less white—does not mean that we can set up numbers that actually *are* hot, sweet, or white. Much less can we use this type of approach to characterize "hotness," "sweetness," or "whiteness." We might just as well affix an esoteric number to "quality" itself. But that is exactly what numerology tries to do. Still, to assign individual numbers to abstractions like "all," "justice," "opportunity," and "perfection" is plain nonsense.[329]

The Pythagoreans, however, thought differently. According to Aristotle, they gave the number 3 to "the Whole" or "All" because it comprised three things: "beginning," "middle," and "end." This, of course, made 3 also the number of the universe.[330] "Justice," on the other hand, was linked to the number 4, because it supposedly was a numerical representation of "reciprocity," which in turn was based on the following concoction: Reciprocity can only be upheld by a square number.[331] Then, the number 7 was associated with the "right time" or the "right season" because the Sun was said to occupy the seventh place among the celestial spheres, and the Sun, naturally, was the cause of seasons.[332] And we have already seen that "per-

---

328 **Guthrie** [43] *HGP* 1.238.
329 Regarding "abstractions," I am alluding to **Guthrie**'s [43] formulation (*HGP* 1.301).
330 **Aristotle**, *On the Heavens* 268a10.
331 **Aristotle**, fr. 203 R. See *Nicomachean Ethics* 1132b23, on the Pythagoreans defining justice as reciprocity. (By other accounts it was the number 9 which stood for justice—also quoted by **Alexander**—as well as the numbers 8, 5, and 3. Cf. **Guthrie** [43] *HGP* 1.304.)
332 See **Aristotle**, fr. 203 R, for "season," while *Metaphysics* 985b28 speaks of "opportunity." On "opportunity" for "right time" or "season," see also **Guthrie** [43] *HGP* 1.301. He explains in 301n3: "This is of course an inadequate translation of *kairos*, but its exact meaning makes no difference here, and it may be allowed to stand as a more convenient term than, say, 'right time.'" On page 303, Guthrie translates again "opportunity" and in 303n4 "the fit and

fection" was equal to the number 10. Obviously, these kinds of speculations belong to numerology, the "study" of the *meaning* of number, and not to mathematics, the study of spatial and numerical relations.

To further differentiate between the two, let us return to Guthrie's assertion that *perceived* physical qualities, such as color, are replaceable by numeric values representing wavelengths. It is true that we can establish by mathematical means what these values are, but this does not suggest that the *number* we have arrived at really possesses the *meaning* or *properties* of the thing we have measured. The problem is exacerbated by the fact that in our measurements, we are commonly dealing with *ranges* of values and not with absolute values that can be represented by one definite number. Thus, the wavelength for the color red is an *approximation:* it ranges between 740 and 620 nm (nanometers), while for yellow it is 585–575 nm.[333] If we still insist, for whatever reason, on determining one single characteristic number for red, we have no choice but to settle on some average value—which, in this case, would be 680 nm—and declare that as absolute red.

But even if we indulge in such a pointless exercise, this still does not imply that the *meaning* of 680 is red, nor that this particular number has red properties. Much less is it implied that everything that could ever amount to 680 in number would automatically be red. To believe such a thing, in spite of the obvious incongruity, is to practice Pythagorean numerology, not science. Six hundred and eighty green pickles only amount to 680 *green* pickles. Let's take another example: we can say that a temperature of 100 degrees is hot, but we are aware that this is just a relative claim. For liquid steel this would be cold, and even more so for the surface of the Sun. Thus, we cannot reserve absolute hotness for the number 100, because this would imply that neither 99 nor 101 degrees could be called "hot." It is obvious then, that numerology does not take into account relativity or a change in conditions. Instead it aims only for a specific meaning, a meaning that must be expressed as an absolute to be recognizable as what it is. We don't say that the number 13 is relatively unlucky, as in "somewhat," or "just a little bit," or "to a certain degree"—we say simply, "Thirteen is unlucky," period.

These problems were cleverly recognized by Aristotle, who rightfully challenges the Pythagoreans, or any other disciple of numerology, to ex-

---

proper season." See also **Burkert** [100] *Lore* 467: " . . . seven is opportunity (kairos) and also Athena, as the 'virginal' prime number. . . . " and also "right time" (40).

333   For values, see *Oxford Dictionary of Physics* [780] 69.

plain what the *good* might be that things obtain from numbers, just because their *composition* is expressible as such.[334] Using an example from both astronomy and astrology, Aristotle makes another strong point: that there are no sacred numbers. He suggests that there is nothing special in the number of stars a constellation might have—such as the Pleiades having seven, or the Bear twelve—because other people may count more stars and still speak of the same constellation.[335] In other words, whether we count six or eight stars in the Pleiades, we are still dealing with the Pleiades. On the other hand, as Aristotle points out, if all things must share in number, many things will end up sharing the very same number, and so things that are quite different would nonetheless appear similar, even identical.[336] Thus, in an effort to match things to each other, or to locate them within a certain order, a numerologist believes that coincidence means analogy. But the fact that things may come together by accident does not suggest that an analogy occurred, in other words, that things were made the same somehow, or that they can stand for each other and hence share the same symbolic number.[337] Aristotle concludes that people who revel in this type of indiscriminate association only pay attention to small resemblances while neglecting the really important ones.[338] Actually, with this statement, Aristotle has given us a useful definition of *irrationality*.

Number Symbolism

Some Pythagorean ideas were nothing less than irrational, indeed bizarre. For example, to the male principle they assigned the number 3, because it was the *first* odd number, but to the female principle the number 2, as it was the first even. (Don't ask.) Of course, 3 plus 2 makes 5, which—and this really shows the boneheadedness of the Pythagoreans—became their number for "marriage." As for 1, it was reserved for the soul, because it was "unchanging, alike everywhere, and a ruling principle," hence, on par with their beloved unit.[339] We are also told that they equated "opinion"

---

[334] **Aristotle**, *Metaphysics* 1092b26.

[335] **Aristotle**, *Metaphysics* 1093a14–20. Cf. **Annas** [621] *Aristotle's Metaphysics Books M and N* 219.

[336] **Aristotle**, *Metaphysics* 1093a2–3 and 1093a9–12. Cf. **Annas** [621] *Aristotle's Metaphysics Books M and N* 129, 218.

[337] Implied by **Aristotle**, *Metaphysics* 1093b16–18.

[338] **Aristotle**, *Metaphysics* 1093a27.

[339] Fr. 203 R. **Aristotle** points out that the soul was called "mind" by the Pythagoreans. See also **Aristotle** on Plato's take on Soul and Number: "Mind Is the Monad." (*On the Soul* 404b22) Noteworthy also is this observation: "Some thinkers declared the soul a self-moving number."

(*doxa*) with the number 2 because it "moved in both directions." This gives us the curious impression that "mind," evidently, had no place in "marriage"; otherwise, the sum would be 6[340] instead of 5, while fickle "opinion," conveniently equated with the female principle, fits perfectly.[341]

"Justice," as we have seen, is "reciprocity"—thus, a "fair and *square*" principle, as expressed by the "square" number 4.[342] However, what may seem just to one person might be unjust to another. In such a case, the reciprocity provision is violated, and, pardon the pun, justice is not a square thing all around. On the other hand, a just verdict may still appear unjust to all sides—which, based on the above reasoning, may again make it square and reciprocal, but only as long as it is *equally* unjust! How beautifully absurd!

All jesting aside, it is important to keep in mind that no matter how numbers are used in numerology, they cannot tell us anything about the individual things themselves. Saying that "woman" is 2 and "man" is 3 cannot reveal to us anything about *this* woman or *that* man, nor, obviously, about a *particular* marriage. They do not tell us whether the marriage will last, if it is happy, horrible, made for convenience, or based on true love. "Man," "woman," and "marriage" are concepts that express general things or universals. To put it differently, "universal man," "universal woman," and "universal marriage" are not particularized or tangible things. They are objects of thought, classifications that we create because they help us to order our thinking and thus manage its inventory. Yet we can, obviously, carry out thinking without pinning a number to everything we think about. In other words, if we fail to assign a number to something we think about, its meaning will still not elude us.

We may ask ourselves what made the Pythagoreans seek refuge in superstitious means if, in fact, they were such great innovators in mathematics?[343] What did they get out of practicing it? There are many religious, cul-

---

(404b28). Cf. **Philip** [163] *PEP* 20n7; also **Burkert** [100] *Lore* 65; Burkert reproduces the following listing for the symbolic numbering: 1 for "mind," 2 for "opinion," 3 for "the number of the Whole," 4 (or 9) for "justice," 5 for "marriage," 7 for "right time," and 10 for "perfect" (*Lore* 40).

340 It seems that the number 6 had no special meaning for the Pythagoreans, at least none that Aristotle preserved. See also **Burkert** [100]: "neither 6 nor 28 play any role." (*Lore* 431)

341 For an ironic account of the kind of epistemic mishmash that is generated by numerology, particularly of the Pythagorean kind, see **Aristotle**, *Metaphysics* 1093a1–1093b6.

342 The number 4 is the first to be divisible into equals, hence, as itself it is equal times equal, i.e., 2 x 2. See **Aristotle**, fr. 203 R; and **Burkert** [100] *Lore* 467.

343 For **Aristotle**'s criticism against creating a hierarchy of abstract concepts based on number (such as opportunity, injustice, mixture), see also *Metaphysics* 990a19; 1091b31; 1093a14.

tural, and magical aspects to this question that, I regret, have no place in this work. However, when we evaluate these needs from a philosophical point of view, the rationale is all too plain. If *counting* numbers will not expose all of the truth, then maybe the so-called *meaning* of said numbers can provide the answers one is seeking. Evidently, the rationalization of number symbolism has not gone out of style in the last 2,500 years, as it still accounts for the notoriety of numbers such as 13, 7, or 3. Yet numbers do not supply people with meaning; rather, it is people who project meaning upon number. That the Pythagoreans were unaware of this "convenience" betrays a lack of self-awareness that is quite unbecoming to anyone who professes to pursue wisdom or truth, even in such early times.[344] The problem of superstition is that it is a "people problem" and not, as in this case, a problem of numbers. In the end, to endow number with meaning is no different than to project human characteristics upon the gods, a habit that was criticized by Xenophanes.[345] People, not numbers, provide answers, even if they like to forget that they do. And when their favorite evidentiary medium proves incapable of fulfilling every demand, it is also people who make up what is missing. They have to; it would seem that the mind needs to complete things if it is to rest.

The Counter-Earth

A good example for this compulsion to make everything symmetrical and neat may have been provided by the Pythagoreans themselves. One of Aristotle's main charges against them was their invention of a "counter-Earth"—supposedly a duplicate of our world, yet obscured from our view because it always travels opposite from us along its orbital path. The center of the Pythagorean cosmos was not occupied by the Sun but by a colossal fire. The spheres of the heavenly bodies moved around this fire, and the Pythagoreans noticed that they were nine in number: Mercury, Venus, Mars, Jupiter, Saturn, the Sun, the Moon, Earth, and an additional one for the fixed stars. (They had relegated all stars to one sphere.)[346] As Aristotle reports, the fact that there were nine such spheres did not conform with the

---

344 Could the same lack of insight have plagued the likes of Heraclitus or Xenophanes? I doubt it.
345 **DK** 21B15 and B16. See Chapter I, subhead "The Search for a Way Out."
346 See **Aristotle**, fr. 203 R. Also **Philolaus**, **DK** 44A16 = **Aetius** 2.7.7. On Plato's ordering of the heavenly bodies versus that of the Pythagoreans, see **Burkert** [100] *Lore* 300, 313, 318, as well as his general discussion, 300–322.]

The Counter-Earth

Pythagorean notion of an ideal ordering of the cosmos. So they devised a "counter-Earth," an additional sphere, which gave them the divine number of their tetractys: the perfect 10. This mirror world was conveniently located on the other side of the central fire, hence invisible to us. Thus, as Aristotle alleges, the Pythagoreans "tweaked" the results of their inquiries to have them match their expectations. Here are Aristotle's accounts in his own words, and his evaluations are quite telling. First, in *On the Heavens*:

> But the Italian philosophers known as Pythagoreans take the contrary view. At the center, they say, is fire, and the earth is one of the stars, creating night and day by its circular motion about the center. They further construct another earth in opposition to ours to which they give the name counter-earth. In all this they are not seeking for theories and causes to account for observed facts, but rather forcing their observations and trying to accommodate them to certain theories and opinions of their own.[347]

And again in the *Metaphysics* he says:

> And all the properties of numbers and scales which they could show to agree with the attributes and parts and the whole arrangement of the heavens, they collected and fitted into their scheme; and if there was a gap anywhere, they readily made additions so as to make their whole theory coherent. E.g. as the number 10 is thought to be perfect and to comprise the whole nature of numbers, they say that the bodies which move through the heavens are ten, but as the visible bodies are only nine, to meet this they invent a tenth—the "counter-earth." [348]

From a philosophical/scientific point of view, Aristotle's criticism of the Pythagoreans' motives was not overly harsh, not if they were trying to "fudge" certain doctrines to make them fit some religious ideal. As I have suggested, if the numbers do not add up, then maybe "meaning" could fill the gaps. In the case of the "counter-Earth" it seems that both meaning and number were used to override observable reality—creating nothing less than a postulated one. Yet without *added* meaning, number alone could not have been used in this capacity; it is not a serviceable medium for counterfeiting what we hold as real. Thus, whenever numerologists give meaning and number to something, they have done nothing more than to give it a name or label, albeit one that suits some present, subjective need, but one which cannot reveal anything about a thing's nature.

---

347 **Aristotle**, *On the Heavens* 293a19–26 (trans. **Stocks, McKeon** [619] (ed.), *The Basic Works of Aristotle* 428).

348 **Aristotle**, *Metaphysics* 986a2–12. See also **Aristotle**, fr. 203 R.

In the final analysis, Pythagorean number theory could not offer us a viable mathematics for the soul. In fact, as we shall see, it was not even an effective means for defending its all-important constituent: the ubiquitous unit. And, in the context of this book, it is that ineffectiveness which is most important to us. Number worship and superstition go hand in hand, and whether we are dealing here with *Mathematikoi* or *Akousmatikoi* in the end makes no difference. The art of speculation was at a crossroad, but it wasn't quite capable yet of fully relinquishing its primitive and irrational roots.

Even Plato's imagination, particularly in his early works, seems captured by Pythagorean mysticism. Dying, resurrection, and the avoidance of worldly things feature prominently in his writings, particularly the notion of "certainty after death," instead of in life. I daresay that for the early pythagorizing Plato, it would have been almost impossible to understand, much less appreciate, what Parmenides was really talking about. It took Plato almost a lifetime to redefine philosophy as a means by which truth can be achieved while still alive, instead of having to die hoping to be rewarded for sinless living with it. As the next chapter will show, this thorough change of heart is evidenced by his most profound dialogue, called not *Pythagoras*, but *Parmenides*. No claim advanced by this remarkable work is to be taken at face value, as Plato demonstrates, but it must be challenged and rechallenged, without compromise or mercy, and from every conceivable angle. That was philosophy. Yet not much in Pythagorean doctrine, and certainly nothing in their superstitious numerology, could stand a chance if ever faced with such a challenge.

CHAPTER IV

Pythagorizing versus Philosophizing

> Q.: Tell us, does the person who knows know something or nothing?
> A.: He knows something.
> Q.: Something that is or something that is not?
> A.: Something that is, for how could something that is not be known?
> Q.: Then we have an adequate grasp of this: No matter how many ways we examine it, what is completely is completely knowable and what is in no way is in every way unknowable?
> A.: A most adequate one.
> —Plato, *Republic*[349]

Truth After Death?

We are told that once, when Plato was asked, "What is philosophy?" he responded that it is "the separation of the soul from the body."[350] This remarkable viewpoint appears supported by one of his most celebrated earlier dialogues, the *Phaedo*, a dramatization of the death of his teacher Socrates. In this work, Plato aims to define philosophy as a preparation for dying.[351] The goal is not only to "survive" death but to achieve a godlike state; as Plato declares, "no one may join the company of the gods who has not practiced philosophy and is not completely pure when he departs from life, no one but the lover of learning."[352] Purification is hampered by corporeal impulses and desires; thus, the philosopher must free his soul from association with the body as much as possible.[353] In fact, the release and sepa-

---

349 **Plato**, *Republic* V.476e–477.
350 **Hippolytus**, *Refutation* 6.25.
351 **Plato**, *Phaedo* 64a, 67e.
352 **Plato**, *Phaedo* 82c.
353 **Plato**, *Phaedo* 65a, 67a.

ration of the soul from the body is his main preoccupation.[354] To achieve this, a philosopher must train himself throughout his life to live in a state as close as possible to death, Plato says, adding: "Those who practice philosophy in the right way are in training for dying and they fear death least of all men."[355] With Socrates' impending execution as a backdrop, he captures the issues confronting a seeker of wisdom with words that are both compelling and astonishing:

> It really has been shown to us that, if we are ever to have pure knowledge, we must escape from the body and observe things in themselves with the soul by itself. It seems likely that we shall, only then, when we are dead, attain that which we desire and of which we claim to be lovers, namely, wisdom, as our argument shows, not while we live; for if it is impossible to attain any pure knowledge with the body, then one of two things is true: either we can never attain knowledge or we can do so after death. Then and not before, the soul is by itself apart from the body. While we live, we shall be closest to knowledge if we refrain as much as possible from association with the body and do not join with it more than we must, if we are not infected with its nature but purify ourselves from it until the god himself frees us. In this way we shall escape the contamination of the body's folly; we shall be likely to be in the company of people of the same kind, and by our own efforts we shall know all that is pure, which is presumably the truth, for it is not permitted to the impure to attain the pure.[356]

As forceful, even sobering, as these remarks may be, it is nonetheless the very same Plato who, in his later dialogues, suggests that a real lover of wisdom strives for truth by seeking the *true being* of things. This is accomplished by coming in touch with the nature of each thing *in itself*, and not as it is believed to be.[357] And the best news is that one does not have to die first to accomplish this goal. What moved Plato to embrace such a fundamental shift in his thinking? Why was it suddenly possible to know truth, to know what things really are, *before* one's death? For an answer, we have to investigate not only Plato's object of inquiry here—true being—but also the means he gradually adopted to secure it.

---

354 **Plato**, *Phaedo* 67d.
355 **Plato**, *Phaedo* 67d–e.
356 **Plato**, *Phaedo* 66d–67b.
357 E.g., **Plato**, *Republic* VI.490a–b. See also 476d on the two states of mind, or types of thinking about things, i.e., thought that is knowledge versus thought that is opinion. And 478a, where knowledge and opinion have different faculties and each is related to a different object. See generally 476–478e. Also **Parmenides**, fr. 1.31–32 for comparison, particularly with 476d.

An Exercise in Apprehending the True Nature of Things

The most abstract, and indeed advanced, use of logical technique can be found in the *Parmenides*, named after the Eleatic thinker, arguably Plato's most demanding dialogue. In fact, some have considered it the most challenging philosophical work of all time, and certain issues it explores have been called the Mount Everest of scholarship.[358] At one point in the dialogue Plato contends that to fully grasp the true nature or essence of a thing is a very difficult task. It is so formidable, in fact, that it can lead the seeker to doubt that anything that profound can exist, or at least to deem it unknowable by human nature.[359] Plato then concludes that only someone who is very gifted can come to know the true being of a thing (that is, its Platonic Form), and that only someone even more gifted will be able to teach it to others, who themselves have to be thoroughly versed in these kinds of problems.[360] These innovative ideas are voiced by Parmenides—the dialogue's titular character—who is in the midst of teaching a young Socrates how to become a seasoned philosopher. Socrates is advised that if, in view of the difficulties involved, one is compelled to deny that for each thing there is true being, or to fail to distinguish one in every case, then there will be nothing toward which to direct one's thought, nothing to grasp or apprehend. Furthermore, if we do not allow each thing to have a character or nature that is *always the same,* we will completely destroy the power or significance of discourse.[361] "What then will you do about philosophy?" asks Parmenides of Socrates. "Where will you turn, while these difficulties remain unresolved?"[362]

After Socrates confesses his perplexity, Parmenides informs him that he is only lacking a very special type of training. Particularly if it is *truth* that he is after, he must be prepared to undergo a most rigorous exercise, albeit one most people regard as useless, viewing it as idle chatter. Yet the purpose of this unusual drill is to go beyond the so-called visible things and investigate the objects of reason, the kind that can only be *apprehended by discourse.* Plato has Parmenides explain to Socrates, "If you want to be trained more thoroughly, you must not only hypothesize, if each thing *is,* and ex-

---

358 Cf. **Sellars** [694] 'Vlastos and the Third Man' 405.
359 **Plato**, *Parmenides* 135a.
360 **Plato**, *Parmenides* 135b.
361 **Plato**, *Parmenides* 135c.
362 Ibid.

amine the consequences of that hypothesis; you must also hypothesize, if that same thing *is not*" (emphasis added).[363]

What is most striking about the above sampling of Platonic ideas is that we are dealing in a sense with two Platos: one whose concerns regarding death, purification, and the rejection of corporeal desires betray an overwhelming Pythagorean disposition, and another, the veteran thinker, who not only redefines a philosopher's vocation regarding "the pursuit of truth," but who also demands a complete subjection to a most rigorous training of reasoning. This training alone is now the determining factor for whether truth is obtainable.

Unlike the *Phaedo*, the *Parmenides* does not claim that we are simple possessions of the gods, confined to our individual prison cell, the body,[364] and its author no longer insists that we must exercise ourselves in dying. Instead, we are advised to train ourselves in reasoning. The main difference between the two approaches to truth is that a Plato under Pythagorean influence sees truth at best as a possibility, only to be attained after death—if at all—while the later Plato asserts quite confidently that truth is available while we are still alive, and that someone who is not trained in ways to secure it should not be considered a philosopher. The shift in Plato's thinking is momentous: the mission of the philosopher is to pursue truth in *life*, and this by his own wits, and not just to wait for death to hand it to him on a silver platter, as a reward, perhaps, for abstaining from corporeal gratification.

What happened to cause this evolution in Plato? Possibly the very same thing that befell a few of the later Pythagoreans, a phenomenon that perchance affected the entire speculative field: once a certain type of thinking was checked by Parmenides' challenge, it matured. Conceivably, this may have been a natural development. When speculation exhausts itself with contemplating such admittedly intriguing motifs as "the afterlife," "reincarnation," "magic," "the supernatural," and the like, where will it go next? Perhaps sooner or later, reason needs to turn to something a bit more graspable or matter-of-fact, something a bit more fulfilling to deliberate upon.

Purification or Reasoning as a Way to Truth?

The "solution" inspired by Pythagorean cultism was illogical and self-defeating, an untrustworthy ordering of words that appears to make sense,

---

363 **Plato**, *Parmenides* 135e–136a.
364 **Plato**, *Phaedo* 62b.

Purification or Reasoning as a Way to Truth?

yet contains numerous traps and contradictions. According to a pythagorizing Plato, death is a categorical separation of body and soul. Yet one may wonder, of what benefit is it to the soul after the body's demise that it has abstained from corporeal pleasures, or that it lived a life emulating death, or that it has undergone countless ritualistic purifications? Death itself is quite obviously the absolute purification. In other words, if we believe that it is the *body* that distorts truth, then no matter what life the soul led *in its company*, once the soul is free, there is nothing further to stand between it and unvarnished truth. The jail cell is broken, the body is gone—as are its senses, its pains, and its passions. What could make a taint or an impurity upon the soul endure under these conditions if the cause of the taint, namely contact with the body, has come to an end? If the soul is still incapable of apprehending truth, then not only must other "factors" be blamed for its blindness, but these "factors" must have survived the death of the body *together with* the soul to be still there in the eternal realm of truth—if only to hinder it further. But how can any distortions survive the demise of the senses, particularly if the senses themselves were the causes of said distortions? Moreover, how can "what is not truth" be brought into the realm of absolute truth, so that it may continue to persevere and plague the soul? And if nothing "detrimental," "untrue," or "impure" can make it to this realm, why bother with purification and abstinence in the first place?

Under rigorous scrutiny, a Pythagorean type of approach to truth collapses into what may be generously called cultic belief. There is no reliable foundation for thinking, no irreducible base from whence to proceed or to which to return.[365] Things are too relative, too dependent upon conjectures that do not guarantee results; there are too many "ifs," "buts," and "maybes." Yet if there is such a thing as "absolute truth"—and reason, apparently, needs to trust that there is—then the whole issue is a simple "is or is not" proposition, ergo, a Parmenidean approach to dilemmas caused by conditionals. (Plato himself makes liberal use of Parmenides' "is or is not" switch; for a sample of this kind of argumentation, see the motto of this chapter.) To debunk precisely these sorts of inconsistencies is the aim of Eleatic methods. Among other things, they reveal the consequences of claims that result in impermissible gradients, particularly when only a cate-

---

365 As opposed to **Parmenides'** doctrine, which is thoroughly based on proof by thinking and discourse; cf. fr. 5: "It is the same to me from what place I begin, for to there I shall come back again."

gorical conclusion is called for. In other words, one should avoid a *conditional* approach if one requires a categorical result.

For example, we are told in the *Phaedo* that we must strive to purify the soul "as much as possible" from corporeal influences. Of course, we may ask, "*How much* purification is enough to ensure that, after death, one has gained access to *complete* truth?" We see that the precondition "as much as possible" is not compatible with anything that ends in "complete" or "absolute." To link the two will cause countless difficulties. For example, will a person who has purified himself for years on end encounter a somewhat "fuller" truth than someone, perhaps, who did not enjoy the same opportunity? Depending on our answer, there are either different degrees of truth—within a state, no less, that is supposed to be absolute—or even the slightest measure of purification will suffice to make all of the truth available. And there is an additional angle: what about an entity who was never sullied by a body—a god, perhaps? Does such a being not entertain a different relationship to truth—never having lost contact with it or seen it distorted in any way—than even the most purified philosopher? If purification is still a factor *after* a soul's escape from the body, god and philosopher shall never share the same truth, which again means there are two truths, not one.

We see that the kind of thinking that may be deemed Pythagorean is not geared to provide *certainty*, but only hope or belief, not exactness but approximation. Accordingly, Plato's pythagorizing statements in the *Phaedo*[366] cannot avoid a measure of vagueness, to wit: "to free one's soul . . . *as far as possible*"; "avoid *as much as we can* all contact with the body"; "it *seems likely* that we shall, only then . . . attain . . . wisdom"; "we shall *probably* be in the company of people of the same kind"; "we shall know all that is pure, which is *presumably* the truth." If we pay attention to the uncertain undertone of Plato's claims, then but one conclusion remains: not even a life lived most ideally can guarantee the seeker the attainment of truth after death. What then? Perhaps, this is the point where, for a Pythagorean, the whole laundering process called the "wheel of rebirth" kicks in: if provided with a new body, one has another chance at completing the purification cycle. In the long run, however, this type of "solution" seems unsatisfactory to Plato. Apparently, the more he pursues the true being of things—his theory of Forms—the more he shuns the notion of degrees of truth in the hereafter.

---

366 I appreciate **Kahn**'s [147] characterization of the *Phaedo*: "As a discourse on immortality in the shadow of Socrates' impending death, the *Phaedo* is the most otherworldly and in this sense the most explicitly Pythagorean of all the dialogues." (*Pythagoras* 52)

Calibrating the Ability to Reason

What is truly remarkable in Plato's change in thinking is that he no longer needs to rely on loaded remarks or images to arouse an inner sense of wonder in his listeners. Noticeably absent are the overt appeals to the perhaps unfulfilled longings for a utopian getaway. Instead, as can be seen in dialogues such as the *Parmenides* and the *Sophist*, he is far more concerned with the *consequences* of statements. In effect, one can trace throughout the *Parmenides*—and particularly in the part that investigates the objects of reason through discourse—the following concerns:

- Is what I have been trying to convey by means of a statement *still true* once the statement has been formulated or expressed?
- Are the consequences of my statement *supportive* of the idea or the meaning I have attempted to impart, or have they defeated the message?

Considerations like these are clearly not Pythagorean, but Parmenidean.

There are further hints in the way the later Plato formulates his metaphysical ideas. We have seen above that he distinguishes between "true being" or "what is" and the things that are merely the objects of opinion.[367] Furthermore, the exercise he calls for is aimed not at the visible things but at the objects of reason—the kind that can be apprehended by discourse, as he puts it.[368] And he also demands that one should investigate both the consequences of the supposition that a thing *is*, and the consequences of supposing that it *is not*. The ideas have an unmistakable affinity to Parmenides' teachings as evidenced by his Poem—for example, the proviso that certain decisions depend only on "is or is not," (Parmenides fr. 8.15–16) or the call to refrain from using one's eyes or ears to verify an argument or refutation that pertains uniquely to an object of thought—not of experience—and that must, therefore, be judged solely by reason (Parmenides fr. 7.3–6).[369] But most important is one particular phrase of Plato, which, when compared to his early pythagorizing, demonstrates how much he has adopted an Eleatic mind-set—that is, that one must isolate *that* character or nature of each thing *that is always the same* if one wants to preserve the capacity or mean-

---

367 E.g., **Plato**, *Republic* VI.490b, also V.476d–478b.
368 **Plato**, *Parmenides* 135e.
369 The decisions in question regard such matters as the coming-to-be or perishing of the object of reason, i.e., the IS for thinking (**Parmenides**, fr. 8.15–16), whose single story to tell (8.1) must be judged by reason and not by eye, ear, and tongue (7.3–6). Accordingly, as an object of inquiry it corresponds to **Plato**'s specifications in *Parmenides* 135e for an object of reason or discourse. (Of course, I don't imply that this makes "it" a Platonic Form.)

ingfulness of discourse.[370] Thus, his Forms share important provisions formulated by Parmenides for his object of rational inquiry—the *esti*, or "that which is," "in which thinking is expressed."[371] Both are exclusively the object of reason, hence equally the object of discourse.[372] And both are always the same; they preserve the sameness or self-identity of their character.[373] This fidelity or faithfulness allows them to be always available to the mind, in contrast to individual sense-experiential things, which are not always the same, nor continuously available to the senses.[374] Consistency provides reliability, a factor that indicates to the mind that it is dealing with truth. Without such verifiable consistency, one cannot formulate an account that is *demonstrably* reliable—Parmenides' unique concept and criterion, and one of the most important philosophical concerns after him.

Rigorous provisions for thinking were sorely lacking in any Pythagorean approach that we know of. Not that the concept of rules was unknown to the followers of Pythagoras, but these were rules for living a pure life, not calibrating reasoning.[375] Setting up and enforcing rules of conduct should not be confused with rules governing philosophical inquiry or logic. Walter Burkert gives a thought-provoking summation on what the Pythagorean way of life must have been like, if indeed they followed to the letter their precepts or *akousmata*:

> To take the *acusmata* seriously means an almost frightening constriction of one's freedom of action in daily life. Whether a Pythagorean gets up or goes to bed,

---

370 **Plato**, *Parmenides* 135c. My argument alludes to the curious "coincidence" that Parmenides' *semata* (fr. 8) can also be applied to a Platonic Form—even if there is a plurality of them. A plurality of theoretical objects does not go against Parmenides, as pointed out by **Curd** [297], who allows a multitude of theoretically basic entities as long as the *semata* apply to each one individually. See *Legacy* 47, 67, 82, 97. Here are two alternate translations of 135c: **Cornford** [282]: "He will have nothing on which to fix his thought, so long as he will not allow that each thing has a character which is always the same; and in so doing he will completely destroy the significance of all discourse." (*Plato and Parmenides* 100) **Gill** and **Ryan** [656]: "He won't have anywhere to turn his thought, since he doesn't allow that for each thing there is a character that is always the same. In this way he will destroy the power of dialectic entirely." (*Plato: Parmenides* 138)

371 **Parmenides**, fr. 8.35.

372 **Parmenides**, frs. 3, 6.1, 8.38, and indirectly 2.8, 7.3–6, 8.8, 8.17.

373 **Parmenides**, fr. 8.29: "Remaining the same in the same it lies by itself and thus fixed in [its] place." This stability makes it able to be apprehended by thought and employed in discourse.

374 E.g., **Parmenides**, fr. 4.

375 If the sources for some of Euclid's definitions are Pythagorean, then they are most likely post-Parmenidean. **Szabó** [772] argues that even the definition of the "unit," commonly attributed to Pythagoras, is in effect Eleatic; see *Beginnings* 261. As far as I am concerned, if any pre-Parmenidean Pythagoreans had "rules for thinking," these probably dealt with numerology, taboos, and other superstitious pursuits.

Calibrating the Ability to Reason 123

puts on his shoes or cuts his nails, stirs the fire, puts on the pot, or eats, he always has a commandment to heed. He is always on trial and always in danger of doing something wrong. No more carefree irresponsibility! Everything he does is done consciously, almost anxiously. The mythical expression of his attitude to life is a world full of souls and daemons, which affect every moment of a person's life. Everywhere are rules, regulations, and an ascetic zeal for discipline.[376]

Yet among all these rules, there is no detached approach to the products of reason, no sensibility for the veridical consequences of discourse—in other words, no demand for thinking and its results to be dependable or error-free. Thus, while the Pythagoreans adopted what they thought was a reliable foundation for their speculations—the unit—they failed to make it unassailable, which never allowed their explanations to rise above mere conjecture and belief. Was their foundation corruptible, or was it not? As we shall find out after becoming acquainted with Parmenides' testing of such things, the answer was not what the Pythagoreans expected. In any case, a "philosophy" that has to advocate *corporeal* purification and death for the potential obtainment of a more reliable insight does not inspire much confidence as a well-thought-out approach. One could not *prove* whether the whole thing actually worked; one had to *believe* that it did. For this reason, Plato, if he wanted certainty in the here and now, had no choice but to turn to Eleatic techniques, particularly if he had to test the results of reasoning based on his version of the perfect premise, the Form. No amount of Pythagorean purification could have provided answers for the sophisticated, logical hypothesis of the *Parmenides*.

We may tentatively conclude that Pythagoreanism was unable to fulfill the requirements for a reliable approach, especially the *evidential* kind demanded by Parmenides; its adherents lacked the methods necessary to calibrate thinking *on its own terms*. Numbers could be endowed with meaning, but this meaning could not be tested by the *means of meaning*. Instead, meaning was simply projected on whatever seemed convenient. And if it was challenged, the outcome was self-defeat and contradiction. In the final analysis, Pythagoreanism had to depend upon purifications of the body to make up for what it lacked in the training of the mind.[377] Perhaps the later

---

376 **Burkert** [100] *Lore* 191.
377 One of the best examples of the two modes of thinking is supplied by the post-Parmenidean Empedocles. Deeply influenced by Pythagoreanism, he bravely holds on to the idea that purification is a must, yet on the other hand he modifies his "roots," i.e., elements, to conform to Parmenidean requirements. See also **McKirahan** [67] *PBS* 262, 266–269.

Plato may still have found some usefulness in such purification practices, but undoubtedly for him, the real benefit for the philosopher—a benefit one could enjoy before dying—was to *exercise* reasoning, if only for reasoning's sake. Prior to Parmenides, such a thing was not conceivable. Hence, it should come as no surprise that this monumental idea is also the key to Plato's *Parmenides* dialogue, a fitting tribute to the Eleatic, as well as to his star pupil Zeno, who himself was deemed the inventor of dialectic by none other than Aristotle.[378] What term can describe the exercising of pure reasoning and discourse better than *dialectic*—"the art of critical examination into the truth of an opinion"?[379]—an art most efficiently performed by such beautifully simple means as an informal conversation.

---

[378] **Aristotle**, fr. 65 R = **D.L.**, 8.57.
[379] OED.

A human being must understand speech in terms of general forms,
proceeding to bring many perceptions together
into a reasoned unity.

—Plato, *Phaedrus* 249b–c

CHAPTER V

Parmenides

THE LAWMAKER

> Besides, we know from Parmenides' life, that he stood in high respect with his fellow-citizens at Elea, whose prosperity must be chiefly ascribed to the laws which Parmenides gave them. We also find in the *pinax* of Cebes [. . .] "a Parmenidean life" used synonymously with a moral life.
>
> —G. W. F. Hegel[380]

Parmenides was a native of Elea, a Greek colony founded c. 535 B.C. on the west coast of Southern Italy.[381] Later known as Velia, the town today is approximately 85 miles south of Naples. The archeological evidence shows that most of the original settlement was built on the side of a hill, framed by two harbors, which used to form a narrow peninsula into the Tyrrhenian Sea. The peculiar shape of the site made access by land very restricted, permitting the inhabitants to bar unwanted intruders. In many ways, Elea—or Hyele, as its founders called it—shared the privileges of a modern gated community, albeit one with fortified walls, guarded towers, and impassable portals. Standing on the top of the hill today, amid the ruins of a once-majestic temple, one still gets the impression of a quiet oasis, sheltered by the glistening sea on all sides, except for the small link to the mainland, which must have allowed its people the luxury of a peaceful, undisturbed existence.

Unfortunately, we know very little of Parmenides' life or the events surrounding it. There is some evidence that his father's name was Pyres, yet the correct date of Parmenides' birth is disputed, and that of his death is un-

---

380 **Hegel** [681] *Lectures on the History of Philosophy*, vol. 1 (trans. **Haldane**) 250.
381 Cf. **Dunbabin** [704] *Western Greeks* 485.

known. However, according to Plato, our most reliable source, Parmenides was around sixty-five years old when he visited Athens for the Great Panathenaea Games of 450 B.C., a famous athletic festival held every four years to honor the goddess Athena.[382] On that occasion, Parmenides is said to have met "a very young" Socrates—perhaps still in his early twenties—and taught the aspiring philosopher a few vital lessons on the subject of speculation. Of course, there is no way to tell how much of the story is reliable fact, or whether it only serves as a dramatic set-up for one of Plato's most ingenious dialogues. But there is not much reason to doubt his description of Parmenides as a man of distinguished appearance, with hair almost white and a calm and dignified demeanor. His characterization of Parmenides in the *Theaetetus* as an awe-inspiring figure of great and noble depth, whose thoughts were even more unfathomable than his words, further shows Plato's great reverence for the Eleatic.[383]

If we can trust Plato's time line, then Parmenides must have been born around 515 B.C., a time when the legendary Pythagoras was still active in Southern Italy and would be heading his mysterious society for perhaps another fifteen to twenty years.[384] This suggests that Parmenides may have been a young child when Sybaris, the richest colony of Greater Greece, was destroyed in 510 B.C. by the Crotonian army under Pythagorean command. We have seen that the fallout from this barbaric event may have led to the first political uprisings against Pythagoreanism within a span of ten to twenty years, as well as, perhaps, to the untimely death of its founder.[385]

Whether Elea was affected by any of these events is not known. Yet it is conceivable; after all, it was only some 80 miles from Sybaris; less than 100 miles from Metapontum, the alleged site of Pythagoras' death; and about 140 miles from Croton, the stronghold of the Pythagoreans and later also

---

382 **Plato**, *Parmenides* 127b. (Cf. also *DNP* 9, under "Panathenaia.") The Great Panathenaea were introduced in 566/5 B.C., which would place the games of the mid–fifth century at around 450/449 B.C. It all hinges on the age of Socrates, who is said to have been "very young" when he met the Eleatic. This oblique statement has been taken by scholars to mean Socrates was around twenty years old. We know that he died in 399 B.C. at seventy; hence, if we take away fifty years we arrive at the mid–fifth century, that is, at c. 450/449 B.C. Cf. **Nestle** [490] *RE* XVIII,4.1554.12; **Guthrie** [43] *HGP* 2.1–2; **KRS** [39] 240; **Stokes** [81] *One and Many in Presocratic Philosophy* 109—11; **Allen** [655] *Plato's Parmenides* 72; **McKirahan** [67] *PBS* 180; **Curd** [297] *Legacy* 15–16.

383 **Plato**, *Theaetetus* 183e–184a.

384 If we take the first anti-Pythagorean revolt of 500–490 B.C. as a *terminus ante quem*. Cf. **von Fritz** [122] *PPSI* 92.

385 Cf. **Minar** [160] *EPP* 9, on the disaster of Sybaris; 53–73 on the first revolt and Pythagoras' death, which he places at 494 B.C. (73); also **Burkert** [100] *Lore* 116–117. See also **Dunbabin** [704] *Western Greeks* 361–365, on the war against Sybaris, and 371–372 on the first revolt.

The Lawmaker

the hub of the revolts against them. Parmenides was probably in his late teens or early twenties when these dramatic events shaped the political landscape of Southern Italy. However, although the influence of the Pythagoreans was seemingly widespread, we are unaware of the extent of their activities in Elea.

There is one rather cryptical report that a member of the order may have befriended Parmenides, stating only that it was "Ameinias the Pythagorean and not Xenophanes" who introduced the young aristocrat to the "peaceful life."[386] Whether this is meant to suggest that Parmenides was inducted into Pythagoreanism, as has been contended, is a bit of a stretch.[387] The sources that allege his link to the movement are simply too wanting, and they are obviously too late chronologically to have had unfettered access to such a nebulous subject as the membership in a secret society, particularly one which had long ceased to exist by the time its history was being written.[388] At the least, we know of no bona fide Pythagorean contemporary of Parmenides who has vouched for his membership. Yet if the account of his connection to Ameinias is accurate, then the Eleatic may have maintained a special kind of friendship with the Pythagorean, who is portrayed as an upright man but also as quite poor. Parmenides, on the other hand, was not only of noble birth but also very wealthy, and this allowed him, as the same report stresses, to honor the elder man with a great shrine after his death. This pretty much concludes any direct link he might have had with the Pythagorean society, at least according to the available evidence.

---

386 **D.L.**, 9.21.
387 Regarding the meaning of "peaceful life," a link has been drawn to **D.L.**, 8.7: "Young men, come reverence in quietude, all these my words," allegedly the beginning of the "Sacred Word," a poem by **Lysis**, the suggestion being that a peaceful or quiet life is that of a student of Pythagoreanism. (However, the poem's source is obscured—it seems to have been originally attributed to Pythagoras—and it is quite likely a forgery. **Burkert** [100] points out that a work by that title is a priori apocryphal, because a "Sacred Word" is that which is not to be revealed to the uninitiated [*Lore* 219–220].) For additional thoughts on the matter, see **Diels** [3] (**DK** I.217n27) and **Gomperz** [352] (*Psychologische Beobachtungen* 33n103) both of whom suggest that a dedication to a "peaceful life" is meant as a withdrawal from political and public life. Cf. also **Burnet** [14] who turns Parmenides into a renegade Pythagorean who founded his own splinter group, *Early Greek Philosophy* 170, 184–185; similarly **Cornford** [282] *Plato and Parmenides* 1, 28–29. See **Minar** [475] on Parmenides' possible links to political Pythagoreanism, 'Parmenides and the World of Seeming' 46–47, 55. **Gallop** [340] also interprets the "quiet life" as meaning a "Pythagorean way of life," (*Parmenides of Elea: Fragments* 104–105, 105n1.) In addition, **Kingsley** [408] recognizes here a reference to "incubation" rituals, (*In the Dark Places of Wisdom* 180–182, 190).
388 E.g., sources like **Sotion** (**D.L.**, 9.21 = **DK** 28A1 = fr. 27, **Wehrli** [666] 'Sotion,' *Schule* Supplementband II = *Doxographi graeci* [1] 147–148), **Strabo**, 6.1.1 (**DK** 28A12), **Proclus**, *Commentary on Plato's Parmenides* 1.619,4 (**DK** 28A4), **Iamblichus**, *VP* 166, 267 (**DK** 28A4), **Photius**,

As for his vocation, we are informed that Parmenides was active as a lawmaker and civil servant.[389] That he composed quite a masterful code of law seems to be attested to by a uniquely Eleatic custom: The citizenry gathered together year after year to repledge all magistrates to Parmenides' constitution.[390] Such practice could only enhance the affluence and stability of the colony, and while the rest of Southern Italy seemed awash with war and political unrest, Elea, like a peaceful island amid a stormy sea, was, as one scholar observed, only known for its philosophers and its well-ordered legal system.[391] Apparently, to lead the kind of ideal existence Parmenides and his fellow citizens enjoyed became eventually something of a proverbial saying, and some have called it a "Parmenidean life."[392]

Naturally, Parmenides' occupation as a lawgiver would have made him ideal recruitment material for the Pythagoreans, who had a preference for legislators, administrators, and politicians. It must be noted, however, that insofar as we can reconstruct the society's motives at that particular time, they seemed to have been largely political. But there are no reports that they might have extended their political machinations to include Elea. Thus, with the sole exception of Parmenides' alleged youthful digression

---

Bibliotheka 249, 439a 36 (**DK** 28A4). (See **Gallop** [340] *Parmenides* 104–123, for proper listing and translations of much of the Parmenidean Testimonia.)

389 Cf. **Speusippus** in **D.L.**, 9.23 (F 3 **Tarán** [667] = **DK** 28A1); **Plutarch**, *Reply to Colotes* 32.1126a (**DK** 28A12). See also **Strabo**, 6.1.1 (**DK** 28A12) on Elea being well-governed because of the influence of Parmenides and Zeno. For further reflections on Parmenides' purported legislative vocation, cf. **Ciaceri** [702] *Storia della Magna Grecia* II 49–50, 114; **Gigon** [40] *Ursprung der griechischen Philosophie* 251, and [41] *Sokrates: Sein Bild in Dichtung und Geschichte* 220; **Untersteiner** [584] *Parmenide: Testimonianze e frammenti* 21–22; **Tarán** [667] *Speusippus of Athens* 237–239, 236n28 (who is somewhat undecided on the issue); and **Minar** [475] 'Parmenides and the World of Seeming,' who sees a connection between Parmenides' legislative and political activities and his rigorous philosophic/logical outlook (44–45, 55). Even **Kingsley** [408], otherwise a diehard advocate of Parmenides' purported shamanism, dedicates one entire, if somewhat speculative, chapter to Parmenides' lawgiving (*In the Dark Places of Wisdom* 204–219). But one of the most fascinating treatments of the subject is by **Capizzi** [252] *La Porta di Parmenide* 46–50, 56, 63–68, 70. Capizzi distills the testimonia to three basic vocations for the Eleatic: ambassador, governor, and legislator, the sum of which begets a fourth, viz. philosopher (48). Furthermore, Capizzi turns a critical eye on the theory that Parmenides was a medical doctor (64n118), a theory that I also find to be groundless.

390 **Plutarch**, *Reply to Colotes* 32.1126a (**DK** 28A12).

391 Cf. **Dunbabin** [704] speaking of the Eleans: "But we hear in this period only of their philosophers and their εὐνομία." (*Western Greeks* 345)

392 **Cebes**, *Tabula Cebetis* 2 (**Coxon** [290] *The Fragments of Parmenides* 120). The origin of this work is shrouded in mystery, but it is likely neo-Pythagorean, albeit possibly incorporating some older passages. According to *RE* XI,1.103.56, it is probably first century A.D., yet the last part of the work—due to its marked difference in style and quality of arguments from the rest—is arguably much older; see 104.56.

The Lawmaker 131

into Pythagoreanism, which I still think is debatable, no member of the society was ever involved in governing his native city.[393]

Barring any additional evidence, we can surmise that the Eleatics were left to pursue their dreams of a Parmenidean life, sheltered by the natural surroundings of their colony together with the incorruptibility of their constitution and the wealth and leisure that ensued from both. If this image of Parmenides' Elea is true, then perhaps only a halcyon sanctuary such as this was able to provide this new art of discourse and reflection a safe place to take hold. Indeed, a new breed of thinkers seems to have found its way to the tranquility of Parmenides' homeland, leading some scholars to postulate the existence of a bona fide Eleatic school. However, whether Parmenides established some sort of institution, or at least a study group, remains an open question. We only know that in antiquity, fewer than a handful of thinkers have been characterized as his immediate pupils or associates. One was Zeno of Elea (born c. 490 B.C.), his confidant and fellow citizen, and another was the Samian admiral Melissus (who defeated the Athenians in 441 B.C.). Occasionally, other Presocratics have been associated with Eleatic thought, such as the Pluralist Empedocles, the Atomist Leucippus, and the Sophist Gorgias. While it stands to reason that they have been strongly influenced by Parmenides, the nature of their relationship, if any, with him or his group is unclear.[394] For the time being, and as an introduction to Parmenides' work, we need to familiarize ourselves only with the ideas of Xenophanes, who is mentioned as both his mentor and friend by reputable sources.[395]

---

393 The one exception is Zeno of Elea, who, as Parmenides' pupil, is automatically invested by later commentators with Pythagorean membership. See **Strabo**, 6.1.1 (**DK** 28A12) and **Proclus**, *Commentary on Plato's Parmenides* 1.619,4 (**DK** 28A4). However, Zeno more likely would have viewed the Pythagoreans as Parmenides' foes, perhaps even writing a book against them; cf. **Plato**, *Parmenides* 128c–e.

394 How reliable the little bits of testimony are is anybody's guess. On Empedocles being Parmenides' pupil, see **D.L.**, 8.56; Leucippus, on the other hand, might have been Zeno's pupil, cf. **D.L.**, 9.30, and **Diels** [25] speculates that Gorgias, after being Empedocles' pupil, adopted the teachings of Zeno, and that his work, "On the Nature of Not-being" was brought about by a period of philosophical doubt and perhaps despair. See 'Gorgias und Empedocles' 359–360.

395 E.g. **Aristotle**, *Metaphysics* 986b23. Also maintained by **D.L.**, 9.21, who might be using the same source or sources.

THE POET'S CHALLENGE AND THE LAWGIVER'S RESPONSE

> The Eleatics, however, in our part of the world, say that things are many in name, but in nature one; this is their mythus, which goes back to Xenophanes, and is even older.
> —Plato, *Sophist*[396]

Xenophanes and the Truth Available to Mortals

What if philosophy as a systematic analytical approach did not find its beginnings in mysticism, shamanism, the arcane arts, or religion, nor in the natural sciences such as geometry, astronomy, or physics—but in lawmaking and justice; in other words, the legal profession? It could have evolved out of a resolute reaction against one of the greatest threats to the concept of knowledge, namely the *relativity* of truth[397] as propounded by Xenophanes of Colophon (c. 570–c. 470 B.C.).[398]

Or if we seek to approach the problem differently, we can ask ourselves: what could have motivated Parmenides, the lawgiver, to create a work so rigorous and abstract that it came to be considered as the first work on logic in the world? For a possible answer, we should find out what kind of sources were available to him, including fellow thinkers who might have made enough impact upon the Eleatic to trigger such a forceful response. Several modern writers have seen his work as a repudiation of Heraclitus (c. 540–c. 480 B.C.); others have sought to demonstrate a strong Pythagorean influence upon it. Yet these theories, while being quite popular, are very difficult to prove. In fact, we have no historical evidence to support a response from Parmenides to these sources—except for the alleged connection to Ameinias the Pythagorean in his youth—but certainly none that links the Eleatic to Heraclitus, the mysterious thinker from faraway Ephesus in Asia Minor. Thus, the only way of proving any connection is by a linguistic examination of the available text, that is to say, by looking for similarities in formulation or choice of words and interpreting these accordingly. But because the surviving material is so meager, the occurrence

---

396 **Plato**, *Sophist* 242d (trans. **Jowett** [654] *The Dialogues of Plato* 4.371).
397 Or rather the unattainability of truth, if truth is viewed as an absolute.
398 **Censorinus**, 15.3X (**DK** 21A7), states that Xenophanes lived more than a hundred years. Yet all evidence is circumstantial; cf. **Guthrie** [43] *HGP* 1.363; **Lesher** [431] *Xenophanes of Colophon* 3; and **McKirahan** [67] *PBS* 59, 59n1.

of few common words here and there cannot establish a credible link between these thinkers, much less prove satisfactorily who influenced whom.[399] On the other hand, it is somewhat odd that today's scholarship questions the possibility of a link between Parmenides and Xenophanes, even though in antiquity they were seen as associates, or even as pupil and teacher.[400] Were Plato, Aristotle, and all the others mistaken? I find that hard to believe. If we focus on the *epistemological* ramifications of their teachings, easy parallels can be drawn between the two without having to distort their core ideas. It is clear that both thinkers are concerned with the question of whether knowledge that is reliable or certain is available to human beings.

An exiled poet who migrated to Sicily, Xenophanes is sometimes associated with the founding of the colony of Elea, mainly because he wrote a poem commemorating this event.[401] A later tradition considers him the originator of the Eleatic branch of philosophy, perhaps on account of Plato's offhand remark that those who believe in the "oneness of all things" trace back to Xenophanes,[402] followed by Aristotle's suggestion that Parmenides was Xenophanes' pupil.[403] Even if we question these observations, there is no reason to doubt that Xenophanes was a familiar figure to the citizens of Elea, and it has been speculated that he moved to the colony for a while for the purpose of teaching there.[404] (His learnedness was famed as far away as Ephesus, in Asia Minor, as attested somewhat disparagingly by one of its most powerful thinkers, Heraclitus.[405]) It can be argued that even if we accept that Xenophanes and Parmenides knew each other, we still do not know whether any influence took place, or who influenced whom. All possibilities have been explored by scholars, including the one that the older

---

399 For a different view, particularly on Parmenides being influenced by Heraclitus, I recommend the informative work of Daniel **Graham** [353] 'Empedocles and Anaxagoras: Responses to Parmenides' 159–180 (an early article, where the issue is only mentioned as a possibility [179n21]), and the later [354] 'Heraclitus and Parmenides' 27–44, which advocates it forcefully. However, the possibility that Parmenides influenced Heraclitus is too easily dismissed by Graham in my view. (Not that I hold this as more plausible than the reverse.) For a more detailed analysis of these issues, see **Hermann** [372] *The Naked IS* (forthcoming).
400 D.L., 9.21.
401 D.L., 9.18, 20.
402 **Plato**, *Sophist* 242d, the so-called "Eleatic tribe." I appreciate **Lesher's** [431] balanced approach on the matter of Xenophanes' Eleaticism (*Xenophanes of Colophon* 6–7).
403 **Aristotle**, *Metaphysics* 986b23.
404 According to **Diels** (DK 21A1), see also D.L. 9.18, trans. **Hicks** [634] Loeb 2.424–425, 424n1.
405 **Heraclitus**, DK 22B40.

thinker may have followed the much younger aristocrat.[406] However, I believe that it was the doubts expressed by Xenophanes regarding the reliability of human knowledge that moved Parmenides to take such a decisive stand.[407]

Yet around Plato's or Aristotle's time, Xenophanes and Parmenides were not regarded as opponents, but as outspoken defenders of an extreme brand of monism—the doctrine that all things are in reality one, or that there is but a single ultimate principle. And admittedly, there is an unmistakable sense of oneness that can be derived from both their works, although in Xenophanes' case, this "one" is God.[408] Thus, when seeking to disassociate their teachings, contemporary interpreters are largely motivated by the need to avert an all-too-close identification of Xenophanes' concept of God with Parmenides' object of discourse. And I concur; there are no hints that they shared the same religious outlook. That does not mean, however, that they could not have entertained similar epistemological concerns.

What is quite striking about Xenophanes' theological ideas is their unaffected originality. His God, as I mentioned in the Introduction, does not resemble man, whether in appearance or in behavior, and thus the deity has nothing in common with the mean-spirited divinities that populate Greek mythology. Not only does Xenophanes criticize Homer and Hesiod for their depiction of the gods, but he faults all of humanity for shaping what is divine in its own image. In a striking passage, Xenophanes demonstrates how different races adopt only gods who bear their individual features.[409] To strengthen the point, he contends that if oxen, horses, or lions had hands, they too would make gods that look like them.[410]

---

406 Cf. **Reinhardt** [520] who proposed this theory (*Parmenides* 103–107, 111–112), and **Popper** [510] who deems it probable, at least, that Xenophanes may have adopted some ideas from Parmenides (*The World of Parmenides* 42–45), but he also speculates that the two may have influenced each other (135, 139).

407 **Popper** [510] thinks along the same lines (*World* 115–117, 121–123). I also value **Long's** [448] reasoned defense of Xenophanes as a first rate thinker, as well as his arguments for the rehabilitation of the tradition that links Xenophanes with Parmenides—which would make the latter respond to the former. ('Parmenides on Thinking Being' 130, 148) And **Cordero** [279] remarks that in regard to the "falsehood of opinion," it is probable that Parmenides had Xenophanes in mind, observing that "for Parmenides there is nothing more dangerous than the plausible, because it is similar to the true, although it is not true," while for **Xenophanes** plausibility and similarity (e.g. **DK** 21B35) were seemingly the only mortal options (*By Being, It Is*, 171–172, forthcoming).

408 Xenophanes, DK 21B23.
409 Xenophanes, DK 21B16.
410 Xenophanes, DK 21B15.

The remarkable thing about Xenophanes' God is not only that he is decidedly unanthropomorphic, but that his other characteristics reveal a freshness of thought in the old poet that surpasses even most modern notions. This God is not just immortal but eternal, meaning that being immortal implies only deathlessness; it does not rule out being born or created. Such ignoble beginnings were commonly attributed to the Olympian gods, who originally were born, a notion condemned by Xenophanes as impiety, because it suggests that there was a time when gods did not exist.[411] Moreover, he seems to think of God as an *inseparable* Unity, because "*all* of him sees, *all* of him thinks, *all* of him hears."[412] Ingenious also is Xenophanes' depiction of deity as causal agent: while being utterly unmoved, because "it is not proper for him to go to different places at different times,"[413] he nonetheless moves all things *without effort*, using only the thoughts of his mind.[414] These revolutionary ideas have contributed to Xenophanes' reputation as the first monotheist.[415]

But leaving his theology aside, the most important aspect of Xenophanes' teachings is his musings on the reliability of knowledge. In this sense, it is not wrong to call the older thinker the father of epistemological inquiry, even though his main contribution was to raise doubts. But he does not condemn mortals to eternal ignorance, bringing up the possibility that by searching, their ability to discover will improve.[416] The key is to figure out how to work on one's beliefs so that they *approximate* truth more closely.[417] If anyone took these ideas seriously, it was certainly Parmenides,

---

411 **Xenophanes**, DK 21A12.
412 **Xenophanes**, DK 21B24.
413 **Xenophanes**, DK 21B26.
414 **Xenophanes**, DK 21B25.
415 However, some of **Xenophanes**' verses refer to "gods" (the plural form), e.g., **DK** 21B23. It seems that he differentiated between the Olympians and his *eis theos*, i.e., One God. For a discussion regarding his use of the singular versus the plural for god, see **Guthrie** [43] *HGP* 1.375. Cf. also **Barnes** [9] *TPP* 89–92; **KRS** [39] 170. Furthermore, for **Aristotle**'s depiction of Xenophanes as the first monist, see *Metaphysics* 986b21–25.
416 **Xenophanes**, DK 21B18, see below. For a good analysis of Xenophanes' alleged skepticism and the juxtaposition of true belief versus true knowledge, see **Barnes** [9] *TPP* 138–143. A must is also **Lesher**'s [431] discussion, *Xenophanes of Colophon* 150–155.
417 **McKirahan** has brought to my attention that my statement on "approximating truth" is not necessarily the only read of **Xenophanes**' "by searching [mortals] discover better," pointing out that mortals may simply "be doing a better job of discovering," and also referring me to **Lesher**'s [431] views on the matter (*Xenophanes of Colphon*). I agree, but I also think that "approximating truth more closely" and "doing a better job at discovering" essentially amount to the same thing. Lesher argues that Xenophanes may have had a "superior approach to discovery" in mind, thinking of his own expertise as superior to those more common attributes that his fellow citizens admire in others (153). In support, Lesher mentions Xenopha-

who not only agreed that one's beliefs should be reworked, but in fact, held that they should be *rephrased* and *tested* before they can be accepted as reliable (Parmenides fr. 1.31–32[418]).

Perhaps I should repeat at this point Xenophanes' monumental statement on a mortal's difficulty in recognizing truth, presented previously in the Introduction: "No man has seen nor will anyone know the truth about the gods and all the things I speak of. For even if a person should in fact say what is absolutely the case, nevertheless he himself does not know, but belief is fashioned over all things."[419]

With this differentiation between godly truth and mortal belief, we have the first hint of the epistemological division that would flower in Parmenides' doctrine and also dominate much of Plato's thinking: the distinction of two classes of knowledge, one expressible as certainty, the other only as opinion or belief. But his words also indicate an intriguing paradox, namely, it is Xenophanes, the *mortal*, who utters them, so by what right can he claim that they are truthful? (This dilemma Parmenides wisely circumvents by putting his truth in the mouth of a goddess.) Nonetheless, Xenophanes seems quite aware of the difficulties inherent in his ideas, and he wisely concludes his writings with the following, rather candid, proviso:

Let these things be believed as resembling the truth.[420]

The idea that mortals are capable of statements that resemble truth is a very important one, and it is also hinted at in Parmenides' work.[421] Further-

---

nes' interest in "hands-on" as opposed to "armchair" discovery, recounting the old poet's extended travels and the geological or biological insights these have brought about, as attested by some of his writings. Accordingly, Xenophanes must have advocated an active and personal involvement in one's inquiries, rather than to passively await for divine "signs" or "revelations" (153–155). In my opinion, there is no better example of a scientific outlook than this, and thus I fully agree with Lesher. However, such a hands-on approach would lead to an increasingly greater discovery of truth, hence each step would constitute a closer and closer approximation of the overall truth, which can be approached only incrementally by mortals. Finally, if Xenophanes really had the notion of the advancement of superior methods in mind, how fitting is this proposition regarding Parmenides' masterful achievements? (This does not suggest however, that Parmenides practiced approximation by his Evidential method; that was reserved for the Plausible approach or Doxa. For further details, cf. Chapter VII, subheads "What Is the Significance of the Proem," and "Doxa, Opinion or Appearance?")

418 Viz. *dokounta* versus *dokimos*.
419 **Xenophanes, DK** 21B34 (trans. **McKirahan** [67] PBS 66–67).
420 **Xenophanes, DK** 21B35 (**Plutarch**, *Table Talk* 9.7.746b, trans. **McKirahan** [67] PBS 67). Resembling truth can also be understood as approximating truth.
421 We are reminded of **Parmenides'** *ta dokounta* (1.31) and the "plausible ordering" (8.60).

more, this resemblance with truth can be improved by man's continuous efforts, as Xenophanes suggests:

> By no means did the gods reveal all things to mortals from the beginning,
> but in time, by searching, they discover better.[422]

In other words, the acquisition of knowledge is an ongoing process for human beings as they strive for better and better approximations of truth. If there ever was a statement that presaged the scientific process, it is this one; no wonder it is viewed as tremendously significant by Karl Popper, who focused so much on science and epistemology.[423] The most important thing about searching, then, is not that it provides us with understanding, but that it *improves our ability to discover*. Thus, "to increasingly approximate truth" may very well be a suitable motto for philosophy itself.

As for why the gods refrained from revealing everything to mortals right away, we are not told, nor do we know whether Xenophanes offered an explanation. Regrettably, even fewer fragments of his work have survived than of Parmenides'. Perhaps there are certain religious implications at work here. After all, if mortals knew everything at once, they would be like the gods. Instead they have to work it out, and if all goes well, they find themselves closer and closer to that state—provided, of course, that they have enough time and never stop searching. It seems that the only factor which hinders them from achieving a godlike state is the limit imposed upon their life span.

Whether Xenophanes would have agreed with my last statement, we do not know. Perhaps for him it was a moot point given the shortness of our lives and the fact that he did not consider God as created or born.[424] God, never having been anything else but God, did not need to undergo a deification process, nor, in fact, any kind of change. God simply *is*—as opposed to mortals, whose very existence is determined by growth, evolution, and the like—in other words, by *becoming*. This circumstance constitutes the gist of our epistemological problem: as long as humans change, what they think they know changes with them, hence, at what point will they have approximated truth well enough to escape the snares of opinion? Consequently, as long as knowledge is a fluid thing, it must continue to be considered belief—at best it is "truth-in-the-making," not truth. Such a chain of

---

422 **Xenophanes, DK** 21B18 (trans. **McKirahan** [67] *PBS* 67).
423 **Popper** [510] *World* 48–50, 116–117.
424 **Xenophanes, DK** 21A12.

reasoning would not be far from Parmenides' reflections, and his Poem reveals that he is aiming for solutions that can close the exact gaps in human understanding that were first pointed out by Xenophanes.

After all, the older poet had managed to unmask a devastating dilemma that would have not only undermined the birth of philosophy but also condemned all knowledge to the twilight of relativity. Considering that Parmenides lived before philosophy had settled into some concrete form, the question of whether or not it would come about was certainly not something that would have concerned him. However, from the point of view of a legislator, the issue of whether all knowledge is relative, provisional, or ambiguous was very much something he would have cared about. The problem was simple enough, but it would prove quite detrimental to the equity of restitution, the allotment of punishment, the immutability and incorruptibility of set law, and thus the judiciary system that had to depend upon such things. Additionally, all fact finding and evidence procurement was in danger, not to mention the reliability of testimony, particularly if said testimony was produced by fellow mortals.

In essence, if all things are susceptible to opinion, then there is nothing that mortals can take as true or dependable, nothing that is immune against distortion and misinterpretation—not even the concepts they might have of the gods. In other words, the very things that are absolute *as themselves* cannot appear equally absolute in the considerations of mortals—no matter how hard mortals want to believe that they are—because, as Xenophanes observes, "belief is fashioned over all things."[425] This consequential comment is also reminiscent of one of Parmenides' most mystifying pronouncements, a line so difficult that there is much debate among scholars regarding its proper rendering. Some of the commonly accepted translations of this passage speak of "the opinions that pervade all things."[426]

In the final analysis, Xenophanes represents a watershed in the fragile beginnings of a science of thinking, one that makes the quest for knowledge itself the object of discourse. McKirahan says it best in his summation of Xenophanes' role:

> Together with his contemporary, Heraclitus, Xenophanes introduces concerns about method and the theoretical limits of human knowledge, which altered

---

425 See above, **Xenophanes**, DK 21B34, as formulated by **McKirahan**. Lesher [431] translates: "But opinion is allotted to all." (*Xenophanes of Colophon* 39)

426 Cf. Cordero, KRS, Coxon, Hölscher, and *mutatis mutandis* for "seeming," DK, Bormann, Gadamer, Barnes, O'Brien, Tarán, Gallop (see bibliography for details).

the course of presocratic thought from speculating about nature to theorizing about the basis for such speculation. In this change of direction we have, in an important sense, the birth of Western Philosophy.[427]

The Need for Reliable Criteria

How do we pierce the veil of opinion if, like a mask, it obscures everything to the point that all is relative, and all is debatable? We can imagine what effect Xenophanes' doubts are capable of having upon any judiciary or legislative system, both of which can function only to the degree that certain things are accepted as true and unchanging. If categorical evidence, eyewitness accounts, sworn testimony, and the like constitute the necessary currency of the legal system, Xenophanes devalued it to the point of worthlessness, because every fact was susceptible to repudiation if one only showed that it was originated by mortals. Indeed, no fact was invulnerable as long as it could be associated with mortals, no matter how remote that association might be. This, of course, was an impossible proposition. Talk about tainting the evidence!

We can imagine a trial in Elea during which the defendant cites venerable Xenophanes, claiming that no one could have seen, much less known, what truth *is*, unless he or she was a god. And what kind of fallout would such contentions have upon the court if the offense was perjury, a most serious crime for the ancient Greeks, and the defense argued with the following words: "As wise Xenophanes taught us, even if a person should in fact say what is absolutely the case, he, nevertheless, will not know that he did—all things being affected by belief.[428] How, then, we ask the court, could the accused have *known* that he did not speak truthfully, when he failed to say what was absolutely the case? In fact, how do *we* know that he did not speak the truth, if we are mortals like he is? Unless we repudiate Xenophanes, and commit impiety to boot, we, as mortals, do not know more truth than the defendant, the injured party, or the witnesses—unless the gods themselves reveal to us what is the case. Until then, we respectfully move that the trial be postponed." How would a court in Parmenides'

---

427 **McKirahan** [67] *PBS* 68.
428 I am aware that in **DK** 21B34 **Xenophanes'** claim is not necessarily intended to be that broad or universal. After all, he said it concerned "the truth about the gods" and "all the things" he spoke of, which arguably are the same subject. In other words, they involve "divine" or "eternal truths" or "things." However, my fictionalized account of a trial is meant as an example of how such a claim can be interpreted. He did say "all" or "all things" twice, and any competent defense would pick up on that, even a fictionalized one.

time react to such an appeal? More importantly, how would Parmenides, the legislator, react? The larger question then must be, "How can errant mortals judge other errant mortals?" (Perhaps it was to avoid a similar dilemma that Parmenides chose a goddess to propound his teachings.[429])

Xenophanes was not glib when he taught that mortal knowledge is not absolute. We are witnessing here the very first steps in what was to become the science of knowing. And naturally, these steps had to be skeptical. They had to shake our convictions to the core, if only to expose them for what they really are: beliefs and opinions *masquerading* as truths. That Xenophanes was nonetheless aware of the need for a reliable standard is evidenced by the following fragment. Speaking of mortals, he contends:

> If god had not created yellow honey,
> they would say that figs are far sweeter.[430]

This comment contains a valuable lesson about how humanity functions. Granted, Xenophanes addressed the relativity of human knowledge, yet he also observed that people seek standards that are absolute—or at least as outermost or ultimate as possible. To take honey as the categorical standard by which sweetness can be judged allows us to differentiate not only the sweet from the nonsweet, but also everything in between. In fact, mortals are so keen on reliable criteria that if they were to be deprived of a standard, they would immediately adopt the next available measure and raise *that* to the ultimate. Hence, figs would be considered not only far sweeter but the epitome of sweetness—if there was nothing sweeter. In other words, not just knowing, but knowing *reliably,* had to be a central concern in all human endeavor. The necessity to calibrate the truths within one's own thinking—as well as with those of other people—was paramount if discourse was to succeed.

To reconcile the mortal demand for an absolute criterion with the inherent relativity of all human knowledge is a need—and as a need, it must

---

[429] In summing up Xenophanes' point of view, **Barnes** [9] makes an interesting observation: "Men's beliefs do not amount to knowledge because they have unsatisfactory causes. The conclusion suggests that true belief will amount to knowledge if its causal antecedents are reputable." (TPP 143) Thus, our human beliefs are the product of circumstance, i.e., there is no causal link between how we have come to our beliefs and the object about which we believe something (142–143). Perhaps Parmenides was aware of the need for reputable causes of knowledge, thus his choice of a deity as the protagonist of his Poem.

[430] Xenophanes, DK 21B38 (Herodian, *On Peculiar Speech* 41.5, trans. **McKirahan** [67] PBS 68).

have had a lasting effect upon Parmenides. This is certainly evidenced in his Poem, particularly by its unprecedented structuring, which delineates two separate yet complementary parts: the first is dedicated to the attainment of trustfulness in reasoning and expression, the other depicts a compromising world as seen through the eyes of mortals, who, by not knowing how to deal with contradiction, only seek to reconcile the irreconcilable through ambiguous pronouncements. Obviously, as we would opt for figs if we did not have honey, we would settle for opinion if certainty were unavailable.[431] While such a solution may not be ideal, we, as mortals, do what we are able, bravely holding our own in a world of compromise.

The Senses, Reason, and Proof

Unable to express the white without the black, mortals create a hodgepodge of the two, often winding up with a murky gray—without realizing that there is no such thing, they get lost in self-refutation. This is particularly true of their take on the sensible world. Because of this, *no* cosmological explanation can be accepted by Parmenides as reliable—this is his main concession to Xenophanes. That is why we find the Eleatic's theories on the cosmos and the heavenly bodies—but also on biology, sense-perception, and procreation—all confined to the latter part of his work, that on mortal opinion.

Yet Parmenides, to his great credit, realized that compromise and uncertainty cannot be allowed to govern all human endeavor. He also recognized that reason, when having to rely only upon itself, was quite able to adopt dependable criteria by which to keep itself in check. There was, however, one requirement: it had to be provided with certain "tools" or "devices" by which to test its assumptions.

Whether Parmenides had an inkling of the abstract as a realm separate from tangible experience—like Plato, for example—we cannot say. But he realized that reason possesses the ability to refute its objects entirely on its own[432]—may these objects be "truths," "facts," "claims," or "beliefs"—without having to experience those facts or depend upon empirical evidence, particularly if none was available. Whether his experience as a law-

---

431 A parallel argument to the subjunctive (*casus irrealis*) read of *khren* in **Parmenides** 1.31–32. See Chapter VII, subhead "What Is the Significance of the Proem," for details.

432 By studying the consequences of Parmenides' use of refutation as a method for securing reliable reasoning by giving it genuine objects (*dokimos*, 1.32), the conclusion seems unavoidable that reason itself is predicated on the ability to refute its objects.

giver played a role here is something we can certainly speculate about. Courts of law generally do not depend on evidence alone, but on people's *interpretation* of that evidence. The tired adage that "the evidence does not lie" has an impressive, even authoritarian sound, yet it is no less a myth. How can evidence lie if it is mute? It certainly does not speak, much less explain itself. Hence, someone to interpret the evidence is always required if it is to be accepted as valid. Accordingly, the maxim is only complete when we say, "Evidence does not lie; people who interpret it do." And this brings us back to Xenophanes' dilemma.

Yet those who dealt with this problem, ages before philosophy was even a dream, had to develop a multitude of techniques to keep it in check. Certainly, the legal profession had no choice but to perfect the art of proving by argumentation alone. What else could it do, particularly in cases where empirical evidence was entirely missing and one had to rely on the self-serving utterances of the interested parties? In such cases, the magistrates or juries had to develop an ear for inconsistences—for accounts that perhaps sounded right, but that when prodded collapsed into nonsensical contradiction and self-refutation. And it is precisely such techniques that we find in the central part of Parmenides' work, known as the Reliable (or Evidential) Account, where method after method is demonstrated, methods not only for proving, but more importantly, for *disproving*. And yet his intention in offering us these techniques continued to be misunderstood.

Throughout the history of philosophy there has been much speculation regarding Parmenides' alleged repudiation of sense-perception. Particularly in antiquity it was a popular conclusion, eternalized by some of the most knowledgeable commentators, such as the Skeptic writer Sextus Empiricus (c. A.D. 200), to whom we owe a considerable part of Parmenides' verse:

> Parmenides rejected opinionative reason . . . and assumed as criterion the cognitive—that is, the inerrant—reason, as he gave up belief in the senses.[433]

However, even if this all too simplistic assessment were accurate, the idea in question was certainly not new, for in a court of law, sense-perception was and still is useless. Whatever the *object of contention* is—be it an overt deed or an omission—the act itself *is* not present, and hence not available to be *experienced* by those in attendance. Regardless of how real it

---

[433] Sextus Empiricus, *Adversus Mathematicos* 1.111, (trans. **Bury** [664]) 57. Cf. also **Gallop** [340] *Parmenides* 95, and **Barnes** [8] *Early Greek Philosophy* 130, for alternative translations.

might have been for anyone directly impacted by it, at trial it is reduced to an abstraction, treated, in other words, as an object of *discourse,* not of sense. And as an object of discourse it has to conform to precise rules that must be observed by all sides. In fact, the principal duty of any presiding arbitrator or magistrate is still the enforcement of strict adherence to these rules, if only to preserve the integrity of the judicial proceedings, in other words, to keep the object of discourse sound and the decision-making process pure.[434]

What other means are available to us when the immediacy of sense-experience is ruled out, and we are restricted to a *re-creation* of events by *discourse?* Naturally, we must look for inconsistencies in the account rendered. We might not have been there when the purported infraction occurred, but we are nonetheless capable of noticing that something is not right with an account when its description of events creates contradiction or discrepancy, particularly when it disagrees with itself. And whenever this occurs, we are justified to deem any claim refuted even if we never had the opportunity to witness the events firsthand. Thus, contradiction is an effective indicator, one that allows us to accept not merely wishy-washiness or ambiguity, but complete *certainty* in regard to the rendering of a state of affairs. It is a negative approach with a positive result: we are finding out how something *is not* as it *supposedly is.* If wielded properly such a method is indeed a powerful tool, especially in the hands of an expert.

It seemed that a door was open for mortals after all: they could have their much-coveted certainty, but only *if* they could find a way of unmasking some inherent contradiction. As I have indicated, this was not a direct approach—one still did not know what the exact truth was—but one at least *knew* what it *was not.* However, if all possibilities could be reduced to only two, then if either one was exposed as false, the other was confirmed as being *necessarily* true. This is precisely what Parmenides was able to accomplish, and it constituted a tremendous achievement.[435] The only question was, how does one go about reducing everything to an "either/or" proposition, in other words, to IS or IS NOT? The demonstration of such techniques occupies the central part of Parmenides' work. With pure genius, he exploits argumentative devices to prove the integrity of his object of discourse, while at the same time confining the listener to the inescapable

---

434 I have here particularly Zaleucus and Charondas, Parmenides' Southern Italian precursors, in mind. **Gagarin** [707] states, "Procedural regulations also were an important part of the work of [...] early lawgivers." (*Early Greek Law* 74–75)

435 **Parmenides**, fr. 8.11, 8.15–16, 8.33. See also Chapter VIII, "Twelve Provisos for the Evidential Account," Proviso 11.

logic of his chain of reasoning. In fact, the inevitability of Parmenides' conclusions conveys almost a sense of predestination, and he often alludes to necessity and fate as if these are causal agencies whose sole task is to determine that what he speaks about *must* be in a certain way and not otherwise—if it is to be at all.

But most importantly, Parmenides' work established one principle that forever changed the landscape of speculative thinking, and without it, logic would have been stillborn. I formulate it as follows: "What can be refuted *must* be refuted; what cannot be refuted *must* be accepted as true." In fact, in one segment he practically dares us to use reason if we want to test his Poem's "much-contested refutations," that is, the logical disproofs offered by the Goddess.[436] Why reason? Because the senses can never provide the kind of irrefutable certainty that reason can muster, particularly in regard to provoking or exposing contradictions. Thus we can say that Parmenides may have saved certainty from the bottomless pit of relativity to which it was banished by Xenophanes.

Early Lawmaking and Analytic Problem Solving

Before there was a systematic approach to reasoning that could be called logic, terminology that focused on evidence, proof, and the challenging of statements—such as we find in Parmenides' Poem—must have been familiar to anyone proficient in matters of law, such as magistrates, legislators, constitutional authorities, and by extension, statesmen, council members, and politicians.[437] The little that we do know of Parmenides' vocation conforms to most, if not all, of these occupations. And, if he indeed provided Elea with equitable laws and a constitution that facilitated its stability and prosperity, we may assume that he had learned his trade by studying the laws and legal precedents of neighboring cities. Fortunately for him,

---

436 **Parmenides**, fr. 7.5.

437 Before logic had adopted symbolic representations—which were unknown to the Greeks—it was largely dependent upon the kind of descriptive terminology we find in Parmenides and **Plato**'s *Parmenides*. See, e.g., Parmenides' use of *pistis alethes* ("true evidence") in 1.30, (cf. also **Verdenius** [585] *Parmenides* 49; and notes 465 , 492); 8.28; *pistis ischus* ("force of evidence") in 8.12; *piston logon* ("evidential/reliable account") in 8.50; *krisis* ("decision") in 8.15; *krinai* ("to judge," "to pronounce that a thing is," cf. **LSJ**); and *poluderis elenchos* ("much-contested disproof"), both in 7.5. Furthermore, *ta dokounta* ("things accepted as true," or "things of opinion") in 1.31 and *dokimos* (as in "genuine" but also "tested," or "proven," from *dokimazo*) in 1.32 may also imply a legal usage. (For a study of *ta dokounta* and *dokimos*, cf. **Mourelatos** [480] *The Route of Parmenides* 201–205. See also Chapter VII, subhead "What Is the Significance of the Proem?" For additional terms see Chapter VIII, subhead "Delimiting the Object of Judgment," and Chapter IX, subhead "Like according to Like." (Also notes 584, 585.)

Southern Italy was blessed with a multitude of laws and constitutions that were very advanced. It was envied, to boot, for bringing forth some of the most renowned lawmakers of antiquity. Its two earliest lawgivers, Zaleucus and Charondas, were already larger-than-life legends in Parmenides' time, and their reputations continued for many centuries. In fact, some have ventured that Parmenides had been influenced by these legislators in both the creation of his famous constitution and his Poem.[438]

According to ancient reports, Zaleucus of Locri (c. 650 B.C.) and Charondas of Catana (end of sixth century B.C.) were not only the first to create written codes of law that survived practically intact for hundreds of years, but they also bolstered these against wanton revision with ingenious devices.[439] For example, while both of their law-codes allowed for emendations, these were regulated within a draconian framework that may be styled as "amendment by noose." It functioned as follows: all citizens had the right to submit a change of law to the assembly, provided they argued their position with a rope around their neck and remained in that unfortunate condition until the magistrates had reached a binding decision.[440] If the suggested amendment was rejected, the petitioner was hanged on the spot. There is a tale that only three pleas had ever been proven successful throughout the centuries when this particular practice was in effect.[441]

---

438 Cf. **Ciaceri** [702] *Storia della Magna Grecia*, II 49–50; **Capizzi** [252] *La Porta di Parmenide* 46–49, 63–66. **Ciaceri** points out that Parmenides' Phocaean ancestors, upon their arrival to Southern Italy—after their forced abandonment of their colony in Corsica—had first found shelter in Reggio (di Calabria), before settling in Elea. As Charondas was the author of Reggio's laws, the Phocaeans' stay and subsequent close relationship with Reggio allowed them to become acquainted with their hosts' constitution. During this period, a strong alliance was forged by the two peoples and Reggio helped the Phocaeans in the founding of Elea. (See *Storia della Magna Grecia*, II 49. Cf. also **Dunbabin** [704] *Western Greeks* 346.) **Capizzi** [252] expands upon these possibilities, also remarking that Parmenides could have modeled his Poem's plot—involving a goddess as his mentor—after a legend depicting Zaleucus as also being inspired by a goddess, namely Athena (*La Porta di Parmenide* 46–48). Furthermore, **Capizzi** sees a connection between law and the philosophy of Parmenides, contending that the immutable nature of the laws of Zaleucus/Charondas may have served as background or model for the immutability of Parmenides' object of discourse (63–67). Perhaps, this immutability, and the methods which secured it, allowed Parmenides to frame an unchangeable constitution without having to defend it by such drastic devices as Zaleucus/Charondas' "amendment by noose." In other words, a constitution defended by logic, not by the threat of execution.

439 See **Aristotle**, *Politics* 1274a23–30 on Zaleucus and Charondas; 1274b7 on Charondas. **Diodorus**, 12.11.4–21.3; **Polybius**, 12.16; also **Demosthenes**, 24.139–141, on the one-eyed-man amendment.

440 Cf. **Diodorus**, 12.17.1–5 on Charondas and the use of the noose for the amendment of laws, and **Polybius**, 12.16, on also using the noose for the reinterpretation of a law of Zaleucus.

441 Three appeals according to **Diodorus**. **Demosthenes** claimed that only one law was changed in 200 years; see **Szegedy-Maszak** [726] 'Legends of the Greek Lawgivers' 207.

One such case concerned itself with the law of retribution (*lex talionis*), colloquially known as "an eye for an eye." The story, preserved by Diodorus Siculus, is that of a man with one eye who had lost that eye at the hands of another, and consequently was made totally blind.[442] According to the prevailing law, the offender, who had regular eyesight, was required to give up one eye, which meant that he still would have remained with one functioning eye. This the blinded man found to be too lenient a penalty, and taking his case to the assembly, he argued that although he lost only one eye, he was made blind by the other's act; hence, it would be only fair and just if the offender was also deprived of his eyesight completely, that is, forced to give up both eyes instead of the obligatory one. After putting the noose around his neck, the blinded man awaited the judgment of the court. The amendment passed, sparing his life, but the assembly had taken an important step: they changed their interpretation of law from the mechanical "eye for an eye" to the more discriminating "eyesight for eyesight." In other words, instead of an obdurate numerical redress, the court decided to move toward the more abstract restitution of a wronged principle.

However, the amendment did not necessarily improve Charondas' law. Ideally, an improvement would have made it universally valid and just—which is exactly what the blinded man charged that it was not. In other words, the new law should have worked in all cases, including the reverse. For example, if we take the same basics, but this time have the one-eyed man taking out one eye of a man with two eyes, and if we adhere to the new interpretation, the outcome would have to be entirely different. Evidently, if we operate within the strict framework the amendment allows us, we would have to let the one-eyed offender go unpunished, because to blind a one-eyed man would be too harsh a punishment if the one he had injured was still able to see. The entire matter serves well as a sophistic as well as a logical exercise, and according to Aristotle, this one-eyed man dilemma was the kind of topic schools of rhetoric explored.[443]

---

442 **Diodorus**, 12.17.1. Whether this particular case can actually be linked with Charondas, or if it is a later neo-Pythagorean invention, we do not know. It has been suggested that Diodorus, or his sources, borrowed this example from the topics debated in schools of rhetoric—perhaps inspired by **Aristotle**'s allusions (*Rhetoric* 1365b16–19)—cf. **Gagarin** [707] *Early Greek Law* 66, 66n63, and **Sealey** [725] *The Justice of the Greeks* 26. However, the fact that Aristotle mentions the one-eyed man dilemma as a fitting exercise for rhetorical training is not enough proof that such a case was never argued in real life, nor that similar cases were not discussed in Parmenides' time.

443 **Aristotle**, *Rhetoric* 1365b16–19.

The Ways of Proof and Disproof

Another example, based on a law of Zaleucus, is the tale of the two men who quarreled over one slave. A man who had owned a slave for some time had to go away for a while, leaving the slave at home. In his absence, another man had come and taken the slave away. Upon returning, the first man angrily went to the house of the other, seized the slave, and took him at once to the magistrates. There he appealed to a law of Zaleucus, which dictated that in a case of disputed ownership, the party from whom the property had been taken away should retain temporary possession of it until the matter had a chance to be resolved in court. However, the second man appealed to the same law and also demanded custody, since the slave had just been removed from *his* house. The magistrates were baffled by this challenge and decided to consult the *cosmopolis* (a kind of chief justice). The experienced arbitrator determined that the law should give preference to the one who had owned the property for an undisputed period of time; thus, he ruled in favor of the first man. The other man objected, denying that this interpretation mirrored the lawgiver's intention, to which the *cosmopolis* replied that they both—the second man and the cosmopolis—could take the matter to the assembly and argue their case with nooses around their necks, so that whoever failed to persuade his listeners would be hanged immediately. Upon hearing this suggestion, the second man declined on the grounds that the arrangement was utterly unfair. After all, he argued, the *cosmopolis* was close to ninety years old, while he himself was still a young man, and thus he had more to lose if he was voted down.

The Ways of Proof and Disproof

We can recognize in the above cases the seeds of the type of logical dilemmas that are not unlike those that preoccupied many of the early thinkers. If unchecked, the law of awarding possession to the one from whom the property was taken away can be readily extended to the absurd. The mother of the slave might argue that he was in her custody before he became the property of another. And if the slave had a voice in all of this, he might argue that he was with God before he was with his mother, or if he was a Pythagorean he might contend that he had been a free man in the previous life and that death and rebirth had unjustly removed his ownership of himself, hence the court should return to him what he was wrongfully deprived of—and so on and so forth. We can see how easy it is to twist the matter into a regressive or nonsensical argument. And simply because the examples are silly does not mean that a defense will not attempt them anyway, especially if it has nothing to lose. No court of justice has ever been exempt from idiotic argumentation.

Whether in a court of law or in philosophy, arguments depend mostly on what is equitable, that is, which things, values, or considerations correspond with each other and which ones do not. If the punishment must fit the crime, then we must have a means of comparison, a standard or gauge that allows us to determine whether such symmetry prevails in every case. We must look for things that are like and learn to recognize and discard the unlike. Thus, when dealing with argumentation, we must seek consistency and reject the inconsistent as false, and hence, self-refuting. In logic and philosophy, this overall principle has gone by many names, such as the simple "Like according to Like" and "Like by Like" (or in the case of coming-to-be from something, "Like *from* Like"), also recast as the Principle of Identity, or respectively, in the reverse, Non-Identity. Yet eons before philosophy, courts of law had to depend upon very similar mechanisms if justice was to be meted out. The case of the one-eyed man is a good example of this, as is the argument on the disparity in age between the *cosmopolis* and the young man. Justice is not considered attained when one side loses more than the other. Thus, a blind man is not equal to or *like* a one-eyed man, just as the latter is not equal to or *like* a man with two eyes.

Equity is achieved if parity is established, and what fails to meet these requirements not only can be refuted but *must* be refuted. It is the categoricalness of the latter approach that most properly characterizes Parmenides' outlook. He was not some blue-eyed speculator who fooled around with possibilities; instead, he was dominated only by what is *necessary*. Thus, there are no moderate positions in the passages that profile his methods, no mediate options or halfhearted solutions; like a stern judge who either approves or rejects, Parmenides divides the conclusions of reasoning only into *what is* or *what is not*. I cannot prove that Parmenides actually knew of the case of the one-eyed man or of the one regarding the disputed slave. Perhaps they happened after his time,[444] but arguably, as a much-valued legislator, he must have studied law and legal proceedings in much the same way as was said of Charondas: "He, after examining the legislations of all

---

444 Cf. **Dunbabin** [704] *Western Greeks* 73; **Oldfather** [633] *Diodorus Siculus*, Loeb 4.396n1; **Gagarin** [707] *Early Greek Law* 62; and **Sealey** [725] *The Justice of the Greeks* 26. However, I see no reason to suppose that judicial dilemmas were unknown to Parmenides or other early lawmakers.

The Ways of Proof and Disproof 149

peoples, singled out the best principles and incorporated them in his laws."[445]

In other words, within the dialectical process required in the making or the interpreting of law, Parmenides could find ample material by which to hone his logical skills. And so we find his work suffused with principles such as Like according to Like, Contradiction, or Non-Contradiction, with enough hints of other logical devices—such as Indirect Proof, Sufficient Reason, Infinite Regress, and the Excluded Third (or Middle)—that we may speculate he invented them. Or perhaps he only adapted these from the argumentative and evidentiary techniques that had been developed in courts of law since the dawn of humankind.

In any case, it helps to keep this legislative background in mind when interpreting the verses of Parmenides, particularly when examining his methods.[446] These plainly fall into two overall categories, namely *proof* and *disproof*. While the *results* of the two appear as opposed as "what is" and "what is not," the *methods* themselves actually complement each other. Why? Because as we shall see, Parmenides considered nothing *as proved* if the reverse possibility was not equally *disproved*. For example, if we want to accept that Like belongs to Like, it is not enough to allot something to its Like, we must also *disprove* any possibility of its being Unlike. That categoricalness, if anything, has turned out to be a lasting legacy of Parmenides, and it constitutes his final answer to Xenophanes' doubts. We may not know what "white" is if we pursue only the "white" and its like. Yet our mind can readily seize upon any contradiction and use it to establish certainty for itself, for if to be likened to "white" creates a *contradiction* with "white" and "like white," then what purports to be "white" is neither "white" nor "like white"—and of *that* we can be certain.

We will see that Parmenides' techniques do actually bring about conclusions that are so profoundly certain that they are utterly inescapable. Of course, whether or not we like this kind of certainty is another matter, and many subsequent thinkers have fought it bitterly—mostly because they mistook his methods for a general thesis about the universe, believing that the stringent provisos for proving advanced by Parmenides eradicated the reality of such physical phenomena as movement, change, and plurality. In

---

445   **Diodorus**, 12.11.4.
446   This link is also recognized by others: **Gigon** [40] *Ursprung* 251; **Untersteiner** [584] *Parmenide: Testimonianze e frammenti* 21–22; **Mansfeld** [455] *Offenbarung* 105, 270–271; **Minar** [475] 'Parmenides and the World of Seeming' 47, 55; **Capizzi** [252] *La Porta di Parmenide, passim*; **Cordero** [279] *By Being, It Is* 145–147 (forthcoming).

many ways, their struggles against the unyielding grip of Eleatic reasoning mark perhaps the most critical phase in the emergence of philosophy. As for Parmenides' "sparring" with the musings of Xenophanes, it seems that, in the end, the lawgiver met the challenge adroitly and on the poet's own terms—namely, by means of a poem.

CHAPTER VI

The Poem of Parmenides

A QUICK GUIDE TO THE POEM'S ORDERING

> At the risk of seeming tedious, I would like to transcribe in this commentary Parmenides' verses on the one being (they are not many), both to justify what I have said about the matter and because of the rarity of Parmenides' treatise.
> —Simplicius (sixth century A.D.)[447]

As far as we know, the teachings of Parmenides are contained in one single work considered philosophical: a terse Poem written in hexameters.[448] In later antiquity, it was sometimes called *Peri Physeos* (or "On Nature"); however, we have no proof that this was its original title.[449] (Throughout this book, I mostly refer to it only as "the Poem," with a capital *P*, to distinguish it from the works of other Presocratic writers.)

What is the Poem about? As I have indicated—and contrary to out-of-date interpretations and the cursory definitions which typify the average works of reference—the Poem is not about the universe, existence, or the oneness-of-it-all. All of these rather lofty objectives are later inventions, even if they have been repeated ad nauseam for the last 2,500 years. Yet the verses themselves bear no evidence that such matters belong to Parmenides' actual concerns. They show, rather, that Parmenides' inquiries were less esoteric, without being less exciting, considering their fundamental ramifications for the integrity of human knowledge and communication, which indeed may also *include* our *knowledge* of the universe, existence, and so forth, and the mode we choose to explain them. Thus Parmenides fo-

---

447 **Simplicius**, *Commentary on Aristotle's Physics* 144.25 (**DK** 28A21). Our only source for the verses known as fr. 8, he explains why he passes Parmenides' words to future generations. The quote is from **Barnes** [8] *Early Greek Philosophy* 134, with one change: the word "prolix" is replaced with "tedious."
448 D.L., 1.16.
449 E.g., **Sextus Empiricus**, *Adversus Mathematicos* 1.111. Cf. **Gallop** [340] *Parmenides* 95.

cused on reasoning and speaking, and how to make both dependable, regardless of what in the end their object may be (as long as it is an expressible object). I like A. A. Long's comment on this issue: "What Parmenides says is a continuous provocation to our own thinking about thinking."[450]

There is a fine but very crucial difference to be made between the advancement of a cosmological theory and the demonstration of techniques of how to make an account reliable. Naturally, such an account may also be used to express a variety of things, including the universe and everything in it, but it is only reliable when such matters are addressed in their *capacity* as objects of thought (see frs. 4 and 7.3–6), and in a form that does not lead to self-contradiction (see fr. 8). In a nutshell, Parmenides' central problem was *how to ensure the reliability of discourse.* Statements had to be defended against self-contradiction as well as against the misleading plausibility of vagueness—regardless, ultimately, of what said statements were about. For both of these vulnerabilities, Parmenides introduces examples and methods to extricate the truth.

Regrettably, the greater part of the Poem is lost in time; after two and a half millennia it is a wonder that we have anything at all. What remains is, perhaps, as much as a third of the original, according to the more optimistic estimates.[451] Here and there in antiquity people have thought to quote from the Poem, usually for their own individual purposes, and so the work has come down to us in bits and pieces, a collection of excerpts, paraphrases, commentaries, and summations. There are twenty such fragments totaling approximately 1,200 words in Greek—with one fragment being preserved only in Latin—that are considered original enough to deem them Parmenides' own. This translates roughly to 160 lines of verse,[452] but so much is gone that it is hard to reconstruct the exact place or context for many of these. This task has been compared to assembling a giant jigsaw puzzle without knowing how many pieces are missing and without having a picture of the finished product to refer to.[453] As we are dealing only with quotations in the works of others, some writers have preserved only a line or even only one word. Throughout this book, whenever I refer to a particular

---

450 **Long** [448] expands on Heidegger's remark about Parmenides' Poem that it "continually deserves more thought." 'Parmenides on Thinking Being' 127.
451 Cf. **Gallop** [340] *Parmenides* 5, on what is extant being perhaps a third of the total; or **Coxon** [290] *Fragments* 9, on "less than a quarter." See also **Diels** [307] *Parmenides Lehrgedicht* 26, on the Aletheia, Doxa estimates.
452 DK (with fr. 7.6 as separate from 8.1) + Cornford Fragment.
453 **Gallop** [340] *Parmenides* 5.

statement or verse, I also include the exact fragment number and line. For example, when referring to fragment 6, line 9, I write it as "fr. 6.9" or simply "6.9."[454]

Most experts distinguish two separate sections in the Poem. The first is called *Aletheia*, which is Greek for "truth"—it is also referred to as "The Way of Truth" or "The Way of Persuasion"—and it encompasses fragment 1 to fragment 8.50. After a short transition, which also serves as an introduction (8.51–61), the second section begins (fr. 9) commonly known as *Doxa*, or "opinion" in Greek, but interpreters use a wide range of designations for it, from "The Way of Opinion" or "The Opinions of Mortals" to "Seeming," "Appearance," "Belief," and even "Illusion."

However, this inconsistency in designation has led to too many confusions, in my belief. I particularly dislike equating Doxa with "appearance" or "seeming," which are all later ideas;[455] nor are such readings supported by the verses themselves.[456] Because of the ambiguous nature of the subject, I think it is best to adhere as much as possible to the words of Parmenides himself—that is to say, of his Goddess.[457] In other words, when I speak of the two parts, I mean two separate *accounts*, one "reliable" or "evidential," the other "a deceptive order of words" or a "plausible ordering." The passages in question are found in fragment 8.50–53:

> Herewith I end for you my *reliable/evidential account* and reasoning about truth. From here on [you shall] learn the opinions of mortals by listening to the *deceptive order of my words*. (Emphasis added)

And in 8.60:

> I disclose to you this *plausible ordering* in its entirety . . .

To further preserve the purity of these differentiations, I rarely use the all too general "Aletheia" for the reliable or evidential account, and mostly in context with those works of other writers who have relied on this partic-

---

454 Naturally, I observe the commonly accepted ordering of Diels/Kranz. While many interpreters specify their **DK** references as, e.g., "**DK** 28B7," or simply "B7," I find this redundant in a work dedicated to Parmenides, and perhaps a bit too distracting. Hence, I will only include this type of referencing when alluding to the fragments of other Presocratics.
455 That is, Platonic.
456 I side with Mourelatos and Cordero on this point.
457 As Parmenides never reveals her name, I usually capitalize the word "Goddess." See also Chapter VII, subhead "What Is the Significance of the Proem?"

ular designation. Worth mentioning also is that some scholars tend to separate the introductory part, or "*Proem*" (1.1–32), from the rest of the Aletheia; thus, they recognize three parts instead of two. Yet I believe it is more useful to distinguish *four* individual parts, in order to avoid confusion over what is talked about in each section, that is, their respective objects of discourse.[458]

In the first part—known simply as the Proem—Parmenides describes the journey to the Goddess, which also includes her reception of him and a brief announcement of the subjects he shall learn, and which, as we shall see, will be treated in the third and fourth parts of the Poem. Then Parmenides is introduced to the so-called "Ways of Inquiry for Thinking"—their differentiation is the central object of discourse of the second part—and only after the Goddess has singled out what approach is inappropriate for her task does she begin the Reliable Account, or third part, whose object of discourse is "that which is." Finally, the Poem concludes with the fourth part, "The Deceptive (or Plausible) Ordering of Words" or "Doxa," whose object is to render an account of mortal opinion, meaning how humans attempt to explain their world as presented to them by sense-experience.

Here, in short, is the structuring of the Poem based on the four central objects of discourse in each section:

1. "The Proem," as the journey to the unnamed Goddess (1.1–32)

2. "The Ways of Inquiry for Thinking" (2.1–7.6)

3. "The Reliable"—or "Evidential"—Account" (8.1–61[459])

4. "Doxa," "The Deceptive Ordering of Words," or "The Plausible Ordering" (9.1–19.3)[460]

What follows next is the Poem itself. Further clarifications of other critical matters, useful perhaps for a proper interpretation of its main points, are offered in the subsequent chapter.

---

458 See also **Gallop** [340] *Parmenides* 5, on the fourfold distinction.

459 Conventionally, the Reliable Account is thought to end at 8.49 or 8.52/3. However, in line 8.54 the Goddess is pointing out to Parmenides that mortals have gone astray in their naming by not doing it right; hence we must assume that her message is to be taken as Reliable. Thus, in fr. 8.53–61 she only explains the foundations of Mortal Opinion but still preserves a critical distance on the matter, in contrast to fr. 9, where she simply performs the Deceptive Account without a further word of caution. **Gallop** [340] *Parmenides* 77, observes the same separation.

460 The Cornford Fragment—if legitimate—should belong to the Reliable Account.

THE POEM, A TRANSLATION

([ ] Brackets signify alternate or implied words, or words added for greater clarity. For a speculative rearrangement of the Ways of Inquiry for Thinking, particularly fragments 5, 6 and 7, see Chapter VII, subhead "Are There Advantages to Rearranging the Fragments?")

The Proem

Fragment 1

1.1 The mares that carry me as far as my spirit might reach
1.2 were escorting me, when guiding they placed me on the much-informing[461]
 road
1.3 of the Goddess [*daimonos*], who leads the man who knows through all
 [. . .][462]
1.4 There I was being carried, brought by wise[463] mares who were
1.5 straining the chariot, while maidens were leading the way.
1.6 The axle's nave shrilled like the bright sound of a pipe,
1.7 sparkling (for it was pushed ahead by two whirling
1.8 wheels at either end), while hastening to escort [me]
1.9 the daughters of the Sun—having left the House of Night
1.10 for the Light—thrust back with their hands the veils from their heads.
1.11 Here are the Gates of the Paths of Night and Day,
1.12 and they are bound together by a lintel and a stone threshold.
1.13 They are high in the sky, blocked by mighty doors
1.14 to which avenging Justice [*Dike*] holds the alternating keys.
1.15 Her the maidens implored with gentle words,

---

461 "Much-knowledge-imparting," or "very-informative." I have taken my cue from **Verdenius** [587] *Parmenides: Some Comments on His Poem* 12; **Deichgräber** [303] *Parmenides' Auffahrt zur Göttin des Rechts* 652; **Gadamer** [39] *Philosophisches Lesebuch*, vol.1, 20; **Tarán** [569] *Parmenides* 10; **Bormann** [232] *Parmenides: Untersuchungen zu den Fragmenten* 29, 58; **Heitsch** [370] *Parmenides: Die Fragmente* 9; **Hölscher** [379] *Parmenides: Vom Wesen des Seienden* 11; et al. However, I like the idea that πολύφημον can also be read as "many signs" or "full of signs"—as proposed by **Lan** [423] and **Cordero** [279]—because it establishes a link to the "single way" of fragment 8, with its many "signs" or "landmarks." (Cf. **Lan** [423] 'Die ΟΔΟΣ ΠΟΛΥΦΗΜΟΣ der Parmenideischen Wahrheit' 376–379; and **Cordero** [279] *By Being, It Is* 28, 199, forthcoming.)

462 I reject the still popular emendation ὥστη or cities. While **Coxon**'s work was valuable in dispelling the emendation, it remains inconclusive regarding an acceptable alternative. (Cf. [289] 'The Text of Parmenides fr. 1.3,' and [290] *Fragments* 158.) **Tarrant**'s [572] interpretation based on Aτη is too conjectural ('Parmenides B1.3: Text, Context and Interpretation' 1–7). See also **Cordero** [279] *By Being, It Is* 28–29 (forthcoming) for a good summarization of the problem—even though I cannot adopt his substitute "there," i.e. "Who leads the man who knows *there*, about everything." (Emphasis added)

463 Or "knowledgeable of the way": πολύφραστοι; cf. **Sider** and **Johnstone** [544] *The Fragments of Parmenides* 8.

1.16 persuading her skillfully to push back the bolted bar
1.17 swiftly from the gates. The doors
1.18 spread open, creating a widening gap, the bronze
1.19 doorposts turning alternately [i.e., back and forth] in their sockets,
1.20 fastened with bolts and rivets. Then, straight through them,
1.21 the maidens kept the chariot and horses on the broad way.
1.22 And the Goddess received me graciously, taking my right hand in hers,
1.23 and addressed me with the following words of counsel:
1.24 "Young man, accompanied by immortal charioteers,
1.25 and the mares who carry you to my abode,
1.26 welcome—for it is not an ill fate which has sent you forth to travel
1.27 this road (though it is far from the beaten [or, customary] path of man),
1.28 but Right and Justice. It is necessary that you learn all things,
1.29 both the unshaking heart of well-rounded [or, persuasive] Truth
1.30 as well as the opinions of mortals, for which there is no true evidence.[464]
1.31 But nevertheless these you shall learn as well: how it would be right for the things of opinion,
1.32 to be provedly things that are altogether throughout.
or,   to be provedly, being entirely [or, in all respects] altogether.[465]

The Ways of Inquiry for Thinking

Fragment 2

2.1 Come now, I will tell you—and preserve my account as you heard it—
2.2 what are the only ways of inquiry for thinking/knowing:
2.3 the one that [states it as] IT IS, and that it cannot NOT BE [as it is],[466]
2.4 is the Way of Persuasion (for it follows the Truth)
2.5 the other that [states it as] it IS NOT, and that it is necessary that it NOT BE [as it is],[467]
2.6 this I point out to you is a completely inscrutable path
2.7 for you cannot know that which IS NOT (for this cannot be done)
2.8 nor can you express it.

---

464 Cf. also 8.28 on πίστις ἀληθής. After much thought, I have decided to go with "true evidence," thus siding with **Heidel** [51] 'On Certain Fragments of the Pre-Socratics' 717–719; **Verdenius** [585] *Parmenides* 49; and similarly **Heitsch** [370] *Parmenides* 13, 29 (i.e., *evidenter Beweis*). Furthermore, I also read πίστος ἰσχύς as "force of evidence" in 8.12, and πιστὸν λόγον as "evidential account" rather than merely a "reliable account" in 8.50. Yet cf. also **Mourelatos** [480] *Route* 150–151, for critical comments on the matter. (See also Introduction, note 32, and Chapter VII, subhead "What Is the Significance of the Proem," and notes 437 and 491.)

465 LSJ: ὄντα: 1. "the things which actually exist"; 2. "reality," "truth." Cf. **Plato**, *Sophist* 263d. For detailed explanations for my rather uncommon rendition of this difficult verse, see Chapter VII, subhead "What Is the Significance of the Proem?"

466 Both "states it as" and "as it is" are conjectures. Cf. Greek text.

467 Again, the same statements—as in 2.3—are conjectures.

Fragment 3

...for "to be thought" and "to be" are the same [thing].[468]
[or, for thinking and being are the same.]

Fragment 4

4.1 Behold things which, although absent, are yet securely present to the mind;
4.2 for you cannot cut off What IS from holding on to What IS;
4.3 neither by dispersing it in every way, everywhere throughout the cosmos,
4.4 nor by gathering it together [or, unifying it].

Fragment 5

5.1 It is the same to me
5.2 from what place [or, whence] I begin, for to there I shall come back again.

Fragment 6

6.1 Speaking and thinking must be of what IS, for it can be,
6.2 but nothing cannot be. I urge you to consider this.
6.3 For first you [will begin] from this way of inquiry...[469]
6.4 But afterward from the one, which mortals who know nothing

---

468 Admittedly, I am taking some liberties here. However, this is how the text is understood by quite a few scholars, often in stark difference to the literal translation. The intended meaning is that to be an object of thought already implies that something is. My understanding of this passage is not essentially different from this version by **McKirahan** [67]: "For the same thing is there for thinking and for being." (*PBS* 152) In other words, something is there for thinking because, above all, it is being. Moreover, as I also consider fr. 3 to be the continuation and completion of the argument in fr. 2, particularly 2.7–8, it is clear that that which IS NOT cannot be known or expressed in any way, because only that which IS can be thought. Thus, from the point of view of that which can be thought, "to be thought" and "to be" are identical. And there is an additional point: It may appear from the above, and perhaps other comments of mine, that I favor what **Long** [448] calls the "mind/being non-identity reading" of Parmenides (cf. 'Parmenides on Thinking Being' 134, and *passim*). However my main intention is to provide a somewhat restricted interpretation of Parmenides—in the context of this work—restricted in the sense that it avoids going into some of the deeper *metaphysical* ramifications of his doctrine (the reasons for this I have stated elsewhere). Yet pondering the identity/non-identity problem of thought and being would have lead in this direction. Nonetheless, I find myself in agreement with many of the points argued by Long in his paper, particularly those regarding fr. 3 and 8.34–36. (See also note 474) Still, I see no need to unequivocally embrace the idea that "Being is Mind." And it can lead to equally self-defeating results as when we say "Being is World."

469 I agree with Cordero and Nehamas in rejecting Diels' εἴργω. However, Cordero's alternate choice, ἄρξει, seems the most appropriate to me, which is why I have followed him. Cf. **Cordero** [277] *Les deux chemins de Parménide* 24, 168–175; **Nehamas** [488] 'On Parmenides' Three Ways of Inquiry' 105. Cf. also **Curd**'s [297] meaningful treatment of these issues, *Legacy* 56–58.

6.5 piece together[470] two-headed[471]; for helplessness in their
6.6 breasts guides their unsteady mind. They are borne along,
6.7 deaf as well as blind, stupefied, hordes without judgment,
6.8 for whom to be and not to be are deemed the same and
6.9 not the same; but[472] the path of all turns back to itself.

Fragment 7

7.1 For things that are not can never be forced to be;
7.2 but keep your thought from that way of inquiry,
7.3 and do not let habit [derived] from much experience force you along this path,
7.4 to direct your unseeing [i.e., unrecognizing] eye and ringing ear
7.5 and tongue; but judge by reasoning [or, discourse] the much-contested disproof
7.6 expounded by me.

The Reliable or Evidential Account

Fragment 8

8.1 ... hereafter a single account
8.2 is left: the way that [states it as] it IS. Yet on this there are landmarks [or, signs]
8.3 aplenty, that What IS is ungenerated and imperishable,
8.4 whole, of one kind, unshakeable [or, immovable] and complete.[473]
8.5 Nor was it before, nor will it be, since it is now, all together,
8.6 one, continuous. For what origin would you seek for it?
8.7 How and whence did it grow? I will not permit you to say
8.8 or to think from What IS NOT; for it cannot be said or thought
8.9 that it IS NOT. What necessity would have impelled it
8.10 to grow later rather than earlier, if it began from nothing?
8.11 Thus it must either wholly be or not be [at all].
8.12 Nor will the force of evidence ever allow [anything] to arise from What IS NOT, [to be]
8.13 alongside it. For this reason, Justice has not allowed it to come to be

---

470 πλάττονται from πλάσσω, as in "to make," "create," "fabricate," or "compose," and not πλάζω "to wander." (Cf. **LSJ**: πλάσσω: I. IV. and V.) I follow here **Cordero**'s [279] line of reasoning (he uses "to make," "create," cf. *By Being, It Is* 136–137, forthcoming) as well as **O'Brien** [493] who opts for "to fabricate" (*Le poème de Parménide* 25, 27). However, I have taken notice of **Sider**'s [543] concerns with πλάσσω (read as "to imagine" [cf. **LSJ** III.]); see 'Textual Notes on Parmenides' Poem' 363–365.

471 Perhaps meaning "of two minds." As pointed out in **Sider** and **Johnstone** [544] *The Fragments of Parmenides* 14, this could be "because such people would need two heads to be able to entertain the contradictory beliefs spelled out below ... "

472 δέ in the strong adversative form, cf. **Denniston** [776] *The Greek Particles* 165–166. See note 570 for additional comments.

473 There are different variations and emendations of the end of this line. Cf. **Sider** and **Johnstone** [544] *The Fragments of Parmenides* 2 and 16, who list ἀτέλεστόν, "without end (in space and time)," instead of the more popular ἠδὲ τελεστόν, "and complete."

The Reliable or Evidential Account

8.14 nor to pass away by easing her bonds,
8.15 but holds firm. The decision in these matters depends on this:
8.16 IS or IS NOT. And it has been decided, just as is necessary,
8.17 to leave one [or, to let go of one as] unthinkable and unnameable (for it is not a true
8.18 route) and the other to be and be true.
8.19 How could What IS be in the future [or, afterwards]? How could it come to be?
8.20 For if it came into being, [then] it IS NOT, nor [IS it] if it is going to be.
8.21 In this way, coming-to-be is extinguished and destruction unheard of.
8.22 Nor is it divisible, since it is all alike [i.e. homogeneous];
8.23 nor is it more here [i.e., in one place], which would prevent it from cohering as one, [lit. "holding together"]
8.24 nor any less, but all [of it] is full of What IS.
8.25 Hence, it is all continuous, for What IS draws close to What IS [or, attracts What IS].
8.26 Yet unmoving [or, changeless] in the limits of great bonds,
8.27 it IS, without beginning or end, since coming-to-be and destruction
8.28 have been driven far off, rejected [or, cast out] by true evidence.
8.29 Remaining the same in the same it lies by itself
8.30 and thus fixed in [its] place, for mighty Necessity
8.31 holds it within the bonds of the limit which encloses it all around,
8.32 because it is not right [or, lawful], for What IS to be incomplete,
8.33 for it is not lacking—but Not Being would lack everything.
8.34 To think and the wherefore [or, the object] of thought are the same [i.e., that for the sake of which there is thought].[474]
8.35 For without What IS, in which it is expressed,
8.36 you will not find thinking/knowing. For nothing else IS or will be
8.37 apart from that which IS—since Fate has bound it
8.38 to be whole and unmoving [or, unchanging]. Which is why *it* has been named all things,
8.39 that mortals have established, persuaded that they are true:
8.40 "coming-to-be" and "passing-away," "to be" and "not [to be],"
8.41 "to change place," and "to alter bright color."
8.42 But since there is an ultimate limit, it is complete,
8.43 from every side well-rounded, like the bulk [or, fullness, curvature] of a sphere,
8.44 equal in every way from the center: for it must be neither more
8.45 nor less, [whether] here or there;
8.46 for neither is there What IS NOT, which might stop it from arriving at [or, reaching]
8.47 its like; nor is What IS such that it might be
8.48 more here and less there than What IS, since it all IS, inviolate;

---

474 I am very impressed by this formulation: "Thinking and that which prompts thought are the same," cited by Long and credited by him to Sedley ("from a forthcoming work"). (Cf. **Long** [448] 'Parmenides on Thinking Being' 136, 136n21) (Perhaps Long had in mind **Sedley**'s [541] 'Parmenides and Melissus,' where Sedley translates "Thinking is identical to that with which thought is concerned." 120.)

8.49 for equal to itself on all sides, it meets its limits uniformly.
8.50 Herewith I end for you my reliable/evidential account[475] and reasoning
8.51 about truth. From here on [you shall] learn the opinions of mortals,
8.52 [by] listening to the deceptive order of my words.
8.53 For they have set their minds on naming [or, identifying] two forms,
8.54 for which to be a unity[476] is not necessary—here they have gone astray—
8.55 and they have differentiated contraries in form [or, constitution] and assigned landmarks [or, signs] to them
8.56 apart from each other: here, on the one hand, the ethereal flame of fire,
8.57 gentle and very light, in every way the same as itself
8.58 but not the same as the other. Yet that one [also], by itself, is the
8.59 reverse: darkest night, a dense and heavy body.
8.60 I disclose to you this plausible ordering in its entirety, so that
8.61 no mortal mind [or, thinking] may ever surpass you.

DOXA—The Deceptive Order of Words, or the Plausible Ordering[477]

Fragment 9

9.1 Yet since all things have been named Light and Night
9.2 and these according to their powers [have been assigned] to one and the other,
9.3 all is full of Light and obscure Night together,
9.4 both equally, since nothing has a share in neither.

Fragment 10

10.1 You shall know the nature of the aether and all
10.2 the signs in the sky and the shining Sun's
10.3 pure torch [and its] destructive effects [lit. deeds], and whence they came into being,
10.4 and you shall learn the revolving deeds of the round-faced Moon,
10.5 and its nature, and you shall also know the heaven which surrounds on both sides,
10.6 whence it grew and how Necessity guided and bound [or, constrained] it
10.7 to hold the limits of the stars.

---

475 For "evidential" see notes 464, 491.

476 Cf. **Schwabl** [537]: "Das (μία) muß die Einheit der (δύο) sein, und so können wir übersetzen: "denn sie legten ihre Meinung dahin fest, zwei Formen zu benennen, von denen eine Eine (d. h. eine einheitliche, die beiden zusammen erfassende Gestalt) nicht notwendig ist; in diesem Punkte sind sie in die Irre gegangen." ('Sein und Doxa bei Parmenides' 54) Similarly **Mansfeld** [455]: "förmliche Einheit." (*Offenbarung* 126) And **Tarán** [569] translates: "a unity of which is not necessary," (*Parmenides* 86) explaining "unity" as: "one" in the sense of a unity of the two μορφαί" (220). **Cordero** [279] speaks of "bringing together" or uniting as a "one." (*By Being, It Is* 167–168, 202, forthcoming). See also note 519.

477 Same ordering as **Gallop**'s [340] *Parmenides* 77. See the beginning of this chapter as to why I distinguish Doxa at this point and not above at 8.51, as is commonly done.

Fragment 11

11.1 ... how Earth and Sun and Moon
11.2 and the common aether and Milky Way and the outermost Olympus
11.3 and the hot force of the stars were impelled
11.4 to come into being.

Fragment 12

12.1 The narrower [bands, or rings?] are full of unmixed Fire,
12.2 those next to them with Night (but a portion of flame is discharged into their midst),
12.3 and in the center is the goddess who governs all things.
12.4 For she rules over hateful birth and intermingling of all things,
12.5 sending the female to unite with male and in turn
12.6 male with female.

Fragment 13

First of all gods she devised Love.

Fragment 14

Shining in the night with a light not of its own, wandering around the Earth.

Fragment 15

Always gazing [searchingly] towards the rays of the Sun.

Fragment 15a

[Parmenides in his verse called the Earth] *rooted-in-water*.

Fragment 16

16.1 For as is at any given moment the mixture of the wandering limbs [or, far-wandering members[478]]
16.2 so also is mind present to humans; for that which thinks [in them],
16.3 [namely] the constitution of their limbs, is the same
16.4 for each and every one; for what preponderates is thought.

---

478 Following **Stratton's** [671] translation of *De Sensibus* in *Theophrastus and the Greek Physiological Psychology Before Aristotle* 68–69. Like Stratton (cf. 67–69 and 158–159), I see in the concept "far-wandering members" an allusion to the "organs of sense-perception." Accordingly, I recognize here a possible if indirect link to fr. 4, if we translate ἀπεόντα as "far-off" or "distant" (as read by Diels, Burnet, Cornford, KRS, Guthrie, Bormann, Heitsch, Hölscher, Gallop, and Curd), thus the manner in which things might appear to the "far-reaching senses" when they are far away.

Fragment 17

> On the right, boys, but on the left, girls . . .

Fragment 18

> 18.1 When a man and a woman mix together the seeds of Love,
> 18.2 a power formed in the veins from the different bloods
> 18.3 produces well-built bodies by preserving the proper proportion.
> 18.4 For if, when the seeds are mixed, the strengths are in conflict
> 18.5 and do not make a unity in the body formed by the mixture, then cruelly
> 18.6 they will afflict the sex of the offspring with double seed.

Fragment 19

> 19.1 Thus, [I tell you] according to opinion, these things have grown and now are,
> 19.2 and then, after growing up, they will reach their end.
> 19.3 And to each humans have assigned a distinctive name.

Cornford Fragment

> Such [or, Alone], changeless, is that for which as a whole the name is: "to be."

CHAPTER VII

The Poem's Most Difficult Points Explained

WHAT IS THE SIGNIFICANCE OF THE PROEM?

> Not everything, but only what is proved should be trusted: the first one is foolish, the other is sound.
> —Democrates[479]

The Realm of the Nameless Goddess

Except for the last five lines (1.28–32), the Poem's Introduction, or Proem, does not give us much to work with, philosophically speaking. The greater part is extremely difficult to interpret, remaining arguably the most mysterious aspect of Parmenides' work. Some writers view the Proem as a symbolic recounting of an initiation of some kind, likening such an allegorical journey to a nameless deity to a spiritual rite of passage, a shamanistic experience, or even a mystic union whereby Parmenides becomes one with "true being," existence, or the universe.[480] I find these theories at least far-fetched if not groundless. Other scholars have spotted in the Proem several parallels to ancient mythological motifs, such as the tales of Homer and

---

[479] Possible **Democritus** (see **DK** 68B67).
[480] On shamanism and Parmenides, cf. **Diels** [307] *Parmenides Lehrgedicht* 14–21; **Meuli** [720] 'Scythica' 171–172; **Cornford** [22] *Principium Sapientiae* 118; **Morrison** [477] 'Parmenides and Er' 59; **Guthrie** [43] *HGP* 11–13; **Mourelatos** [480] *Route* 42–44; **Kingsley** [408] *In the Dark Places of Wisdom* 62, 72–73; **Henn** [371] *Parmenides of Elea* 7, 9. On *unio mystica* see **Fränkel** [29] *Early Greek Poetry and Philosophy,* particularly 351–352, 352n9, 365–369, 366n41a. Similar takes are found in **Verdenius** [585] 'Parmenides' Conception of Light' 121–123, 125, 128, and [585] *Parmenides* 67–68; and in **Vlastos** [594], 'Parmenides' Theory of Knowledge,' *passim.* (See *TAPA* 77 [1946]: 76, on Parmenides' philosophy being a "strange blend of mysticism and logic.")

164   WHAT IS THE SIGNIFICANCE OF THE PROEM?

Hesiod or the creation legends of Babylon and Mesopotamia, and admittedly these particular studies can provide one with much food for thought.[481] However, no one has been able to explain why Parmenides insists on such minutiae like the chariot's wheels, axles, and hubs, or the sockets, pivots, and bolts of the ethereal doors. Speculations on whether certain words may conceal a secret meaning have been generally unfruitful, and some conclusions have been outright embarrassing, as, for example, Sextus Empiricus' commentary, which sees veiled references to Parmenides' doctrine in every detail. Sextus considers the "road of the Goddess" (1.2–3) to be the method of philosophical inquiry available to reason, likening the latter to a divine guide that directs us toward universal knowledge.[482] While some of this may sound reasonable, he also believes that the horses pulling the chariot stand for the soul's irrational desires, and that the Sun Maidens represent the visual senses, while the two rounded wheels remind him of the round shape of our ears. Of course, speculation of this kind does not make the verses in question more intelligible or their purpose transparent.

But neither have other, seemingly more accessible concepts been adequately explained, concepts like the "man who knows" (1.3), "the House of Night" (1.9), or "the paths of Night and Day" (1.11). In fact, scholars cannot even agree upon such simple matters as the direction of the route: is it from Night to Light or the other way around, or possibly to a realm beyond such distinctions? Interpreters with a Platonic disposition may hold that Parmenides is advancing from Darkness to Light, and some have considered his journey a parable for an initiatory passage, one that takes the initiate—also known as the "man who knows"—from the depths of shadowy ignorance to the bright light of wisdom.[483] However, one of the things this theory does

---

481 On interpreting the Proem in a mythological light, see **Havelock** [713] *The Greek Concept of Justice* 270–71, and [363] 'Parmenides and Odysseus' 133–143, *passim;* **Deichgräber** [303] *Parmenides' Auffahrt* 6–11, 23–43, 85–86; **Burkert** [246] 'Das Proömium des Parmenides und die Katabasis des Pythagoras' *Phronesis* 14 (1969): *passim;* **Pellikaan-Engel** [504] *Hesiod and Parmenides, passim;* **Steele** [555] 'Mesopotamian Elements in the Proem of Parmenides? Correspondence Between the Sun-God Helios and Shamash' 583–588. See also **Henn** [371] who seeks to establish links to Zoroastrianism. (*Parmenides of Elea* 39–46) Intriguingly **Capizzi** [252] interprets the Proem both allegorically and as an actual topographical travelogue to the top of Elea's headland, cf. *La Porta di Parmenide* 31–38. (See also below, plus note 486.)

482 **Sextus Empiricus**, *Adversus Mathematicos* 1.112–113. See **Gallop** [340] *Parmenides* 95. For further comments on the "Way of the Goddess," see Chapter IX, subhead "Like According to Like."

483 Cf. **Sextus Empiricus**, *Adversus Mathematicos* 1.112–113; **Diels** [307] *Parmenides Lehrgedicht* 50; **Kranz** [417] 'Über Aufbau und Bedeutung des Parmenideischen Gedichtes' 1163–1165; **Gigon** [40] *Ursprung* 247; **Deichgräber** [303] *Parmenides' Auffahrt* 11, 28–30; **Fränkel** [29] *Early Greek Poetry* 352n9; **Guthrie** [43] *HGP* 2.9; **Brumbaugh** [13] *The Philosophers of Greece* 50.

not explain is why Parmenides is already such a "knowing man" *before* he embarks on his voyage.

Other scholars see Parmenides moving in the opposite direction, not from wisdom to ignorance, of course, but from the everyday Light of the mortal realm toward the eternal Night of an Orphic Underworld.[484] This particular view takes into account the older myths, which often speak of a mystical passage to Hades—such as the ones of Odysseus, Orpheus, and Pythagoras—and this does seem more in character with Parmenides' time. Yet our difficulties in making sense of the direction lie with the text itself. The verses only say that the Daughters of the Sun have left the House of Night for the Light (1.9), thus we are not told whether they left the Night in order to pick up Parmenides in the mundane Light—before returning home to the hallowed Dark—or if they found him in the Darkness of not-knowing and now are coming back to the Light of knowledge.

A third group of interpreters believe that it is inconsistent with the rest of the Poem to designate either Light or Night as the final realm of the Goddess, especially as Doxa, as the Mortal Account, is treating both as elementary counterparts—constituents by which mortals construe all things (8.56–59, 9.1–4). Moreover, the verses speak of the Gates of the Paths of Night and Day (1.11), hence we must assume that the paths lead to the gates and end there, and that neither one continues past these without the other. Bound by these considerations, I count myself among those who think that the realm of the Goddess resides beyond such differentiations as Light and Night or dark and bright, in other words, beyond the realm of sense-experience.[485] And there is one further if remote possibility, namely that Parmenides' travelogue is nothing more than the concealed description of an actual route and not an allegorical one, perhaps even to the sacred grounds of the colony itself, which—due to its cul-de-sac-like seclusion on top of the Eleatic headland, and safeguarded by "high in the sky gates" toward the back—can be said to "lay far from the beaten track of men," as verse 1.27 declares, that is, far from the roads and settlements of the valleys beyond (or the seaports below).[486] But all of this is wanton speculation of course, and I also

---

484 Cf. **Morrison** [477] 'Parmenides and Er'; **Burkert** [246] 'Das Proömium des Parmenides und die Katabasis des Pythagoras' 8–12; **Kingsley** [408] *In the Dark Places of Wisdom* 50–51, 64–71, 75, 94–97.

485 Cf. **Schwabl** [538] 'Der Forschungsbericht *Parmenides*' 145; **Cornford** [282] *Plato and Parmenides* 30, **KRS** [39] 244; **Burkert** [246] 'Das Proömium des Parmenides und die Katabasis des Pythagoras' 15–16; **Mansfeld** [455] *Offenbarung* 246–247.

486 Cf. **Capizzi** [252] *La Porta di Parmenide* 28–40, 45, or **Rizzo** [524] *La Voce delle Pietre* 23–24, in regard to *Porta Arcaica*, the old gate—in mere ruins today—situated at the top of the

admit to having strong sympathies with the scholarly view that contends that "the topography of the journey is blurred beyond recognition," meaning that we have no way of telling which way the chariot is going.[487]

As to the identity of Parmenides' Goddess, we have no real clue who she might be, although there have been a number of hypotheses about her function or name.[488] None are convincing, however, and most are groundless, particularly when she is identified as Aletheia, the goddess of truth, or Dike, the goddess of justice.[489] The latter is clearly distinguished as the guardian of the gates from which the path to the abode of Parmenides' divine mentor leads (1.11–21). Thus, she remains nameless, but as a substitute for a name I have opted to refer to her as "the Goddess" with a capital G, if only to differentiate her from other female deities. In regard to the Goddess' role in the Poem, it is important to note that the verses never imply that we are witnessing a mystic union between God and man.[490] The Goddess does not take over Parmenides' body, nor does he function as her avatar. In fact, quite the opposite is true: a continuous distance is studiously maintained between instructor and listener. The Goddess argues matter-of-factly, not unlike an advocate who thoughtfully elaborates the evidence in court or a magistrate who sums up the findings.[491] One may even wonder what may have moved Parmenides to use a goddess for his protagonist, if the answer

---

promontory of Elea/Velia. Of course, the validity of any hypothesis that views it as analogous to the Gates of Night and Day of Parmenides' Proem (1.11–20) hinges largely on its actual age, which we must postulate as being of late sixth century or early fifth century B.C. However, as of my last visit, on-site archeologists have voiced doubts regarding this theory, and speculate that Porta Arcaica was built around the fourth century B.C.

487 As **Mourelatos** [480] poignantly observed, cf. *Route*, 15–16. Cf. also **Tarán** [569] *Parmenides* 24, and **Curd** [297] *Legacy* 19.

488 On the special significance of her road being identified as that of the *daimonos* or "daemon" (1.2–3) see Chapter IX, subhead "Like according to Like."

489 On the Goddess being Aletheia see **Heidegger** [364] *Parmenides*. However I agree with **Diels** [307] who defends her anonymity as intentional, cf. *Parmenides Lehrgedicht* 9. We will return to the question regarding her nature when we examine the unique function she performs for Parmenides; see Chapter IX, subhead "Like according to Like."

490 Cf. **Mansfeld** [455] *Offenbarung* 252–259, who criticizes the *unio mytica* interpretation convincingly. Mansfeld likens Parmenides' methodology not to a mystic journey but to a progressive logical process or procedure. (259).

491 **Cordero** [279] makes a similar observation. He states that "her sentences, like lawyer's submissions, are supported by "arguments" (*logoi*)." (*By Being, It Is* 31, forthcoming, cf. also 145–147.) **Heidel** [51] uses the term "forensic argumentation" for the Goddess' evidentiary presentation ('On Certain Fragments of the Pre-Socratics' 718); and **Mansfeld** [455] refers to same as "forensic rhetoric" (*Offenbarung* 105). (See also Introduction, note 32.) **Verdenius** [585] points out that *pistis* (1.30, 8.28, etc.,) "may be best rendered by 'evidence,'" in which sense it is often used to denote a convincing legal argument." (*Parmenides* 49) (For further possible legal aspects or terms, cf. notes 437, 464, 584, 585).

would not be so extraordinarily intriguing and equally unheard of: after introducing her attentive pupil to the ways that are available for proper inquiry, the Goddess bids him to use reasoning to judge her arguments, which she herself calls "contentious" (frs. 2, 6, and 7). When has a deity ever asked a mortal not to accept his or her godly statements on faith, but to scrutinize them carefully, even to render judgment? The Goddess seems to assure Parmenides that he possesses at least one faculty that brings him on par with the gods: *his ability to reason*. Has there ever been a message that, while being purportedly divine, is nonetheless less mystical, or conversely, more rational than this?

The Curriculum

Philosophically most significant are the Proem's last lines, but regrettably they are also not easy to interpret, particularly because we encounter a textual problem in the last line (1.32). What we can be sure of is that Parmenides is introduced to a curriculum of sorts:

1.28 It is necessary that you learn all things,
1.29 both the unshaking heart of well-rounded [or, persuasive] Truth
1.30 as well as the opinions of mortals, for which there is no true evidence.
1.31 But nevertheless these you shall learn as well: how it would be right [*khren*] for the things of opinion [*ta dokounta*]
1.32a to be provedly [*dokimos einai*] things that are altogether throughout [*dia pantos panta per onta*].

or,

1.32b to be provedly, by being entirely [or, in all respects] altogether.[492]

Not only is Parmenides advised that he must learn all things, but, seemingly, these are assigned to two separate categories, the first being the "unshaking heart of well-rounded Truth" (which some manuscripts preserve as "persuasive Truth"), and secondly, the unreliable "Opinions of Mortals." The Goddess insists that even if there is no "true evidence" for these he still must learn them, which is very interesting as it underscores the importance of including Doxa in the Poem—or in any study program that concerns itself with teaching "all things." However, the Goddess adds

---

492 Following **Mourelatos** [480], version 1.32b uses *onta* as a "circumstantial participle of manner ("by being") depending on δοκοῦντα." (*Route* 215n63)

a necessary qualifier regarding these "things of opinion" (*ta dokounta*, 1.31) and this is sadly where the cryptic ordering of words in line 1.32 fails us. We can gather that Parmenides must learn how the "things of opinion"—which the Goddess had just in the previous line stressed as unproven—could nonetheless reliably or provedly be, but we do not know what condition or factor may ever allow us to judge opinion that way, meaning as actually reliable. Our problem is with the available source material, which is transmitted in different versions, one preserving the very last word in line 1.32 as the Greek *peronta*, meaning "to pervade" or "to pass through," while the other splits the word into *per onta*, which signifies "just [or, indeed] the things which actually exist," as in what is true or real.[493] Thus, the more popular translations of 1.31–32 give us either, "But nonetheless you shall learn these things too, how what is believed would have to be assuredly, pervading all things throughout,"[494] or, "But nevertheless you will learn these too—that the things that appear must genuinely be, being always, indeed, all things."[495]

How Opinion Would Be Judged If Truth Did Not Exist

Whether the "things of opinion" pervade all things or whether they are real because they are in fact "all things," as notions they lead essentially to similar if troublesome conclusions. At first glance, it does appear that the Goddess classifies belief either as equal to truth or as something that may have been originally a substitute for truth, but which by now has managed to supplant it in every conceivable way. Of course such a view must negate just about everything in Parmenides' Poem. It gives a power or authority to opinion that should be rightfully reserved for truth itself; after all, in fr. 2.4 the Goddess has persuasion following *truth*, not belief. To save the Poem's overall message while keeping our initial interpretation of 1.31–32 intact, we must limit or qualify the above statement somehow, and this is precisely what most scholars have done. Thus, the majority confine the import of 1.31–32 to the mortal point of view, and explains it as follows: mortals, due to their ignorance of fact, are compelled to believe that whatever *appears* to

---

493 For *per onta*, see **Mourelatos** [480] *Route* 212–215, 214n60 and 61; **Zafiropulo** [615] *L'école Éléate* 133, 294–297; **Owen** [496] 'Eleatic Questions' 85–89; **Guthrie** [43] *HGP* 2.9; **Brague** [238] "les réalités," 'La vraisemblance du faux: Parménide fr. I, 31–32,' *Études sur Parménide*, Vol. 2. 57; **McKirahan** [67] *PBS* 152; **Curd** [297] *Legacy* 21. See **LSJ** on ὄντα: 1. "the things which actually exist"; 2. "reality," "truth."

494 **KRS** [39] 243.

495 **McKirahan** [67] *PBS* 152.

How Opinion Would Be Judged If Truth Did Not Exist 169

them as real or true, *is* genuinely real or true. Some interpreters even go so far as to suggest that the Goddess advances a hypothetical conclusion that depends on having truth be nonexistent. Thus, if one reads the mood of the Greek verb that in 1.32 expresses "necessity" (*khren*) as subjunctive, the line can be translated in this manner: "Yet, nevertheless these things you will also learn: how it *might have been necessary* (*khren*) that the things that *seem* true, really *are* true . . . " to which one must add "provided that the *actually true* did not exist."[496] The provision in the end must be supplied for the hypothetical reading to work. The implication is that the things of opinion would be judged rightfully, indeed unavoidably, as being genuine and true, *if* actual truth was not available. Mortals, without the possibility of knowing better, would have to settle on the next best thing, namely opinion, in a kind of epistemological opportunism that is reminiscent of Xenophanes' remarks about what role honey plays in the assessment of sweetness.[497] If, as in Xenophanes' view, mortals would judge figs far sweeter if they did not have honey, so, one could argue, they would trust opinion far more if they did not have truth. In fact, they would trust opinion absolutely, as the above reading implies.

Interpreters who prefer the hypothetical read share a dismissive attitude toward Doxa, something I also classify as a "negative reading."[498] It implies, depending on the interpreter's point of view, that Doxa is just a fantasy, a collection of empty words, a falsehood, an illusion, a counterfeit cosmology, a sham. Indeed, most scholars, even if they do not support the hypothetical reading, reject the Mortal Account in some form or another. The problem with this general view is, as I will show, that if we dismiss Doxa as a fraud, there is nothing to stop us from invalidating it entirely, meaning we will have to equate it to that which is not, or to nonexistence. But in that case the whole point of the Poem becomes redundant: there is no one to give an account, no one to receive it, and nothing to give an account about. Whatever is left, may this be Being, Truth, or who knows what, does

---

496 The example I am using is a modified version of **Cordero's** [279] translation (*By Being, It Is* 37, 199, forthcoming). Cf. **Kranz** [417] who observes that while the way is unreal for the Goddess, she does know, being omniscient, the beliefs of mortals ('Über Aufbau und Bedeutung des Parmenideischen Gedichtes' 1170); and also **Falus** [315] 'Parmenides-Interpretationen' 286–287, for a supporting read. See also **Zafiropulo's** [615] discussion of the issue, but in regard to *per onta* (*L'école Éléate* 296–297).

497 **Xenophanes, DK** 21B38. I have also argued this point in Chapter V, "The Poet's Challenge and the Lawgiver's Response."

498 Indeed, **Cordero** [279] refers to Doxa as "the negative part of the thesis" of Parmenides (*By Being, It Is* 163, forthcoming), or "the negation of the thesis" (135).

not have to give an account of itself to itself, much less learn the lessons of the Poem. But all of these possibilities are absurd, and it only exemplifies, in my view, why much of the interpretation available on Parmenides, when tested by his own methods, is provably at a deadlock on these matters.[499] (This will be discussed in greater detail below, and also in "Doxa: Opinion or Appearance?")

Dokimos—What is Genuinely Reliable Because Proven as Such

Returning to the question of 1.31–32, I think we must dig deeper if we want to reveal the more thought-provoking aspects of this mystifying but critical verse. Thus we should discuss some of the words used by Parmenides, as well as their arrangement, in greater detail. This is, after all, the end of the Goddess' introduction, and we must assume that with what she says, she is attempting to set the tone and direction for the lessons to come; she may even give us a clue for a possible resolution of the mortal dilemma. We will see that in the process of thinking about 1.31–32 many philosophical points can be touched upon.

Now, if the lines in question are really suggesting that the things of opinion have fully subverted the things of truth, then perhaps in some ways we have here a play on another idea expressed by Xenophanes, namely that "belief is fashioned over all things."[500] In this case we may ask ourselves whether mortals have a realistic chance of ever overcoming this far-reaching dilemma. If opinion is indistinguishable from reality, if in fact it *is* all of reality, where, then, may we look for truth? Surely it cannot hide out there somewhere among the things of opinion and sense-perception, if these are all that is. Absolute opinion would be just as unescapable as a prison cell without an outside beyond its walls. But if we study the rest of the Poem, the outlook is not that bleak. We find a number of significant

---

499 A purely dismissive or negative read of Doxa cannot resolve **Owen's** [496] "notorious deadlock" ('Eleatic Questions' 88). (Owen's own solution is simply an upgrade of **Kranz's** [417] reading of 1.31-32, which appeals to a modified form of *casus irrealis* for *khren*, as Kranz himself indicates, and which he takes literally as pointing to the "Unreality of Mortal Belief." Cf. 'Über Aufbau und Bedeutung des Parmenideischen Gedichtes' 1170.) (See also note 503) **Owen** [496], however, seems to want to avoid a categorical dismissal of Doxa, deeming it a dialectical exercise ('Eleatic Questions' 85, 89).

500 **Xenophanes, DK** 21B34. Cf. also **Mourelatos** [480] who says that one should interpret 1.31-32 against the background of **Xenophanes** B34 (*Route* 217). However, the point that he makes is slightly different than mine. **Long** [446] speaks of the "omnipresence" of the appearances (however, without reference to Xenophanes). (Cf. 'The Principles of Parmenides' Cosmogony' 93.) (See also note 506)

details that can justifiably give hope to mortals. While it is true that the "things of opinion" are not to be deemed as genuine per se—on a par with or as reliable as the "heart of truth"—there are sufficient indications that, provided one follows certain rules or perhaps techniques, statements about them can be arranged in a dependable way. Indeed, a few interpreters see in lines 1.31–32 allusions to a test of some sort that the "things of opinion" have to go through in order to be judged as "resting on evidence."[501] And such a test is actually mentioned in fragment 7.5, termed as a "much-contested disproof."

Very important in this context is the word *dokimos* in line 1.32. *Dokimos* has links to "reliably," "really," "truly," and "genuinely" in the adverbial sense, as found here, but it is also related to "testing," "proving," "assaying," and "approving."[502] Thus, if we return to the text keeping the above in mind, we could attempt a different approach to translating the passage—a rough one, perhaps, but we are easing our task by splitting the essential proposition into a simple question and answer (while leaving a peculiar word grouping toward the end of the verse, for later). Question: "How or in what way should (*khren*[503]) the things of opinion be, if they are to be taken as reli-

---

501 E.g., **Lesher** [429]: "But nonetheless you will also learn these, how the things that are believed had to genuinely be, all of them passing through all [tests]." ('Parmenides' Critique of Thinking: The *poludēris elenchos* of Fragment 7' 19–20) Lesher shows that whether one emends *dokimōs* to *dokimōsai* like Diels, or takes it as *dokimōs einai*, as given by Simplicius, the idea is the same, namely that of a test or *elenchos* (19n21). Lesher explains: "Although the proem . . . contains as many, if not more difficulties than Fragment 7, the concluding couplet of the proem calls for the kind of certification procedure that the *elenchos* has delivered," adding, "it does seem that we are going to learn something about *ta dokounta*, 'the things believed'; namely, how they had to *dokimōs einai*, how they had to assuredly, genuinely, certifiably be." (19) Furthermore, "we must still acknowledge that being *dokimos*, or being in a way which is *dokimōs*, involves some sort of *dokimasia*, and some process of *dokimadzein*. Whether we are dealing with a process of certification of civic officials, or the assaying of gold for purity, or the testing of a warrior for battle, or a witness for veracity, the method for *dokimadzein* remains the same: each must be put to the *elenchos*"(19–20). Cf. also **Davidson** [300]: " . . . that every opinion needs must pass through the ALL, and vanquish the test with approval" ('Parmenides' 4). And **Freeman** [32]: " . . . how one should go through all the things-that-seem, without exception, and test them" (*Ancilla to the Pre-Socratic Philosophers* 42). See also **Mourelatos'** [480] comments on *doxa* and *dia pantos*, "under all tests" (*Route* 205) and **Curd** [297] on the test aspect (*Legacy* 22).

502 **LSJ**: δοκιμασία: "examination," "scrutiny"; II. δοκιμή: "proof," "test"; 2. δόκιμος: "tried" or "approved," "acceptable"; 3. Adv. δοκίμως: "really," "genuinely."

503 This also works if *khren* is a strict necessity, i.e., how *must* they be? Cf. **Mansfeld** [459] (trans.), *Parmenides: Über das Sein* 7 (Ed. **von Steuben** [558]); also **McKirahan** [67] *PBS* 152. If required, this also works in the past tense, as demanded by **Tarán** [569] *Parmenides* 213–215, **Barnes** [8] *Early Greek Philosophy* 131, and many others. But in that case it probably works better as a *casus irrealis*, as read by **Kranz** [417] 'Über Aufbau und Bedeutung des Parmenideischen Gedichtes' 1170; **Falus** [315] 'Parmenides-Interpretationen' 286; and more recently **Cordero** [279] *By Being, It Is* 37 (forthcoming), see above and note 499. But in my view it works

able, or in a proven manner (*dokimos*)?" Answer: "[They should be] the things that really are, that actually exist (*onta*)." The soundness, indeed obviousness, of this demand has convinced me to favor the *per onta* reading, that is to say, the "things that really exist" version, as opposed to the "pervade everything" version.[504] Moreover, the latter read can force us to interpret lines 1.31–32 all too pessimistically. Yet I prefer a positive reading of this verse, meaning that in contrast to most scholars I do not see the Goddess denigrating Mortal Opinion here. In fact, I see her alluding to a possible redemption or rehabilitation of the unreliable things. She patently demonstrates later in the Poem what mistaken considerations cause the mortal approach to be untrustworthy in the first place, thus she could be giving Parmenides a hint at this point about how the "things of opinion" would have to be to deserve one's trust. She might even go so far as to suggest that they have to be formulated or organized in a *unified* way—as opposed to a contradicting one—if they are to be judged as fully dependable. But I am getting ahead of myself.

Doxa: the Positive Versus the Negative Read

If I can take a moment to revisit the difference between a positive and a negative interpretation of Doxa in general, and of these crucial lines in particular, as it might help us to get a better grasp of the unity of the Poem and, consequently, of its lessons. First of all, it is difficult to understand how having the things of opinion pervade everything makes them reliable in any way.[505] Our only option is to take this statement in a negative way, which, incidentally, is how most scholars read it. The consensus is that mortals have no choice but to confuse opinion with fact or appearance with re-

---

best in a stronger form, like **Mourelatos'** [480] "it was proper" or "appropriate," (*Route* 207) or "it would be [or 'would have been'] right," (210, 216). (See his general discussion, *Route* 205–210). **KRS** [39] opts for "would have to be" (243); and **O'Brien** [493] for "would have to have real existence" (*Le poème de Parménide* 8), both of which work well.

504 Aside from the fact that *per onta* seems to be better attested than *peronta*. Cf. **Owen** [496] 'Eleatic Questions' 85–86, 89; **Guthrie** [43] *HGP* 2.9; **Mourelatos** [480] *Route* 214; **Brague** [238] 'La vraisemblance du faux: Parménide fr. I, 31–32,' *Études sur Parménide*, Vol. 2, 46–51, 56, 60. (The *per onta* reading is also observed by **McKirahan** [67] *PBS* 152, and **Curd** [297] *Legacy* 21, 113n48, 114n52, and favored by **Engelhard** [313] *Die Sicherung der Erkenntnis bei Parmenides* 126.)

505 Unless we think that with "pervading everything" the Goddess means that the things of opinion must "pass through the whole process of being tested" (cf. **Lesher** [429] 'Parmenides' Critique of Thinking: The *poludēris elenchos* of Fragment 7' 20). However, this interpretation—while being the only attractive reason for choosing *peronta*—is regrettably not mainstream. Of course, neither is mine.

ality because of a variety of reasons, one of them being that they lack the faculties to determine which is which. Thus, unaware that they are being deceived, mortals take their impressions of the world for granted.[506] And once this fundamental error has been committed—described by Karl Reinhardt as "a kind of cognitive original sin"[507]—everything else follows: conviction reinforces conviction, and mortals behave as if they know the truth (in other words, as if the things of opinion have genuine existence), but in reality, their opinions are only backed up by other opinions. Whether we think that Parmenides blames a primordial fall from grace for the predicament of mortals, the fact is that they have nothing to compare their opinions to that is not just some other opinion, and in consequence, they are unable to revise their beliefs. This is why they are *forced* to think that what they believe in is real. Of course, there is nothing they can do about it, aside from renouncing all of their beliefs outright. But in favor of what alternative? If truth is utterly inaccessible, then mortals are left with nothing, not even the notion that they themselves exist. This is the gist of the negative interpretation, and its conclusions are inescapable.

Admittedly, on the surface a dismissive take on Mortal Opinion seems somewhat legitimate, as it appears consistent with the overall approach in the Poem of separating the reliable from the deceptive. However, a purely negative interpretation that categorically rejects Doxa will create its own unsurmountable problems, and no scholar who supports this view has been able to explain why the account of Mortal Opinion is included in the Poem if it is so hopelessly deceptive. It would have sufficed to have the Goddess indicate that there is the "unshaking heart of well-rounded truth" in contrast with the opinions "for which there is no evidence or trust"—as she does just a couple of lines before 1.32—and to leave it at that, without having to explain anything more about such irredeemably treacherous things. But then Parmenides might just as well have given up at that point. Why continue with the rest of the Poem if there is no chance that a mortal will find something useful in its lessons? The problem is that if we do not apply the Goddess' evidentiary techniques to the "the things of opinion" because we have considered them "groundless nothingnesses," then of what use is it to learn both the methods *and* the deceptive account? Certainly whatever

---

506 Cf. **Tarán** [569] *Parmenides* 215; **Bormann** [232] *Parmenides* 6869; **Engelhard** [313] *Die Sicherung der Erkenntnis bei Parmenides* 123–128. As **Long** [446] poignantly observed: "Owing to their omnipresence, the goddess seems to be saying, the appearances had to be accorded genuine existence in mortal accounts." ('The Principles of Parmenides' Cosmogony' 93)

507 **Reinhardt** [520] *Parmenides* 26.

is true does not need a validating treatment of any kind, particularly if it remains steadfastly out of the reach of mortals. As for the opinions, if those are all mortals have had right from the start, they do not need to be reminded of them by Parmenides, much less by a deity. But if this is the case, then the whole Poem must be accepted as an exercise in futility.

It is quite interesting how even the most die-hard critics of the Mortal Account seek to avoid this last logically unavoidable step in their interpretations. For example, Leonardo Tarán, who strongly objects to granting Doxa any sort of reality (on grounds which we shall revisit shortly) and who also argues that for Parmenides "the sensible world is absolute non-Being," concedes nonetheless in his otherwise meticulous book on the Eleatic that "if a human being is told the truth, he can learn it."[508] This is all well and good in my opinion, but of what use is it to a human being to learn the truth, if he must conclude in the process that by belonging to the sensible he is just as nonexistent as the rest of the sensible world?[509] Without a question, this type of reasoning turns the Poem's teaching on its head.

To make sense of the above, we should reduce this arguably most fundamental problem in interpreting Parmenides into an "either/or" proposition—just as he would. The problem hinges on the postulated gap between truth and belief, that is to say, on the perceived incompatibility between the reliable things and the things of opinion. Regardless of how wide or deep we may think this gap is, we either maintain that it is utterly unbridgeable or we believe that it can be overcome—at least in regard to some things—and this in a nutshell is the difference between a negative or a positive interpretation of the Poem as a whole, and the role of Doxa in particular. Personally, I have no choice but to adopt the positive position.

A Call for a Unified Approach?

Embarking on a positive route, we are nonetheless confronted by a formidable difficulty, namely how do we get from one to the other, from fickle

---

508 **Tarán** [569] *Parmenides* 202–230 and *passim,* on the unreality of Doxa. The partial quote on the sensible world is from 209 (see also 230 on Doxa being the way of non-Being); for the quote on a human's ability to learn the truth, together with supporting references from the Poem, see 215–216, and also 209.

509 **McKirahan** [67] asks that if Parmenides can dismiss the mortals and their beliefs, together with his own corporeal existence—as they are all part of the unreal world of opinions—then how about his own mind, or his thoughts? (*PBS* 178) This is a very valid point, and it indicates an interesting solution. McKirahan's distinction cuts an important Gordian knot in interpretation, because it does not do away with Parmenides the thinker of IS, but only with his impressions of his corporeal existence; in other words, with the somatic aspects of his being

A Call for a Unified Approach?

opinion to factual truth? There can be only one solution: we do it by using an evidential procedure to prove whether or not a thing is real, that is to say, whether an *account* of it is reliable or true. Applied to the lines of 1.31–32, this conclusion still requires an adaptation to the surviving text. I have already offered a rough translation of the first half of the statement found in these lines, in the form of a question and answer. The result was that if the things of opinion are to be considered reliable, they would have to be "the things that really are, that actually exist." So far, so good, but we have not yet been told something useful or practical that would allow us to differentiate one from the other, and consequently to test, adjust, or reformulate the things of opinion until reliability is achieved. The rest of 1.32—the peculiar word grouping I have left out before—may give us what we need, keeping in mind that we are dealing with the most difficult line in the Poem. As the adverb *dokimos* means "really," "reliably," "genuinely"—while having links to "examined," "proved," and "approved"—we should seek a formula that can faithfully frame or describe that which is "reliably being." Remarkably, we find exactly such a structuring in the last half of 1.32, a rather mysterious and powerful, indeed mantra-like, chaining of words: *dia pantos panta per onta*.[510] It has been noted that the use of *dia pantos panta* is intended to bring forth the universality of the subject in question.[511] Some scholars translate this phrase quite literally as "altogether throughout," but also as "all in all," or "all through all," or "all completely," or "all of them altogether," while a different group prefers a temporal reading such as "always all," or "whole and continually," or "forever everything." (In either case, it is irrelevant whether or not the "pervading" reading is adopted.) However, the consensus among most who prefer the alternative to the "pervading" theory is that Parmenides speaks here of "all things," or "the whole of things," or something to that effect.[512] But adopting such a read does not necessarily imply that a positive indication of how the things of opinion should be has been gleaned from these verses. In fact, it has been

---

that necessarily belong to Doxa, but not to the cognitive "part." The dilemma therefore is avoided: there still is a thinker, hence thought that is expressed in the IS, while questions regarding the body can be relegated to where they belong, i.e. opinion.

510 I have already stated the reasons for rejecting *peronta* or "pervading."

511 Cf. **Mansfeld** [455] *Offenbarung* 160. Mansfeld has Doxa's Light and Night in mind, speaking of "der Universalität der Elemente." Cf. also **Deichgräber** [303] *Parmenides' Auffahrt* 709, 709n1. **Mourelatos** [480] *Route* 214, speaks of "universal-and-total-being."

512 Cf. **Owen** [496] 'Eleatic Questions' 88; **Mourelatos** [480] *Route* 214–216; **McKirahan** [67] *PBS* 152; **Engelhard** [313] *Die Sicherung der Erkenntnis bei Parmenides* 126; **Curd** [297] *Legacy* 21–22.

argued that mortals mistake the things of opinion for "the whole of things," and that it is this error that the Goddess rebukes at this juncture.[513] While I agree that mortals mistake their opinions for truth, and that anything and everything can serve as the object of these opinions, I do not think that the Goddess has this kind of universality in mind when she finishes introducing her curriculum to Parmenides. In fact, I believe that she indirectly criticizes the "things of opinion" for not being universal enough. They could have been formulated by mortals in a way that reflects what a true universality has to be, namely, *a perfect unity*. But they did not, and that is their error.

Granted, the things of opinion—being essentially the objects of sense-experience—fill out the universe, and so one can say, at least superficially, that they constitute a whole. But that is not the kind of wholeness the Goddess takes issue with. It is not the problem of quantity that the Goddess addresses but a *problem of definition*.[514] The things of opinion are not perfect unities *in themselves*, or at least mortals do not speak of them in such a manner. We learn in the beginning of the Doxa that according to mortals, all things are composed of contradictory elements, and that they have identified these as Light and Night (8.53–59, 9.1–4). But most important is the claim that mortals have *named* all things in accordance to these "contraries in form or constitution" (8.55, 9.1–2). Now when Parmenides speaks of *naming* there is no evidence that he has in mind the act of referring to some thing by means of an epithet or designation; it is not just the labeling of a thing or the giving of a call sign, but the *formulation* of what something is by using a specific ordering of words. Thus, every time the Goddess engages in this activity we see her *describing* her object of discourse in a way that can only be judged as an early attempt of giving a *definition* of something. For Parmenides this must be part of what *to give an account* means. We see that the Way of Persuasion (2.4)—also referred to as the "Way that it IS" (8.2) or the Reliable/Evidential Account (8.50)—relies on the use of so-called *semata*, signifying "signs" or "landmarks" that accompany it (8.2–3). These are not

---

513 E.g., **Curd** [297] *Legacy* 22. Curd does point out, however, that Parmenides "must learn both the criteria for reliability and the tests that will allow him to investigate and to evaluate various claims for trustworthy and reliable being, or what-is"—an assessment with which I could not agree more. (See also **Owen** [496] 'Eleatic Questions' 88–89.)

514 However, my read does not preclude a more metaphysical interpretation in the manner of, e.g., **Curd** [297] *Legacy*. I will take up this subject in **Hermann** [372] *The Naked IS* (forthcoming).

just labels or arbitrary designations, but precise indications of the characteristics, indeed properties, of the object under investigation. Parmenides uses them to demonstrate what the object of inquiry *is*, and they attest to its identity and self-consistency. Assembled properly, they provide proofs that the object under consideration is represented faithfully and accurately *as it is*. We can also say that they demonstrate the inherent unity of a thing, which is expressed in the form of a unifying formula.[515]

However, the same term *semata*, for "signs" or "landmarks," is not foreign to the Mortal Account (8.55). Its role, once again, is to point to the characteristics or properties of the objects of discourse, but with one significant difference: there are *two* sets of landmarks laid out by the Goddess, one for each of the primary principles, Light and Night. The first is described as an "ethereal fire, gentle and light"; the other as "darkest night, a dense and heavy body" (8.56–59). These descriptions are clearly definitions, not merely designations. Yet of tremendous importance is the fact that individually, each principle is said to be "in every way the same as itself but not the same as the other"; thus they are true to themselves but the reverse of each other (8.57–59). Alone, each principle is a perfect unity, as perfect as the object of a Reliable Account. Only in *relation* to the other is each formula necessarily and entirely the contrary of the other. The trouble starts whenever we attempt to combine such formulas in order to produce the account of a sensible thing. By pointing out that mortals have named all things in accordance to Light and Night, and that therefore all is full of Light and Night both equally and together (fr. 9), the Goddess implies that mortals have attempted to represent or comprehend all things on the basis of mutually negating formulas.[516] This means that if anyone attempts to explain anything, self-contradiction is an absolute must; it cannot be avoided.

---

515 In some ways, my read shares certain ideas expressed by **Curd** [297] in her arguments for what she calls a "predicational unity," as in "Whatever genuinely is must be a predicational unity" (*Legacy* 66 and *passim*). I certainly agree with this assessment: "Parmenides is committed to and argues for the internal unity of each thing that is (so there can be no internal differences in each thing that is)" (96). For further arguments on "unity," cf. *Legacy* 69, 82, 105–106. However, I do not support the idea of a "predicational monism" on Parmenides' part, as Curd has championed, largely because I find the notion of a Parmenidean monism unfounded, no matter how we characterize such monism.

516 Cf. **Curd** [297] on the subject (*Legacy* 105–109). I agree with many of her conclusions, particularly her assessments of the *semata* of Light and Night. However, I have a different view of 8.53–54 (see below), even though I accept her alternative interpretations (109–110) as valid considerations. What is quite compelling is one of her versions according to which that what is rejected in 8.54 is the postulation of both forms. For an entirely different view than my take on the criticism of the two mutually negating formulas in Doxa, see **Nehamas** [489] 'Parmeni-

The Problem of Contradictory Formulas

What is admittedly laudable about the mortal effort is that the necessity for creating consistent definitions seems to have been recognized. However, to call this task demanding is to understate it. One of the first stumbling blocks that confronted an inquirer into such matters was how to account for all the opposites presented by a sense-experiential world, namely "hot and cold," "dark and light," "dense and rare," "wet and dry," "far and near," and so forth. This issue was as old as the cosmological speculations of the Milesians, and may have still preoccupied some Pythagoreans in Parmenides' time. One method that must have seemed quite clever initially was to organize these characteristics according to their mutual affinities or kinships, while contrasting them to what appeared unsupportive or reverse. In other words, characteristics were assembled according to a Like to Like versus an Unlike to Unlike approach. "Hot," "bright," "rare," and "light" could be grouped together on one side, with "cold," "dark," "dense," and "heavy" on the other. A good example is the Pythagorean table of opposites preserved by Aristotle[517]:

limit	unlimited
odd	even
one	plurality
right	left
male	female
at rest	moving
straight	bent
light	darkness
good	evil
square	oblong

---

dean Being/Heraclitean Fire' 62–63. His interpretation is no less revolutionary, and is indeed unprecedented. He calls Doxa "Parmenides' glory," arguing that the duality outlined in the Mortal Account is a great achievement and a direct critical response against the liabilities of Milesian monism. However, I have worked occasionally within Nehamas's framework, and find that our reads are not mutually exclusive. For example, I agree with Nehamas that, as he puts it, "Parmenides believes both that mortal opinions are deceptive and that his cosmology is correct," although from a somewhat different point of view. But I can be persuaded and will continue to study this fascinating problem.

517 **Aristotle**, *Metaphysics* 986a22. The table is reproduced from **McKirahan** [67] *PBS* 107. McKirahan also provides a useful and to-the-point analysis of the subject (108). For a more elaborate treatment, cf. **Guthrie** [43] *HGP* 1.245–248, 252; and **Burkert** [100] *Lore* 51–52, 52n119, 60, 282–283. In this context, however, I am not implying that Parmenides is replying in any way to the Pythagoreans. It is possible, indeed attractive as a hypothesis, but nothing more. Thus, until additional research proves otherwise, I must agree with Burkert's assessment on the chronology in question: "There is nothing to impel us to insert, between the Ionians and the philosopher from Elea, a specifically Pythagorean doctrine of opposites." (*Lore* 283)

Attempts like the above are a good exercise, but difficulties had to arise whenever mortals tried to explain the things themselves without paying attention to the problem that in the process the two essential but opposing formulas became mixed. By attributing the contradictory characteristics of Light and Night to all things, error was provenly unavoidable, as were the resulting inconsistencies in definition. Some illustrations of such inconsistencies can be found in what little is preserved of the Mortal Account. For example, fr. 10.2–3 speaks of "the shining Sun's pure torch and its destructive effects." Now, quite obviously, the Sun belongs to the Light principle; indeed, it is about as close to being the principle itself as any physical object can be. From time immemorial it has been considered divine, the source of all light, warmth, growth, life, and so forth. And yet Parmenides reminds us that its rays can also be very harmful: they can cause drought, burn the crops or the skin, cause pain, or bring about blindness if someone stares too long at their source.[518] But how are such detrimental effects compatible with something belonging to a principle that was initially described as "gentle and very light" (8.57)? Where would the harshness or heaviness that must be present to account for its destructive properties come from? In a universe composed of two contrary principles, what is "ungentle" must come from the opposite of Light, thus from the "dense and heavy body" that is Night (8.59). But is it not a contradiction to say that the Sun—which by its very nature and function is only associable with Light and Day—must also belong to Night to a certain degree, if we want to have all of its effects accounted for?

Another example of such inconsistency in formulation is indicated by the short fragments 14 and 15, which refer to the Moon. In fr. 14, the Moon is described as "shining in the night with a light not of its own." In other words, the Moon must belong essentially to what are "dark, dense and heavy bodies." And yet in order to be distinguished at night, an important characteristic that pertains to some *other* thing must be associated with the Moon. Thus, to account for it at all, we need to include the provision that the *light* of the Moon is not really its own; indeed, this light cannot belong to the formula for "dark and heavy bodies" but to something whose for-

---

518 Cf. also **Mourelatos** [480] *Route* 237–240, who makes some similar observations regarding 10.2–3 and even points to the contradictory characterization of the Sun and its overpowering or detrimental effects, as well as to the paradoxical representation of both Sun and Moon in the Doxa. However, as far as I can tell, Mourelatos does not interpret these passages as indicative of the need for unity in formula, and his hypothesis that Parmenides is rejecting Heraclitus' doctrine of coincidence of opposites here, I cannot support.

mula is "ethereal flame, gentle and very light" (8.56–57). But here again we have the dependency of one formula upon the opposite of itself, and thus the *formula Moon* must "always gaze searchingly" toward the *formula Sun* (fr. 15) in order to plausibly account for what is Moon. This demonstrates that neither the Sun nor the Moon can be explained independently of one another, or more precisely, independently of the opposite formula of the principle that they generally belong to. This mixing of mutually exclusive characteristics, without exerting the additional effort necessary for the attainment of a non-contradictory or unified account of something, is what Parmenides regards as a critical mistake.

The Goddess refers to this fundamental error right at the start of Doxa. It is the very first thing she directs Parmenides' attention to, just as it is—as I contend—the very last thing she mentions in line 1.32 at the end of her introduction. Here is the whole passage, including the points regarding the differentiation of contraries in form or constitution and the assigning of characteristics that are on the one side consistent, and on the other mutually excluding:

8.53 For [mortals] have set their minds on naming two forms,
8.54 for which to be a unity[519] is not necessary—here they have gone astray—
8.55 and they have differentiated contraries in form [or, constitution] and assigned landmarks [or, signs] to them
8.56 apart from each other: here, on the one hand, the ethereal flame of fire,
8.57 gentle and very light, in every way the same as itself
8.58 but not the same as the other. Yet that one [also], by itself, is the
8.59 reverse: darkest night, a dense and heavy body.

These verses contain not only a compelling analysis of the problem of mortal naming, but also indicate a possible solution to the enigma of 1.32: mortals have created two sets of formulas for which *to be a unity was not deemed necessary* by them, and that is, if you will, their "original cognitive sin"—the error that will make all their accounts untrustworthy. At best, they can hope to achieve a *plausible* explanation of things (8.60), that is, an approximation of truth; however, when challenged by the appropriate evidentiary procedures offered by the Reliable Account, even their best constructs must collapse into a heap of self-contradiction. But the methods

---

519 On *mian* as "unity" or "oneness," cf. **Schwabl** [537] 'Sein und Doxa bei Parmenides' 53–54; **Mansfeld** [455] *Offenbarung* 126; **Tarán** [569] *Parmenides* 220, 224–225. See **Cordero** [279] on "bringing together." (*By Being, It Is* 167–168, forthcoming.) Cordero however, has in mind the bringing together—as one—of the two mortal viewpoints about the forms, and not the forms themselves. (On *mian* see also note 476 above.)

outlined by that same Reliable Approach could equally straighten out an account by ridding it of contradictory elements that would sabotage the unity of definition one was seeking. And arguably, it was this very unity, integrity, or wholeness—in what is being formulated or expressed—that was Parmenides' primary concern. Interestingly, this fact is attested by none other than Aristotle, usually a stern, largely unfair critic of the former. In a rare moment of genuine discernment regarding Eleatic doctrine, Aristotle differentiates the older legislator's teachings from those of his younger follower Melissus by pointing out that "Parmenides seems to fasten on that which is one in formula, Melissus on that which is one in matter."[520]

A Unity of Formula

Returning one last time to the lines of 1.31–32, we may have found a key for the enigmatic phrasing *dia pantos panta per onta* and for the kind of universality that is intended here. Not for the principle of cosmological wholeness does the Goddess make her appeal, but for the principle of a logical/veridical unity. Thus, if we expand our original question—but this time with a more acute reformulation—we get the following: "How or in what way would it be appropriate for the things of opinion to be provedly those things that actually are?" Our answer can only be: "They would have to be entirely or in every respect altogether, whole, complete."[521] In other words, we are seeking a perfect unity. But why, one may ask, use the word "provedly" for *dokimos*, instead of just "reliably" or "genuinely?"[522] As we are dealing with the things of opinion here—and due to the general mixing of contraries and inconsistencies in regard to such things—if they are to be

---

520 **Aristotle**, *Metaphysics* 986b19. See also note 534.
521 **Mourelatos** [480] said it best when he remarked that for Parmenides to be *dokimos* is to be *pampan* (cf. 8.11) or *dia pantos*, i.e., "altogether" (*Route* 205). See also note 523.
522 In addition to my general arguments above, the *OED* defines "proved" as: "1. tried, tested; hence, That has stood a trial or test; approved, trustworthy, trusty. 2. Shown to be true, or to be as stated; demonstrated. Hence 'provedly' *adv.*" This definition I find very much appropriate to the adverbial δοκίμως, especially to its roots and links. Much of this has been argued also by others; cf. **Mourelatos** [480] (*Route* 199–200, 204–205), even though he adopts "acceptably" for *dokimos* (199–200, 216). **Mansfeld**'s [455] "annehmbar" is very similar (*Offenbarung* 162; however, in *Parmenides: Über das Sein*, he translates it as "gültig"). My general read is not that far from both, particularly from **Mourelatos** [480] who translates as follows: "how it would be right for things deemed acceptable to be acceptably: just being all of them altogether." But if I understand Mourelatos correctly, what he means by "all of them" is not the sense-experiential things or the opinions about them, which should be "altogether," but the primary principles themselves, Light and Night. I may be wrong, but this seems to me to be the outcome of his arguments. (Cf. *Route* 216–221, particularly 220–221.)

elevated to the point of reliability, they must be shown to be internally consistent. This, in effect, means proving them. Thus, by subjecting things to such methods as are exemplified by fr. 8, their exact characteristics will be brought out. Nothing more can be brought out, and anything less will not represent our subjects faithfully. In fact, they have to "*wholly* be, or not be at all," as 8.11 reiterates, another provision that reinforces the unity principle we are after.[523]

But does all this talk about unity suggest that the subject of our considerations must also be *physically* altogether? The question does not apply to our concerns here; in fact, it can be answered any way one wants, with one important restriction, namely, that whatever we give an account of is not the subject of differentiable contraries in form or constitution (8.55) and does not have characteristics assigned to it that are the reverse of each other (8.55–56).[524] In other words, we have to be *consistent*. And to be consistent, the components—words, terms, characterizations, etc.—we use in our account must also create a consistent whole. That is all. If we, in contrast to Doxa's mortals, do recognize that a unity in formula is necessary when expressing a thing (8.54), and if we adhere to principles and methods that can ensure this unity by preventing contradiction, we can talk about whatever we want. Once we know the rules and the proper techniques—which is precisely what the Poem has to offer—it is up to us to figure out a way to express a subject in a manner that is consistent with itself without having to violate its internal unity, so to speak. We must express it as being, in Parmenides' words, "in every way the same as itself," without having it be at the same time the "reverse of itself." (Thus, the opposite of how mortals approach such matters, "for whom to be and not to be are deemed the same and not the same," as fr. 6.8–9 points out.)

In summary, the above reading allows us to conclude that Parmenides' curriculum includes not only the proven or evidentiary things, but also a method of how to turn belief into certainty. The method itself is demonstrated in the Reliable Account of fr. 8, which, as will be shown further on,

---

523   The kinship between *dia pantos* as "altogether throughout" and "*pampan*" as "altogether" in 8.11 is also noted by **Mourelatos** [480] (*Route* 205, 211–212). See also note 521.

524   I like the way **Curd** [297] frames the issue, putting all cosmological/existential questions in a proper perspective: "There is reason not to take Parmenides as concerned with Existence, Being, or 'the all,' but rather as concerned with what it is to be the genuine nature or character of a thing. Parmenides is thus discussing the internal unity of an entity, and not the relations among entities." (*Legacy* 82) However, I do believe that essentially a relation is also a unity or can be reduced to one. But that is another subject, belonging to a discussion of **Plato's** *Parmenides*.

is an evidentiary argumentative procedure. We can call it an Evidential Account. As for the status of Doxa, whether one considers the Poem in general, or lines 1.31–32 in particular, there is a clear sense that the Opinions of Mortals cannot be accepted or judged as equally true as the Evidential Account. (The main difference being that the latter is proven, while the former is only conjecture—and it remains so up to the point where it is subjected to proving.) But already in that pre-evidentiary state the ordering of words that constitutes Doxa follows certain rules. For example, it does not allow Nothingness or Void to participate as a constituent in things alongside Light and Night. And it also observes an ordering according to the Principle of Like to Like (see fr. 16, for example). In other words, Mortal Opinions do not constitute just senseless noise, or unintelligible babble; they are conveying something, some message or information. It seems that the reason Parmenides must learn the "things of opinion"—together with the rules and methods for an Evidential Account—is so he can find ways of making explanations like these worthy of genuine acceptance. (This does not mean that he will always succeed; certain things may remain unprovable in an absolute way. See Einstein's observations on mathematics in Chapter XI, "Mind and Universe.") If the above interpretation reflects the true message of the last lines of the Proem, as I hope it does, then perhaps we have found a way to make them more consistent with the rest of the Poem.

"*ESTI*" OR "IS": THE PARMENIDEAN OBJECT

> Without the fact of being there would not be things that are...
> and that is the reason why [Parmenides'] thinking starts from an
> analysis of the notion of the fact of being, which is reached from
> the evidence that "is" is occurring.
> —Néstor-Luis Cordero[525]

Verb or Subject?

What is Parmenides' main object of discourse in the so-called Aletheia section, particularly, in lines 8.1–49? This is without a doubt the most difficult question that confronts the interpreter—who is not helped by the fact that most philosophical works of reference perpetrate misleading and old-fashioned definitions or interpretations. When directly referring to this elusive object, Parmenides uses the Greek word *esti*, which, strictly translated to English, corresponds to our "is," that is, the third person singular present indicative of the verb "to be." Of course, what is here referred to as being is the big question, and it causes much disagreement among scholars. Some speak of it as "reality" or "existence," others are more explicitly cosmological and see it as "the world" or "the universe." A different group treats the object as an ontological device and calls it "Being," "One Being," or "the One," and a few see it as "Mind" or "Truth."[526] More recent interpretations have opted for less graphic and thus more appropriate terms, referring to it as "that which is" or "what is." But there are certain specifications preserved in the verses that must override all considerations: The Goddess links *esti* with the "ways of inquiry *for thinking*" in a manner that makes *esti* the only conceivable object for these kinds of ways (actually, for one of the ways).[527]

---

525 **Cordero** [279] *By Being, It Is* 64 (forthcoming). The quote is from uncorrected page proofs, so I cannot vouch for the accuracy of the wording.)

526 "Reality": **Fränkel** [29] who equates it with "Being" and "Truth," *Early Greek Poetry* 353, also **Robinson** [526] 'Parmenides on the Real in Its Totality' 56. "The World," "The Universe," "Cosmos": **Popper** [510] *World* 114 and *passim*. "The One": **Plato**, *Parmenides* 137b. "Being": **Tarán** [569] *Parmenides, passim*. "One Being": **Cornford** [282] *Plato and Parmenides* 29. "Mind": **Vlastos** [594], 'Parmenides' Theory of Knowledge' 72. "Mind" as "cognitive capacity": **Long** [448] 'Parmenides on Thinking Being' 126, and *passim*. Long also sees Parmenides as investigating "veridical thinking." (126) "Truth": **Kahn** [395] 'The Thesis of Parmenides' 700–724. "IT is": **McKirahan** [67] *PBS* 171.

527 Regarding *esti, eon,* or *einai*—Parmenides' object of discourse—**Owen**'s [496] 'Eleatic Questions' is very important (*Studies in Presocratic Philosophy*, ed. **Allen** and **Furley** 2.59–61) as well as **Kahn**'s [392] 'The Greek Verb "To Be" and the Concept of Being,' *passim*; and [394] 'The Thesis of Parmenides' 707–712. See also **Cordero** [272] 'Les deux chemins de Parménide dans

Verb or Subject?

But how can a verb function as an object or subject? Is it not more proper to speak of *esti* or "to be" as *having* a subject—or even as not having one—instead of *being* a subject? The questions of whether *esti* has a subject or not, or whether the subject is not expressed, or if we should seek it elsewhere in the Poem, or whether its subject is even the way itself are issues that have been tirelessly discussed for more than a century by modern scholars. There is no need to join this debate at the moment. It suffices to lay out my position as follows: I believe that *esti* is intrinsic to thought. On its most basic level, it is simply the recognition of "that which is." Whether we view this as a function, a cognitive phenomenon, a methodical way of reasoning, or a state—such as the state of being—or indeed all of the above, is a matter of interpretation depending largely on the field of inquiry to which one applies Parmenides' teachings. Furthermore, these are for the most part metaphysical issues that can be set aside for a later discussion.[528] What is important in our present context is this: thought understands that things *are*, and it understands the things *that* are. In other words, thought understands being, and it understands *by way* of being. *Esti* is basically the indication *that* something *is*. This "fact of being"—or *esti*—can also be revealed.[529] A properly conducted reasoning process will make this "fact of

---

les fragments 6 et 7′ 1–32; and *By Being, It Is* 47–68 (forthcoming). Furthermore: **Austin** [199] *Parmenides, Being, Bounds, and Logic* 11–40; **Barnes** [9] *TPP* 160–163; **Bormann** [232] *Parmenides* 1–8, 181–182; **Calogero** [249] *Studien über den Eleatismus* 1–27; **Casertano** [256] *Parmenide: il metodo; la scienza l'esperienza* 92–93, 95–98; **Cassin** [260] *Parménide: Sur la nature ou sur l'étant* 31–47, 163–164; **Collobert** [268] *L'Être de Parménide ou le Refus du Temps* 77–82; **Cornford** [282] *Plato and Parmenides* 33–34, 42–43; **Coxon** [290] *Fragments* 19–21,193–195; **Curd** [297] *Legacy* 34–42; **Deichgräber** [304] *Das Ganze–Eine des Parmenides* 5–6, 10–12; **Fränkel** [29] *Early Greek Poetry* 353, 353n13; **Gallop** [339] '"IS" or "IS NOT"?' 1 and *passim*, also [334] *Parmenides* 7–10; **Gómez-Lobo** [351] *El Poema de Parménides* 48–55, 198–206; **Guthrie** [43] *HGP* 2.14–20; **van Hagens** [361] *Parmenide* 41–44, 52–55; **Heitsch** [365] *Gegenwart und Evidenz bei Parmenides* 7–8, 21–26; **Hölscher** [379] *Parmenides* 77–82, 126–129; **Imbraguglia** [383] *L'Ordinamento assiomatico nei frammenti Parmenidei* 14–17, 25, 154; **KRS** [39] 245–246; **Mansfeld** [455] *Offenbarung* 82–92; **McKirahan** [67] *PBS* 160–163, 170–172; **Meijer** [469] *Parmenides Beyond the Gates* 85–95; **Mourelatos** [480] *Route* 47–71; **O'Brien** [493] *Le poème de Parménide* 160–169, 228–237, 253–277, 312–314; **Popper** [510] *World* 114, 151; **Tarán** [569] *Parmenides* 179–180, 191–193, 197–199; **Verdenius** [585] *Parmenides* 31–44; **Wiesner** [607] *Parmenides: Der Beginn der Aletheia* 201–232.

528 Many of these questions become clearer when one understands what a categorical role truth plays in Parmenides' epistemology, and how What IS NOT is contrasted with What IS. (See "What Does the Concept of Truth Signify for Parmenides?" and "The Question of IS NOT," both in this chapter.) I also agree with the way **Long** [448] addresses this subject: "Parmenides' first call on us is not to think about Being but to *think about thinking Being* ... He is not purely or primarily a metaphysician. He is investigating mind, from the starting-point that something is there—Being or truth—for mind to think." ('Parmenides on Thinking Being' 127.)

529 When I use the term "revealed" I do not have in mind some kind of mystical experience, but only the result of a logical or systematic reasoning process. Then, one may ask, why

being" evident, and thus thought seizes upon the *esti* or "is" of things; it is that which makes them *intelligible*.

Way or Destination?

Now for a few remarks on the relation between the reasoning process and its outcome, that is to say, between the "way of *esti*" and *esti* as "confirmed fact": As noted by Cordero (see the motto at the beginning of this section), for the analysis of the notion of the "fact of being," there must be evidence, in his words: "evidence that 'is' is occurring." The evidence is supplied by the way that reveals or expresses "what is," namely the "many signs" or "landmarks" that belong to it (8.1–3). And this confirms, according to Cordero, "that the way and its content have fused," that "*estin* is inseparable from the subject that it itself has produced."[530] This unity of way and subject is not different from the unity of *esti* and thought explained in fr. 8.34–36:

> 8.34 To think and the wherefore [or, the object] of thought are the same,
> 8.35 For without What IS, in which it is expressed,
> 8.36 you will not find thinking/knowing.

In this sense, *esti* should be considered the "noetic 'that which is,'"[531] or thinking's "what is there to be thought." Technically, from a logical and epistemological point of view, it is *that "is" which reasoning determines as being the case*.

And there are some additional observations we can make that support the above: first, there is the concept of the "unshaking heart of well-rounded Truth" introduced in verse 1.29. Thus when Parmenides soon mentions "the Way of Persuasion (for it follows the Truth)" (2.4) as one of

---

use the term at all? Because a "revealed" or "revealing *esti*" echoes the notion of *aletheia* as the "unconcealed" or "unveiled" truth, an idea I find conducive to a deeper understanding of What IS.

530 **Cordero** [279] *By Being, It Is* 181 (forthcoming). Cf. also **Deichgräber** [303] (*Parmenides' Auffahrt* 676); furthermore **Stenzel** [80] (*Metaphysik des Altertums* 50–53), and **Snell** [79] (*Die Ausdrücke für den Begriff des Wissens in der vorplatonischen Philosophie* 53–54) on the complete identity between thinking and being, or cognition and the object of cognition.

531 *noetic* = def.1a.: "Of or pertaining to mind or intellect"; 2.: "Originating or existing in the mind or intellect, purely intellectual or abstract." (*OED*) In a similar vein, **Deichgräber** [303] speaks of *esti* or IS as "the beingness of a noetic existence" ("das Sein einer noetischen Existenz"). (*Parmenides' Auffahrt* 676)

the "ways of inquiry for thinking" (2.2), he must mean the way to the unshaking heart. Accordingly, if the way to the heart of truth is a way for *thinking*—and not for perceiving or experiencing—then the heart cannot be less or other than the way that leads to it. In other words, it is not an object of sense-experience but of reason.

This particular point is missed by interpreters with a cosmological bent, who must see the cosmos or the universe in everything Parmenides says. Yet if the "*is* for thinking" is identical with the "heart of truth," then we are talking about something veridical and epistemological—ergo a thing pertaining to truth and knowledge—and not some existential or cosmological object. In Charles Kahn's words, it is "the object of knowing, what is or can be known."[532] It is quite helpful to keep this concept in mind whenever Parmenides' verses seem unclear or confusing. As can be demonstrated, the conclusions of the Reliable/Evidential Account (fr. 8) will only make sense if we accept that they pertain exclusively to an intelligible object and not to some physical thing.

Nonetheless, this interpretation does not rule out knowledge about existential or cosmological objects, provided, of course, that what we know about them satisfies the criterion of reliability demanded by the Poem. To understand what reasoning underlies this criterion, we should attempt to reconstruct Parmenides' thoughts on the matter, which may have been as follows: a useful way of inquiry needs a corresponding object of inquiry; thus, a reliable way requires a reliable object. To be reliable, a way of inquiry must be performed by reason, not by using one's unsteady senses. And if a rational way calls for a rational object, then only when we approach the object of inquiry, whatever it may be, from its noetic angle can we fulfill the reliability requirement. This is reiterated by fragment 4, which stresses the steadfastness and dependability aspect of things when looked upon in such a way—that is, as intelligible—because, even when absent, they are nevertheless present to thought or mind. In the case of an existential or cosmological thing, this means that we are not investigating it per se, but only what is being thought and said about it, that is, its *esti* in the sense of "that which can be known and reliably expressed." (Naturally, only a purely abstract object can be considered as investigated per se.)

---

532 **Kahn** [395] 'The Thesis of Parmenides' 710. Kahn also refers to it as "the knowable, the object of cognition" (712–12). See also **Long** [448]: "When Parmenides talks about "thinking" (veridical thinking, I mean), his words refer to cognition." ('Parmenides on Thinking Being' 145–146)

The Object of Judgment

Having established that *esti* points to or represents the "object of knowledge"—and wanting to be most discerning and precise regarding such matters, thus also allowing for a more technical formulation for scholars—we can narrow *esti* down even further by defining it as the *result of a deliberative process*, that is to say, a *determination of what is the case brought about by an act of critical judgment*. To substantiate this conclusion we need merely to review the pivotal function *esti* has in Parmenides' system, which, only for the sake of his unusual demonstration, becomes a twofold one: while *esti*—or that which IS—is generally the criterion that an account must meet, if it is to be judged as reliable, in fragment 8, it itself becomes the *object of judgment* of said account, hence the outcome of an evidentiary method. It is this unprecedented approach by means of "forensic argumentation"[533] that seizes upon the "is" or *esti* of a thing, the overriding factor that makes it rationally coherent by allowing the *unity of its formula* to be expressed.[534] This formula or definition consists of the abovementioned corresponding characteristics or "landmarks" (*semata*, 8.1–3), which conform to the Principle of Non-Contradiction—a principle not observed by mortals regarding their objects of opinion, thereby forgoing the kind of unity that reliability necessitates (see 8.53–54). (We shall return to these difficulties and the principle in-

---

533 Heidel's [51] formulation ('On Certain Fragments of the Pre-Socratics' 718). **Mansfeld** [455] speaks of "forensic rhetoric" (*Offenbarung* 105).

534 Arguably, this could be what **Aristotle** had in mind when he differentiated Parmenides' object of inquiry from that of Melissus, cf. *Metaphysics* 986b19. In *Physics* 185b19, however, Aristotle misinterprets the requirement for the "unity of definition"—that of corresponding *semata* or landmarks—censuring all Eleatics indiscriminately for their alleged doctrine of Oneness, saying that it inadvertently supports Heraclitus' unity of opposites. (Cf. also **Cherniss** [17] *Aristotle's Criticism of Presocratic Philosophy* 66n270 and generally 63–67.) However, the "oneness in formula" should not be taken as implying one homogeneous and wholesale definition for all of the things that make up the universe, thereby forcing opposites such as good and bad, hot and cold, etc., to be identical or same. The oneness and uniqueness of *esti* is not to be read as exclusionary in a physical sense, to the detriment of anything else. (E.g. Aristotle, who regards Eleatic Being as a "unified concept in the physical world," ibid. 65.) If *esti* is the standard for reliability, as indicated by the correspondence among *semata* or landmarks, then any collection of landmarks that does not violate Like to Like (i.e., Identity and Non-Contradiction) attests that the object being judged is expressed as it IS. (Conceivably, each thing, if properly thought and spoken of, may have its own formula of agreeable, nonconflicting landmarks. This does not mean, however, that there might be different kinds or pluralities of What IS. An account must be true regardless of what it is about, as long as the restrictions for reliability are followed. When this occurs, we recognize it as true, meaning not as *a* truth among *many* truths, but that a very specific—indeed absolute—standard of veracity has been met. In short, there is only one truth. Thus, even when dealing with a plurality of things, we cannot account for them as parts of pluralities, but must address each thing on its own terms, i.e., express its own unity of definition. If we succeed, the IS is expressed, and the standard was met.)

volved.) I therefore believe that for Parmenides the *method of critical judgment* must reveal only one *object of critical judgment*—the *oneness in formula*—and that is precisely the "heart of truth": the *esti* or the "that which is" of what is being judged. Of course, what is being judged can be anything, as I have indicated above. We find no restrictions imposed by the Goddess upon what may qualify as the object of judgement—except for "What IS NOT," which cannot be thought or expressed in such a manner.

The Naked IS

A few remarks on the metaphysical implications of the Parmenidean object: If we take this "object of cognition" and entify it (that is, define it as an entity, which it obviously must be already, being an object) and then take one further step in the revolutionary direction suggested by Patricia Curd—which, intriguingly, was also opted for by such post-Parmenidean Presocratics as the Pluralists or the Atomists—we can have a myriad of such entities—as many as there are objects of thought.[535] Curd, in her critical work *The Legacy of Parmenides* considers the *esti* or "IS" an "informative identity claim, an assertion that, when true, reveals the nature of a thing, saying just what something is."[536] She theorizes that Parmenides explored the nature of theoretically basic entities, meaning the essential nature of objects of thought. Depending on context, I like to think of the essential "that which IS for thinking"—the elemental model for any object of reason—as the "Naked IS." This shorter designation signifies a theoretically basic entity—à la Curd—in its most simple, unadulterated form, not yet adorned with those designations or attributes by means of which we keep track of our objects of reason.[537] (See the Preface for the analogy to a Christmas tree with all of its ornaments removed.) In any case, even if entified, *esti* is not

---

535 Yes, I am aware that the post-Parmenideans also took the model presented by Parmenides' noetic object in a cosmological vein, but this should come as no surprise; after all, the Eleatic showed them how to reconcile this: he gave them Doxa. The Pluralists and the Atomists were apparently much more impressed with the cosmological model advanced by the Doxa, which they could retool for their own purposes, than they were with the purely noetic approach of the Evidential Account. In truth, they profited from both. (Not to mention the Sophists whose outlook was entirely Doxa oriented.)

536 **Curd** [297] *Legacy* 39; cf. also 97. On "theoretically fundamental entities," see 47, 67, 82; and "metaphysically basic entities" 123.

537 Cf. **Madden** [450] and **Sachs**: "To be a Parmenidean individual is to be precisely an entity to which no quality terms, not even primary ones, are applicable and hence to be an entity wholly characterized by what it can do." ('Parmenidean Particulars and Vanishing Elements' 153)

the universe or the world, but the object of thought in its most basic, most essential form. It is the *bookend* for thinking, the "last thinkable thing." However, these notions lead us to the rather convoluted subject of Parmenidean metaphysics. (Not that he intended to write on that subject; instead, I refer to the kind of metaphysics that others have gleaned from Parmenides' verses.[538]) But this is not the place to explore the more hypothetical consequences of Parmenides' doctrine; in-depth studies on the matter will be released in the future in separate works, one titled *The Naked IS,* and the other, which examines Plato's *Parmenides,* titled *Above Being.*

For the sake of clarity or simplicity, I generally prefer a simple "IS" or "the IS" for Parmenides' *esti,* written in capital letters for instant recognition (and sometimes adding "What" to "IS" for fluency).

---

[538] To a certain degree I agree with **Capizzi**'s [252] observation that Parmenides' doctrine was not necessarily a metaphysic theory but a "philosophy of law" (cf. *La Porta di Parmenide* 108). However, I do not subscribe to all parts of his premise. While I can see the Poem as a linguistic exercise, among other things, to say that its purpose was to offer a "linguistic analysis of Parmenides' political constitution," as Capizzi does, is pure speculation. While the idea is intriguing, and Cordero and I have reflected much on the subject, it remains nonetheless unprovable—at least until some archeologist somewhere digs up a piece of this long-lost legislation. For my part, I believe that while Parmenides' teaching had obvious metaphysical implications, these could not have been foremost on his mind. Most, if not all, metaphysical aspects were developed after him, first by the post-Parmenidean Presocratics, and ultimately by Plato, Aristotle, and Plotinus.

THE IS AS THE UNIVERSE: AN OLD MISCONCEPTION

> The world consists, in reality, of one huge, unmoving, homogenous, solid block of spherical shape in which nothing can ever happen; there is no past or future.
> —Karl Popper[539]

The Dead World

It is hard to understand why so many commentators believe that Parmenides' object of discourse is the tangible world, the universe, or all of reality. The verses in question are simply too explicit. And yet some of the most brilliant minds in philosophy have argued differently. For example, Karl Popper is certain that Parmenides theorizes about the universe, a cold, dark, and bleak universe at that, so extremely dense and dead that there is no room for anything else, not even space. In Popper's own words: "[For Parmenides,] the real world is full: it is a spherical block of continuous matter," thus "there can be no movement. Nothing ever happens."[540] (See also the motto, above.) Yet Popper is also a strong admirer of Parmenides' work, calling it well-articulated but pessimistic, while acknowledging, nonetheless, that the Eleatic must have been aware of "life in all its warmth and movement and beauty and poetry." However, Parmenides seems to have had no choice but to repudiate these impressions, having realized that, as Popper says, "the icy truth is death." I dare say that it is not Parmenides but Popper whose outlook is rather pessimistic, and that for this grim view of the object in question there is not one word in the Poem, nothing that advocates that the universe is a dead, solid block of matter. Just because the object of thought is not affected by motion—which is, after all, a physical phenomenon—does not suggest that the outer world is spaceless so as to prevent such phenomena.

The point is that if we merge all of the characteristics of Parmenides' object of discourse and apply them to a physical thing, we will only gain contradiction and absurdity. Yes, we can say that scarcity is impossible (8.32–33) because everything that ever *was*, still is. Just as everything that ever *will be* has always been here. But in fact we have said nothing meaningful. Nor have we said something meaningful if we call it a solid block of matter. The trouble with such an impenetrable mass is that nothing really

---

539 **Popper** [510] 79–80.
540 Ibid., 69.

can be said about it. Yet this conflicts with Parmenides because he demonstrates that it can be the object of a detailed Evidential Account.

But the biggest contradiction is when we try to resolve the problem of thought and the exclusiveness that such a solid mass requires. If it is all there is, then thought would be a second thing in addition to the mass, unless we think that the mass is thought. But Parmenides is clear that thought cannot be expressed without it (8.35–36). If our object is a solid, indivisible mass of matter, or even Being—whatever that may be—then no thought can ever be expressed without violating its indivisibility, homogeneity, and existential monopoly. On the other hand, if we do not want to lose thought as a factor, then our object would have to be that thought absolutely, meaning being both originator and the object toward which thought is directed—if every thought must have an object—a formula which already implies a duality of some kind. However, there is no indication in the Poem that the object of discourse is pure, self-absorbed Mind.[541] And even if we accept such a bizarre idea, it would defeat any cosmological notion of the *esti* as world or universe. Finally, if no thought is possible, then there is no thinker, no Parmenides, mortals, or goddesses, a theory some scholars have seriously suggested.[542] But then there is also no such thing as a Reliable Account if no one is there to give or to receive it. Yet if we accept such an idea, we have virtually murdered Parmenides. Thus, all speculations that make his object of discourse a material mass violate the heart and soul of his Poem. It seems, therefore, far less problematic to accept this object as the object of reason, which can be inquired into and accounted for by the ways for thinking, just as he promised (fr. 2).

A Fateful Misunderstanding?

Unfortunately, the cosmological interpretation of Parmenides goes as far back as Aristotle, and is largely due to a few careless remarks on his part.[543] Indeed, some of Plato's musings about the Eleatic object also fall

---

541 Cf. **Vlastos** [594], 'Parmenides' Theory of Knowledge' 72, 72n41, 73, who implies that Being and Mind are one.

542 Cf. **Tarán** [569] who actually argues that neither Parmenides, nor the Goddess, nor thought, for that matter, can exist *for* Parmenides; see *Parmenides* 193–194, 198–199, 230. Or see **Coxon**'s [290] statement: "The paradox of Parmenides' philosophy, in which human beings and human experience are nothing [. . .]." (*Fragments* 21)

543 It has been argued that the fault lies with Melissus, who seems to be the first to treat the Eleatic object of inquiry as the world or the universe (cf. **Cordero** [278] 'Una Tragedia Filo-

back on cosmological imagery, and many subsequent thinkers have taken such a narrow read quite seriously. And yet it remains unworkable, as Plato would be the first to admit; after all, he did concede that Parmenides' words—and even more their meaning—may have not been properly understood.[544] The trouble with a cosmological reading is that it only makes sense if we think of Parmenides as a bumbling idiot, who either did not realize or did not care that he was contradicting himself. Indeed, Aristotle seems so irritated at one point that he speaks of Eleatic belief as being next door to madness, suggesting that Parmenides and his followers may be worse than lunatics.[545]

Perhaps it was the same kind of unflattering judgment of Parmenides that had a century before Aristotle prompted Zeno of Elea to defend his teacher against the criticisms of unnamed others. It is very unfortunate that the identity of the group in question has remained unknown. Plato only describes them as "those who try to make fun of Parmenides' argument" and also as "those who assert the many"—that is, "plurality"—but not much else is explained.[546] It has been speculated that they might have been the Pythagoreans, and that Zeno only attacked the plurality upon which their mathematics rested, but the subject is a source of much controversy for scholars—particularly because some doubts have been raised whether Pythagorean mathematics was sufficiently developed at Zeno's time to warrant his attacks.[547] However, while we do not know the identity of his critics, there is no reason to doubt that the essential misreading of the object of Parmenides' inquiry had already begun to take hold.

We see that neither what Parmenides investigated nor the methods he employed were taken as demonstrations of "how to prove and disprove the

---

sófica: Del "Se Es" de Parménides al Ser-Uno de Meliso' 283–293). Also suggested by **KRS** [39] (395) on behalf of Plato's and Aristotle's take on Eleatic "monism." A different view is elaborately argued by **Barnes** [9] TPP 180–185, 194–198, 200–230. See also **Vlastos** [595] on the incorporeality of Melissus' Being ('Raven's 'Pythagoreans and Eleatics,' Studies in Greek Philosophy 1.186–188).

544 **Plato**, Theaetetus 184a.
545 **Aristotle**, On Generation and Corruption 325a18–23.
546 **Plato**, Parmenides 128c–d.
547 Pro: **Cornford** [282] Plato and Parmenides 58–61; **Raven** [516] Pythagoreans and Eleatics 3–5, 55–56, 68, 70–77. Con: **Owen** [495] disputes that Zeno is attacking Pythagorean mathematics: "For first, the picture of Pythagorean mathematics, to the extent that it is intelligible, rests on quite inadequate evidence. And secondly . . . if there were such a stage in the history of mathematics, Zeno's arguments would not be directed primarily at it." ('Zeno and the Mathematicians' 212) Cf. also **Vlastos** [595] 'Ravens's 'Pythagoreans and Eleatics' 182–185, who contests that the Pythagoreans possessed a notion of "number-atomism"; and **van der**

rightness of an account by reasoning and discourse alone." Instead, his logical proofs were mistaken as statements about the world, which is, as I have already indicated, a very odd way of misunderstanding him, because he himself shows that all cosmological explanations are tied to the realm of the senses, about which we can venture only untrustworthy opinions. And yet whenever Parmenides attempted to prove that "movement" and "change" were considerations that did not apply to his object of judgment, people thought that he tried to convince everyone that there is no such thing as movement and change in the *universe*. Admittedly, by trying to square the Eleatic's uncompromising conclusions with the observable world, much worthwhile philosophy has been created, but what if everyone was barking up the wrong tree?

It is quite interesting, however, that Zeno does not seem at all perturbed by this general misjudgment. Instead, he uses the most cunning argumentative mechanisms to destabilize such critique on its very *own* terms. Plato compares this practice to not only paying people back in their own currency, but also having change to spare.[548] Thus, Zeno attacks arguments about motion with arguments *for* and *against* motion, and arguments about plurality with arguments *for* and *against* plurality, thereby creating paradoxes, a most powerful refutative tool. His skill for arguing on both sides of an issue—which he picked up from Parmenides—strongly influenced both Socrates and Plato and earned him the title of inventor of dialectic from Aristotle.[549] As a technique, it was a surefire way to achieve contradiction, which, as we will see further on, frees the speculator from having to prove positively that something is the case if the reverse is exposed as impossible or absurd.

Proving Motion Versus Proving a Proper Understanding of Motion

There is also a little anecdote regarding Zeno that may underscore how deep the misconception of Eleatic ideas was: we are told that when Antisthenes the Cynic first heard Zeno's arguments against motion, unable to answer them in kind, he simply got up and walked away. It was an act that

---

Waerden [598] 'Zenon und die Grundlagenkrise der griechischen Mathematik' 141–161, who argues that the fundamental crisis of Greek mathematics was not brought about by the refutation of infinitesimals, but by the discovery of irrationals, which according to van der Waerden occurred after Zeno's time.

548 **Plato**, *Parmenides* 128d.
549 **Aristotle**, fr. 65 R; **D.L.**, 8.57 and 9.25 (**DK** 29A1).

has found much acclaim among some commentators, because it supposedly indicates that *proof by action is more persuasive than any refutation by logic.*[550] However, the only thing Antisthenes proved convincingly is that he failed as a *thinker*. Any child can get up and walk away, but this deed does not establish the child's philosophic credentials. Nor can such an approach disprove Zeno, particularly because what he demonstrated only concerned our ability to reason and some of its shortcomings. For example, the mind will often have problems with reconciling the impressions it obtains from sense-experience with the type of categorizations it must base its judgments upon—a difficulty typically addressed by the Eleatics. Thus, Antisthenes, by trying to refute a purely rational proof by physical means, mixed two approaches that should not be mixed, a misstep already pointed out by Parmenides, who warns that a refutative argument should not be judged by the use of the senses, but only by applying reason (7.3–6).

In fact, if we examine Zeno's work, we cannot find any conclusive statements about the state of the world or of the things that form it. Mostly what Zeno shows is that if we think in a certain way, we will inevitably arrive at problems, and if we attempt to avoid these by thinking differently, more often than not we will still arrive at the same problems. His paradoxes do not offer solutions—no proper paradox can—but they do prove that *if* we follow some of our assumptions to the end, we may be surprised by the absurdity of the result. Zeno's book is supposed to have contained forty such brainteasers, yet sadly, only a handful have been preserved—and without Aristotle we would not have even that many. Each one is a formidable example of "disproof by argument alone," proving what is perceived by the senses is often incompatible with the expectations set up by reason, and that a problem posed by the mind should be solved by the mind.

In summary, there is no evidence that Zeno or Parmenides denied the existence of change, or movement per se. Some may argue that Parmenides must have spoken of the physical universe, because abstract or intelligible things had not yet been discovered in his time. However, I would like to remind the reader of the message of fragment 4:

4.1 Behold things which, although absent, are yet securely present to the mind;
4.2 for you cannot cut off What IS from holding on to What IS;
4.3 neither by dispersing it in every way, everywhere throughout the cosmos,
4.4 nor by gathering it together.

---

550 **Elias**, *Commentaria in Aristotelem Graeca* 18.109, 6 (**DK** 29A15); cf. **Barnes** [9] *TPP* 296.

As these verses show, Parmenides was well-acquainted with the intelligible aspect of things, reminding us that, as objects of thought, they are always available—thus, *present*—in the mind, regardless of what might happen to their sensory-experiential counterparts—which may, after all, be absent. Not so, he says, for the things of mind, which is why we should give preference to this particular aspect when focusing on things in general. To be secure and present means to be immune against change, because the mind is not a domain where physical phenomena apply—with all their discrepancies and contradictions—which, again, for Parmenides, were the kind of things that afflict only the objects of sense-experience.

It is very clear that Parmenides *does* accept change—as long as it relates to the object of sense, not mind. Otherwise, he could have never spoken of the two latter options above that can both be characterized as change of place, that is, "dispersing" (4.3) and "gathering together" (4.4). He does not say that you cannot cut off "What IS" from holding on to "What IS" because it is an impossible operation as such—meaning there is no such thing as dispersion or gathering. He says, specifically, that even if you *do* disperse or gather it, you still won't manage to cut off "What IS" from "What IS."

Julian Barbour's The End of Time

One final word on Parmenides' object of inquiry and physical reality or existence: I do not claim that Parmenides' principles or landmarks have absolutely no bearing on what we may discover about the universe. My interpretation is not intended to discourage research into the possible parallels between the elements of his doctrine and their applicability to cosmological, even cosmogonical, inquiry. The intention of this work is to focus on what appears to be Parmenides' immediate concerns, namely the reliability of discourse and the adoption of a noetic/argumentative approach to proving—which we call logic—instead of depending on some empirical procedure. But Parmenides also gave us Doxa, which, in spite of its professed deceptiveness, was nonetheless an early systematic, indeed scientific, account of the outer world. It is not out of the question that the principles Parmenides discovered may have some relevance regarding how the universe functions in ways no one suspected, and science may still find one day that all movement and change is illusion. And perhaps it already has. Intriguingly, the best book on the subject is written not by a philosopher, but most fittingly by the physicist Julian Barbour [775]. In *The End of Time: The Next Revolution in Physics,* Barbour compares some basic cosmological ideas distinguished as Heraclitean and Parmenidean, bringing them in context with the theories of Galileo, Newton, and Einstein, and even those of contemporary physicists such as Stephen Hawking. The book is very accessible, and its ideas are well-presented, venturing into such subjects as a timeless, changeless universe—which the author calls Platonia—as well as time capsules, quantum cosmology, black holes, general relativity, time as the measure of difference, the improbability of history, "the Now" as the very essence of the physical world, even time travel, and whether free will exists in Platonia. I highly recommend it.

WHAT DOES THE CONCEPT OF TRUTH SIGNIFY FOR PARMENIDES?

> The notion of truth claim presupposes the notion of truth... For Parmenides, the primary veridical notion is that of fact or state of affairs, what obtains 'out there,' independently of what we say or think, and what makes what we say or think true or false.
> —Charles Kahn.[551]

The Poem indicates a close affinity between the concepts of Truth, or Aletheia, and the object of discourse itself, in other words, *esti* or IS. I have mentioned that a few interpretations have suggested that *esti* stands for truth. Most notable is again Charles Kahn's, as proposed in his seminal essay, "The Thesis of Parmenides."[552] The idea that Parmenides' use of *esti* is largely veridical is very exciting, particularly because it opens the door to a comprehensive interpretation that reconciles all parts of the Poem without creating the kind of inconsistencies or contradictions that mark the existential or cosmological read. Thus, Kahn has laid one of the most important foundations for the future of Parmenidean interpretation.

However, I would like to go one step further and pose the following question: if Parmenides' use of *esti*, or IS, is veridical, which means it stands for "is true" or "is the case,"[553] then what exactly does this truth signify for Parmenides in the context of his differentiation between two ways of rendering an account, one evidential and the other plausible/deceptive? I contend that it is *certainty*. And I do not mean certainty in the form of a personal conviction, but in its strongest form, that is to say, *infallibility*. It is the kind of ultimate certainty explicitly denied to mortals by Xenophanes, namely, *to saphes*, "the *'clear and certain truth'* no man has seen."[554] Obviously, the way sought by Parmenides could not have been aimed at a lesser

---

551   **Kahn** [400] 'Parmenides and Plato' 84.
552   See also **Kahn**'s [392] papers, 'The Greek Verb "To Be" and the Concept of Being,' and [396] 'Why Existence Does Not Emerge as a Distinct Concept in Greek Philosophy' 323–334, for further elaborations on the theory of the veridical "IS." Another valuable contribution to the subject is **Long**'s [448] 'Parmenides on Thinking Being.' E.g.: "As Parmenides' readers, we are being invited to learn to think correctly by assimilating our minds to the knowledge and thought which pertain to truth as such." (143)
553   This is **Kahn**'s [397] precise formulation; see 'Why Existence Does Not Emerge as a Distinct Concept in Greek Philosophy' 328.
554   **Lesher**'s [431] formulation for τὸ σαφὲς, *Xenophanes of Colophon* 155, 156. Cf. **Guthrie** [43] *HGP* 1.395: "certain truth"; **KRS** [39] 179: "the complete truth"; **Heitsch** [369] *Xenophanes: Die Fragmente* 77: "das Genaue"; **Barnes** [8] *Early Greek Philosophy* 94: "the clear truth"; **McKirahan** [67] *PBS* 67: "What is absolutely the case."

truth, not if it was to dispel the doubts expressed by Xenophanes. To demonstrate this point effectively, the notion of certainty, as well as its match, the Reliable/Evidential Account, had to be contrasted with ambiguity and Mortal Opinion. What made the difference, and thus surpassed all previous attempts to attain a greater, more dependable insight, was simply a *methodical approach*. And that is precisely what Parmenides provided: the Methods of Proof and Disproof—to be examined later—a step-by-step technique that allowed one to take any opinion, belief, or "plausible ordering" (8.60) and submit it to a test. This examination was carried out as a logical argument; in essence, it was a succession of assertions and refutations. But it was a succession of assertions and refutations about *something*. Then the expressed opinion about that something either passed the test and was proven as true, or it did not and was exposed as a contradiction—in other words, the *opinion* was either validated or exposed, not the thing itself. Either way the outcome is certainty: certainty that a thing IS—and that it is expressed *as* IT IS—or certainty that it IS NOT expressed as IT IS—meaning, not expressed, period.

THE QUESTION OF IS NOT

> When you've seen Nothing, you've seen everything.
> —Buddy Kenworthy,
> Mayor of Nothing, Arizona, pop. 4

That we are dealing with the object of knowledge in the Reliable Account is particularly evident when we try to relate it to the reverse of what it is, namely, "What IS NOT" or *ouk esti* in Greek. Even though Parmenides declares that "What IS NOT" cannot be a legitimate object of discourse or thought, we can refer to it, as I do now. This apparent inconsistency has stirred much controversy. But this dilemma is also resolvable when we remind ourselves that Parmenides has the object of *knowledge* in mind. It is rather evident that "that which IS NOT" can never be *known;* hence, it is in *this* particular capacity that it can never serve as a legitimate object for speech and thought. Why does Parmenides venture this view? Aside from the obvious—that knowledge must be about *something,* and without it there is nothing to know—Parmenides does have some special concerns. As we can see, for him reason and discourse have a specific role to play, and that is *to give an account.*

Why was this so important to him? To find an answer, we must first pose another question: how can one get to know an object of reason, an abstraction for instance? It seems that the only means available is to *give some kind of account*—in short, we must speak of it, as quite obviously, we cannot apply our eyes or ears to observe this type of object, nor can we experience it in any way. Consequently, we must rely on the account and the way that it is given (meaning the *ordering* of words used) as the only means for becoming acquainted with such intangible subjects. For example, an infringement of law, or the breach of an obligation for which there was no further evidence than the words of a witness, could also fall into such a category.

These considerations can provide us with a reason as to why Parmenides required an account to be as reliable as possible: there was no other way to assess what is purely intelligible or discursive. We can see how particularly relevant this might be to someone with a legal background, who must evaluate the veracity of statements because that is all he has to work with. In Parmenides' day, there were no crime scene investigators, crime labs, or genetic fingerprints, and even if there had been, someone would still be needed to interpret the evidence and to offer an *account* of it to the court. The deciding magistrates or jury do not collect and examine the evidence themselves; they must rely on the way it is presented to them by others. Hence, their real responsibility is to determine not only if the account offered is consistent with itself, which is a must, but whether it can be *forced* into contradiction, and thus self-refutation. If the latter succeeds, whatever the account intended to express has been discredited; there is no heart of truth.

We can make the following comparison: if the "that which IS" is the well-rounded or persuasive heart of truth, then contradiction must be at the heart of rejection, the opposite of persuasion. In other words, it is "that which IS NOT"—as in *that* which cannot be known or thought—because there is nothing there to know or to grasp by thought. Of course, this also denotes that there is nothing there that can be *positively* expressed or spoken of (see 2.7–8, 6.1–2, and 8.17). In short, no ordering of words, no matter how sophisticated or simple it may be, can convey knowledge about What IS NOT, regardless of whether we are dealing with the IS NOT of self-negation, contradiction, nonbeing, or the unthinkable in general.

It is not even appropriate to think of IS NOT as a navigable route on par with *esti*, (see fragment 2) because, as the Goddess declares, it is not a true route (8.17–18). It is certainly not an account of any kind, not even a deficient one like Doxa. This suggests that to be a genuine route of inquiry, an approach must have a suitable, corresponding object; thus, a true route would have a true object. Conversely, what conforms to the notion of an unthinkable, unnameable route (8.17) can only be what is equally unthinkable and unnameable, which is tantamount to saying that, as a route, IS NOT lacks any sort of expressible object—much less a feasible destination.[555] As all thinking, knowing, and naming are exclusively linked to the IS—nothing else being available—it winds up being the only object for these activities, including the designations that appeal to mortals (8.35–41). (However, which of the designations survive the *method of critical judgment* is a different matter. Ultimately, it will be those that comply to the criteria exacted by the method, i.e., that facilitate the *unity of formula*.) In any case,

---

555 **Capizzi** [252] points out that the Goddess does not introduce Parmenides to "what are the only ways for searching" but to "what only ways of searching are thinkable." Also what is denied is not the thinkability, per se, of the way that says "it is not," because we are dealing with an "unexplorable path but not an unthinkable path. Unthinkable is alone its point of arrival" (*La Porta di Parmenide* 77). In other words, the end of the path or the result of the method is incogitable; we are left without a concrete object of thought. See also Capizzi regarding fr. 8.15–16 on the decision being that one of the two ways bears the unthinkable and inexpressible, as opposed to the real and certain way, but as a way, the former is just as thinkable as the latter. (79)

all the non-contradictory characteristics (*semata*, or landmarks, 8.2) that a way of inquiry for thinking requires of its object must be present and available for testing. All other possibilities—the ambivalent, duplicitous, and conjectural—are simply relegated to Doxa or Mortal Opinion. (See also fr. 19.)

What, then, if anything, "belongs" to IS NOT, announced as the "second way of inquiry" in fragment 2? As I have suggested above, the answer is *contradiction*. It indicates an unintelligible, indiscriminating fusion of being and not being, predicated on the utter negation of the Principle of Non-Contradiction.[556] As ways, the difference between the first and the second is both subtle and severe, hinging only on the choice between two little words: "or" versus "and." Thus "IS *or* IS NOT" is the hallmark of the first approach (8.11, 8.15), as opposed to "IS *and* IS NOT," which is that of the second. The first way gets us someplace by allowing us to distinguish and discriminate—it is, as we shall see, an exercise in *separation*. The second way is the exact opposite: it leads nowhere because it obscures and confuses, making everything unintelligible.

There is one interesting detail that can be missed when dealing with the difficult subject of IS NOT, but it highlights the strange idiosyncracy of deeming it a way, and conversely strengthens the claim of the first way to be the *only* legitimate *method of judgment*: after the Goddess informs us that the decision regarding the "coming-to-be" or the "passing-away" of What IS depends on "IS or IS NOT," she also reveals that "it has been decided, just as is necessary, to leave one unthinkable and unnameable (for it is not a true route) and the other to be and be true" (8.15–18). The message here is clear and unambiguous: a definitive judgment *has already been rendered* regarding IS NOT—notice the explicit use of the past tense—but we, as mortals, are not told by whom. But the decision-maker could only have been a divine agency, perhaps Justice herself—who has been just mentioned in 8.13 as the preventer of generation and destruction—or maybe she has ordained such matters in accordance to mighty Necessity—also cited in this context—whose unyielding demands not even the gods can set aside. In any case the judgment is a final one, and thus mortals are foreclosed from

---

[556] This is also **Cordero's** [279] position and formulation (*By Being, It Is* 141–143, forthcoming). Cordero finds that the "content of the second way," as he puts it, "consists in the affirmation of a negation, and the negation of an affirmation," which denotes it as "a mixture of being and not-being in which each notion is attributed to its contrary." (143) He further remarks (on fr. 6.8–9) that to assert "that that which is *and* that which is not are the same *and* not the same assumes that two contradictory judgments are possible at the same time," which shows that mortals do not respect the Principle of Non-Contradiction. (Ibid.)

ever revoking it. In fact, this is a case of an "unbreakable law"; not even the most cunning can make use of IS NOT as a traversable route.[557] As IS NOT is for all times prevented from getting us anyplace, it can never bring us *to* an *object of judgment*—all in all it amounts only to the indirect indication that such an object has been refuted. Thus, the management of the object of judgment belongs exclusively to its counterpart, the IS, which is both the route by which to judge, and the destination of said route.

As with *esti* or IS, my approach to Eleatic technical terms is to adhere as much as possible to Parmenides' way of formulating something; thus, when alluding to IS NOT, I do it in much the same way as when he writes *ouk esti* or *ouk estin* (e.g., 8.9, 8.16), except that I write it in capital letters, again, for better discernment (and as can be seen above, at times I will add "What" to the IS NOT so as to maintain fluency).

---

557 Cf. **Curd** [297] on the decision against IS NOT standing for all time (*Legacy* 31). Gorgias may have been aware of the implication of an irrevocable decision on this matter, because if anyone tried to contravene the impassability of IS NOT, it was he, in his work "On What Is Not."

DOXA: OPINION OR APPEARANCE?

> "[Parmenides] calls this account apparent and deceptive, meaning not that it is absolutely false, but that the perceptible has fallen away from intelligible truth to what is apparent and seeming."
>
> —Simplicius[558]

The nature of Doxa, or the Deceptive Ordering of Words, and its justification for being included in the Poem is a very controversial issue. As an account, it is more of an explanation than a deductive method of proof, unlike its counterpart, the Reliable/Evidential Account. The subject it addresses is a number of cosmological, astronomical, and biological theories, all assembled under the broad heading called Mortal Belief. What makes it different from the Evidential Account is that, as an explanation of things, it alludes to or expresses their *mixed nature*.[559] The entities that populate the outer universe are all portrayed as composites, that is, they are made from different components that are reducible to two elementary but contradictory forms or formulas: Light and Night. Consequently, all things share some of the characteristics of each of these elements, and when accounted for, they are presented as combinations of two separate formulas, that if taken as a whole, are mutually exclusive. No other principle is involved in the mix, not even nothingness; "it" obviously has no characteristics, hence no formula. But the available mixtures are never uniform: things are composed of *varying* proportions of Light and Night. This factor alone distinguishes them from each other because of the variations in their blend ratios. In other words, each individual thing has its very own, very unique share of Light and Night.

The reason the Mortal Account is deceptive is that it tries to express these differing mixtures in a way that they do not allow themselves to be expressed, that is, as unambiguous or certain. Composite things are not sta-

---

558 **Simplicius**, *Commentary on Aristotle's Physics*. 9.39. 10–12 (DKA34). Trans. **Barney** [10] 'Socrates Agonistes: The Case of the *Cratylus* Etymologies' 91.

559 Regarding Doxa as mix or mixture, cf. **Reinhardt** [520] *Parmenides* 73–76; **Verdenius** [585] *Parmenides* 24–26; **Gigon** [40] *Ursprung* 264, 273–274, 281; **Minar** [475] 'Parmenides and the World of Seeming' 52–53; **Vlastos** [594] 'Parmenides' Theory of Knowledge' 68; **Coxon** [288] 'The Philosophy of Parmenides' 142–43; **Finkelberg** [318] '"Like by Like" and Two Reflections of Reality in Parmenides' 408: "*Opinion*, or knowledge of reality as a mixture of light and darkness, is characteristic of mortals"; **Hölscher** [379] *Parmenides* 108: "Der Gedanke der Mischung beherrscht nun die ganze Kosmologie des Parmenides"; also **Meijer** [469] *Parmenides Beyond the Gates* 156; and **Wiesner** [607] *Parmenides: Der Beginn der Aletheia* 64–73.

ble as the mix varies constantly. Things come to be, change, move, and pass away because their components, being opposites, are in a continuous flux. The kind of account that must take these changes into consideration can only be called opinion, not truth, because the situation it describes is never settled. It does not reach a point where we can consider it stabilized or decided; thus we can never give a final account. I have indicated before that in contrast to the Evidential Account, whose domain is certainty, Mortal Opinion must operate in a world of approximations and estimates. It is therefore far more Pythagorean or Heraclitean than Parmenidean, because it can never capture a concrete state of affairs. This is why the Goddess declares the subjects of "change," "coming-to-be," and "growth" to be matters of opinion not pertaining to the Evidential Account, because the latter focuses on objects that are not susceptible to these kinds of phenomena:

19.1 Thus, according to *opinion,* these things have grown and now are,
19.2 and then, after growing up, they will reach their end. (Emphasis added.)

We can appreciate how much affinity Parmenides' thought processes have with those of Albert Einstein, 2,500 years later: Both thinkers differentiate two objects in their respective fields—the fields being knowledge for Parmenides and mathematics for Einstein. Both consider one object as certain and the other as variable. Both associate the former with the speculative realm, and the latter with the outer world.[560] For Parmenides, the object of knowledge is certain; therefore, the world of sense-experience cannot be expressed by it. For Einstein, as we shall see further on, the statements of theoretical mathematics are certain; therefore, they do not refer to reality. Conversely, as reality can only be expressed by uncertain statements in Einstein's view, so in Parmenides' view can the world of sense-experience only be expressed by opinion. That is precisely what Doxa is—the world expressed not as a certain ordering but as a plausible one—and this explains why Doxa has a legitimate, even indispensable place in the Poem.

Some interpreters equate Doxa not with opinion but with "appearance," "seeming," or "illusion" in the belief that Parmenides alludes here to a distortion of reality caused by the deficient sense-perception of mortals. In other words, it represents a world that only *appears* to be real because our

---

560   See the motto of Chapter XI, "Mind and Universe," i.e., **Einstein's** [741] remark: "Insofar as the statements of mathematics refer to reality, they are not certain, and insofar as they are certain, they do not refer to reality."

lying senses tell us that it is, but that cannot be as real as the one offered by thought.

Of course, this line of reasoning convinces many of the same interpreters to deny *any* sort of reality to Doxa—and accordingly deny it a legitimate place in Parmenides' doctrine—a charge that is commonly built around two complementary arguments: (1) what seems or appears to be is not the same as What IS, and (2) because it is not the same as reality, it must be illusion. Furthermore, by appealing to a phrase in the Poem that speaks of "IS or IS NOT" (8.16), some of these writers aim to deprive Doxa *entirely* of validity—not even allowing it to be an approximation of "what is the case"— because they hold that Parmenides approved only two options, either "all" or "nothing." This principle is called the Law of the Excluded Third, or the Excluded Middle.[561] Yet Parmenides mentions "IS or IS NOT" only as criterion or determinant by which to decide whether coming-to-be or perishing is applicable to What IS (8.13–16), and not as a means of total negation, by which to repudiate the existence of everything that deviates from "pure Being," as some have suggested.[562] Leonardo Tarán, one of the advocates of this theory, remarks that reality does not come in differing degrees for Parmenides; thus, if Doxa is an erroneous account of something, instead of being a reliable one, it must be an account of nothing, because "Parmenides did not believe in degrees of error."[563]

However, in order to denigrate Doxa we must perform a few subtle alterations within Parmenides' doctrine. We have to quietly assume that regarding the IS, he does not have "that which is for thinking" in mind, but some sort of tangible reality—even if we choose to call this reality "Being" or "existence." Such proposition would automatically make any account of said reality that does not mirror it absolutely and continuously, a lesser account—no matter how slight or fleeting the differences may be. If we accept something as being less than totally accurate, then it must be all the way false, as the Law of the Excluded Third demands—there is no middle

---

561 Also *tertium quid*, i.e., "some third thing"; cf. **Tarán** [569] *Parmenides* 192, 202, 209, 221n51; or *tertium non datur*, as in "no third possibility exists." Cf. **Furth** [334] 'Elements of Eleatic Ontology' 121, 127; **Gallop** [339] '"IS" or "IS NOT"?' 68.

562 **Loew** [442] 'Das Verhältnis von Logik und Leben bei Parmenides' 2, 10; **Tarán** [569] *Parmenides* 38, 192–193, 207–210, 221n51; and [570] 'Alexander P. D. Mourelatos' The Route of Parmenides' 665–666; **Furth** [334] 'Elements of Eleatic Ontology' 121–122, 127; **Heitsch** [370] *Parmenides* 90; **Brumbaugh** [13] *The Philosophers of Greece* 56–57; **Meijer** [469] *Parmenides Beyond the Gates* 136–138 (only implied).

563 See **Tarán** [569] *Parmenides* 207, also 221n51, 223; or that difference is not real for Parmenides, 218.

ground—which means that the object it describes is not reality at all, but illusion. And if it is illusion, then it is absolute existential nothingness, because, again, following the "all or nothing" provision, illusion is not tangible reality.

The trouble with such an oversimplified interpretation of Parmenides is that there are numerous very pivotal aspects that are glossed over or ignored. The difficulty with most interpretative approaches is that they are piecemeal, even fractional. The focus is all too often on bringing a few verses at a time into rapport with each other, without paying attention to the fact that in the end the whole construct may have become distorted. None of the interpreters who discount the Deceptive Ordering of Words has given satisfactory answers as to why the Goddess insists that Parmenides should learn *all things*, not only the evidential way of giving an account but also the gist of Mortal Opinion. They have not explained why he must be fed all kinds of lies, distortions, and illusions if he has already been given the full, unadulterated truth—a truth, for that matter, as some of the same interpreters insist, that must imply that neither he, nor the bearer of such "good news," the Goddess herself, exists. Why? Because if reality or Being is all there is, there can be nothing less or other than it; again, it is a question of "all or nothing."[564] Of course, all these attempts to eliminate Doxa can only result in far greater absurdities than may ever be drawn from the verses themselves.

Doxa is neither illusion nor appearance. It is an account of something, just as much as the Evidential Account is an account of something. But the Evidential Account is reliable because it is a method of proving the veracity of its object by assembling and reproducing those characteristics that are like each other—meaning agreeable or consistent—hence, the characteristics that define it as an object of reason, not sense. In contrast, the Deceptive Ordering of Words attempts to bring together and thus reconcile a whole group of factors that are *unlike*, disharmonious, and incompatible. The account is still an account of something, but the ordering—because it employs many opposing elements that vie for supremacy—can never be as homogeneous or consistent as the evidential one. Moreover, its object is not one of reason, but a cross section of the disjointed stimuli offered by sense-experience, which is why it is only in this part of the Poem that Parmenides speaks of the world, the cosmos, life, death, procreation, and so forth. If the universe is a volatile mix, so must be our account of it, even though it is

---

564 **Tarán** [569] *Parmenides* 193–194, 230.

only an approximation of what we think is going on out there and thus not as reliable as when we speak of an object of reason.

In summary, why must Parmenides learn all things? Because if one cannot distinguish between a reliable and an unreliable account, one may confuse the one for the other. Mortal Opinion can be quite deceiving—if we forget to demand proof. Indeed, we have seen Parmenides indicate that one should know this merely "plausible" or "likely-seeming" construction in its entirety, lest one is bested by it (8.60–61). It is useful to remind ourselves here of the distinctions drawn by Xenophanes: a mortal may very well stumble upon the truth and speak it without, of course, knowing that he did.[565] But his lack of insight regarding the factuality of his speech does not automatically make the object of his account an illusion, even more so because he may have *actually spoken the truth*—including the truth regarding illusions. In other words, what makes an account of an object unreliable for Parmenides is only the ordering of words, and not the object or even the means employed in its initial apprehension. The important thing is to hone one's ability to distinguish one way of putting words together from another. We should learn not only to know that it is *truth* that has been assembled whenever consistent, non-contradictory statements are used—the coveted unity of formula—but also to recognize when we are not dealing with the same *because* incompatibles were introduced. In this manner, Xenophanes' doubt-generating considerations have been trumped by Parmenides. We can speak the truth, and *know* that we did, but also know *when we did not*, as is the case with Doxa, where we are aware that we have only expressed something plausible at best.[566] That is why the Deceptive Ordering of Words has to be included in the Poem, because to recognize it as such answers and checks Xenophanes' negative epistemology. And of course, Parmenides had to be provided by the Goddess with something to work upon. He had to find out for himself how the "things of opinion"—as we know from 1.31–32—would have to be, if they are to be accepted as reliable, namely, by being *made* that way.

---

565 **Xenophanes**, DK 21B34.
566 Cf. **Heitsch** [370] *Parmenides* 137, on a mortal cosmology: "The [Goddess] knows that fundamentally, this topic allows only suppositions and probability statements, because the nature of the thing makes evidentiary proofs impossible." (My translation.)

ARE THERE ADVANTAGES TO REARRANGING THE FRAGMENTS?

The position of some of the fragments is not at all a definite thing. In particular, the places of fragments 3 to 7 are very much undecided. Even the ordering of the verses themselves may be erroneous, because they may have been taken out of context, or have gaps, or perhaps even contain corrupted words. This, arguably, is the case with fragments 6 and 7. It is not at all clear, for example, that the ordering of fragment 6 should be as now assumed, because line 6.3 contains a gap of indeterminate size. Hermann Diels chose to fill this gap with the word "bar" ("for first I bar you") which he thought appropriate, and most interpreters were willing to follow his lead.[567] Other scholars, particularly Néstor-Luis Cordero and Alexander Nehamas, have offered convincing, indeed revolutionary, arguments as to why line 6.3 should be translated differently than the generally accepted version.[568] I have adopted this new reading, as can be seen in the Poem above. In doing so, and while studying other works on rearranging the verses, it has come to my attention that line 6.3 fits perfectly after 7.6, and line 7.1 after 6.2.[569] After pondering these matters for quite a while, I also became swayed that fragment 5 dovetails quite nicely between 6.9 and 8.1, if one translates one little but crucial word differently. The word in question, *de*, appears in line 6.9 and is commonly translated as "and" instead of "but."[570] Here is the whole rearrangement, which I have bookended with

---

567 **Diels** [307] *Parmenides Lehrgedicht* 68. More extensive comments on these factors, and scholarly considerations regarding my proposed ordering, can be found in my other Parmenidean work, **Hermann** [372] *The Naked IS* (forthcoming).

568 Cf. **Cordero** [277] *Les deux chemins* 24, 168–175; **Nehamas** [488] 'On Parmenides' Three Ways of Inquiry' 105.

569 Neither Cordero nor Nehamas advocate rearrangement. For repositioning of 7.1–2 after 6.2, I follow **Sprague**'s [552] suggestions; however, without (a) dropping 7.2, nor by (b) following it with the rest of 6—both proposed by Sprague—but with the rest of 7 (cf. 'Parmenides: A Suggested Rearrangement of the Fragments in the "Way of Truth"' 124–126).

570 In accordance to **Denniston** [776] *The Greek Particles* 165–166, I have opted for the strong adversative "but" for δέ in 6.9: "πάντων δέ παλίντροπός ἐστι κέλευθος." However, I am grateful to Stanley **Lombardo** for his input on the subject, even if he disagrees with my read. He graciously exemplified how δέ can be used as a strong adversative at times, as opposed to a weak adversative. Yet even as a weak adversative, δέ would work in this context, because as Denniston points out, instead of eliminating the opposing idea in its strong form, δέ as a weak adversative may balance two opposing ideas (165). Thus, the only ideas to be balanced here are "to be and not to be are the same and not the same" and "the path of all turns back on itself." Either way, δέ distinguishes them as opposing, and not complementary as most interpreters believe. I guess the difference is whether we believe that a race car—as Lombardo puts it—must return to its starting line by going forward and around the track, or whether it shifts to *reverse* in order to drive *backward* to the start. Contrary to most interpreters, I believe that the race car here goes forward and around the track, instead of going in reverse.

fragment 2 and, respectively, the beginning of fragment 8 for a comprehensive picture—with the exception of fragment 4, whose place in the Poem still remains to be determined. (I have kept Diels/Kranz's line numbering for better discernment):

2.1 Come now, I will tell you—and preserve my account as you heard it—
2.2 what are the only ways of inquiry for thinking/knowing:
2.3 the one [that states it] as IT IS, and that it cannot NOT BE [as it is],
2.4 is the Way of Persuasion (for it follows the Truth),
2.5 the other [states it] as it IS NOT, and that it is necessary that it NOT BE [as it is],
2.6 this I point out to you is a completely inscrutable path
2.7 for you cannot know that which IS NOT (for this cannot be done)
2.8 nor can you express it . . .
3.0 . . . . for "to be thought" and "to be" are the same [thing].
6.1 Speaking and thinking must be of what IS, for it can be,
6.2 but nothing cannot be. I urge you to consider this.
7.1 For things that are not can never be forced to be;
7.2 but keep your thought from that way of inquiry,
7.3 and do not let habit [derived] from much experience force you along this path,
7.4 to direct your unseeing eye and ringing ear
7.5 and tongue; but judge by reasoning the much-contested disproof
7.6 expounded by me.
6.3 For first you [will begin] from this way of inquiry . . .
6.4 But afterward from the one, which mortals who know nothing
6.5 piece together two-headed; for helplessness in their
6.6 breasts guides their unsteady mind. They are borne along,
6.7 deaf as well as blind, stupefied, hordes without judgment
6.8 for whom to be and not to be are deemed the same and
6.9 not the same; but the path of all turns back to itself.
5.1 [Thus,] it is the same to me
5.2 from what place I begin, for to there I shall come back again.
8.1 . . . hereafter a single account
8.2 is left, the "way" [that states it] as it IS. Yet on this there are landmarks . . .

Naturally, I do not advocate a permanent change of the Diels/Kranz arrangement, which has become quite an orthodoxy for interpreters. Nonetheless, I hope the reader can appreciate how well the message flows in this particular ordering: one by one, the ways are addressed and dealt with, without repetition or redundancy. As the Goddess has made known to Parmenides, she circles from the IS to IS NOT, and then to the Mortal Account, only to return to the IS, which subsequently becomes the object of demonstration of the only method that can do justice to it. (Fr.8)

CHAPTER VIII

Guidelines for an Evidential Account

DELIMITING THE OBJECT OF JUDGMENT

> For mighty Necessity holds it within the bonds of the limit which encloses it all around.
> —Parmenides 8.30–31

I have argued that Parmenides' central problem was how to ensure the reliability of discourse. To facilitate this end, he had to develop certain rules or restrictions—the necessary "bonds" or stipulations that must delimit statements if they are to be dependable, and not self-refuting. This chapter will focus on those provisions that can be gleaned from what is left of his verses and that may help us understand what it takes to achieve reliability. Now, it did not matter whether a given account was one's own or someone else's. The essential difficulty—as we have seen in light of Xenophanes' objections—was the same: not only will I have a hard time assessing whether another person's account is trustworthy and true, but how can I know—as a human being prone to error—whether my own explanations are accurate, if all things are subject to belief?[571] How can I find something, anything, that is unconditionally impervious to distortion, a criterion, perhaps, that is immune to opinion? Because if whatever it is I must rely upon remains susceptible to corruption or misrepresentation, I evidently cannot trust it, regardless of whether in a particular case it may indeed be true. Moreover, how can I differentiate one case from the other? How can I tell that a statement about something is not colored by belief at this moment, as opposed to later, when it might be? Essentially, what factor or gauge can indicate to

---

571 Xenophanes, DK 21B34.

me—beyond a shadow of doubt—that an account I have given or received was absolutely accurate, meaning opinion-free?

These questions are precisely the kind that must have bothered Parmenides deeply, but he did manage to isolate an important part of the problem and to develop interesting and indeed workable solutions. I have mentioned that an account had to be made impervious against two dangers: on one hand, *contradiction,* which turned a statement inside out, supplanting something with nothing; and on the other, *a deceptive plausibility,* which stems from the kind of ambiguity that typifies all mortal explanations—if we recall in this context the error of trying to account for things by combining two contradicting formulas. (8.53–56)

Parmenides realized that he had to establish certain criteria or rules that could separate the wheat from the chaff, so to speak—the formulas in question—that is to say, he had to weigh those characterizations that support the expression of something certain against those that do not and thus undermine such an endeavor. That, in a nutshell, is what the Poem is about. It is an *exercise in separation,* the separation of what is incompatible with or self-defeating to the core of a message—to its "heart of truth."[572] It is this exercise in separation that is intrinsically connected to Parmenides' legal background.[573] Even a cursory investigation of his work reveals that it is replete with terminology that is not poetic but technical, much of it with legal or juridical implications. Some phrases are quite obvious, such as "true evidence" (1.30, 8.28), "force of evidence" (8.12), "evidential account" or "faithful speech" (8.50),[574] not to mention his meaningful references to Dike, the goddess of justice (1.14, 1.28, 8.14). The term *dike* was also used for "trial" or "lawsuit" and in connection with "restitution" and "atonement." L. R. Palmer, in his fascinating study on the subject, demonstrates how *dike* in its origins was related to "limits," "boundaries," "landmarks," "marks as characteristics," or "marks or signs by which to show, or point out something."[575] This particular meaning reminds us of Parmenides' *semata,* the

---

572 See **Gigon** [40] *Ursprung* 263, on separation by methodical elimination, i.e., negative proof, which characterizes the whole structure of the Poem. Cf. also **Mansfeld** [455] *Offenbarung* 43.

573 Cf. **Heidel** [51] 'On Certain Fragments of the Pre-Socratics' 718; **Gigon** [40] *Ursprung* 251; **Mansfeld** [455] *Offenbarung* 270–271; **Cordero** [279] *By Being, It Is* 146 (forthcoming).

574 See also Introduction, note 32; Chapter VI, note 464; Chapter VII, "What Is the Significance of the Proem," note 491. For additional comments and terms see, Chapter V, subhead "The Poet's Challenge and the Lawgiver's Response," note 437. Also notes 584, 585, this chapter.

575 **Palmer** [722] 'The Indo-European Origins of Greek Justice' 149–168. Cf. also **Sealey** [725] *The Justice of the Greeks* 141. For further reflections on *dike* as goddess as well as the term,

Delimiting the Object of Judgment 213

"landmarks" or "signs" that mark the single way that expresses the IS (8.2). They indicate the IS by constraining it within its limiting demarcations, thereby excluding from its formula what did not belong there. (See, for example the *sphere* simile for the IS, 8.42–43, which was held by an "ultimate limit." The association of delimiting with "chaining" or "bonding" is a recurring theme in Parmenides, which we will revisit shortly.) Palmer explains that literally "the just man" means someone who "remains within his marks or limits," and that these limits constitute "his proper portion or allotment."[576] Here, once again, we find imagery that is strikingly Parmenidean. Eventually *dike* became associated with the transgression of accepted boundaries or limits, together with the reparation for these transgressions.[577] It came to stand for "judgment," yet as demonstrated by Raphael Sealey in his informative work *The Justice of the Greeks*, *dike* was not merely a pronouncement or assertion, it represented a "mode of proof"; its main purpose was to resolve disputes by means other than bloodshed.[578] Many of these solutions had to rely largely upon the proper formulation of oaths, as well as the refinement of various means of persuasion. We understand how critical the right formulation of oaths is for any society, particularly if its very existence depends upon nonviolent redress or the avoidance of conflict altogether.[579] The techniques for creating a Reliable/Evidential Account come to mind, that is, the trustworthy *ordering* of words—which must have played an important role for Parmenides also in the structuring of Elea's constitution, and which arguably represents the link between his legislation and the Poem. But the oaths themselves were undoubtedly a powerful element in the public and political life of his fellow citizens, as attested by the yearly repledging of their magistrates to Parmenides' laws.[580]

---

see **Ehrenberg** [705] *Die Rechtsidee im frühen Griechentum* 54–102; **Wolf** [87] *Vorsokratiker und frühe Dichter*, Griechisches Rechtsdenken, vol. 1, 288–296; **Fränkel** [327] 'Studies in Parmenides' 6–14; **Cornford** [21] *From Religion to Philosophy* 54, also on Dike "keeping individuals in their places" (82), and Dike as "Way" (172ff); **Mansfeld** [455] *Offenbarung* 261–271, (however, I disagree that Parmenides' mentor, the unnamed Goddess, is Dike, as also proposed by **Deichgräber** [303] *Parmenides' Auffahrt*); and **Gagarin** [707] *Early Greek Law* 100, 107. See also **Vlastos** [728] on the role of *dike* in Parmenides ('Equality and Justice in Early Greek Cosmologies' *Studies in Greek Philosophy*, Vol. I: *The Presocratics*. 63–64, 69, 83).

576 **Palmer** [722] 'The Indo-European Origins of Greek Justice' 162.
577 After **Peters** [784] *Greek Philosophical Terms* 38.
578 **Sealey** [725] *The Justice of the Greeks* 100–105, 138–141. Cf. also **Gagarin** [707] *Early Greek Law* 106, 106n19.
579 For further information of the function and importance of oaths, see **Gagarin** [707] *Early Greek Law* 43, 43n66, 74, 82–84, 89–92, 97; **Sealey** [725] *The Justice of the Greeks* 51–52, 92–101, 146–148.
580 **Plutarch**, *Reply to Colotes* 32.1126a (**DK** 28A12).

Worth mentioning in this context is also the concept of "speaking a straight *dike*" in a court of law. As Michael Gagarin points out, it "involves both telling the truth, which may be guaranteed in some cases by the swearing of an oath, and proposing a settlement that will be acceptable to both parties, which may require the rhetorical ability to persuade them to accept it."[581] Ideally in a dispute, as Gagarin also observes, if all parties agree to keep their accounts straight, what comes out is a straight *dike*. Noticeably, several of the factors just mentioned seem familiar to the student of Parmenides, not only the speaking of truth, but also persuasion, acceptance, just settlements or decisions, and even rhetorical ability. Together with the aforesaid oaths, these things are only possible when one knows how to choose words carefully and place them in a rightful order.

Another "mode of proof" made famous by Parmenides was *disproof*, announced by the Goddess in 7.5 as *poluderis elenchos*, "much-contested disproof" (translated by others also as "refutation," "test," "proof," or "challenge"[582]). The exact nature or application of this disproof is a much-debated issue among interpreters, yet beyond question, fragment 8 is a collection of refutative exercises. As contradiction is Parmenides' weapon of choice for putting statements to the test, I believe we must look no further than these demonstrations. (More on this subject will be presented in subsequent chapters.)

The Poem preserves additional terms that are important in our context, such as *doxa*, *ta dokounta*, and *dokimos*, familiar to us from the Proem (1.30–32). Alexander Mourelatos, in *The Route of Parmenides*—truly one of the most indispensable works on the Eleatic—has pointed to the close relationship these words have with each other and how they are inherently linked with the concepts of "seeming," "expectation," and "acceptance."[583] Essentially, what constitutes mortal opinion is what *seems* true to them, what they have come to *expect* as true (by custom, habit, and so forth; remember 7.3, "habit from much experience"); in other words, what mortals have agreed

---

581   **Gagarin** [707] *Early Greek Law* 107, cf. also 21–22.

582   For "disproof," see also **Gallop** [340] *Parmenides* 63. For "refutation," see **KRS** [39] 248; **Guthrie** [43] *HGP* I.21; **Mansfeld** [459] (trans.), *Parmenides: Über das Sein* 9; **McKirahan** [67] *PBS* 153. For "test" or "testing," see **Coxon** [290] *Fragments* 58; **Curd** [297] *Legacy* 61–62. For "proof," see **Burnet** [14] *Early Greek Philosophy* 173; **Cornford** [282] *Plato and Parmenides* 32; **Cordero** [279] *By Being, It Is* 200 (forthcoming). For "challenge," see **Austin** [199] *Parmenides, Being, Bounds, and Logic* 163; and **Lombardo** [444] *Parmenides and Empedocles* 14; **Cerri** [261] *Parmenide di Elea* 151. **Tarán** [569] has "argument" (*Parmenides* 73).

583   **Mourelatos** [480] *Route* 197–205. Cf. also **LSJ**, under the root word δοκέω, i.e., "expect," "seem." On *ta dokounta*, and *dokimos*, see also Chapter VII, "What Is the Significance of the Proem," and notes 437, 501, 522.

Delimiting the Object of Judgment 215

among themselves to *accept* as true. But there are differences in what kind of acceptance we speak of, for example, whether we have in mind *ta dokounta*, (literally, "the things commonly accepted" or "the things generally held as true") or rather *dokimos*—with its ties to "assaying," "examining," or "passing muster"—hence, in regard to "things that are provedly true or real" because they passed a test. The latter then are worthy of genuine acceptance, not by convention but by proof. And *doxa* itself, while still linked with "expectation," pertains also to "notion," "opinion," and "judgment," the latter—as outlined by Liddell and Scott's Greek-English Lexicon—"whether well grounded or not."

Well-grounded judgment is best represented by the word *krisis* or "decision," (8.15)—one of the most important terms in Parmenides' vocabulary—together with the verb *krinai* (7.5, "to judge," "to decide," "to pronounce that a thing is"). They are both linked with juridical usage, that is, court decisions, the passing of sentences, the rendering of judgments, and so forth.[584] Most importantly, these concepts derive from "to separate" or "to divide." The idea of separation allows one not only "to distinguish" or "to discern"—which are secondary usages of the same verb—but also "to allocate, to impart to each its proper due."[585] Bestowing upon each side its rightful share was not only a magistrate's duty, but above all it was the prerogative of the gods in meting out one's fate—a fate, I might add, that was the epitome of justice, because it represented one's indisputably individual share in the world.[586] Fate was neither punishment nor reward; one simply had to do one's part, since it was the only part one got. Thus, the allotment "to each its own" was a governing principle, one strenuously observed by Parmenides throughout his Poem, and without it we could not make sense of the evidentiary "landmarks" or characteristics that belong to "that which IS" (fr. 8) and which distinguish it from "that which it IS NOT," or from Doxa. This principle, as I have mentioned, is Like by Like, or Like according to Like. In the next chapter we will examine how Parmenides uses *krisis* or judgment to *separate* mixtures of contradicting concepts by distinguishing what notions belong to the object of his demonstration—that is, to its for-

---

584 Cf. **Cordero** [279] *By Being, It Is* 146 (forthcoming). (Also *kekritai* "has been decided" (8.16) and *ekrinanto* "judged," "differentiated" (8.55) belong to the abovementioned category. I am indebted to Cordero for pointing this out.)

585 Cf. **Ehrenberg** [705] *Die Rechtsidee im frühen Griechentum* 97–98; **Wolf** [87] *Vorsokratiker und frühe Dichter, Griechisches Rechtsdenken*, vol. 1, 288, 290; and **Mansfeld** [455] *Offenbarung* 263–264, 269: "For the Greek sense of language (*Sprachempfinden*) 'separation' has become the factor that characterizes the nature of judicial *procedure*." (264, my translation)

586 Cf. **Ehrenberg** [705] *Die Rechtsidee im frühen Griechentum* 57–60.

mula—and what notions do not.[587] This was logic in its original form: the rendering of a judicial determination, not *only* upon matters of law, but expanding their utilization, or "mandate," if you will, upon other matters which also required a critical/rational approach.

For this to work, however, additional laws had to be established—not dissimilar from the ones in court—yet this time for the "court of reasoning," the mind. These were rules for thinking in accordance to which "the man who knows" (1.3) them would be able to distinguish the reliable from the plausible (8.60), to separate what did or did not belong together (fr. 8), and to judge after proving and disproving (7.5) what single truth remained to represent "What IS" (8.1–2). And these were not just any kind of rules, but precisely those that had the power to fasten reasoning to truth. Parmenides regularly alludes to these as "chains" or "bonds" (8.14–15, 8.26, 8.31, 8.37, 10.6) or "limits" (8.26, 8.31, 8.42, 8.49, 10.7) and often both concepts in tandem, such as "the limits of great bonds," or "the bonds of the limit." These images are alternately associated with the three goddesses "Justice," "Necessity," and "Fate," which either hold the respective object of discourse down or bind it, as if to secure it against escaping or being altered[588] (see 8.13–14, 8.30–31, and 8.37–38). Obviously, if the IS for thinking were allowed to become otherwise than it is, it would elude reasoning. This general idea we find emulated by Plato, who speaks of the need to tie "true opinion" to the mind by raising it to knowledge.[589] Plato laments that "true opinion," while being generally beneficial and worth striving for, nonetheless has the tendency to flee all too quickly from a person's mind. To prevent this, one has to tie it down by finding the reason for why something is as it is, that is, by apprehending the governing principles beyond the things, or as Guthrie put it, "the logical reason for a necessary consequence."[590] By

---

587 Echoing 7.5, **Mansfeld** [455] characterizes the *elenchos* (disproof) as a "separation by logos," *Offenbarung* 43.

588 Cf. **Vlastos** [728]:"We know that in Parmenides *Ananke* and *Dike* perform the same function of holding Being fast 'in the bonds of the limit.' We may thus infer that 'mighty oath' in Empedocles, like 'strong *Ananke*' in Parmenides, alludes to the orderliness of existence conceived under the aspect of justice." ('Equality and Justice in Early Greek Cosmologies,' *Studies in Greek Philosophy*, vol. 1, 63) See also **Mourelatos** [480] "many-faced" divinity (Mourelatos recognizes four divine forces, including "Persuasion") and its bonds or shackles, *Route* 25–29, 160.

589 **Plato**, *Meno* 97d–98a. I believe that Plato may have Parmenides' distinction between *ta dokounta* and *dokimos* in the back of his mind (1.31–32) when he contrasts "true opinion" with "knowledge." If so, it also seems that he understood the possibility of converting the former to the latter, much like Parmenides' Goddess indicates.

590 **Guthrie** [43] *HGP* 4.261.

Delimiting the Object of Judgment

understanding the why or the principles that apply, "true opinion" turns into knowledge, and knowledge perseveres. As Plato concludes, what makes knowledge more valuable is that it is secured in such fashion, in other words, it is "hardwired" to the mind. As we can see, this analogy is undoubtedly Parmenidean. Parmenides attributed a similar inescapable linkage between thinking and the IS known by it—provided the intellect followed strictly its own rules, that is, the rules that govern it and its very own objects.

For the rest of this chapter, I shall attempt to present a condensed overview of these guidelines or provisos, put in place not only with the intent of defending the integrity of the object of discourse but also to assure the reliability of the method used in such defense.[591] Thus, before we turn to the methods themselves—taken up in the next chapter—we must acquaint ourselves briefly with each one of these points. Together they provide the methods with a well-defined field to operate within. Some of these restrictions we have already met, so here and there we may revisit familiar ground. However, it is best to view them together, or as a whole. One may consider them to be the pillars on which Parmenides' doctrine rests—this is, if you will, the essential Parmenides.

---

591 On the necessary correspondence between object and method, **Deichgräber** [303] remarks: "Method and the concept of IS (*Seinsbegriff*) are not separable." (*Parmenides' Auffahrt* 676) Cf. **Cordero** [279] *By Being, It Is* 181, (forthcoming). See also Proviso 5, below.

TWELVE PROVISOS FOR THE EVIDENTIAL ACCOUNT

GENERAL GUIDELINE:

When investigating or creating an account, the elements used must be provable as being consistent or in agreement with each other, as well as with the overall object at issue. The guiding principle is Like according to Like—that is, *correspondence, agreeability, commensurateness*. If any element or part violates this principle then the integrity of the formula we are after is compromised and the reliability of the whole account is called into question. The account may still be plausible, but it is disproved as being *certain*.

PROVISO 1:

The method of inquiry is for thinking and speaking (fr.2).

In other words, the examination is to be performed by purely rational/discursive means—reasoning expressed as a chain of arguments. As Kahn points out, this is not "*thinking* in some vague psychological sense," but *cognitive reasoning*.[592] It is reason's unempirical approach for testing or demonstrating the validity, meaning, and *consistency* of its objects and statements (2.1–8).

PROVISO 2:

There are *two* ways of giving an account: one reliable/evidential, the other deceptive/plausible (fr. 8.50–52, 8.60).

The evidential one corresponds to reason's independent way of achieving validation and certitude, that is, it expresses the IS. The other may aim for the same, but it is dependent upon the input of sense-perception for support or validation. Accordingly, the latter is only as accurate as the information it receives—and

---

592 Kahn [395] 'The Thesis of Parmenides' 712.

much of this information can contradict itself. Therefore, it is deemed a Deceptive Order of Words, or a Plausible Ordering.

PROVISO 3:

One must learn both the reliable/evidential and the deceptive/plausible way of ordering words (frs. 1.28–32, 8.60–61).

One must recognize which approach is which, or know which to avoid. This allows us not to be fooled when the latter masquerades as the former. It may, after all, appear quite credible (8.60)—if left unchecked (1.31–32) (in other words, if *ta dokounta*, "the things of opinion," are not tested to the point of being confirmed as genuine, *dokimos*).

PROVISO 4:

What is reliable/evidential is entirely agreeable—thus *persuasive*—because all the things that can be said about it correspond with each other (fr. 8).

See the above general guideline on Like according to Like, that is, the result is an agreeable whole if all its "landmarks" or characteristics confirm each other—without ever negating or contradicting each other or the whole—meaning, without becoming *unlike* each other or the whole. In short, the essential unity of formula is attained.

PROVISO 5:

Not only must the characteristics of a thing be consistent with each other—that is, compatible, corresponding, of the same kind—but the method for testing this must also be consistent with these characteristics. Thus, the object of an inquiry must be examined by means that do justice to its formula, and ultimately, its nature (frs. 4, 7.3–6).

This again is conform to the general principle of correspondence, that is, Like according to Like. Thus, the means that depend on sensory input—eye, ear, and so on—must not be brought in when judging what IS of reason alone. One should not mix methods or objects (7.3–6). This is reiterated by fragment 4, which urges us to always give *preference* to the method that is independent of empirical validation, if a thing's IS or *esti* is our aim. This applies also to the things of sense-experience, if certainty is at stake. We have no choice but to view *all things* from reason's perspective if we aim to secure what is stable or reliable about them. When viewed through the senses, the same things may appear different from when they are viewed by reason (4.1–4). Also, the senses can be separated from their object, that is, the eye may go blind, the ear become undiscerning (7.4). However, reason and its object—the "that which is there to be thought"—are inseparable (3, 6.1, 8.34–37).

PROVISO 6:

Ultimately, for the object of discourse to be accepted as reliably proved, the test it must withstand is *disproof* (fr. 7.5, 8.3–11, 8.19–20).

For an account to be made immune against disproof, its object has to pass such a test. While Parmenides had an early notion of the Law of the Excluded Third, he did not have a modern understanding of it. He applied it in a sense that did not allow uncertainty, conditionality, and other-dependency for the object of the Evidential Account. He did not like half-measures. Thus, his grasp of the principle might be formulated as follows: "What can be proved, *must* be proved; what can be disproved, *must* be disproved." If the object was not subjected to disproof, the ordering of its landmarks—even if it obeyed Like according to Like absolutely—remained nonetheless only a proposition, a hypothesis. Thus, the object of inquiry had to be tested both ways: assertively or positively, and also in the reverse, negatively or whether it was "otherwise than it is." If it passed the latter, then what was originally positively asserted or claimed could be accepted as confirmed (*dokimos*). This process of "IS*ing* and IS-NOT*ing*" the object of inquiry—if I may turn these concepts into verbs—made a great impression upon Plato, and much of his logical examinations are patterned after it (see some of the argument in the *Sophist* and above all the hypotheses of the *Parmenides*).

PROVISO 7:

One cannot know What IS NOT, neither through thinking nor speaking (fr. 2.7–8).

It follows then, that What IS NOT cannot be expressed by either account, meaning that it is not enough of a factor or constituent in anything to be expressible as a "something," not even by the most Deceptive Ordering of Words (9.4). Thus, it plays no role in Doxa's system, as all its things are composed only according to the formulas of Light and Night, excluding Nothingness (9.4). In short, there is no formula for What IS NOT, and no formula can be modified enough to reflect it. (However, two mutually excluding formulas can result in What IS NOT if pitted against each other in their entirety, meaning point by point. The outcome is no formula at all, hence What IS NOT.[593])

PROVISO 8:

What is self-refuting lacks the IS. Lacking the IS, it is just IS NOT (fr. 8.9–11, 8.20, 8.33).

Thinking or speaking cannot express a self-refutation in an objectified form. While we may form the words, we are not conveying anything—think of Meinong's/Russell's "round-square." Or, if IS NOT is "predicateless," and "predicateless" is a predicate, then IS NOT is not even "predicateless"—this is McKirahan's example. He concludes that IS NOT is unintelligible because noth-

---

[593] Doxa's saving grace must be that no thing is composed of each and every characteristic of Light and Night, and that in equal measure. The result would be equivalent to being in every conceivable way a "round-square."

ing can be meaningfully asserted *or denied*.[594] However, to have nothing be assertable or deniable, denotes just as much the unintelligible, as to have everything—or the same thing—be assertable *and* deniable, as in the case of contradiction. But what is contradictory must be proven or *judged* as self-refuting, otherwise it is conceived as it appears to mortals: for example, they hold that "to be and not to be are the same and not the same" (6.8), without ever noticing the contradiction.[595] Why? Because they have not exercised judgment (6.7). And barring that, there is certainly nothing "there" to be picked up by their senses. Thus, without a discernible/expressible IS, there is simply nothing available for naming (6.1–2, 8.16–18), hence, there is no object of thought and speech (2.7–8, 7.1, 8.7–9, 8.35–36), and consequently no object of judgment.

PROVISO 9:

As nothing else is available for naming, it is "that which IS for thinking" that ends up being named *all things* or *names* thought up by mortals as being appropriate or true (fr. 8.38–41) But mortals believe that they are naming everything in accordance with the *sensory* impressions they have of things—i.e., conform to the contradictory characteristics of "Light" and "Night" (8.55–59, 9.1–2, 19.1–4)—instead of recognizing that a unity in naming would be necessary to express the IS of things. (8.53–54)

Conformity in naming is the crux of the problem, which also depends upon what ordering of words one chooses. The difference between a true unified formula and a tentative or superficial one, is determined largely by how the question of ordering is approached. This is why distinguishing between an evidential way

---

594 **McKirahan** [67] *PBS* 162. He also makes the following remark: "If nothing is true of the nonexistent, it is not even true that it does not exist." This is typical of the kind of paradoxes Parmenides' IS NOT generates, and explains why I feel justified to equate it with self-refutation or contradiction, and not with "nothingness" or "not-being," not to mention "void."

595 Regarding the mortals of the same passage (6.7–9), **McKirahan** [67] makes a similar observation, stating that they are unable to tell that they are following the unintelligible (*PBS* 164).

of doing so (8.50) and a merely plausible way (8.60) is necessary. Furthermore, the sheer fact that "that which IS NOT" is not nameable, expressible, or knowable is also a factor that gives us absolute certainty in proving—albeit a negative one.

PROVISO 10:

The construction and/or examination of an Evidential Account is an exercise in separation of concepts or designations (i.e., landmarks) that prevent the integral unity of such Account. It follows the Principle of Like according to Like and avoids contradiction (fr. 8).

The Evidential Account in fragment 8 demonstrates the separation of what is *like* the IS for thinking (the characteristics that delimit the object and equivalent of reason) from what is *unlike* it (i.e., the characteristics of the objects of sense-experience). It shows that if one includes or mixes some of the latter with the former, *and tests the conclusions or consequences which ensue for both,* contradictions will be made apparent. (See, for example, the contradictions that are generated by having What IS come about from What IS NOT [8.8–10].) Essentially, what is being cleansed in fragment 8 is the formula of the IS, by exposing and removing from it those characteristics that contravene its unity.

PROVISO 11:

Accordingly, the *measure* of an Evidential Account is this: *it is the same where one begins—when embarking on one—because to that point one will return again* **(fr. 5.1–2; possibly 6.9).**

This is the standard of calibration that reasoning must implement for its deductions, and it is also applicable to any account that expresses a true state of affairs. Proving must orient itself according to the original premise, if only to return to it and find it still valid and true. If that is the case, then it was successful. And the reverse is true of any method of disproof: if it was effective, then the original premise has been destroyed. Consequently, the only way to test whether there is a "heart of truth" in the approximative mix that is the Plausible/Deceptive Ordering of Words is to reduce it either to a "that which IS" or a "that which IS NOT" (8.15–16)—a self-refutation. If something survives, then that is a "that which IS"—or the "heart"—as opposed to "that which IS NOT," which, by being exposed as contradictory, eliminates itself. Only then is certainty restored (1.31–32).

PROVISO 12:

When the two, *like* and *unlike*, are expressed as *one* account, a mix of two unlikes results: thus, we have *opinion*.

Technically, opinion is any mix of the incongruous, be it a mix of the characteristics of the object of reason with those of sense-experience—as critiqued in fragment 8—or a combination of the basic yet opposing elements that are contained in the formulas of the objects of sense-experience, for example, Light and Night and their derivatives: hot and cold, light and heavy, dense and rare, and so forth (8.57–59). Either way, mortals, being untrained in or ignorant of how to manage the objects of reason, habitually regard both thought-objects and world-objects as unions of opposites. However, their explanations only amount to a Deceptive Ordering of Words—which may be plausible at best because it attempts to express the Unlike as being Like, in other words, as a conglomerate of "agreeable incompatibles" (8.53–59, 9.1–4, 12.1–6, 16.1–4). Essentially, Doxa is an attempt to reconcile the Like and the Unlike—which is of course the Unlike with the Unlike—by considering both as being like and unlike at the same time, that is, "the same and not the same." But a forced reconciliation of incompatibles is not a true unity.

CHAPTER IX

Methods of Proof and Disproof

LIKE ACCORDING TO LIKE

> The majority of general views about sensation are two: some make it of like by like, others of opposite by opposite. Parmenides, Empedocles and Plato say it is of like by like, the followers of Anaxagoras and of Heraclitus of opposite by opposite.
> —Theophrastus[596]

The Way of the Daemon

Why does Parmenides resort to an anonymous deity for the demonstration of his methods? Why did he not perform his exercises as himself—just by simply showing us how to organize a Reliable/Evidential Account? An answer may be found in a function carried out by the Goddess that originally was thought to be uniquely divine—unique, that is, until magistrates or judges were charged to perform the same within a court of law—and that is, to right what was wronged by reestablishing *dike* or justice. When Parmenides mentions the deity for the first time, he does so in connection with her "much-knowledge-imparting" road, which he calls the "way of the *daimonos*," and not of "*thea*" or "goddess" (1.3). Originally, the concept of *daimon* had not much to do with its modern, utterly corrupted counterpart "demon," denoting an evil spirit or devil.[597] (In literature, the former is

---

 596 **Theophrastus**, *De Sensibus* 1 (**DK** 28A46); trans. **KRS** [39] 261.

 597 According to **Burkert** [701], it was Plato's pupil Xenocrates, along with Plato to a certain degree, who were responsible for this negative take on *daemon*. (Cf. *Greek Religion* 179, 332–333.) For some examples of **Plato**'s use of the term—and its various translations as "guarding," "guiding," or "tutelary spirit," as well as "guardian angel" and "genius"—see *Phaedo* 107d; *Republic* X.617d–e, 620d–e; *Timaeus* 90a–c; *Laws* 732c, 877a. Cf. also **Dodds** [703] on the three types of *daemon* (*The Greeks and the Irrational* 40–43) and on the occasional practice (as exemplified by the *Iliad* and *Odyssey*) of attributing divine monition or intervention to a

often written as *daemon* to differentiate it from the latter.) It meant "god," "goddess," or any individual "deity" or "divine being." Even though such entities represented the quintessential invisible divine force—or as Burkert remarked, "the veiled countenance of divine activity"[598]—some Pythagoreans claimed for themselves the ability to actually see these supernatural beings, and acted surprised if no one else could.[599] The term *daimon* however is rooted in "to divide," "to apportion," or "to distribute"; thus, a *daimon* was a "divider of things" and sometimes a "distributer" of what was partitioned.[600] *Daimones* dispensed destinies or individual fates, sometimes wealth, and also punishment and retribution, particularly when the crime was against the set order of things. Such an act was a "transgression" in the original sense of the word, i.e. an act of "going over prescribed bounds," thus a violation of divinely allotted "borders" or "limits."[601] Considering these unique divine functions, we may better appreciate why Parmenides is compelled to call upon an unnamed *daimon* to perform the godly act of separation and redistribution of that which was unduly mixed by ignorant mortals. These are, as it turns out, the landmarks or characteristics of the IS, the way and object of reason, which have been almost irreparably blended with the characteristics of the objects of sense-experience, and it takes a divine act to draw the boundaries anew, to reapportion what belongs to what, and what is *like* in accordance to *like*. (This is one more proof of the indispensability of Doxa.) And so fragment 8 is nothing but a record of this divine interference, the act of separating the landmarks of the "what there IS for thinking" from the "what there is for experiencing or perceiving," as in "what there is to have opinions about." By giving the IS its due share—as she "cleans up"

---

nameless or anonymous *daemon*, rather than to a specific anthropomorphic deity (11–13, 40–41). See **Cornford** [21], for four types of *daemon*. (*From Religion to Philosophy* 100) Cf. Cornford's general discussion of the subject (35–39, 95–100). **Gigon** [40] speculates that the "Daemonology," which played such a great role in the old Academy, may have had its beginning in Parmenides' Doxa (*Ursprung* 282).

598 **Burkert** [701] *Greek Religion* 180.
599 **Aristotle**, fr. 193.
600 Cf. **Palmer** [722] 'The Indo-European Origins of Greek Justice' 166–167; **Dodds** [703] *The Greeks and the Irrational*, 23n65; **Mansfeld** [455] *Offenbarung* 265–266; **Burkert** [701] *Greek Religion* 180, 420n3. See also **Cornford** [21] on *Moira's* or Fate's role in partitioning lots among gods and men, meaning "allotted portion," or "part"—even "status" (*From Religion to Philosophy* 15–17). (Incidentally, **Loew** [441] postulates a categorical distinction between the goddesses of Aletheia and the divinities of Doxa—only the latter are characterized by him as *daimones*. [Cf. 'Die Götterwesen bei Parmenides' 620–624.] I disagree, see fr. 1.2.)

601 Cf. **Palmer** [722] 'The Indo-European Origins of Greek Justice' 166–168; **Mansfeld** [455] *Offenbarung* 265–266. Furthermore, cf. **Cornford** [21] on the "moral frontier" or "boundaries of moralities" of a society (*From Religion to Philosophy* 59).

Aiming for Conceptual Correspondence

the corresponding landmarks which state it as it is—the Goddess does justice or *dike* to the IS in the original sense of the word: she restores to the IS its designative limits, that is, she *re-landmarks* it until its internal unity and integrity are fully manifested. At that point, the complete restitution of both integrity and limit—which, obviously, go hand in hand—is underscored by an analogy that at first seems peculiar yet ultimately is very fitting, namely, the image of a perfect sphere. Here are the considerations that accompany this simile, which also signal the culmination of the process, meaning the conclusion of the Reliable/Evidential Account:

8.42 But since there is an ultimate limit, it is complete,
8.43 from every side well-rounded, like the bulk [or, fullness] of a sphere,
8.44 equal in every way from the center: for it must be neither more
8.45 nor less, [whether] here or there;
8.46 for neither is there What IS NOT, which might stop it from arriving at
8.47 its like; nor is What IS such that it might be
8.48 more here and less there than What IS, since it all IS, inviolate;
8.49 for equal to itself on all sides, it meets its limits uniformly.

What better words than these to describe how both "unity" and "limit" complement each other, and how in the end they are indispensable for securing the equally "well-rounded" heart of truth (1.29)? Yet the decisive factor in all of this is the discriminating method employed by the Goddess in her quest for reliable discourse. By learning this "well-landmarked solitary way" (8.1–2) we realize that—in true Parmenidean fashion—we have been brought full circle back to the *daimon's* "much-informing road" announced at the start of the Poem,[602] and we too can be individuals "who know." (1.3) What is there to be known? How things can be properly distinguished, ordered, or made to fit so that they can be expressed *reliably*.

Aiming for Conceptual Correspondence

In this sense, the Principle of Like according to Like must remain the indispensable golden thread that prevails throughout the whole Poem, displaying the Goddess' touch, her separating guidelines—regardless of whether we are dealing with the Evidential Account or Doxa. While Theophrastus (c. 371–c. 287 B.C., a pupil of Aristotle to whom we owe fragment

---

602 The idea that the two ways are one and the same was suggested by **Lan** [423] 'Die ΟΔΟΣ ΠΟΛΥΦΗΜΟΣ der Parmenideischen Wahrheit' 376–379; and **Cordero** [279] *By Being, It Is* 28, 199, (forthcoming).

16 and the motto of this chapter) correctly observes that Parmenides adheres to Like by Like in his theory of perception, it is wrong to conclude that it applies only to Doxa.[603] In fact, the principle is so indispensable to the Eleatic approach that Parmenides cannot allow even the Plausible Ordering to be absolutely baseless, otherwise it would be neither plausible nor ordered. As we can see that it is governed, we can realize that it is *governable*; the same, obviously, cannot be said of What IS NOT, for which Like according to Like is irrelevant. Thus, even if Doxa does not allow Parmenides to attain the same fidelity as the Evidential Account—nor obviously, does he willfully pursue the untruth—he at least aims for *equivalence*—if only, perhaps, as a substitute for total unity. Equivalence, it seems, is the closest thing for him to genuine truth in this world, and it provides his system with an overall rationale. This is also noticed by Gregory Vlastos who addresses what he calls "the deductive system which is Parmenides' norm of truth." Vlastos explains: "In such a system (to use the language of a later logic), every proposition expresses an equivalence, and every difference masks an identity."[604]

What makes the Mortal Account plausible as an ordering is precisely the arrangement of things according to their affinities for each other, in other words, hot belongs to the hot, and cold to the cold. In fragment 16 we see that human thought is determined in the same way; what counts is a preponderance of one basic element over the other. As Theophrastus understands Parmenides, human thought varies according to whether the hot or the cold prevails, meaning Light or Night. This basic law also applies to perception; this is demonstrated by Theophrastus' other comment regarding Parmenides' theory that a corpse cannot perceive light, heat, or sound because of its own deficiency of fire, which, however, does not hinder it

---

603 I fully agree with **Finkelberg**'s [318] observations: "Our examination of the implications of the principle of cognition of like by like within the framework of the general Parmenidean doctrine leads to the conclusion that it is not merely a doctrine about the nature of perception, as it was taken by Theophrastus and is usually understood by modern scholars, rather, it constitutes the basis of the entire Parmenidean teaching: the Parmenidean dualism arises from it and it is on the basis of this principle that the dichotomy is resolved." ('Like by Like and the Two Reflections of Reality in Parmenides' 408) See also **Reinhardt** [520] who concludes that Parmenides must be the originator of the "Like is recognizable by Like" reasoning, because as a theory, it cannot be older than the concept of mixture. And Reinhardt considers Parmenides as the first one to raise mixture to a bona fide principle, a need born out of his rigorous, anti-empirical logic (*Parmenides* 73–76). It is also noted by **Hölscher** [379] that before Parmenides there were teachings neither about mixture, nor about opposites (*Parmenides* 108). Further comments on fr. 16, Like by Like and mixture, cf. **Verdenius** [585] *Parmenides* 14–27.

604 **Vlastos** [728] 'Equality and Justice in Early Greek Cosmologies,' *Studies in Greek Philosophy*, vol. 1, 66.

from perceiving the contraries of fire, in other words, cold, silence, darkness, and so on.[605]

What is also important in this context is Theophrastus' brief remark that, according to Parmenides, "everything that exists has some measure of knowledge." In other words, if Like is known by Like, then not only will the preponderance of one element over another in a mix affect human thought and its affinities (e.g., "dark" thoughts will have a bias toward dark things), but also the things themselves will "know" those things that have a similar or corresponding composition. In this sense, the cold and dead eye will "know" cold and dead things. This correlation between knowledge and perception, which is characteristic for the Deceptive Ordering of Words, we find underscored by Aristotle in his commentaries on older thinkers, hence he often cites Empedocles, who, as we know, was strongly influenced by Parmenides.[606] Thus, we find Empedocles saying:

For by earth we see earth, by water, water,
by aither, divine aither, by fire, destructive fire....[607]

Another example of Empedocles' Like according to Like orientation can be found in the following verses:

Thus sweet catches hold of sweet, bitter rushes towards bitter,
sour goes to sour and hot rides upon hot.[608]

It is remarkable that even though Parmenides completely dismisses sense-experience as a means of inquiry germane to the Evidential Account, in the Doxa, the rational Principle of Like according to Like is nonetheless preserved. This suggests, in light of the preference he gives to the Evidential Account as well as to its noetic object (see fr. 4), that the idea of an ordering according to Like is inherent to it, and that it is, if you will, only lent to the Doxa as a guideline by which common yet untested opinion (*ta dokounta*, 1.31) can be arranged acceptably/reliably (*dokimos*, 1.32), that is, as plausible as possible (8.60). (Of course, if they pass the Test of Disproof [7.5, 8.6–11, 8.19–20] they can be considered evidential or genuine, i.e., truly *dokimos*.)

---

605   **Theophrastus**, *De Sensibus* 1.3 (**DK** 28A46).
606   **Aristotle**, *On the Soul* 409b25–410a2, 427a20–427b5; *Metaphysics* 1009b13–25.
607   **Empedocles**, **DK** 31B109 (trans. **McKirahan** [67] *PBS* 250).
608   **Empedocles**, **DK** 31B90 (trans. **McKirahan** [67] *PBS* 250).

A Unity of Corresponding Landmarks

If there is no reliance upon sense-experience for the Evidential Account, what then may be ordered according to the Principle of Like to Like? The answer, as we have seen, is the so-called landmarks or signs of the object of inquiry. Parmenides makes use of these to demonstrate that whenever we express a particular attribute or characteristic regarding an object that is being judged, corresponding attributes *must* follow if our account of it is to be deemed reliable.[609] Thus, Parmenides takes advantage of the mind's propensity to identify or classify things, yet in a purely abstract or logical context, as we would say today; a milestone in the history of philosophy. Interestingly, there is a force at work here, often referred to by Parmenides as necessity, that compels all distinctions (or features) of an object of reason to be agreeable, hence *like*. This appeal is also indicated in this statement: "For what IS *draws close* to what IS" (8.25).

Parmenides proves that once we have established a distinctive attribute for an object of discourse—meaning, once we have *said* something about it, such as that "it is *present* "—a certain order of distinctions must follow that relate to what we have said in a *like* manner—namely, "if it is present, it *cannot be absent*" (fr. 4). Another example would be that if "it" is "ungenerated," "it" is also "imperishable" (8.3, 8.21). Why? Because the same "factor" that determines "it" as ungenerated *by necessity* requires "it" to be equally imperishable. In other words, to be ungenerated is *like* being imperishable, an equilibrium that for Parmenides signifies fairness or justness.

---

609 This requirement is all too often ignored in interpretation. While many scholars refer to the *semata* (landmarks) as "attributes" (e.g., **McKirahan** [67] *PBS* 166; **Gallop** [340] *Parmenides* 12) or "characteristics" (**Curd** [297] *Legacy* 75) and "predicates" (e.g., **Coxon** [290] *Fragments* 193), what is frequently not emphasized is that each of these landmarks needs to be grouped exclusively with kindred landmarks, meaning only landmarks that do not initiate contradiction. (**Curd** [297] belongs to the exceptions, stating that "characteristics are explored that are *consistent* with the route" [*Legacy* 75, emphasis added].) However, that is precisely the indicator of what constitutes proof: whether we have distilled the subsequent landmarks as being *agreeable*—i.e., not mutually negating. If we have, our construct stands and the object of discourse is expressed as consistent with reason. However, if we have picked an unsuitable signpost or landmark, our account is reduced to the self-refuting or absurd. Thus, we are dealing here with an exercise in identity or Like to Like, and not mere attribution, let alone, the rebuttal of Heraclitus. I favor **Mourelatos**' [480] approach, which views the landmarks as intrinsically linked to proofs, not merely as names, but as an outline of a program (*Route* 94–95). On the *semata* as proofs, see also **Cordero** [279] *By Being, It Is* 28, 180–182, 201 (forthcoming). (Cf. also **Deichgräber** [303] *Parmenides' Auffahrt* 676–677, 676n1 on method.) (On landmarks as a program, see also **Owen** [496] 'Eleatic Questions' 93, 97, 101; and **Gallop** [340] *Parmenides* 12–13. As a "table of contents," see **McKirahan** [67] *PBS* 166. However, it is a table of non-contradictory or compatible contents.)

Accordingly, the goddess of justice is put in charge of such affairs as coming-to-be or perishing, allowing neither option for the IS by "holding it fast" (8.13–14).

What is true of "ungenerated" and "imperishable" is also true for the rest of the landmarks. They also can be derived from each other or have each other as consequences. What Parmenides demonstrates is that the landmarks of his object of discourse all belong to the same class of concepts—the implied oneness in formula. Naturally, the overriding category is provided by the object of discourse itself, the IS. Moreover, the landmarks can be proven by the same agency, reason, and can all be subjected to the very same methods. And they are contradicted by the same *unlike* assemblage of distinctions that mark the objects of experience. Thus, we are dealing here with a dichotomy of two opposing Likes, the Like for reason and the Like for sense-experience, which can be ordered as two separate formulas:

The Like Landmarks for the Objects of Reason:	The Like Landmarks for the Objects of Sense-Experience:
ungenerated	generated
imperishable	perishable
whole	part
of one kind	of many kinds
immovable, changeless	movable, changeable
complete, not lacking	incomplete, lacking
now all together	never all together now, but in the future and/or past
one	more or less than one
continuous	discontinuous, intermittent

We can see the correspondence each landmark has with the rest of its group. To recognize this fittingness is to recognize the necessity that guides thinking to group things on an "either/or" basis: its own objects (or their landmarks) *either* belong together, *or* they do not—in which case they are not its objects. However, the same uncompromising "either/or" approach cannot be used with the objects of sense-experience. Even though their landmarks seem the exact opposite of those of the objects of reason, in reality the objects of sense-experience can as themselves have contradicting characteristics, thus their landmarks can belong to Light as well as to Night. Such composite things may appear to adopt even the landmarks of the objects of reason, while still displaying those of sense-experience. A changing thing may seem changeless, or a moving thing unmoving. It may seem one while being many, or look complete and yet be incomplete. Thus, the object of sense-experience is both like and unlike itself, while a reliable object is never unlike itself.[610]

What Do Falling Millet Seeds Have in Common?

Keeping this in mind, the task of putting together a reliable formula or account is not a difficult one: what is "like" or "same" can be ordered with its "like" or "same." This constitutes a proof—a very simple one, but a proof no less. Whatever can be said of things or states of affairs must correspond and be consistent in order to be accurate and true. Once we recognize the pattern, whatever does not fit the ordering is revealed as unsuitable, because it is Unlike. It distorts or misrepresents the accepted ordering and consequently the rest of the Like. To uncover it, we must use other methods—methods that do not just prove consistency as in Like according to Like, but that have the capacity to reveal a hidden Unlike. The goal is to isolate the unfitting, incongruent, or incompatible. Thus, the methods of disproof favored by the Eleatics feast on the Unlike. A good example is Zeno's "Millet Seed" argument:

Zeno: "Tell me, Protagoras, does a single millet seed make a noise when it falls, or one ten-thousandth of a millet seed?"
Protagoras: "No."
Zeno: "Does a bushel of millet seeds make a noise when it falls, or doesn't it?"
Protagoras: "It does."
Zeno: "But isn't there a ratio between the bushel of millet seeds and one millet seed, or one ten-thousandth of a millet seed?"
Protagoras: "Yes there is."
Zeno: "So won't there be the same ratios of their sounds to one another? For

---

610 Applying Like or Unlike to What IS NOT is pointless: there is nothing there, no landmarks or objects of any kind. Thus, What IS NOT is not *like* anything in both categories above, e.g., it is *neither* ungenerated *nor* generated. And what is in all respects *neither* Like *nor* Unlike cannot be expressed. **Plato** recognized this, as shown by the First Hypothesis of the *Parmenides* dialogue: "It will be neither like nor unlike anything, either itself or another" (139e, see also 140a–b). Hence: "No name belongs to it, nor is there an account or any knowledge or perception or opinion of it. . . . Therefore it is not named or spoken of, nor is it the object of opinion or knowledge, nor does anything that is perceive it." (142a) This matches Parmenides, and it reflects his insistence that What IS NOT is unnameable and inexpressible (2.7–8, 6.1–2, 8.17). Without landmarks or characteristics nothing can be organized into a formula or account—not even an erroneous one. This detail is commonly overlooked by interpreters who equate Doxa with What IS NOT. But "neither/nor" does not apply to Doxa; it only applies to What IS NOT—in fact, it is the only thing that can be accurately said of What IS NOT.

> as the things that make the noise <are to one another>, so are the noises <to one another>. But since this is so, if the bushel of millet seeds makes a noise, so will a single millet seed and one ten-thousandth of a millet seed."[611]

In our context, Zeno likens the fall of millet seeds with the noise they make, observing that while sound and the fall of a bushel of millet seeds are items that belong together, the fall of a single one does not belong, because no sound can be heard. Zeno specifically addresses what he calls the "same ratios" that must exist between a bushel and a single millet seed. Thus, the question that is implied is as simple as it is devastating: how many millet seeds does it take for millet seeds to become *unlike* millet seeds? In other words, how can sameness be lost if we are only dealing with the very same thing, in this case, millet seeds—without introducing extraneous factors?

These are important questions, the kind that spawned the discipline of logic. Yet Zeno's example seems not quite proper because it also introduces sense-perception, in this case "hearing," as one of its main criteria. And sense-perception does not produce reliable results, or at least, not the kind that logic demands. Thus, the fault does not lie with the millet seeds—they do not actually become unlike themselves. It is only our senses that make them appear that way. Nonetheless, we can use this approach as a starting point from which to check for further inconsistencies in reasoning.

In a nutshell, early attempts to prove what a thing was focused on securing its like. That is, to establish those factors that, by belonging together, reveal a thing's essential nature, and thus define or delimit it. Naturally, what did not correspond or belong had to be brought out and eliminated. Because Parmenides' object of discourse was not one of sense-experience, all he had to work with was conceptual correspondence, that is, whether a given concept in an ordering of concepts matched the rest of the ordering or whether it distorted or repudiated it. It seems that Parmenides wisely realized that a thing's true nature cannot be considered as proven until everything that might contravene or misrepresent this nature was purged from the account. Hence, proof had to go hand in hand with disproof, as the next section will show.[612]

---

611 **Simplicius**, *Commentary on Aristotle's Physics* 1108.18–25 (**DK** 29A29), trans. **McKirahan, Curd** [24] (ed.), *A Presocratics Reader* 77.

612 Cf. **Austin** [202]: "For Parmenides to prove is to negate." ('Parmenides, Double-Negation, and Dialectic' 99)

SUFFICIENT REASON, CONTRADICTION, AND INFINITE REGRESS

> Our reasoning is founded on two great principles: The first is the principle of *contradiction*, by virtue of which we consider as false what implies a contradiction and as true what is the opposite of the contradictory or false.
> The second is the principle of *sufficient reason*, in virtue of which we hold that no fact can be true or existing and no statement truthful without a sufficient reason for its being so and not different. (Emphasis added.)
> —Gottfried Wilhelm Leibniz, *Monadology* #31 and #32[613]

Right from the start of Parmenides' fragment 8, where the bulk of his methods are preserved, it is quite obvious what kind of examination the Goddess alluded to in fragment 7, the so-called "much-contested disproof" to be judged exclusively by reasoning. As the grouping of *corresponding* landmarks (*semata*) beginning in 8.3 suggests—see the previous section—her method of testing the account of the IS relies on the ordering of its characteristics according to the Principle of Like according to Like. She shows us that concepts such as "ungenerated," "imperishable," "whole," "of one kind," "complete," and so forth not only belong together, but most importantly—because they create a coherent category—they exclude the possibility of contradiction. In contrast, the mishmash of expressions used by mortals to describe the makeup of their sensible world cannot achieve the same coherency, and accordingly, their explanations are not conducive to conveying reliable truths.

Language itself—or in a Parmenidean sense, the *way we are ordering our words*—can be a serious impediment if we aim to secure *non-contradictory conclusions*. As a way out of this dilemma, Parmenides offers techniques for us to use in our reasoning process that help to disentangle some of its notions by stripping away what is incompatible, contradictory, or self-refuting. Incidentally, such a *technical* approach to thought and discourse was absolutely unprecedented, which is why Parmenides should be considered the first true philosopher. With fragment 8, he demonstrates that we must separate the true landmarks of the IS from all those other landmarks that

---

613 **Leibniz** [684] *Monadology and Other Philosophical Essays* (trans. **Schrecker** and **Schrecker**) 153.

would turn it into its own refutation, that is, into what *it* IS NOT.[614] Thus, he is trying to teach us how to unmix a mix of incompatible concepts. As we have already seen, such a mix for the IS constitutes an ordering of words that make it appear both *like* and *unlike* itself. Thus, everything about Parmenides' approach has to do with disentanglement.[615] That is his number one strategy, and, conceivably, his response to Xenophanes' challenge.

To put it bluntly, Parmenides recognized that even if the landmarks of the IS are mixed with the landmarks derived from sense-experience—"growing," "decaying," and so forth—this will not turn the IS into an object of the senses, but into its very own contradiction, ergo IS NOT. It was an astonishing observation of tremendous depth, an observation at the birth of logic and metaphysics whose consequences are still not entirely mapped out by modern philosophy.

Now, one may argue that if we are dealing exclusively with the IS for thinking, and not with an existential or cosmological understanding of it, then conversely the IS NOT of the Poem must also be the IS NOT for thinking. But would such an idea not clash with Parmenides' claim that What IS NOT is unthinkable and unutterable? No, it would not, as can be demonstrated if we take IS NOT as the reverse of what is *expressible*, in other words, as an approach that must lead to self-refutation. As I have suggested previously, if we expand Parmenides' analogy of the IS as the heart of persuasive truth, then we may also say that IS NOT is at the heart of every contradiction.

We should remember in this context fragment 2.5, where this negative approach is portrayed as the one that states something "as it IS NOT, and that it is necessary that it NOT BE"—as it is. Obviously, we cannot provide an accurate statement about something if we state it *as it is not*. Technically, in such a case, we have not expressed the IS of a thing, thus rendering it unintelligible—following Parmenides' dictum of 8.35–36: "For without What IS, in which it is expressed, you will not find thinking." Accordingly, we may just as well say: "For without *non-contradiction* you will not find thinking, because it cannot be expressed by means of contradiction." Thus, the reason why IS NOT cannot be thought out is certainly not because it is void or nothingness—as both are demonstrably thinkable—but because *What IS*

---

614 As **Capizzi** [252] observes, one cannot force What IS to "coexist" with opposing or negating predicates, i.e., with predicates which contradict it (*La Porta di Parmenide* 105).
615 This is also the determining factor in Doxa. However, as observed by **Mourelatos** [480] (*Route*, 221) the "decision, separation" on which Doxa is based is not radical enough.

does not allow itself to be expressed in the form of a contradiction, or by means of one.

This rule of the nonthinkability of IS NOT has broader consequences in Parmenides' mind, because it may also apply to concepts or statements that can—by a chain of reasoning—be *associated* with IS NOT and consequently become exposed as contradictions, concepts like "coming-to-be" and "passing-away." Clearly both notions, when applied to What IS, must necessitate an inconsistency that results in self-refutation, because they link the IS to the reverse of what it IS. And that is precisely what constitutes the so-called error of mortals: as they allow themselves to speak of perceptible things in contradictory arrangements of words, so will they speak about the object of thought as a contradictory thing. But when they do, they can never arrive at a definitive judgement. In short, they are liable to use a mix of landmarks that make the IS not only seem like a negation of itself, but as if it were both: that which IT IS *and* that which IT IS NOT. Or, as the Goddess puts it when speaking of the mortal outlook: "for whom to be and not to be are deemed the same and not the same" (6.8–9). Again, what better statement to describe contradiction as an illegitimate mix, one that is made up of the self-refuting or incongruous?

In the end, while IS NOT is unthinkable as an *object* in its own right, "it" seems thinkable enough for us to postulate "coming-to-be" from it. We can simply bookend a series of "becomings" with IS NOT—preferably at both ends—and not think about it further. In other words, we can claim that any sequence of things that are brought about by generation and growth must have initially begun in nothingness—which is not only an absence of generation and growth but also an absence of the things themselves. And just as easily we can claim that such a sequence eventually exhausts itself, thereby returning again to nothingness. Thus, it is quite possible for us to muse that existence erupted out of a void—by means of a Big Bang, for example—without having to worry about some preexisting cause. We do not have to account for what might have "lit the fuse" to an exploding universe, much less whether such a "fuse" would also constitute a nothingness, because, obviously, that is what precedes a somethingness. In fact, a number of modern physicists are seriously contemplating this "all from nothing" theory.[616] However, for Parmenides, considerations of this kind are ratio-

---

616 See **Kaku** [781] *Beyond Einstein: The Cosmic Quest for the Theory of the Universe* 189, who mentions theories that fascinate physicists, such as the entire universe being "created as a 'vacuum fluctuation,' a random quantum leap from the vacuum into a full-fledged universe." Kaku defines "nothing" as "pure space-time, without matter or energy," but he does not ex-

nally inconsistent, at least insofar as the object of thought is concerned. Perhaps it was all right for mortals to opine that "things have grown and now are, and then after growing up they will reach their end" (fr. 19), but excluding sense-experience, such an explanation violates certain laws of thinking—particularly if the object of contemplation is the IS.

In Parmenides' view, anyone advocating that What IS has suddenly sprung from What IS NOT is offering a Deceptive Ordering of Words, not an Evidential Account, because for What IS to pull this off, "becoming" is required and "becoming" belongs to Doxa (fr. 19). Thus if we associate the IS with "becoming" we are treating it as a sensible object and not an object of reason. Or as we might call it today, this is not advancing a logical claim but an existential/empirical one. And if our claim is existential, then what it implies is that there once was a time without What IS, which might just as well be saying that there once was a time without a *now*. In fact, we would have to say that there once was a time without past or present but only with future. But then we would have to accept that somehow, mysteriously, this peculiar—indeed unthinkable—circumstance has led to the creation of a first now, to be followed by a succession of nows, which eventually gave us the past, present, and future as we know it.

It is no wonder that subsequent philosophers, such as Aristotle, found these kinds of ideas intolerable, preferring instead to suppose an eternal universe, absorbed in eternal motion, effectuated by an eternal mover, in other words, God. Then, even if we are forced to concede that there once was a time without movement, and that everything must have had a beginning, with God we finally have an agency that can be exempted from such requirements. We may be willing to accept that there once was a now without the universe, if we can be assured that there *never* was a now without God.

Again, for the mind, an expressible construction—whatever that may be—is always preferable to the unexpressible or unthinkable, because only that which can be grasped as an object by thought can play a role in an explanation (see 6.1–2, 8.35–36, 38–41). And it is this particular function of reason that Parmenides seized upon. For better or worse, as long as what we say or think is consistent within itself, we have something to work with—be this in science, religion, politics, or a court of law.

---

plain what the qualifier "pure" stands for, or how *it* came about, nor does he tell how anything can be said to exist, much less come about, without a relation to something else. But I understand that these are problems of logic and not necessarily of physics.

While we may never know Parmenides' views on God or the universe, we do know his concerns regarding the *integrity* of discourse, as well as that of its object. To preserve it, Parmenides needed to *unmix* all those landmarks that would make the object of reason appear to be fused with the object of sense-experience, as only in regard to the latter could mortals have enough justification to believe that it was *both* being and not being (by being, for instance, hot and not hot, far and not far, etc.). What this meant for the IS for thinking was that it had to be divested of any kind of affiliation with what it was not, as well as any association with impressions derived from sense-experience, such as coming-to-be or passing-away. This certainly excluded any possible role for What IS NOT to be progenitor or final fate for What IS. But this was not all. In order to rule out coming-to-be as categorically as possible, if only to fulfill all that thinking required of the IS, Parmenides had to absolve it from *any and all* generation, meaning neither from *itself*, nor from some *other* IS, could it be said to have come. (How far he went, and whether all of these options are supported by the surviving verses, is a disputed subject among scholars.) I shall attempt, as far as it is possible, to reconstruct his overall refutation of generation.

One thing is certain: as Parmenides could not prove an ungenerated IS by empirical means, he had to attempt an *indirect*, hence, purely rational, approach. This fact alone defines precisely what kind of object we are dealing with in the Evidential Account, namely, an absolute object of thought. The rational IS should never under any circumstances be confused with an object of sense-experience. Thus, the technique of Indirect Proof, also known as *reductio ad absurdum*, is the nonempirical approach par excellence,[617] and the question of the IS being generated—whether from IS or IS NOT—addresses a purely rational dilemma. The problem is plain: can we really think of the IS—regardless of what we conceive it to be—as being truly capable of coming-to-be, without having to contradict ourselves? We may not be able to. (The same, of course, would also apply to perishing.)

To recognize that this dilemma lay at the core of thought, representing perhaps one of the most fundamental truths—or idiosyncracies—of the human mind, was without a doubt a great achievement for Parmenides. Considering the surefooted strategy he pursued, it is likely that he analyzed the ramifications of this phenomenon for quite some time before framing it as a poem. If only to ensure the intelligibility of his object—so critical in bringing about a correct judgment—Parmenides was forced to stack his argu-

---

617 Cf. **Szabó** [772] *Beginnings* 215, 218–219.

Sufficient Reason, Contradiction, and Infinite Regress 239

ments in ways that revealed any inherent or ensuing contradictions or absurdities. In any case, the verses in question are a pure philosophical masterpiece. Speaking of the IS, we have seen the Goddess first establishing its Like according to Like landmarks, which are then used as a backdrop for her logical refutations. Here again is the passage:

> 8.3 [...] What IS is ungenerated and imperishable;
> 8.4 whole, of one kind, unshakeable and complete.
> 8.5 Nor was it before, nor will it be, since it is now, all together,
> 8.6 one, continuous. For what origin would you seek for it?
> 8.7 How and whence did it grow? I will not permit you to say
> 8.8 or to think from What IS NOT; for it cannot be said or thought
> 8.9 that it IS NOT. What necessity would have impelled it
> 8.10 to grow later rather than earlier, if it began from nothing?
> 8.11 Thus it must either wholly be or not be.
> 8.12 Nor will the force of evidence ever allow [anything] to arise from What IS NOT, [to be]
> 8.13 alongside it. For this reason, Justice has not allowed it to come to be.[618]

Thus, after informing us of what it takes to be the IS—which is to have landmarks agreeable with nonempirical objects—Parmenides suddenly plays devil's advocate and asks what kind of birth we would seek for such an object (8.6). For Indirect Proof to work, we need to pretend that the reverse is true. Let's assume then that the IS is not an object of reason but one of sense-experience. As we are told by Parmenides, this kind of an object has grown and now is, and then after growing up will come to an end (19.1–2). Now, by adopting this qualifier for our test object, the setup for a reduction to the absurd—that is, the uncovering of the inherent contradiction in our assumption—is in place.[619] Furthermore, we can recognize two additional devices that may have assisted him in his disproof. These are known as Sufficient Reason and Infinite Regress. (Parmenides does not explicitly outline each one per se, but these strategies are evident and have been individually deduced by numerous scholars.[620]) Simply speaking, if

---

618 The correct translation of 8.12–13—with or without emending "from IS NOT" to "from IS"—is a debatable subject.

619 Cf. on Indirect Proof: **Mourelatos** [480] *Route* 98–100; **Szabó** [772] *Beginnings* 218; **Popper** [510] *World* 77n4: "The old pre-Aristotelian formal proof was, it seems, mainly the indirect proof, the *elenchos* (*reductio ad absurdum*). Parmenides mentions it by name in B7: 5. It is good that there can be no doubt about its meaning, as it derives from *elencho* ('to disgrace,' 'scorn,' 'dishonour'; in this case, to dishonour an assertion)." See also **Gigon** [40] on the "is" being proved in a negative way, by revealing the other contrary possibilities as absurd, *Ursprung* 263.

620 See **Popper** [510] on *reductio* and Contradiction: *World* 86, 102–103, 160; **Owen** [497] on Sufficient Reason: 'Plato and Parmenides on the Timeless Present' 326, 329, on Infinite Re-

we want an explanation to work, it is necessary to pay attention to these three factors: (1) we should always have a Sufficient Reason that can back up any fact or part of our claim; (2) we must not allow Contradiction—which we expose or prevent by means of Indirect Proof—and (3) we should rule out Infinite Regress by staying away from fraudulent solutions.

In our case, it is exactly these factors—when avoided as difficulties—that dictate that the IS must be ungenerated. I will take up each point individually and examine what type of generation is ruled out—that is, whether from IS or IS NOT—and if from the IS, then whether from itself or another IS. Let's begin first with Sufficient Reason, the most obvious of the three.

Sufficient Reason

An important arrow in Parmenides' quiver is what is called the Principle of Sufficient Reason—formulated as such by the German philosopher G. W. Leibniz (1646–1716) (see the motto of this chapter). An adaptation of it implies that nothing *comes to be* without there also being some *reason* for it to come to be.[621] That Parmenides had some awareness of this principle may be deduced from the way he constructs his arguments. However, we should take note that Parmenides seeks no grounds—or sufficient reason—for the *being* of that which IS or the *not-being* of that which IS NOT. These distinctions he treats as self-evident and necessary, namely that What IS is, or that What IS NOT is not.[622] If Parmenides really demands a *sufficient rea-*

---

gress: 326, on *reductio*: 326–329; **Tarán** [569] on *reductio*: *Parmenides* 201; **Mourelatos** [480] *Route* 98–100 on Sufficient Reason, Infinite Regress, and *reductio*; **Kahn** [395] on Sufficient Reason: 'The Thesis of Parmenides' 715, on *reductio*: 707; **Szabó** [772] on Contradiction and Indirect Proof: *Beginnings* 218 and *passim*; **Barnes** [9] on Sufficient Reason: *TPP* 187–188; **Lloyd** [717] on Sufficient Reason and *reductio*: *Magic, Reason and Experience* 70–71; **KRS** [39] on Sufficient Reason: 250; **Gallop** [340] on Sufficient Reason: *Parmenides* 15; **Austin** [198] on Sufficient Reason: 'Parmenides and Ultimate Reality' 222, 231, on *reductio*: 224, on Non-Contradiction: 228, 231; **McKirahan** [67] on Sufficient Reason: *PBS* 167, on *reductio*: 181n5; **Curd** [297] on Sufficient Reason: *Legacy* 76n30, 77, on Infinite Regress: 76–77; **Tejera** [82] on Regress: *Rewriting the History of Ancient Greek Philosophy* 52.

621   Leibniz [684] *Monadology* #32 and 36. Also important is this remark from the Fifth Paper to Clarke, paras. 125–129, G 7.419–420: L 717: "The principle in question, is the principle of the want of a sufficient reason; in order to anything's existing. In order to any event's happening." (**Jolley** [682] ed., *The Cambridge Companion to Leibniz* 194). One of the reasons Leibniz adopted this principle is to prove God's prerogative as the overall Sufficient Reason for what exists. This principle was particularly useful in proving a monotheistic deity, i.e., one God suffices (*Monadology* #39). Obviously, the definition of what God is does not necessarily exclude other gods, it just makes them superfluous. One God should be enough to run one universe.

622   Regarding What IS NOT, the case for "self-evidence" is not as explicit as for What IS. The Goddess points out that some kind of—perhaps godly—decision was necessary to rule

son for something, then, conceivably, it is only for deviations from the self-evident and necessary, that is, for *digressions* from What IS or What IS NOT. In other words, he requires that notions such as "change," "coming-to-be" or "passing-away," "birth," "growth," "decay," and so forth be justified if they are to apply to the IS. The way he addresses the subject necessitates that we concede that if there is no sufficient reason for something to come to be, *it will not come to be,* period. The rational implications are obvious: if we cannot conceive of a sufficient reason for something to come to be, we cannot *understand* it as coming to be—whether it may do so or not.

In this context, it is helpful to remind ourselves that Parmenides' methods are categorically *independent* of sense-experience. Whatever his intention may have been, in the final analysis it gave us the epitome of a nonempirical approach: techniques by which reason can evaluate its objects on its own terms and by its own means. In effect, reason can evaluate its own understandings—be they of its functions or its objects. Thus, left to its own devices, it is one thing for reason to apprehend its object as *being* in a certain way and not otherwise; however, it is quite another thing to accept that something *changed* from being in one way to being in a *different* way. In such a case, thinking must be provided with a satisfactory reason for the change. In other words, reason seeks to know *why* something is becoming otherwise than it is (or why something is to be *understood* as being otherwise than it has been hitherto understood).

Therefore, it is crucial for the rendering of an Evidential Account that any *change* be disallowed regarding the object of discourse, if a sufficient reason cannot be established for said change—which would also include change in the form of coming-to-be or perishing. For example, if we argue that What IS comes from What IS, we may not be able to back up this claim, because why would that which IS come from that which IS, if it *already is*? There is simply no good reason for what already IS being to come about from itself. It is also absurd, because it would have to have been in existence *before* it came into being.[623]

Accordingly, if we must have What IS come from What IS, we are obliged to include the proviso that "the IS comes from a *different* or *other* IS." (However, this option can also be defused, if by a separate argument; see Infinite Regress, below.) The Principle of Sufficient Reason is also appli-

---

IS NOT as unthinkable and unnameable (8.16–18). See also Chapter VII, subhead "The Question of IS NOT" and note 557.

[623] Pointed out by **Szabó** [772] *Beginnings* 218.

cable to growth, that is, there is no reason for What IS to grow if it is already *all together and complete* (8.4–7). And even more compelling is the need for a sufficient reason, if the IS is presumed to have grown from IS NOT.

Contradiction

Can that which IS come from that which IS NOT? Attempts to satisfy this question usually turn out as futile exercises, because any *assertive* or *affirmative* treatment of IS NOT inadvertently "turns" it into an IS—meaning an object of thought and discourse. This must teach us an important lesson, perhaps the most fundamental in Parmenides, namely, that all thought is essentially affirmative. Thus, even in a strict existential sense if we ask of IS NOT to be a *source* of something, it would, quite obviously, have to *be* a something, and that makes it its own opposite. Such a contradiction begs to be refuted by Indirect Proof, and, interestingly, it may also provide us with a lean formula for what it takes to have being, proficiently observed by Owen Goldin in his essay "Parmenides on Possibility and Thought":

> [Regarding] Parmenides' argument for the thesis that only what is can be an object of reference or thought. Parmenides asserts without argument that whatever can be thought can be. He argues that what is not cannot be ... on the basis of a reductio ad absurdum argument: If we assume that the nonbeing can be, then it already has the status of something whose being is present insofar as it is available. As such, it is, which contradicts the premise that it is not. Hence *no nonbeing can be an object of thought; if something is an object of thought, it is a being.*[624] (Emphasis added.)

Clearly, if we can defeat the notion of the IS being "generated from the IS" because of lack of a sufficient reason to generate itself if it already IS, then the notion of "generation from IS NOT" is equally moot, because if we subject IS NOT to a reasoning process, we cannot avoid treating "it" as the IS. To demonstrate this point, Parmenides opts to indulge a bit in such fallacious reasoning. We can follow this strategy through verses 8.7–10. First, he stirs our memory of earlier verses with allusions to the dictum that What IS NOT cannot be spoken or thought.[625] Yet he adapts the idea to include the

---

624 **Goldin** [346] 'Parmenides on Possibility and Thought' 32.
625 **Parmenides**, fr. 2.7–8: "For you cannot know that which IS NOT ... nor can you express it"; implied by 8.7–9: "I will not permit you to say or to think <that it grew> from What IS NOT; for it cannot be said or thought that it IS NOT." Echoed again in 8.17: "unthinkable and unnameable."

Contradiction

IS having to *grow* from IS NOT, something that would violate its thinkability, and which, obviously, is forbidden because it puts IS on par with IS NOT. Evidently, the thinkable cannot have its roots in the unthinkable, meaning that the thinkable is not essentially unthinkable in order to become thinkable. Parmenides then follows his admonition with one of the most beautiful twists of reducing such fallacy to absurdity:

> What necessity would have impelled it to grow later rather than earlier, if it began from nothing?[626]

This formulation exploits various conclusions from previous points in order to utterly crush the idea of generation from IS NOT. For example, for something to grow it must have a means and a point of origin, a "*how* and a *whence*" (8.7). Neither can play the role of IS NOT—by being a manner and source both are unequivocally IS. Furthermore, for something to grow, there must be a need that compels or instigates that growth. Yet not even necessity can be harbored by What is NOT.[627] A necessity is a something, is it not? And even if we assert that necessity is not a something, but rather a *lack* of something, and that it is such want (or privation) that compels something to grow—that is, its sufficient reason—we still have not achieved a satisfactory solution. This can be retraced in the artful way Parmenides switches the somethingness question from the IS to necessity, as evidenced by the ingenious introduction of the temporal proviso "later rather than earlier": if growth must be prompted, then something must act as a prompter. This again cannot be the IS itself, lacking sufficient reason, hence it must be the lack or absence of IS, in other words, necessity. But if this is the case, what might have impelled necessity itself to suddenly stir into action? Not only are we running into the phenomenon of Infinite Regress at this point—which will be further demonstrated below—but what made necessity grow the IS at that particular point in time and not earlier, if nothing was there to stand in the way of such growth? If necessity itself was exempt from coming about, hence always was, why did it not compel the IS to begin growing *immediately* instead of at a later point? Again if no sufficient reason can be found *why* the IS rose *when* it did—if only What IS NOT prevailed—then we must deny that any such generation occurred.[628]

---

626 **Parmenides**, fr. 8.9–10.
627 Cf. **KRS** [39] 250, linking "how" to Sufficient Reason, and "need" with a "principle of development" contained by what comes to be, yet not containable within the nonexistent.
628 Cf. **Gallop** [340] *Parmenides* 15; **Curd** [297] *Legacy* 76n30; and **Barnes** [9] *TPP* 187–188.

But that is not all: not only must we be able to explain why something occurred at a particular time—and not at a different time—if we claim that it occurred at all,[629] but by introducing such explanations "into" What IS NOT we must stomach the absurdity of having to deal with *two* What IS NOTS. If IS began from IS NOT, it must have begun at a certain point, the point where necessity started to make its influence count. But then we have an *earlier* IS NOT—before the stirring of necessity—and a *later* IS NOT, which marks the commencement of growth, because it is evidently from *this* What IS NOT—and not the former—that the IS sprung. Yet what could have intervened "within" IS NOT to separate it into "earlier" and "later"? Or into being both nonsource and then source? (These kinds of absurd speculations constitute typical examples of mortal reasoning. Recall the Goddess' evaluation of mortals: "For whom both to be and not to be are judged the same and not the same" [6.8]. In the case outlined above, IS NOT would have to be considered as both IS NOT and IS, ergo, the same and not the same as itself.)

If there is no such dividing factor "within" What IS NOT—particularly because it cannot possess or harbor any factors, properties, or dispositions—then there is no reason or necessity for the IS to have begun at some point, regardless of this being later or earlier. Richard McKirahan relates this principle poignantly:

> Since there is no time at which IT should come into existence rather than at any other time, and since IT cannot come into existence at all times, there is no reason to suppose that IT came into existence at all.[630]

In summary, any combination of the concepts "growth,"[631] "IS," and "IS NOT" can only result in contradiction.

Infinite Regress

One avenue remains open: we may speculate that if the IS cannot come to be from itself, nor from its contrary IS NOT, it still might be able to come

---

629 Cf. **Mourelatos** [480] *Route* 100, on Sufficient Reason and time, fr. 8.10–11. Likewise **McKirahan** [67] *PBS* 167.

630 **McKirahan** [67] *PBS* 167.

631 I do not draw a sharp distinction between "growing" and "coming-to-be" in Parmenides, primarily because I do not think the Poem warrants it. For this position I have found eloquent support in **Barnes** [9] *TPP* 184, who states: "I find nothing in the subsequent lines that reflects such a distinction, and I take 'grow' as a picturesque synonym for 'come into being.'"

from another IS. However, if we embrace this additional possibility, we will not be able to escape this question: from where, then, did this *other* IS come from? As we again cannot say "from itself" or "from IS NOT," we must assume that it came to be from yet another IS—a third, even earlier version, if you will. But then we will need a fourth IS to explain that, then a fifth, and so on, without end. Such an explanation requires the IS to come to be an infinite number of times in order to come to be *once*. That is the anatomy of Infinite Regress,[632] a "lapse of reason" that occurs whenever we attempt to solve a problem with a solution that only duplicates the problem, requiring in turn a duplicate of the same solution, and so forth to infinity. "Explanations" of this kind are self-defeating.

In our case, we are left with two possibilities: (1) either the IS did not come about from a previous IS, or (2) if it did, then there must have been some earliest representative of the IS—a *bookend* IS, so to speak, to the series—for which, however, the very conditions that facilitated this chain of becoming *did not apply*. In other words, for the first IS to be the *IS*, it did not have to come about from a previous IS, a circumstance that corresponds precisely to the first option above. Yet if this prototype did not need to come about in order to be, why then should our initial IS have needed to? Hence, why not assume right away that there is no series of becoming, meaning that the first option can apply directly to our original object of discourse, namely that IS which made us start our inquiry? Therefore, the solution we must adopt in order to bookend the series might just as well apply to our present IS, thereby rendering the entire series moot. And if no *series* of becomings is possible, then there is no such thing as coming-to-be from an earlier IS.

Thus, if we only take Sufficient Reason, Contradiction, and Infinite Regress into consideration, then the IS can come neither from itself, another IS, or IS NOT.[633]

Summation of Parmenides' Doctrine

We see that Parmenides does not have to provide any practical or empirical proof that the IS is ungenerated. This is an impossible task anyhow,

---

632 Whether the regress is "vicious" or "benign" I need not explain further. It is obvious that in this particular case of a "solution substitute," it is commonly considered vicious.
633 I am sure that for some interpreters, the question remains whether this threefold conclusion is fully preserved by the available verses. This is a controversial subject, and it depends largely on how we translate the lines 8.12–13. This question is addressed in **Hermann** [372] *The Naked IS*, "Alternate Interpretations of Lines 8.12–13" (forthcoming).

as no one can go backward in time in order to witness first hand whether it has a beginning. Clearly, sense-experience is utterly unfit to resolve such matters. All Parmenides has to do is demonstrate that there *are no sound or compelling reasons for What IS to have come about.* (In other words, even if some reasons are *thinkable*—let's say, on a purely speculative basis—the problems these would ultimately create would disqualify them as possible solutions.) Thus, to establish an unimpeachable rationale—as in ground, motive, or need—is the key to accepting change, regardless of whether we assume that something comes from something or from nothing. We can't help it; this is the way our mind works. Perhaps this is the very definition of mind itself: the urge, even compulsion, to search for a rationale.

If no rationale can be found, then no change can be assumed.[634] In the case of the IS, it should suffice to say that it is continuously "all together," "one," and "complete" in the "now" (8.4–6) because this is tantamount to saying that it has no reason to grow, or add to itself, much less to become what it already is. This should constitute sufficient positive proof, a proof that does not violate the homogeneity or "alikeness" of its landmarks. However, the mind is not quite satisfied with that: it balks at grasping the obvious conclusion, namely that the IS must be ungenerated. Hence, Parmenides feels obligated to demonstrate what consequences ensue if the reverse were true: he must engage the negative path, the one of IS NOT, to show that it does not lead anywhere (2.6; 8.17–18). In fact, our pursuit can only lead us back to where we began (fr. 5), that is, to the original statement. Consequently, to achieve this return as a confirmation of his initial claims, Parmenides complements positive proof with negative proof—or, *disproof*—to attain a "well-rounded" decision about such matters, hence truth (8.14–15).[635] Only when this argumentative balancing succeeds—reminding us of the function of Justice—are we provided with an unimpeachable rationale, and our minds can rest.

The above exercises are highly beneficial for analytical thinking. They can teach us one very important, very Parmenidean point: when inquiring into a subject, if any of our considerations creates contradictions, we must continue to strive for a solution that does not create them—no matter how improbable the solution may otherwise seem. As with any chain of reason-

---

634 Also **Lloyd** [717]: "If no cause can be adduced, or no explanation given, to account for the universe coming to be at one time rather than at any other, then we may consider this an argument for rejecting the notion that it came to be at all." (*Magic, Reason and Experience* 71)

635 Similarly **Gigon** [40] *Ursprung* 263, on the IS being proved negatively, by eliminating other options.

ing, we must rearrange the links—or replace them—until all unlikeness or disparity that might stand in the way of having a tenable chain is removed. This is what the gathering of landmarks in fragment 8 suggests, despite the unusual outcome we may obtain when we order them in a compatible way.

It is such ordering, as a "compatible way," that Parmenides had in mind when he spoke of "the Way of Persuasion" that makes us adhere to the Truth (2.4). And we are also told that this truth has an unshaking heart (1.29). Unshaking, it is stable. In other words, it is a trustworthy, reliable result of a chain of reasoning, regardless of how incredible such an outcome may seem to anyone who has not tested the chain. Those who do, however, have no choice but to accept it. Undoubtedly, such was the outlook of the Eleatics, who, I believe, were the ultimate pragmatists. Neither Parmenides nor Zeno attacked common sense; instead, they both used it to prove inconsistencies in reasoning and speaking, just like a skilled martial arts instructor makes use of the momentum of his students. Accordingly, we may use common sense to arrive at some very uncommon conclusions.

Through his unusual approach of "legislating" rational judgment, together with his even less common object of inquiry, the IS for thinking, Parmenides has shown that certain principles, such as "a proper ordering of words," the "avoidance of contradiction," and "having a good reason for something"—all fundamental to philosophy and logic, but also to law—will allow us to map out a terrain where sense-experience is irrelevant. Thus we may boil down his methodology to these three essential lessons:

(a) Any non-contradictory statement—which, demonstrably, can only pertain to the object of thought—expresses the IS of a thing. To have its truth expressed is what distinguishes the *object of judgment*. Conversely, no statement that incorporates IS NOT as part of what it tries to express can avoid contradiction, because it will inadvertently end up asserting that "to be and not to be are the same and not the same"—the credo of those who lack judgment (6.7–9) and who therefore cannot express the truth of a thing. In the end, What IS NOT cannot be objectified (6.2; 7.1), neither by affiliation with What IS nor by supplanting it in any way.

(b) Any untested, approximative statement is Doxa or opinion—even if it is accepted by everyone as plausible or true (*ta dokounta*, 1.31). If such a statement can be brought to a point where it contradicts itself—exposing the inherent "IS NOT"—it must be discarded (8.15–18). On the other hand, if it can be freed from contradiction—or immunized against it—it is elevated to a Reliable/Evidential Account (again, the outcome of 8.15–18). But if this operation succeeds, the object of such an account is once again an object of thought, meaning an *object obtained by rational judgment*.

(c) Doxa prevails only so long as mortals accept certain statements as sufficiently credible, even though they lack genuine verification. Thus, such statements are to be judged as at best plausible descriptions of the sensory-experiential domain (8.60), and not as pronouncements about rational things. (This distinction will become very important in the next chapters. And perhaps mortals should not be blamed indiscriminately for such a faux pas. While having to navigate a universe that is more experiential than rational, they may be confronted with things that elude rigorous testing. Thus they may be forced to settle on the plausible rather than the true—at least until by searching, as Xenophanes said, they discover better.[636])

Now that we have become acquainted with Parmenides' mode of thinking, his methods, and his critical distinction between the reliable and the approximate, we can investigate what impact this might have had upon a newly emerging field of speculative reasoning, particularly upon the designs of later Pythagoreanism. We have finally arrived at the crossroads where both approaches can be compared, keeping in mind that certainty and proof are the sole criteria, and only insofar as they are pursued by non-empirical means.

---

636 Xenophanes, DK 21B18.

For Parmenides, thought—genuine thought—is univocal and indissolubly attached to truth, knowledge, and reality. By presenting his arguments as the gift of a divine revelation, Parmenides presumes that human beings can (at least momentarily) think the thoughts that the divine thinks.

—A. A. Long [448] 148

CHAPTER X

Irrationals and the Perfect Premise

> Some say the supernatural power took revenge on those who published Pythagoras' teachings. The man who revealed the construction of the "twenty-angled shape" was drowned at sea like a blasphemer. (He told how to make a dodecahedron, one of the "five solid figures," into a sphere.) Some say this fate befell the man who told about irrationality and incommensurability.
> —Iamblichus[637]

Philosophy: An Exercise in Infallibility

I have approached the next two chapters as the *pièce de résistance* of this book, a place where Parmenideanism and late Pythagoreanism converge, but also as a battleground for certain fundamental ideas that have had much to contribute to ancient philosophy, especially to the birth of logic and metaphysics.

To improve our appreciation of the types of factors capable of breaking Pythagoreanism's back as a reliable approach—even though it was based on arithmetic and geometry, both considered exact—we should review a few important aspects. As Plato observed, the critical requirement for any object of speculative inquiry is *to be discernible by thought*.[638] I call this "Plato's Parmenidean criterion." In other words, we need a thinkable thing toward which to turn or direct our thoughts—a graspable, imaginable something, essentially characterized by its capability of being objectified by reasoning. Indeed, regardless of what our speculations are about, their object must be made *more* intelligible by our speculations, not less intelligible.[639] That, if

---

637 **Iamblichus**, *VP* 247.
638 **Plato**, *Parmenides* 135b–c.
639 Meaning not to pursue "inconceivables," like "surds," "irrationals," etc. See **Pappus** (c. A.D. 300), *The Commentary of Pappus on Book X of Euclid's Elements* I.2. (**Junge-Thomson** [651]) 64.

anything, should be philosophy's primary task. Basically, it must provide people with something to think about. Next, one must recognize that the object of speculative inquiry is an object of reason, and that it must be approached differently than the object of sense-experience (remember fr. 4 and 7.3–6). This requires the object of reason to be discernible and provable entirely through intellectual means, that is to say, only by thinking and discourse.

Philosophically speaking, what reason should probe are the *consequences* of its activities, that is, the consequences that ensue upon our comprehension of a particular object if we subject it to a chain of reasoning or express it by discourse. The question is, can our understanding of something change if we simply think or speak about it in a certain way? And if there are consequences, how does this affect our understanding of *other* concepts or objects of reason? Do they become more or less intelligible, or do they change altogether? The demonstration provided by Parmenides, for example, explores what befalls our notion of IS or IS NOT if we say that IS comes from IS NOT. Does IS remain IS, or does IS NOT remain IS NOT? The lesson here is that in a chain of reasoning, each link must hold its own. Then it remains true to itself, as well as the chain, so that we may have reasoning and discourse that is dependable. Accordingly, the object of reason must be always the same as *itself*, that is, it has to be *true to itself*.

In a Platonic sense, this might *represent* a nonabstract individual, such as a particular apple, which obviously is liable to change, but the *thought-object* "apple" must remain the same regardless of what happens to its physical counterpart (see again Parmenides fr. 4). Only what is stable in itself, unconditional, and complete can be used as a *noetic* criterion, and—as we have seen with Parmenides' fragment 5—it may serve as a starting point from where reasoning and discourse can proceed or to which they can return.[640] (See also Proviso 11 in "Twelve Provisos for the Evidential Account" in Chapter VIII.)

---

640 **Parmenides**, fr. 5; cf. **Proclus** [662] *A Commentary on Plato's Parmenides* 1.708. Proclus uses this fragment to disprove the view that Parmenides was advocating monism for the "intelligible world." He says that this and other passages (8.25, 8.44) show that Parmenides postulates many "intellectual beings" and that he orders them by priority. While the last comment may be a Neoplatonic spin, comparable to Plotinus' hypostases, the overall import shows that fr. 5 allows the Goddess to visit a multitude of objects of reason in her discourse—i.e., in a chain of reasoning as, e.g., fr. 8—as long as she never forsakes where she began. Proclus also cites a similar principle for mathematics. Paraphrasing Porphyry, he states: "We must understand that all mathematical arguments proceed either from or to the starting-points." (*In Euclidem* 255.12–14, Friedlein, trans. **Morrow** [663] *A Commentary on the First Book of Euclid's Elements* 198)

A Perfect Premise

What we attempt to convey by means of a statement should *still be true* after the statement has been formulated or expressed. That is to say, the *consequences* of a statement must support the idea or meaning one has sought to convey, and not undermine it in any way. Conclusions that defeat the intended message have to be ruled out or rendered impossible. For example, the *consequences* of expressing that "apple exists," should not turn out as meaning that "not-apple exists" or "apple does not exist." If the *consequences* of the idea we have meant to express have not defeated it, we have succeeded in rendering an Evidential Account.[641] The same principle must underlie any attempt to prove something through a nonempirical approach—if we remember that this is what Pythagoras failed to observe in the parable of the shield of Euphorbus, when he did not provide a reasoned or logical proof for his previous existence.

By "proof only by thinking" I mean any *speculative* method by which we can ascertain that the *result* of a speculative process is correct or factual. It also assures us that a chain of reasoning will hold. As we learn from Plato's *Parmenides*, only when philosophy is practiced as a most rigorous discipline can we be sure that our thinking is accurate. And furthermore, it is the task of the philosopher to figure out the means or techniques for such calibration while attempting at the same time to make an object of thought as graspable as possible so that it may be taught to others. The key to speculative pursuit is to have confidence in one's methods. Only then can we trust our conclusions, being assured that they are the result of a properly conducted reasoning process.

What kind of methods can help us tune our thinking? Essentially, these are *exercises in infallibility*, which, if we follow Plato's lead, should be carried out by discourse. He champions this idea convincingly not only in the *Parmenides* but whenever he spoke of dialectic. He seems convinced that no one but the philosopher can come up with the appropriate workouts. There is no doubt that in this, Parmenides was the first to succeed, yet it remains to be seen how his approach applies to the Pythagorean problem.

A Perfect Premise

Since to supply reason with a discernible object is imperative, we must aim for concepts—to be utilized in discourse—that reduce the risk of con-

---

[641] **Parmenides**, fr. 8.50.

tradition or self-refutation, or, ideally, eliminate it altogether.[642] If we fail in this matter—perhaps by not ensuring that our object has a character that is always the same—then we will have nothing to turn our thought to, as Plato says, and consequently, discourse will become defunct, as its objects lose their significance.[643] (Remember Parmenides: "For without What IS, in which it is expressed, you will not find thinking" [8.35–36], which underlies the above.) To avoid this, the thinker must learn how to adopt something dependable, some valid concept from whence to proceed—essentially, a thought-object that remains true to itself, no matter what. We see some of this echoed by Aristotle in the *Topics*:

> Those things are *true and primary* which get their trustworthiness through themselves rather than through other things (for when it comes to scientific starting-points, one should not search further for the reason why, but instead each of the starting-points ought to be trustworthy in and of itself).[644]

Consequently, we are obliged in our deliberations to proceed from a solid or reliable foundation, a *self*-evident truth, a premise. Of course, as Aristotle suggests, the premise, being prime, cannot itself be tested. However, this does not mean that we must accept every premise as suitable for the task.[645] But then, how do we know we have the appropriate premise? As I have pointed out, we must examine the *consequences* that ensue—the consequences from relying upon it in our reasoning process. If we cannot subject the self-evident to testing, we can at least test what we have done with it. That is, we can test our conclusions and explanations, those elaborate constructions that are built on said premise. The question is, will our explanations leave our premise intact, or will they alter or modify the premise in ways that cannot support the explanations, therefore rendering it moot? In short, does the premise allow the conclusion, or will the conclusion—if ac-

---

642 The aim of reducing the possibility of contradiction altogether explains Parmenides' frugality; his statements are almost digital in their starkness. However, as he himself also shows, it is a nearly impossible task. Language is still not as precise as philosophers need it to be.

643 **Plato**, *Parmenides* 135b–c. That Plato had his Forms in mind is beside the point. In terms of intelligibility they were governed by the same principles as, e.g., Parmenides' object of reason or discourse. See Chapter IV, "Pythagorizing Versus Philosophizing."

644 **Aristotle**, *Topics* 100b17 (trans. **Smith** [625] *Aristotle Topics: Books I and VIII* 1).

645 I do not believe that in Parmenideanism there is such a thing as a false or fraudulent premise, but only an inappropriate or misapplied premise. Technically, two contradictory assumptions have become unduly mixed, resulting in opinion or belief. However, this is a matter for a different book, one that deals with the consequences of Parmenidean logic.

A Perfect Premise

cepted—alter the premise beyond recognition? We will know that our base is the proper one when it has remained solid and true, being neither changed nor affected by the speculative process that depended on it.

To return to the arithmetical example used in the Introduction, any given number can serve as our speculative base, and after all the additions, subtractions, and so forth that we can perform, we can expect the number itself not to have been irreparably altered by the process. Thus, if we want to test the process by reversing it, we should arrive at the exact number from where we began. If everything works out, we can have confidence in our conclusions. All that we need to establish, therefore, are a suitable base and the right rules of how to proceed and/or return. We can then take comfort in the fact that as long as we obey these rules, our thinking is properly calibrated. (Incidentally, the further development of said "rules for thinking" eventually gave us *definitions,* that is, the "marking off" or the "delimiting" of a subject, thereby making it intelligible. Defining a subject became essential for the exercise of dialectical discourse.[646] All this began, as we have seen, with Parmenides' prototype for definitions, the unified formula, or the coherent account.)

I have indicated that philosophy itself is a quest for such reliable foundations, each one a coveted halt on our speculative journey—be they the Pythagorean Unit, Heraclitus' *Logos,* Empedocles' Elements, Leucippus and Democritus' Atoms, Plato's Forms, Aristotle's First Principles, Plotinus' Ineffable One, or others. The trademark of practically every thinker is some fundamental idea upon which to build the remainder of his constructions. Regardless of how dissimilar each individual outlook might be—or what final abstraction, principle, or entity they may settle upon in their explanations—all philosophers have one thing in common: the need to come up with a *perfect premise.*[647]

---

646 Cf. **Szabó** [772] *Beginnings* 256.

647 **McKirahan** has pointed out to me that while I speak of a perfect *premise,* the things I have mentioned above are not premises, as in statements found in arguments, but entities. My answer is that that is a correct observation, to which I might add that *now* they are entities. However, I believe that such statements can evolve into objects of thoughts themselves, i.e., they become "entified." There is the Pythagorean Monad, for example, which in all probability began with considerations about unity and limit, as opposed to the unlimited. Even clearer is the evolution of Parmenides' *esti*: initially a verb, it becomes criterion, premise, and way, then root or element, then world and atom, and by the time Plato comes around, it is One or Being, both bona fide entities. In fact, this process of entification underlies the Naked IS theory, as I call it—namely that philosophy evolved from *esti,* Parmenides' object of discourse—and explains why it was more usable or dependable than the Pythagorean unit, which is the overall

Naturally, the difficulty in formulating any principle that purports to be universal is that it has to gain everyone's acceptance; it has to be "all things to all people." And this is best achieved if it is *internally consistent*. It must also be *adaptive* but *stable*, meaning *compatible*, without losing its identity or distinction. And it must be very *simple*, but able to take part in the most complex structures imaginable. Only then will it gain the widest acceptance, because it can be used by anyone to explain anything. (Incidentally, this may be why the premise of God has worked so well, for so many, for such a long time.)

But the most important demand of such a perfect premise—in this the Pythagoreans and Parmenides seem to be in agreement—is the ability to be used as a reliable standard or criterion against which all things, all theories and speculations, can be measured. The perfect premise, then, helps us calibrate our thinking, because if we lose sight of everything else, we have it to fall back upon. For Parmenides, this was the IS for thinking—the most basic of basics, without which thinking cannot find expression. Number, as we have seen, served in a similar capacity for the Pythagoreans, and it was just as much an object of thought as Parmenides' *Thought-IS*. However, the Pythagorean version of the perfect premise had a built-in flaw that no one could foresee: it had nothing in common with the universe it supposedly explained.

To Drown in a Sea of Non-Identity

How close did the Pythagoreans get to finding the perfect premise? Close, no doubt, but no cigar. Their "base for thinking"—the unit—failed to remain immune to the effects of a particular speculative treatment. Of course, each "number-unit," or integer, was supposed to have the ability to serve in a variety of capacities or functions without losing its identity. We expect 1 to remain essentially 1 regardless of what is done with it, arithmetically speaking. This is why it is supposed to be a reliable standard by which to perform speculative calibrations. Whether we use it as the beginning of a number series or its end, or as a component in a calculation or the result of same, 1 must remain 1 and not be suddenly more, less, or something entirely different. And it should certainly never occur that when us-

---

message of this present work. Eventually this same *esti*, by being subjected to an extended dialectical process, "matured" into a variety of metaphysical entities. However, we cannot say that Parmenides originally intended it as a solution for a *metaphysical* problem, much less that he conceived it as a *metaphysical* entity.

ing 1, we suddenly discover that we have lost it, and no calculation we perform can return it. But that is precisely the fate that befell the Pythagorean unit. How was this possible?

The answer is as intriguing to us as it was unsettling to the ancient Greeks: the fault, as it turns out, lies with the unit, or more accurately, with the Pythagorean concept of it. What they demanded of the unit, it could not deliver. Although deemed *identical* with the geometric and numerical 1, under certain conditions, the unit could be used to produce something akin to an anti-unit, that is, something not expressible in units.

I have mentioned this in the Introduction, when I touched upon the phenomenon of irrational numbers and incommensurable magnitudes. These kinds of values denote spatial relationships (i.e., ratios) that cannot be expressed as finite terms but only as random, never-ending sequences of digits.[648] Thus, to the surprise of the early thinkers, not every time they proceeded from unit did they manage to arrive at unit. This made their base for thinking not only unreliable, but occasionally unspeakable, even unthinkable. Obviously, if "one" is our answer for everything, whenever a "result" cannot be expressed in terms of "ones," *it cannot be expressed at all*. It cannot be thought or communicated. Consequently, discourse is impossible, we have *no object to train our mind on,* and Plato's prerequisites for a proper philosophical inquiry are not met.

And once again, it is poor Hippasus of Metapontum whose name has been linked to this ominous find. According to legend, he either discovered these "forbidden" ratios or he revealed them to the outside world, thereby undermining the movement's reputation. Suddenly, it seems, the universe of the Pythagoreans was not the orderly place it purported to be, a realm where all things could be brought into harmony because they had the unit in common. Instead, it looked messy, even unruly, and to make matters worse, it seemed grounded on the *inconceivable*. According to some versions of the legend, the unfortunate discoverer was met by an untimely death: he

---

648 Here is a sample of some of the most poignant definitions of irrational numbers I could find: **Courant, Robbins, Steward** [737] *What Is Mathematics?* 60: "An irrational number represents the length of a segment incommensurable with the unit." **Niven** [764] *Numbers: Rational and Irrational* 39: "Any real number which cannot be expressed as the ratio a/b of two integers is called an irrational number." **Szabó** [772] *Beginnings* 330: "*Rational* numbers can be written as *fractions* or *ratios* (m/n), whereas *irrational* ones cannot." **Russell** [769] *Introduction to Mathematical Philosophy* 72: "An 'irrational number' is a segment of the series of ratios which has no boundary. A 'rational real number' is a segment of the series of ratios which has a boundary." For an in-depth discussion, see **Manning** [759] *Irrational Numbers and Their Representation of Sequences and Series,* chapter I.II, 'Definition of Irrational Numbers' 5–14.

was either drowned at sea by the gods for impiety or by his fellow Pythagoreans for treason.[649] The mathematical commentator Pappus (third century A.D.) considers the story a Pythagorean morality tale against preoccupation with what cannot be grasped by thought. He provides us with this account in his commentary on the tenth book of Euclid's *Elements* (Arabic version):

> Indeed the sect (or school) of Pythagoras was so affected by its reverence for these things that a saying became current in it, namely, that he who first disclosed the knowledge of surds[650] or irrationals and spread it abroad among the common herd, perished by drowning: which is most probably a parable by which they thought to express their conviction that firstly, it is better to conceal (or veil) every surd, or irrational, or inconceivable in the universe, and, secondly, that the soul which by error or heedlessness discovers or reveals anything of this nature which is in it or in this world, wanders [thereafter] hither and thither on a sea of non-identity (i.e., lacking all similarity of quality or accident), immersed in the stream of the coming-to-be and passing-away, where there is no standard of measurement.[651]

Once again, we can recognize a warning against violating Plato's Parmenidean criterion for an object of thought: any absence of a stable discernible thing condemns one to the unintelligibleness of non-identity; hence, there is nothing to distinguish or to figure out.

Even if the actual events that led to this momentous discovery are shrouded by legend, why did many of the ancient commentators—to whom we owe the story and who probably embellished it—consider irrationals such a terrible find that they associated the Pythagoreans with this unreasonably cruel punishment of one of their best thinkers? For a possible answer, we need to recapitulate briefly some of the qualities of the unit and compare it to the prerequisites for a "reliable base for thinking" listed at the beginning of this chapter. (See section "Philosophy: An Exercise in Infallibility.") Perhaps this may help us understand why some Pythagoreans may have been persuaded of its indispensability.[652]

---

649 Or perhaps they only erected a gravestone or tomb for the betrayer of secrets, effectively declaring him dead to the society, see **Iamblichus**, *VP* 246–247.

650 "Surd" from Latin *surdus*—deaf, silent, mute, indistinct. Surds are another name for irrational numbers or incommensurable magnitudes, cf. OED.

651 **Pappus**, *The Commentary of Pappus on Book X of Euclid's Elements* I.2 (**Junge-Thomson** [651]) 64. Also **Heath** [636] *Euclid: The Elements* 3.1: ". . . hinting that everything irrational and formless is properly concealed, and, if any soul should rashly invade this region of life and lay it open, it would be carried away into the sea of becoming and be overwhelmed by its unresting currents." Cf. also **Burkert** [100] *Lore* 457–458.

652 Perhaps such thinkers as the post-Parmenidean Philolaus, arguably one of Aristotle's main sources for Pythagorean doctrine.

On the face of it, the study of number is the study of relations. But actually, it is the study of certain rules for thinking and their consequences upon other rules for thinking. Reasoning recognizes relationships and sets up the rules necessary to govern certain associations or differentiations. And to function as bona fide rules, these relations or ratios are set up to be invariable. The ruling principle of the later Pythagoreans was that of limit, which imposes boundaries upon the unlimited—including invariability. Limit *unitizes* the unlimited, and so the building blocks of the universe, *as we understand it,* are formed.[653] Existence itself was composed of sets of units, in unitary relationships, regulated by unitizing principles. Thus, at the core of everything stood the unit, the perfect premise.

Number can also be defined as a "plurality of units."[654] Not only does the number series proceed from said unit, but the things themselves have to be expressed in *unitary,* meaning *commensurable,* relations. In this sense they were *rational,* not irrational; in other words, they stood for unitary ratios or relationships, not nonunitary ones. Essentially, things had to be unitary compositions: made by finite units to be themselves finite units, and having finite unitary relationships with other finite units. That is the key to their existence, if we use unit as existential criterion: to be a unit is to be, to not be a unit is not to be.

The unit's counterpart, the *point,* was also important: in fact, it was considered as the unit's manifestation in space. The unit and the point were deemed identical, except for one difference: one had a location, the other did not. Thus, a unit was defined as a "point without position," and a point as "a unit having position."[655] This distinction alone should have indicated that the realm of the unit is the mind, while that of the point is the physical universe. A critical oversight.

Even if "taken apart," the principle of unit is not lost, or so it was believed, because the resulting fractions retain their characters as numbers—being odd or even—and when we put them together again we have restored the original unit. Thus, fractions of units were deemed just as rational and

---

653 These principles are largely found in the fragments of Philolaus. The act of studying quantities and magnitudes is in itself an exercise in making the infinite finite. See **Proclus**: "For [the Pythagoreans] say that the sciences study the finite in abstraction from infinite quantities and magnitudes, since it is impossible to comprehend infinity in either of them." (*In Euclidem* 36 [Friedlein], trans. **Morrow** [663] *A Commentary on the First Book of Euclid's Elements* 30)

654 **Morrow** [663] *A Commentary on the First Book of Euclid's Elements* 128n140.

655 **Aristotle**, *Metaphysics* 1084b26: "For the unit is a point without position," and *On the Soul* 409a6: "For a point is a unit having position."

commensurable as the units themselves and their relations.[656] Whether it was used as base, fountainhead, or constituent, the unit facilitated every conceivable combination or function. Things got their individuality from it, and groups their identity. Without it, nothing could be recognizable, much less ordered in any fashion. Even the cosmos would lose its structure without it.

Here, arguably, was the ultimate premise. And so whoever put their stock in it never saw it coming. The wake-up call arrived in the most irritating form: certain calculations revealed "fractions" that refused to be unitized. Chaos loomed if some quick fix could not be found to reconcile these unruly inconceivables with the acceptable order. But everyone who saw the unit as the "answer to everything" had made a tragic mistake: they never realized that *the universe did not share the mind's concept of what a unit is.*

Irrationality and the Pythagorean Theorem

Whether it was really Hippasus who poured cold water on Pythagorean aspirations, we cannot say for certain.[657] It seems that the difficulties first appeared in geometry, when no common measure could be found for certain magnitudes—at least not one expressible in terms of units. The ratios for *pi* (π) and $\sqrt{2}$ are both irrational, and it is the latter that is more interesting in our context, because as an exercise, it demonstrated quite indisputably the fallibility of the Pythagorean unit.

If we do not have a last term in a number series, we are confronted with two major difficulties: we cannot determine whether the "number" is odd or even—thus, per the Pythagoreans, it cannot be a number—nor can we find some way to express it in a comprehensive manner. We can obviously neither think it through, speak it, nor write it down because it is incom-

---

656 There are certain idiosyncracies regarding the unit's special status in Pythagorean doctrine: on the one hand, it was the starting point of the number series; on the other hand, it was not part of it, because for any regular number to be a *valid number* it had to be *either* odd or even. Yet strangely, for some unnamed Pythagoreans (perhaps the *Akousmatikoi*), the unit itself, as the *source* of all numbers, was *both* odd and even. Cf. **Aristotle**, *Metaphysics* 986a19.

657 For pro: **von Fritz** [120] 'The Discovery of Incommensurability by Hippasus of Metapontum' 242–264; **Boyer** [733] *A History of Mathematics* 72, 76, 611. For contra: **Junge** [750] (primarily against Pythagoras or early Pythagoreans as the discoverers of irrationals), 'Wann haben die Griechen das Irrationale entdeckt?' 221–264; **Vogt** [773] 'Die Entdeckungsgeschichte des Irrationalen' 97–155; **Philip** [163] *PEP* 29–32. For general comments: **Heath** [636] *Euclid: The Elements* 1.411–414; **Burkert** [100] *Lore* 455–460; **Sinnige** [78] *Matter and Infinity in the Presocratic Schools and Plato* 76–78; **Szabó** [772] *Beginnings* 33–36; **van der Waerden** [183] *Pythagoreer* 71–75, 398–399; **Guthrie** [43] *HGP* 1.320–322; **McKirahan** [67] *PBS* 98–99; **Zhmud** [187] "Mathematici and Acusmatici," in **Boudouris** (ed.), *Pythagorean Philosophy* 245–246.

Irrationality and the Pythagorean Theorem 261

plete. Consequently, the all-important principle of limit is abolished, and with it all relationship. What remains has nothing to do with units per se, thus, one may ask, what are these "numbers" or "magnitudes" doing in a universe that supposedly consists of units and is ordered according to units? No doubt irrationals were a major headache for some of the early thinkers.

Unfortunately, we are not sure what impact this discovery might have had upon Pythagorean doctrine, although much has been written about the subject. Indeed, some German scholars have spoken of a *Grundlagenkrise*, a crisis of fundamental proportions for the society.[658] We may speculate that if the legends are true regarding these unwelcome revelations, then the issue could be quite embarrassing for a cult that could not afford to be wrong in the eyes of the public—particularly after the political fiascos it had endured. At least, this impression may be gleaned from the various theories put forth by other commentators who link the order with this disconcerting, if accidental, find.[659]

To add insult to injury, it was the Pythagorean theorem, of all things, that played a pivotal role in the discovery of the "forbidden numbers." We all know the famous theorem from school: "In a right-sided triangle, the square of the hypotenuse is equal to the sum of the squares of the other two sides," also known as $a^2 + b^2 = c^2$, with c being the hypotenuse. This theorem works beautifully when side a represents three units and side b four, giving us five units for side c; thus, when we square a and b we arrive at a commensurable hypotenuse for c: $3^2 + 4^2 = 5^2$ (see the left diagram below):

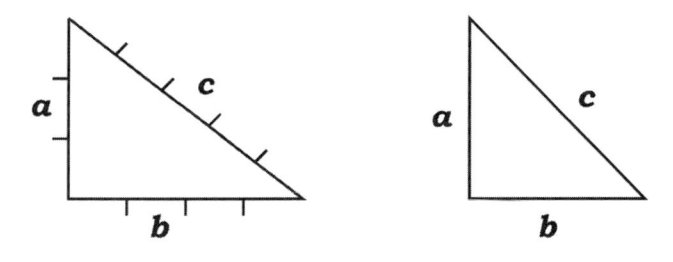

---

658 See **Hasse** and **Scholz** [128] *Die Grundlagenkrisis der griechischen Mathematik* 3–12. For a synopsis, cf. **Burkert** [100] *Lore* 455–462, 455n42, 455n43.

659 **Von Fritz** [120]: "The discovery of incommensurability must have made an enormous impression in Pythagorean circles because it destroyed with one stroke the belief that everything could be expressed in integers, on which the whole Pythagorean philosophy up to then had been based." ('The Discovery of Incommensurability' 406–407) Also **Hasse** and **Scholz** [128] *Die Grundlagenkrisis der griechischen Mathematik*; **Heath** [636] *Euclid: The Elements* 1.351, 411–414, 3.1–3, and [745] *A History of Greek Mathematics* 1.154–157; **Burnet** [14] *Early*

However, if, as in the diagram on the right, sides *a* and *b* are of equal length—each representing *one* unit—and we then perform the very same operation of squaring *a* and *b*, the hypotenuse, or diagonal side, *c* is not commensurable to the sides. As it cannot be expressed in terms of units, it is unmeasurable if we aim for an exact value. For example, if each side is 1 inch long, the length of the diagonal will be the square root of 2 inches[660]—$\sqrt{2}$—which is a sum we can only *begin* to express as 1.41421356237309504880168887242097 . . . and the digits after the decimal proceed infinitely, without pattern or repetition. This "value" should not be confused with a fraction, which, being complete, can be complemented by other fractions to make up a unit again. Hence, we are dealing here not with an exact account of something, but only with an approximation.

Yet coming close is not a satisfactory outcome for any science that considers itself exact, like mathematics—and why shouldn't philosophy strive to be just as accurate? As Parmenides' Poem demonstrates, that is precisely what he was aiming for: a method that makes reasoning rigorous and its results flawless. But did his "only way of inquiry for thinking"[661] have the capacity to provide proofs that were at least as accurate as those of arithmetic, perhaps even succeeding where the latter failed? Might his unusual techniques be of use to mathematicians, perhaps providing them with the kind of infallibility their own methods were not yet able to? Árpád Szabó thought so (see *The Beginnings of Greek Mathematics*), and after much soul-searching, I have come to agree.

The Indirect Proof of Odd Being Even

If, for example, an irrational number is infinite, and thus not able to be grasped by thought, what other means can tell us accurately that we are dealing with an irrational, and not an extremely long, yet finite, fraction? Clearly, we cannot measure it with a ruler, nor can we think it through infinitely in order to find out whether or not it has a last term. We would have to invent a different approach, a method that does not try to chase down in-

---

Greek Philosophy 105; **Maziarz** and **Greenwood** [761] *Greek Mathematical Philosophy* 49–55, 64; **Russell** [769] *Introduction to Mathematical Philosophy* 4, 66–67; **Boyer** [733] *A History of Mathematics* 72–73, 88: "logical scandal" 113; **Kline** [752] *Mathematics for the Nonmathematician* 66, 68; **Maor** [760] *e: The Story of a Number* 189–190; **Clawson** [735] *Mathematical Mysteries: The Beauty and Magic of Numbers* 85.
    660 Example is by **Russell** [769] *Introduction to Mathematical Philosophy* 4, 67.
    661 **Parmenides**, fr. 2.2.

finity—which is impossible—but that seizes upon some other factor, which perhaps is reducible to an either/or proposition.

And using Indirect Proof is exactly how we can approach $\sqrt{2}$—that is, the problem posed by the hypothenuse of a right-sided triangle with equal sides (i.e., the diagonal of "the one unit square"). Now, as it is useless to focus on the interminable aspect of such a "number," we can take up another aspect: for example, the problem of odd versus even, as a rational or real number has to be one or the other. Perhaps we can check whether we can make our mystery value conform to this stringent demand. If we succeed, then it is evident that we have probed a very long, but nonetheless finite, number, which consequently can be expressed in unitary form. However if we fail, we have discovered something just as certain, namely, that we are dealing with an irrational.

The principle underlying the test we need to perform is the same as the one behind Parmenides' approach, which the previous chapters have shown. Referred to as the Principle of Non-Contradiction, as well as the Law of Contradiction, it is one of the fundamentals of logic, demanding that a thing cannot be both itself and its very own contrary. We can also say that something cannot be the opposite of itself and still be itself. We have seen how much Parmenides abhorred mixing contradictories and how his method of disentanglement was specifically designed to eliminate self-refuting combinations—such as the generation of IS from IS NOT, which makes IS be IS NOT, and IS NOT be IS. As a reminder, the way Indirect Proof works is not by establishing a positive—that something *is* the case—instead, it demonstrates that if the *opposite* is accepted as being the case, it will lead to absurd or impossible conclusions—absurd or impossible, of course, according to commonly accepted premises.

And if the commonly accepted premise is that a real number has to be either odd or even, then any value that is proven to be *both* cannot pass for such a number—numbers being something distinct, not indeterminate. And this is exactly what the Parmenidean method allows us to establish when applied to the problem of distinguishing irrationals: it makes these kinds of values appear to be both odd and even, thereby exposing their impossibility. That Aristotle was aware of this technique—particularly as it applies to the one-unit square—is evident from a couple of brief references in the *Prior Analytics*.[662] He points out that if the diagonal of such a square is assumed to be commensurate with its side, then odd numbers come out

---

662 **Aristotle**, *Prior Analytics* 41a23, and 50a37.

equal to even numbers. Thus, if we can find some way of determining that a number has to be odd in order to be even, and vice versa, we have determined that it is irrational.

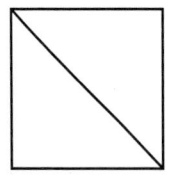

To summarize the above, we note that if positive proof is not feasible, we must reach for the reverse approach. If we cannot prove, then we must disprove. Because we are assuming (for the sake of an indirect approach) that our value is *either* odd *or* even—as any rational number would be—it is precisely that assumption that is subjected to a test.[663] If a contradiction ensues, then certainty is inescapable: we *know* the value is not rational but irrational. Our certainty is so complete that it cannot be lesser than that of the gods.

The only difference is that we have to rely on a systematic approach. It alone allows us to determine with *absolute certainty* that our number is irrational and infinite, not because we have actually measured it in any way, which we can't do, but because we can *show* that if we treat it as rational and finite we reap only contradictions.[664]

---

663 Cf. **Heath** [636] *Euclid: The Elements* 3.2, on the proof formerly known as Euclid X.117.

664 We have no reliable evidence that the Pythagoreans—whether early, late, or wannabe—were actually fazed by the discovery of incommensurability, or by the proof that makes odd be even. As I have indicated, it makes a compelling story; however, when or by whom the Indirect Proof of $\sqrt{2}$ was formulated is simply unknown. Yet the coincidence of having the Eleatic technique of Indirect Proof be the one that resolves the question of the irrationality of $\sqrt{2}$ remains intriguing. However, even if the proof that "odd numbers come out equal to evens" was known substantially before Aristotle, say, sometime during the fifth century B.C., those Pythagoreans who believed that the one was both odd and even (**Aristotle**, *Metaphysics* 986a19) might not have been disturbed by the fact that the Pythagorean theorem—when applied to the unit square—produced a result that was as odd and even as the unit itself. Actually, they might have rationalized this result as proof of the unique position of the monad as the fountainhead of the number series. Ardent adherents of numerology, like the *Akousmatikoi*, would not have been above such justifications. Perhaps even a serious thinker like **Philolaus** would have seen nothing wrong with a proof that establishes a mix of odd and even; after all, he said, "Number, indeed, has two proper kinds, odd and even, and a third from both mixed together, the even-odd" (**DK** 44B5, trans. **Huffman** [135] *Philolaus* 178). Huffman suggests that with the even-odd, Philolaus has numbers in mind, which consist of even and odd integers combined in ratios, e.g., 2:1, 4:3, etc. (190) However, is it out of the question that Philolaus was thinking of irrationals? This is pure speculation, of course, but the discovery of $\sqrt{2}$ is thought to fall within his time, and Indirect Proof was known since Parmenides.

While gods may know instantaneously "What IS" or "What IS NOT" the case, with a little time and a reliable method, we will not only discover better, as Xenophanes believed, but we may even reach a level of knowledge that is neither inferior nor less certain.

The field of speculation was off to a promising start.

CHAPTER XI

Mind and Universe: Two Realms, Two Separate Approaches

> Insofar as the statements of mathematics refer to reality, they are not certain, and insofar as they are certain, they do not refer to reality.
>
> —Albert Einstein[665]

Two Ways of Looking at Things

The problem of irrationality and incommensurability would have lasting effects on ancient Greek thinking, leading to an un-Pythagorean rift between geometry and arithmetic that remained unbridged for thousands of years. Scholars believe that for mathematicians in general, and the later Pythagoreans in particular, these would be bitter lessons to be learned. Having to confront the reality of unexpressible proportions, such difficulties were soon confined to geometry, if only to preserve the ideal of an exact discipline in the realm of rational numbers.[666] In other words, geometry was delimited to spatial magnitudes, meaning the outer universe, while mathe-

---

665   **Einstein** [741] *Geometrie und Erfahrung* 3–4: "Insofern sich die Sätze der Mathematik auf die Wirklichkeit beziehen, sind sie nicht sicher, und insofern sie sicher sind, beziehen sie sich nicht auf die Wirklichkeit." Cf. **Popper** [690] *The Logic of Scientific Discovery* 314n4.

666   **Boyer** [733]: "The world of continuous magnitudes was a thing apart from number and had to be treated through geometric method," and "Greek mathematics tended to avoid proportions." (*A History of Mathematics* 88, 113) **Maor** [760]: "This distinction between arithmetic number and geometric magnitude, which in effect contradicted the Pythagorean doctrine that number rules the universe, would henceforth become an essential element of Greek mathematics." (*e: The Story of a Number* 190) **Maziarz** and **Greenwood** [761]: "A rift was opened between arithmetic and geometry." (*Greek Mathematical Philosophy* 51) **Kline** [752]: "Although [the Greeks] recognized that quantities exist which are neither whole numbers nor fractions, they were so convinced that the concept of number could not comprise anything else than whole numbers or fractions that they did not accept irrationals as numbers." (*Mathematics for the Nonmathematician* 69) See also **Pappus**, *The Commentary of Pappus on Book X of Euclid's Elements* I.3 (**Junge-Thomson** [651]) 64–65, below.

matics was elevated to the higher, less uncooperative realm of abstraction. In a sense, this differentiation is not dissimilar to that made by Parmenides, who, when aiming for reliability, prefers the objects of thought, which, interestingly, is a view echoed by Einstein (as illustrated by the quote above).

A sure way of preventing contradiction is by avoiding a mix of incompatible things. This essentially Parmenidean consideration must have been on the mind of those who began to believe that geometry and arithmetic lacked a common ground.[667] In other words, a perfect premise was missing. Numbers could be absolved of irrationality if the phenomenon was confinable to magnitudes. For instance, one could maintain that numbers themselves are ruled most rigorously and without exception by the unit, while magnitudes and proportions are so ruled only sporadically or under certain conditions. A similar take is preserved in Pappus' summation of the problem, for he presents an interesting distinction: numbers have a minimum but no maximum, magnitudes have no minimum but a maximum. In both cases, it is the *unit* that provides closure, but at opposite "ends": as a minimum, it is the "one" for the number series, as a maximum it is the "whole" for magnitudes:

> Numbers, progressing by degrees, advance by addition from that which is a minimum, and proceed to infinity (or indefinitely); whereas the continuous quantities begin with a definite (or determined) whole and are divisible (or subject to division) to infinity (or indefinitely). If, therefore, a minimum cannot be found in the case of the continuous quantities, it is evident that there is no measure (or magnitude) which is common to all of them, as unity is common to the numbers.[668]

Pappus highlights an important principle that has been at the core of much of Greek philosophy, namely the distinction between things that are reducible (or divisible) to an irreducible minimum—such as the basic unit—and things that are infinitely divisible, without ever coming upon that one ultimate irreducible term that can function as a bookend, putting a halt to the reduction process. It also explains the abhorrence of the Greeks for accepting the infinite *as a base for thinking* and perhaps the disinclination

---

667 Perhaps irrationals were excluded from arithmetic because the Greeks had no way of expressing such "values"—and symbolic notation had not yet been introduced. This suggestion is by **Heath** [746] *The Manual of Greek Mathematics* 54–55, 246.

668 **Pappus**, *The Commentary of Pappus on Book X of Euclid's Elements* I.3 (**Junge-Thomson** [651]) 64–65.

to adopt anything akin to zero as the foundation of a number series.[669] But most important, the notion that perfection and exactness belonged exclusively to the realm of mind—and not the messy universe—gained strength and conviction, particularly through the works of Plato, which represented a distinct departure from the Pythagorean stab at a unified theory.

But again, it is Parmenides who seems to have inaugurated the trend. After all, it is his differentiation between two types of objects, those of truth versus those of opinion, equivalent to the intelligible on one side and the sensible on the other—and most significant, of the two ways of accounting for each, one certain, the other plausible/approximative—that was to pave the way for a bifurcated approach to inquiry. It allowed the "coexistence" of otherwise irreconcilable differences that distinguish the objects of reason from those of sense-experience.[670] Each could be addressed on its own terms without having to negate the other.

What We Think Fits with What We Think, but Not Necessarily with the Universe

Based on the above considerations, we may surmise that the objects of reason are *necessarily* commensurable—not because of some innate predilection, but because *the mind cannot do otherwise than to create conformable things*. This is why, for example, for the later Pythagoreans, the *unpositioned unit* as an object of reason was identical to the *positioned point*, the object of sense-experience. However, theirs was a cardinal mistake: just because the objects of reason are commensurable with each other does not mean that they have to have matching counterparts in the physical universe—and if they do, that the imagined commensurability they possess is able to survive a transition to the sensible world.

Particularly when dealing with the absolute, the perfect, and the ideal—or the mathematically certain, according to Einstein—no field of in-

---

669 Zero is not an irreducible unit. Perhaps there was a psychological aversion against having a bona fide number series be based on "nothing." Cf. **Guthrie** [43] *HGP* 1.240: "The reason why the unit occupies such an anomalous position in Greek thought is no doubt that zero was unknown." For further discussions on zero, see **Kaplan** [751] *The Nothing That Is* 14–27. For the term "zero" being derived from the Arabic *zephirum*, see **Boyer** [733], *A History of Mathematics* 254.

670 Of course a monistic interpretation of Parmenides does not allow the formulation of his doctrine as above. But after all the advances in Parmenidean interpretation within the last thirty years such a one-sided view has become tedious if not untenable. What is commonly ignored is the fact that before Parmenides, a twofold approach to inquiry was unheard of, yet after him it was an indispensable device for most philosophical directions.

terest has a mandate over reality, regardless of whether it is geometry, mathematics, or carpentry. Once more, we can turn to Pappus, who, in his own way, almost two millennia before Einstein, came to similar conclusions; in fact, he summarizes the lessons that even earlier thinkers had to learn, all of whom had a similar inkling of two not quite conformable "realities":

> We must recognize what the ultimate nature of this matter consists in, namely, that a common measure exists naturally for the numbers, but does not exist naturally for the continuous quantities on account of the fact of division which we have previously set forth, pointing out several times that it is an endless process. On the other hand it (i.e. the measure) exists in the case of the continuous quantities by convention as a product of the imaginative power. We assume, that is, some definite measure or other and name it a cubit or a span or some such like thing. Then we compare this definite unit of measurement which we have recognized, and name those continuous quantities which we can measure by it, rational, whereas those which cannot be measured by it, we classify as irrationals. To be rational in this sense is not a fact, therefore, which we derive from nature, but is the product of the mental fancy which yielded the assumed measure. All continuous quantities, therefore, cannot be rational with reference to one common measure. For the assumed measure is not a measure for all of them; nor is it a product of nature but of the mind.[671]

While a strong Platonic influence is undoubtedly present in Pappus' commentary, he seems to go here one step further: order is the product of the mind, the individual, yes, even the *human* mind.[672] It is we who define what the standard of measurement is and then act surprised whenever the universe does not slavishly conform to our designs. Yet commensurability, hence *finitude,* is not something derived from nature but a peculiarity that, at best, is exported from us to it. Sometimes things will appear to conform and sometimes they will not.

In fact, the mind's relationship with the universe is somewhat one-sided. What comes from the universe, the mind can take and make fit to its own designs. On the other hand, the mind cannot readily export its norms to the universe and have them equally accepted. Thus, geometrically speak-

---

671 **Pappus**, *The Commentary of Pappus on Book X of Euclid's Elements* I.5 (**Junge-Thomson** [651]) 68–69.

672 There are Neoplatonic parallels as well as a curious debt to Parmenides. Pointed out astutely by **Kahn** [395]: "It is through its Aristotelian reformulation that the Parmenidean identification of knowing and Being has exerted its historical influence. This identification is firmly established in Neoplatonism, where the Platonic Forms themselves lose their independent status and are ultimately indistinguishable from νοῦς, the noetic principle which guarantees their unity." ('The Thesis of Parmenides' 723)

ing, if we are looking for a common principle, not all possible segmentations offered by the universe may fit all possible segmentations[673]—at least not according to our understanding of what fitting should mean.[674]

Hence, when we define the objects of reason, we may be inspired by the things of the universe, which does not mean, however, that the reverse is also true. Another mistake is to think that whenever we are studying an abstraction we are actually studying the *object* of our abstraction. Jonathan Barnes offers us an interesting oxymoron regarding the natural scientist, even venturing a quite scary proposition: can physics be the study of the unreal?

> Natural scientists regularly study idealized entities: the objects of their theories are not the rough and ready physical bodies of our mundane world, but ideal approximations to them; they study frictionless surfaces, not ordinary tables or desks; they talk of an isolated system, not of a piece of our messy world. Physics is the most unreal of sciences.[675]

Whatever we convert from universe to an idealized form is just that: an idealized form. The critical question is this: is the universe in an *idealized form* still the universe? Those who study it like to think so, yet with Parmenides a new idea has emerged, namely, the more reliable *our account* of the universe is, the less it is an account of the universe known to us by *experience*. We must therefore recognize that if we are dealing with the universe there must be room for error, yet when we are dealing with thinking, there cannot be. In fact, if error is excluded, we can be certain of one thing: we are not dealing with reality. As a formula, this has been poignantly framed by Karl Popper, who thought to retool Einstein's remark on the unreality of certainty as follows:

> Insofar as a scientific statement speaks about reality, it must be falsifiable: and insofar as it is not falsifiable, it does not speak about reality.[676]

While the falsifiability of how we both register and express reality is an intriguing subject, more important in our context is the reverse: the *incorruptibility of the object of reason*. It may not be entirely commensurate with

---

673 **Boyer** [733]: "The discovery of the incommensurable had shown that not all line segments could be associated with whole numbers; but the converse statement—that numbers can always be represented by line segments—obviously remains true." (*A History of Mathematics* 114)

674 The rift between geometry and arithmetic was eventually healed by Descartes, but that is another story.

675 **Barnes** [9] *TPP* 172.

676 **Popper** [690] *The Logic of Scientific Discovery* 314.

the object of sense-experiential reality, but how commensurate can anything be with something that must be falsifiable to pass for real? Simply because Einstein observed that exact mathematical statements are at odds with reality does not mean that to strive for certainty is wrong, or that it doesn't have a vital calibrating function for the mind.

To what other criteria may we turn when we need to tune our thinking, if not only our grasp of reality is falsifiable, *but also our reasoning*? Existence would be a chaos beyond our imagination. Thus, we have no choice but to set rational parameters or standards, and if these standards are met we have certainty. This is an essential Parmenidean message, even though it was often misunderstood or ignored.

But Parmenides did not stop there: while he demanded that reason's account be rigorously reliable, he allowed for its counterpart, the description of sense-experience, to fulfill a precisely definable minimum of fidelity in its ordering of words. Plausibility is not irrefutable fact, but it has its merits when addressing the object of sense. Accordingly, one of the Eleatic's greatest achievements is to allow error in our dealings with sense-experience—particularly if we try to explain it—but to categorically reject such an approximative approach when dealing with thinking. In fact, he even encourages us to learn what the errors are, so that we may not be fooled by plausible accounts into thinking that they are dependable (8.60–61).

In the final analysis, incommensurability occurs when reality and the norms set up by thinking collide, revealing a startling incompatibility, a mystery no one has yet managed to explain. Those who bargained on the unit to be the golden premise that could link the inner world with the outer had to discover, much to their dismay, that units govern not the universe, but only what little sense we make of it. In the end, the objects of thought and those of experience will continue to bear a certain incongruence so long as no common measure is found to which both can be subjected. If Parmenides attempted anything, then it must have been a completely new approach to this dilemma. This was his shot at the perfect premise. After all, instead of adopting something like the numerical unit, he went deeper, finding the "that which IS for thinking" to be the ultimate measure of commensurability.[677] In this sense, he was forced to redefine what is real not as what is sensible or plausible, but as what is *reasoned*, hence true, because it was fully verifiable—the persuasive solution to Xenophanes' dilemma.

---

677 Even though What IS is unitary. This aspect of it was exploited by **Plato** in the *Parmenides*.

But was Parmenides' approach sufficiently useful, if not in setting up a common standard, then at least for the management of both the objects of mind *as well as* those of sense-experience? There are enough indications that this new system was capable of also accommodating the latter acceptably (viz. *dokimos*, 1.32). Thus one may speculate that such integration was the real purpose of Doxa, a factor that may have played a role in the plausibility of its ordering. However, whether the attempt was successful, we do not know; too little of the Doxa survived. But if we study the remnants carefully, we realize that this is neither a perfunctory nor a haphazard representation of the outer world. It is too orderly in its arrangement,[678] too compliant to some of the provisos of the Evidential Account—for example, the exclusion of the existential version of IS NOT (that is, void) from participating as one of the basic elements, alongside Light and Night (9.4). Still, a Deceptive Ordering of Words is certainly not the same as a Reliable or Evidential Account. So Doxa is something in between after all: sufficiently consistent in its composition to be *plausible*, yet compromising or approximative enough to be *untrustworthy*.

And so the question remains: do we have sufficient grounds to conclude that Doxa's purpose was to bring the objects of sense-experience more in accord with those of reason, to create a bridge, perhaps, between the two worlds, or to be part of the solution for some common system? Maybe future interpretations can answer this question definitively. For now, my reflections on the issue must suffice, although I hope to have opened a few new possibilities in interpretation. What remains is to provide a brief summarization, a final comparison between a Pythagorean and a Parmenidean approach to understanding.

Renouncing Thinking's Dependency upon Sense-Experience

Surely the biggest breakthrough for any science of thought was its liberation from the clutches of sense-experience. (We don't have to have the experience of putting a man on the Moon, in order to figure out how to put a man on the Moon.) However, I do not think that Parmenides was advocating an all-out anti-empiricism, much less that he was a consummate idealist, as some interpreters believe. I think that he attempted to strike a balance between the two epistemological realms, because he focused strongly

---

678 Cf. **Barney** [10] "The *Doxa* is, for all its originality, represented as a rational reconstruction of human opinion." ('Socrates Agonistes' 93)

on some of the laws he thought they had in common. Thus, we need to strike a similar balance when interpreting him, as when we philosophize in general. The key is the same as it was 2,500 years ago, namely, to harmonize the knowledge created by reason with the information gathered by the senses. If humanity had relied only on experience, none of us would have left our caves. There was always someone who had to speculate on what may lie beyond the horizon before anyone actually went there and checked. However, going out there and checking was just as necessary as was dreaming about it.

For myself, one of Parmenides' greatest contributions is the idea that thinking can be managed or controlled. The Goddess, his mentor, constantly urges him to "think this" or "don't think that," and like a good teacher, she also teaches by example. What purpose do rules for thinking have? What benefit? Above all, they define the object of reason. Rules make things intelligible by imposing certain limits upon how they are and how we may think of them. They demand us to think "this" and "not that," or think "so" and "not otherwise." Thus, when the Goddess encourages Parmenides to think something or bars him from thinking something else, she teaches him where to set the limits to what is being thought; indeed, how to ascertain the boundaries of any object of judgment. We have learned that there is "an ultimate limit" (8.42), and that our object is held "within the bonds of the limit which encloses it all around" (8.31), and also that it must be a perfect unity (8.23, 8.49, 8.54) and that "it must either wholly be or not be at all" (8.11), and so forth. The outright restrictions are far too numerous to be repeated here, but we have also seen that the greater part of Parmenides' Poem has more affinity with a lawbook than a philosophical treatise. Yet these kinds of rigorous "rules for thinking" are missing in any kind of philosophical direction before Parmenides.

Admittedly, the Pythagoreans were the first to search for a unified theory, and for most of us their grandest questions are still not categorically resolved. No one really *knows* whether there is such a thing as preexistence or afterlife. At least the Pythagoreans dared to dream of immortality. However, for all their tentative steps into inquiry they were burdened by the legacies of proto-civilization, such as magic, cultism, soothsaying, and mysticism, which, paradoxically, are "paths of inquiry" that have a greater affinity for what can be experienced, sensed, or perceived rather than for the exercise of passionless reason. Thus, Pythagoreanism resided largely in the twilight of wisdom, before the sun of philosophy had cleared the experiential horizon. This goes hand in hand with Walter Burkert's conclusion: "The significance of Pythagoras is to be sought not in the realm of philosophy proper but in the approaches to it, in his position as an intermediary between old and new."[679]

If Pythagoras was an intermediary, then Parmenides could only belong to the new. In his repudiation of sense-experience as a standard by which to test the object of reason or judgment, we can recognize a first attempt to emancipate thinking and make it self-reliant. His pioneering ideas have allowed not only philosophy—as the art of coordinating thought and discourse—to shed the bonds of empirical dependency, but also benefited other fields of inquiry. I have mentioned, for instance, the mathematicians and the problem of incommensurable magnitudes. But where did these thinkers get the idea that a purely rational approach proves anything? Numbers, as we have seen, were not regarded as abstract entities by the earliest thinkers, nor, as Eurytus' "pebble-arithmetic" shows, were they treated any differently than the sensible things. And, apparently, accountants, architects and surveyors were proud of the fact that the outcome of their work was verifiable by actual calculation or measurement.[680]

Árpád Szabó has argued that neither anti-empiricism nor the method of Indirect Proof could have arisen out of mathematics, but that mathematicians must have been inspired by an outside influence—a philosophical debate, perhaps, between the Eleatics and Pythagoreans. Why else, he asks, would "a predominantly empirical mathematical tradition suddenly and for no apparent reason become anti-empirical and anti-visual?"[681] He also points out that in Greek mathematics, the first demonstrations of indirect argument coincided with the emergence of non-experiential ideas.[682] Thus, Szabó concludes:

> It was the teaching of Parmenides and Zeno which (in the first half of the fifth century, most probably) induced mathematicians to turn away from empiricism and to adopt the view that mathematical objects *exist only in the mind*. The method of indirect proof, so typical of mathematical reasoning, and the theoretical *foundations* of mathematics had their origins in Eleatic dialectic. Furthermore, all the terms which were used to denote fundamental mathematical principles came from there as well. Indeed, as we have seen, Euclid's very first

---

679 **Burkert** [100] *Lore* 192.
680 **Szabó** [772] *Beginnings* 216.
681 Ibid., 217.
682 Ibid., 219. Enter Parmenides, who ultimately aimed for that principle which, as **de Santillana** [532] puts it, "'holds all together ...' And this implies no longer visualizing, but an *abstract* representation." (*Prologue to Parmenides* 23)

arithmetical definition (VII.1) presupposes the 'theory of the One' (*Republic* VII.525), which is in a sense identical with Parmenides' doctrine of 'Being.'[683]

There is an undeniable Eleatic undertone in Plato's argumentation in *Republic* VII 524e–525, where he states that the study of unity "will be one of the studies that guide and convert the soul to the contemplation of true being." And the nonempirical import of *Republic* 526 is even more compelling. The question is raised as to what kind of numbers are of such oneness that "each unity is equal to every other without the slightest difference and admitting no division into parts." The answer given is: "Units which can only be conceived by thought, and which it is not possible to deal with in any other way."[684] We see that the notion of two objects—one exclusively of reason, to be distinguished from the one of sense-experience—was so firmly established in Plato's time that the issue was capable of being elaborated from various points of view, including mathematics. Yet as much as Plato accomplished in detailing the subject, he himself did not *invent* this twofold distinction; Parmenides did.

We have come full circle, in the spirit of Parmenides' Goddess, and perhaps we have a better appreciation as to why Parmenides did not deal with the world but with our understanding of "what there is for thinking"—and that alone secured the object of reason a place in philosophy.

Whether Pythagoreanism failed because it neglected to distinguish between the objects of reason and those of sense-experience, we can only speculate. They certainly deserve credit for aiming for a unifying theory that would make sense of all things, regardless of their nature or apparent differences. And theirs would not be the last attempt of this kind.

It should give us pause that, so far, no one has managed to find that common measure which can do justice to mind and universe alike. There is certainly a mystery here that apparently not even Einstein could resolve. While he points out the disparity between certainty and reality, he offers no reason for it, nor the possibility of a solution. And maybe such a thing is impossible, and other attempts will fail just like the Pythagoreans did if no clear-cut distinction is made between the objects of reason and the objects of sense.

---

683 **Szabó** [772] *Beginnings* 304–305. See also 257–261, which lays the groundwork for this conclusion.

684 I believe that it is this passage, i.e., *Republic* 526a, that **Szabó** [772] has in mind when he refers to *Republic* 525. Cf. *Beginnings* 258–259.

Whether, perhaps, Parmenides learned from their failures or uncovered such misconceptions on his own is something we can muse about but not prove either way. Yet he lived in a time and place where, as fate would have it, these exact problems came to a head. Eventually, someone had to realize that, in a manner of speaking, the unit had to be separated from the point, that it had to relinquish a position in space and time to be confined where it belonged—to a presence in the *mind*. And that, in the end, was the final answer to Xenophanes, because as the Goddess indicates, there was one kind of commensurability that was nevertheless possible, not necessarily between mind and sense-experience, but between the reality known to the gods and the reality known to mortals—after all, they *both* had reason in common. And that, even old Xenophanes would have agreed, was the best of all premises.

Paradoxically, this newly discovered kinship with the divine seems to have allowed humankind a tentative independence from same. At least more and more people no longer required that all of their truths be spelled out by gods, opting to trust—as Parmenides' Goddess urged—their inherent reasoning faculties, rather than await extraneous direction. Free to acquire the means, the checks, and the balances to pursue our own answers and designs, we have increasingly relied on that particular discipline that so far has proven best suited for the management of human knowledge, namely science. Of course, for us—whether now, or 2,500 years ago—the journey on the "much-informing road of the Goddess" has just begun.

Appendix

The Info to Certainty Sequence, Part I

Objective:
   Introduction to a Simple Method for Assessing Pythagorean Lore

Subject Under Consideration:
   The Cross-Referencing of the Raw Data on Pythagoras' Life as a Demonstration of the INFO TO CERTAINTY SEQUENCE

What is there to be known regarding Pythagoras' life and death, the anti-Pythagorean revolts in Southern Italy, and the eventual fate of the order? Very little that is conclusive. The next two sections outline a system of classifying raw data so that better estimates can be achieved as to the plausibility of the accounts offered by ancient commentators. But first I will address the "INFO TO CERTAINTY SEQUENCE" itself.

How to Transform Raw Data, Remarks, Bits of Lore— "Info"—to Reliable Knowledge

The goal of the sequence is to establish or attain certainty. The sequence is subdivided into five sections, each one marking a specific state of affairs or phase of action. The sequence begins with a sort of *first contact* with our subject, in which we take notice or become aware of a piece of information—a bit of lore, for example. The accumulated data are then whittled down through various steps, such as from *possible* to *probable*, then further reduced to what can be *confirmed* or authenticated, and lastly, the remainder may be classified as *certain*.

Thus, for the classification of the reliability of information, each step is defined per the following criteria in a descending order:

- **CERTAINTY** represents irrefutable proof.
- **CONFIRMED** applies to data that are corroborated or verifiable, meaning that we either have one dependable source—one that we know and can predict because we have confirmed its reliability before, perhaps on other subjects—or we have a multitude of independent sources. The latter we might not know well, but if they are independent of each other and offer us corresponding accounts of something, we may feel assured that the sources are confirming a fact because *they confirm each other*. Of course, they might still be collectively wrong, which is why the information does not rise to the level of **CERTAINTY** until *irrefutability* is established. Thus, to qualify something as **CONFIRMED** one must overcome or eradicate all reasonable contradictions. To raise it to **CERTAINTY** is to make it utterly impervious. To be unchallengeable is the key to irrefutability.
- **PROBABLE** suggests that the information is about as accurate as it can be without sufficient or satisfactory cross-referencing that would qualify it as **CONFIRMED**. It may also be the case that the information is independently substantiated but incomplete, and we are lacking those crucial details that would confirm it. Thus, the hallmark of **PROBABLE** is that something *decisive* is missing. The information might come from sources that are either too few or unknown to us, or they do not support each other adequately, or their own credibility has not been sufficiently tested. Yet a **PROBABLE** account also suggests that there are acceptable grounds that something may *reasonably* be so. In other words, based on the current information and sources available—even though we are lacking some corroborative elements—we can find no reason to assume that if we *could* find such corroborative elements in the future, these would not confirm what we now only *assume to be likely*. In short, as long as the data is **PROBABLE**, we must continue to pursue corroboration. Yet the best way to do this is to seek without mercy *any* conceivable factor or element that can undermine or negate our information. In other words, the main task of the **PROBABLE** phase is to hunt for contradictions that could undermine raising the data to **CONFIRMED**.
- **POSSIBLE**, in contrast to **PROBABLE**, suggests only that an account, or the state of affairs described, possesses the *capability* of being or having occurred as suggested. For example, no known law of nature stands in the way of something having transpired as reported. The category of **POSSIBLE** is very much connected with potentiality or capacity; however, the *ability* of something to be in a particular way must not necessarily come to fruit or withstand testing. Thus, in regard to *reliable knowledge*, a piece of data that belongs to **POSSIBLE** cannot assure us that something actually occurred in the way suggested, but only that there was no other factor—that we know of—which could have prevented it from occurring in the fashion described. Hence, in the **POSSIBLE** phase we begin to assemble our first arsenal of tests, witnesses, and other evidentiary means with which to begin authenticating our information in the subsequent steps.
- And finally, **INFO**—the initial phase—represents the unqualified collection of raw data, including anecdotes, allegations, rumor, gossip, myths, lore, or fable, and even outright lies, fabrications, and forgeries. Of course, some of these unqualified data

might eventually be turned into **CONFIRMED** fact. But until the possibility and probability is determined for such a fact, until it is tested, and corroborated, everything remains only a story. Hence, in the **INFO** phase we simply collect everything we can get our hands on, indiscriminately. What is important is that nothing gets ruled out in the **INFO** phase—regardless of how far-fetched it may seem.

Thus, if we are to classify in a more cogent fashion the various bits of lore available about Pythagoras or the Pythagoreans, we should subject them to a system like the INFO TO CERTAINTY SEQUENCE. What follows is an example of how the Sequence works on behalf of some general information on Pythagoras—before we proceed to the outcome of this method as applied to the story of his death and the Pythagorean revolts.

It is very important that we initially approach no subject as if any part of it belongs a priori to a higher classification than **INFO**. In other words, every scrap of information must be subjected to the sequence, and we must not skip any of the steps.

Lore About Pythagoras—Life, Activities, and the Pythagorean Order:

First and foremost, whenever we carry out this type of investigation, the general goal is to establish the answer to this question: is there information that can be brought up through the sequence all the way to **CERTAINTY**? (For the purpose of this presentation, it must be noted that I have already executed the sequence for myself and that I am offering here only the *results* of this exercise; thus, I begin with **CERTAINTY**. Obviously, a point-by-point demonstration of the execution of the entire sequence would begin with **INFO**, but, naturally, such a demonstration would require another book.)

Is the fact that an influential sage named Pythagoras actually existed as the figurehead of a movement around the second part of the sixth century *incontestible*? We do not have *irrefutable proof* in support of this claim—not in its entirety. As pointed out by Walter Burkert: "It is only in post-Aristotelian sources that biographical and historical details regarding Pythagoras and the Pythagoreans are to be found"[685] (in other words, our first sources are Aristotle's pupils, Aristoxenus and Dicaearchus, and the rest come well

---

685 **Burkert** [100] *Lore* 109. Also **Philip** [163] *PEP* 194: "Our best attested evidence . . . is of fourth century origin." And that is based on oral tradition up to 150 years old.

after his death in 322 B.C.). This means that as long as no better or more immediate sources turn up in the future, not to mention some sort of *physical* proof, we can only make do with the many independent accounts and traditions. Thus, so far we have to conclude: there are no certainties when dealing with the subject of Pythagoras. So we can skip **CERTAINTY**.

What information may be deemed *confirmable*? (Again, the following classifications are intended as an illustration of how I have applied the INFO TO CERTAINTY SEQUENCE—rendered here in reverse because it represents the result of an executed sequence. Furthermore, this is not a comprehensive categorization of *all* the Pythagorean lore. For information regarding Pythagoras' death and the revolts, see the next section. Thus, what we will be examining here is information on Pythagoras' life, activities, and the Pythagorean order.)

The following information can be classed as **CONFIRMED** by a variety of independent sources:

CONFIRMED:

- The existence of a sage named Pythagoras—two independent contemporaries (sixth century) speak of him by name (albeit unfavorably), namely, Xenophanes (c. 570–470 B.C.) and Heraclitus (c. 540–480 B.C.).[686] The fifth-century historian Herodotus (485–424 B.C.) refers to Pythagoras as "hardly the weakest intellect in Greece," yet has no more to add by way of a historical account.[687] There is also numismatic evidence, e.g., the coins of Adbera, which portray a bearded head and the inscription *PUTHAGORES*.[688]
- There are, as far as we can tell, numerous independent reports stating that Pythagoras emigrated to Southern Italy and that his base was the city of Croton.[689]

---

686 Xenophanes, **DK** 21B7; **Heraclitus**, 22B40. Another probable reference to Pythagoras is **Empedocles'** affectionate ode, **DK** 31B129, yet without mentioning his name.

687 **Herodotus**, *The Histories* 4.95–96, only mentions the spurious tale of Pythagoras' slave Zamolxis, who was in fact a Thracian deity. Even Herodotus voices his doubts about the story. However meager our evidence may be, scholars infer that it suffices to prove the existence of Pythagoras. As **Burkert** [100] concludes: "The oldest sources show Pythagoras, unlike Orpheus, as a tangible personality of the historical period." (*Lore* 131)

688 As to the numismatic evidence and the *Puthagores* coins, see **Burkert** [100] *Lore* 110n2. See also **de Vogel**'s [180] general discussion of Pythagorean coins, *Pythagoras* 6, 28–39, 49, 52–57. And **von Fritz** [122] *PPSI* 6.70, 80–86, 99, on coins as evidence of Croton's dominance. See **Philip** [163] for a more cautious view regarding the *Puthagores* coin's link with Pythagoras (*PEP* 194). See **Minar** [160] *EPP* 77–78, on coin evidence and the downfall of Croton in 460 B.C. or after.

689 **Justin**, 20.4.1–5; 17–18. This account is supposedly from **Timaeus**. Furthermore, **Diodorus**, 12.9; **DK** 14,14. On the establishment of Pythagoras in Croton, see **Dicaearchus**, fr. 33 (Wehrli) = **Porphyry**, *VP* 18, **DK** 14,8a; **Iamblichus**, *VP* 28–30. For more references, see **Dicaearchus**, fr. 34; **Porphyry**, *VP* 54–57. Additionally, there is **Aristoxenus**, fr. 18 (Wehrli); **Iamblichus**, *VP* 248–251; **DK** 14,16. Also Aristotle, fr. 191 R, and **D.L.**, 8.3, 21, 38–39.

- There are various independent (again, as far as we can tell) reports that the movement he inspired was mystical, religious, and speculative in nature, and that *its* central beliefs focused on the transmigration of the soul and the leading of a decent or virtuous life.[690]

PROBABLE:

What, then, belongs to *PROBABLE*?

- Pythagoras lived between approximately 570 and 500 B.C.[691]
- Samos is Pythagoras' place of origin. This cannot be unconditionally confirmed—there are simply too many separate accounts that say otherwise. Nonetheless, Samos is the most widespread belief: thus, it is sufficiently cross-referenced to make it **PROBABLE**.[692]

---

690   See **Aristotle**, frs. 192 (R), 196, 197, 201, 203; **Dicaearchus**, fr. 33 (Wehrli) = **Porphyry**, *VP* 18–19 (**DK** 14,8a). Also **D.L.**, 8.4, on metempsychosis, and 8–25 on general precepts. On the transmigration of the soul, see also **Diodorus**, 10.6. In my view, this subject is most poignantly defined by **Barnes** [9] *TPP* 103: "The doctrine of metempsychosis, or the transmigration of souls, is on any account characteristic of Pythagoreanism; on Dicaearchus' account, to which I assent, it is the chief constituent of that small body of theory which we are justified in ascribing to Pythagoras. And it is enough ... to secure a place for Pythagoras among the philosophers." However, regarding the so-called Pythagorean life, I am quite uneasy with giving its precepts the same rank as metempsychosis. We cannot confirm that they originate with Pythagoras himself. Thus, what I have pointed out is that the *movement's* focus was on these beliefs; these may have been originally his, or subsequent adoptions. Be that as it may, on "cultivating the simple life," see **Diodorus**, 10.7. As for **Iamblichus** and **Porphyry**, everything in their *VPs* constitutes a relevant reference (e.g., **Porphyry**, *VP* 19; **Iamblichus**, *VP* 134). Additionally (according to **Aristoxenus**, fr. 15 [Wehrli] = **D.L.**, 8.7), Pythagoras received his moral teachings from the priestess of Delphi. Of course, this piece of lore belongs to **POSSIBLE**.

691   See **Lévy** [155] *Sources* 1–5, on the difficulties of reconciling the two main yet contradicting versions. Lévy points to a discrepancy between Aristoxenus' account, which fixes Pythagoras' date of birth around 570 B.C.—based on the assumption that he was forty years old when Polycrates came to power in Samos—and other accounts that have him been born in the last quarter of the sixth century B.C., in order to be, e.g., Empedocles' teacher. Lévy points out that the modern scholarship relies unanimously on Aristoxenus (*Sources* 5). See also **von Fritz**'s [122] discussion of the inconsistencies in **Timaeus**' version, *PPSI* 47–51, and his time line including the second revolt and exodus (*PPSI* 92). A sample of dates from other authors: 571/0–497/6 B.C.: **Jacoby** [617] based on **Apollodorus** (*Apollodor's Chronik* 215–227; see also **Philip** [163] *PEP* 195, for the short version); c. 570–480 B.C.: *DNP* 10 (**Riedweg** [167]); c. 570–503/490 B.C.: **de Vogel** [180] *Pythagoras* 23–25.

692   According to **Hermippus**, **D.L.**, 8.1. The same passage also recounts Aristoxenus' report on Pythagoras being a Tyrrhenian, i.e., Etruscan. See also **Diodorus**, 10.3, on Samos, and also on accounts on being Tyrrhenian (*Loeb* 4.55). See **Porphyry**, *VP* 1, on "some think he was a Samian, while Neanthes ... says he was a Syrian from the city of Tyre." In *VP* 2, "Neanthes says that others held [Pythagoras'] father for a Tyrrhenian." Nonetheless even **von Fritz** is compelled to assert: "Daß Pythagoras in Samos geboren war und seine Jugend dort verbracht hat, besteht keinerlei Grund zu bezweifeln." (*RE* XXIV.185.28–29) See **Minar** [160] mentioning Samian and Etruscan descent, also Phlius, and even Apollo as progenitor (*EPP* 3).

- The same applies to Pythagoras' study of number, proportion, and harmony, which seems to have inspired others to busy themselves with geometry, arithmetic, and music.[693]
- It is also **PROBABLE** that Pythagoras gave guidance and advice to people. However, the notion that he was the sole author of the teachings observed by the movement belongs rightfully to **POSSIBLE**. The same applies to the subject of his teachings, about which we can only speculate. As Dicaearchus says: "Now the content of his teaching to his associates no one can describe reliably, for the secrecy they maintained was quite exceptional."[694]
- And also **PROBABLE** is that Pythagoras and his followers exercised some political influence upon the community at large.[695]

POSSIBLE:

What, then, belongs to **POSSIBLE**?

- Pythagoras invented several geometrical and mathematical theorems.[696]
- Pythagoras gave public and private lectures on various subjects, such as right living, virtuous conduct, etc., or that he issued precepts for the observance of spiritual and corporal purification.[697]
- Pythagoras authored books (which never became known to outsiders).[698]

---

693 **Aristotle**, *Metaphysics* 985b23–986a6 and fr. 203 R. See also **Diodorus**, 10.6.4 on **Callimachus**' quote on Phrygian Euphorbus, i.e., Pythagoras, as well as **Callimachus**, *Oxyrhyrchus Papyri* 1011 (**Hunt** [ed.], trans. **Oldfather** [633] *Diodorus Siculus*, Loeb 4.62). On music and harmony, see also **Plutarch**'s general comments in *On Music* (*Moralia* 1144.37, 1147.44). On followers, see, e.g., Philolaus, Archytas, and Eurytus; also note below.

694 **Dicaearchus**, fr. 33 (Wehrli) = **Porphyry**, *VP* 19 (DK 14,8a. **Burkert** [100] *Lore* 122). For the **POSSIBLE** content of his **POSSIBLE** public lectures, see the note below on Teachings.

695 A sample is **Iamblichus**, *VP* 33. See the extensive exposition by **Dunbabin** [704] *Western Greeks* 73, 93, 360–362, 366–367, 369, 371–373, 385. Naturally, the entirety of **von Fritz's** [122] *PPSI* is a must, particularly the chapter on "Pythagorean Rule," 94–102. The same goes for **Minar's** [160] *EPP*, which is utterly indispensable. An example of conspiratory political machinations is **Justin**, 20.4.14. See below.

696 See **D.L.**, 8.11: "[Pythagoras] brought geometry to perfection... and [he] spent most of his time upon the arithmetical aspect of geometry." Also, that he sacrificed an ox after the discovery of the famous theorem named after him (**D.L.**, 8.12). According to **Diodorus**, Callimachus claimed Pythagoras discovered some of the problems of geometry himself, while other ones he was the first to introduce from Egypt to Greece (**Diodorus**, 10.6.4). Furthermore, according to **Aristoxenus**, Pythagoras was the first to introduce weights and measures into Greece; cf. fr. 24 (Wehrli) = **D.L.**, 8.14.

697 Teachings: **Diodorus**, 10.6–10. For samples of *akousmata*, see **Porphyry**, *VP* 42–44. **D.L.**, 8.8–10, 12, 17–19, 22–24, 32–36. On purification, a sample: The air is full of souls, i.e., daimones and heros. They are the causes for disease and health, and it is to them that the purifications are directed (**D.L.** 8.32–34). Likewise, **Iamblichus'** *VP* is fraught with purported instructions. For a sample of teachings, see the "four speeches," **Iamblichus**, *VP* 35–58, although the prospect that he actually gave these exact speeches is at best barely **POSSIBLE**. The same applies to almost all teachings. Most are post-Pythagorean in origin.

698 **D.L.**, 8.6–8. A claim deemed spurious by scholars.

The Info to Certainty Sequence, Part I 285

- Some of Pythagoras' medical precepts or methods actually made people well.[699]
- Pythagoras' followers advanced *his* ideas to the point that they themselves made valuable contributions to the sciences.[700]
- It is **POSSIBLE** that Pythagoras genuinely intended to educate and reform society—or simply better it any which way he could—just as it is also **POSSIBLE** that he only aimed to set up a dictatorship. *Both* versions are accounted for.[701]

INFO:

Lastly, what kind of information belongs to **INFO**, that is, what do we simply *take notice of*?

- Pythagoras appeared in two places at the same time.[702]
- Pythagoras was the son of Hermes.[703]
- Or the son of Apollo.[704]
- Or Pythagoras was *himself* Apollo and/or the Hyperborean Apollo.[705]
- Pythagoras was Euphorbus in a previous life.[706]

---

699 Pythagoras created songs for the diseases of the body, and cured the sick (**Porphyry**, *VP* 33). **Iamblichus** gives a lengthy account of Pythagoras' musical healing methods (*VP* 64, 68), which includes methods like "arrangements" and "treatments" ("touchings"), as well as the blending of diatonic, chromatic, and enharmonic melodies, which supposedly reversed the maladies of the soul. See **de Vogel** [180] for extensive comments on music and healing (*Pythagoras* 162, 164–166, 232–235). However, Pythagoras could not heal his teacher from being inflicted with lice, a condition which killed him eventually; cf. **Porphyry**, *VP* 55; **Iamblichus**, *VP* 252.

700 On contributions by Pythagoras' followers, see material on Hippasus (**DK** 18), also Philolaus' fragments, e.g., **DK** 44B4–6 and 11, and Eurytus (**DK** 45). On Archytas, see **DK** 47A14 and A15 on doubling of the cube, as well as 47B1 and B2. Furthermore, see **Heath** [745] *A History of Greek Mathematics* 1.143–169, for a detailed account and commentary.

701 On the order's anti-democratic stance and conspiratorial takeover of Croton, see **Justin**, 20.4.14, **D.L.**, 8.39, and **Iamblichus**, *VP* 257–261, particularly Ninon's accusation that Pythagoreanism was essentially a conspiracy against democracy. See **Burkert**'s [100] comments: "Theopompus must have said that the secret, but genuine, goal of the philosophy introduced by "the excellent Pythagoras" . . . was tyranny" (*Lore* 118, 118n55), and **Dunbabin** [704] who speaks of "the weakness of the democratic feeling in the west and the authoritarian tendency evident also in the Pythagorean reverence for the Master." (*Western Greeks* 385) Cf. the *akousmata* on avoiding beans, which can be read as a political instruction to abstain from democratic voting. Beans were used to cast votes (see **Aristotle**, fr. 195 R = **D.L.**, 8.34; also **Guthrie**'s [43] brief explanation, *HGP* 1.185). For an opposing view on Pythagoras, check **Iamblichus**, *VP* 33, which paints the sage as a champion for freedom and against tyranny.

702 **Aristotle**, fr. 191 R; **Porphyry**, *VP* 27; **Iamblichus**, *VP* 134.

703 Source is **Heraclides Ponticus**, according to **D.L.**, 8.4.

704 Cf. **Iamblichus**, *VP* 5 and 8, where he states that the soul of Pythagoras must have been sent to mankind from Apollo's domain.

705 **Aristotle**, fr. 191 R, and **Iamblichus**, *VP* 30, 91, 135.

706 **Dicaearchus**, fr. 36 (Wehrli); **Callimachus**, fr. 191 (cf. *Callimachus, Iambi*, Loeb 109, also **Diodorus**, 10.5.4 and 10.5.2 on the "Shield of Euphorbus" tale); **Porphyry**, *VP* 26 and 45; **Iamblichus**, *VP* 63.

- Pythagoras had a thigh made of gold.[707]
- When crossing a river, it greeted him in a loud voice, saying, "Good morning, Pythagoras."[708]
- Pythagoras killed a poisonous snake by biting it first.[709]
- There are three classes of rational entities: gods, mortals, and beings like Pythagoras.[710]

Again, I have listed mere samples of the lore we possess on Pythagoras and his movement, but as we shall see, it helps if we qualify each piece of data according to the above categories. I refer to this ordering as being a *sequence* because each classification is not intended as a permanent label. In fact, one of the principal tasks to be performed by a researcher is to convert raw or unqualified data to *certain knowledge*. One must look for corroborating and/or refuting evidence until it can be confirmed that something *is* or *is not* the case (incidentally, we owe this method to Parmenides). If we can actually achieve **CERTAINTY**, so much the better, but this is a luxury rarely afforded to the investigator of such distant events. Nonetheless, even the most ancient histories are not immune to new discoveries. Archeology moves on, and the numismatic evidence, for example, has boosted many ideas and deflated others. The ground still holds much undiscovered proof that may move a piece of data from **PROBABLE** to **CONFIRMED**—or even to **CERTAINTY**.

---

707 **Aristotle**, fr. 191 R; **D.L.**, 8.11; **Porphyry**, *VP* 28; **Iamblichus**, *VP* 92.
708 **Aristotle**, fr. 191 R; **Porphyry**, *VP* 27; **Iamblichus**, *VP* 134.
709 **Aristotle**, fr. 191 R.
710 **Aristotle**, fr. 192 R = **Iamblichus**, *VP* 31.

The Info to Certainty Sequence, Part II

Objective:
Use of the INFO TO CERTAINTY SEQUENCE to Further Classify Pythagorean Lore with a Focus on the Death of Pythagoras and the Revolts

Subject Under Consideration:
Pythagoras' Death, the Anti-Pythagorean Revolts, and the Demise of Organized Pythagoreanism in Southern Italy

Regarding the questions surrounding Pythagoras' death and the undoing of Pythagoreanism, how may we classify the various bits of lore according to the INFO TO CERTAINTY SEQUENCE?

CERTAINTY:

- Regrettably, there is hardly anything we know for certain regarding Pythagoras' death that can be proved beyond refutability.[711] Obviously, even to surmise that he must have died if he had lived may be a conjecture in Pythagoras' case, because we are told that he belonged to a third category of rational beings—i.e., "beings like Pythagoras"—and we are not informed whether or not they die. This piece of lore rightfully belongs to **INFO**. We certainly do not have a body to point to or establish a genetic match with. Be that as it may, it is, I believe, far more rewarding to move on to **CONFIRMED**.

CONFIRMED:

- The city of Croton, traditionally considered the home base of the Pythagoreans, defeated the rival city of Sybaris in 510 B.C.[712]
- Afterward, Croton gained a predominant status among other Southern Italian cities, until about 450 B.C.[713]

---

711 See **Philip** [163]: "We do not know, and we cannot discover, the dates of Pythagoras' life." (*PEP* 196) And, "we do not know the circumstances of Pythagoras' death." (*PEP* 192)

712 **Diodorus**, 11.90, 12.9.5–10.4; **Dunbabin** [704] *Western Greeks* 362–365; **Burkert** [100] *Lore* 115. See **von Fritz**'s [122] chronological remarks, *PPSI* 49–51. **Minar** [160] *EPP* 8–14, examines the situation of Croton and Sybaris, stating that the destruction of Sybaris was the worst disaster in Greek history (see also 9 and 9n42; the same is asserted by **Dunbabin** [704] *Western Greeks* 364). And yet the commanding general was a Pythagorean, Milo by name. This according to **Diodorus**, 12.9.5. On Milo as a Pythagorean, see also **Strabo**, 6.1.12

713 **Diodorus**, 12.11.3 (generally, 12.9–10); D.L., 8.39. **Polybius**, 2.39.7, talks about a league established by Croton, yet the exact date is unclear, as Sybaris is listed as one of the par-

- There was at least one rebellion against Pythagoreanism within the first half of the fifth century B.C. Croton also became the center for the persecution of the Pythagoreans.[714]
- A few Pythagoreans escaped the pogroms and emigrated to other lands, such as the Greek mainland.[715]
- At some time, the political climate improved for the Pythagoreans, compelling some to return.[716]
- Around 400 B.C. a sudden surge in expatriation occurred and soon certain "Pythagorists" began to emerge within the Greek world in noticeable numbers.[717]
- The next-generation Pythagoreans (perhaps the *Mathematikoi, Akousmatikoi,* Last Pythagoreans, Pythagorists, et al.) were living in small communities or families, keeping to themselves, preferring anonymity rather than life in the mainstream. Eventually, they died out.[718]
- Additional difficulties encountered by the remainder of the order in Italy led to the eventual exile of just about every (prominent?) Pythagorean by about 400 B.C.—with

---

ticipants, and this account follows his report on the burning of Pythagorean meetinghouses (2.39.1). See **Burkert** [100] *Lore* 115 and 115n41 on numismatic evidence; also elucidations by **de Vogel** [180] *Pythagoras* 24–25, 54–57; and **Dunbabin**'s [704] general account, *Western Greeks* 365–370: "Kroton ruled a solid block of territory between Metapontion and Lokroi" (368), "unquestionably the first power in south Italy for a generation" (367). See **von Fritz**'s [122] discussion of the Crotonite Alliance coins and their discontinuation after 453 B.C., with the rebuilding of Sybaris, *PPSI* 80–86; also 73–74, 93, on the downfall of the alliance. See **Minar** [160] who recognizes the Pythagoreans as the driving force behind Croton's expansion and eventual predominance in Southern Italy, up to the coincidental downfall of the society mid-century (*EPP* 36–49).

714 **Aristoxenus**, fr. 18 (Wehrli) = **Iamblichus**, *VP* 250; **Porphyry**, *VP* 55–56; **D.L.**, 8.39; **Justin**, 20.4.14–18; **von Fritz** [122] *PPSI* 12, 92; **Minar** [160] *EPP* 64, 70; **Guthrie** [43] *HGP* 1.178–179; **Dunbabin** [704] *Western Greeks* 366–367; **de Vogel** [180] *Pythagoras* 22–25; **Zeller** [91] *Outlines of the History of Greek Philosophy* 35 and [89] *DPdG* I/1.416–417.

715 **Aristoxenus**, fr. 18 (Wehrli); **Porphyry**, *VP* 55; **Iamblichus**, *VP* 250 (on Lysis fleeing to the Peloponnese and then Thebes); on other Pythagoreans fleeing to Rhegium, then later leaving Italy altogether, see **Iamblichus**, *VP* 251). See also **Diodorus**, 10.11.2 on Lysis in Thebes, and **Plutarch** (*De Genio Socratis* 583 A) on Gorgias reporting to a Sicilian circle of Pythagoreans that he had met Lysis by chance in Thebes. (Plutarch is considered not very reliable on his Pythagorean accounts.) See comments, **von Fritz** [122] *PPSI* 79.

716 I am not fully convinced this piece of lore is really confirmable. There is, nonetheless, sufficient consensus among many modern interpreters. The reference is **Iamblichus**, *VP* 263–264 ("the citizens of Croton ... were reconciled with the exiles"), probably from **Timaeus** (see **Minar** [160] *EPP* 82–83). On the other hand, **Polybius**, 2.39, does not mention that the Pythagoreans returned and reconciled their situation. Interpretations that believe in the return and even the expansion of the political influence of the surviving Pythagoreans are found in **Minar** [160] *EPP* 80–84; **Philip** [163] *PEP* 180; **Guthrie** [43] *HGP* 1.179; **von Fritz** [122] *PPSI* 91–92, 99–100; **KRS** [56] 224; **McKirahan** [67] *PBS* 79; and **Dunbabin** [704] *Western Greeks* 367.

717 **Von Fritz** [122] *PPSI* 75–76; **Philip** [163] *PEP* 20, 180: "When Dionysius II began to extend his dominion over Magna Graecia, 'Pythagorists'—in what numbers we cannot guess—took refuge in Attica." See **Burkert** [100] *Lore* 198–202, 198n25, for references for *Pythagoristai*. See **Van der Waerden** [183] *Pythagoreer* 64–65, for a comprehensive listing of terms or classes of Pythagoreans.

718 **Porphyry**, *VP* 58–59; **Iamblichus**, *VP* 252–253, via Nicomachus and Neanthes. See **Guthrie** [43] *HGP* 1.180; and **Minar** [160] *EPP* 34: "Those who were driven from Croton and other cities ... maintained themselves in small exclusive groups for a number of years." Check also **Aristoxenus**, fr. 18 (Werhli) = **Iamblichus**, *VP* 248–252, particularly 251. Aristoxenus

the exception of Archytas of Tarentum, who was still the leader of his city when Plato visited Sicily.[719]

PROBABLE:

- The Pythagoreans had played an important part in the politics of Croton as far back as the destruction of the city of Sybaris in 510 B.C. Or in Pythagoras' case, even as early as his arrival in Croton.[720]
- The downfall of the Pythagorean order commenced from a political power struggle, conceivably as a reaction against its influence, partisanship, or even its anti-democratic tendencies.[721]
- Two catastrophic episodes ensued—usually characterized as revolts—against the leading members of the society or Pythagoreanism as such. The first occurred around the beginning of the fifth century, the other fifty to sixty years later, about 450 B.C.[722]

---

probably referred to the Last Pythagoreans. Of course there is also **Plato**, on the Pythagoreans of Phlius (*Phaedo* 57a) and Thebes (*Phaedo* 61e).

719 Possibly there were difficulties with the tyrant Dionysius (**von Fritz** [122] *PPSI* 77, 98–99; **Philip** [163] *PEP* 180). For general reference: **Aristoxenus**, fr. 18, i.e., **Iamblichus**, *VP* 251. See **Plato**'s *Seventh Letter* and **D.L.**, 8.79. (D.L., 8.82, preserves Aristoxenus' account that Archytas was never defeated as commander-in-chief of Tarentum's army.) See **von Fritz** [122] *PPSI* 15, 28, 75–76, for analysis on Archytas' political role and time-span. See also **DK** 47A13 on Aristotle supposedly writing a work on Archytas.

720 On Pythagoras' political activity and Croton, see **Dicaearchus**, fr. 33 (Wehrli); **Justin**, 20.4.6–18 (source: **Timaeus** on early Pythagorean political rule and the conspiracy of the young Pythagorean men: *FGrHist* 566F44–45); also **Porphyry**, *VP* 18 (**DK** 14,8a), and **Diodorus**, 10.3, 9, 11 (see **DK** 14,14), and 10.23 on Sybaris. For a detailed account of the Croton versus Sybaris war and Pythagoras' role, see **Diodorus**, 12.9–10. General parallels on these topics are in **Iamblichus**, *VP* 33, 133, 177, 255, and **Porphyry**, *VP* 9, 18–22, 54–57. Also **Polybius**, 2.39.1–7. For comments on Sybaris, see **von Fritz** [122] *PPSI* 91 and all of *PPSI* on politics, particularly the chapter "Pythagorean Rule," 94–102: "These [Pythagorean] societies tried to acquire political influence and seem to have taken a strong hand in active politics as far back as the great struggle between Kroton and her mighty neighbor Sybaris in 510." (99) Furthermore, all of **Minar**'s [160] *EPP* is a must-read. Likewise, **Guthrie** [43] *HGP* 1.175–178; also **Burkert** [100] *Lore* 115–116. See **Philip** [163] *PEP* 143–145, 179–180, on earlier political activity, and last, see **Dunbabin**'s [704] *Western Greeks* 93, 359–367, for the historical perspective.

721 **Porphyry**, *VP* 54–55; **Iamblichus**, *VP* 248, 255; **Diodorus**, 10.11.1; **Polybius**, 2.39.1–4; **Aristotle**, fr. 191 R; **D.L.**, 8.39: "The inhabitants of Croton [were] anxious to safeguard themselves against the setting up of a tyranny." Comments: **von Fritz** [122] *PPSI* 97–100; **Minar** [160] *EPP* 50–86; **Guthrie** [43] *HGP* 1.176–181; **Dunbabin** [704] *Western Greeks* 360–361, 366–367, 371–372.

722 **Von Fritz** [122] *PPSI* 87, 92, 98–100: "We have, then, to assume that Timaios mentioned two rebellions, one in the early part, the other in the middle, of the fifth century." (87) See also **Minar** [160] *EPP* 52–53, who sees the revolts as "in fact only single aspects of a long struggle"; "however, in at least two separate cases, the opposition forces attained temporary success," i.e., these two "successes" account for there having been *two* revolts. See **Burkert** [100]: "Probably two anti-Pythagorean movements have been combined, one in Pythagoras' lifetime and another about 450." (*Lore* 117) On the first revolt, **Philip** [163] is cautious: "We have no independent historical tradition for the earlier uprising." (*PEP* 192) See also **Dunbabin** [704] *Western Greeks* 366–367, 371–372, e.g.: "The details related of the earlier revolt are

- The first revolt had a political/anti-cult motivation that targeted the Pythagoreans for their secretive ways, their unwelcome political meddling, and the unjust redistribution of the land seized in the war against Sybaris.[723]
- The consensus among scholars is that the first revolt was limited to Croton, and that while other cities did not participate, they also did not come to the rescue of the persecuted Pythagoreans.[724] However, this assessment has some risks. If we are to distinguish the first struggles from the second, then it is best said that the first were more limited in scope and intensity than the second. After the first troubles, the Pythagoreans were probably able to recuperate their losses and/or influence, yet after the second they were doomed.
- Pythagoras had foreseen the difficulties arising in Croton and moved away to Metapontum.[725]

---

unreliable." (366) As an aside, everyone seems to forget that the first murderous episode against the order was the slaughtering of certain Pythagorean citizens of Sybaris as part of the revolt that brought the tyrant Telys to power. This episode played a role in Pythagoras' motivations to drive the Crotonians to a war with Sybaris (**Iamblichus**, *VP* 133, 177). See **Minar** [160] *EPP* 13–14, for elucidations. However, practically all the ancient commentators were ignorant of the fact that there were two revolts and not one, e.g., Porphyry and Neanthes. See **van der Waerden** [183] *Pythagoras* 214; **Minar** [160] *EPP* 52.

723   **Iamblichus'** account of the struggles begins at *VP* 248. See *VP* 255 on the unhappiness with the Sybarite land distribution (probably from **Timaeus** via **Apollonius**, **Minar** [160] *EPP* 54, 54n14). Comments: **von Fritz** [122] *PPSI* 87, 91–92; **Dunbabin** [704] *Western Greeks* 366; **Minar** [160] *EPP* 53–55, e.g.: "The citizens began to believe that the Pythagorean meetings were part of a conspiracy against themselves" (55) and "But the decisive factor in bringing the discontent to a head was the refusal of the ruling oligarchy (controlled by the Pythagoreans) to divide the newly-acquired territory according to the pleasure of the populace." (61)

724   Limited to Croton, according to **Aristoxenus**, fr. 18 (Wehrli) = **Iamblichus**, *VP* 248–251 (see assessment by **von Fritz** [122] *PPSI* 78, and also 87: "The first of them is restricted to Kroton, is caused by a common suspicion on account of the secrecy of the meetings of the Pythagoreans."). However, the disinterest of the cities recorded by Iamblichus is in reference to what we can recognize as the events of the *second* revolt (**Iamblichus**, *VP* 250). This is in direct contradiction with their active role in the persecution preserved by **Dicaearchus**, fr. 34 (Wehrli) = **Porphyry**, *VP* 56, namely that "the revolts took place everywhere," as well as the burning of the *synedria* (meetinghouses) all over Italy according to **Polybius**, 2.39.1–4 (possibly from Timaeus; see doubtful comments by **Minar** [160] *EPP* 75n86). This suggests that the revolt confined to Croton is the first, and the widespread one is the second. However, Aristoxenus, along with all other sources, knew practically nothing of value of the first revolt. See **von Fritz** [122] *PPSI* 30–32, for a juxtaposition of the incongruous accounts of Dicaearchus and Aristoxenus. Von Fritz then surmises that Aristoxenus must be considered most reliable for the period after about 450 B.C. This is a contradiction, in my opinion, that is overlooked by all relevant scholars, because this suggests that no one knew anything decisive of the first revolt. Thus, Dicaearchus and Aristoxenus contradict each other on behalf of the *same* event, i.e., the *second* revolt. Even if the usual explanation suffices that Aristoxenus attempted to minimize the anti-Pythagorean struggles to make the movement look good—which is why he omits that the revolt was widespread—he is *then* omitting Dicaearchus' "everywhere uprisings" and **Polybius'** "burning of the synedria (plural) of the Pythagoreans in Magna Graecia." Yet both statements pertain to the second revolt—ergo, we know nothing of the first, not even enough to say whether it was or was not limited to Croton.

725   **Aristotle**, fr. 191 R. Also hinted by **Aristoxenus**, fr. 18 (Wehrli) = **Iamblichus**, *VP* 249, and **Apollonius** in **Iamblichus**, *VP* 255. (See **Burkert** [100] *Lore* 117n46.) According to **Pompeius Trogus**, he moved to Metapontum (voluntarily) after spending twenty years in

- Pythagoras met an untimely death that was somehow connected to or that resulted from the anti-Pythagorean rebellions.[726]
- Pythagoras died in Metapontum, between c. 500 and 490 B.C.[727]
- The second revolt ensued around 450 B.C. Bloodier than the first, it was not limited only to Croton, but spread to other cities as well.[728]
- As an organized political entity, the Pythagorean society is annihilated around 454–450 B.C.[729]
- At the same time there was a strong democratic movement under way that ultimately terminated Croton's hold on other cities, rendering the colony weak and insignificant.[730]

Croton. (**Justin**, 20.4 [**Philip** [163] *PEP* 144]) Thus, **Minar** [160] calls Pythagoras' flight to Metapontum "a well attested fact." (*EPP* 59)

726   **D.L.**, 8.39–40; **Dicaearchus**, frs. 34, 35 (Wehrli); **Aristoxenus**, fr. 18 (Wehrli); **Porphyry**, *VP* 56–57; **Iamblichus**, *VP* 249. See **Zeller** [89] *DPdG* I/1.418–420, who sees the main troubles manifesting after Pythagoras' death, yet concedes that the opposition could have emerged within Pythagoras' lifetime, and could account for his relocation to Metapontum.

727   **Dicaearchus**, fr. 35; **Aristoxenus**, fr. 18 (Wehrli); **Porphyry**, *VP* 57; **Iamblichus**, *VP* 249; **D.L.**, 8.40. Cicero, when visiting Metapontum, even went to the place where Pythagoras is said to have died: "To see the very place where Pythagoras breathed his last and the seat he sat in." (**Cicero**, *De finibus bonorum et malorum* 5.2.4) For speculations on the date of death, see **von Fritz** [122] "490 B.C.," *PPSI* 49; **de Vogel** [180] *Pythagoras* 21–24, relates "509 B.C.," respectively, "503" (Lenormant) and "490 B.C." (von Fritz); **Philip** [163] *PEP* 195–196 (following **Jacoby** [617]) opts for **Apollodorus'** chronology, i.e., "497/6 B.C." We should discount one of Iamblichus' versions, i.e., 470 B.C.—based on Timaeus—according to the general consensus. (See **von Fritz**, *PPSI* 49–50, 55.)

728   **Dicaearchus**, fr. 34 (Wehrli) = **Porphyry**, *VP* 56; **Polybius**, 2.39; **Plutarch**, *De Genio Socratis* 583. **Von Fritz** [122] *PPSI* 87: "The second rebellion... starts spontaneously in a great many different places." **Zeller** [89] *DPdG* I/1.419–420 "Daß... die Parteikämpfe mit den Pythagoreern in den großgriechischen Städten zu verschiedenen Zeiten sich wiederholt haben." See **Minar** [160] *EPP* 74–79, for analysis.

729   According to **Aristoxenus**, fr. 18 (Wehrli) = **Iamblichus**, *VP* 250, who mentions that the Pythagoreans abandoned their involvement in politics due to the failure of the cities to avert the disaster and because too many of their political leaders were killed. **Polybius**: "... the leading citizens of each city having thus unexpectedly perished, and in all the Greek towns of the district murder, sedition, and every kind of disturbance were rife." (2.39) **Porphyry** (*VP* 57–59): "When this catastrophe seized upon the men, the knowledge likewise came to an end with them, since it had been kept as a secret in their breasts until that time." **Minar** [160]: "Around 454 the society in Croton was shattered." (*EPP* 34) **Dunbabin** [704]: "The Pythagoreans were expelled from Kroton and other cities by party strife." (*Western Greeks* 372) **Philip** [163]: "Their domination came to an end about the middle of the fifth century, when they were killed, exiled, or dispersed. After that, though there may have been some Pythagorean activity in Magna Graecia of which we know nothing, it is unlikely to have been scientific activity." (*PEP* 25)

730   **Von Fritz** [122]: "The disappearance of Krotonian Alliance coins and the appearance in the second half of this century of independent coins of several cities which up to that time had had their coins in common with Kroton indicates a strong decrease if not a complete breakdown of her power." (*PPSI* 85) Also: "The second rebellion... is caused by democratic opposition to the oligarchic policy of the Pythagoreans." (87) See **de Vogel** [180]: "Not until 450–40 is there a large-scale democratic reaction in Southern Italy and a break-away from Croton." (*Pythagoras* 26) **Dunbabin** [704]: "The government by Pythagorean clubs had in it elements of a genuine aristocracy of merit. Unfortunately, neither of these experiments was successful." (*Western Greeks* 372) See **Burkert** [100] on reports that the Pythagoreans were antidemocratic or even secretly tyrannical, and that the revolts were a democratic reaction against

- Some of the fleeing Pythagoreans who had survived gathered at Rhegium, although the worsening political climate had driven practically all Pythagoreans out of Southern Italy by 400–390 B.C., with the exception of Archytas of Tarentum. Rhegium must also have been abandoned eventually.[731]
- Various subgroups of Pythagoreans emerged. Due to the inevitable separation peculiar to a life in exile, as well as the pursuit of separate interests, the surviving members and their descendants began to form separate societies. Pythagoreans began to be referred to by a variety of names—at least by others, such as commentators, historians, biographers, and playwrights. Hundreds of years later, Porphyry and Iamblichus recognized two principal orientations of the Pythagoreans, calling them the *Akousmatikoi* and the *Mathematikoi*—those who listen and those who study or learn.[732]

POSSIBLE:

- Pythagoras died in the Temple of the Muses in Metapontum after forty days of starvation.[733]
- Pythagoras may also have died of natural causes in Metapontum.[734]

---

their increasing oppression. (*Lore* 118–119) As mentioned by **D.L.**: "The citizens of Croton were anxious to protect themselves against the setting up of tyranny." (8.39)

731 **Aristoxenus**, fr. 18 (Wehrli). **Iamblichus**, *VP* 251: The surviving Pythagoreans assembled in Rhegium to live there together. Eventually the political climate worsened, and they left Italy, with the exception of Archytas of Tarentum. Comments: See **von Fritz** [122] *PPSI* 74–77, who views the strengthening of the influence of the tyrant Dionysius as the cause of the final exodus from Italy, except from Tarentum, which never came under his control (76–77). **Wehrli** [626] supports the Dionysius theory (*Schule* II *Aristoxenus* 52–53). See also **de Vogel** [180] *Pythagoras* 26–27, for a good synopsis; and **Minar** [160] *EPP* 84–86; **Dunbabin** [704] *Western Greeks* 367; and **Guthrie** [43] *HGP* 1.179, for a brief mention.

732 Here are a list of designations of those associated with Pythagoreanism: *Esoterikoi* (**Hippolytus**, *Refutation* 1.2.4; **Iamblichus**, *VP* 72.15); *Exoterikoi* (**Hippolytus**, *Refutation* 1.2.4); *Oikonomikoi* (**Iamblichus**, *VP* 72.11); *Politikoi* (**Iamblichus**, *VP* 72.11); **Photius**, *Bibliotheka* 438 b 22); *Pythagoreioi* (**Iamblichus**, *VP* 80; **Photius**, *Bibliotheka* 438 b 25); *Pythagoristai* (**Iamblichus**, *VP* 80; **Photius**, *Bibliotheka* 438 b 26—see "beggar *Pythagoristai*," Schol. Theocr. 14.5 according to **Burkert** [100] *Lore* 192n2); *Akoustikoi* or *Auditors* and *Physikoi* (**Gellius**, *Attic Nights* I.9); *Mathematikoi* (**Gellius**, *Attic Nights* I.9; **Photius**, *Bibliotheka* 438 b 23; **Iamblichus**, *VP* 81.26; **Porphyry**, *VP* 37); *Pythagorikoi* (**Photius**, *Bibliotheka* 438 b 24); *Sebastikoi* (**Photius**, *Bibliotheka* 438 b 20); *Akousmatikoi* (**Iamblichus**, *VP* 30.1, 81.25, 82.5, 87.8; **Porphyry**, *VP* 37); *Pythagoristes* (**Aristophon**'s title and frs. 9, 12, 13); *Pythagorikós* (**Antiphanes**, fr. 160); *Pythagóreios* (**Alexis**, fr. 196); and *Phythagorizontes* (**Alexis**, fr. 220). (Some of these references are from **van der Waerden** [183] *Pythagoreer* 64–65, and **Burkert** [100] *Lore* 192–202, particularly 198n25.) Further designations are **Aristoxenus**' "Last Pythagoreans" (fr. 19, Wehrli = **D.L.**, 8.46) and **Aristotle**'s "so-called Pythagoreans" (*Metaphysics* 985b23, 989b30). (See *On the Heavens* 293a19 for "the Italian philosophers known as Pythagoreans.") **Photius** explains certain distinctions as follows: *Sebastikoi* is for those disciples who are devoted to contemplation; *Politikoi* are those engaged in business; *Mathematikoi* is for those who studied geometry and astronomy; *Pythagorikoi* are those who associated personally with Pythagoras; and *Pythagoristai* are those who imitated his teachings (*Bibliotheka* 438 b 19–27).

733 **Dicaearchus**, fr. 35b (Wehrli), **D.L.**, 8.40.

734 According to **Pompeius Trogus**, 20.4.16–18: "Pythagoras, after having spent twenty years in Croton, moved to Metapontum and died there. The veneration for him was so great

- Cylon, a representative of the non-Pythagorean aristocracy, was the architect of the first revolt.[735]
- Ninon, the speaker for the democratic masses, was the instigator of the second revolt.[736]
- It is also **POSSIBLE** that Cylon and Ninon collaborated on the same revolt, each repre-

---

that they made a temple of his home and treated him as a god." (**Philip** [163] *PEP* 144). There is some indication by **Aristoxenus** (fr. 18; **Iamblichus**, *VP* 248–249) that Pythagoras went to Metapontum not as a result of the revolt but before it. And **Aristotle** (fr. 191 R) reports that Pythagoras foresaw the coming political difficulties—so he left Croton—but not that he had to suffer them. He could have foreseen problems far in the future, for example, even after his death, and might have left as a precaution or maybe to sidestep an untimely occurrence. **Zeller** [89] (*DPdG* I/1.420, 420n2) specifically maintains the possibility that Pythagoras died of natural causes in Metapontum—"die letzte Zeit seines Lebens unangefochten in Metapont zugebracht hat"—i.e., uncontested by opposition or strife, and that the Cylonian uprisings occurred after Pythagoras was long dead.

735 **Aristoxenus**, fr. 18 (Wehrli); **Iamblichus**, *VP* 248; **Porphyry**, *VP* 54; **Diodorus**, 10.11; **Plutarch**, *De Genio Socratis* 583 A. On Cylon's uprising being the first revolt: **Guthrie** [43]: "The rebellion of Cylon, which must have taken place about the turn of the sixth and fifth centuries ..." (*HGP* 1.179); **Dunbabin** [704]: "This [Cylonian] revolt against the Pythagoreans is confused in the Pythagorean tradition with the great revolt of some fifty years later...." (*Western Greeks* 366–367); **von Fritz** [122]: "Kylon, one of the most outstanding figures of the epoch, was firmly dated in the lifetime of Pythagoras" (*PPSI* 64), meaning he could not have been present at the second revolt. On the other hand, **Philip** [163] (*PEP* 191–192) sees no proof that there even was a first revolt but only the great debacle mid-century. That the anti-Pythagorean faction ended up as the "Cylonians" may have nothing to do with any historical Cylon, or he "may be a person constructed after the name of the party." (*PEP* 192) Another possibility is **Corssen**'s [106] assessment ('Die Sprengung des pythagoreischen Bundes' 340–341) of the differing accounts between Iamblichus-Nicomachus and Porphyry. While according to Porphyry, Cylon's plea for membership was rejected by the Pythagoreans, Iamblichus-Nicomachus treat the subject as if he was expelled after being a member. There is also the reference in **Olympiodorus**' scholia of *Phaedo*, p. 61D, according to which a *Gylon* (Cylon?) sought revenge for being kicked out of the Pythagorean auditorium. This is also mentioned by **Zeller** [89] (*DPdG* I/1. 420n2, 422–423); and **Corssen** [106] ('Die Sprengung des pythagoreischen Bundes' 343–344). Their hypothesis is that **Iamblichus**, *VP* 74, 250, 252, and **Porphyry**, *VP* 49, and the scholia on the *Phaedo*, p. 61D, are all based on an anonymous report on the fate of the Pythagorean order which is more reliable than the other account, yet which agrees with **Polybius**, 2.39, and **Plutarch**, *De Genio Socratis* 583 A. According to this theory, the so-called Cylonian movement was the result of an internal power struggle within the Pythagorean order that was caused by Cylon's expulsion. If we may speculate, why should Cylon *not* have been a member, if he was (1) part of the aristocracy—the group closest to the Pythagorean political outlook—hence, their favorite recruiting pool for adherents, and (2) the governor of the defeated Sybaris, and thus, warden of the spoils and the land distribution. (**Iamblichus**, *VP* 74 calls him "commander" of Sybaris.) Moreover, if it was a Pythagorean, i.e., general Milo, who defeated Sybaris, why then would the Pythagoreans allow the administration of the spoils to go to a political enemy? **Minar** [160] *EPP* 69–70, speculates that the Cylon from Sybaris may not be the same Cylon, the Crotonian aristocrat. Or if he indeed governed Sybaris, as a Pythagorean with high ambitions of power, he could have sided against them in the redistribution of land, thereby provoking his expulsion. Be that as it may, **Zeller** [89] and **Corssen** [106] ('Die Sprengung des pythagoreischen Bundes' 344) conclude that when all this occurred, Pythagoras was long dead.

736 *RE* Supp. IX.461.57 (**von Fritz**). Synopsis: The proverb "we do not live in Ninon's times anymore," which was popular in the later half of the fifth century, proves that such a man actually had lived. Thus, the proverb itself must be coupled to the time of the ultraviolent anti-Pythagorean movement that affected a great number of cities in Southern Italy, i.e., the

294   APPENDIX

senting a different side of interest: Cylon, the (non-Pythagorean) aristocrats, and Ninon, the democratic commoners.[737]
- Pythagorean meetinghouses (*synedria*) were burned throughout Southern Italy (in the second revolt).[738]
- During the second revolt, Lysis and Archippus were the only Pythagoreans to escape the burning of the meetinghouse in Croton.[739]

INFO:

Additional lore regarding the death of Pythagoras:

- As Pythagoras sat among his followers in the house of Milo, it was set on fire by enemies of his order.[740]
- Pythagoras' disciples made a bridge over the fire with their own bodies, allowing their master to escape the holocaust. They perished in the process. Pythagoras was so distraught at the loss of his friends that he either died of grief or opted for a voluntary death.[741]

---

middle of the fifth century. That Cylon became linked to the later conflicts is the result of the erroneous combination of early fifth-century events with mid-century ones.

737 This is the traditional account compiled by **Iamblichus**. Probably he was relying on Apollonius—wholeheartedly (*VP* 258–264). Our difficulty is that this account is the only version of events that includes Ninon's alleged anti-Pythagorean, i.e., pro-democratic activities. Thus, as **von Fritz** rightfully concludes: "The particulars on Ninon which Iamblichus reports have no warranty" (i.e., cannot be substantiated). (*RE* Supp. IX.461.65) In any case, certain scholars, when recounting the events of the Cylonian revolt—i.e., the first, approx. 500 B.C.—routinely include Ninon in their evaluations. See **Minar** [160] *EPP* 56–61; **Guthrie** [43] *HGP* 1.178; **van der Waerden** [183] *Pythagoras* 210–211. However, after stating that Apollonius-Iamblichus' source must have used Timaeus' account, **van der Waerden** [183] speculates that Iamblichus expanded it to a full-blown drama by means of his own imagination (*Pythagoras* 211).

738 Polybius, 2.39.1–4 (probably from **Timaeus**). There are similarities with **Pompeius Trogus**, where one meetinghouse gets burned with sixty members trapped inside (**Justin**, 20.4.15–16) and **Dicaearchus**: "Forty of his companions were caught together sitting in someone's house." (Fr. 34 = **Porphyry** *VP* 56) **Aristoxenus** specifies that it was Milo's house that got torched (Fr. 18, Wehrli = **Iamblichus**, *VP* 249), and he also mentions that only Lysis and Archippus escaped. In **Porphyry**, the latter is repeated by Neanthes, who also specifies Lysis' and Archippus' escape from the fire (**Porphyry**, *VP* 55, probably from **Aristoxenus**, referenced above). **Nicomachus** is credited with the phrase "those the Pythagoreans had given up as hopeless and exposed to ridicule, attacked them and set them on fire everywhere." (**Iamblichus**, *VP* 252; this account may have been originally from Neanthes—as indicated by **Minar** [160] *EPP* 68). D.L. preserves a number of versions, one of which was that the house of Milo was set on fire with Pythagoras inside, who escaped (probably Dicaearchus' account, 8.39). He also says that forty disciples were murdered (8.39, again Dicaearchus' version). And then there is **Porphyry**'s tale of the disciples forming a bridge with their own bodies over the flames, allowing Pythagoras to escape (*VP* 57—maybe from Neanthes). Comments: On the burning of meetinghouse(s), **Minar** [160] surmises: "The destruction *by fire* and all subsequent details belong properly to the second great catastrophe." (*EPP* 68, 68n 64)

739 According to **Aristoxenus**, fr. 18 (Wehrli) in **Iamblichus**, *VP* 248–251; **DK** 14,16; Neanthes in **Porphyry**, *VP* 55; and D.L., 8.39.

740 D.L., 8.39, and **Porphyry**, *VP* 57.

741 **Porphyry**, *VP* 57.

- Trying to escape his pursuers, Pythagoras came upon a field of beans, and refusing to cross it, he was captured and had his throat cut.[742]
- Pythagoras went to Metapontum and chose to starve to death, because upon his return to Italy (after the revolt) he saw Cylon (the instigator of the uprising) give a luxurious banquet. After this, he saw no point in living any longer.[743]
- Pythagoras was not in the country during the riots, having traveled abroad on an errand.[744]
- Pythagoras and his disciples joined the war against Syracuse by siding with Agrigentum. When their line was overrun by the enemy, he was killed by the Syracusans when he sought to avoid a field of beans.[745]

Other lore regarding the revolts:

- It was Cylon's followers who surrounded Milo's house, setting it on fire and stoning and burning the assembled Pythagoreans. After being stoned and "set on fire everywhere," the dead Pythagoreans were thrown out and left unburied.[746] (Here again, events pertaining to separate revolts have become merged.)
- The aristocrat Cylon was denied membership to the order because Pythagoras, after studying the other's outward appearance, had judged his character violent and tyrannical. This made Cylon so mad that he whipped up instant support from those friendly to him and launched a catastrophic revolt against the Pythagoreans.[747]
- Gylon is Cylon, who was expelled from the Pythagorean auditorium and sought revenge for his expulsion from the order. This would make Cylon a disenchanted Pythagorean.[748]
- Ninon, in his anti-Pythagorean speech at the assembly, possessed an illegal copy of Pythagoras' mysterious writing called the "Sacred Discourse" (*Logos Hieros*, or "Mystical Logos"[749]). Quoting from it, he attempted to prove that the Pythagoreans were in fact anti-democratic. The sample cited is an alleged *akousmata* admonishing the members of the order to honor each other like gods, yet to treat outsiders as if they were wild beasts.[750]
- The book, "Sacred Discourse," was a forgery written by Hippasus to defame Pythagoras.[751]

---

742 **D.L.**, 8.39.
743 **Heraclides Ponticus**, D.L., 8.40.
744 **Nicomachus** in **Iamblichus**, *VP* 251, to nurse his dying teacher Pherekydes on Samos. In **Porphyry**, *VP* 55, he visits his teacher in Delos, not Samos.
745 **Hermippus**, D.L., 8.40.
746 **Porphyry**, *VP* 55, and **Iamblichus**, *VP* 252, who cites **Nicomachus**.
747 **Aristoxenus**, fr. 18 (Wehrli); **Iamblichus**, *VP* 248; **Porphyry**, *VP* 54–55.
748 **Olympiodorus'** scholia on the *Phaedo*, p. 61D, according to **Corssen** [106] 'Die Sprengung des pythagoreischen Bundes' 343.
749 "Sacred Discourse": **Minar** [160] *EPP* 56; "Mystical Logos" and "Sacred Logos": **Guthrie** [43] *HGP* 1.320. Also "Sacred Book" and *Hieros "Logos"*: **Clark** [639] *Iamblichus* 40n90, 108.
750 **Iamblichus**, *VP* 258–259.
751 Called *"On the Mysteries"*: **D.L.**, 8.7. Comments: Most informative is **Philip** [163] *PEP* 28, citing Diels; **Guthrie** [43] *HGP* 1.320.

- Ninon's speech inflamed the audience to the point that when the Pythagoreans had gathered by a temple to sacrifice to the Muses, there was a mass attack by an unruly mob. The fleeing Pythagoreans sought refuge in an inn.[752]

And after the riots and exile, the further fate of the Pythagoreans is described with moving words by Porphyry, *VP* 57–59, and Iamblichus, *VP* 252–253. For an exact quote from Porphyry, see Chapter II, subhead "The Revolts Against the Pythagorean Political Elite."

---

[752] Iamblichus, *VP* 261.

Subdivided Bibliography

I. ANCIENT TEXTS—ORIGINAL TEXTS COLLECTIONS

II. GENERAL PRESOCRATIC STUDIES
Translations of Texts, and/or Commentaries

III. PYTHAGORAS AND THE PYTHAGOREANS
Including Philolaus and Later or Neo-Pythagoreans

IV. PARMENIDES AND THE ELEATICS
Including Xenophanes, Zeno of Elea, and Melissus

V. INDIVIDUAL ANCIENT AUTHORS AND SOURCES
Original Texts and/or Translations

VI. PHILOSOPHY AFTER THE PRESOCRATICS
Plato, Aristotle, Neoplatonism; also General
and Modern Philosophy

VII. ANCIENT GREEK HISTORY, POLITICS, LAW,
RELIGION, AND SCIENCE

VIII. GEOMETRY AND MATHEMATICS
With a Focus on Incommensurable Magnitudes,
Irrational Numbers, and/or Indirect Proof

IX. MISCELLANEOUS

I. ANCIENT TEXTS—ORIGINAL TEXTS COLLECTIONS

(For individual texts, see also under "Individual Ancient Authors," e.g., Elias, Iamblichus, etc.)

[1] *Doxographi graeci*. Hermann Diels. 2nd ed. Berlin: de Gruyter, 1929.
[2] *Die Fragmente der Griechischen Historiker (FGrHist)*. Felix Jacoby. Leiden: E. J. Brill, 1923–58.
[3] *Die Fragmente der Vorsokratiker: griechisch und deutsch* (DK). Hermann Diels, and Walther Kranz. 6th ed. 3 vols. 1951. Reprint, Zurich: Weidmann, 1996.
[4] *Greek Philosophy: A Collection of Texts Selected and Supplied with Some Notes and Explanations*. Cornelia J. de Vogel. Vol. 1. Leiden: E. J. Brill, 1957.
[5] *Lexicographi Graeci*. 5 vols. *Suidae Lexicon*. Ed. Ada Adler. Sammlung Wissenschaftlicher Commentare. Munich: Saur, 2001.

II. GENERAL PRESOCRATIC STUDIES
Translations of Texts, and/or Commentaries

(These works may offer translations and/or commentaries on both Pythagoreanism and Parmenides—in addition to other Presocratics, and a few related works on Socrates. For readers interested in some of the many translations of Parmenides' Poem, the works that contain complete or (largely complete) versions of it are marked with a single asterisk [*]. See also the section on "Parmenides and the Eleatics." Articles on the Presocratics with special focus on Parmenides/Eleatics are also listed under "Parmenides and the Eleatics." For additional entries with a broader focus on Greek culture, history, law and religion—but which may also contain Presocratic material—see "Ancient History, Politics, Law, Religion, and Science.")

[6] Banu, Ion. 'La philosophie de Gorgias: Une ontologie du *Logos* 1.' *Philologus* 131 (1987): 231–244.
[7] Banu, Ion. 'Structure Théoretique de la philosophie grecque préclassique évidenciée dans la pensée des Ioniens.' In *Studies in Greek Philosophy. No 1: Ionian Philosophy*. Athens: International Association for Greek Philosophy, 1989, 41–48.
[8] * Barnes, Jonathan. *Early Greek Philosophy*. London: Penguin Books, 1987.
[9] Barnes, Jonathan. (*TPP*): *The Presocratic Philosophers*. Rev. ed. New York: Routledge, 1982, 1996.
[10] Barney, Rachel. 'Socrates Agonistes: The Case of the *Cratylus* Etymologies.' *Oxford Studies in Ancient Philosophy* 16 (1998): 63–98.
[11] Bernays, Jacob. 'Heraklitische Studien.' *Rheinisches Museum für Philologie*, n.s. 7 (1850): 90–116. Reprinted in *Gesammelte Abhandlungen von Jacob Bernays*. Ed. H. Usener. Vol. 1. Berlin: Wilhelm Hertz, 1885.

[12] Boswell, Foster Partridge. *A Primer of Greek Thought*. Geneva: Humphrey, 1923.
[13] Brumbaugh, Robert S. *The Philosophers of Greece*. Albany: State University of New York Press, 1981.
[14] * Burnet, John. *Early Greek Philosophy*. 4th ed. London: Adam & Charles Black, 1930.
[15] Burnet, John. *Greek Philosophy: Thales to Plato*. London: Macmillan, 1914.
[16] * Capelle, Wilhelm. *Die Vorsokratiker: Die Fragmente und Quellenberichte übersetzt und mit einer Vorbemerkung versehen*. Berlin: Akademie, 1958.
[17] Cherniss, Harold. *Aristotle's Criticism of Presocratic Philosophy*. Baltimore: John Hopkins Press, 1935.
[18] Cherniss, H. F. 'The Characteristics and Effects of Presocratic Philosophy.' In *Studies in Presocratic Philosophy*. Eds. David J. Furley, and R. E. Allen. Vol. 1. London: Routledge, 1970, 1–28.
[19] Consigny, Scott. *Gorgias: Sophist and Artist*. Columbia: University of South Carolina Press, 2001.
[20] Copleston, Frederick S. J. *A History of Philosophy*. Vol. 1. London: Burns and Oats, 1943. Reprint, New York: Image-Doubleday, 1993.
[21] Cornford, Francis Macdonald. *From Religion to Philosophy: A Study in the Origins of Western Speculation*. New York: Harper & Brothers, 1957.
[22] Cornford, Francis Macdonald. *Principium Sapientiae: A Study of the Origins of Greek Philosophical Thought*. Ed. W. K. C. Guthrie. Cambridge: Cambridge University Press, 1952. Reprint, New York: Harper & Row, 1965.
[23] Cornford, Francis Macdonald. 'Anaxagoras' Theory of Matter.' In *Studies in Presocratic Philosophy*. Eds. R. E. Allen, and David J. Furley. Vol. 2. Atlantic Highlands: Humanities Press, 1975, 275–322.
[24] * Curd, Patricia, ed., and Richard McKirahan, Jr., trans. *A Presocratics Reader: Selected Fragments and Testimonia*. Indianapolis: Hackett Publishing, 1996.
[25] Diels, Hermann. 'Gorgias und Empedocles.' *Sitzungsberichte der Königlich Preussischen Akademie der Wissenschaften* 28.1 (1884): 343–368.
[26] Dixsaut, M., and A. Brancacci. *Platon: Source des Présocratiques*. Paris: Librairie Philosophique J. Vrin, 2002.
[27] Favento, Sergia Rossetti. 'Logos: The Sense of word and its use in Ancient Sources.' In *Philosophy of Logos*. Ed. K. I. Boudouris. Vol. 2. Athens: International Center for Greek Philosophy and Culture, 1996, 65–77.
[28] * Fairbanks, Arthur. *The First Philosophers of Greece*. London: Kegan Paul, Trench, Trübner, 1898.
[29] * Fränkel, Hermann. *Early Greek Poetry and Philosophy*. Trans. Moses Hadas, and James Willis. New York: Harcourt Brace Jovanovich, 1975.
[30] Franz, Michael. 'Fiktionalität und Wahrheit in der Sicht des Gorgias und Aristoteles.' *Philologus* 135 (1991): 240–248.
[31] Freeman, Kathleen. *The Pre-Socratic Philosophers: A Companion to Diels, Fragmente der Vorsokratiker*. 2nd ed. Cambridge, MA: Harvard University Press, 1966.
[32] Freeman, Kathleen. *Ancilla to the Pre-Socratic Philosophers: A complete translation*

of the Fragments in Diels, Fragmente der Vorsokratiker. 1948. Reprint, Cambridge, MA: Harvard University Press, 1983.

[33] von Fritz, Kurt. 'ΝΟΤΣ, NOEIN, and Their Derivatives in Pre-Socratic Philosophy (Excluding Anaxagoras). Part 1: From the Beginnings to Parmenides.' Classical Philology 40 (1945): 223–242.

[34] von Fritz, Kurt. 'ΝΟΤΣ, NOEIN, and Their Derivatives in Pre-Socratic Philosophy (Excluding Anaxagoras). Part 2: The Post-Parmenidean Period.' Classical Philology 41 (1946): 12–34.

[35] * Fülleborn, Georg Gustav. *Beyträge zur Geschichte der Philosophie*. Rev. ed. I und II. Stück. Züllichau: Frommann, 1796. (For the fragments of Parmenides' Poem and translation see VI. Stück, 1795, 35–96)

[36] Fuller, B. A. G. *History of Greek Philosophy: Thales to Democritus*. Vol. 1. Westport: Greenwood Press, 1923, Reprint 1968.

[37] Furley, David J. *The Greek Cosmologists*. Vol. 1. Cambridge: Cambridge University Press, 1987.

[38] Furley, David J. *Cosmic Problems: Essays on Greek and Roman Philosophy of Nature*. Cambridge: Cambridge University Press, 1989.

[39] * Gadamer, Hans-Georg. *Philosophisches Lesebuch*. Vol. 1. Frankfurt am Main: Fischer Bücherei, 1965.

[40] Gigon, Olof. *Der Ursprung der griechischen Philosophie: Von Hesiod bis Parmenides*. Basel: Benno Schwabe, 1945.

[41] Gigon, Olof. *Sokrates: Sein Bild in Dichtung und Geschichte*. Bern: A. Francke, 1947.

[42] Gomperz, Theodor. *Greek Thinkers: A History of Ancient Philosophy*. Vol. 1. 1901. London: John Murray, 1955.

[43] * Guthrie, W. K. C. (*HGP*): *A History of Greek Philosophy*. 6 vols. Cambridge: Cambridge University Press, 1962–81. (* For Parmenides' Poem, see vol. 2.)

[44] Hasper, Pieter Sjoerd. 'The Foundations of Presocratic Atomism.' Oxford Studies in Ancient Philosophy 17 (1999): 1–14.

[45] Havelock, Eric A. *Preface to Plato*. Cambridge, MA: Belknap Press of Harvard University Press, 1963.

[46] Havelock, Eric A. 'Pre-Literacy and the Presocratics.' Institute of Classical Studies 13 (1966): 7–82.

[47] Havelock, Eric A. 'The Linguistic Task of the Presocratics.' Language and Thought in Early Greek Philosophy (1983): 7–82.

[48] Havelock, Eric A. *Alle Origini della Filosofia Greca: Una Revisione Storica*. Roma: Editori Laterza, 1996.

[49] Heidel, William Arthur. 'Qualitative Change in Pre-Socratic Philosophy.' Archiv für Geschichte der Philosophie 19 (1906): 333–379.

[50] Heidel, William Arthur. 'Περὶ Φύσεως. A Study of the Conception of Nature among the Pre-Socratics.' Proceedings of the American Academy of Arts and Sciences 45 (1909): 79–133.

[51] Heidel, William Arthur. 'On Certain Fragments of the Pre-Socratics: Critical Notes and Elucidations.' Proceedings of the American Academy of Arts and Sciences 48.19 (1913): 683–734.

[52] Hölscher, Uvo. *Anfängliches Fragen: Studien zur frühen griechischen Philosophie*. Göttingen: Vandenhoeck & Ruprecht, 1968.

[53] Hussey, Edward. *The Presocratics*. New York: Charles Scribner's Sons, 1972.
[54] Kalogerakos, Ioannis G. *Seele und Unsterblichkeit: Untersuchungen zur Vorsokratik bis Empedokles*. Stuttgart: B. G. Teubner, 1996.
[55] Kirk, G. S. 'Popper on Science and the Presocratics.' In *Studies in Presocratic Philosophy*. Eds. David J. Furley, and R. E. Allen. Vol. 1. London: Routledge, 1970, 154–177.
[56] * Kirk, G. S., J. E. Raven, and M. Schofield. (KRS): *The Presocratic Philosophers*. 2nd ed. Cambridge: Cambridge University Press, 1983.
[57] Kranz, Walther. 'Vorsokratisches 1.' *Hermes* 69 (1934): 114–119.
[58] Kranz, Walther. 'Vorsokratisches 2.' *Hermes* 69 (1934): 226–228.
[59] Kranz, Walther. 'Vorsokratisches 3.' *Hermes* 70 (1935): 111–119.
[60] Kranz, Walther. *Die griechische Philosophie: Zugleich eine Einführung in die Philosophie überhaupt*. 3rd ed. Birsfelden: Schibli-Doppler, 1955.
[61] * Kranz, Walther. *Vorsokratische Denker: Auswahl aus dem Überlieferten*. Hildesheim: Weidmann, 1939, 1974.
[62] Mackenzie, Mary Margaret. 'The Moving Posset stands still: Heraclitus Fr. 125.' *American Journal of Philology* 107 (1986): 542–551.
[63] Mansfeld, Jaap. 'De Melisso, Xenophane, Gorgia: Pyrrhonizing Aristotelianism.' In *Studies in the Historiography of Philosophy*. By Jaap Mansfeld. Assen: Van Gorcum, 1990.
[64] Mansfeld, Jaap. 'Historical and Philosophical Aspects of Gorgias' "On What Is Not."' Reprinted in *Studies in the Historiography of Greek Philosophy*. By Jaap Mansfeld. Assen: Van Gorcum, 1990.
[65] * Mansfeld, Jaap, trans. *Die Vorsokratiker: Griechisch-Deutsch*. Vol. 1. Stuttgart: Reclam, 1995.
[66] McDiarmid, J. B. 'Theophrastus on the Presocratic Causes.' *Studies in Presocratic Philosophy*. Eds. David J. Furley, and R. E. Allen. Vol. 1. London: Routledge, 1970, 178–238.
[67] * McKirahan, Richard, Jr. *(PBS): Philosophy Before Socrates*. Indianapolis: Hackett Publishing, 1994.
[68] * Nahm, Milton C. *Selections from Early Greek Philosophy*. 4th ed. New York: Appleton-Century-Crofts, 1964. (With a translation of Parmenides' Poem by Richard Lattimore, 91.)
[69] Nietzsche, Friedrich. *The Pre-Platonic Philosophers*. Translated from the German and Edited with an Introduction and Commentary by Greg Whitlock. Urbana: University of Illinois Press, 2001.
[70] Ortega y Gasset, José. *The Origin of Philosophy*. Trans. Toby Talbot. New York: Norton, 1967. Reprint, Urbana: University of Illinois Press, 2000.
[71] Perpeet, Wilhelm. *Von der Eigenart der griechischen Philosophie: Ausgewählte Studien*. Bonn: Bouvier Verlag, 1998.
[72] Popper, Karl R. 'Back to the Presocratics.' In *Studies in Presocratic Philosophy*. Eds. David J. Furley, and R. E. Allen. Vol. 1. London: Routledge, 1970, 130–153.
[73] Reedy, Jeremiah. 'Mythos, Logos, and the Birth of Philosophy.' In *Philosophy of Logos*. Ed. K. I. Boudouris. Vol. 2. Athens: International Center for Greek Philosophy and Culture, 1996, 163–173.

[74] Sambursky, Shmuel, ed. *Physical Thought from the Presocratics to the Quantum Physicists: An Anthology*. New York: Pica Press, 1975.
[75] Sandywell, Barry. *Presocratic Reflexivity: The Construction of Philosophical Discourse c. 600–450 BC*. Vol. 3. London: Routledge, 1996.
[76] * De Santillana, Giorgio. *The Origins of Scientific Thought: From Anaximander to Proclus, 600 B.C. to A.D. 500*. New York: Mentor Books, 1961.
[77] Shibles, Warren A. *Models of Ancient Greek Philosophy*. London: Vision Press, 1971.
[78] Sinnige, Theo Gerard. *Matter and Infinity in the Presocratic Schools and Plato*. Assen: Van Gorcum, 1968.
[79] Snell, Bruno. *Die Ausdrücke für den Begriff des Wissens in der vorplatonischen Philosophie*. 1924. Reprint, Zurich: Weidmann, 1992.
[80] Stenzel, Julius. *Metaphysik des Altertums*. Munich: Oldenburg, 1931.
[81] Stokes, Michael C. *One and Many in Presocratic Philosophy*. Washington, DC: Center for Hellenic Studies, 1971.
[82] Tejera, V. *Rewriting the History of Ancient Greek Philosophy*. Westport: Greenwood Press, 1997.
[83] Thomson, George. *The First Philosophers. Studies in Ancient Greek Society*. Vol. 2. London: Lawrence & Wishart, 1955.
[84] * Waterfield, Robin, trans. *The First Philosophers: The Presocratics and the Sophists*. Oxford World's Classics. Oxford: Oxford University Press, 2000.
[85] * Wheelwright, Philip, ed. *The Presocratics*. Upper Saddle River, NJ: Prentice-Hall, 1966.
[86] * Wilbur, J. B., and H. J. Allen, eds. *The Worlds of the Early Greek Philosophers*. Buffalo, NY: Prometheus Books, 1979.
[87] Wolf, Erik. *Vorsokratiker und Frühe Dichter. Griechisches Rechtsdenken*. Vol. 1. Frankfurt a. M.: Klostermann, 1950.
[88] * Wright, M. R. *The Presocratics: The main fragments in Greek with introduction, commentary and appendix; containing text and translation of Aristotle on the Presocratics*. Bristol: Bristol Classical, 1985.
[89] Zeller, Eduard. (*DPdG*): *Die Philosophie der Griechen in ihrer geschichtlichen Entwicklung*. 6 vols. 2nd reprint of the 6th ed. (Leipzig 1919), Hildesheim: Georg Olms, 1990.
[90] Zeller, Eduard. *A History of Greek Philosophy: From the Earliest Period to the Time of Socrates; with a General Introduction (Zeller's Presocratic Philosophy)*. Trans. S. F. Alleyne. 2 vols. London: Longmans, Green, 1881.
[91] Zeller, Eduard. *Outlines of the History of Greek Philosophy*. 13th ed. 1931. Reprinted in Key Texts: Classic Studies in the History of Ideas. Bristol: Thoemmes Press, 1997.

III. PYTHAGORAS AND THE PYTHAGOREANS
Including Philolaus and Later or Neo-Pythagoreans

(For original material on Pythagoreanism as preserved by individual ancient sources such as Aristoxenus, Dicaearchus, Hippolytus, Diogenes Laertius,

Iamblichus [*De vita Pythagorica*], Porphyry [*Vita Pythagorae*], etc., see also "Individual Ancient Authors and Sources." Works that deal with Pythagoreanism in context with Eleatic doctrine are listed in section "Parmenides and the Eleatics." For additional works with special focus on geometry, mathematics, incommensurable magnitudes, and irrational numbers, see "Geometry and Mathematics.")

[92] Anderson, Graham. *Philostratus: Biography and Belles Lettres in the Third Century* A.D. London: Croom Helm, 1985.

[93] Anton, John P. 'The Pythagorean Way of Life: Morality and Religion.' In *Pythagorean Philosophy*. Ed. K. I. Boudouris. Athens: International Center for Greek Philosophy and Culture, 1992, 28–38.

[94] Bauer, Wilhelm. *Der ältere Pythagoreismus: Eine Kritische Studie*. 1897. Reprint, Hildesheim: Georg Olms, 2001.

[95] Becker, Oskar. 'Die Aktualität des pythagoreischen Gedankens.' In *Die Gegenwart der Griechen im Neueren Denken*. Tübingen: J. C. B. Mohr (Paul Siebeck), 1960.

[96] Boudouris, K. I. 'The Pythagorean Community: Creation, Development and Downfall.' In *Pythagorean Philosophy*. Ed. K. I. Boudouris. Athens: International Center for Greek Philosophy and Culture, 1992, 49–69.

[97] Brisson, Luc. 'Platon, Pythagore et les Pythagoriciens.' In *Platon: Source des Présocratiques*. Eds. Dixsaut, M., and A. Brancacci. Librairie Philosophique J. Vrin, 2002, 21–46.

[98] Burkert, Walter. 'Platon oder Pythagoras? Zum Ursprung des Wortes "Philosophie."' *Hermes* 88 (1960): 159–177.

[99] Burkert, Walter. 'Hellenistische Pseudopythagorica.' *Philologus* 105 (1961): 16–43, 226–246.

[100] Burkert, Walter. *Lore and Science in Ancient Pythagoreanism*. Cambridge, MA: Harvard University Press, 1972.

[101] Cardini, Maria Timpanaro. *Pitagorici: Testimonianze e frammenti*. Biblioteca di Studi Superiori 28. Firenze: Nuova Italia, 1958.

[102] Centrone, Bruno. 'The Theory of Principles in the Pseudopythagorica.' In *Pythagorean Philosophy*. Ed. K. I. Boudouris. Athens: International Center for Greek Philosophy and Culture, 1992, 90–97.

[103] Colavito, Maria Maddalena. *The Pythagorean Intertext in Ovid's Metamorphoses: A New Interpretation*. Studies in Comparative Literature. Vol. 5. Lewiston: Edwin Mellen Press, 1989.

[104] Cornford, Francis Macdonald. 'Mysticism and Science in the Pythagorean Tradition.' *The Classical Quarterly* (1923): 1–12. Reprinted in *The Presocratics: A Collection of Critical Essays*. Ed. Mourelatos. Garden City, NY: Anchor Press, 1974. Reprint, Princeton: Princeton University Press, 1993.

[105] Corssen, P. 'Die Schrift des Arztes Androkydes. ΠΕΡΙ ΠΥΘΑΓΟΡΙΚΩΝ ΣΥΜΒΟΛΩΝ.' *Rheinisches Museum für Philologie* 67 (1912): 240–263.

[106] Corssen, P. 'Die Sprengung des pythagoreischen Bundes.' *Philologus* 71 (1912): 332–352.

[107] Delatte, Armand. *Études sur la Litérature Pythagoricienne*. Paris: Honoré Champion, 1915.
[108] Delatte, Armand. 'La chronologie pythagoricienne de Timée.' *Musée Belge* 1 (1920): 5–13.
[109] Delatte, Armand. 'Faba Pythagore cognata.' *Serta Leodiensia* 44 (1930): 3–57.
[110] Delatte, Armand. *La Vie de Pythagore de Diogène Laërce*. 1922. Reprint, New York: Arno Press, 1979.
[111] Delatte, Armand. *Essay sur la Politique Pythagoricienne*. Liège-Paris, 1922. Reprint, Genève: Slatkine Reprints, 1979.
[112] Deubner, Ludwig. *Bemerkungen zum Text der Vita Pythagorae des Iamblichos*. Berlin: Akademie der Wissenschaften, 1935.
[113] Diels, Hermann. 'Ein gefälschtes Pythagorasbuch.' *Archiv für Geschichte der Philosophie* 3 (1980): 451–472.
[114] Dillon, John. *The Middle Platonists: 80 B.C. to A.D. 220*. Ithaca, NY: Cornell University Press, 1977.
[115] Döring, A. 'Wandlungen in der pythagoreischen Lehre.' *Archiv für Geschichte der Philosophie* 5 (1892): 503–531.
[116] Festugière, A. J. 'Les "Mémoires Pythagoriques" cités par Alexandre Polyhistor.' *Revue des études grecques* 58 (1945): 1–65.
[117] Flinterman, Jaap-Jan. *Power, Paideia and Pythagoreanism: Greek Identity, Conceptions of the Relationship Between Philosophers and Monarchs and Political Ideas in Philostratus' Life of Apollonius*. Amsterdam: Gieben, 1995.
[118] Frank, Erich. *Plato und die sogenannten Pythagoreer: Ein Kapitel aus der Geschichte des griechischen Geistes*. 2nd ed. Tübingen: Niemeyer, 1962.
[119] Freitag, Willy. 'Ein Bruderschaftsbund vor Jahrtausenden: Das pädagogisch-politische Problem der Pythagoreer.' *Zeitschrift für Geschichte der Erziehung und des Unterrichts* 2 (1933): 83–112.
[120] von Fritz, Kurt. 'The Discovery of Incommensurability by Hippasus of Metapontum.' *Annals of Mathematics* 46 (1945): 242–264. Reprinted in *Studies in Presocratic Philosophy*. Eds. David J. Furley, and R. E. Allen. Vol. 1. London: Routledge, 1970.
[121] von Fritz, Kurt. *Mathematiker und Akusmatiker bei den alten Pythagoreern*. Munich: Bayerische Akademie der Wissenschaften, 1960.
[122] von Fritz, Kurt. *(PPSI): Pythagorean Politics in Southern Italy: An Analysis of the Sources*. New York: Octagon Books, 1977.
[123] Gorman, Peter. 'Pythagoras Palaestinus.' *Philologus* 127 (1983): 30–42.
[124] Guthrie, Kenneth Sylvan. *The Pythagorean Sourcebook and Library: An Anthology of Ancient Writings Which Relate to Pythagoras and Pythagorean Philosophy*. Ed. David R. Fideler. Grand Rapids: Phanes Press, 1987.
[125] Guthrie, Kenneth Sylvan, trans. *Porphyry's Launching-Points to the Realm of Mind: An Introduction to the Neoplatonic Philosophy of Plotinus*. Grand Rapids: Phanes Press, 1988.
[126] Guthrie, W. K. C. 'Pythagoras and Pythagoreanism.' In Paul Edwards, ed., *The Encyclopedia of Philosophy*, unabr. ed. New York: Simon & Schuster Macmillan, 1996.

[127] Hare, R. M. 'Plato and the Mathematicians.' In *New Essays in Plato and Aristotle*. London: Routledge, 1965, 21–38.
[128] Hasse, Helmut, and Heinrich Scholz. *Die Grundlagenkrisis der griechischen Mathematik*. Charlottenburg: Kurt Metzner, 1928.
[129] Heidel, William Arthur. 'Πέρας and "Άπειρον in the Pythagorean Philosophy.' *Archiv für Geschichte der Philosophie* 14 (1901): 384–399.
[130] Heidel, William Arthur. 'Notes on Philolaus.' *American Journal of Philology* 28 (1907): 77–81.
[131] Heidel, William Arthur. 'The Pythagoreans and Greek Mathematics.' *American Journal of Philology* 61 (1940): 1–33.
[132] Heller, Siegfried. *Die Entdeckung der stetigen Teilung durch die Pythagoreer*. Berlin: Akademie, 1958.
[133] Huffman, Carl A. 'The Role of Number in Philolaus' Philosophy.' *Phronesis* 33 (1988): 1–30.
[134] Huffman, Carl A. 'Philolaus' Cosmogony.' In *Studies in Greek Philosophy. No 1: Ionian Philosophy*. Athens: International Association for Greek Philosophy, 1989, 186–194.
[135] Huffman, Carl A. *Philolaus of Croton: Pythagorean and Presocratic. A Commentary on the Fragments and Testimonia with Interpretive Essays*. Cambridge: Cambridge University Press, 1993.
[136] Huffman, Carl A. 'The Pythagorean Tradition.' In *The Cambridge Companion to Early Greek Philosophy*. Ed. A. A. Long. Cambridge: Cambridge University Press, 1999, 66–87.
[137] Huffman, Carl A. 'The Philolaic Method: The Pythagoreanism Behind the Philebus.' In *Essays in Ancient Greek Philosophy*. Vol. 6. Ed. Anthony Preus. Albany: State University of New York Press, 2001, 67–86.
[138] Huffman, Carl A. 'Doubling the Cube: Plato's Criticism of Archytas.' 6th Annual Colloquium in Ancient Philosophy. Tucson, 2001.
[139] Jacoby, Felix. "Juba II. (2)," *RE* IX,2.2384–2395 (particularly 2387.60).
[140] Jäger, Hans. *Die Quellen des Porphyrios in seiner Pythagoras-Biographie*. Diss. Universität Zürich. Chur: Sprecher, Eggerling, 1919.
[141] von Jan, Carl. 'Die Harmonie der Sphären.' *Philologus* 52 (1893): 13–37.
[142] Jauhiainen, T., and V. Häkkinen. 'Further Considerations of the Euclidean-Pythagorean Structure and Quadratic Metrics in the Perceptual Manifold of the Sense of Hearing.' *Annales Academiae Scientiarum Fennicae* Ser. A5: Medica 106/20 (1964): 3–20.
[143] Junge, Gustav. 'Die pythagoreische Zahlenlehre.' *Deutsche Mathematik* 5 (1940): 341–357.
[144] Junge, Gustav. 'Die Sphären-Harmonie und die pythagoreisch-platonische Zahlenlehre.' *Classica et Mediaevalia* 9 (1947–48): 183–194.
[145] Junge, Gustav. 'Von Hippasus bis Philolaus: Das Irrationale und die Geometrischen Grundbegriffe.' *Classica et Mediaevalia* 19 (1958): 41–72.
[146] Kahn, Charles H. 'Pythagorean Philosophy Before Plato.' In *The Presocratics: A Collection of Critical Essays*. Ed. Mourelatos. Garden City, NY: Anchor Press, 1974. Reprint, Princeton: Princeton University Press, 1993, 161–185.

[147] Kahn, Charles H. *Pythagoras and the Pythagoreans: A Brief History*. Indianapolis: Hackett Publishing, 2001.
[148] Kerényi, Karl. *Pythagoras und Orpheus: Präluden zu einer zukünftigen Geschichte der Orphik und des Pythagoreismus*. 3rd ed. Zurich: Rhein-Verlag, 1950.
[149] Krüger, Manfred. *Ichgeburt: Origenes und die Entstehung der christlichen Idee der Wiederverkörperung in der Denkbewegung von Pythagoras bis Lessing*. Hildesheim: Georg Olms, 1996.
[150] Kucharski, P. 'Aux frontières du Platonisme et du Pythagorisme. A propos d'un passage *De Anima* d'Aristote.' *Archives de Philosophie* 19 (1955–56): 7–43.
[151] Kusayama, Kyoko. 'Pythagoreanism in Plato's Cosmology.' In *Pythagorean Philosophy*. Ed. K. I. Boudouris. Athens: International Center for Greek Philosophy and Culture, 1992, 102–109.
[152] Lappan, Glenda, James T. Fey, William M. Fitzgerald, Susan N. Friel, and Elizabeth Difanis Phillips. *Looking for Pythagoras: The Pythagorean Theorem*. Teacher's ed. Palo Alto, CA: Dale Seymour, 1998.
[153] Lautner, Peter. 'Pythagorean and Aristotelian Elements in the Theories of Perception in the Later Athenian Commentators.' In *Pythagorean Philosophy*. Ed. K. I. Boudouris. Athens: International Center for Greek Philosophy and Culture, 1992, 110–116.
[154] Lévy, Isidore. *Recherches esséniennes et pythagoriciennes*. Geneva: Librairie Droz, 1965.
[155] Lévy, Isidore. *Recherches sur les Sources de la Légende de Pythagore*. Paris: Ernest Leroux, 1926. Reprint, Ann Arbor: UMI, 2001.
[156] Lionel, Frédéric. *Das Vermächtnis des Pythagoras*. Grafing: Aquamarin, 1990.
[157] Lloyd, William. *A chronological account of the Life of Pythagoras and of other famous men his contemporaries, with an epistle to the Rd. Dr. Bentley about Porphyry's and Iamblichus's lives of Pythagoras*. London: H. Mortlock & J. Hartley, 1699.
[158] McClain, Ernest G. *The Pythagorean Plato: Prelude to the Song Itself*. 1978. Reprint, York Beach: Nicolas-Hays, 1984.
[159] Mead, G. R. S. *Apollonius of Tyana*. Montana: Kessinger, n.d.
[160] Minar, Edwin L. Jr. (*EPP*): *Early Pythagorean Politics*. Baltimore: Waverly Press, 1942. Reprint, Ann Arbor: UMI, 2001.
[161] Oliver, George. *The Pythagorean Triangle, or The Science of Numbers*. Secret Doctrine Reference Series. 1875. Reprint, Minneapolis: Wizards Book Shelf, 1975.
[162] O'Meara, Dominic J. *Pythagoras Revived: Mathematics and Philosophy in Late Antiquity*. Oxford: Clarendon Press, 1989.
[163] Philip, J. A. (*PEP*): *Pythagoras and Early Pythagoreanism*. Toronto: University of Toronto Press, 1966.
[164] Pike, Albert. *Morals and Dogma of the Ancient and Accepted Scottish Rite of Freemasonry*. Rev. ed. Richmond: Jenkins, 1950.
[165] Pike, Albert. *Pythagoras and Hermes*. Edmonds, WA: Holmes Publishing, n.d.
[166] Rhode, Erwin. 'Die Quellen des Jamblichus in seiner Biographie des Pythagoras.' *Rheinisches Museum für Philologie* 26, 27 (1871): 554–576, 23–61.
[167] Riedweg, Christoph. 'Pythagoras [2],' in *Der neue Pauly: Enzyklopädie der*

Antike. Ed. Hubert Cancik, and Helmuth Schneider. Vol. 10. Stuttgart: J. B. Metzler, 1996.

[168] Riedweg, Christoph. *Pythagoras: Leben, Lehre, Nachwirkung; Eine Einführung.* Munich: C. H. Beck, 2002.

[169] Rowe, N., trans. *Commentary of Hierocles on the Golden Verses of Pythagoras; From the French of André Dacier.* Rev. ed. 1906. Reprint, London: Theosophical Publishing House, 1971.

[170] Rowe, N., trans. *The Golden Verses of Pythagoras with the Commentary of Hierocles.* Santa Barbara: Concord Grove, 1983.

[171] Schuré, Edouard. *Pythagoras and the Delphic Mysteries.* London: Philip Wellby, 1906. Reprint, Mokelume Hill, CA: Health Research, 1964.

[172] Shrine of Wisdom. *The Golden Verses of the Pythagoreans: A New Translation; Commentary by the Editors of the Shrine of Wisdom.* Surrey: Shrine of Wisdom, n.d.

[173] Staab, Gregor. *Pythagoras in der Spätantike: Studien zu De Vita Pythagorica des Iamblichos von Chalkis.* Beiträge zur Altertumskunde 165. Munich: Saur, 2002.

[174] Stanley, Thomas. *Pythagoras: His Life and Teachings.* 1687. Reprint, Los Angeles: Philosophical Research Society, 1970.

[175] Suzuki, Teruo. 'Philolaus: Epistemologist or Ontologist?' In *Pythagorean Philosophy.* Ed. K. I. Boudouris. Athens: International Center for Greek Philosophy and Culture, 1992, 205–219.

[176] Taylor, Christopher W. 'The Arguments in the *Phaedo* concerning the Thesis that the Soul is a *Harmonia.*' In *Essays in Ancient Greek Philosophy.* Eds. Anton, John P., and Anthony Preuss. Vol. 2. Albany: State University of New York Press, 1983, 217–231.

[177] Taylor, Thomas, trans. *Ocellus Lucanus on the Nature of the Universe; Taurus, the Platonic Philosopher on the Eternity of the World; Julius Firmicus Maternus of the Thema Mundi; Select Theorems on the Perpetuity of Time, by Proclus.* 1831. Reprint, Los Angeles: Philosophical Research Society, 1976.

[178] Thesleff, Holger. *An Introduction to the Pythagorean Writings of the Hellenistic Period.* Åbo: Åbo Akademi, 1961.

[179] Thesleff, Holger, ed. *The Pythagorean Texts of the Hellenistic Period.* Acta Academiae Aboensis Ser. A: Humaniora 30.1. Åbo: Åbo Akademi, 1965.

[180] De Vogel, Cornelia J. *Pythagoras and Early Pythagoreanism: An Interpretation of Neglected Evidence on the Philosopher Pythagoras.* Assen: Van Gorcum, 1966.

[181] Vogt, Heinrich. 'Die Geometrie des Pythagoras.' *Bibliotheca Mathematica* 3.9 (1908): 15–54.

[182] van der Waerden, B. L. 'Die Harmonielehre der Pythagoreer.' *Hermes* 78 (1943): 163–199.

[183] van der Waerden, B. L. *Die Pythagoreer: Religiöse Bruderschaft und Schule der Wissenschaft.* Zurich: Artemis, 1979.

[184] van der Waerden, B. L. *Die gemeinsame Quelle der erkenntnistheoretischen Abhandlungen von Iamblichos und Proklos.* Sitzungsberichte der Heidelberger Akademie der Wissenschaften. Heidelberg: Winter University Press, 1980.

[185] Watters, Hallie. *The Pythagorean Way of Life: With a Discussion of the Golden Verses.* Adyar: Theosophical Publishing House, 1926.

[186] Whittaker, John. 'Neophythagoreanism and Negative Theology.' *Symbolae Osloenses* 44 (1969): 109–125.
[187] Zhmud, Leonid. 'Mathematici and Acusmatici.' In *Pythagorean Philosophy*. Ed. K. I. Boudouris. Athens: International Center for Greek Philosophy and Culture, 1992, 240–249.
[188] Zimmern, Alice, trans. *Porphyry's Letter to His Wife Marcella: Concerning the Life of Philosophy and the Ascent to the Gods*. Grand Rapids: Phanes Press, 1986.

IV. PARMENIDES AND THE ELEATICS
Including Xenophanes, Zeno of Elea, and Melissus

(For additional listings of works that also offer the Poem of Parmenides—marked by a single asterisk [*]—see "General Presocratics.")

[189] Abraham, William E. 'The Nature of Zeno's Argument against Plurality in DK 29 B1.' *Phronesis* 17 (1972): 40–52.
[190] Albert, Karl. 'Zum Lehrgedicht des Parmenides.' *Der Altsprachliche Unterricht* 12 (1969): 30–50.
[191] * Albertelli, Pilo. *Gli Eleati: Testimonianze e frammenti*. Bari: Gius. Laterza & Figli, 1939.
[192] Anderson, Daniel E. 'The Paradox of Parmenides.' *Southern Journal of Philosophy* 1–3 (1963): 20–29.
[193] Anscombe, G. E. M. 'Parmenides, Mystery and Contradiction.' *Proceedings of the Aristotelian Society* 69 (1968–69): 125–132.
[194] Anscombe, G. E. M. *From Parmenides to Wittgenstein: The Collected Philosophical Papers of G. E. M. Anscome*. 2 vols. Minneapolis: University of Minnesota Press, 1981.
[195] Aubenque, Pierre, Rémi Brague, Barbara Cassin, Néstor-Luis Cordero, Lambros Couloubaritsis, Monique Dixsaut, Jean Frère, et al. *Études sur Parménide: Problèmes d'interprétation*. Vol. 2. Ed. Pierre Aubenque. Paris: Librairie Philosophique J. Vrin, 1987.
[196] Austin, Scott. *The Method of Parmenides*. Diss. University of Texas. 1979. Ann Arbor: UMI, 2001.
[197] Austin, Scott. 'Genesis and Motion in Parmenides: B8.12–13.' *Harvard Studies in Classical Philology* 87 (1983): 151–168.
[198] Austin, Scott. 'Parmenides and Ultimate Reality.' *Ultimate Reality and Meaning* 7 (1984): 220–232.
[199] * Austin, Scott. *Parmenides: Being, Bounds, and Logic*. New Haven: Yale University Press, 1986.
[200] Austin, Scott. 'Parmenides' Reference.' *The Classical Quarterly* (1990): 266–267.
[201] Austin, Scott. 'Parmenides and the Closure of the West.' *American Catholic Philosophical Quarterly* 74 (2000): 287–301.
[202] Austin, Scott. 'Parmenides, Double-Negation, and Dialectic.' In *Presocratic Philosophy: Essays in Honour of Alexander Mourelatos*. Ed. Victor Caston and Daniel W. Graham. Burlington: Ashgate, 2002, 95–100.

[203] Aznar, José Camón. 'Parménides y el Clasicismo Griego.' *Revista de Ideas Esteticas* 31 (1973): 3–7.
[204] Ballew, Lynne. 'Straight and Circular in Parmenides and the *Timaeus*.' *Phronesis* 19 (1974): 189–209.
[205] Barnes, Jonathan. 'Parmenides and the Eleatic One.' *Archiv für Geschichte der Philosophie* 61 (1979): 1–21.
[206] Basson, A. H. 'The Way of Truth.' *Proceedings of the Aristotelian Society* 61 (1960–61): 73–86.
[207] * Beaufret, Jean. *Parménide: Le Poème*. Paris: Presses Universitaires de France, 1955. Reprint, Quadrige, 1996.
[208] Becker, Ottfrid. 'Das Bild des Weges und verwandte Vorstellungen im frühgriechischen Denken: Parmenides.' *Hermes* 4 (1937): 139–143.
[209] Becker, Oskar. 'Drei Abhandlungen zum Lehrgedicht des Parmenides.' *Kant-Studien* 55 (1964): 255–259.
[210] Bedoya, Orlando. 'Verdad y Opinion: Estudio gnoseolócigo des poema *Sobre la Naturaleza*, de Parménides.' *Franciscanum* 7 (1965): 63–83.
[211] Benedum, J., and M. Michler. 'Parmenides Uliades und die Medizinschule von Elea.' *Clio Medica* 6 (1971): 295–306.
[212] Bicknell, P. J. 'Zeno's Argument on Motion.' *Acta Classica* 6 (1963): 81–105.
[213] Bicknell, P. J. 'Aristotle's Comments on the Parmenidean One.' *Acta Classica* 7 (1964): 108–112.
[214] Bicknell, P. J. 'Dating the Eleatics.' *For Service to Classical Studies. Essays in Honour of F. Letters.* (1966): 1–14.
[215] Bicknell, P. J. 'Parmenides' Refutation of Motion and an Implication.' *Phronesis* 12 (1967): 1–5.
[216] Bicknell, P. J. 'Parmenides, Fragment 10.' *Hermes* 96 (1968): 629–631.
[217] Bicknell, P. J. 'Parmenides, DK 28 B4.' *Apeiron* 13 (1979): 115.
[218] Bicknell, P. J. 'Parmenides, DK 28 B5.' *Apeiron* 13 (1979): 9–11.
[219] Bidez, J. 'Observations sur quelques fragments d'Empédocle et de Parménide.' *Archiv für Geschichte der Philosophie* 9 (1896): 298–309.
[220] Blank, David. 'Faith and Persuasion in Parmenides.' *Classical Antiquity* 1 (1982): 167–177.
[221] Bloch, Kurt. 'Über die Ontologie des Parmenides.' *Classica et Mediaevalia* 14 (1953): 1–29.
[222] Boeder, Heribert. 'Parmenides und der Verfall des kosmologischen Wissens.' *Philosophisches Jahrbuch* 74 (1966–67): 30–77.
[223] Böhme, Robert. *Die verkannte Muse: Dichtersprache und Geistige Tradition des Parmenides*. Bern: Francke Verlag, 1986.
[224] Bodnár, Istvan M. 'Contrasting Images—Notes on Parmenides B5.' *Apeiron* 19 (1985): 57–63.
[225] Bollack, Jean. 'Sur deux fragments de Parménide (4 et 16).' *Revue des Études Grecques* 70 (1957): 56–71.
[226] Bollack, Jean, and Heinz Wismann. 'Le moment théorique. Parménide fr. 8,42–49.' *Revue des Sciences Humaines* 39 (1974): 203–212.
[227] Bollack, Jean. 'La Cosmologie parménidéenne de Parménide.' In *Herméneu-*

tique et Ontologie: Mélanges en hommage à Pierre Aubenque. Paris: Presses Universitaires de France, 1990, 17–53.

[228] Boodin, J. E. 'The Vision of Parmenides.' *The Philosophical Review* 52 (1943): 578–589.

[229] Booth, N. B. 'Were Zeno's Arguments a reply to attacks upon Parmenides?' *Phronesis* 2 (1957): 61–65.

[230] Booth, N. B. 'Were Zeno's Arguments Directed Against the Pythagoreans?' *Phronesis* 2 (1957): 90–103.

[231] Booth, N. B. 'Did Melissus believe in Incorporeal Being?' *American Journal of Philology* 79 (1958): 61–65.

[232] * Bormann, Karl. *Parmenides: Untersuchungen zu den Fragmenten*. Hamburg: Felix Meiner, 1971.

[233] Bormann, Karl. 'The Interpretation of Parmenides by the Neoplatonic Simplicius.' *The Monist* 62 (1979) 30–42.

[234] Bosley, Richard. 'Monistic Argumentation.' *Canadian Journal of Philosophy* Suppl. Vol. 2 (1976): 23–44.

[235] Bostock, David. 'Plato on "Is Not" (Sophist, 254–9).' *Oxford Studies in Ancient Philosophy* 2 (1984): 89–119.

[236] Boussoulas, N. I. 'La structure du mélange dans la pensée de Parménide.' *Revue de Métaphysique et de Morale* 1 (1964): 1–13.

[237] Bowra, C. M. 'The Proem of Parmenides.' *Harvard Studies in Classical Philology* 32 (1937): 97–112.

[238] Brague, Rémi. 'La vraisemblance du faux: Parménide fr. I, 31–32.' *Études sur Parménide*. Ed. Pierre Aubenque. Vol. 2. Paris: Librairie Philosophique J. Vrin, 1987, 44–68.

[239] Bröcker, Walter. 'Gorgias contra Parmenides.' *Hermes* 86 (1958): 425–440.

[240] Bröcker, Walter. 'Parmenides.' *Archiv für Begriffsgeschichte* 9 (1964): 79–86.

[241] Bröcker, Walter. 'Parmenides' ΑΛΗΘΕΙΑ.' *Hermes* 106 (1978): 79–86.

[242] Bröcker, Walter. 'Heidegger's letztes Wort über Parmenides.' *Philosophische Rundschau* 29 (1982): 72–76.

[243] Broemser, Ferdinand. 'ΛΟΓΟΣ und ΈΠΟΣ bei Heraklit und Parmenides.' In *Festschrift zur Fertigstellung der Schulgebäude*. Staatliches Kurfürst Salentin-Gymnasium Andernach. Andernach: Gebrüder Wester, 1957.

[244] Brzoska, Andreas. *Absolutes Sein: Parmenides' Lehrgedicht und seine Spiegelung im Sophistes*. Münster: Lit. Verlag, 1992.

[245] Bultmann, Rudolf. 'Zur Geschichte der Lichtsymbolik im Altertum.' *Philologus* 97 (1948): 1–36.

[246] Burkert, Walter. 'Das Proömium des Parmenides und die Katabasis des Pythagoras.' *Phronesis* 14 (1969): 1–30.

[247] Bux, Ernst. 'Gorgias und Parmenides.' *Hermes* 76 (1941): 393–407.

[248] Calogero, Guido. 'Parmenide e la genesi della logica classica.' *Annali della Reale Scuola Normale Superiore di Pisa* 5 (1936): 143–185.

[249] Calogero, Cuido. *Studien über den Eleatismus*. Trans. Wolfgang Raible. Hildesheim: Georg Olms, 1970.

[250] Campbell, R. 'Sur une interprétation de Parménide par Heidegger.' *Revue Internationale de Philosophie* 5 (1951): 390–399.

[251] Capizzi, Antonio. 'Recenti studi sull' eleatismo.' *Rassegna di Filosofia* 4 (1965): 205–213.
[252] Capizzi, Antonio. *La porta di Parmenide: Due saggi per una nuova lettura del poema*. Filologia e critica: Collana diretta da Bruno Gentili 14. Rome: Edizioni dell'Ateneo, 1975.
[253] Capizzi, Antonio. 'A proposito di Parmenide e Socrate demistificati.' *Rivista Critica di Storia della Filosofia* 32 (1977): 401–405.
[254] Capizzi, Antonio. 'Eliadi, Meleagridi, Pandionidi. Osservazioni sulla metafora mitica in Parmenide.' *Quaderni Urbinati di Cultura Classica* 32 (1979): 149–160.
[255] Capizzi, Antonio. 'Tracce di una polemica sulla scrittura in Eraclito e Parmenide.' *Giornale Critico della Filosofia Italiana* 58 (1979): 106–130.
[256] * Casertano, Giovanni. *Parmenide: il metodo; la scienza l'esperienza*. Skepsis: Collana di testi e studi di filosofia 5. Napoli: 1978. Reprint, Napoli: Loffredo, 1989.
[257] Casertano, Giovanni. 'Parmenides—początki myśli filozoficnej i naukowej.' *Przegląd Filozoficzny* 38 (2001): 125–133.
[258] Casertano, Giovanni. 'Parménide, Platon et la vérite.' In *Platon: Source des Présocratiques*. Eds. Dixsaut, M., and A. Brancacci. Librairie Philosophique J. Vrin, 2002, 67–92.
[259] Cassin, Barbara. *Si Parménide: Le traité anonyme de Melisso Xenophane Gorgia*. Lille: Presses Universitaires, 1980.
[260] * Cassin, Barbara. *Parménide: Sur la nature ou sur l'étant; La langue de l'être?* Paris: Éditions du Seuil, 1998.
[261] * Cerri, Giovanni. *Parmenide di Elea: Poema sulla natura; testo greco a fronte*. 2nd ed. Milan: Rizzoli, 2000.
[262] Chalmers, W. R. 'Parmenides and the Beliefs of Mortals.' *Phronesis* 5 (1960): 5–22.
[263] Cherniss, H. F. 'Parmenides and the *Parmenides* of Plato.' *American Journal of Philology* 53 (1932): 122–138.
[264] Chitas, Eduardo. 'Sobre a questão da unidade do método e da realidade (Parmenides; Hegel).' *Vertice* 27 (1967): 676–691.
[265] Clark, R. J. 'Parmenides and Sense-Perception.' *Revue des Études Grecques* 82 (1969): 277–293.
[266] Classen, C. J. 'Licht und Dunkel in der frühgriechischen Philosophie.' *Studium Generale* 18 (1965): 97–116.
[267] Classen, Joachim C. 'Xenophanes and the Tradition of Epic Poetry.' In *Studies in Greek Philosophy. No 1: Ionian Philosophy*. Athens: International Association for Greek Philosophy, 1989, 91–103.
[268] * Collobert, Catherine. *L'Être de Parménide ou le Refus du Temps*. Paris: Kimé, 1993.
[269] * Conche, Marcel. *Parménide: Le Poème; Fragments*. Épiméthée: Essais Philosophiques. Paris: Presses Universitaires de France, 1996.
[270] Constantineau, Philippe. *Parmenides und Hegel über das Sein: Zur Interpretation des Anfangs der Hegelschen Logik*. Diss. Universität Heidelberg. n.p.: Akad., 1985.
[271] Constantineau, Philippe. 'La question de la verité chez Parménide.' *Phoenix* 41 (1987): 217–240.

[272] Cordero, Néstor-Luis. 'Les deux chemins de Parménide dans les fragments 6 et 7.' *Phronesis* 24 (1979): 1–32.

[273] Cordero, Néstor-Luis. 'Joseph Scaliger y el poema de Parmenides.' *Atlas del Tercer Congreso Nacional de Filosofia* 2 (1982): 117–122.

[274] Cordero, Néstor-Luis. 'La version de Joseph Scaliger du poème de Parménide.' *Hermes* 110 (1982): 391–398.

[275] Cordero, Néstor-Luis. 'Zénon d'Élée, Moniste ou Nihiliste?' *La Parola del Passato* 43 (1983): 100–126.

[276] Cordero, Néstor-Luis. 'L'histoire du texte de Parménide.' *Études sur Parménide*. Ed. Pierre Aubenque. Vol. 2. Paris: Librairie Philosophique J. Vrin, 1987, 3–24.

[277] * Cordero, Néstor-Luis. *Les deux chemins de Parménide*. (1984) 2nd ed. Paris: Librairie Philosophique J. Vrin, 1997.

[278] Cordero, Néstor-Luis. 'Una Tragedia Filosófica: Del "Se Es" de Parménides al Ser-uno de Meliso.' *Revista Latinoamericana de Filosofia* 25 #2 (1999): 283–293.

[279] * Cordero, Néstor-Luis. *By Being, It Is*. Las Vegas: Parmenides Publishing, forthcoming [2004]. (The page references in the text may not be accurate as they refer to uncorrected page proofs.)

[280] Cornford, Francis Macdonald. 'Parmenides' Two Ways.' *The Classical Quarterly* 49 (1933): 97–111.

[281] Cornford, Francis Macdonald. 'A New Fragment of Parmenides.' *The Classical Review* 4 (1935): 122–123.

[282] * Cornford, Francis Macdonald. *Plato and Parmenides*. 1939. Reprint, New York: Humanities Press, 1951.

[283] Cosgrove, Matthew R. 'The ΚΟΥΡΟΣ Motif in Parmenides B1.24.' *Phronesis* 19 (1974): 81–94.

[284] * Couloubaritsis, Lambros. *Mythe et Philosophie chez Parménide; En Appendice: Traduction du Poème*. Bruxelles: Ousia, 1986.

[285] Covotti, A. 'Intorno alla finitezza dell'essere Parmenideo nel testo Simpliciano.' *I Presocratici* (1934): 122–125.

[286] Covotti, A. 'Intorno alla seconda parte del poema di Parmenide.' *I Presocratici* (1934): 130–136.

[287] Covotti, A. 'La "Verita Afisica" di Parmenide e l'"Aiuto" di Zenone.' *I Presocratici* (1934): 97–113.

[288] Coxon, A. H. 'The Philosophy of Parmenides.' *The Classical Quarterly* 28 (1934): 134–144.

[289] Coxon, A. H. 'The Text of Parmenides fr. 1.3.' *The Classical Quarterly* 18, (1968): 69.

[290] * Coxon, A. H. *The Fragments of Parmenides*. Assen: Van Gorcum, 1986.

[291] Croissant, Jeanne. 'Le début de la ΔΟΞΑ de Parménide.' In *Mélanges offerts a A.-M. Desrousseaux*. Paris: Libraire Hachette, 1937, 99–104.

[292] Crystal, Ian. 'Parmenidean Allusions in *Republic V*.' *Ancient Philosophy* 16 (1996): 351–363.

[293] Crystal, Ian. 'The Scope of Thought in Parmenides.' *The Classical Quarterly* 52 (2002): 207–219.

[294] Curd, Patricia. 'Parmenidean Monism.' *Phronesis* 36 (1991): 241–264.
[295] Curd, Patricia. 'Deception and Belief in Parmenides' Doxa.' *Apeiron* 25 (1992): 109–133.
[296] Curd, Patricia. 'Eleatic Monism in Zeno and Melissus.' *Ancient Philosophy* 13 (1993): 1–22.
[297] * Curd, Patricia. *The Legacy of Parmenides: Eleatic Monism and Later Presocratic Thought*. Princeton: Princeton University Press, 1997.
[298] Curd, Patricia. 'Eleatic Arguments.' In *Methods in Ancient Philosophy*. Ed. Jyl Gentzler. Oxford: Clarendon Press, 1998, 1–28.
[299] Dalfen, Joachim. '"Dasselbe ist Denken und Sein." Ist es dasselbe? Die Ontologie des Parmenides als philologisches Problem.' In *Liebe zum Wort. Beiträge zur klassischen und biblischen Philologie*. Salzburg: Otto Müller Verlag, 1993, 13–32.
[300] * Davidson, Thomas. 'Parmenides.' *Journal of Speculative Philosophy*. Vol. 4: 1–16. St. Louis, MO: R. P. Studley, 1870.
[301] D'Avino, Rita. 'Parmenide e il linguaggio (B8.53–54).' *Helikon* 5 (1965): 296–317.
[302] de Rijk, L. M. 'Did Parmenides reject the Sensible World?' *Papers in Medieval Studies* 4 (1983): 29–53.
[303] Deichgräber, Karl. *Parmenides' Auffahrt zur Göttin des Rechts: Untersuchungen zum Prooimion seines Lehrgedichts*. Abhandlungen der Akademie der Wissenschaften und der Literatur: Geistes- und Sozialwissenschaftliche Klasse 11. Wiesbaden: Franz Steiner, 1958.
[304] Deichgräber, Karl. *Das Ganze–Eine des Parmenides: Fünf Interpretationen zu seinem Lehrgedicht*. Abhandlungen der Akademie der Wissenschaften und der Literatur: Geistes- und Sozialwissenschaftliche Klasse 7. Wiesbaden: Franz Steiner, 1983.
[305] Detel, Wolfgang. 'Zeichen bei Parmenides.' *Zeitschrift für Semiotik* 4 (1982): 221–239.
[306] Diels, Hermann. 'Gorgias und Parmenides.' *Sitzungsbericht der Königlichen Akademie der Wissenschaften zu Berlin* 1 (1884): 343–368.
[307] * Diels, Hermann. *Parmenides Lehrgedicht*. Berlin: Georg Reimer, 1897.
[308] Dillon, John. 'Proclus and the Forty Logoi of Zeno.' *Illinois Classical Studies* 11 (1986): 35–41.
[309] Dolin, Edwin F. 'Parmenides and Hesiod.' *Harvard Studies in Classical Philology* 66 (1962): 93–98.
[310] Ducci, E. 'Il τό ἐόν parmenideo nella interpretazione di Simplicio.' *Angelicum* 40 (1963): 313–327.
[311] Ebert, Theodor. 'Wo Beginnt der Weg der Doxa?' *Phronesis* 34 (1989): 121–138.
[312] Ebner, Pietro. 'Parmenide Medico ΟΥΛΙΑΔΗΣ.' *Giornale di Metafisica* 21.1 (1966): 103–114.
[313] Engelhard, Hans Peter. *Die Sicherung der Erkenntnis bei Parmenides*. Problemata 138. Stuttgart: Frommann-Holzboog, 1996.
[314] English, Robert B. 'Parmenides' Indebtedness to the Pythagoreans.' *TAPA* 42 (1912): 81–94.
[315] Falus, R. 'Parmenides-Interpretationen.' *Acta Antiqua Academiae Scientiarum Hungaricae* 8 (1960): 267–294.

[316] Faris, J. A. *The Paradoxes of Zeno*. Aldershot: Ashgate, 1996.
[317] Ferrara, Vincent J. 'Some Reflections on the Being-Thought Relationship in Parmenides, Anselm and Hegel.' *Analecta Anselmiana* 3 (1972): 95–111.
[318] Finkelberg, Aryeh. '"Like by Like" and the Two Reflections of Reality in Parmenides.' *Hermes* 114 (1986): 405–412.
[319] Finkelberg, Aryeh. 'The Cosmology of Parmenides.' *American Journal of Philology* 107 (1986): 303–317.
[320] Finkelberg, Aryeh. 'Parmenides: Between Material and Logical Monism.' *Archiv für Geschichte der Philosophie* 70 (1988): 1–14.
[321] Finkelberg, Aryeh. 'Parmenides' Foundation of the Way of Truth.' *Oxford Studies in Ancient Philosophy* 6 (1988): 39–67.
[322] Finkelberg, Aryeh. 'Studies in Xenophanes.' *Harvard Studies in Classical Philology* 93 (1990): 103–167.
[323] Finkelberg, Aryeh. 'Xenophanes Physics, Parmenides' Doxa and Empedocles' Theory of Cosmogonical Mixture.' *Hermes* 125 (1997): 1–16.
[324] Floyd, Edwin D. 'Why Parmendes wrote in Verse.' *Ancient Philosophy* 12 (1992): 251–265.
[325] Fränkel, Hermann. 'Parmenides: Some Comments on his Poem, by Willem Jacob Verdenius.' *Classical Philology* 41 (1946): 168–171.
[326] Fränkel, Hermann. *Wege und Formen frühgriechischen Denkens*. Munich: Verlag C.H. Beck, 1955.
[327] Fränkel, Hermann. 'Studies in Parmenides.' Reprinted in *Studies in Presocratic Philosophy*. Eds. R. E. Allen, and David J. Furley. Vol. 2. Atlantic Highlands: Humanities Press, 1975, 1–47.
[328] Fränkel, Hermann. 'Zeno of Elea's Attacks on Plurality.' Reprinted in *Studies in Presocratic Philosophy*. Eds. R. E. Allen, and David J. Furley. Vol. 2. Atlantic Highlands: Humanities Press, 1975, 102–142.
[329] Frère, Jean. 'Parménide et l'ordre du monde: Fr. VIII, 50–61.' *Études sur Parménide*. Ed. Pierre Aubenque. Vol. 2. Paris: Librairie Philosophique J. Vrin, 1987, 192–212.
[330] Furley, David J. 'Notes on Parmenides.' *Phronesis* 1 (1973): 1–15.
[331] Furley, David J. 'Anaxagoras in Response to Parmenides.' In *Essays in Ancient Greek Philosophy*. Eds. John P. Anton, and Anthony Preus. Vol. 2. Albany: State University of New York Press, 1983, 70–92.
[332] Furley, David J. 'Melissus of Samos.' In *Studies in Greek Philosophy, No 1: Ionian Philosophy*. Ed. K. I. Boudouris. Athens: International Association for Greek Philosophy, 1989, 114–122.
[333] Furley, David J. 'Truth as what survives the Elenchos.' In *Cosmic Problems*. Ed. David Furley. Cambridge: Cambridge University Press, 1989, 38–46.
[334] Furth, Montgomery. 'Elements of Eleatic Ontology.' *Journal of the History of Philosophy* 6 (1968): 111–132. Reprinted in *The Presocratics: A Collection of Critical Essays*. Ed. Mourelatos. Garden City, NY: Anchor Press, 1974. Reprint, Princeton: Princeton University Press, 1993.
[335] Furth, Montgomery. 'A 'Philosophical Hero'? Anaxagoras and the Eleatics.' *Oxford Studies in Ancient Philosophy* 9 (1991): 95–129.

[336] Gadamer, Hans-Georg. 'Kurt Riezler: Parmenides. Frankfurt a.M.: Klostermann 1934. 99 S. 6 M. (Frankfurter Studien zur Religion und Kultur der Antike. 5.)' *Gnomon* 2 (1936): 77–86.

[337] Gadamer, Hans-Georg. 'Retraktionen zum Lehrgedicht des Parmenides.' *Varia Variourum* (1952): 58–68.

[338] Gadamer, Hans-Georg. 'Parmenides oder das Diesseits des Seins.' *La Parola del Passato* 43 (1988): 143–176.

[339] Gallop, David. '"IS" or "IS NOT"?' *The Monist* 62 (1979): 61–80.

[340] * Gallop, David. *Parmenides of Elea: Fragments; A Text and Translation with an Introduction.* Toronto: University of Toronto Press, 1984.

[341] Garotti, Loris Ricci. 'Parmenide B3 et 6 (D.K.) in alcune interpretazioni Heideggeriane.' *Studi Urbinati* 35 (1961): 160–172.

[342] Gershenson, Daniel E. 'Aristotle confronts the Eleatics: Two Arguments on "The One."' *Phronesis* 7 (1962): 137–151.

[343] Gigante, M. 'Parmenide e i Medicini nelle nuove iscrizioni di Velia.' *Rivista di Filologia e di Instuzione Classica* 95 (1967): 487–490.

[344] Gilbert, Otto. 'Die δαίμων des Parmenides.' *Archiv für Geschichte der Philosophie* 20 (1907): 25–45.

[345] Gilbert, Otto. 'Ionier und Eleaten.' *Rheinisches Museum für Philologie* 64 (1909): 185–201.

[346] Goldin, Owen. 'Parmenides on Possibility and Thought.' *Apeiron* 26 (1993): 19–35.

[347] Gómez-Lobo, Alfonso. 'La vias de Parménides.' *Revista Latinamerica de Filosofia* 3 (1977): 269–281.

[348] Gómez-Lobo, Alfonso. 'Parménides: Las puertas de la noche y el dia.' *Revista Latinamerica de Filosofia* 3 (1977): 185–188.

[349] Gómez-Lobo, Alfonso. 'Retractacion sobre el Proemo de Parmenides.' *Revista Latinamerica de Filosofia* 7 (1977): 253–260.

[350] Gómez-Lobo, Alfonso. 'El Proemio de Parménides y sus intérpretes Alemanes.' *Revista de Filosofia* 23–24 (1984): 59–76.

[351] * Gómez-Lobo, Alfonso. *El Poema de Parménides: Texto griego, traducción y comentario.* 2 vols. Santiago: Editorial Universitaria, 1999.

[352] Gomperz, Heinrich. *Psychologische Beobachtungen an griechischen Philosophen.* Vienna: Internationaler Psychoanalytischer Verlag, 1924.

[353] Graham, Daniel W. 'Empedocles and Anaxagoras: Responses to Parmenides.' In *The Cambridge Companion to Early Greek Philosophy.* Ed. A. A. Long. Cambridge: Cambridge University Press, 1999, 159–180.

[354] Graham, Daniel W. 'Heraclitus and Parmenides.' In *Presocratic Philosophy: Essays in Honour of Alexander Mourelatos.* Ed. Victor Caston, and Daniel W. Graham. Burlington: Ashgate, 2002, 27–44.

[355] Granger, Herbert. 'The Cosmology of Mortals.' In *Presocratic Philosophy: Essays in Honour of Alexander Mourelatos.* Ed. Victor Caston, and Daniel W. Graham. Burlington: Ashgate, 2002, 101–118.

[356] Groarke, Leo. 'Parmenides' Timeless Universe, again.' *Dialogue* 26 (1987): 549–552.

[357] Guérard, Christian. 'Parménide d'Élée chez les Néoplatoniciens.' *Étude sur*

Parménide. Ed. Pierre Aubenque. Vol. 2. Paris: Librairie Philosophique J. Vrin, 1987, 294–313.

[358] Günther, Hans-Christian. *Aletheia und Doxa: Das Proömium des Gedichts des Parmenides*. Philosophische Schriften 27. Berlin: Duncker & Humblot, 1998.

[359] Günther, Hans-Christian. *Grundfragen des griechischen Denkens: Heraklit, Parmenides und der Anfang der Philosophie in Griechenland*. Würzburg: Königshausen, 2001.

[360] Gurtler, Gary M. '"Parmenides" by Alfonso Gómez-Lobo.' *Ancient Philosophy* 5 (1990): 274–276.

[361] van Hagens, Bernardo. *Parmenide*. Brescia: "La Scuola" Editrice, 1945.

[362] Hankinson, R. J. 'Parmenides and the Metaphysics of Changelessness.' In *Presocratic Philosophy: Essays in Honour of Alexander Mourelatos*. Ed. Victor Caston, and Daniel W. Graham. Burlington: Ashgate, 2002, 65–80.

[363] Havelock, Eric A. 'Parmenides and Odysseus.' *Harvard Studies in Classical Philology* 63 (1958): 44–67.

[364] Heidegger, Martin. *Parmenides. Gesamtausgabe Band 54*. Frankfurt a. M.: Klostermann, 1992.

[365] Heitsch, Ernst. *Gegenwart und Evidenz bei Parmenides*. Abhandlungen der Akademie der Wissenschaften und der Literatur: Geistes- und Sozialwissenschaftliche Klasse 4. Wiesbaden: Franz Steiner, 1970.

[366] Heitsch, Ernst. 'Sein und Gegenwart im frühgriechischen Denken.' *Gymnasium* 78 (1971): 421–37.

[367] Heitsch, Ernst. 'Evidenz und Wahrscheinlichkeitsaussagen bei Parmenides.' *Hermes* 102 (1974): 411–419.

[368] Heitsch, Ernst. *Parmenides und die Anfänge der Erkenntniskritik und Logik*. Donauwörth: Ludwig Auer, 1979.

[369] Heitsch, Ernst. *Xenophanes: Die Fragmente*. Munich: Artemis, 1983.

[370] * Heitsch, Ernst. *Parmenides: Die Fragmente*. Munich: Heimeran, 1974. 3rd ed. Zurich: Artemis & Winkler, 1995.

[371] * Henn, Martin J. *Parmenides of Elea: A Verse Translation with Interpretive Essays and Commentary to the Text*. London: Praeger, 2003.

[372] Hermann, Arnold. *The Naked IS*. Las Vegas: Parmenides Publishing, (forthcoming).

[372a] Hermann, Arnold. *Above Being*. Las Vegas: Parmenides Publishing, (forthcoming).

[373] Hershbell, Jackson P. 'Parmenides and *Outis* in *Odyssey* 9.' *The Classical Journal* 68 (1972): 178–180.

[374] Hershbell, Jackson P. 'Plutarch and Parmenides.' *Greek, Roman, and Byzantine Studies* 13 (1972): 193–208.

[375] Hershbell, Jackson P. 'Parmenides' Way of Truth and B16.' In *Essays in Ancient Greek Philosophy*. Eds. John P. Anton, and Anthony Preus. Vol. 2. Albany: State University of New York Press, 1983, 41–58.

[376] Hinze, Oscar Marcel. 'Parmenides' Auffahrt zum Licht und der tantrische Yoga.' *Symbolon* 7 (1971): 53–79.

[377] Hölscher Uvo. 'Grammatisches zu Parmenides: Fragment 4 Vers 1.' *Hermes* 84 (1956): 385–397.

[378] Hölscher, Uvo. *Der Sinn von Sein in der älteren griechischen Philosophie*. Heidelberg: Carl Winter University Press, 1976.
[379] * Hölscher, Uvo. *Parmenides: Vom Wesen des Seienden; Die Fragmente, griechisch und deutsch*. Frankfurt am Main: Suhrkamp, 1986.
[380] Hösle, Vittorio. *Wahrheit und Geschichte: Studien zur Struktur der Philosophiegeschichte unter paradigmatischer Analyse der Entwicklung von Parmenides bis Platon*. Stuttgart-Bad Cannstatt: Friedrich Frommann Verlag. Günther Holzboog, 1994.
[381] Hoy, Roland C. 'Parmenides' complete Rejection of Time.' *Journal of Philosophy* 91 (1994): 573–598.
[382] Ihde, Don. 'Parmenidean Puzzles.' *Southern Journal of Philosophy* 4 (1966): 49–54.
[383] * Imbraguglia, Giorgio. *L'Ordinamento assiomatico nei frammenti Parmenidei: Per uno studio sulla genesi dell'assiomatica astratta nel processo di formazione delle teorie scientifiche*. Pubblicazioni dell'Istituto di Filosofia Facoltà di Magistero dell'Università di Genova 22. Milan: Marzorati, 1974.
[384] Isnardi Parente, Margerita. 'Parmenide e Socrate demistificati. Questioni di metodo a proposito di alcuni recenti studi di filosofia antica.' *Rivista Critica delle Filosofia* 31 (1976): 422–436.
[385] Jackson, Henry. 'On Parmenides 52 (60).' *Journal of Philology* 21 (1893): 73–74.
[386] Jaeger, Werner. 'Ein verkanntes Fragment des Parmenides.' *Rheinisches Museum für Philologie* 100 (1957): 42–47.
[387] Jameson, G. '"Well-rounded Truth" and Circular Thought in Parmenides.' *Phronesis* 3 (1958): 15–30.
[388] Jantzen, Jörg. *Parmenides zum Verhältniss von Sprache und Wirklichkeit*. Munich: C. H. Beck, 1976.
[389] Jones, Barrington. 'Parmenides "The Way of Truth."' *Journal of the History of Philosophy* 11 (1973): 287–298.
[390] Jucker, Hans. 'Zur Bildnisherme des Parmenides.' *Museum Helveticum* 25 (1968): 181–185.
[391] Jüngel, Eberhard. *Zum Ursprung der Analogie bei Parmenides und Heraklit*. Berlin: De Gruyter, 1964.
[392] Kahn, Charles H. 'The Greek Verb "To Be" and the Concept of Being.' *Foundations of Language* 2 (1966): 245–265.
[393] Kahn, Charles H. 'Parmenides: Text, Transl., Comm. and Critical Essay by Leonardo Tarán, Princeton, N.J.: Princeton UP 1965. XV, 314 S.' *Gnomon* 40 (1968): 123–133.
[394] Kahn, Charles H. 'More on Parmenides—A Response to Stein and Mourelatos.' *Review of Metaphysics* 23 (1969): 333–340.
[395] Kahn, Charles H. 'The Thesis of Parmenides.' *Review of Metaphysics* 22 (1969): 700–724.
[396] Kahn, Charles H. 'The Verb "Be" in Ancient Greek.' Part 6 of *The Verb "Be" and Its Synonyms: Philosophical and Grammatical Studies*. Ed. John W. M. Verhaar. Foundations of Language. Supplementary Series. Vol. 16. Boston: D. Reidel, 1973.

[397] Kahn, Charles H. 'Why Existence Does Not Emerge as a Distinct Concept in Greek Philosophy.' *Archiv für Geschichte der Philosophie* 58 (1976): 323–334.
[398] Kahn, Charles H. 'Retrospect on the Verb "To Be" and the Concept of Being.' *The Logic of Being* 28 (1986): 1–28.
[399] Kahn, Charles H. 'Being in Parmenides and Plato.' *La Parola del Passato* 43 (1988): 237–261.
[400] Kahn, Charles H. 'Parmenides and Plato.' In *Presocratic Philosophy: Essays in Honour of Alexander Mourelatos*. Ed. Victor Caston, and Daniel W. Graham. Burlington: Ashgate, 2002, 81–94.
[401] Kember, Owen. 'Right and Left in the Sexual Theories of Parmenides.' *Journal of Hellenic Studies* 91 (1971): 70–79.
[402] Kerferd, George B. '"Parmenides through his Fragments" by Bohrmann, Karl.' *The Classical Review* 23 (1973): 129–131.
[403] Kerferd, George B. 'Charles Kahn: The Verb "Be" in Ancient Greek (The verb "be" and its synonyms, philosophical and grammatical studies edited by John W. M. Verhaar, Part 6 = Foundations of Language, Supplementary Series Vol. 16.) Dordrecht, D. Reidel 1973.' *Archiv für Geschichte der Philosophie* 58 (1976): 60–64.
[404] Kerferd, George B. 'Parménide. Critical Note.' *Phronesis* 34 (1989): 227–231.
[405] Kerferd, George B. 'Aristotle's Treatment of the Doctrine of Parmenides.' *Oxford Studies in Ancient Philosophy*. Supplementary Volume (1991): 1–7.
[406] Kern, Otto. 'Zu Parmenides.' *Archiv für Geschichte der Philosophie* 3 (1980): 13–176.
[407] Ketchum, Richard J. 'Parmenides on What There Is.' *Canadian Journal of Philosophy* 20 (1990): 167–190.
[408] Kingsley, Peter. *In the Dark Places of Wisdom*. Inverness: Golden Sufi Center, 1999.
[409] Kirk, G. S., and M. C. Stokes. 'Parmenides' Refutation of Motion.' *Phronesis* 5 (1960): 1–4.
[410] Kirwan, Christopher. '"Parmenides" by Leonardo Tarán.' *MIND* 79 (1970): 308–310.
[411] Klowski, Joachim. 'Zum Entstehen der Begriffe Sein und Nichts in der Weltentstehungs- und Weltschöpfungstheorien im strengen Sinne, Part 1.' *Archiv für Geschichte der Philosophie* 49 (1967): 121–148.
[412] Klowski, Joachim. 'Zum Entstehen der Begriffe Sein und Nichts in der Weltentstehungs- und Weltschöpfungstheorien im strengen Sinne, Part 2.' *Archiv für Geschichte der Philosophie* 49 (1967): 225–254.
[413] Klowski, Joachim. 'Die Konstitution der Begriffe Nichts und Sein durch Parmenides.' *Kant-Studien* 60 (1969): 404–416.
[414] Klowski, Joachim. 'Zum Entstehen der logischen Argumentation.' *Rheinisches Museum für Philologie* 93 (1970): 111–141.
[415] Klowski, Joachim. 'Charles Kahn: The verb "Be" in Ancient Greek / Dordrecht-Boston: Reidel 1973.' *Gnomon* 47 (1975): 737–746.
[416] Klowski, Joachim. 'Parmenides' Grundlegung seiner Seinslehre B2–7 (Diels-Kranz).' *Rheinisches Museum für Philologie* 120 (1977): 97–137.

[417] Kranz, Walther. 'Über Aufbau und Bedeutung des Parmenideischen Gedichtes.' *Sitzungsberichte der Königlich Preussischen Akademie der Wissenschaften* 35 (1916): 1158–1175.
[418] Kullmann, Wolfgang. 'Zenon und die Lehre des Parmenides.' *Hermes* 86 (1958): 157–172.
[419] Kuspit, Donald B. 'Parmenidean Tendencies in the Epoché.' *Review of Metaphysics* 18 (1964–65): 739–770.
[420] Lacey, A. R. 'The Eleatics and Aristotle on Some Problems of Change.' *Journal of the History of Ideas* 26 (1965): 451–468.
[421] Lafrance, Yvon. 'Le Logos Présocratique dans le Parménide de Platon.' In *Philosophy of Logos*. Ed. K. I. Boudouris. Vol. 1. Athens: International Center for Greek Philosophy and Culture, 1996, 129–147.
[422] Laks, André. 'The "More" and the "Full": On the Reconstruction of Parmenides' Theory of Sensation in Theophrastus, *De Sensibus*, 3–4.' *Oxford Studies in Ancient Philosophy* 8 (1990): 1–18.
[423] Lan, Eggers C. 'Die ΟΔΟΣ ΠΟΛΥΦΗΜΟΣ der Parmenideischen Wahrheit.' *Hermes* 88 (1960): 376–379.
[424] Langan, William J. 'Parmenides and Mystical Reason: A Metaphysical Dilemma.' *Modern Schoolman* 60 (1982–83): 30–47.
[425] Lascaris, Constantino. 'Parmenides. Sobre la Natura Naturaleza.' *Revista de Filosofia de la Universidad Costa Rica* 13 (1975): 1–55. (Re'ed. San José, Costa Rica, 1982, 52p.)
[426] Lear, Jonathan. 'A Note on Zeno's Arrow.' *Phronesis* 26 (1981): 91–104.
[427] Lee, H. D. P. *Zeno of Elea: A Text, with Translation and Notes*. Cambridge: Cambridge University Press, 1936.
[428] Lesher, J. H. 'Xenophanes' Scepticism.' In *Essays in Ancient Greek Philosophy*. Eds. John P. Anton, and Anthony Preus. Vol. 2. Albany: State University of New York Press, 1983, 20–40.
[429] Lesher, J. H. 'Parmenides' Critique of Thinking: the *poludēris elenchos* of Fragment 7.' *Oxford Studies in Ancient Philosophy* 2 (1984): 1–30.
[430] Lesher, J. H. 'Xenophanes on Inquiry and Discovery: An Alternative to the "Hymn to Progress" Readings of Fr. 18.' *Ancient Philosophy* 11 (1991): 229–248.
[431] Lesher, J. H. *Xenophanes of Colophon*. Toronto: University of Toronto Press, 1992.
[432] Lesher, J. H. 'The Significance of κατὰ κάντ' ἄ<σ>τη in Parmenides Fr. 1.3.' *Ancient Philosophy* 14 (1994): 1–20.
[433] Lloyd, G. E. R. 'Parmenides' Sexual Theories—A Reply to Mr. Kember.' *Journal of Hellenic Studies* 92 (1972): 178–179.
[434] Loenen, J. H. M. M. *Parmenides, Melissus, Gorgias: A Reinterpretation of Eleatic Philosophy*. Assen: Van Gorcum, 1969.
[435] Loew, Emanuel. 'Ein Beitrag zum heraklitisch-parmenideischen Erkenntnisproblem.' *Archiv für Geschichte der Philosophie* 31 (1917): 63–90, 125–152.
[436] Loew, Emanuel. 'Zu Parmenides 1 31,32.' *Philologische Wochenschrift* 44 (1924): 300–302.
[437] Loew, Emanuel. 'Das Lehrgedicht des Parmenides.' *Philologische Wochenschrift* 48 (1928): 605–608.

[438] Loew, Emanuel. 'Das Lehrgedicht des Parmenides -Gliederung und Gedankengang.' *Rheinisches Museum für Philologie* 78 (1929): 148–165.
[439] Loew, Emanuel. 'Die Ausdrücke φρονεῖν und νοεῖν bei den Vorsokratikern.' *Philologische Wochenschrift* 6 (1929): 426–429.
[440] Loew, Emanuel. 'Das Lehrgedicht des Parmenides—Eine Kampfschrift gegen die Lehre Heraklits.' *Rheinisches Museum für Philologie* 79 (1930): 209–214.
[441] Loew, Emanuel. 'Die Götterwesen bei Parmenides.' *Philologische Wochenschrift* 20 (1930): 620–624.
[442] Loew, Emanuel. 'Das Verhältnis von Logik und Leben bei Parmenides.' *Wiener Studien* 53 (1935): 1–37.
[443] * Lombardo, Stanley. 'Parmenides: The Road to Being.' *Tōkaidō* (1982): 30–36.
[444] * Lombardo, Stanley. *Parmenides and Empedocles: The Fragments in Verse Translation*. San Francisco: Grey Fox, 1982.
[445] Long, A. A. 'Die Offenbarung des Parmenides und die menschliche Welt. By J. Mansfeld.' *Philosophical Quarterly* 16 (1966): 269–270.
[446] Long, A. A. 'The Principles of Parmenides' Cosmogony.' *Phronesis* 8 (1963): 90–107. Reprinted in *Studies in Presocratic Philosophy*. Eds. R. E. Allen, and David J. Furley. Vol. 2. Atlantic Highlands: Humanities Press, 1975.
[447] Long, A. A. '"Melisso" by Giovanni Reale.' *Gnomon* 48 (1976): 645–650.
[448] Long, A. A. 'Parmenides on Thinking Being.' *Proceedings of the Boston Area Colloquium in Ancient Philosophy* 12 (1996): 125–162.
[449] Mackenzie, Mary Margaret. 'Parmenides' Dilemma.' *Phronesis* 27 (1982): 1–12.
[450] Madden, Edward H., and Mendel Sachs. 'Parmenidean Particulars and Vanishing Elements.' *Studies in History and Philosophy of Science* 3 (1972): 151–166.
[451] Mader, Johann. *Von Parmenides zu Hegel*. 2nd ed. Vienna: WUV-Universitätsverlag, 1996.
[452] Makin, Stephen. 'Zeno on Plurality.' *Phronesis* 27 (1982): 223–238.
[453] Malcolm, John. 'On Avoiding the Void.' *Oxford Studies in Ancient Philosophy* 9 (1991): 75–94.
[454] Manchester, P. B. 'Parmenides and the Need for Eternity.' *The Monist* 62 (1979): 81–106.
[455] Mansfeld, Jaap. *Die Offenbarung des Parmenides und die menschliche Welt*. Assen: Van Gorcum, 1964.
[456] Mansfeld, Jaap. 'Parmenides Fr. B2,1.' *Rheinisches Museum für Philologie* 109 (1966): 95–96.
[457] Mansfeld, Jaap, 'Bad World and Demiurge: A "Gnostic" Motif from Parmenides and Empedocles to Lucretius and Philo.' Reprinted in *Studies in Later Greek Philosophy and Gnosticism*. By Jaap Mansfeld. London: Variorum Reprints, 1989.
[458] Mansfeld, Jaap. 'Hesiod and Parmenides in Nag Hammadi.' Reprinted in *Studies in Later Greek Philosophy and Gnosticism*. By Jaap Mansfeld. London: Variorum Reprints, 1989.
[459] * Mansfeld, Jaap, trans. *Parmenides: Über das Sein: Griechisch-Deutsch*. Ed. Hans von Steuben. Rev. ed. Stuttgart: Reclam, 1995.

[460] Marcovich, Miroslav. 'Xenophanes on Drinking-Parties and Olympic Games.' *Illinois Classical Studies* 3 (1978): 1–26.
[461] Mason, Richard. 'Parmenides and Language.' *Ancient Philosophy* 7 (1988): 149–166.
[462] Matson, Wallace I. 'Parmenides Unbound.' *Philosophical Quarterly* 2 (1980): 345–360.
[463] Matson, Wallace I. 'Zeno Moves!' In *Essays in Ancient Greek Philosophy*. Ed. Anthony Preus. Albany: State University of New York Press, 2001, 87–108.
[464] Matthen, Mohan. 'A Note on Parmenides' Denial of Past and Future.' *Dialogue* 25, 3 (1986): 553–557.
[465] McCoy, Matthew K. 'Xenophanes' Epistemology: Empiricism leading to Skepticism.' In *Studies in Greek Philosophy, No 1: Ionian Philosophy*. Athens: International Association for Greek Philosophy, 1989, 235–240.
[466] McGibbon, D. 'The Atomists and Melissus.' *Mnemosyne* 17 (1964): 248–255.
[467] Medicus, Fritz. 'Zur Physik des Parmenides.' *Philosophische Abhandlungen Max Heinze zum 70. Geburtstag*, Berlin (1906): 137–145.
[468] Meijer, P. A. 'Das Methodologische im 5. Fr. des Parmenides.' *Classica et Mediaevalia* 30 (1969): 102–108.
[469] Meijer, P. A. *Parmenides Beyond the Gates: The Divine Revelation on Being, Thinking and the Doxa*. Amsterdam Classical Monographs 3. Amsterdam: Gieben, 1997.
[470] Meixner, Uwe. 'Parmenides und die Logik der Existenz.' *Grazer Philosophische Studien* 47 (1994): 59–75.
[471] Mena, Jóse Lorite. 'Parménide: La parole entre la vérité et le soupçon.' *Revue de Métaphysique et de Morale* 83 (1978): 289–307.
[472] Miller, Ed. L. 'Parmenides the Prophet?' *Journal of the History of Philosophy* 6 (1968): 67–69.
[473] Miller, Fred D. Jr. 'Parmenides on Mortal Belief.' *Journal of the History of Philosophy* 5 (1977): 253–265.
[474] Miller, Mitchell. 'Parmenides and the Disclosure of Being.' *Apeiron* 13 (1979): 12–35.
[475] Minar, Edwin L. Jr. 'Parmenides and the World of Seeming.' *American Journal of Philology* 70 (1949): 41–55.
[476] Mondolfo, Rudolfo. 'Discussioni su un testo parmenideo (Die Fragmente der Vorsokratiker, 28B8, versi 5–6).' *Rivista Critica di Storia della Filosofia* 19 (1964): 810–815.
[477] Morrison, J. S. 'Parmenides and Er.' *Journal of Hellenic Studies* 75 (1955): 59–68.
[478] * Mourelatos, A. P. D. *The Philosophy of Parmenides*. Diss. Yale University. 1963. Ann Arbor: University Microfilms, 2001.
[479] Mourelatos, A. P. D. 'The Real, Appearances and Human Error in Early Greek Philosophy.' *Review of the Metaphysics* 19 (1965): 346–365.
[480] * Mourelatos, A. P. D. *The Route of Parmenides: A Study of Word, Image, and Argument in the Fragments*. New Haven: Yale University Press, 1970.
[481] Mourelatos, A. P .D. 'Mind's Commitment to the Real Parmenides.' *Essays in Ancient Greek Philosophy*. Eds. Anton, John P., and George L. Kustas. Vol. 1. Albany: State University of New York Press, 1971, 59–80.

[482] Mourelatos, A. P. D. 'Heraclitus, Parmenides, and the Naive Metaphysics of Things.' *Phronesis*. Supplementary Volume 1 (1973): 16–48.
[483] Mourelatos, A. P. D. 'Determinancy and Indeterminancy, Being and Non-Being in the Fragments of Parmenides.' *Canadian Journal of Philosophy*. Supplementary Volume 2 (1976): 45–60.
[484] Mourelatos, A. P. D. 'Some Alternatives in Interpreting Parmenides.' *The Monist* 62 (1979): 3–17.
[485] Mourelatos, A. P. D. '"Nothing" as "Not-Being": Some Literary Contexts that bear on Plato.' *Essays in Ancient Greek Philosophy*. Eds. John P. Anton, and Anthony Preus. Vol. 2. Albany: State University of New York Press, 1983, 59–69.
[486] Mugler, Charles. 'Der Schatten des Parmenides.' *Hermes* 103 (1975): 144–154.
[487] Napoli, Mario. *Guida degli Scavi di Velia*. Luglio: Di Mauro Editore, 1972.
[488] Nehamas, Alexander. 'On Parmenides' Three Ways of Inquiry.' *Deucalion* 33/34 (1981): 97–111.
[489] Nehamas, Alexander. 'Parmenidean Being/Heraclitean Fire.' In *Presocratic Philosophy: Essays in Honour of Alexander Mourelatos*. Ed. Victor Caston, and Daniel W. Graham. Burlington: Ashgate, 2002, 45–64.
[490] Nestle, Wilhelm. "Parmenides." *RE* XVIII,4.1553–1559.
[491] Nussbaum, Martha Craven. 'Eleatic Conventionalism and Philolaus on the Conditions of Thought.' *Harvard Studies in Classical Philology* 83 (1979): 63–108.
[492] O'Brien, Denis. 'Temps et Intemporalité chez Parménide.' *Études Philosophiques* 3 (1980): 257–272.
[493] * O'Brien, Denis. *Le poème de Parménide: Texte, traduction, essay critique. Études sur Parménide*. Ed. Pierre Aubenque. Vol. 1. Paris: Librairie Philosophique J. Vrin, 1987.
[494] O'Brien, Denis. 'L'être et l'éternité.' In *Études sur Parménide*. Ed. Pierre Aubenque. Vol. 2. Paris: Librairie Philosophique J. Vrin, 1987, 135–162.
[495] Owen, G. E. L. 'Zeno and the Mathematicians.' *Proceedings of the Aristotelian Society* 58 (1957): 199–222. Reprinted in *Logic, Science and Dialectic: Collected Papers in Greek Philosophy*. Ed. Martha Nussbaum. Ithaca, NY: Cornell University Press, 1986.
[496] Owen, G. E. L. 'Eleatic Questions.' *The Classical Quarterly* 10 (1960): 84–102. Reprinted in *Logic, Science and Dialectic: Collected Papers in Greek Philosophy*. Ed. Martha Nussbaum. Ithaca, NY: Cornell University Press, 1986.
[497] Owen, G. E. L. 'Plato and Parmenides on the Timeless Present.' *The Monist* 50 (1966): 317–340. Reprinted in *Logic, Science and Dialectic: Collected Papers in Greek Philosophy*. Ed. Martha Nussbaum. Ithaca, NY: Cornell University Press, 1986.
[498] Owens, Joseph. *The Physical World of Parmenides*. Essays in Honor of Charles Pegis. Toronto: Pontifical Institute of Medieval Studies, 1974.
[499] Owens, Joseph. 'Naming in Parmenides.' In *Kephalaion. Studies in Greek Philosophy and its Continuation*. Eds. J. Mansfeld, and L. M. De Rijk. Assen: Van Gorcum, 1975, 16–25.
[500] Owens, Joseph. 'Knowledge and *Katabasis* in Parmenides.' *The Monist* 62 (1979): 15–29.

[501] Patin, A. *Parmenides im Kampfe gegen Heraklit.* Jahrbücher für classische Philologie. Supplementband 25. Leibzig: B. G. Teubner, 1899.

[502] Patinella, Valeria. 'Parmenide: dalla mitologia alla logica.' *Quaderni di Filosofia* 2 (1979): 91–18.

[503] Peck, Arthur L. 'Plato Versus Parmenides.' *The Philosophical Review* 71 (1962): 159–184.

[504] Pellikaan-Engel, Maja E. *Hesiod and Parmenides: A New View on Their Cosmologies and on Parmenides' Proem.* Amsterdam: Adolf M. Hakkert, 1974.

[505] Perry, Bruce Millard. *Simplicius as a Source for and an Interpreter of Parmenides.* Diss. University of Washington, 1983. Ann Arbor: University Microfilms, 1984.

[506] Peterson, Sandra. 'Zeno's second Argument against Plurality.' *Journal of the History of Philosophy* 16 (1978): 261–270.

[507] Pfeiffer, Horand. *Die Stellung des Parmenideischen Lehrgedichtes in der epischen Tradition.* Bonn: Rudolf Habelt, 1975.

[508] Phillips, E. D. 'Parmenides on Thought and Being.' *The Philosophical Review* 64 (1955): 546–559.

[509] Platt, Arthur. 'Parmenides Fragment 1.37.' *The Classical Quarterly* 5 (1911): 253–257.

[510] Popper, Karl R. *The World of Parmenides: Essays on the Presocratic Enlightenment.* London: Routledge, 1998.

[511] Prauss, Gerold. 'Hegels Parmenides-Deutung.' *Kant-Studien* 57 (1966): 276–285.

[512] Preti, Giulio. 'Sulla Logica degli Eleati.' *Rivista Critica di Storia della Filosofia* 31 (1976): 82–84.

[513] Prier, Raymond Adolph. *Archaic Logic: Symbol and Structure in Heraclitus, Parmenides, and Empedocles.* The Hague: Mouton, 1976.

[514] Rauschenberger, Walther. 'Heraklit und die Eleaten.' *Archiv für Geschichte der Philosophie* 32 (1919): 108–112.

[515] Rauschenberger, Walther. 'Parmenides und Heraklit.' *Jahrbuch der Schoppenhauer-Gesellschaft* 28 (1941): 134–150.

[516] Raven, J. E. *Pythagoreans and Eleatics: An Account of the Interaction Between the Two Opposed Schools During the Fifth and Early Fourth Centuries* B.C. Chicago: Ares Publishers, 1966.

[517] Reale, Giovanni. *Melisso: Testimonianze e frammenti.* Firenze: Nuova Italia, 1970.

[518] * Reale, Giovanni. *Parmenide: Poema sulla natura: I frammenti e le testimonianze indirette. Saggio introductivo e Commentario filosofico di Luigi Ruggiu.* Collana: I Classici del Pensiero. Milan: Rusconi, 1991.

[519] Reich, Klaus. 'Parmenides und die Pythagoreer.' *Hermes* 82 (1954): 287–294.

[520] Reinhardt, Karl. *Parmenides und die Geschichte der griechischen Philosophie.* 4th ed. Frankfurt a.Main: Klostermann, 1985.

[521] Reinhardt, Karl. 'The Relation between the Two Parts of Parmenides' Poem.' In *The Presocratics: A Collection of Critical Essays*, Ed. Mourelatos. Garden City, NY: Anchor Press, 1974. Reprint, Princeton: Princeton University Press, 1993.

[522] * Rietzler, Kurt. *Parmenides: Übersetzung, Einführung und Interpretation.* Ed. Hans-Georg Gadamer. 3rd ed. Frankfurt a.Main: Klostermann, 2001.

[523] Rist, J. M. 'Parmenides and Plato's *Parmenides.*' *The Classical Quarterly* 20 (1970): 221–229.
[524] Rizzo, Antonio. *La voce delle Pietre*. Ascea: Pro.Sys, 1999.
[525] Robinson, T. M. 'Parmenides on the Ascertainment of the Real.' *Canadian Journal of Philosophy* 4 (1975): 623–633.
[526] Robinson, T. M. 'Parmenides on the Real in Its Totality.' *The Monist* 62 (1979): 54–60.
[527] Robinson, T. M. 'Parmenides and Heraclitus on what can be known.' *Revue de Philosophie Ancienne* 7 (1989): 157–167.
[528] Rohatyn, Dennis Anthony. 'A Note on Parmenides B19.' *Apeiron* 5 (1971): 20–23.
[529] Rosen, Stanley. 'Commentary on Long's "Parmenides on Thinking Being."' *Proceedings of the Boston Area Colloquium in Ancient Philosophy* 12 (1996): 125–162.
[530] Salmon, Wesley C., ed. *Zeno's Paradoxes*. Indianapolis: Bobbs-Merrill, 1970. Reprint, Indianapolis: Hackett Publishing, 2001.
[531] Sanders, Visvald. *Der Idealismus des Parmenides*. Diss. Philosophische Fakultät Munich. Munich: Straub, 1910.
[532] De Santillana, Giorgio. *Prologue to Parmenides*. Lectures in Memory of Louise Taft Semple. Cincinnati: University of Cincinnati, 1964.
[533] Schick, Thomas. 'Check and Spur: Parmenides' Concept of (What) Is.' *The Classical Journal* 60 (1965): 170–173.
[534] Schmitz, Hermann. *Der Ursprung des Gegenstandes: Von Parmenides bis Demokrit*. Bonn: Bouvier Verlag, 1988.
[535] Schmitz, Hermann. 'Nachlese zu Parmenides.' *Hermes* 129 (2001): 459–466.
[536] Schofield, Malcolm. 'Did Parmenides discover Eternity?' *Archiv für Geschichte der Philosophie* 52 (1970): 113–135.
[537] Schwabl, Hans. 'Sein und Doxa bei Parmenides.' *Wiener Studien* 66 (1953): 50–75.
[538] Schwabl, Hans. 'Der Forschungsbericht *Parmenides.*' *Anzeiger für die Altertumswissenschaft* 9.3 (1956): 129–156.
[539] Schwabl, Hans. 'Hesiod und Parmenides. Zur Formulierung des parmenideischen Prooimions (28B1).' *Rheinisches Museum für Philologie* 106 (1963): 134–142.
[540] Sedley, David. 'Two Concepts of Vacuum.' *Phronesis* 27 (1971): 175–193.
[541] Sedley, David. 'Parmenides and Melissus.' In *The Cambridge Companion to Early Greek Philosophy*. Ed. A. A. Long. Cambridge: Cambridge University Press, 1999, 113–133.
[542] Sellmer, Sven. *Argumentationsstrukturen bei Parmenides: Zur Methode des Lehrgedichts und ihren Grundlagen*. European University Studies. Series 20. Vol. 577. Frankfurt a.Main: Peter Lang, 1998.
[543] Sider, David. 'Textual Notes on Parmenides' Poem.' *Hermes* 113 (1985): 362–366.
[544] * Sider, David, and Henry W. Johnstone. *The Fragments of Parmenides*. Bryn Mawr: Bryn Mawr Commentaries, 1986.
[545] Slonimsky, H. *Heraklit und Parmenides*. Philosophische Arbeiten 7.1. Gießen: Töpelmann, 1912.

[546] Solmsen, F. 'Parmenides and the Description of Perfect Beauty in Plato's *Symposium*.' *American Journal of Philology* 92 (1971): 62–70.

[547] Solmsen, F. 'The Tradition about Zeno of Elea re-examined.' *Phronesis* 16 (1971): 116–141.

[548] Solmsen, F. 'Light from Aristotle's Physics on the Text of Parmenides B8 DK.' *Phronesis* 22 (1977): 10–12.

[549] Solomon, J. H. M. 'Parmenides and the Gurus.' *Platon* 30 (1978): 157–173.

[550] Songe-Möller, Vigdis. *Zwiefältige Wahrheit und zeitliches Sein: Eine Interpretation des parmenideischen Gedichts*. Epistemata: Würzburger Wissenschaftliche Schriften; Reihe Philosophie. Vol. 3. Würzburg: Königshausen & Neumann, 1980.

[551] Spangler, G. A. 'Aristotle's Criticism of Parmenides in *Physics 1*.' *Apeiron* 13 (1979): 92–103.

[552] Sprague, Rosamond Kent. 'Parmenides: A Suggested Rearrangement of the Fragments in the "Way of Truth."' *Classical Philology* 50 (1955): 124–26.

[553] Sprague, Rosamond Kent. 'Parmenides, Plato and I Corinthians 12.' *Journal of Biblical Literature* 86 (1967): 211–213.

[554] Stannard, Jerry. 'Parmenidean Logic.' *The Philosophical Review* 69 (1960): 526–533.

[555] Steele, Laura. 'Mesopotamian Elements in the Proem of Parmenides? Correspondence Between the Sun-God Helios and Shamash.' *The Classical Quarterly* 52.2 (2002): 583–588.

[556] Steinhart, Carl. 'Geschichte der Philosophie. *Die Philosophie der Griechen. Eine Untersuchung über Charakter, Gang und Hauptmomente ihrer Entwicklung* von Dr. Eduard Zeller. 1. Theil: Allgemeine Einleitung. Vorsokratische Philosophie 8. (18 Bogen) Tübingen, Fues. 1844.' *Allgemeine Literatur Zeitung* 2.259–260 (1845): 881–886, 889–896.

[557] Steinhart, Carl. 'Parmenides.' In *Allgemeine Enzyklopädie der Wissenschaft und Künste*. Eds. J. S. Ersch, and J. G. Gruber. Leibzig: Brockhaus, 1839, 233–244. Reprinted Graz: Akademische Druck- und Verlagsanstalt, 1989.

[558] * Steuben, Hans von, ed. *Parmenides: Über das Sein: Griechisch-Deutsch*. Rev. ed. Stuttgart: Reclam, 1995. (Poem translation by Jaap Mansfeld.)

[559] Stevens, Annick. *Postérité de l'être: Simplicius interprète de Parménide*. Cahiers de philosophie ancienne 8. Bruxelles: Ousia, 1990.

[560] Stewart, D. 'Contradiction and the Ways of Truth and Seeming.' *Apeiron* 14 (1981): 1–14.

[561] Stokes, Michael C. 'Parmenides, Fragment 6.' *The Classical Review* 10 (1960): 193–194.

[562] Stough, Charlotte. 'Parmenides' Way of Truth, B8.12–13.' *Phronesis* 13 (1968): 97–107.

[563] Strohal, R. 'Parmenides und das "Sein."' In *Innsbrucker Beiträge zur Kulturwissenschaft, 'Erkenntnis und Wirklichkeit.'* Innsbruck: I. Kohler, H. Windischer, 1958.

[564] Susemihl, Fr. 'Zum Zweiten Theile des Parmenides.' *Philologus* 58 (1899): 205–214.

[565] Szabó, Árpád. 'Eleatica.' *Acta Antiqua* 3 (1953/54): 67–103.

[566] Szabó, Árpád. 'Zum Verständnis der Eleaten.' *Acta Antiqua* 2 (1953/54): 243–289.

[567] Szabó, Árpád. 'Die Philosophie der Eleaten und der Aufbau von Euklids Elementen.' *Philosophia* 1 (1971): 195–228.

[568] Tarán, Leonardo. 'El significado de Noein en Parménides.' *Anales de Filologia Classica* 7 (1959): 122–139.

[569] * Tarán, Leonardo. *Parmenides: A Text with Translation, Commentary and Critical Essays*. Princeton: Princeton University Press, 1965.

[570] Tarán, Leonardo. 'Alexander P. D. Mourelatos: The Route of Parmenides.' *Gnomon* 48 (1977): 651–666.

[571] Tarán, Leonardo. 'Perpetual Duration and Atemporal Eternity in Parmenides and Plato.' *The Monist* 62 (1979): 43–53.

[572] Tarrant, Harold. 'Parmenides B1.3: Text, Context and Interpretation.' *Antichton* 10 (1976): 1–7.

[573] Tarrant, Harold. 'Moderatus and the Neophytagorean Parmenides.' In *Pythagorean Philosophy*. Ed. K. I. Boudouris. Athens: International Center for Greek Philosophy and Culture, 1992, 220–225.

[574] Tegtmeier, Erwin. *Zeit und Existenz: Parmenideische Meditationen*. Philosophische Untersuchungen 3. Tübingen: Mohr Siebeck, 1997.

[575] Teloh, Henry. 'Parmenides and Plato's *Parmenides* 131a—132c.' *Journal of the History of Philosophy* 14 (1976): 125–130.

[576] Thanassas, Panagiotis. 'From the Prehistory of Logos: Parmenidean Being as "Monon Legomenon."' In *Philosophy of Logos*. Ed. K. I. Boudouris. Vol. 2. Athens: International Center for Greek Philosophy and Culture, 1996, 206–215.

[577] * Thanassas, Panagiotis. *Die erste "zweite Fahrt": Sein des Seienden und Erscheinen der Welt bei Parmenides*. Munich: Wilhelm Fink Verlag, 1997.

[578] Tilghman, B. R. 'Parmenides, Plato, and logical Atomism.' *Southern Journal of Philosophy* 7 (1969): 151–160.

[579] Theodoracopoulos, J. N. 'La filosofia de Parménides.' *Folia Humanistica* 6 (1968): 109–117.

[580] Townsley, Ashton L. 'Some Comments on Parmenidean Eros.' *EOS* 64 (1976): 153–161.

[581] * Trabattoni, Franco, trans. *Parmenide: I Frammenti*. Prefazione di Carlo Sini. I Presocratici: Collana diretta da Franco Trabattoni. Milan: Marcos y Marcos, 1985.

[582] Tugwell, Simon. 'The Way of Truth.' *The Classical Quarterly* 14 (1964): 36–41.

[583] Untersteiner, Mario. 'L'ΟΔΟΣ di Parmenide come via all' EON.' *Studi Urbinati* 29 (1956): 22–69.

[584] * Untersteiner, Mario. *Parmenide: Testimonianze e frammenti*. Firenze: Nuova Italia, 1958.

[585] Verdenius, W. J. 'Parmenides' Conception of Light.' *Mnemosyne* 2 (1949): 116–131.

[586] Verdenius, W. J. 'Parmenides B2, 3.' *Mnemosyne* 15 (1962): 237.

[587] Verdenius, W. J. *Parmenides: Some Comments on His Poem*. Amsterdam: Adolf M. Hakkert, 1964.

[588] Verdenius, W. J. 'Der Logosbegriff bei Heraklit und Parmenides, 1.' *Phronesis* 11 (1966): 81–98.

[589] Verdenius, W. J. 'Der Logosbegriff bei Heraklit und Parmenides, 2.' *Phronesis* 12 (1967): 99–117.
[590] Verdenius, W. J. 'Opening Doors (Parm. B1, 17–18).' *Mnemosyne* 30 (1977): 287–288.
[591] Verdenius, W. J. 'Opening Doors again.' *Mnemosyne* 33 (1980): 175.
[592] Vick, George R. 'Heidegger's Linguistic Rehabilitation of Parmenides' "Being."' *American Philosophical Quarterly* 8 (1971): 139–150.
[593] Viola, Coloman Étienne. 'Aux origines de la Gnoséologie: Réflections sur les sens du Fr. IV du poème de Parménide.' *Études sur Parménide*. Ed. Pierre Aubenque. Vol. 2. Paris: Librairie Philosophique J. Vrin, 1987, 69–101.
[594] Vlastos, Gregory. 'Parmenides' Theory of Knowledge.' *TAPA* 77 (1946): 66–77. Reprinted in *Studies in Greek Philosophy*. Ed. Daniel W. Graham. Vol. 1. Princeton: Princeton University Press, 3rd printing 1996, 153–163.
[595] Vlastos, Gregory. 'Ravens's Pythagoreans and Eleatics.' *Gnomon* 25 (1953): 29–35. Reprinted in *Studies in Presocratic Philosophy*. Vol. 2. Eds. R. E. Allen, and David J. Furley. Atlantic Highlands: Humanities Press, 1975. Also reprinted in *Studies in Greek Philosophy*. Ed. Daniel W. Graham. Vol. 1. Princeton: Princeton University Press, 3rd printing 1996, 180–188.
[596] Vlastos, Gregory. 'Plato's Testimony concerning Zeno of Elea.' *Journal of Hellenic Studies* 95 (1975): 136–162.
[597] Vollenhoven, D. H. 'Methode-Perikelen bij de Parmenides-Interpretatie.' *Philosophia Reformata* 30 (1965): 63–112.
[598] van der Waerden, B. L. 'Zenon und die Grundlagenkrise der griechischen Mathematik.' *Mathematische Annalen* 117 (1940–1941): 141–161.
[599] Vos, H. 'Die Bahnen von Nacht und Tag.' *Mnemosyne* 16 (1963): 18–34.
[600] de Waehlens, A. 'Le poème de Parménide.' *Revue Internationale de Philosophie* 10 (1956): 496–503.
[601] Wardy, R. B. B. 'Eleatic Pluralism.' *Archiv für Geschichte der Philosophie* 70 (1988): 125–146.
[602] * Welzk, Stefan. *Die Einheit der Erfahrung: Eine Interpretation der parmenideischen Fragmente*. Munich: Carl Hanser, 1976.
[603] Wheeler, Samuel C. 'Megarian Paradoxes as Eleatic Arguments.' *American Philosophical Quarterly* 20 (1983): 287–295.
[604] Whittaker, John. 'Parmenides 8,5.' *Symbolae Osloenses* 44 (1969): 109–125.
[605] Wiesner, Jürgen. 'Die Negation der Entstehung des Seienden. Studien zu Parmenides B8.5–21.' *Archiv für Geschichte der Philosophie* 52 (1970): 125–146.
[606] Wiesner, Jürgen. 'Überlegungen zu Parmenides B8.34.' *Études sur Parménide*. Ed. Pierre Aubenque. Vol. 2. Paris: Librairie Philosophique J. Vrin, 1987, 170–191.
[607] * Wiesner, Jürgen. *Parmenides: Der Beginn der Aletheia*. Berlin: De Gruyter, 1996.
[608] Wilamowitz-Möllendorff, U. V. 'Lesefrüchte.' *Hermes* 34 (1899): 203–230.
[609] Wilson, John R. 'Parmenides, B8.4.' *The Classical Quarterly* 20 (1970): 32–34.
[610] Wiśniewski, Bohdan. 'La Théorie de la Connaissance de Parménide.' *Studi Italiani di Filologia Classica* 35 (1963): 199–204.

[611] Wolf, Erik. 'Dike bei Anaximander und Parmenides.' *Lexis* 2 (1949): 16–24.
[612] Woodbury, Leonard. 'Parmenides on Names.' *Harvard Studies in Classical Philology* 63 (1958): 145–160.
[613] Woodbury, Leonard. 'Parmenides on Naming by Mortal Men: Fr. B8.53–56.' *Ancient Philosophy* 6 (1986): 1–13.
[614] Yamakawa, Hideya. 'Ο ΖΗΝΩΝ ΠΥΘΑΓΟΡΙΖΕΙ.' In *Pythagorean Philosophy*. Ed. K. I. Boudouris. Athens: International Center for Greek Philosophy and Culture, 1992, 226–239.
[615] * Zafiropulo, Jean. *L'école Éléate: Parménide—Zénon—Mélissos*. Paris: Belles Lettres, 1950.
[616] Zeppi, S. 'La concepzione parmenidea della limitatezza speziale dell'ente e la teologia parmenidea.' *Studi sulla Filosofia Presocratica* (1962): 57–66.

V. INDIVIDUAL ANCIENT AUTHORS AND SOURCES
Original Texts and/or Translations

Apollodorus

[617] Jacoby, Felix. *Apollodor's Chronik: Eine Sammlung der Fragmente*, Philologische Untersuchungen 16. 1902. Reprint, New York: Arno Press, 1973.

Aristotle

[618] Barnes, Jonathan, ed. *The Complete Works of Aristotle: The Revised Oxford Translation*. 2 vols. Princeton: Princeton University Press, 1991.
[619] McKeon, Richard, ed. *The Basic Works of Aristotle*. New York: Random House, 1941.

Physics:

[620] Graham, Daniel. *Aristotle Physics Book VIII*. Clarendon Aristotle Series. Oxford: Clarendon Press, 1999.

Metaphysics:

[621] Annas, Julia, trans. *Aristotle's Metaphysics Books M and N*. Clarendon Aristotle Series. Oxford: Clarendon Press, 1976.
[622] Furth, Montgomery, trans. *Aristotle: Metaphysics Books VII–X; Zeta, Eta, Theta, Iota*. Indianapolis: Hackett Publishing, 1984.
[623] Madigan, Arthur, trans. *Aristotle: Metaphysics Book B and Book K 1–2*. Clarendon Aristotle Series. Oxford: Clarendon Press, 1999.
[624] Ross, W. D. *Aristotle's Metaphysics*. 2 vols. Oxford: Clarendon Press, 1924.

Topics:

[625] Smith, Robin, trans. *Aristotle Topics: Books I and VIII*. Clarendon Aristotle Series. Oxford: Clarendon Press, 1997.

Aristoxenus

[626] Wehrli, Fritz. *Die Schule des Aristoteles: Texte und Kommentar*. Heft II. Basel: Benno Schwabe, 1945.

Cicero

[627] Caplan, Harry, trans. *Rhetorica ad Herennium*. Loeb Classical Library. Vol. 1. Cambridge, MA: Harvard University Press, 1954.
[628] Falconer, W. A., trans. *Cicero: De Divinatione*. Loeb Classical Library. Vol. 20. Cambridge, MA: Harvard University Press, 1923.
[629] King, J. E., trans. *Tusculan Disputations*. Loeb Classical Library. Rev. ed. Vol. 18. Cambridge, MA: Harvard University Press, 1945.
[630] Rackham, H., trans. *Cicero: De finibus bonorum et malorum*. Loeb Classical Library. 2nd ed. Vol. 17. Cambridge, MA: Harvard University Press, 1931.
[631] Shackleton, Bailey D. R., trans. *Cicero: Letters to Atticus*. Loeb Classical Library. 4 vols. Cambridge, MA: Harvard University Press, 1999.

Dicaearchus

[632] Wehrli, Fritz. *Die Schule des Aristoteles: Texte und Kommentar*. Heft I. Basel: Benno Schwabe, 1944.

Diodorus Siculus

[633] Oldfather, C. H., trans. et al. *Diodorus Siculus: The Library of History*. Loeb Classical Library. 12 vols. Cambridge, MA: Harvard University Press, 1933–1967.

Diogenes Laertius

[634] Hicks, R. D., trans. (D.L.): *Diogenes Laertius: Lives of Eminent Philosophers*. Loeb Classical Library. 2 vols. Cambridge, MA: Harvard University Press, 1925.

Elias

[635] Busse, Adolfus, ed. *Eliae in Porphyrii Isagogen et Aristotelis Categorias*. Vol. 18, Part 1 of *Commentaria in Aristotelem Graeca*. Berlin: Georg Reimer, 1900.

Euclid

[636] Heath, Thomas L. *The Thirteen Books of Euclid's Elements: Translated with Introduction and Commentary*. 3 vols. 2nd ed. New York: Dover Publications, 1956.

Gellius

[637] Rolfe, John C., trans. *Aulus Gellius: The Attic Nights*. Loeb Classical Library. 3 vols. Cambridge, MA: Harvard University Press, 1927.

Hippolytus

[638] Osborne, Catherine. *Rethinking Early Greek Philosophy: Hippolytus of Rome and the Presocratics*. Ithaca, NY: Cornell University Press, 1987.

Iamblichus

(Listed here are mainly original texts and/or translations of Iamblichus' writings. For further collections of translations of Pythagorean material, which may include Iamblichus—such as Guthrie [124])—see the section on "Pythagoras and the Pythagoreans.")

[639] Clark, Gillian, trans. *Iamblichus: On the Pythagorean Life*. Liverpool: Liverpool University Press, 1989.
[640] Deubner, Ludwig, ed. *Iamblichus: De vita Pythagorica*. Stuttgart: B. G. Teubner, 1975.
[641] Dillon, John, and Jackson Hershbell, trans. *Iamblichus: On the Pythagorean Way of Life*. Atlanta: Scholars Press, 1991.
[642] De Falco, Victorius, ed. *[Iamblichi]: Theologumena arithmeticae*. Stuttgart: B. G. Teubner, 1975.
[643] Festa, Nicolaus, ed. *Iamblichus: De communi mathematica scientia*. Stuttgart: B. G. Teubner, 1975.
[644] Johnson, Thomas, trans. *Iamblichus: The Exhortation to Philosophy Including the Letters of Iamblichus and Proclus' Commentary on the Chaldean Oracles*. Ed. Stephen Neuville. Grand Rapids: Phanes Press, 1988.
[645] Pistelli, Hermenegildus, ed. *Iamblichus: Protrepticus*. Stuttgart: B. G. Teubner, 1996.
[646] Taylor, Thomas. *Iamblichus on the Mysteries of the Egyptians, Chaldeans, and Assyrians; Life of Pythagoras; Ethical and Political Fragments of Ancient Pythagorean Writers*. 1818–22. Reprint, The Thomas Taylor Series. Vol. 17. Somerset: Prometheus Trust, 1999.
[647] Waterfield, Robin, trans. *The Theology of Arithmetic: On the Mystical, Mathematical and Cosmological Symbolism of the First Ten Numbers. Attributed to Iamblichus*. Grand Rapids: Phanes Press, 1988.

Nicomachus of Gerasa

[648] D'Ooge, Martin L., trans. *Introduction to Arithmetic by Nicomachus*. Ed. Mortimer J. Adler, and Philip W. Goetz. Great Books of the Western World. 2nd ed. Vol. 10. *Euclid, Archimedes, Nicomachus*. Chicago: Encyclopædia Britannica, 1990.

[649] Levin, Flora R. *The Manual of Harmonics of Nicomachus the Pythagorean: Translation and Commentary*. Michigan: Phanes Press, 1994.

Olympiodorus

[650] Busse, Adolfus, ed. *Olympiodori Prolegomena et in Categorias*. Vol. 12, Part 1 of *Commentaria in Aristotelem Graeca*. Berlin: Georg Reimer, 1902.

Pappus

[651] Thomson, William, and Gustav Junge, trans. *The Commentary of Pappus on Book X of Euclid's Elements*. Cambridge, MA: Harvard University Press, 1930.

Plato

[652] Cooper, John. *Plato: Complete Works*. Indianapolis: Hackett Publishing, 1997.
[653] Hamilton, Edith, and Cairns Huntington, eds. *The Collected Dialogues of Plato: Including the Letters*. Bollingen Series LXXI. Princeton: Princeton University Press, 1961.
[654] Jowett, B. *The Dialogues of Plato*. 3rd ed. 5 vols. London: Oxford University Press, 1924.

Parmenides:

[655] Allen, R. E. *Plato's Parmenides*. Rev. ed. New Haven: Yale University Press, 1997.
[656] Gill, Mary Louise, and Paul Ryan. *Plato: Parmenides*. Indianapolis: Hackett Publishing, 1996.

Plutarch

[657] Einarson, Benedict, and Phillip H. De Lacy, trans. *Plutarch: Moralia*. Loeb Classical Library. Vol. 14. Cambridge, MA: Harvard University Press, 1967.

Polybius

[658] Paton, W. R., trans. *Polybius: The Histories*. Loeb Classical Library. 6 vols. Cambridge, MA: Harvard University Press, 1922–27.

Pompeius Trogus (Justin)

[659] Yardley, J. C. *Justin: Epitome of the Philippic History of Pompeius Trogus*. Atlanta: Scholars Press, 1994.

Porphyry

(The works listed here preserve the original text and/or translations of *The Life of Pythagoras*. For further studies or commentaries on Porphyry see the section on Pythagoras and the Pythagoreans.)

[660] Hadas, Moses, and Morton Smith. *Heroes and Gods: Spiritual Biographies in Antiquity*. New York: Harper & Row, 1965.
[661] Sodano, Raffaele, and Giuseppe Girgenti. *Porfirio: Vita di Pitagora; Testo greco e arabo a fronte*. Milan: Rusconi, 1998.

Proclus

[662] Morrow, Glenn R., and John M. Dillon, trans. *Proclus' Commentary on Plato's Parmenides*. Princeton: Princeton University Press, 1987.
[663] Morrow, Glenn R. *Proclus. A Commentary on the First Book of Euclid's Elements*. Princeton: Princeton University Press, 1992.

Sextus Empiricus

[664] Bury, R. G., trans. *Sextus Empiricus: Against the Logicians*. Loeb Classical Library. Vol. 2. Cambridge, MA: Harvard University Press, 1935.
[665] Flückiger, Hansueli, trans. *Sextus Empiricus: Gegen die Dogmatiker = Adversus mathematicos libri 7–11*. Sankt Augustin: Academia, 1998.

Sotion

[666] Wehrli, Fritz. *Die Schule des Aristoteles: Texte und Kommentar*. Supplementband II. Basel: Benno Schwabe, 1978.

Speusippus

[667] Tarán, Leonardo. *Speusippus of Athens: A Critical Study with a Collection of the Related Texts and Commentary*. Philosophia Antiqua: A Series of Monographs on Ancient Philosophy. Ed. W. J. Verdenius, and J. C. M. Van Winden. Vol. 39. Leiden: E. J. Brill, 1981.

Stobaeus

[668] Taylor, Thomas. *Political Fragments of Archytas, Charondas, Zaleucus and Other Ancient Pythagoreans Preserved by Stobaeus; Ethical Fragments of Hierocles*. Chiswick: Whittingham, 1822.
[669] Taylor, Thomas. *Fragments of the Ethical Writings of certain Pythagoreans in the Doric Dialect; and a Collection of Pythagoric Sentences from Stobaeus and Others: Translated from the Greek*. N.d. Reprint, Edmonds, WA: Alexandrian Press, 1983.

Strabo

[670] Jones, Horace Leonard, trans. *Strabo: Geography*. Loeb Classical Library. 8 vols. Cambridge, MA: Harvard University Press, 1917–32.

Theophrastus

De Sensibus

[671] Stratton, George Malcolm. *Theophrastus and the Greek Physiological Psychology Before Aristotle*. London: George Allen & Unwin, 1917.

VI. PHILOSOPHY AFTER THE PRESOCRATICS
Plato, Aristotle, Neoplatonism; also General and Modern Philosophy

[672] Annas, Julia. 'Becoming like God: Ethics, Human Nature, and the Divine.' *Platonic Ethics, old and new. Cornell Studies in Classical Philology* 57 (1999): 52–71.

[673] Biffle, Christopher. *Landscape of Wisdom: A Guided Tour of Western Philosophy*. Mountain View: Mayfield Publishing, 1999.

[674] Burnyeat, M. F. 'Idealism and Greek Philosophy: What Descartes Saw and Berkeley Missed.' *Philosophy* 13 (1982): 19–50.

[675] Chattopadhyaya, P. D. 'On the ways of knowing what is there: Being and Knowing.' *Proceedings of the Twentieth World Congress of Philosophy* 2 (1999): 187–194.

[676] Coope, Ursula. 'Why does Aristotle say that there is no Time without Change?' *Proceedings of the Aristotelian Society* 101 (2001): 359–367.

[677] Denyer, Nicholas. *Language, Thought and Falsehood in Ancient Greek Philosophy*. London: Routledge, 1991, 1993.

[678] Dodd, Julian. 'Is Truth supervenient on Being?' *Proceedings of the Aristotelian Society* 102 (2002): 69–85.

[679] Fontaine, Piet F. M. *The Light and the Dark: A Cultural History of Dualism*. Vol. 3. Amsterdam: J. C. Gieben, 1988.

[680] Goldberg, David W. 'The Power of Logos.' In *Philosophy of Logos*. Ed. K. I. Boudouris. Vol. 1. Athens: International Center for Greek Philosophy and Culture, 1996, 110–119.

[681] Hegel, Georg Wilhelm Friedrich. *Lectures on the History of Philosophy*. Bison ed. Vol. 1. Trans. S. E. Haldane. Lincoln: University of Nebraska Press, 1995. First published London: Kegan Paul, Trench, Trübner, 1892.

[682] Jolley, Nicholas, ed. *The Cambridge Companion to Leibniz*. Cambridge: Cambridge University Press, 1995.

[683] Keefe, Rosanna. 'When does circularity matter?' *Proceedings of the Aristotelian Society* 102 (2002): 275–292.

[684] Leibniz, Gottfried Wilhelm. *Monadology and Other Philosophical Essays*. Trans. Paul and Anne Martin Schrecker. Indianapolis: Bobbs-Merrill, 1965.

[685] Lewis, David. 'Tensing the Copula.' *MIND* 111 (2002): 1–13.

[686] Mansfeld, Jaap. *Studies in Later Greek Philosophy and Gnosticism*. London: Variorum Reprints, 1989.

[687] Mansfeld, Jaap. *Prolegomena mathematica: From Apollonius of Perga to Late Neoplatonism; With an Appendix on Pappus & the History of Platonism*. Leiden: E. J. Brill, 1998.

[688] Nails, Debra. *The People of Plato: A Prosopography of Plato and Other Socratics.* Columbia: Hackett Publishing, 2002.
[689] Perelmuter, Ze 'Ev. 'The Logos of Opinion and Knowledge. How does the Logos of Opinion differ from that of Knowledge?' In *Philosophy of Logos.* Ed. K. I. Boudouris. Vol. 1. Athens: International Center for Greek Philosophy and Culture, 1996, 169–175.
[690] Popper, Karl R. *The Logic of Scientific Discovery.* 1959. Reprint, London: Routledge, 2000.
[691] Russell, Bertrand. *A History of Western Philosophy.* New York: Simon & Schuster, 1945.
[692] Santos, J. G. T. 'ΛΟΓΟΣ, Knowledge and the Forms in Plato.' In *Philosophy of Logos.* Ed. K. I. Boudouris. Vol. 2. Athens: International Center for Greek Philosophy and Culture, 1996, 174–181.
[693] Sedley, David. 'The Ideal of Godlikeness.' *Plato 2: Ethics, Politics, Religion, and the Soul.* Ed. Gail Fine. Oxford: Oxford University Press, 1999, 309–328.
[694] Sellars, Wilfrid. 'Vlastos and the Third Man.' *The Philosophical Review* 64 (1955): 405–437.
[695] Stoehr, Kevin L. 'The Virtues of Circular Reasoning.' *The Proceedings of the Twentieth World Congress of Philosophy* 5 (2000): 159–171.
[696] Yamakawa, Hideya. *Greek Philosophy and the Modern World.* Athens: Ionia Publications, 1998.

VII. ANCIENT GREEK HISTORY, POLITICS, LAW, RELIGION, AND SCIENCE

(For special focus on the Presocratics, see also section "General Presocratic Studies.")

[697] Agard, Walter R. *What Democracy Meant to the Greeks.* Madison: University of Wisconsin Press, 1942.
[698] Bell, Catherine. *Ritual: Perspectives and Dimensions.* New York: Oxford University Press, 1997.
[699] Burkert, Walter. 'ΓΟΗΣ—Zum Griechischen Schamanismus.' *Rheinisches Museum für Philologie* 105 (1962–63): 36–55.
[700] Burkert, Walter. *Structure and History in Greek Mythology and Ritual.* Berkeley: University of California Press, 1979.
[701] Burkert, Walter. *Greek Religion.* Cambridge, MA: Harvard University Press, 1985.
[702] Ciaceri, Emanuele. *Storia della Magna Grecia.* Vol. 2. Milan: Dante Alighieri di Albrighi, Segati, 1927.
[703] Dodds, E. R. *The Greeks and the Irrational.* Sather Classical Lectures 25. 1951. Reprint, Berkeley: University of California Press, 1984.
[704] Dunbabin, T. J. *The Western Greeks: The History of Sicily and South Italy from the*

Foundation of the Greek Colonies to 480 B.C. Oxford: Clarendon Press, 1948. Reprint, London: Sandpiper, 1999.
[705] Ehrenberg, Victor. *Die Rechtsidee im frühen Griechentum*. Leipzig: S. Hirzel, 1921.
[706] Eliade, Mircea. *Shamanism: Archaic Techniques of Ecstasy*. Bollingen Series LXXVI. Trans. Willard R. Trask. Princeton: Princeton University Press, 1972.
[707] Gagarin, Michael. *Early Greek Law*. Berkeley: University of California Press, 1989.
[708] Gosepath, Stefan. 'The Global Scope of Justice.' *Metaphilosophy* 32 (2001): 135–159.
[709] Guthrie, W. K. C. *The Greeks and Their Gods*. Boston: Beacon Press, 1955.
[710] Guthrie, W. K. C. *Orpheus and Greek Religion: A Study of the Orphic Movement*. London: Methuen, 1952. Reprinted with a new foreword by Larry J. Alderink. Princeton: Princeton University Press, 1993.
[711] Hack, Roy Kenneth. *God in Greek Philosophy: To the Time of Socrates*. New York: Burt Franklin, reprinted 1970.
[712] Hamburger, Max. *The Awakening of Western Legal Thought*. London: George Allen & Unwin, 1942.
[713] Havelock, Eric A. *The Greek Concept of Justice: From Its Shadow in Homer to Its Substance in Plato*. Cambridge, MA: Harvard University Press, 1978.
[714] Heidel, William Arthur. *The Heroic Age of Science: The Conception, Ideals, and Methods of Science Among the Ancient Greeks*. Baltimore: Williams & Wilkins, 1933.
[715] Jaeger, Werner. *Paideia: The Ideals of Greek Culture*. Trans. Gilbert Highet. 2nd ed. Vol. 1. New York: Oxford University Press, 1945.
[716] Jaeger, Werner. *The Theology of the Early Greek Philosophers: The Gifford Lectures 1936*. Trans. Edward S. Robinson. Oxford: Oxford University Press, 1947.
[717] Lloyd, G. E. R. *Magic, Reason and Experience: Studies in the Origin and Development of Greek Science*. Cambridge: Cambridge University Press, 1979.
[718] Magee, Bryan. *The Story of Philosophy*. London: Dorling Kindersley, 1998.
[719] Mansfeld, Jaap. 'Myth Science Philosophy: A Question of Origins.' Reprinted in *Studies in the Historiography of Greek Philosophy*. By Jaap Mansfeld. Assen: Van Gorcum, 1990.
[720] Meuli, K. 'Scythica.' *Hermes* 70 (1935): 121–176.
[721] Nestle, Wilhelm. *Vom Mythos zum Logos: Die Selbstentfaltung des griechischen Denkens von Homer bis auf die Sophistik und Sokrates*. 2nd ed. Stuttgart: Alfred Kröner, 1942.
[722] Palmer, L. R. 'The Indo-European Origins of Greek Justice.' *Transactions of the Philological Society* (1950): 149–168.
[723] Rawls, John. *A Theory of Justice*. Rev. ed. Cambridge: Harvard University Press, 1971. Reprint, Cambridge: The Belknap Press of Harvard University Press, 2003.
[724] Rutter, N. K. *The Greek Coinages of Southern Italy and Sicily*. London: Spink, 1997.
[725] Sealey, Raphael. *The Justice of the Greeks*. Ann Arbor: University of Michigan Press, 1994.

[726] Szegedy-Maszak, Andrew. 'Legends of the Greek Lawgivers.' *Greek Roman and Byzantine Studies* 19 (1978): 199–209.

[727] Vidal-Naquet, Pierre. *The Black Hunter: Forms of Thought and Forms of Society in the Greek World*. Trans. Andrew Szegedy-Maszak. Baltimore: Hopkins University Press, 1986.

[728] Vlastos, Gregory. 'Equality and Justice in Early Greek Cosmologies.' Reprinted in *Studies in Greek Philosophy*. Ed. Daniel W. Graham. Vol. 1. Princeton: Princeton University Press, 3rd printing 1996, 57–88.

[729] Zielinski, Thaddeus. *The Religion of Ancient Greece*. Trans. George Rapall Noyes. Chicago: Ares Publishers, reprinted 1975.

VIII. GEOMETRY AND MATHEMATICS
With a Focus on Incommensurable Magnitudes, Irrational Numbers, and/or Indirect Proof

[730] Becker, Oskar. 'Die Lehre vom Geraden und Ungeraden im Neunten Buch der Euklidischen Elemente.' *Quellen und Studien zur Geschichte der Mathematik, Astronomie und Physik* 3 (1936): 533–553.

[731] Becker, Oskar. *Grundlagen der Mathematik in geschichtlicher Entwicklung*. Freiburg: Karl Alber, 1954.

[732] Becker, Oskar. *Das mathematische Denken der Antike*. 2nd ed. Göttingen: Van den Hoeck, 1966.

[733] Boyer, Carl B. *A History of Mathematics*. 2nd ed. Revised by Uta C. Merzbach. New York: John Wiley & Sons, 1991.

[734] Brown, James Robert. *Philosophy of Mathematics: An Introduction to the World of Proofs and Pictures*. London: Routledge, 1999.

[735] Clawson, Calvin C. *Mathematical Mysteries: The Beauty and Magic of Numbers*. Cambridge: Perseus Books, 1999.

[736] Colerus, Egmont. *Von Pythagoras bis Hilbert: Die Epochen der Mathematik und ihre Baumeister; Geschichte der Mathematik für Jedermann*. Berlin: Karl H. Bischoff, 1944.

[737] Courant, R., H. Robbins, and I. Steward. *What Is Mathematics? An Elementary Approach to Ideas and Methods*. 2nd ed. Oxford: Oxford University Press, 1996.

[738] Davis, Philip J., and Reuben Hersch. *The Mathematical Experience*. With an introduction by Gian-Carlo Rota, 1981. Reprint, Boston: Mariner Books, 1998.

[739] Devlin, Keith. *Mathematics: The Science of Patterns*. New York: Scientific American Library, a division of HPHLP, 1994.

[740] Dunlap, Richard A. *The Golden Ratio and Fibonacci Numbers*. Singapore: World Scientific, 1997.

[741] Einstein, Albert. *Geometrie und Erfahrung*. Berlin: Julius Springer, 1921.

[742] Frege, Gottlob. *The Foundations of Arithmetic: A logico-mathematical enquiry into the concept of number*. 2nd ed. Evanston, IL: Northwestern University Press, 1980.

[743] George, Alexander, and Daniel J. Velleman. *Philosophies of Mathematics*. Oxford: Blackwell, 2002.
[744] Gullberg, Jan. *Mathematics: From the Birth of Numbers*. New York: W. W. Norton, 1996.
[745] Heath, Thomas L. *A History of Greek Mathematics*. 2 vols. Oxford: Clarendon Press, 1921. Reprint, New York: Dover Publications, 1981.
[746] Heath, Thomas L. *The Manual of Greek Mathematics*. Oxford: Oxford University Press, 1931. Reprint, New York: Dover Publications, 1963.
[747] Heiberg, I. L. *Geschichte der Mathematik und Naturwissenschaften im Altertum*. Vol. 5. Section 1. Part 2. Munich: C. H. Beck, 1975.
[748] Hintikka, Jaakko, ed. *The Philosophy of Mathematics*. Oxford Readings in Philosophy. Oxford: Oxford University Press, 1969.
[749] Huntley, H. E. *The Divine Proportion: A Study in Mathematical Beauty*. New York: Dover Publications, 1970.
[750] Junge, Gustav. 'Wann haben die Griechen das Irrationale entdeckt?' *Bibliotheca Mathematica* 7.3 (1907): 1–44.
[751] Kaplan, Robert. *The Nothing That Is: A Natural History of Zero*. Oxford: Oxford University Press, 2000.
[752] Kline, Morris. *Mathematics for the Nonmathematician*. New York: Dover Publications, 1967.
[753] Körner, Stephan. *The Philosophy of Mathematics: An Introductory Essay*. London: Hutchinson, 1960. Reprint, New York: Dover Publications, 1986.
[754] Lavine, Shaughan. *Understanding the Infinite*. Cambridge, MA: Harvard University Press, 1994.
[755] Lawlor, Robert. *Sacred Geometry: Philosophy and Practice*. London: Thames & Hudson, 1982.
[756] Lines, Malcolm E. *A Number for Your Thoughts: Facts and Speculations About Numbers from Euclid to the Latest Computers*. Bristol: Institute of Physics Publishing, 1986.
[757] Livio, Mario. *The Golden Ratio: The Story of Phi, the World's Most Astonishing Number*. New York: Broadway Books, 2002.
[758] Mankiewicz, Richard. *The Story of Mathematics*. Princeton: Princeton University Press, 2000.
[759] Manning, Henry Parker. *Irrational Numbers and Their Representation by Sequence and Series*. New York: John Wiley & Sons, 1906.
[760] Maor, Eli. *e: The Story of a Number*. Princeton: Princeton University Press, 1994.
[761] Maziarz, Edward A., and Thomas Greenwood. *Greek Mathematical Philosophy*. New York: Frederick Ungar, 1968.
[762] Morrell, Charles. *The Squaring of the Circle: Comprising the Rectification with a Different Ratio from π, Based on Euclid I, 47, Called the Pythagorean Proposition; and The Equalization*. Chicago: Hesperan Ve, 1924.
[763] Nagell, Trygve. *Introduction to Number Theory*. New York: John Wiley & Sons, 1951.
[764] Niven, Ivan. *Numbers: Rational and Irrational*. New York: Random House, 1961.

[765] Oystein, Ore. *Number Theory and Its History*. New York: McGraw Hill, 1948. Reprint, New York: Dover Publications, 1988.
[766] Rademacher, H., and O. Toeplitz. *Von Zahlen und Figuren: Proben mathematischen Denkens für Liebhaber der Mathematik*. Berlin: Julius Springer, 1930. Reprint, Berlin: Springer Verlag, 1968.
[767] Reidemeister, Kurt. *Das exakte Denken der Griechen: Beiträge zur Deutung von Euklid, Plato, Aristoteles*. Hamburg: Claassen & Goverts, 1949.
[768] Runion, Garth E. *The Golden Section*. Palo Alto, CA: Dale Seymour Publications, 1990.
[769] Russell, Bertrand. *Introduction to Mathematical Philosophy*. 1919 ed. Reprinted with a new introduction by John G. Slater. London: Routledge, 1993.
[770] Seife, Charles. *Zero: The Biography of a Dangerous Idea*. New York: Penguin Books, 2000.
[771] Szabó, Árpád. 'Wie ist die Mathematik zu einer deduktiven Wissenschaft geworden?' *Acta Antiqua* 4 (1956): 109–112.
[772] Szabó, Árpád. *The Beginnings of Greek Mathematics*. Budapest: Akadémiai Kiadó, 1978.
[773] Vogt, Heinrich. 'Die Entdeckungsgeschichte des Irrationalen nach Plato und anderen Quellen des 4. Jahrhunderts.' *Bibliotheca Mathematica* 3.9 (1908—1909): 97–155.
[774] van der Waerden, B. L. *Science Awakening*. Trans. Arnold Dresden. 4th ed. Vol. 1. Leyden: Noordhoff International, 1975.

IX. MISCELLANEOUS

[775] Barbour, Julian. *The End of Time: The Next Revolution in Physics*. Oxford: Oxford University Press, 2000.
[776] Denniston, J. D. *The Greek Particles*. 2nd ed. Revised by K. J. Dover. Indianapolis: Hackett Publishing, 1996.
[777] Edwards, Paul, ed. *The Encyclopedia of Philosophy*. Unabr. ed. New York: Simon & Schuster Macmillan, 1996.
[778] Flew, Anthony, ed. *Dictionary of Philosophy*. 2nd ed. New York: St. Martin's Press, 1984.
[779] Glugston, M. J., ed. *The New Penguin Dictionary of Science*. London: Penguin Books, 1998.
[780] Isaacs, Alan, ed. *Dictionary of Physics*. 3rd ed. Oxford: Oxford University Press, 1996.
[781] Kaku, Michio, and Jennifer Thompson. *Beyond Einstein: The Cosmic Quest for the Theory of the Universe*. Rev. ed. New York: Anchor Books, 1995.
[782] Martin, Robert M., ed. *The Philosopher's Dictionary*. 2nd ed. New York: Broadview Press, 1984.
[783] Mautner, Thomas, ed. *Dictionary of Philosophy*. Cambridge: Blackwell, 1996.
[784] Peters, F. E. *Greek Philosophical Terms: A Historical Lexicon*. New York: New York University Press, 1967.

[785] Reese, William L., ed. *Dictionary of Philosophy and Religion: Eastern and Western Thought.* 2nd ed. Atlantic Highlands, NJ: Humanities Press, 1996.
[786] Sacks, David. *A Dictionary of the Ancient Greek World.* New York: Oxford University Press, 1995.
[787] Sandys, John Edwin. *A History of Classical Scholarship.* 3rd ed. 3 vols. 1920. Reprint, Mansfield Center, CT: Maurizio Martino, 1998.

Index Locorum

Aelianus
   4.17   84n 254, 84n 256
Aetius
   2.1, 1   99n 305
   2.7.7   112n 346
Alexander
Commentarius in Metaphysica
   39.20–23   94n 288
   39.22–40.9   103n 317
Alexis
Fragments
   fr. 196   292n 732
   fr. 220   292n 732
Antiphanes
   fr. 160   292n 732
Apollonius
historiae mirabiles
   6   34n 77
Aristophon
Fragments
   fr. 9   292n 732
   fr. 12   292n 732
   fr. 13   292n 732
Aristoxenus
Fragments
   fr. 1   35n 82
   fr. 15   283n 690
   fr. 16   41n 102
   fr. 17   35n 83
   fr. 18   282n 689, 288n 714,
                         288n 715, 288n 718,
                         289n 719, 290n 724,
                         290n 725, 291n 726,
                         291n 727, 291n 729,
                         292n 731, 292n 734,
                         293n 735, 294n 738,
                         294n 739, 295n 747
   fr. 19   21n 52, 292n 732
   fr. 43   35n 83, 82n 241
   fr. 67   18n 39, 35n 82
   fr. 68   18n 39, 35n 82
   fr. 118   21n 52
   fr. 120a   21n 52
Aristotle
Fragments
   fr. 65 R   124n 378, 194n 549
   fr. 191 R   18n 38, 34n 77,
                         75n 213, 282n 689,
                         285n 702, 285n 705,
                         286n 707, 286n 708,
                         286n 709, 289n 721,
                         290n 725
   fr. 192 R   18n 38, 58n 156,
                         283n 690, 287n 710
   fr. 193   226n 599
   frs. 194–197   19n 44
   fr. 195 R   59n 168, 59n 169, 285n
                         701
   fr. 196 R   48n 124, 283n 690
   fr. 197 R   283n 690
   fr. 199   100n 308
   fr. 201 R   100n 308, 100n 310,
                         2836n 690
   fr. 203 R   94n 288, 101n 311,
                         103n 317, 108n 331,
                         108n 332, 110n 339,
                         111n 342, 112n 346,
                         113n 348, 283n 690,
                         284n 693
On Generation and Corruption
   325a18–23   9n 26, 193n 545
On the Heavens
   268a10   108n 330
   284b7   33n 74

290b12	101n 311	1092b15	107n 325
293a19–26	113n 347	1092b26	110n 334
293a19	292n 732	1093a1–1093b6	111n 341
Metaphysics		1093a2–3	110n 336
982b12	2n 11	1093a5	101n 311
983b20	3n 12	1093a9–12	110n 336
983b29–984a4	3n 12	1093a14–20	110n 335
984a5	3n 12	1093a14	111n 343
985b23	23n 58, 33n 74, 91n 284, 107n 326, 292n 732	1093a27	110n 338
		1093b2	101n 311
985b23–986a6	95n 292, 284n 693	1093b16–18	110n 337
985b28	108n 332	*Nicomachean Ethics*	
986a2–12	83n 243, 113n 348	1132b23	108n 331
986a2	101n 311	*Physics*	
986a7	94n 290	185b19	188n 534
986a8	96n 296	203a10	100n 308
986a18–21	100n 308	203a10–15	100n 310
986a19	260n 656, 264n 664	203a11	100n 308
986a20	16n 35, 100n 308	213b22	100n 310
986a22	178n 517	*Politics*	
986a30	33n 73	1274a23–30	145n 439
986b19	181n 520, 188n 534	1274b7	145n 439
986b21–25	135n 415	*Prior Analytics*	
986b23	131n 395, 133n 403	41a23	263n 662
987a15–20	100n 308	50a37	263n 662
987a20	8n 25	*Rhetoric*	
989b29	33n 74	1365b16–19	146n 442, 146n 443
989b30	23n 58, 96n 293, 292n 732	*On the Soul*	
		404b22	110n 339
990a12–22	98n 300	404b28	110n 339
990a19	111n 343	409a6	259n 655
1009b13–25	229n 606	409b25–410a2	229n 606
1053b14	3n 12	427a20–427b5	229n 606
1080b17–21	96n 293	*Topics*	
1080b19	96n 295	100b17	254n 644
1080b32	96n 293	**Athenaios**	
1083b7–19	98n 300	*Deipnosophistai*	
1083b11	16n 35, 96n 293	12.521	64n 185
1084b26	259n 655	**Cebes**	
1091a13–20	99n 306	*Tabula Cebetis*	
1091a15	100n 309, 100n 310	2	130n 392
1091a18	100n 308	**Censorinus**	
1091a23	100n 308	15.3X	132n 398
1091b31	111n 343	**Chalimachus**	
1092a32	99n 306	fr. 191	286n 706
1092b8–25	98n 300	*Oxyrhyrchus Papyrus*	
1092b10	97n 298	1011	284n 693

Index Locorum

Clemens
Stromateis
    2.21.130, 3   98n 303
    2.84   84n 257
    2.84 st.   98n 303

Cicero
De Divinatione
    2.58.119   59n 168
De Finibus Bonorum et Malorum
    5.2.4   xvii n 1, 76n 215, 291n 727
Letters to Atticus
    22 (II.2)   35n 87
    305 (XIII.32)   35n 87
    309 (XIII.33)   35n 87
On the Republic
  Scipio's Dream
    VI.18.19   104n 319
Rhetorica ad Herennium
    4.17.24   84n 258
Tusculan Disputations
    1.10.19   21n 52
    1.22.51   21n 52

Demosthenes
    24.139–141   145n 439

Dicaearchus
Fragments
    fr. 33   35n 86, 41n 101, 282n 689, 283n 690, 284n 694, 289n 720
    fr. 34   35n 86, 50n 130, 282n 689, 290n 724, 291n 726, 291n 728, 294n 738
    fr. 35   291n 726, 291n 727
    fr. 35a+b   76n 215
    fr. 35b   292n 733
    fr. 36   286n 706

Diodorus Siculus
    4.24.7   65n 189
    8.18–20   64n 181
    8.18   64n 182
    8.32   42n 107
    10.1.2   78n 222
    10.3   283n 692, 289n 720
    10.3.3   47n 122
    10.5.1–3   25n 60
    10.5.1   59n 167
    10.5.2   286n 706
    10.5.4   286n 706
    10.6–10   284n 697
    10.6   283n 690
    10.6.4   284n 693, 284n 696
    10.7   283n 690
    10.7.4   72n 205, 72n 205
    10.9   289n 720
    10.11   73n 209, 289n 720, 293n 735
    10.11.1   289n 721
    10.11.2   288n 715
    10.23   289n 720
    11.90   287n 712
    12.9–10   64n 183, 287n 713, 289n 720
    12.9   64n 184, 282n 689
    12.9.1–2   63n 179
    12.9.2   63n 180
    12.9.5–10.4   287n 712
    12.9.5–10.1   65n 187
    12.9.5   287n 712
    12.11.3   287n 713
    12.11.4–21.3   145n 439
    12.11.4   149n 445
    12.17.1–5   145n 440
    12.17.1   146n 442
    15.76.4   22n 53, 79n 224

Diogenes Laertius
The Lives of Eminent Philosophers
    D.L., 1.12   1n 8, 5n 18
    D.L., 1.16   151n 448
    D.L., 2.40   2n 10
    D.L., 2.349–351   19n 44
    D.L., 3.37   18n 39, 35n 82
    D.L., 8.1   283n 692
    D.L., 8.3   51n 136, 52n 138, 282n 689
    D.L., 8.4–5   15n 33, 18n 38
    D.L., 8.4   283n 690, 285n 703
    D.L., 8.6–8   18n 40, 285n 698
    D.L., 8.7   129n 387, 283n 690, 295n 751
    D.L., 8.8–25   283n 690
    D.L., 8.8–10   284n 697
    D.L., 8.8   5n 18

D.L., 8.9	20n 46	II	86n 270
D.L., 8.11	284n 696, 286n 707	IV	87n 274
D.L., 8.12	284n 696, 284n 697	(Scholium 42)	86n 270
D.L., 8.14	284n 696	VII.1	275–276
D.L., 8.15	82n 241	IX. 21–34	86n 270
D.L., 8.17–19	284n 697	X.117	264n 663
D.L., 8.19	59n 168, 72n 205	**Eudemus**	
D.L., 8.20	19n 45, 72n 205	fr. 137	87n 273
D.L., 8.21	282n 689	**Gellius**	
D.L., 8.22–24	284n 697	*Attic Nights*	
D.L., 8.22	20n 47	I.9	292n 732
D.L., 8.24	100n 308	**Heraclides Ponticus**	
D.L., 8.27	20n 48	fr. 44	84n 257, 98n 303
D.L., 8.32–36	284n 697	**Herodian**	
D.L., 8.32–34	284n 697	*On Peculiar Speech*	
D.L., 8.34–36	19n 44	41.5	140n 430
D.L., 8.34	59n 168, 84n 255, 285n 701	**Herodotus**	
		Histories	
D.L., 8.38–39	282n 689	4.95–96	282n 687
D.L., 8.39–40	291n 726	5.44	65n 188
D.L., 8.39	52n 137, 285n 701, 287n 713, 288n 714, 289n 721, 292n 730, 294n 738, 294n 739, 294n 740, 295n 742	**Hippolytus**	
		Refutation	
		1.2.2	99n 304
		1.2.4	292n 732
		6.25	115n 350
D.L., 8.40	76n 215, 291n 727, 292n 733, 295n 743, 295n 745	6, 154 W 27.5	59n 169
		Iamblichus	
		De Communi Mathematica Scientia	
D.L., 8.46	21n 52, 292n 732	25	81n 234, 89n 280, 83n 286
D.L., 8.48	16n 34, 99n 305		
D.L., 8.56	131n 394	*Protrepticus*	
D.L., 8.57	124n 378, 194n 549	21.104.27	82n 240
D.L., 8.79	78n 219, 289n 719	21.105.6	82n 240
D.L., 8.82	78n 219, 289n 719	21.106.8	82n 240
D.L., 9.18	133n 401, 133n 404	21.107	85n 262
D.L., 9.20	133n 401	21.107.6	84n 248
D.L., 9.21	129n 386, 129n 388, 131n 395, 133n 400	21.108.3	84n 249
		Theologumena Arithmeticae	
D.L., 9.23	130n 389	82.10ff.	96n 297
D.L., 9.25	194n 549	*De vita Pythagorica*	
D.L., 9.30	131n 394	VP 5	37n 94, 285n 704
Elias		VP 8	285n 704
Commentaria in Aristotelem Graeca		VP 28–30	282n 689
18.109.6	195n 550	VP 30	18n 38, 23n 57, 43n 110, 81n 234, 85n 265, 90n 282, 285n 705
18.128.5	33n 70		
Euclid			
The Elements			
Books I–IV	86n 270	VP 30.1	292n 732

Index Locorum

VP 31	18n 38, 56n 156, 286n 710	VP 91	285n 705
VP 33	35n 83, 284n 695, 285n 701, 289n 720	VP 92	286n 707
		VP 94	52n 140, 72n 205
		VP 95	61n 178
VP 35–38	284n 697	VP 96–100	56n 154
VP 36	43n 109	VP 97	80n 229
VP 37	43n 110, 44n 114	VP 100	58n 164, 72n 205
VP 45	45n 116, 61n 176	VP 103–105	82n 240
VP 48	46n 117	VP 104	35n 83, 72n 203, 72n 205
VP 50	46n 117		
VP 51	46n 118	VP 105	56n 153, 72n 203, 84n 246
VP 54	46n 119		
VP 56	47n 120	VP 108–109	90n 282
VP 63	25n 61, 286n 706	VP 108	80n 229
VP 64	285n 699	VP 108.16 80n	230
VP 68	72n 205, 285n 699	VP 109	59n 168
VP 70–74	52n 140	VP 115–121	93n 287
VP 71	53n 142, 53n 143	VP 129	80n 229
VP 72	53n 144, 54n 146, 60n 173, 72n 206, 80n 229, 81n 235	VP 130	35n 83
		VP 132	46n 117
		VP 133	289n 720, 289n 722
VP 72.11–12	54n 145	VP 134	19n 42, 283n 690, 285n 702, 286n 708
VP 72.11	292n 732		
VP 72.15	292n 732	VP 135	285n 705
VP 73	54n 147, 61n 178	VP 137	57n 158
VP 74	54n 147, 61n 178, 71n 202, 73n 209, 293n 735, 293n 735	VP 140	83n 245
		VP 149	72n 205
		VP 150	80n 229, 81n 234
VP 80	81n 235, 292n 732	VP 165	59n 167
VP 81	17n 36, 81n 234, 89n 280, 90n 282	VP 166	129n 388
		VP 168	60n 173
VP 81.25	292n 732	VP 171	58n 164
VP 82–86	83n 245	VP 174–175	58n 162
VP 82	19n 44, 81n 234, 82n 239, 83n 242, 85n 265	VP 174	57n 159
		VP 177	64n 185, 289n 720, 289n 722
VP 82.5	292n 732	VP 187	69n 196, 69n 196
VP 83	84n 247	VP 196–198	72n 205
VP 84	49n 127, 85n 262	VP 197–198	72n 205
VP 85	19n 44, 21n 51, 48n 125	VP 197	72n 204
		VP 200	55n 152
VP 86	19n 44	VP 203	58n 163
VP 87	81n 234, 86n 267	VP 223	58n 164
VP 87.8	292n 732	VP 225–226	72n 205
VP 88	81n 234	VP 226	72n 205
VP 89	54n 146, 56n 157, 81n 232, 81n 235, 89n 281	VP 227	72n 203
		VP 228	84n 259
		VP 232	70n 198, 70n 199

VP 246–247	258n 649	20.3.5–6	42n 105
VP 247	251n 637	20.4	290n 725
VP 248–258	73n 209	20.4.1–5	282n 689
VP 248–252	288n 718	20.4.1	42n 108
VP 248–251	283n 689, 290n 724, 294n 739, 295n 750	20.4.4	51n 136
		20.4.10–12	44n 112, 47n 120
VP 248 –249	292n 734	20.4.6–18	289n 720
VP 248	289n 721, 290n 723, 293n 735	20.4.6–12	47n 121
		20.4.14–18	288n 714
VP 249	290n 725, 291n 726, 291n 727, 294n 738	20.4.14	50n 131, 61n 176, 284n 695, 285n 701
VP 250	78n 220, 88n 278, 288n 714, 288n 715, 290n 724, 291n 729, 293n 735	20.4.15–16	294n 738
		20.4.16–18	292n 734
		20.4.17–18	282n 689

Olympiodorus
Comentaria in Aristotelem Graeca

VP 251	21n 52, 79n 224, 79n 226, 288n 715, 288n 718, 289n 719, 292n 731, 295n 744	12.13.13	33n 70

Scholia on the *Phaedo*

		p. 61D	73n 209, 293n 735, 295n 748
VP 252–253	288n 718, 296		

Pappus
Commentary on Book X of Euclid's Elements

VP 252	54n 148, 71n 202, 285n 699, 293n 735, 294n 738, 295n 746	I.2	251n 639, 258n 651
		I.3	267n 666, 268n 668
VP 253	79n 225	I.5	270n 671

Parmenides
The Poem

VP 254	54n 148, 55n 151, 56n 154, 56n 155, 73n 208	fr. 1	155–156
		frs. 1–8.50	155–162
VP 255–257	71n 200	fr. 1.1–32	155–156
VP 255	54n 148, 71n 201, 289n 720, 289n 721, 290n 723, 290n 725	fr. 1.2–3	155, 166n 488
		fr. 1.2	226n 600
VP 256	59n 167	fr. 1.3	164, 216, 225, 227
VP 257–261	285n 701	fr. 1.9	164, 165
VP 257	54n 145, 54n 148, 60n 173, 72n 206, 89n 279	fr. 1.11–21	166
		fr. 1.11–20	165n 486
		fr. 1.11	164, 165
VP 258–264	294n 737	fr. 1.14	212
VP 258–259	295n 750	fr. 1.27	165
VP 259	54n 148, 74n 210	fr. 1.28–32	163, 164, 219
VP 260	54n 148, 59n 169	fr. 1.28–32a	167
VP 261	54n 148, 296n 752	fr. 1.28	212
VP 262	54n 148	fr. 1.29	xix, 186, 227, 247
VP 263–264	288n 716	fr. 1.30–32	214
VP 267	23n 57, 129n 388	fr. 1.30	144n 437, 166n 491, 212

Justin
Epitome of Pompeius Trogus' "Historiae Philippicae"

20.2.12–3.8	42n 107	fr. 1.31–32	116n 357, 136, 141n 431, 167, 168, 170, 170n 499,

		170n 500, 171, 172, 175, 181, 183, 208, 216n 589, 219, 224	fr. 6.8	222, 244
			fr. 6.9	153, 209, 210, 223
			fr. 7	155, 158, 167, 171n 501, 209, 209n 569, 209n 570, 234
fr. 1.31	136n 421, 144n 437, 167, 229, 247		
fr. 1.32	136n 421, 144n 437, 167, 167, 169, 171, 173, 175, 175, 180, 229, 273	fr. 7.1–6	210
		fr. 7.1–2	209n 569
		fr. 7.1	209, 222, 247
fr. 1.32b	167, 167n 492	fr. 7.2	209n 569
frs. 2.1–7.6	154	fr. 7.3–6	30n 65, 121, 121n 369, 122n 372, 152, 195, 219, 252
fr. 2	156, 157n 468, 167, 192, 202, 210, 218		
fr. 2.1–8	210, 218	fr. 7.3	214
fr. 2.2	xix, 187, 262n 661	fr. 7.4	220
fr. 2.3	156n 467	fr. 7.5	xix, 144n 436, 144n 437, 171, 214, 215, 216, 220, 229, 239n 619
fr. 2.4	168, 176, 186, 247		
fr. 2.5	235		
fr. 2.6	246		
fr. 2.7–8	157n 468, 201, 221, 222, 232n 610, 242n 625	fr. 7.6	152n 452, 209
		fr. 8	xviii, 12n 32, 122n 370, 151n 447, 152, 155n 461, 158–160, 182, 187, 188, 210, 214, 216, 219, 223, 224, 226, 234, 247, 252n 640
fr. 2.8	122n 372		
frs. 3–7	209		
fr. 3	122n 372, 157, 157n 468, 210, 220		
		fr. 8.1–61	154
fr. 4	122n 374, 152, 157, 161n 478, 195, 210, 219, 229, 230, 252	fr. 8.1–49	184
		fr. 8.1–3	186, 188
		fr. 8.1–2	210, 216, 227
fr. 4.1–4	220	fr. 8.1	121n 369, 152n 452, 210
fr. 4.1	xix		
fr. 4.3	195	fr. 8.2–3	176
fr. 4.4	195	fr. 8.2	xviii, 176, 202, 213
fr. 5	119n 365, 156, 157, 210, 246, 252, 252n 640	fr. 8.3–13	239
		fr. 8.3–11	220
		fr. 8.3	230, 234
fr. 5.1–2	210, 223	fr. 8.4–7	242
fr. 6	155, 157–158, 167, 209, 209n 569	fr. 8.4–6	246
		fr. 8.6–11	229
fr. 6.1–2	201, 210, 222, 232n 610, 237	fr. 8.6	239
		fr. 8.7–10	242
fr. 6.1	xix, 122n 372, 220	fr. 8.7–9	222, 242n 625
fr. 6.2	210, 209n 569, 247	fr. 8.7	243
fr. 6.3	209, 210, 209n 569	fr. 8.8–10	223
fr. 6.4–9	210	fr. 8.8	122n 372
fr. 6.7–9	222n 595, 247	fr. 8.9–11	221
fr. 6.7	222	fr. 8.9–10	xiii, 243n 626
fr. 6.8–9	182, 202n 556, 236	fr. 8.9	203

fr. 8.10–11	244n 629
fr. 8.11	143n 435, 181n 521, 182, 182n 523, 202, 274
fr. 8.12–13	239n 618, 245n 633
fr. 8.12	144n 437, 156n 464, 212
fr. 8.13–16	206
fr. 8.13–14	216, 231
fr. 8.13	202
fr. 8.14–15	216, 246
fr. 8.14	212
fr. 8.15–18	202, 247
fr. 8.15–16	121, 121n 369, 143n 435, 201n 555, 224
fr. 8.15	144n 437, 202, 215
fr. 8.16–18	222, 240n 622
fr. 8.16	203, 206, 215n 584
fr. 8.17–18	201, 246
fr. 8.17	201, 122n 372, 232n 610, 242n 625
fr. 8.19–20	220, 229
fr. 8.20	221
fr. 8.21	230
fr. 8.23	274
fr. 8.25	230, 252n 640
fr. 8.26	216
fr. 8.28	144n 437, 156n 464, 166n 491, 212
fr. 8.29	122n 373
fr. 8.30–31	211, 216
fr. 8.31	216, 274
fr. 8.32–33	191
fr. 8.33	143n 435, 221
fr. 8.34–37	220
fr. 8.34–36	157n 468, 186
fr. 8.35–41	201
fr. 8.35–36	xix, 192, 222, 235, 237, 254
fr. 8.35	122n 371
fr. 8.37–38	216
fr. 8.37	216
fr. 8.38–41	222, 237
fr. 8.38	122n 372
fr. 8.42–49	227
fr. 8.42–43	213
fr. 8.42	216, 274
fr. 8.44	252n 640
fr. 8.49	154n 459, 216, 274
fr. 8.50–53	153
fr. 8.50–52	218
fr. 8.50	12n 32, 144n 437, 156n 464, 176, 212, 223, 253n 641
fr. 8.51–61	153
fr. 8.51	160n 477
fr. 8.52/3	154n 459
fr. 8.52	8n 25, 12n 32
fr. 8.53–61	154n 459
fr. 8.53–59	176, 180, 224
fr. 8.53–56	212
fr. 8.53–54	177n 516, 188, 222
fr. 8.54	154n 459, 177n 516, 182, 274
fr. 8.55–59	222
fr. 8.55–56	182
fr. 8.55	176, 182, 215n 584
fr. 8.56–59	165, 177
fr. 8.56–57	180
fr. 8.57–59	177, 224
fr. 8.57	179
fr. 8.59	179
fr. 8.60–61	208, 219, 272
fr. 8.60	136n 421, 153, 180, 199, 216, 218, 219, 223, 229, 247
frs. 9.1–19.3	154
fr. 9	153, 154n 459, 160, 177
fr. 9.1–4	165, 176, 224
fr. 9.1–2	176, 222
fr. 9.4	221, 273
fr. 10	160
fr. 10.2–3	179, 179n 518
fr. 10.6	216
fr. 10.7	216
fr. 11	161
fr. 12	161
fr. 12.1–6	224
fr. 13	161
fr. 14	161, 179
fr. 15	161, 179, 180
fr. 15a	161

Index Locorum

fr. 16	161, 183, 227–228, 228n 603, 228	140a–b	232n 610
		142a	232n 610
fr. 16.1–4	224	*Phaedo*	
fr. 17	162	57a	78n 221, 288n 718
fr. 18	162	59c	78n 221
fr. 19	162, 202, 237	61e	78n 221, 288n 718
fr. 19.1–4	222	62b	118n 364
fr. 19.1–2	205, 239	64a	115n 351
Cornford fr.	152n 452, 154n 460, 162	65a	115n 353
		66d–67b	116n 356
Photius		67a	115n 353
Biblioteka		67d–e	116n 355
249	129n 388	67d	116n 354
438 b 19–27	292n 732	67e	115n 351
438 b 19–23	80n 229	82c	115n 352
438 b 20	292n 732	86d	21n 52
438 b 22	292n 732	88d	21n 52
438 b 23	292n 732	107d	225n 597
438 b 24	292n 732	*Phaedrus*	
438 b 25	292n 732	249b–c	125
438 b 26	292n 732	249c	v
Philolaus		*Republic*	
fr. 4	98n 302	V.476–478e	116n 357
Plato		V.476d–478b	121n 367
Laws		V.476e–477	115n 349
VIII.732c	225n 597	V.476d	116n 357
IX.856b–c	58n 165	V.478a	116n 357
IX.877a	225n 597	VI.490a–b	116n 357
Meno		VI.490b	121n 367
97d–98a	216n 589	VII.524e–525	276
Parmenides		VII.525	276, 276n 684
127b	128n 382	VII.526	276
128c–d	193n 546	VII..526a	276n 684
128c–e	131n 393	X.600b	33n 72
128d	194n 548	X.617b	83n 243, 101n 311, 102n 315
133b–134c	7n 23		
133b–c	5n 20	X.617d–e	225n 597
134a–c	5n 20	X.620d–e	225n 597
134d–e	5n 20	*Sophist*	
135a	117n 359	242d	132n 396, 133n 402
135b–c	251n 638, 254n 643	263d	156n 465
135b	117n 360	*Theaetetus*	
135c	117n 361, 117n 362, 122n 370	176b	13
		183e–184a	116n 383
135e–136a	118n 363	184a	193n 544
135e	121n 368, 121n 369	*Timaeus*	
139e	232n 610	90a–c	225n 597

349

Plutarch
De Genio Socrates
  583   291n 728, 293n 735
  583A   288n 715
Moralia
  583.B   78n 220
  On Music
  1144.37   284n 693
  1145.37   94n 291
  1147.44   105n 324, 284n 693
Reply to Colotes
  32.1126a   130n 389, 130n 390,
               213n 580
Table Talk
  9.7.746b   136n 420
Polybius
The Histories
  2.39   50n 130, 77n 217,
               288n 716, 291n 728,
               291n 729, 293n 735
  2.39.1–7   289n 720
  2.39.1–4   36n 89, 289n 721,
               290n 724, 294n 738
  2.39.1   287–288n 713
  2.39.7   287n 713
  12.16   145n 439, 145n 440
  12.28.5–7, 405   36n 92
Porphyry
Vita Pythagorae
  VP 1   283n 692
  VP 2   283n 692
  VP 9   289n 720
  VP 10   37n 94
  VP 18–22   289n 720
  VP 18–19   283n 690
  VP 18   41n 101, 282n 689
               289n 720
  VP 19   11n 30, 283n 690,
               284n 694
  VP 20   85n 265
  VP 21–22   35n 83
  VP 22   60n 171
  VP 25   43n 109
  VP 26   286n 706
  VP 27   25n 61, 285n 702,
               286n 708
  VP 28   286n 707
  VP 32   56n 153
  VP 33   60n 173, 84n 252,
               285n 699
  VP 35   72n 205
  VP 37   17n 36, 81n 234,
               82n 239, 86n 268,
               292n 732
  VP 41–45   84n 261
  VP 41–42   82n 240
  VP 41   48n 124, 84n 260
  VP 42   19n 44, 56n 153
  VP 42–44   284n 697
  VP 43–44   59n 168
  VP 45   286n 706
  VP 49   293n 735
  VP 53   18n 39, 35n 82
  VP 54–57   282n 689, 289n 720
  VP 54–55   73n 209, 289n 721,
               295n 747
  VP 54   292n 732
  VP 55–56   288n 714
  VP 55   285n 699, 288n 715,
               294n 738, 294n 739,
               295n 744, 295n 746
  VP 56–57   291n 726
  VP 56   35n 86, 50n 130,
               76n 214, 290n 724,
               291n 728, 294n 738
  VP 57–59   291n 729, 295n 744,
               296
  VP 57–58   79n 225
  VP 57   72n 203, 76n 215,
               291n 727,
               294n 738, 294n 740,
               294n 741
  VP 58–59   288n 718
Proclus
Parmenides Commentary
  1.619,4   129n 388, 131n 393
  1.708   252n 640
In Euclidem
  I.32   87n 271
  I.36   259n 653
  I.44   87n 273
  255.12–14   252n 640

Index Locorum

Sextus Empiricus
Adversus Mathematicos
    1.111   142n 433, 151n 449
    1.112–113   164n 482, 164n 483

Simplicius
Commentary on Aristotle's Physics
    9.39.10–12   204n 558
    144.25   151n 447
    1108.18–25   233n 611

Speussipus
    F28   96n 297

Stobaeus
    Fl. 43.132, fr. 2c   57n 161
    fr. 18   60n 172

Strabo
    6.1.1   129n 388, 130n 389, 131n 393
    6.1.12   287n 712

Timaeus
    fr. 9   64n 181
    fr. 44   73n 207

Theophrastus
Metaphysics
    6a19   97n 298
De Sensibus
    1   225n 596
    1.3   229n 605

General Index

A

acceptance. *See* dokimos
afterlife. *See also under* immortality, centrality of to Pythagorean teachings, 18–21
agreeability. *See* Like according to Like
akousmata, 82, 122–123, 284n 697
    defined, 82
    examples of, 83–85
Akousmatikoi/Akoustikoi/auditors, 81, 88
    defined, 82
    Hippasus' role in formation, 88–89
    not relevant to genuine philosophical ideas in Pythagoreanism, 90–91
    "outside the veil"/Listeners, 81
    rejection of innovation, 85
    split of Pythagoreanism into *Akousmatikoi* and *Mathematikoi*, 89
    teaching of by passwords, tokens, and maxims, 82–86
Aletheia
    Parmenides' concept of Truth, 198–199
    goddess of truth, Parmenides' Goddess as, 165–167
    section of Parmenides' Poem, 153, 154–157
alikeness. *See* Like according to Like
Ameinias, the Pythagorean, 129, 132
Ananke, 216n 588
Anaximander, 3, 6n 22
Anaximenes, 3
Annas, Julia, 11
anti-democracy. *See also* dictatorship
    anti-majority and, 55–56
    beans and, 59–60, 74–75
    Ninon on 74–75, 285n 701
    political outlook of Pythagoreans, 39, 51–52, 60–61
    Pythagoreanism as xvi, 51–52, 54–56
    secrecy and, 55–56
anti-empiricism, 275–276
Antisthenes, 194–195
Anton, John P., 55n 150
apartness, Pythagorean, 56
appearance. *See* Doxa
approximating/approximation, 109, 247–248. *See also* Doxa
Archytas of Tarentum
    as commander-in-chief, 77–78, 289n 719
    as a philosopher, 22
    as benign and wise Pythagorean, 77
    on ruler *vs.* ruled, 57
    as student of Philolaus of Croton, 78
"argument too strange" (Plato), 5n 20
aristocrats
    Pythagoras' recruitment of, 61
    Pythagorean, 64
    role in early Pythagoreanism 52, 60–61
    Sybarite, 63–64, 68
Aristotle
    on cosmology, 2–3
    criticism of Pythagorean counter-Earth invention, 112–113
    and the dawning of philosophy, 2–3
    on Eleatic belief, 193
    epistemological aspects of his teachings, 133
    on the eternal universe, 237
    On the Heavens, 101, 113
    Metaphysics, 100, 113
    methodical speculation, 3
    on numbers, 263–264
    as preserver of Pythagoreans' genuine philosophical ideas, 56, 90
    on Pythagoras, 33n 73

Aristotle (*continued*)
    on Pythagorean belief of reducing all things to numbers, 107–110
    on Pythagorean table of opposites, 178–179
    on Pythagoreans, 23, 34n 78, 96, 107–108, 113
    on the sound of the stars, 102
    "Those Called Pythagoreans," 33, 90–91
    on Zeno, 194
Aristoxenus of Tarentum
    attitude of toward Aristotle and Plato, 35
    Dicaearchus compared with, 35
    falsities in writings, 35
    knowledge of last Pythagoreans, 34–35, 78–79
    as source for Pythagorean tradition, 34–35
    use of his writings, 37–38
arithmetic, 107, 267, 275–276. *See also* mathematics; number(s)
asceticism/ascetics (Pythagorean), 69, 79, 122–123
Atomists, 189
attributes/attributing/attribution, 230. *See also semata*
Austin, Scott, xxvi, 184n 527, 214n 582, 239n 620

B

Barbour, Julian, *The End of Time: The Next Revolution in Physics*, 196–197
Barnes, Jonathan
    on Aristotle's Pythagorean views, 34n 78
    metempsychosis/transmigration of souls, 283n 690
    on the natural scientist, 271
    on Parmenides' "growing" and "coming-to-be," 244n 631
    on Xenophanes' viewpoint, 140n 429
Barney, Rachel, 204n558, 273n 678
base for thinking, 256–260, 268
    "discernible by thought," 251–252
    as premise, 254–256
    as "true being of things," 116–117

"true to itself," 252–253
    as Pythagorean unit, 257
beans, Pythagorean ordinance against, 59–60, 74, 82, 90, 285n 701
Becker, Oskar, 86n 270
being(s)/beingness
    Aristotle's classification of rational beings, 56
    evidence of, 186
    interpretations of, 185
    Parmenidean, 185n 528
    as tangible reality, 206
belief. *See also* certainty(ies); *dokounta*, Doxa; opinion
    gap between truth and, 174
Big Bang, 236
Bonds/bonding, as recurrent theme of Parmenides, 213, 216, 274
Bormann, Karl, 138n 426, 184n 527
Boudouris, Konstantine I., 50, 51n 135, 54n 149
boundaries/bounds
    associations with *dike*, 212, 213–214
    Goddess setting, 274
    transgression, 226
Boyer, Carl B., 267n 666, 271n 673
Brague, Rémi, 168n 493, 172n 504
Brumbaugh, Robert S., 164n 483
Burkert, Walter, xvii, xix, xxii
    on Aristotle, 33n 72, n 73
    on daimon, 226
    on Iamblichus, 53n 141
    on lack of biographical information on Pythagoras, 282n 687
    on life of Pythagoras, 29n 64, 36
    Lore and Science in Ancient Pythagoreanism, xvi
    on Mathematikoi, 86
    on music and the soul, 104
    on plausible account of Pythagoras' life, 38–39
    on politics and cultism, 50–51, 291n 730
    on Parmenides and Pythagorean doctrine, 178n 517
    on the Pythagorean way of life, 122–123
    on science and Pythagoreans, 19n 43
    on significance of Pythagoras, 274–275

on *symbola*, 82
    on Tauromenium, 36
Burnet, John, 21n 52, 129n 387
Bury, R. G., 142n 433

C

calibrating/calibration
    ability to reason, 121–124, 167
    cognitive, 218
    relying on, 26–29
Callimachus, 284n 693
Calogero, Cuido, 184n 527
Capizzi, Antonio
    on factuality of the Proem, 164n 481
    La Porta di Parmenide, 145n 438, 190n 538
    origin of plot of Poem, 145n 438
    on Parmenides as medical doctor, 130n 389
    on Parmenides' doctrine, 190n 538
    Parmenides' Phocaean ancestors' link with Reggio, 145n 438
    on Parmenides' vocations, 130n 389
Casertano, Giovanni, 184n 527
Cassin, Barbara, 184n 527
Cerri, Giovanni, 214n 582
certainty. *See also* knowledge; truth
    after death, 114
    contrasted with ambiguity and Mortal Opinion, 198–199
    contradiction and, 143, 144, 149
    difficulty achieving, 286
    Einstein on unreality of, 267, 271, 276
    Pythagorean attitude to, 119–120
    senses *vs.* reason, 144
    turning belief into, 182
chain of reasoning, 252–253
change (and Parmenides), 195, 205, 241
Charondas of Catana
    as "follower" of Pythagoras, 35
    law of retribution/*lex talionis*, 145–146
    legendary early lawmaker, 145
    in list of *Mathematikoi*, 23n 57
    process for incorporating laws, 148–149
Cherniss, H., 188n 534
chord (musical), 94–95
Ciaceri, Emanuele, 145n 438

Cicero, xvi–xvii, 34n 80, 35, 84n 258, 104n 319
Clark, Gillian, xxvi, 81n 235
Clawson, Calvin C., 262n 659
Collobert, Catherine, 184n 527
coming-to-be (from IS)
    Goddess' declarations on, 202, 205
    vs. "growing," 244n 631
    from IS NOT, 236
    Parmenides' refutation of generation, 238, 240–241
commensurability/commensurateness
    as human creation, 270
    lack of, between thought and reality, 272
    measure of, 272
    of objects of reason, 269
    Pappus' commentary on, 270
    as proviso for investigating evidential account, 217
    "that which IS for thinking" as ultimate measure of, 272
    unitary ratios, 259
communism, aristocratic, 61
conceptual correspondence, 227–229, 233. *See also* Like according to Like
consistency, in logic and philosophy. *See* Like according to Like
contradiction(s). *See also* self-contradiction
    avoidance of, 247
    certainty and, 149, 221–222
    Goddess' use of, 236, 244
    Indirect Proof and, 240
    IS NOT and, 201, 221–222, 235–236
    persuasion, rejection, and, 201
    Parmenides' use of to determine truth, 7–8, 143–144, 212
    principle of, 234
    role of in Parmenides' refutation of generation for IS, 241–244
    test of, 9, 180, 182
contradictory formulas, problem of, 177–182
contraries, 176
Cooper, John, xxvi
Cordero, Néstor-Luis, xv, xvii, xxii, 184
    analysis of "way of *esti*" and *esti* as "confirmed fact," 186

Cordero, Néstor-Luis (*continued*)
    on ἄρξει in fr. 6.3 instead of Diels'
        εἴργω, 157n 469, 209, n 568
    By Being, It Is, 184
    on Doxa, 134n 407, 153n 456, 169n 498
    on *"esti denudé,"* xviii
    on fusion of way and content, 186,
        217n 591
    on *khren*, 171n 503
    legal aspect in Parmenides, xvii, 149n 446,
        166n 491, 212n 573, 215n 584
    on Parmenides and Xenophanes,
        134n 407
    Principle of Non-Contradiction,
        202n 556
    on *semata* as proofs, 230n 609
Cornford, Francis Macdonald, 122n 370,
    226n 597
Cornford fragment, 154n 460, 162
Corssen, P., 73n 209, 293n 735
cosmological model, advanced by Doxa,
    189n 535
cosmological interpretation of Parmenides,
    192–194
cosmology. *See also* existential/cosmological
    matters
    Aristotle on, 2
    epistemology *vs.* cosmology, 187
    harmony, 101–104
    Music of the Spheres, 101–104
    order and disorder, 101–104
cosmos. *See also* universe
    inner and outer, 105
    music as a bridge for, 105
    as order *vs.* chaos, 99–101, 105–106
    Pythagoreans' use of the word, 16, 99
    song of the, 105
counter-Earth, 112–114
Courant, R., 257n 648
Coxon, A. H., 155n 462, 192n 542
Crathis/Crati (river), 63, 66
Croton, 41–42, 42–44, 47. *See also* Pythago-
    rean political elite, revolts against
    political climate in, 61–62
    Pompeius Trogus' account of Pythago-
        ras in, 47
    before Pythagoras, 41–42

    Pythagoras' arrival in, 21, 41, 47
    Pythagoras' departure from, 292, n 734
    Pythagoras' motivation of the citizens
        of, 42–43
    revival of, 43–44
    Sybaris contrasted with, 69–70
    war with Locri, 41–42
    war with Sybaris, 44, 62–70
cultic belief, 119
cultism/cults
    defined, 23
    political power and, 54–55, 60–61, 61–62
    potential effect of irrationals on, 261
    Pythagoreanism as, xvi, 20–21, 22–23,
        50–52, 72, 118–119
    Walter Burkert on, 50–51
Curd, Patricia, xvii, xxiii, 182n 524, 189,
    230n 609
    on cosmological and existential ques-
        tions in Parmenides, 182n 524
    on *esti*/IS, 189
    on IS NOT, 203n 557
    on landmarks/characteristics in Parmen-
        ides, 230n 609
    The Legacy of Parmenides, xvii, xxiii, 189
    on metaphysical implications of Par-
        menidean object, 189
    Parmenides and criteria and tests for re-
        liability, 176n 513
    per onta, 168n 493
    on predicational unity and monism,
        177n 515
    on *semata* of Light and Night,
        177n 516
    on theoretically fundamental entities,
        xvii–xviii, 122n 370, 189, n 536
Cylon/Gylon, 293, n 735, 294, n 736
    role of in anti-Pythagorean revolts, 73

D

daemon/daimon/daimonos
    defined, 225–226
    as "divider" and "distributer," 226
    functions of, 226
    Parmenides' Goddess as, 225–226
    much-informing road of, 225, 227
    Plato's use of the term, 225n 597

General Index

darkness. *See* Light and Night
Daughters of the Sun/Sun Maidens, 164–165
Davidson, Thomas, 171n 501
death, 54, 118–119
    knowing truth after (Plato), 115–116, 118–119, 120
    purification, 118–120
    separation of body and soul, 118–119
    symbolic, 54
Deceptive Order/Ordering of Words (Doxa). *See* Doxa
deceptiveness, 212. *See also* plausible/deceptive
Deichgräber, Karl, 184n 527
    on "beingness of a noetic existence," 186n 531
    on object, method, and IS, 217n 591, 230n 609
    thinking and being, 186n 530, n 531
deity(ies). *See also* God, god(s)/divinity
    abstraction of concept of, 4
    concept of in ancient Greece, 1–2
    E. L. Minar on, 57n 160
    as eternal *vs.* immortal, 135
    kinship of with truth, 5
    Parmenides' Goddess as, 225–227
    Xenophanes' concept of, 134–135, 137
Delatte, Armand, 38n 99, n 100, 52n 139, 57n 161, 58, n 165, 82n 239
    structure of Pythagorean society, 80 n 228, n 230
delimiting, of a subject, 255
Democritus/Democrates, 163, 255
demonstration, 24, 25
Denniston, J. D., 210n 570
dia pantos panta per onta, (fr. 1.32) 167, 171n 501, 175, 181, 182n 523
dialectic(s)
    defined, 124
    defining a subject, 255
    Eleatic influence on, 275–276
    Parmenides' use of, 149
    process of making or interpreting law, 149
    Zeno as inventor of, 124, 194
    Zeno's skill at, 194
Dicaearchus, as source of Pythagorean tradition, 34, 35

dichotomies, 56. *See also* opposites
dictatorship, 74. *See also* anti-democracy
Diels, Hermann, xxv, 129n 387, 209, n 567
Dike, goddess of Justice, 166, 213, n 575
dike, 212–214, 225, 227
Diodorus Siculus
    "an eye for an eye" story, 146
    as commentator on Pythagorean historical tradition, 34n 80
    on government, 74, 146
    on luxury and wealth, 47, 63, 64
    on Pythagoras' claim to have been Euphorbus, 25
    on Pythagorean practice of reporting on fellow members, 59
Diogenes Laertius, biographer of philosophers, 37
discourse, reliability of, 152, 196. *See also* Parmenidean object of discourse
    role of as "to give an account," 200–201
disproof. *See also* poluderis elenchos
    of Goddess, 144
    Indirect Proof and, 239–240
    methods of, in Parmenides' Reliable Account, 142
    positive and negative proof and, 246
    test of, 220–221, 229
    use in Sufficient Reason and Infinite Regress, 239–240
    ways of proof and, 147–149
Dodds, E. R., 225n 597
dokimos (dokim, dokimadzein, dokimasia, dokimazo), 144n 437, 167
    meaning/translation of, 171, 175, 181, 214–215
    passing Test of Disproof, 229
    what is reliable because proven as such, 170–172
dokounta (ta), 144n 437, 167, 168, 214, 219, 229
Doubling of the Cube, 87, 285n 700
Doxa (Mortal Account, Mortal Opinion, Deceptive Order of Words, Plausible Ordering), 154, 160–162. *See also* opinion
    attempt to reconcile Like and Unlike in, 224, 229
    vs. certainty, 198–199

Doxa (*continued*)
    contrasted with "that which IS" and "that which IS NOT," 215
    correlation between knowledge and perception as characteristic of, 226
    cosmological model advanced by, 189n 535
    defined, 247
    dokounta (*ta*) as, 215, 219, 229, 247
    equated with What IS NOT, 232n 610
    in contrast to Evidential Account, 205
    vs. Reliable / Evidential Account, 204, 207, 273
    importance of, 167, 226
    lacking unity in formula, 182
    Light and Night, 176
    nature of, 204, 273
    negative reading of, 169, 172–174
    Alexander Nehamas on, 177n 516
    as opinion or appearance, 170, 204–208
    plausibility of as an ordering, 225
    positive *vs.* negative reading of 172–174
    Like according to Like and, 178, 183, 215, 224, 226, 227–229
    purpose of, 154, 273
    integration of objects of mind and sense-experience as, 273
    semata and, 176–177
    sense-experience as object of, 207
    Leonardo Tarán on, 174
    truth and, 208
    untested statement as, 247–248
doxa, 214
dualism/duality, 177n 516
Dunbabin, T. J.
    on Council of the Thousand at Croton, 45n 115
    on Pythagoras and moral regeneration of Crotonians, 43n 111
    on Southern Italian history, 31
    on Sybaris and archeological promise, 66

E

Earth as a prison, 47–49, 69
education
    vs. concern for the body, 45
    of Crotonians by Pythagoras, 44
    Iamblichus on admission to, 52
    of the masses, 55
    Pythagorean ruling class and, 61
Ehrenberg, Victor, 212n 575, 215n 585, n 586
einai, 167, 171n 501, 184n 527
Einarson, Benedict, 94n 291, 105n 324
Einstein, Albert, 7
    Parmenides compared with, 205
    on reality, 267, 268, 269–270
        disparity between certainty and reality, 276
    Karl Popper and, 271
    on the unprovable, 183
    on the unreality of certainty, 271
ekrinanto, 215n 584
elders, respecting, 44, 46
Elea/Velia
    description of, 127, 128, 130
    Xenophanes and, 133
Eleatics
    doctrine of Oneness, 188n 534
    mind-set, 121
    peaceful life of, xvi, 131
    Plato on, 132
    as pragmatists, 247
elenchos
    derivation of meaning, 239n 619
    descriptive terminology in logic, 144n 437
    disproof, 214
        indirect, 239n 619
        poluderis elenchos, 144n 437, 171n 501, 172n 505, 214
    separation by logos, 216n 587
    test of, 171n 501
    "things of opinion" and, 172n 505
emotional expression, 72
Empedocles, 131
    Like according to Like orientation, 228–231
empirical inquiry, 28, 251–252
empiricism/*empeiria*, 275
End of Time, The (Barbour), 196–197
Engelhard, Hans Peter, 172n 504, 175n 512
entification, 255n 647
entity, theoretically fundamental, xvii–xix, 122n 370, 189, n 536

Epaminondas, 37n 96, 75, 78, n 222
epistemology. *See* knowledge; truth
equity, in law, 148–149
equivalence, as the closest thing to truth for Parmenides, 228
esoterics/*esoterikoi*, 20, 81, 90
esti/*estin*. *See also* IS
    affinity between truth and, 198
    Cordero on, 186
    disagreement on meaning of, 184
    evolution of, from verb to entity, 255n 647
    relation between "way of *esti*" and *esti* as "conformed fact," 185–190
    as "that which is," 184, 185–186, 188, 189
    as verb *vs.* subject, 184–185
    as way *vs.* destination, 186–187
Euclid, 86–87, 258, 275–276
Euphorbus, 25, 29
Euphorbus' shield, 25–26
Eurytus, 78–79, 97, 275
Even-odd
    indirect proof, 262–265
    irrationality and, 260
    meanings and numbers, 110–111
    principle of unit, 259
    reasoned proof and, 103
Evidential Account. *See also* Reliable Account
    twelve provisos for 218–224
    Mortal Opinion in contrast to, 205
    object of knowledge in, 200
Excluded Third/Excluded Middle/*tertium quid*/*tertium non datur*, 149, 206
exercises in infallibility, 251–253
existence. *See* being(s)/beingness
existential/cosmological matters, 182–183, 187
Exoterikoi, 292n 732
"eye for an eye," 146

F

faith, 82
falsifiability, 271. *See also* disproof
Fate, 215
Fiammenghi, Dot.ssa Antonella, xxiii
Finkelberg, Aryeh, 204n 559, 228n 603

forensic argumentation, 12n 32, 188
Four Speeches, of Pythagoras at Croton, 44–47
Fränkel, Hermann, 184n 526
Freeman, Kathleen, 87n 275
Friedlein, G., 252n 640
friendship (Pythagorean), 45, 60n 173, 74
von Fritz, Kurt, 287n 713, 294n 737
    on incommensurability, 261n 659
    on Pythagorean order, 61n 175, 65n 186, 289n 720
    on Pythagorean politics, 61n 175, 65n 186, 289n 720
    on revolts, 128n 384, 289n 722, 290n 724, 291n 730, 293n 736
Furley, David J., 184n 527
Furth, Montgomery, xviii, 206n 561, n 562

G

Gadamer, Hans Georg, 155n 461
Gagarin, Michael, 214
Gallop, David, 129n 387, 130, 154n 458–459
Gassner, Verena, xxiii
geometry, 86, 267–268, 284n 696
    and Pythagoras, 284n 696
    rift between arithmetic and, 267–268
Gigon, Olof, 212n 572, 225n 597, 239n 619, 246n 635
Gill, Mary Louise, 122n 370
God
    according to Aristotle, 237
    E. L. Minar on, 57n 160
    eternal *vs.* immortal, 135
    Xenophanes' concept of, 134–135, 137
Goddess, in Parmenides' Poem
    on *esti*, 184
    as daemon, 225–226
    on "problem of definition," 176
    identity of, 165–167,
    journey to, 154
    and "mortal opinion," 167, 172, 173, 175–176
    realm of, 163–167
    Reliable Account, 154
    role of in Poem, 166, 225
    setting of boundaries, 274

god(s)/divinity
    characterization of Greek gods, 134
        by Pythagoras, 45
    government by, in Pythagoreanism,
        56–58
    immortal *vs.* eternal, 135
    mortals relationship to, 118–119
    origins of philosophy and, 1–5
    Pythagoras as, 58
    Pythagoras as a son of, 18
    worshiping, 44
Goldin, Owen, 242
Gómez-Lobo, Alfonso, 184n 527
Gomperz, Heinrich, 129n 387
Gorgias, 10, 131n 394
Graham, Daniel, 133n 399
Greco, Dot.ssa Giovanna, xxiii
Greenwood, Thomas, 262n 659
Grundlagenkrise (Pythagorean). *See* Incommensurability
Guthrie, W. K. C.
    on ban on beans, 60
    on dating of Pythagoreanism, 34n 78
    on philosophy as eternal salvation,
        19n 43
    on Pythagorean followers, 80
    on numbers applied to qualities, 108,
        109
    on zero, 244n 669

H

Hammill, Peter, xiii–xiv, xxiv
harmonia, 21n 52
harmony
    cosmic, 102
    laws of proportion, 103
    numbers and, 93–96
    Pythagorean doctrines, 56
    and the soul, 104–107
Harmony of the Spheres. *See* Music of the Spheres
Hasse, Helmut, 261n 658, n 659
Havelock, Eric A., 164n 481
Hawking, Stephen, 197
Hearers. *See Akousmatikoi/Akoustikoi/*auditors
Heath, Thomas L., 258n 651
Hegel, Georg Wilhelm Friedrich, 127

Heidegger, Martin, 166n 489
Heidel, William Arthur, 166n 491
Heitsch, Ernst, 155n 461, 184n 527, 198n 554
    Doxa and probability statements,
        208n 566
    "evidenter Beweis," 156n 464
Henn, Martin J., 163n 480
Heraclides Ponticus, 285n 703
Heraclitus, xvi, 26n 62
    Parmenides' work as a reaction against,
        132, 133n 399
Hermann, Arnold, 133n 399, 176n 514,
    209n 567, 245n 633
Hermes, 15, 18n 38, 26
Hesiod, 134
    tales of, 4
hetaireia, 23n 56
Hicks, R. D., 82n 241
Hippasus of Metapontum, 21n 50,
    22n 55, 39, 62, 74, 88, 89,
    89n 280, 257–258
    as all-around thinker, 88–90
    "forbidden ratios," 257
    as member of one Pythagorean faction,
        74
    "Sacred Discourse," 295
    uncertainty of claims, 260
Hippolytus, 99
Hölscher, Uvo, 155n 461, 184n 527, 204n 559,
    228n 603
Homer
    tales of, 4
    "shepherd of the people," 74
    Xenophanes' theological criticism of,
        134
Huffman, Carl A., 11n 31, 87n 276–277,
    91n 285, 264n 664
Hyele. *See also* Elea/Velia
    description, 127, 128
    Xenophanes and, 133

I

Iamblichus, 37
    on *akousmata*, 83–86
    on *Akousmatikoi, Mathematikoi* 89n 280
    Burkert on, 53n 141
    on Hippasus 89n 279, n 280

General Index

on Pythagoras, 251
On the Pythagorean Life, 37, 52, 71
on Pythagoreans' view of public opinion, 55
on veil; separation of insiders, outsiders, 56, 81n 232, 90n 281, n 282
image of the perfect sphere (Parmenides), 227
Imbraguglia, Giorgio, 184n 527
immortality, 21
    unresolved questions, 274
incommensurability, 264n 664
    discovery of, 271n 673
        as destroying base of Pythagorean philosophy, 261n 659
    Grundlagenkrise (Pythagorean), 193n 547, 261, n 658, n 659
    line segments, 271n 673
    occurrence of, 272
    problem of, leading to rift between geometry and arithmetic, 267, 271n 674
Indirect Proof (*reductio ad absurdum*), 149, 238, 239n 619
    Arpád Szabó, 275
    contradiction and, 239–240
    of odd being even, 262–265
    of $\sqrt{2}$, 262–263, 264n 663, n 664
    use of by Parmenides, 8
        refutation of generation for IS, 238
infallibility
    philosophy as exercise in, 251–253
    significance for Parmenides, 179
Infinite Regress (principle of), 149, 234
    use of by Parmenides' disproof of generation of IS, 239, 244–245
infinity
    mathematics and, 267–268
    units and, 99, 259
Info to Certainty Sequence
    Part I, 279–286
    Part II, 287–296
irrational numbers/irrationals
    confinement of magnitudes, 268
    exclusion from arithmetic, 268n 667
    morality tale against preoccupation with, 268
    Pythagorean Theorem and, 260–262
    rift between geometry and arithmetic, 267
    spatial relationships and, 257
irrationality
    defined, 110
    problem of, 267
    and the Pythagorean Theorem, 260–262
irrefutability, 144, 280
IS (*esti*), 230–231
    associating of with "becoming," 236
    certainty and, 198
    coming-to-be of from another IS, 244–245
    coming-to-be of from IS, 241–242
    coming-to-be of from IS NOT, 236–237, 242–244, 252
    Charles Kahn on, xix, xix n 7, 187, n 532, 198, n 551, n 552, n 553
    contradiction and, 222, 242–244
    Evidential/Reliable Account and, 158–160, 223
    Infinite Regress and, 244–245
    landmarks/*semata* of, 212–213, 215, 234, 239
    meaning, 198
    must be ungenerated, 240, 246
    Parmenides and, 196
    Parmenides' doctrine and, 206. *See also* coming-to-be; Parmenidean object; Thought-IS
    Patricia Curd on, 189
    re-landmarking to designative limits, 226
    reducing things to, 143
    Richard McKirahan on, 244
    sense-experience and, 235, 238
    separation of from landmarks of objects of sense-experience, 226
    Sufficient Reason and, 240–242
    truth and, 198
    as the universe, 191–194
    as verb *vs.* subject, 184–186
    "Way that it IS," 176
    as way *vs.* destination, 186–187
    and ways of inquiry for thinking, 156
    what is self-refuting lacks the, 221

IS NOT. *See also* coming-to-be; IS; Parmenidean object
   cannot be objectified, 247
   contradiction and, 200–203, 242–244
   as contradiction of IS, 235
   Néstor-Luis Cordero on, 202n 556
   Evidential/Reliable Account and, 158–160, 223–224
   existential version of, 273
   IS as coming from, 242–244
   one cannot know what, 221
   Patricia Curd on, 203n 557
   Plato and, 232n 610
   question of, 200–203
   reducing things to, 143
   Richard McKirahan on, 221–222
   rule of nonthinkability of, 235
   Sufficient Reason and, 240–242
   and ways of inquiry for thinking, 156–158
   what is self-refuting, 221
"ISing" the object of inquiry, 220–221

J

Jacoby, Felix, 283n 691
Johnstone, Henry W., xxvi
Jowett, B., 132n 396
judgment. *See also* object of judgment
   method of, 201, 202
Junge/Junge-Thomson, Gustav
   arithmetic numbers and geometric magnitude, 267n 666
   The Commentary of Pappus on Book X of Euclid's Elements, 258n 651
justice, 111. *See also* dike
   goddess of. *See* Dike
Justin (Pompeius Trogus), 34n 80, 42n 105
   "insider club" (Pythagorean), 51
   Pythagoras and Croton, 47, 292n 734
   on *synedria* (Pythagorean meetinghouses) 77, 290n 724, 294

K

Kahn, Charles, xix, xix n 7, 33n 71, 101n 310, 270n 672
   attempt to reconcile contradictions surrounding Pythagoras, 20n 49, 38n 97
   on *esti*, 184n 527, 187
   on *esti* and truth, 198–199,
   neoplatonic parallels to Parmenides, 270n 672
   "object of knowing," "object of cognition," xix, 187, n 532
   Parmenidean inquiry as "cognitive reasoning," 218
   on *Phaedo*, 120n 366
Kaku, Michio, 236n 616
Kant, Immanuel, xi
Kaplan, Robert, 269n 669
kekritai, 215n 584
khren, 141n 431, 167, 169, 170n 499, 171, n 503
King Juba II of Mauretania, 33
Kingsley, Peter, 129n 387, 130n 389, 163n 480, 165n 484
Kirk, G. S., 18n 40
Kline, Morris, 267n 666
knowing, science of, 137, 138, 140
knowledge. *See also* certainty(ies); object of cognition/object of knowledge
   Aristotle and, 3
   human *vs.* divine, 1, 5
   methodical form of speculation, 3
   quest for, 2
   truth and, 4
   Xenophanes on, 135–140
   two classes of, 136
Kranz, Walther, 169n 496, 170n 499, 171n 503
krisis (judgment), 215–216

L

Laertius, Diogenes, 37
   as biographer, 37
   on Crotonian's view of Pythagoreanism, 52
   on Pythagoras and memory, 15
   on Pythagoras and philosophy, 1
   on Pythagorean tradition, 34
Lan, Eggers C., 155n 461, 227n 602
landmarks, (*semata*, signs/signposts), xviii, 188, 212–213, 236
   as characteristics of that which IS, 188n 534, 212–213, 215, 234, 239
   as evidence of the fact of being, 185–186, 196

General Index

for Light and Night in Mortal Account, 177–180
for the objects of reason, 176–177, 186, 188, 219, 223, 231
for the objects of sense-experience, 176–180, 220, 231
reliance of Way of Persuasion on, 176–177
role of in inquiry, 202, 215, 227, 230, n 609, 234–239
unity of corresponding, 230–232, 246
Last Pythagoreans, 22, n 53, 23, 34–35, 78–79, 90n 283, 292n 732
law(s), 7, 138, 142, 148
"amendment by noose," 145, n 439, n 440
equity in, 148
logic and (common origin and methodology), 216, 226, 247
Pythagoreans and, 35, 57–59, 60, 70, 74, 75–76, 85, 90
Parmenides and, 7, 127, 130, 133, 144, 148, 149, 190n 538, 200, 213, 274
punishment, 145–147
of retribution (*lex talionis*), 146
of Southern Italy, Zaleucus, Charondas, 145, n 438, n 441, 146, 147, 148–149
"unbreakable," 202–203, n 557
war (as lawful), 70
Law of Contradiction, 263
Law of the Excluded Third, 149, 206
lawgiver/lawmaker/legislator. *See under* Parmenides
lawlessness, 58. *See also* anarchy
lawmaking, early pre-logic, 144–147
Learners. *See* Mathematikoi
Leibniz, Gottfried Wilhelm, 234
formulator of Principle of Sufficient Reason, 240
Lesher, J. H., 135n 417, 171n 501
Leucippus, 100n 308, 131
Levin, Flora R., 94n 289
Lévy, Isidore, 283n 691
life, purpose of, (Pythagorean view) 47–49
Light and/or Night
contradictory characteristics, 179
each as perfect unity, 176–177

Goddess and, 164, 176
hot *vs.* cold and, 228
naming sensory impressions, 222–223
destination of chariot's journey, 164–165
Sun and Moon, 179–180
things consisting of (mixtures of), 177, 180, 204, 221
Like according to Like, 148, 225–233
aiming for conceptual correspondence, 227–229
as central thread of Parmenides Poem 227–229
Doxa and, 178, 183, 215, 224, 226, 227–229, 231, 232n 610
Goddess and *semata*, 234
as one of Parmenides' methods, 226–229, 234–235, 246–248
not applicable to IS NOT, 232n 610
provisos for Evidential Account and, 218–219, 223–224
unity of corresponding landmarks, 230–232
"way of the daemon," 225–227
Zeno's "Millet Seed" argument, 232–233
Like by Like/Like from Like. *See* Like according to Like
limit, principle of, 103
limits/limiters/limiting
daimones, 212
dike, 212
Guthrie, 99n 307
how unity and, complement each other, 227
Listeners. *See* Akousmatikoi
Lloyd, G. E. R., 246n 634
Loew, Emanuel, 226n 600
logic, Parmenides as father of, 8, 144
Lombardo, Stanley, xxiii, 209n 570
Long, A. A.
on Being, 185n 528
defense of Xenophanes, 134n 407
on fr. 8.34, 159n 474
identity/non-identity problem, 157n 468
on mind, "veridical thinking," 184n 526, 185n 528, 187n 532, 198n 552
on "omnipresence" of appearances, 170n 500, 173n 506

Long, A. A. (*continued*)
  on what Parmenides' Poem is about, 152
  on Parmenides thinking "the thoughts that the divine thinks," 289
  veridical/noetical approach, xix n 7,
luxury (and Pythagoreanism), 21, 42, 43, 44, 47–48, 60, 61, 64, 69, 84n 250
Lysis, 37n 96
  burning of meeting houses and, 75
  end of movement and, 78
  Epaminondas and, 78
  escape with Archippus, 294

M

Madden, Edward H., 189n 537
Manning, Henry Parker, 257n 648
Mansfeld, Jaap,
  against "*unio mystica*," 166n 490
  "annehmbar," *dokimos*, 181n 522,
  "forensic rhetoric," 12n 32, 166n 491, 188n 533
  legal aspect in Parmenides, 149n 446, 212n 573, 215n 585
  method, separation, 166n 490, 212n 572, 216n 587, 226n 600
  universality of Light and Night, 175n 511
Maor, Eli, 267n 666
mathematics, 16, 23, 29
  achievements of, 86–88
  defined, 108–109
  influence of Parmenides and Zeno on, toward anti-empiricism, 274–276
  outside influence, 274–276
  Zeno and, 193, n 547, 275
Mathematikoi, 81, 86–91, 288, 292
  as developers of number theory, 17
  emergence of, 86–91
  "inside the veil," or Learners, 81, 90n 281
Maziarz, Edward A., 262n 659, 268n 666
McKirahan, Richard, xv, xviii, xxii, 82n 239, 135n 417
  on *Akousmatikoi*, 85
  on entities, 255n 647
  on immortality, 19n 43

  on IS NOT, 221–222, n 594, n 595, 244
  on IT is, 184n 526, 244
  per onta, 168n 493
  Philosophy Before Socrates, xv–xvi, xxii
  on whether Parmenides thinks of himself as real, 174n 509
  table of opposites, 178, n 517
  on Xenophanes, 6 (trans), 137 (trans), 138–139, 198n 554
Meijer, P. A., 184n 527, 204n 559, 206n 562
Melissus, 181
  as Parmenides' pupil, 131
metaphysics
  Parmenidean, 190
  Plato on, 120–121
Metaphysics (Aristotle)
  criticism of Pythagoreans' motives, 113
  on the point, 259n 655
  Ross on, 34n 78
  on unity of definition, 188n 534
  the unlimited, 100
metempsychosis, 29n 64, 283n 690
  as central feature of Pythagoras' teachings, 19
Meuli, K., 163n 480
mian (unity, oneness), 160n 476, 180n 519
Milesians, xvi, 177n 516. *See also* Anaximander; Anaximenes; Thales
  Aristotle on, 3
  vs. Xenophanes, 6–7
Miller, Mitchell, xxiii
"Millet Seed" argument, 232–233
Milo (Pythagorean), 65, 287n 712, 293n 735, 294, n 738, 295
Minar, E. L.
  burning meeting houses, 75n 211
  on Parmenides and Pythagoreanism, 129n 387, 130n 389
  on Pythagoras' teaching, 50n 131
  on Pythagorean Society, 48n 123, 58, 61n 176, n 177, 290n 723
  on revolts against Pythagoreans, 71n 201
  on rule of silence, 53n 144
  on rulers and God, 57n 160
mind
  perfection and exactness belonging to, 269
  relationship of with the universe, 270

mixture, 228n 603
    avoiding (incompatibles), 268
    Doxa as, 204–205, 207, 224, 226, 229, 254n 645
    of Light and Night, 179, 180–181, 204
    mixing methods, 195, 220, 223, 236
    separation of 215, 226, 235, 238, 263
Moira, 226n 600
Monad, 100n 308, 255n 647. *See also* unit(s)
    as Pythagoreans' base for everything, 16
money. *See* luxury
monism, 134, 177n 515, 177n 516, 192n 543
    predicational, 177n 515
    unfounded in Parmenides, 177n 515, 269n 670
monotheism, 5
    Xenophanes', 135
Moon (in Parmenides), 179–180
Morrison, J. S., 163n 480
Morrow, Glenn R., 252n 640, 259n 653
Mortal Account, Mortal Opinion, 155. *See* Doxa, opinion
Mortal Belief, as subject of Doxa, 204
mortal naming, problem of, 180
motion, proving
    vs. proving proper understanding of motion, 194–195
Mourelatos, Alexander
    on *dia pantos panta per onta*, 175n 511, n 512
    on *dokimos*, 181n 521, n 522
    on *doxa, ta dokounta*, and *dokimos*, 144n 437, 171n 501, 214
    on *khren*, 171n 503
    on landmarks, 230n 609
    onta, 167, n 492
    on *panpam*, 181n 521, 182n 523
    on *per onta*, 168n 493, 172n 504
    on Sufficient Reason, Infinite Regress, and *reductio*, 239n 620
    on Sun and Moon in the Doxa, 179n 518
    on topography of Parmenides' journey being blurred, 166, n 487
    on Xenophanes and Parmenides' fr. 1.31–32, 170n 199
Moynahan, Patrick, 26n 62

music, 93–94
    effect of on the soul, 104–105
    Pythagoras' study of, 93–94
Music of the Spheres, 99–106
    ordering the unlimited, 99–101
    connection with the soul, 104–106
    order and proportion, 102–104
    sound of order, 101–102

N

Naked IS, xvii, 189–190, 255n 647
Neanthes, 34n 80, 37n 96, 294n 738
Nehamas, Alexander,
    Doxa as "Parmenides' glory," 177n 516
    rejection of εἴργω in fr. 6.3, 157n 469, 209, n 568
Nestle, Wilhelm, 128n 382
Nicomachus, 266n 738
Night. *See* Light and Night
Ninon, 293–295
    role of in anti-Pythagorean revolts, 74
Niven, Ivan, 257n 648
noetic/noetic-IS, 189n 535. *See also* Thought-IS
Non-Contradiction, Principle of
    elimination of self-refuting combinations, 263
    esti and, 188
    negation of, 202
    Parmenides' use of, in lawmaking, 149
Non-Identity, 148, 256–260
nonbeing/not-being. *See* IS NOT
number symbolism, 110–112
number-unit/number-atomism
    "base for thinking" for Pythagoreans, 256
    individual entity, 95
    irrationality and, 260
    overview of, 95–98
    "plurality of units," 259
    "point" and, 259
    relationships to other entities, 95
number(s), 103
    Aristotle on, 96, 109–110, 263
    avoidance of disorder and, 103
    as basic constituent of music, 94–95
    confusing of with things, 106–110

number(s) (*continued*)
    constructing whole universe out of, 96–98
    defined, 259
    deriving philosophy from, 106–114
    music and Pappus on, 268–269
    Pythagoreans' study of, 15–17, 24
number theory, *Mathematikoi* as developers of, 17
numerology
    classification based on, 56
    and the counter-Earth, 112–114
    defined, 108–109
    evolution of number theory into, 106–114
    vs. mathematics, 109
    number theory and, 259, 264n 664

O

oaths, 213
object of cognition/object of knowledge, 187–190, 205
object of discourse. *See* Parmenidean object of discourse
object of judgment, 188–189, 202, 222, 247
    delimiting, 211–217
object of opinion, 8, 169, 170, 198–199, 216–217, 224. *See also* Doxa, *dokounta*
object of reason, aspects of, 251–254
object(s) of sense-experience, 196, 238–239, 269. *See also* sense-experience
    as both like and unlike itself, 232
    characteristics of, 222–224
    IS as, 239
    separation of from IS, 226–227
    things of opinion as, 176
objects of thought, 95, 252, 258, 277
O'Brien, Denis, 158n 470, 171n 503, 184n 527
occult, 20–21, 91, 118–119
odd being even, indirect proof of, 262–265
oikonomikoi, 54n 145, 292n 732
oligarchy, 74
Olympians, relationship of to truth, 4
one. *See* unit
one-eyed-man dilemma, 146n 442, 146–149
oneness, 133, 134, 180n 519, 184, 188n 534. *See also* unity

onta, 167n 492, 168n 493, 172
opinion, 199, 216–217, 224. *See also* Doxa
    gap between truth and, 5n 20
    how it would be judged if truth did not exist, 168–170
    as one of two classes of knowledge, 136–137
    technique for examining, 7–8
    "things of," 170–171, 172, 173–176
Opinions of Mortals, 182–183. *See also* Doxa
opposites, 178–179, 188n 534. *See also* dichotomies
order, 22–23, 69–70, 102. *See also* law
    cosmic, 99
    laws of proportion ensuring, 101–104
    Pythagoreans' study of, 16
    units and, 16
ordering of words, 200, 201, 213. *See also* Doxa, *vs.* Evidential/Reliable Account
Osborne, Catherine, 59n 169
otherness, 51, 241
ouk esti. See IS NOT
Owen, G. E. L., 184n 527,
    on *per onta*, 168n 493, 172n 504
    "notorious deadlock," 170n 499
    disputes that Zeno attacks Pythagorean mathematics, 193n 547

P

Palmer, L. R., 212–213
pampan, 181n 521, 182n 523
panta, 167, 175, 181
pantos, 167, 171n 501, 175, 181
Pappus, 258, 268–271
    "sea of non-identity," 258
    summation of the problem of incompatibilities, 268–271
paradoxes, 194–195
parents, honoring, 44
"Parmenidean life," 127, 131
Parmenidean object of discourse, 122, 184–190
    approach to accurate testimony of, 7–8
    metaphysical implications of, 189–190
    misunderstanding the, 191–197

Parmenides, xv. *See also specific topics*
    on change and motion, 194–196
    concept of consistency of, 122
    concept of the divine of, 4
    cosmological interpretation of, 192–194
    disentangling incompatible objects, 234–235
    early lawmaking and analytic problem solving, 144–147
    as first true philosopher, 234
    influence of on logical skills, 147–150
    as lawmaker, 127–131
    link to Pythagoreans, 128–129, 130
    Poem. *See* Poem of Parmenides
    poet's challenge and lawgiver's response, 132–150
    on preserving the integrity of discourse, 238
    reason and, 141–142, 144
    refutation of generation, 237–240
        indirect, 238
    and reliability of discourse, 211
    repudiation of sense-experience of, 141–144
    truth according to, 26, 198–199
    twofold approach to inquiry of, 269n 670, 272, 274
    Xenophanes' influence on, 132–150
Parmenides' doctrine, 245–248
    three essential lessons of, 247–248
Parmenides (Plato), xv, 117–118, 121–122, 253–254
    key to, 124
    literature on, 190
    logical hypothesis of, 123
    logical technique in, 117
passing-away, 202, 238, 241. *See also* coming-to-be
passwords, 82, 89
    teaching by, 82–86, 284n 697
Paton, W. R., 77n 217
pebble arithmetic, 78, 97–98, 275
peira, 28
Pellikaan-Engel, Maja E., 164n 481
per onta (*vs. peronta*), 167, 168, 172, 175, 181
peras, 100n 308

perfect premise, 15–17, 253–256
perfect sphere, image of, 227
peronta. *See per onta*
persuasion, 10, 176, 219, 247
    contradiction and, 202
Peters, F. E., 99n 305
Phaedo (Plato), 115–116, 118–120
Philip, J. A., 22n 56, 23n 59, 255n 685
Philolaus of Croton, 22, 87, 264n 664
    author of book on Pythagorean doctrine, 11
    as teacher of Last Pythagoreans, 78–79
philosopher(s)
    Mathematikoi as, 86
    Thales, Anaximander, and Anaximenes as earliest natural, 3–4
    task of, 253
philosophy, 2–3, 23, 24, 26
    birth of, 2–3
        in argumentative means, 10
    defined, 2–3, 275
    deriving from number, 107–114
    how and why it came about, xiv
    nature of, 115
    and other fields of study, 27
    pioneers of, 3
    search for the perfect premise, 15
    Pythagoreanism as, 24
Phocaean/Phocaeans, 145n 438
physics, 196–197, 271
physikoi, 292n 732
pistis, 144n 437
piston logon, 144n 437
Plato, 11n 28, 39, 48n 126, 123, 257
    "argument too strange," 5n 20
    on classes of knowledge, 136, 216–217
    on Eleatic object, 192
    on Eleatics, 132
    "Greatest Difficulty," 5
    metaphysics, 120
    Parmenidean criterion on object of thought and, 258
    Parmenides' influence on, 194
    on philosophy, 115–116
    on Pythagoras, 33
    and Pythagorean mysticism, 114
    on truth, two approaches to, 118

Plato (*continued*)
    twofold distinction of, 276
    writings. *See also* Parmenides
        Phaedo, 115–116, 118–120
        Republic, 115–116, 276
        Sophist, 132–133
        Theaetetus, 128
plausible account, 38, 39, 272–273. *See also* Doxa
plausible/approximate. *See* Doxa
plausible/deceptive, 153, 198, 212, 218, 224
Plotinus, xxiii, 190n 538, 252n 640, 255
plurality, 193, 259
Plutarch, 94, 288n 715
    on music, 105
Poem of Parmenides, xiii, 9, 121, 138, 155–162
    advantages to rearranging the fragments, 209–210
    contradictions of cosmological or existential reading of, 192–197
    guide to the ordering of, 151–154
    Like according to Like as central thread of, 227–229
    sections of, 152–154
    significance of Proem in, 163–183
    terminology in, 212–217
point-atoms, 98n 301. *See also* atom/atom-points-units
points, 259
political conspiracy (Pythagorean), 49–52
politics (Pythagorean), 41, 45, 46
    beans and, 59–60
    religion and, 47, 54
politikoi, 80–81, 88, 89
poluderis elenchos, 144n 437, 171n 501, 172n 505, 214, 239n 619
    derivation of meaning, 239n 619
    descriptive terminology in logic, 144n 437
    separation by logos, 216n 587
    test, 171n 501
    "things of opinion" and, 172n 505
Polybius, 34n 80, 36n 89, n 92, 50n 130, 73n 208, 77, 288n 716, 290n 724
Pompeius Trogus. *See* Justin
Popper, Karl, 7, 134n 406, n 407, 137, 239n 619, 271
    on Einstein's remark on the unreality of certainty, 271
    on Parmenides' *esti* as solid block of matter, 191
Porphyry, 41, 59–60, 81
    akousmata of, 84
    on final days of Pythagoras' disciples, 79
    Life of Pythagoras, 37, 41
    as source of Pythagorean lore, 34
    on "walk on highways" saying, 55
predicateless, 221. *See also* Naked IS
predicational unity, 177n 515
premise (perfect), 15–17, 253–256
Presocratics, 3, 189
    Parmenides' impact on, xv
Principle of Identity. *See* Like according to Like
Principle of Non-Contradiction, 263
Proclus, 252n 640, 259n 653
Proem, 154, 155–156
    call for a unified approach, 174–177
    curriculum in, 167–168
    how opinion would be judged if truth did not exist, 168–170
    problem of contradictory formulas, 178–181
    realm of the nameless Goddess, 163–167
    significance of, 163, 183
    unity of formula, 181–183
    what is genuinely reliable because proven as such, 170–172
proof, 181n 522, 253. *See also dokimos*; Indirect Proof
    by action, 194
    and disproof, 214, 232, 263
    ways of, 147–150, 199
    need for, 82
    noetic/argumentative approach to, 196
    search for, 25–30
    the senses, reason, and, 141–144
properties. *See semata*
property (communal, Pythagorean), 60
proportion, 56, 99, 105
    drinking and eating, 20n 46
    irrationals, incommensurables and, 267n 666, 268, 284

musical, 94
numerical, 93, 102
   position of astral bodies in accordance with, 101–103
Parmenides and, 162, 205, 228–229
principle of, 105–106
Protagoras, 232–233
provedly. *See dokimos*
proviso(s), 218–224
punishment (Pythagorean), 48, 69, 72n 204, n 205
purification, 52, 115, 123, 284n 697
   as a way to truth, 118–120
Pythagoras. *See also specific topics*
   Aristotle on, 33–35
   concept of the divine of, 4
   cultism, deification of, xvi, 22
   death of, 37n 96, 75–76
      certainty about, 287
      information about, 294
      possible facts about, 292
      probability about, 290–291
      relationship of to uprisings, 31–33
   four speeches, 44–47
   idea of unit in, 16–17
   involvement of in Croton's war with Sybaris, 63, 67–68
   as lecturer and miracle-worker, 42–44
   life and activities, 281–286
   past lives, 25–26, 65
   Plato on, 33
   purported divine origin of, 18
   seeker of wisdom, 5, 17–21
   tradition *vs.* historical account of the life of, 31–40
      commentators on historical tradition, 34n 80
      conflicting reports and forgeries, 31–33
      in Plato and Aristotle, 33–34
      sources of tradition, 34–40
      works, counterfeit, 32–33
Pythagorean agenda
   Croton before Pythagoras, 41–42
   Earth regarded as a prison, 47–49
   the Four Speeches, 44–47
   Pythagoras as lecturer and miracle-worker, 42–44
"Pythagorean life," 33, 47
Pythagorean lore
   main sources of, 34–40
   method for assessing, 279–296
Pythagorean number theory, 7, 114
Pythagorean monad, 255n 647
Pythagorean organizations, 20, 22, 30, 50, 88
Pythagorean political elite, 23, 52, 55, 60–62, 69, 80–82
   revolts against, 287–296. *See also* Pythagoreanism
      first revolt, 73–75
      gradual end of the movement, 78–79
      growing hatred of non-Pythagoreans, 71–73
      return to power and second revolt, 77–78
      split in the order, 80–82
Pythagorean precepts and maxims. *See also akousmata*, 82–86
Pythagorean society, 22–23, 48n 123
   becoming a member in, 52–55
   structuring of, 80–81
Pythagorean table of opposites, 178
Pythagorean theorem, 86, 87
   irrationality and, 260–262
Pythagorean thinking, lack of rigorousness of, 121–124
Pythagorean writings, 32
Pythagoreanism
   anti-Pythagorean uprisings, 38. *See also* Pythagorean political elite, revolts against
   demise of, in Southern Italy, 287, 291
   history of, 21–24
   politics of, 23, 50–62. *See also* anti-democracy
      as anti-democratic, 52
      beans and politics, 59–60
      becoming a member in the Pythagorean society, 52–55
      gods and ruling of the many by the few, 56–58
      making of a religious political conspiracy, 50–52

Pythagoreanism (*continued*)
    Pythagorean police state, 58–59
    Religious-political-economic dictatorship, 60–62
  secrecy of, 11, 18, 50–51, 55–56, 71–73
    mistrust of the masses, 55–56
    practice of apartness, 56
  split in the order, 80–82
    Listeners. *See also* Akousmatikoi, 82–86
    Learners. *See also* Mathematikoi, 86–88
  stages of, 21–24
  unit, as perfect premise, 256
  women in, 23n 57, 41, 43n 110
Pythagoreans
  daily life of, 19
  emergence of scientist, 86–88
  Last. *See* Last Pythagoreans
  love of law of, 58–59
  study of number, 15–17
  tradition *vs.* historical account, 31–40
    conflicting reports and forgeries, 31–33
  unified theory of, 12, 15

R

rational/discursive means, 218
rational numbers, 257n 648, 259, 260
rational object, 187
Raven, J. E., 18n 40, 96n 294
reason, 141, 142, 251–252
  ability to, Pythagorean *vs.* Parmenidean, 121–124
  as a means to proof, 141–142
  object of, 224, 226, 230, 238
  Principle of Sufficient, 149, 234, 240–242
  role of consisting of, to give an account, 200
reasoning
  ability to reason, 167
    calibrating the ability, 121–124
  chain of, 216, 247, 252, 253
  cognitive, 218
  relying on, 27–29
reductio ad absurdum. *See also* Indirect Proof, 238, 239, 242
refutation, 144
reincarnation of Pythagoras, 25–26, 73n 208

Reinhardt, Karl, 20n 49, 134n 406, 173, 204n 559, 228n 603
reliability, 152, 280. *See also dokimos*; Reliable or Evidential Account
  as a benchmark of truth, 27–28
  of information, classification of, 280–281
Reliable Account. *See also* Evidential Account, 154, 158–160
  vs. Deceptive Ordering of Words, 273
  vs. Doxa, 204, 273
  IS, IS NOT, and, 158–159
  in Poem, 153–154, 158–160, 180–183, 191–192, 199, 200
  sense-experience and, 229
  techniques for creating, 213
retribution, law of, 145–146
revolts, anti-Pythagorean. *See under* Pythagorean political elite
Rhegium (Reggio di Calabria), xvi, 77, 145n 438
right-angled triangle/right-sided triangle, 261
Rizzo, Antonio, 165n 486
road (or, way) of the Goddess (much-informing/much-knowledge-imparting)
  beginning of journey, 277
  daimon and, 226
  structure of the Poem, 154
  unity and limit, 227
Robbins, H., 257n 648
Robinson, T. M., 184n 526
Ross, W. D., 34n 78, 81
round-square, 221
Russell, Bertrand, 221, 257n 648
Ryan, Paul, 122n 370

S

Sachs, Mendel, 189n 537
Sacred Discourse ("Sacred Logos"), 74, 295n 749
sameness (Like according to Like)
  aiming for conceptual correspondence, 227–229
  Goddess and *semata*, 234
  provisos for Evidential Account and, 218–221, 222–224
  unity of corresponding landmarks, 230–232
  way of the *daemon*, 225–227

Santillana, Giorgio de, 275n 682
saphes (to), 198
Schofield, M., 18n 40
Schrecker, Anne Martin, 234n 613
Schrecker, Paul, 234n 613
Schwabl, Hans, 160n 476
sea of non-identity, 256–258
Sealey, Raphael, 213n 578
secrecy and secret societies. *See under* Pythagoreanism, politics of
Sedley, David, 159n 474
seeming, 214
self-contradiction, 152, 177. *See also* contradiction(s); self-refutation
self-control, 45, 53
self-defeating, 157n 468, 212, 245
self-refutation, 201, 221, 224, 235, 236
Sellars, Wilfrid, 117n 358
semata. *See* landmarks
sense-experience, 220, 226, 246, 272, 273. *See also* object(s) of sense-experience
    Evidential Account and, 229
    landmarks of the IS mixed with landmarks derived from, 234–235
    Like landmarks for objects of, 231
    object of knowledge and, 205
sense-experiential world, 178
sense-perception, 205
    Parmenides' repudiation of, 141–144
separation,
    Pythagorean, 56, 61. *See also* veil
    exercise in (Parmenidean), 202, 212n 572, 215–216, 223, 235
    characterizes judicial procedure, 215n 585
    Doxa and, 235n 615
    godly act, 226–227
    by logos (elenchos), 216n 587
Sextus Empiricus, 142, 151, 164
sexuality, 46
shamanism, 163
Sider, David, xxv
signs/signposts. *See* landmarks
silence, Pythagorean rule of, 51n 134, 53n 144, 72, 81
Simplicius, 151, 204
Sinnige, Theo Girard, 260n 657

Snell, Bruno, 186n 530
Socrates, 39, 55n 151, 116, 117
    Parmenides and, 128, 194
    view of deity of, 2n 10
Sophists, 10, 221
soul, 110, 115, 119–120
    music of the spheres' connection with, 104–106
    purification of by Pythagoreans, 20
    transmigration of, 19, 26
sound, 94–95, 101–104
Spartan *Dioscuri*, 42n 106
Speusippus, 96n 297, 130n 389
spheres. *See also* perfect sphere, image of
    heavenly, 101–103
Sprague, Rosamond Kent, 209n 569
Steele, Laura, 164n 481
Stenzel, Julius, 186n 530
Steuben, Hans von, 171n 503
Steward, I., 257n 648
Stobaeus, 60
Stokes, Michael C., 128n 382
Stratton, George Malcolm, 161n 478
subjunctive mood (*casus irrealis*), 141n 431, 169
suffering, 48–49. *See also* Earth as a prison; punishment
Sufficient Reason (Principle of), 149, 234
    use of by Parmenides in disproof of generation of IS, 240–242
Sun (in Parmenides), 179n 518, 180
Sun Maidens/Daughters of the Sun, 164–165
superstition, 90, 93, 112, 114
surd(s), 251n 639, 258. *See also* irrational numbers/irrationals
    defined, 258n 650
Sybaris, xvi
    as antipode of Pythagoreanism, 63–65
    contrasted with Croton, 68–69
    reason for destruction of, 67–69
    ruins, 66–67
    war with Croton, 44, 64–70, 128
symbola. *See* akousmata
symbolism. *See also* akousmata
    number, 110–112
synedria, 77, 290n 724, 294

Szabó, Árpád, 122n 375, 241n 623, 255n 646
   on empirical proof in mathematics, 11n 29, 275
   Indirect Proof, 238n 617, 239n 620, 275
   irrational numbers, 257n 648
   Eleatics and non-empirical proof, 262, 275–276
Szegedy-Maszak, Andrew, 145n 441

T

taboos. *See akousmata*
Tarán, Leonardo, xxv, 184n 527, 192n 542
   on Being, 184n 526
   on Doxa, 174, 206
   on the Excluded Middle, 206
   on *reductio*, 240n 620
   on unity, 160n 476
Tarrant, Harold, 155n 462
Tauromenium, 36
Taylor, Hubert, xxiv
Taylor, Thomas, 48n 125, 49n 127, 82n 238
Taylor, Virginia, xxiv
teaching by passwords, tokens, and maxims. *See also akousmata*, 80–86
Tejera, V., 240n 620
testing, 254, 280. *See also* proof, and disproof
   the account of the IS, 234
   methods of, 219
   opinions, 7, 8, 171–172, 213–215, 218–220
test(s)
   to become member of Pythagorean society, 52, 82
   of contradiction, 9
tetractys, 83, 96, 113
Thales, 3
Theages, 74
Theophrastus, 34n 80
   observations of on Parmenides' Like by Like, 225, 227, 228
theos (*eis*), 135n 415
Thesleff, Holger, 32–33n 68–71
thinking, 122–123, 138. *See also* Ways of Inquiry
   base for, 256
   idea that it can be managed/controlled, 274

renouncing its dependence upon sense-experience, 273–277
   role of contradiction in, 8
   ways of inquiry for, 155–158
thought
   objects of, 95, 252, 258
   problem of, 191–192
Thought-IS, 256. *See also* noetic/noetic-IS
Thought-object, 95, 252, 258
Timaeus (the historian), 23n 56, 37n 96
   as source of Pythagorean history, 34, 35–36
true nature of things, apprehending (Plato), 115–118
truth, 8, 167, 184. *See also* certainty(ies); IS; knowledge; object of cognition/object of knowledge; Parmenidean object
   absolute *vs.* relative, 4–5, 6–8, 11. *See also* knowledge, human *vs.* divine
   according to Parmenides, 26, 196–197
   affinity between *esti*/IS and, 196–197
   defined, 26
   gap between belief and, 174
   goddess of. *See* Aletheia
   gods/deity and, 5–6
   gods *vs.* mortals- access to, 1, 7–9, 139–140
   heart of, as a way of thinking, 187
   how opinion would be judged if truth did not exist, 168–170
   knowing whether one is speaking, 139–140
   linkage of deity, 4
   mortals' difficulty in recognizing, 136
   nature of, 26
   Olympians and, 4
   Plato on, 115–116, 118
   pure, 4
   purification *vs.* reasoning as a way to, 118–120
   relativity of, 132
   reliable criteria, need for, 139–141
   types/classes of, 4, 5, 6, 7, 8
   Xenophanes on, 135–139
      approximating, 135n 417

General Index

U

unified theory, 16, 269
    call for a unified approach, 174–177
    numbers and, 106
    Pythagoreans', 11, 16, 274
unio mystica, 163n 480
unit-seed/unitary/unitize, 99, 106
unitizing, 100, 259
    numbers as aid to, 95
unit, 260–265. *See also* number-unit/number-atomism
    concept/principle of, 16–17, 259
    conversion of unlimited to unity by, 99–101, 259
    defense of integrity of, 106
    as foundation of creation, 99, 259
    functions and nature of, 99, 258–259
    as providing closure, 268
    as Pythagoreans' base for everything, 16, 256–261
    as Pythagoreans' perfect premise, 256
    relation of with other things, 106
    that can be conceived only by thought, 276
    two Pythagorean views of, 100n 308
unity, 180. *See also* oneness
    of formula/definition, 181–183, 188n 534, 201, 208, 219
    how limit and complement each other, 227
    predicational, 177n 515
universe, 104, 184, 187, 194
    as dead world, 191–192
    IS as, 191–197
    music-producing, 101–102
    source code of, 93–98
Unlike, 232
unlimited, 104
    conversion of to unity, 100–101
unmix/unmixed, 238
"unshaking heart of well-rounded truth"/"heart of truth," xix, 156, 167, 171, 173, 186, 187, 189, 201, 212, 224, 227, 235, 247
Untersteiner, Mario, 130n 389

V

van der Waerden, B. L., 38n 99, 43n 111, 294n 737
    on Pythagoras/Pythagoreans responsibility for Sybaris' destruction, 67n 193
    on Zeno and the crisis of Greek mathematics, 193n 547
van Hagens, Bernardo, 184n 527
veil/"inside the veil," 54, 55n 151, 56, 81, 88, 89–90
Verdenius, W. J., 166n 491
veridical/noetical, xv, xix, 252, 270n 672
Vidal-Naquet, Pierre, 78n 222
Vlastos, Gregory, 1, 195n 588
    on *dike* in Parmenides, 212n 575, 216n 588
    esti as mind, 184n 526, 192n 541
    on Parmenides' deductive system, 228
de Vogel, Cornelia J.
    on contradictions in argument for Pythagoras as public educator, 55, n 150, n 151
    on Pythagoras as "founder of all political education," 49n 128
    on Pythagoras' education of the people, 43n 111, 55n 150
    on secrecy and separation of Pythagorean political elite, 56

W

war (Pythagorean) as holy struggle, 70
Ways of Inquiry for Thinking, 153–154, 156–158
what-is. *See* IS
wheel of rebirth, 120
Wiesner, Jürgen, 184n 527, 204n 559
wisdom, dual approach to, 5
Wolf, Erik, 212n 575
women, 69
    of Croton, Pythagoras' speech to, 46
    Pythagorean, 23n 57
    Sybarite *vs.* Crotonian, 69
wording. *See* Doxa, *vs.* Evidential/Reliable Account; ordering of words
world, 107, 184, 187, 194
    as dead world, 191–192
    source code of, 93–98

world-objects, 196, 224, 231–232, 238–239, 269
    characteristics, 222–224, 226
    IS as, 239
    things of opinion as, 176

X

Xenocrates, 34n 80
Xenophanes of Colophon
    on belief, 170
    concept of God of, 134–136, 137
    dilemma of, 136, 137, 142
        solution to, 272
    on the divine, 3–4, 5, 198–199
    as first monotheist, 135
    honey and sweetness, 169
    influence of on Parmenides, 132–150
    negative epistemology, 6–7, 208
    on truth, 132–139, 198–199, 208
        need for reliable criteria, 139–141
        on the reliability of knowledge, 135–139
    on twofold distinction of knowledge/truth, 6–7

Y

Yount, David, xxiii
youth, 45–46

Z

Zafiropulo, Jean, 168n 493, 169n 496
Zaleucus of Locri
    as "follower" of Pythagoras, 35
    on list of *Mathematikoi*, 23n 57
    legendary early lawmaker, 144–147
Zamolxis, 282n 687
Zeller, Eduard, 91n 285, 288n 714, 291n 726, n 728, 292n 734, 293n 735
Zeno of Elea
    arguments against motion, 194–195
    defense of Parmenides, 193, 194
    as inventor of dialectic, 124, 194
    on mathematics and plurality, 193, 275
    "Millet Seed" argument, 232–233
    as Parmenides' pupil, 131
    use of paradox, 194–195
zero, disinclination of Greeks to adopt as foundation of a number series, 269n 669
Zhmud, Leonid, 260n 657